MW00581972

THE PURSUIT OF EUROPE

ANTHONY PAGDEN

THE

PURSUIT
of EUROPE

A HISTORY

OXFORD
UNIVERSITY PRESS

OXFORD
UNIVERSITY PRESS

Oxford University Press is a department of the University of Oxford.
It furthers the University's objective of excellence in research, scholarship,
and education by publishing worldwide. Oxford is a registered trade mark of
Oxford University Press in the UK and certain other countries.

Published in the United States of America by Oxford University Press
198 Madison Avenue, New York, NY 10016, United States of America.

Cataloging-in-Publication data is on file at Library of Congress

ISBN 978–0–19–027704–8

1 3 5 7 9 8 6 4 2

Printed by Sheridan Books, Inc.,
United States of America

For Giulia
Semper eadem

Acknowledgments

Earlier iterations of some of the ideas to be found in this book were tried out on audiences at the University of Oradea, Romania; at the Centro de Cultura Contemporánea de Barcelona, Spain; at the Centro de Estudios Políticos y Constitucionales, Madrid; at the Kreisky Forum for International Dialogue, Vienna, Austria; and at the Universities of Helsinki, Bolzano and the Hebrew University of Jerusalem. In 2015, the University of Arhus, Denmark, kindly invited me to give the Annual Slok Lecture in the History of Ideas, on "Reinventing Europe 1815–1919", and the University of Copenhagen, to deliver the inaugural lecture for their Project on European Enlightenment, on "Cosmopolitanism, Patriotism, Nationalism: Europe's Uncertain Future". I would like thank all those who were present on these occasions for their interest, their suggestions, and their sometimes vigorous objections. I owe a special debt of gratitude to the Axel and Margaret Ax:son Johnson Foundation which was kind enough to ask me to participate in the 2012 Engelsberg Seminar, in Stockholm, Sweden on "The Pursuit of Europe: Perspectives from the Engelsberg Seminar", which became the inspiration for so much of what evolved into the subject of this book. They also gave me my title. I have also benefited from conversations over the years on aspects of this subject with Quentin Skinner and Susan James, with David Armitage, with the late Tzvetan Todorov, with Lionel Jospin (on the subject of Napoleon), with José María Hernández, Joan-Pau Rubies, and Roberto Farnetti, and with my colleagues at UCLA, in particular Davide Panagia, and Kal Raustiala.

I am, as always, indebted to my editor Mathew Cotton at Oxford University Press for his support, his patience, and his careful pruning, and to Kizzy Taylor-Richelieu and to Bala Shanmugasundaram for guiding the book through the various stages of its production, with such care and attention. I am also greatly indebted to Donald Watt and Henry MacKeith, who read the final manuscript with scrupulous care and saved me from numerous errors and oversights.

I would like to express my gratitude to Andrew Wylie, the best of all possible literary agents, for his guidance, his patience, his support, and his encouragement, which have now accompanied me for the best part of two decades.

To Mike Rapport I owe a very special debt of gratitude. He read the original proposal for the book, offered a number of helpful comments, and reminded me, among other things, of the central role played by Christianity in the formation of "Europe" down to and including the creation of the European Union. He then read the final version with immense care and attention, making numerous suggestions for improvement, most of which, I hope, I have been able to follow, and saving me from a number of egregious errors and careless slips. From all of this, the present version has, I hope, benefited immeasurably.

As with every book I have written over the past twenty years, this one owes much of its initial inspiration and a great many of its insights to conversations with my wife Giulia Sissa—she who is the very best of Europeans. She has over the years helped me to think more clearly about the Europe to which we both belong and the European Union to which she—fortunate that she is—still belongs. She has done much to clarify the overall argument of this book, and it was she who suggested that I use the image of "Allegory of Justice and Peace" by Corrado Giaquinto which appears on the cover and which captures so eloquently what modern Europe now stands for. To her, as always, for her support, her generosity, her encouragement, her wisdom, and her love, I owe more than I can ever express or hope to repay.

Castellaras le Vieux, Mouans-Sartoux

Contents

A Note on Citations and Translations

All Greek and Latin sources have been cited in the traditional manner, without reference to any particular edition. In the case of modern works for which there exist large numbers of editions, I have, where possible, used book, chapter, or paragraph numbers instead of page numbers. In some cases I have singled out a particular edition. Wherever possible, I have used the most accessible and reliable English translation for works in languages other than English, although I have sometimes changed them slightly. Where no English-language edition is cited, the translation is my own.

It is not the interests of the many (the peoples), as is no doubt claimed, but above all the interest of certain princely dynasties and certain classes of business and society, that impel to this nationalism; once one has recognized this fact, one should not be afraid to proclaim oneself simply a *good European* and actively to work towards the amalgamation of all nations.

Friedrich Nietzsche, *Human, All Too Human*

Introduction

I

This is the story of an ambition, of a dream, of, some would say, an illusion. It is the story of a project, of a long, tortuous bid to unite groups of varied, diverse, and heterogeneous peoples, to give them a collective identity without robbing them of their individual identities—to make it possible to speak meaningfully, as the English scientist, philosopher, and loyal servant of the British crown Francis Bacon did in the seventeenth century, of "We Europeans"—*nos Europai*.[1] "Europe" is a metaphor and an allegory. It is also, of course, more obviously a place, a continent, a small and indeterminate one, what the French poet Paul Valéry in 1924 called a "Peninsula of Asia," whose frontiers have changed constantly, expanding and contracting over the centuries, ever since the word first began to be used by the Greeks in about 500 BCE.[2] They understood it to be little more than the Greek islands and mainland, and all the obscure unexplored landmass that lay behind it. No one could be certain how extensive it was or quite where it ended. But for all that its known frontiers dissolved, sometimes imperceptibly, into Asia to the east and into Africa to the south, for all that these frontiers were human, political, cultural, and sometimes religious, they were nevertheless very real. "A man seems to take leave of our world... before he cometh to Buda," wrote the English traveler Edward Brown in 1669 on crossing the border into Hungary, then under Ottoman rule. "He seems to enter upon a new stage of the world, quite different from that of the Western countries."[3]

But Europe, as the great French historian Lucien Febvre told an audience at the Collège de France in the final years of World War II—when any sense of what Europe had been, or might be again, except for a scene of seemingly endless carnage, had all but vanished—had throughout its history always been far more than a mere place. Its geography was meaningless. "For there are no Eastern limits to Europe," he said, "no impassable river, no insurmountable mountain chains, no arm of the sea, no great lake, no deserts of burning sands or glacial stones." There is only history. "Europe is an ideal, a dream," he went on, "for which men have been killed by the millions. Europe is a cultural idea (but to speak of culture today is almost to speak of dreams). Europe is an expanse of territory, of ever-expanding territory."[4] Febvre was reaffirming, at a particularly dark moment, a conviction which had been, in one way or another, a part of European history since antiquity.

It was in the eighteenth century, however, during what has come to be called the Enlightenment, that the idea that Europe could be understood as something more than a simple indeterminate geographical expression or a collective noun came slowly into being. "Europe" was a shared space, a single culture, which stood midway between the narrow and possibly perilous attachment to one's "nation" or one's "patria" and the imprecise amorphous identity called "humanity." This, for instance is how the great jurist and political theorist Charles-Louis de Secondat, baron de Montesquieu, in one of the jottings he called his "thoughts"—which I shall have cause to quote again—understood it. "If I knew something useful to me and harmful to my family", he wrote:

> I would reject it from my mind. If I knew something useful to my family and not to my country, I would try to forget it. If I knew of something useful to my country and harmful to Europe, or useful to Europe and harmful to Mankind, I would look upon it as a crime.[5]

A patriot, wrote the English historian Edward Gibbon in 1776, in a similar vein, has the obligation to "promote the exclusive interest and glory of his native country; but a philosopher may be permitted to enlarge his views, and to consider Europe as one great republic whose various inhabitants have attained almost the same level of politeness and cultivation." Gibbon was writing in the still turbulent wake of the Seven Years War of 1756–63, once called by Winston Churchill the real "First World War," which, at one time or another had involved all of the great powers of Europe and their overseas empires. Yet even what Gibbon calls, almost dismissively, "these partial events" did not "essentially injure our general state of happiness, the system of arts, and laws, and manners, which so advantageously distinguish above the rest of mankind, the Europeans and their colonies."[6]

By the late eighteenth century this sense that, despite almost perennial conflict, there existed a common European territory, some kind of common European identity, and common European interests, and that ultimately the individual states of Europe could not survive without each other, had become something of a commonplace. "Things are such in Europe" wrote Montesquieu, always the most acute political observer of his day, "that the states depend upon each other. Europe is one state made up of many provinces."[7] The great eighteenth-century French poet, playwright, historian, and philosopher François-Marie Arouet, better known by his sobriquet Voltaire, imagined Europe to be as a "kind of great republic, embracing several states ... all having one and the same religious basis, the same principles of public law, the same political ideas, all of them unknown in other parts of the world." What the Anglo-Irish jurist and political theorist Edmund Burke called, significantly, "the great vicinage of Europe" was, he claimed, despite his attachment to his own "little platoon," "virtually one great state, having the same basis of general law, with some diversity of provincial customs and local establishments.... The whole of the polity and economy of every country of Europe has been derived from the same sources" to the point that "no European can be a complete exile in any part of Europe."[8]

Even the German philosopher and historian Johann Gottfried Herder, who had a very strong sense of the individualities of all the different cultures and "Fatherlands" of which Europe was now composed, believed that:

> In no one quarter of the Globe have nations been so intermingled as in Europe; in no one have they so often and so completely changed their abodes, and with them their way of life and manners.... In the course of ages the ancient family stamp of many European nations has been softened down and altered by a hundred causes, and without this the *general spirit* of Europe could not easily have been excited.[9]

There are many things which have, over the centuries, been identified as specific, if not unique to Europe. Two, however have been more enduring than all others, and have made the very idea of the unity of all its many different peoples ultimately possible. The first is something of a commonplace, if a highly fraught and contested one. As the eminent Italian jurist Aldo Schiavone has argued, of all the things which modern Europe has inherited from classical antiquity, two have been of lasting political significance: the idea of representative government—"the Greek paradigm of politics as popular sovereignty"—and the Roman conception of rule under a common law "defined by reason." It is, however, modern Europe which, through a long series of convulsions, revolutions, and reforms has succeeded, if only ever imperfectly, in uniting the two.[10] The actual forms of government adopted by the different peoples of the continent have, of course, varied widely. But all have subscribed to the idea a of "civil society," by which is meant a life lived under the protection of a universal system of law to which all its peoples might be supposed to have given their consent. It is a belief which, although—and in part because—it was so brutally suppressed in so many places throughout so much of the twentieth century, constitutes the main intellectual and ideological support on which the European Union now rests.

The other is perhaps less obvious. Europe, said the Greek geographer Strabo in the first century CE, was unique in being able to provide for itself all "the fruits that are best and that are necessary for life and all the useful metals," and needed to import only luxury goods, "spices and precious stones" which, he said dismissively, "make the life of persons who have a scarcity of them fully as happy as those who have them in abundance."[11] But only *Europe* as a continent, crisscrossed by trade routes from east to west, could do this, and never one alone of the many disparate peoples of the Mediterranean. Because, that is, life was so difficult for each of them individually that they could only survive by developing the great commercial networks which were to become the basis of their future expansion far beyond the limits of Europe. They were also, because of the intense competition which persisted amongst them, all forced from time to time into political unions, and were from time to time compelled to develop systems of alliance, federations, and leagues. In historical reality the Europeans were, of course, by no means the only peoples to recognize the value of cooperation. But few peoples have needed to cooperate with one another quite so often over quite such a long period of time. Leagues, or rather the ability to form leagues, came to be thought of as one of the features of the European peoples, and one of the sources of their success. The Persians, those great "others" of classical antiquity, conquered their neighbors. The Greeks may have done the same to theirs; but they also knew how to form alliances with them. The most famous of these leagues were the amphictyonies—the "leagues of neighbors"—of the ancient Greek city states, originally intended as alliances to provide protection for the sacred shrines around the Mediterranean. The best-known, the Delian or Great Amphictyonic League, was believed to have been founded after the Trojan War to protect the

Temple of Apollo on the island of Delos, but it was still in existence in the second century CE. These became a point of reference for many later generations of Europeanists eager to see in these remote classical origins the possibilities for the creation of a new and more enduring pan-European league. Leagues, like federations and confederations, offered simultaneously both individual freedom and collective security.

"The cities of Ancient Greece," wrote Gibbon of the origins of his "one great republic,"

> were cast in the happy mixture of union and interdependence which is repeated on a larger scale, but in a looser form, by the nations of modern Europe—the union of religion, language, and manners which renders them spectators and judges of each other's merits; the independence of government and interests which asserts their separate freedoms and excites them to strive for pre-eminence in the career of glory.[12]

It was on this belief in the creative force of "union and interdependence" perhaps more than any other conviction that the possibility of a future European union rested. "Let us, however, immediately insist," Lucien Febvre concluded his Collège de France lecture, "that European unity is not uniformity."[13] "Unity in diversity," as the motto of the European Union has it.

II

Most of the authors of these generalized claims were aware that although they all made much of the diversity of the modern European states, the unity of Europe, this "*general spirit*" as Herder phrased it, had already been "undesignedly prepared" by the one thing which he, at least, most despised: the Roman Empire.[14] Like Herder, Gibbon too was convinced that in his day it had been precisely the "division of Europe into a number of independent states connected, however, to each other by the general resemblance of religion, language and manners" that had been responsible for the "most beneficial consequences to the liberty of mankind."[15] But, unlike Herder, he was also convinced that the Roman Empire in the age of the Antonines, of the "Five Good Emperors" as they have come to be known—from Nerva (reigned 96–8 CE) until Marcus Aurelius (161–80 CE)—had been the "period in the history of the world during which the condition of the human race was the most happy and prosperous," and which, of course, extended well beyond the frontiers of modern Europe to include "the fairest part of the earth and the most civilized portion of mankind."[16]

That, however, had all begun to disintegrate after the succession of the
Emperor Marcus Aurelius' son Commodus in 177, at which point the empire
"fell into the hands of a single person [and] the world became a safe and
dreary place for his enemies" until, slowly but ineluctably, in Herder's words,
"the machine *fell apart* and *covered* all nations of the Roman world in wreck-
age."[17] In 476, after more than two centuries of this agony, the German
chieftain Odoacer deposed the last of the emperors, Romulus—referred to
contemptuously as "Augustulus," "Little Augustus"—and the Roman
Empire in the West collapsed into a squabbling succession of fiefdoms, principalities, duchies, city states, and bishoprics.[18] What remained, what still
remains in many places to this day, is an image of ancient Rome as that
moment when everyone in what we now call "Europe" lived a relatively
safe, relatively stable, and prosperous life under the auspices of the Roman
law. "It was their custom," wrote Francis Bacon of the Romans, in 1605:

> to give a speedy denization, and in the highest degree; that is, not only a right
> of commerce, of marriage and inheritance, but also the right of suffrage, and
> of candidature for places and honors. And this not only to particular persons;
> but they conferred it upon entire families, cities, and sometimes whole nations
> at once. Add to this their custom of settling colonies, whereby Roman roots
> were transplanted in foreign soil. And to consider these two practices together,
> it might be said, that the Romans did not spread themselves over the globe,
> but that the globe spread itself over the Romans.

It was, he concluded, "the securest method of extending an empire."[19] It
was also, of course, at many levels a carefully nurtured illusion fostered and
propagated by the Roman state itself, and has subsequently been made to
serve a number of narrowly sectarian and nationalistic ambitions. But for all
that, it was, as we shall see, to become a valuable imaginative resource for the
future builders of European unity. For, in this vision of Rome, which Cicero,
the last great orator and jurist of the Roman Republic, had tellingly described
as being more like "a protectorate [*patrocinium*] than an empire of the
world,"[20] it was possible to create the image of a league made up of free
states bound together by a single body of law and a common citizenship in
which a large number of diverse cultures and systems of belief could flourish
unhindered, so long as they offered no threat to the common good. All of
those from Bacon to the Russian-born French philosopher Alexandre
Kojève (of whom more later), who between 1945 and his death in 1968
worked in the French Ministry of Economic Affairs and exercised a considerable if hidden influence over the French involvement in the creation of

the European Economic Community, knew full well that the realities of
Roman imperial government and of life under the empire, even before the
demise of the Republic in 27 BCE, had never been quite so benign or ecumenical. They knew that the empire had been acquired for the most part
through conquest. They knew too that even if those conquests had often been
carried out "in the interests of allies," many of those allies had been chosen
in order to enable expansion by defending them, so that, as Cicero himself
recognized, "our nation has gained control of the entire world through
defending its allies."[21] They also knew, of course, that the much-vaunted
Roman grandeur had been built upon slave labor, and that because of this,
as the great eighteenth-century philosopher David Hume remarked, "to
one who considers coolly on the subject it will appear that human nature,
in general, really enjoys more liberty at present in the most arbitrary government of EUROPE than it ever did during the most flourishing period
in ancient times."[22] They knew that women had very little standing or social
independence from their fathers or their husbands under Roman law and
that fathers could exercise the power of life and death over their children.
They were fully aware of all this, as they were of the gruesome brutality of
the games, and of the cruelty and depravity of so many of the Roman imperial households. But the historical reality was not to the point. What mattered was the ambition, the objective, the perception of what a true
confederation of peoples, of what Kojève would call a "true empire,"
could be.

At the end of the eighth century, Charles I, king of the Franks, known
as Charlemagne, "Charles the Great," set out to recreate at least a part of
what he knew of all this. In 800, having conquered much of southern and
central Europe, he had himself crowned by Pope Leo III as "Emperor of
the Romans." The Carolingian Empire covered most of central Europe,
parts of northern Spain, as far east as what is now Poland, and a large part
of northern Italy. It was, of course, far smaller than the Roman Empire had
been at its height, and it lasted less than a century. But it was the founding
state of what would become the Holy Roman Empire—or after 1512, the
"Holy Roman Empire of the German Nation"—which would survive
until brought to an ignominious end by Napoleon in 1806, and which was
to have immense political significance, if not real political power, for later
generations. It was also responsible for providing the initial political cohesion which would make all of Europe throughout the Middle Ages
synonymous with what Pope Leo the Great in the fifth century designated

the *orbis Christianus*, or, as it would be called in the European vernaculars, simply "Christendom."

Unlike its predecessor, however, which had, since the reign of the Emperor Antonius Pius, claimed (at least) to be a world empire, the Carolingian Empire was explicitly European, and Charlemagne himself was referred to, from the early nineteenth century, as *Pater Europae*, the "Father of Europe." Over the centuries he came to represent the possibility of reuniting the French and German peoples—who have always been at the core of the geographical vision of Europe—and thereby of finally creating a single united Europe. The European Union has also taken up this legacy. One of the buildings of the European Commission in Brussels is called "the Charlemagne Building," and ever since 1950 Charlemagne's capital, the city of Aachen—or Aix-la-Chapelle—has annually awarded a prize to those peoples—or things, as in 2002 it was awarded to the euro—who have contributed most to the "voluntary union of the European peoples without constraint." The first laureate was the eccentric European federalist, the Austrian–Japanese Count Richard von Coudenhove-Kalergi. In his acceptance speech in 1950 he called for a "Union Charlemagne," that is, "the renewal of the Empire of Charlemagne as a confederacy of free nations . . . to transform Europe from a battlefield of recurring world wars to a peaceful and blooming worldly empire of free people!" Coudenhove-Kalergi's characterization of the legacy of Charlemagne, and the EU's embrace of it, is, however, deeply problematical. For the Carolingian Empire was clearly not, as most subsequent projects for European integration down to and including the EU have been, at least in the first instance, an attempt to bring an end to the incessant warfare between the various states of Europe and to restore to the continent a universal realm of justice. It was, instead, a bid by a powerful tribal ruler to appropriate for himself the status and the glory of the former Roman Empire in the West. If the objective of integration is to bring the peoples of Europe together "without restraint," then, clearly, it has to be achieved by some means other than conquest.

III

Coudenhove-Kalergi was, however, right about one thing. Every attempt at creating a unified Europe has been, initially at least, a response to a crisis which in one way or another has touched all the European peoples, and, until very recently, most of those crises have been caused by war.[23] The most extensive and certainly the most devastating of all the wars that the European peoples have fought amongst themselves before World War I were the prolonged, often civil wars which followed the religious Reformation of the sixteenth century. In most of these, for the first time in their history, the combatants were not struggling over dynastic claims or for land or to defend the supposed rights of their rulers. They were fighting over beliefs.[24] The wars, which had begun in the Holy Roman Empire in 1546, spread steadily across the whole of Europe, bringing ever-increasing internecine conflict in their wake. They included the French Wars of Religion from 1562 until 1598, the English Civil War of 1642–9, and what the Spanish called the "Dutch Revolt" and the Dutch "the Eighty Years War" between 1566 and 1648. The final stage of this conflagration, which began in 1618 and lasted uninterrupted until 1648, came to be known as the "Thirty Years War." It raged across the whole of central and eastern Europe, drawing into its maw at one time or another all the major states of the continent, from Spain to Sweden. The huge armies that it created left behind them vast tracts of the continent in smoldering ruins. When it was finally over, a third of the population of central Europe was dead. As Voltaire remarked in astonishment on rereading his own description of all this butchery: "Is it the history of snakes and tigers which I have just written? No, it is that of men. Tigers and snakes do not treat their own kind in that manner."[25]

The series of agreements which brought all this, and with it all confessional conflict within Europe, finally to an end were signed between some two hundred Catholic and Protestant powers in the Westphalian cities of Osnabrück and Münster between May and October 1648, and were known collectively as the "Peace of Westphalia." This was, in effect, the first modern treaty. It was the first treaty between sovereign nations which aimed at creating a lasting peace and not merely, as all previous treaties had, a temporary ceasefire. It was also the first truly international gathering of European states, and the first formally to recognize the existence of two new states, the United Netherlands, which had in effect established its independence from Spain forty years earlier, and the Swiss Confederation, which now became a sovereign republic, independent of the Habsburg Empire. From 1648, the disordered, divided monarchies of Europe slowly began to transform themselves into the modern nation states which most of them still are to this day.

The Peace of Westphalia had been one lastingly consequential solution to the crisis. The other, which was scattered, imprecise, and initially inconsequential, took the form of a series of projects for a perpetual peace in Europe through the creation of a political union among the various European states. Although there are earlier proposals for a unified Europe going all the way back to Dante Alighieri's *De Monarchia* of 1313 (which in effect only envisages a stronger, more centralized version of the Holy Roman Empire extended to the whole of Europe), the earliest of these to have any lasting significance was *Le Grand Dessein* (*The Grand Design*) composed by the Duc de Sully, finance minister to King Henri IV of France, between about 1617 and 1630, which was still being cited approvingly by the highly influential Swiss jurist Johann Caspar Bluntschli as late as 1878.[26] It exists, however, only in fragments in Sully's *Mémoires* printed in 1638, and until the nineteenth century was widely assumed to have in fact been written, as Sully indeed claims it was, by the king himself—which, perhaps more than its content, explains the frequent admiring allusions to the work. The *Design* proposed that the Habsburg monarchy—which at the time encompassed both Spain and Portugal and their respective overseas empires, and which Sully, unsurprisingly, looked upon as the prime cause of conflicts within Europe—be reduced to "the sole Kingdom of Spain," and that Europe should thereafter be divided into fifteen states, as nearly equal as possible in both territorial extent and military power. These would preserve the political forms—both monarchical and republican—and the religions—Catholic and Protestant—of their originals, and would be governed by a General Council composed of four delegates from the greater powers and two from the lesser which would exercise ultimate legislative authority over all the member states. There would be freedom of trade; and the customs barriers between the states, if not their borders, would be abolished. Presiding over it all, however, would, unsurprisingly perhaps, have been Henri IV himself, who, having brought the Wars of Religion in France to an end in 1598, would now go on to lead the rest of Europe toward a future of perpetual peace and renewed prosperity.[27] What Sully and Henri had seen was that if France were to emerge from the civil and religious conflict that had divided the kingdom since 1562, and if a now religiously divided Christendom were to be able to resist the rising power of the Ottoman Empire, then Europe would have to rebuild, if not as another Roman Empire, then as something far closer to a federation of states.

In 1623, an obscure French monk named Éméric Crucé, with no connection to Sully, published a similar, if yet more ambitious project, *Le Nouveau Cynée* (*New Cyneas*), offering "the best occasions and methods for

establishing a general peace and freedom of commerce for the whole world."
This laid out elaborate plans for a world federation—although Crucé was,
in fact, concerned predominantly with Europe and its perpetual conflict
with the Ottoman Empire—governed by a permanent conference of delegates based in Venice, a convenient gateway, geographically and culturally,
between Europe and the Ottomans. These would have represented not only
all the nations of Europe, but also the Ottoman Empire itself, Persia, China,
"Ethiopia," Africa, and Russia. They would have arbitrated between these
regions and might also have been allowed to use force against any dissident
member (although where this force was to come from Crucé does not say).
The Pope would have been the president and the Sultan his deputy. There
was to be a common currency, standardized weights and measures, and free
trade. It was an early outline, as some have seen it, of the League of Nations,
the United Nations, and the European Union, all somehow rolled into one.[28]

As the European states continued to battle mercilessly with one another,
even after the Treaty of Westphalia had seemingly put an end to any future
possibility of confessional conflict, a steady flow of proposals for the final
abolition of war, some pragmatic, most impossibly improbable, followed in
the trail of the *Grand Design* and the *New Cyneas*. They included William
Penn's *An Essay towards the Present and Future Peace of Europe* of 1693; *Some
Reasons for a European State* of 1710, by Penn's friend and fellow Quaker John
Bellers; the *Declaration for a Lasting Peace in Europe* by the "Old Pretender"
(known to his followers as King James III of England and VIII of Scotland)
of 1722; the *Scheme of A "Perpetual Diet" for Establishing the Public Tranquillity*
of 1736 (which was more of a proposal for conquering the Ottoman Empire)
by Giulio Alberoni, skilled social climber and cardinal in the service of
Philip V of Spain; a parody by Voltaire in 1770, which is in reality a plea for
universal religious toleration; the *Project for Perpetual Peace between the
Sovereigns of Europe and their Neighbours* by a former galley slave, Pierre-
André Gargaz, which so impressed Benjamin Franklin that in 1782 he
printed it on the press he had set up on his estate at Passy outside Paris; and
Jeremy Bentham's *A Plan for a Universal and Perpetual Peace* of 1789, which,
among other things, called for the dissolution of the European overseas
empires, which he denounced as "violations of common sense" and
"bungling imitations of miserable [Greco-Roman] originals."[29]

Many of these, however, owed rather more than their titles to a bulky,
ponderous work by Charles-Irénée Castel, abbé de Saint-Pierre, *A Project for
Establishing a Perpetual Everlasting Peace in Europe*, written in 1713, a text

whose influence, attenuated but perceptible, has carried down through the centuries, via the pioneer socialist Claude-Henri de Saint-Simon in the nineteenth century to the founders of the European Union—a term which Saint-Pierre seems to have been the first to use. Saint-Pierre—the "pacific philosopher, a friend of the human race," as he called himself—was, in many respects, a remarkable and remarkably prescient man, and his project, although it is unwieldy, prolix, and presents itself merely as commentary on the *Grand Design*, not only was far more radical than any of its predecessors, and some of it successors, but also in some respects comes far closer to describing the kind of quasi-federation which Europe has subsequently become. A diplomat who had been a negotiator of the Treaty of Utrecht in 1712–13 which had ended the War of the Spanish Succession, and who had been expelled from the Académie française in 1718 for denouncing the rule of its patron, Louis XIV, Saint-Pierre devised plans for a graded tax system—virtually unthinkable in the early eighteenth century—and for free education for all, both men and women. His *Project* envisaged a future European federation drawn together through the beneficial effects of trade, bound by a "treaty of European Union" but ruled not as individual states are, by a single sovereign, but by a council or diet on which the princes of every member state would sit, and by which all the disputes that arose across the continent would be resolved, without, or so he believed, seriously damaging the authority of the monarchs of the individual states. This, Saint-Pierre was convinced, would eliminate warfare, except as a means of last resort, and thus bring the greatest happiness to the greatest number, and finally demonstrate to princes that their true interests lay not in conflict but in what he called *bienfaisance*, or "beneficence," which was an expression of that "sympathy" which all human beings were supposed, as individuals, to share with one another.[30]

Saint-Pierre hoped that one day it would be possible to extend this federation to Asia, Africa, and America, but he reflected that any such proposal at this date would make his plan seem absurdly unrealistic. Even without attempting to embrace the entire world, the *Project* was duly mocked by most of those who read it. Voltaire dismissed it as "a chimera which could no more exist among princes than it could among elephants and rhinoceroses, or wolves and dogs."[31] Gottfried Wilhelm Leibniz, ironical as ever, remarked that it reminded him of a "device in a cemetery with the words: *Pax perpetua* [Perpetual peace]; for the dead do not fight any longer: but the living are of another humour; and the most powerful do not respect tribunals at all." [32] (Leibniz, himself, however, had his own project for Europe as a kind of revitalized Holy Roman—and hence German—Empire.) In 1756 Jean-Jacques Rousseau wrote a brief "Judgment" on the *Project* (the only thing of substance that emerged from what was intended to be an edition of Saint-Pierre's entire *oeuvre*), and although he acknowledged that many would toss it aside, as they would any such utopian project, as mere "vain speculation," it was, he believed, nevertheless a demonstration of the "general and particular utility" of "moral truth." [33] He disagreed, however, with the idea that a federation could achieve peace (historically, as he pointed out, most had been created for the purposes of war). Nor did he believe that commerce encouraged harmony and cooperation, but that in reality it only increased the sources for competition between states and thus the grounds for war. In the end he came to the conclusion that the kind of federation of states Saint-Pierre had conjured up out of his overly optimistic imagination would require a situation in which "the sum of particular interests did not overpower the common interest and . . . each one sees in the good of all, the greatest good which he could hope for himself." The only possible way to bring that about would, in his view, be a revolution. And if that were the case, then "who among us would dare to say whether the European League were more to be feared than desired?" [34]

The person who substantially transformed the idea that the only way to bring about perpetual peace was by means of a league of nations was Immanuel Kant. In the wake of the Treaty of Basle on April 5, 1795—which had ended the War of the First Coalition between the monarchical states of Europe and Revolutionary France, and which had ceded to France all territory West of the Rhine, and allowed Russia, Austria, and Prussia to carve up Poland between them—Kant laid out his own project for ending warfare. He called it *Toward Perpetual Peace, a Philosophical Sketch.* In 1795 Kant was 71 years old and widely admired throughout Europe as perhaps the most important, the most ambitious European philosopher since Aristotle.

Toward Perpetual Peace is, its title makes clear, a contribution to an as yet unfinished project. It is a proposal, a mere "philosophical sketch" which will lead "toward" a condition that can only be realized in future times. Perhaps for that reason it is written, unpromisingly, in the form of a series of articles—and Kant's lengthy reflections on the meaning of each one—for a hypothetical universal peace treaty. It is, however, a treaty unlike any which had hitherto existed and, in Kant's mind, was the only one which could ensure the future, and inescapably cosmopolitan development of the human race. Its conclusions were to have a powerful and widespread, if also diffuse, influence well beyond the confines of professional philosophy. It has left its mark on many later generations, and its presence can still be seen not only in contemporary discussions about global governance and global justice, but also in the creation of the universal institutions intended to sustain them, in the League of Nations, in the United Nations, and, perhaps most clearly of all, in the European Union.

As Saint-Pierre, whom Kant cited frequently, had acidly observed, the sovereign powers of Europe as they were currently constituted were no different from "the little kings of Africa, the unhappy Caciques, or the little sovereigns of America." There existed among them nothing which could be described as a "sufficiently powerful and permanent society." The closest they had come was the Swiss Federation or the states of the Netherlands. As a consequence, all the other powers were ceaselessly driven to war to resolve their differences.[35] Kant agreed. Every treaty organization by which the states of Europe had sought to bind themselves—including the one con- cluded at Basle—had been nothing other than a "mere truce, a suspension of hostilities, not a *peace*," since none of them had ever aimed at a "stable, permanent condition."[36] Saint-Pierre's project may have been illusory and without any practical value, since all such proposals have always been "ridiculed by great statesmen, and even more by heads of state, as pedantic, childish, and academic ideas," but that, in Kant's view, was probably only because Saint-Pierre had believed that "its execution was too near."[37] His basic claim, however, that perpetual peace, within Europe or beyond, could only be brought about by some kind of federation was inescapable. The only way, Kant insisted, to bring an end to the current condition of unstructured barbarism between the states of the world was for all of them to form "a general league of nations, establish a public legislation, define a public authority to appropriate national prerogatives, and thereby make possible a universal peace."[38] Kant's own project was far more ambitious than those of any of his predecessors; and it was an attempt not so much to resolve a problem, however pressing, within Europe as it was to transform the entire international order.

The question for Kant, the question which Saint-Pierre and most previ- ous propagandists for perpetual peace had singularly failed to answer, was how the kinds of international communities that had been envisaged were to be brought into being in such a way that they would not collapse under the slightest pressure. As Rousseau had observed, when it came to means

Saint-Pierre "reasoned like a child." He imagined "naively that it would be enough to assemble a Congress, suggest some articles, have them signed, and then all would be done."[39] But as both Rousseau and, with even greater urgency, Kant fully realized, to create Saint-Pierre's "European Union," it would first be necessary to transform utterly the kind of relationship which existed between states. Individual societies were bound together by a pact between rulers and their citizens or subjects. The same, however, clearly did not apply between states, where the only contracts that had ever existed had taken the form of treaties—what Kant called a "peace pact (*pactum pacis*)"—and these had only ever put an end to a "current war...but not a condition of war, of always finding pretexts for a new war."[40] If these unsatisfactory arrangements were to be replaced by anything more binding, then nations would have first to change their own political identities. In this Saint-Pierre and Rousseau had been looking in the right place, but even Rousseau had failed to grasp the full implication of his own claim that nothing resembling Saint-Pierre's project could come into existence unless each state created a form of government in which "the sum of particular interests did not overpower the common interest."

Kant's project was markedly different from those of all his predecessors. They had worked with the assumption that a lasting peace might be achieved between the states of Europe—and in some cases the entire world—while both the structure of government within each nation and the legal order to which each belonged remained unchanged. Kant took a radically different view. Peace—perpetual peace—could only be achieved through the creation of an entirely new international legal order, one which would be capable only of bringing peace between nations but also of creating an order of justice amongst them. For peace without justice could only ever be ephemeral.

Unlike all his predecessors, Kant had seen that only states which shared the same political form would be able to enter into a lasting peaceful union with one another. The kind of union which Sully had imagined, in which monarchies and republics were supposed to cooperate happily together, was in practice unthinkable. (The same is still broadly true, one might argue, of the United Nations.) Furthermore, the only political form under which such a union was possible was what he famously called a "representative republic." This he defined as a society in which no individual should be constrained by any external—that is, purely human—law except for "those to which I could have given my consent."[41] In Kant's view, only in a republic in which the legislator was obliged to pass laws "in such a way that they *would have been able* to arise from the united will of an entire people" and which was thus a "*system representing* the people in order to protect its rights in its name" would the individual, "even if he is not good in himself... nevertheless be compelled to be a good citizen."[42] Such a republic was also the only one which "offers a prospect of attaining the desired result, i.e. Perpetual Peace," since only when they were the ultimate arbitrators of the law would the citizens be in a position to "give their free assent, through their representatives, not only to the waging of war in general, but also to each particular declaration of war."[43] Only in a truly representative republic do the base interests of the individual coincide with the interests of the state as a whole.[44] For the citizens of a state, going to war inevitably means not only "taking upon themselves all the hardships of war"; it also means being compelled, once the war is over, to assume the "burden of debt that embitters peace itself, and that can never be paid off because of new wars always impending," thereby making their "cup of troubles overflow."[45] In a situation in which it is *they* who decide whether to take up arms or not, they are only likely to do so if they are certain there can be no solution *other* than war. Although Kant himself forcefully denied that his "representative republic" was a "democracy"—since what he understood by "democracy" was the regime of ancient Athens, and possibly of Revolutionary France during the Terror—it does meet the requirements of what today would be called a "liberal democracy."[46]

The representative republic was not, however, only the means of ensuring that justice be extended to all its citizens. It was also the only form of government which was capable of creating what Kant called the "lawful condition" in which a union of states might be created. This he called variously a "world-republic," a "league of peoples," a "state of nations," an "international state," a "universal union of peoples," a federation, a confederation, a partnership, and a permanent state congress.[47] The model to which Kant returned most often—a model to which, as we shall see, many others would also later return—was that of the Amphictyonic Leagues of ancient Greece. But no matter what form this might take, it would be a peaceful, consensual body, and all those who joined it would do so because they perceived it to be in their particular interests, and they would do so of their own volition, and once joined, "every state, even the smallest could expect its security and rights not from its own might, or its own juridical judgment, but only from this great federation of nations."[48] What Kant was advocating, however, was no superstate—or what he calls a "state of nations"—much less an empire, that "graveyard of freedom," but a free association which would lead to an "increasing culture and the gradual approach of human beings to greater agreement in principles."[49]

When this happened, a new form of interstate law—what he famously called the "cosmopolitan right" (*ius cosmopoliticum* or *Weltbürgerrecht*)—would come to replace the old law of nations (*ius gentium*), which in Kant's opinion had always been an utterly ineffectual code, since between states, as they then existed, there was no "common external constraint."[50] But this would be far more than a simple law. It would be an entire *order of justice*.

For Kant the realization of the new league and of the "cosmopolitan right" to which it would give birth still lay far in the future. It was, he admitted, a "dream of perfection," but like all such ideas it should not abandoned, as he had said of the Platonic republic, "under the very wretched and harmful pretext of its impracticability."[51] So long as we are free—morally and intellectually—we can only go on hoping that some kind of cosmopolitan world will be achieved. His objective had always been to obtain what he calls "a history of future times, i.e. a predictive history."[52] For although animals, if left to themselves, reach their "complete destiny" as individuals, humans can only do so as a species, and they can, therefore, get there only "through *progress* in a series of innumerably many generations."[53] The "complete destiny" of man always remains a distant but attainable goal, which makes it the duty of all beings "to work toward this (not merely chimerical) end"[54]; and while the human race may experience many setbacks on its long journey through time, and although "the *tendency* to this final end can often be hindered, it can never be completely reversed."[55] Kant, despite his initial reliance on Saint-Pierre, was offering a solution to what he saw as a human, not a narrowly European, problem. His league would be a union of *world* states. But there can be no doubt that not only could the conditions for the formation of the new amphictyonic league only arise in Europe, but they would, in all probability, and possibly for innumerable centuries, have to remain there.

Kant has left his mark on almost all thinking about the possibility of some future world order, from his own day to this. All the international institutions, from the creation of the League of Nations in 1919, of the United Nations in 1945, to that of the European Union between the Treaty of Rome in 1957 and the Treaty of Lisbon in 2009, bear some trace of the idea that, although we are still very far from achieving anything resembling a universal league of peoples, we may indeed be said to have reached the stage at which "a violation of rights in one part of the world is felt everywhere."[56] The United Nations, wrote the idiosyncratic Sir Alfred Zimmern, classicist and a key policymaker during World War I who exercised a powerful influence on its ideological formation, was "the *res-publica* with which it is our duty to concern ourselves" and which "extends to the ends of the earth."[57] It was to be, in time, the expression of Kant's "cosmopolitan right."

What Kant's optimistic vision of the future notably lacked, however, was an explanation of how his new international order was to be organized and governed. Only once does he suggest that the "permanent congress of states" would be a Europe-wide court of arbitration which would allow the minsters of the individual states to look upon "the whole of Europe as a single federated state which they accepted as an arbiter, so to speak, in their public disputes."[58] But what institutional form this would take he does not say.

The year before the appearance of *Perpetual Peace*, Marie-Jean-Antoine-Nicolas de Caritat, marquis de Condorcet, a champion of equal rights for women and for all peoples of all races, and an abolitionist who devised the world's first state education system, looked forward into what he believed to be an imaginable future, when "the peoples [of the world] will learn that they cannot become conquerors without losing their liberty, that perpetual confederations are the only way to preserve their independence; that they should seek for security not for power." When that time arrived, nations would be driven by politics and morals to "share the goods created by nature and industry," and thereby finally bring to an end those "national hatreds," and in that distant epoch, "institutions, better conceived than those projects for perpetual peace which have occupied the leisure time and consoled the minds of certain philosophers, will accelerate the progress of this fraternity of nations."[59]

Both Kant and Condorcet lived in the shadow the French Revolution. Kant thought that he had seen in it, despite the horrors of the Terror, proof of the apparent progress of the human will.[60] Condorcet, who died in mysterious circumstances in a Jacobin cell in March 1794, despite being one of its most notable victims, believed it to be the culmination of "a revolution in the destinies of the human race." Both recognized that the Revolution had changed the political landscape not only of France, but of the whole of Europe, if not of the entire world; that it had, in Condorcet's words, embraced "the whole economy of society, to change all social relations, to penetrate to the smallest link of the political chain." Both too believed, for very different reasons, that the French had, in effect, succeeded in creating the world's first truly "representative republic," that the revolutionaries had been, in Kant's words:

> [the] first to dare, in a great nation...to maintain in the people their rights of sovereignty, that to obey only those laws whose mode of creation, even if it has been entrusted to their representatives, has been legitimated by their immediate approbation, and which, should [those representatives] threaten their rights or interests, they may always secure their reform, by a regular act of [their] sovereign will.[61]

The creation of the French Republic in 1792 had done all that. Kant, however, insisted that Louis XVI's decision to call the Estates General on May 5, 1789, so as to pass on the burden of an "embarrassment of large state debts" to his people had constituted a legitimate transfer of power, as a consequence of which the "monarch's sovereignty wholly disappeared...and passed to the people." The dissolution of the monarchy, the creation of the Republic, and all the revolutionary violence which followed had been a result of Louis's unwarranted attempt to wage war on his own people in order to recover what he had freely and voluntarily contracted away. In this the French Revolution had, therefore, been no revolution at all, but the unintended consequence of Louis's: "very serious error of judgment." It had also, although this was not something Kant makes comment on, created the French nation, the idea of which the French would subsequently seek to export to the rest of Europe.[62] France therefore had, in a few short years, created a model for the kind of state, united, democratic, and dependent upon a single source of shared political authority, out of which the future united Europe would eventually be built.

What Kant had not foreseen, however (he died in 1804), was that it would also be responsible for unleashing twenty-three years of warfare across most of Europe, as the new French Republic first fought off an alliance of European monarchies bent on its destruction and then, under Napoleon, set about uniting as much of Europe as it could conquer in order to transform the continent into a new French Empire. Like the Wars of Religion of the sixteenth and seventeenth centuries, these too were ideological wars, and they too would create a crisis, the response to which would also mark the beginning of a new project to unite the peoples of the "great republic of

Europe." It is a project that is still unfinished. But the European Union as
it is today is not, as it has so often been represented, the haphazard outcome
of a sometimes desperate bid to rescue the nations of the European continent
from the consequences of the devastation inflicted upon them by World War
II. The objectives, the aspirations, and the ideals which have driven its
"founders" and their successors—those are the creation of a long historical
process. This book is an attempt to tell their story.

1

Remaking the Great
European Family

I

On November 11, 1816, in the drawing room of Longwood House on the island of St Helena, Napoleon Bonaparte told his loyal follower, the former atlas-maker turned imperial amanuensis Emmanuel de Las Cases, that his "greatest idea" had been "the agglomeration the concentration of the same geographical peoples which revolutions and politics had broken down. I would have liked," he claimed, "to make of each of these peoples one and the same national body." Then, he went on, it would have been possible to:

> conceive of a chimera of a beautiful ideal of civilization. For under such conditions one would have more chance of distributing everywhere a unity of laws, of opinions, of sentiments, of points of view and interests. Then, perhaps, with the aid of an enlightenment diffused throughout the continent it would have been possible to dream for the great European family, the application of the American Congress or of the Amphictyonies of Greece.[1]

We need not, of course, entirely believe him. By the winter of 1816 Napoleon had already spent nearly a year of enforced inactivity on St Helena, a volcanic outcrop in the mid-Atlantic, and one of the remotest places on earth, to which he had been exiled in perpetuity after his final defeat at Waterloo, and where he was to die, in somewhat mysterious circumstances, on May 5, 1821. His great victories were now far behind him, and in the long conversations he held with Las Cases, he was doing his best to create an elevated impression of his career and what he saw (or imagined to have been) his calling and objectives. This, he hoped, was how history would remember him: not as Samuel Taylor Coleridge's "upstart Corsican" but as the great unifier, pacifier, and ultimately the liberator of a fragmented, disordered, bellicose Europe. Las Cases, who had followed him from Waterloo and who was nothing if not devoted to preserving, when not enhancing, his master's image, was also not above putting high-sounding words into his mouth.

We need not believe him; but neither should this claim be attributed to simple self-aggrandizement. It is easy enough to dismiss Napoleon as an opportunist, a cynical pragmatist willing to depict himself as a new Solomon or a new Mohammed (or a new Alexander, a new Caesar) or a new Charlemagne to win the allies he needed, or more mundanely to secure lucrative positions for members of his close family.

It is easy, too, to deny him any substantial political vision beyond a simple primordial quest for personal grandeur. Even his vision of a new Amphictyonic League was ultimately directed towards securing his own personal ambitions. "The first sovereign," he told Las Cases, "who in the midst of the first great conflict embraces the cause of peoples in good faith, will find himself at the head of all Europe, and will be able to attempt whatever he pleases."[2] "He wished to create nothing but his own fame," wrote the writer, philosopher, politician, diplomat, and historian François René de Chateaubriand, who believed that he had good reason to dislike him. "He seemed to understand that his mission would be brief; that a torrent that came from such a height would soon run dry. He was in a great hurry to enjoy and abuse his own glory as fleeting youth."[3] He was a "fantastic creature made up of lies."[4] But then, as Chateaubriand recognized, had that really been all he was, he would never have been what he had already become by the the 1840s, when Chateaubriand was writing, "a legendary figure made up of the whims of poets, the calculations of soldiers and people's tales," a sort of latter-day Alexander or Charlemagne. And it was, Chateaubriand insisted, "this fantastic hero who has become the real person while all the other depictions of him disappear."[5] Goethe too, who had a brief interview with him in 1808—on which he wryly commented, "In an attempt to flatter the Germans, to whom he was obliged to do so much harm, he had learned a little about our literature"—wrote of him after his encounter that "It might well be said of him, that he was found in a state of continual enlightenment. On this account, his destiny was more brilliant than any the world had seen before him, or perhaps will ever see after him."[6] He was, in the view of Georg Wilhelm Friedrich Hegel, who had seen him riding past in Jena in 1806, and famously called him this "world soul [Weltseele] on horseback," the "living instrument of the world mind," the supreme example of those whose "individuality," while always acting for purely individual ends, nevertheless succeeds in achieving universal ones.[7]

It is easy, too, to concede, as even his most dogged opponents were pre-pared to do, that he was a brilliant strategist and charismatic leader ("I can hardly conceive of anything greater," wrote the Duke of Wellington, half in admiration, half in despair, "than Napoleon at the head of an army") who, by employing mass conscription for the first time, utterly transformed what had once been a conflict between rulers into a massive confrontation between entire peoples. Napoleon had understood that if the people of France were finally to become the "nation" the Revolution had proclaimed them to be, then one, possibly the only means by which this could be achieved was by transforming them into an army. No one had seen what the future consequences of this would be more clearly than the greatest of all the modern theoreticians of war, the Prussian Carl von Clausewitz. After witnessing the destruction of his homeland at the battle of Jena in 1806, he wrote, part in anger, part in awe, that now it was no longer "the King who wars on a king, not an army which wars on an army but a people which wars on another, and the king and army are contained in the people."[8] Napoleon changed the nature of warfare, and in doing so he changed the relationship between civil society and the armed forces created to defend and extend it. Conscription now became inseparable from the right each citizen was supposed to hold as a member of the nation.[9] He also dramati-cally and decisively changed the nature of all future relationships between the states of Europe. And despite himself he transformed utterly the shape and structure of those nations themselves. From the battle of Marengo in 1800 between Revolutionary France and Austria until the surrender of Nazi Germany in 1945, European identity and the struggle for European unity would be played out as a dual response to war and the nationalism which warfare had created. And the originator of this conflict was Napoleon Bonaparte.

II

Certainly Napoleon was quixotic and protean. His actions, if not his words, paralleled in seven years the trajectory of the Roman Republic over five hundred. In 1796, when he took command of the army of Italy, he was a convinced republican, the champion of the rights of man and the broader principles of the Revolution keen to export them throughout Europe and even beyond. He remained a loyal republican even after the coup of 18 Brumaire (November 9, 1799) which disposed of the ineffective Directory (the five-man executive council which had taken power after the end of the Thermidorian Convention in October 1795) had elevated him to the position of "First Consul" and de facto absolute ruler of France. In August 1802, however, he made himself, in imitation of Julius Caesar, "Consul for Life" and, two years later, by means of a rigged plebiscite, transformed the "one and indivisible French Republic" into a hereditary empire, with himself as emperor. The analogy was not lost on contemporaries; nor was its possible outcome. In November 1800, Napoleon's brother Lucien Bonaparte, then minister of the interior—presumably in preparation for 1802—commissioned a pamphlet comparing Napoleon warmly to Caesar and warning against the inevitably disastrous consequences that any repetition of the Ides of March would inflict upon the French.[10] In making this move from consul to emperor, Napoleon changed dramatically the political order of Revolutionary France and effectively put an end to the Revolution as such. He was, in the words of the English historian E. H. Carr, writing in 1945— shortly after the fall of what he hoped would be the last—"in many senses the first 'popular' dictator."[11] His political career was indeed not unlike those of the charismatic leaders we have subsequently come to call "populists;" and like most populists his actions are hard to evaluate from any one political perspective. He encouraged a form of refeudalization, tried unsuccessfully to reconquer Haiti and to reintroduce slavery, created a new hereditary aristocracy of service, concluded a concordat with the Church (but refused to provide his armies with priests), and cajoled Pope Pius VII to attend his imperial coronation in Notre Dame on December 2, 1804 (but only as a bystander). He was, said Chateaubriand, the "greatest organiser of aristocracy within democracy" there has ever been.[12]

Yet, for all that, the policies which he implemented, or attempted to implement, were never merely reactionary, nor ever entirely self-serving. The new French empire was to be an empire in name, but it was never to be a monarchy as it had been understood under the *ancien régime*. Despite the transformation from First Consul of the Republic into "Emperor of the French," he remained for many, as he had been for Thomas Carlyle, "our last Great Man"—even if not so great as Cromwell—even if, in the end, he "apostatized from his old faith in Facts, took to believing in Semblances, strove to connect himself with Austrian Dynasties, Popedoms, with the old

Feudalities which he once saw clearly to be false."[13] Or, rather more prosaically and rather more precisely, in Ralph Waldo Emerson's words, he was:

> the agent or attorney of the middle class of modern society; of the throng who fill the markets, shops, counting-houses, manufactories, ships, of the modern world, aiming to be rich. He was the agitator, the destroyer of prescription, the internal improver, the liberal, the radical, the inventor of means, the opener of doors and markets, the subverter of monopoly and abuse.[14]

He was, perhaps, all of these things. But he also, *pace* Chateaubriand, did have a vision of a future not only for himself, not only for France, but also, as he repeated time and again, for Europe. True, it took various forms and was never anything as far-reaching as he told Las Cases. But he spoke often, if sporadically, throughout his career, of his desire to unite—or, as he seems often to have seen it, reunite—what he called the "European family." "With very slight shades of variety," he told Louis Antoine Bourrienne, his private secretary and at one time his chief of police, in 1802, "France, Spain, England, Italy, and Germany, have the same manners and customs, the same religion, and the same dress.... With the exception of Turkey, Europe is merely a province of the world, and our warfare is but civil strife." Three years later, on February 15, 1805, he announced to the *Corps législatif:* "It is my task, our task, the task of the most gentle, most enlightened, most human of peoples to remind the civilized nations of Europe that they are part of one family and that the energies they engage in their civil conflicts are a blow to the common prosperity."[15]

Later, while in exile on St Helena, Napoleon would reflect that, although he had perhaps gone about achieving these ends in the wrong way, and certainly had not fully succeeded in realizing what he persisted in calling his "system," "never was a project so favourable to the interests of civilization conceived with more disinterested intentions, or so near being carried into execution."[16] In his own estimation of himself, he had been the prime mover who had roused from their torpor the peoples of Europe buried for centuries beneath monarchical tyranny. His conquests and reforms, incomplete and piecemeal though they were, had, in his view, set in motion a process which could now never be reversed. "The agglomeration [of the peoples of Europe] will take place in the course of events," he informed Las Cases; "the first impetus has been given, and I do think that after my fall and the disappearance of my system, there will be no other great equilibrium possible, than the agglomeration and confederation of the great peoples [of Europe]."[17] As a prediction, it was overstated and exaggerated. But it was far from being entirely wrong. He had seen clearly what, within a century, would become for many an obvious commonplace: "The nations of Europe have every reason in the world to put an end to their wars and to create a federation. Europe is a province of the world, and war among Europeans is a civil war."

It is unsurprising that one of the most insistent of the champions for European unity in the period after 1919, the quixotic, eccentric, but also widely influential creator of the Pan-Europa movement, the Austrian–Japanese Count Richard von Coudenhove-Kalergi (of whom more later), should have used this quotation as an epigraph for his book *A United Europe* of 1939. "Napoleon," he wrote, "was the Emperor of Europe. Had Napoleon won at Leipzig, Europe would in all probability have been a federation today." The French Empire, he knew, would not have survived Napoleon, but he was firmly convinced that the "political and economic union of the Continent" would.[18]

III

Napoleon's claim was always that his armies were armies of liberation, that his objective had always been to free the peoples of the various nations of Europe from their despotic monarchs. Like most of the would-be liberators of mankind before and since, he was convinced that, at heart, all peoples, once they had been sufficiently enlightened, could not possibly want but for one thing. In this case it was his own peculiar version of "enlightened absolute monarchy," legitimated by the (supposed) consent of the people.[19] As he told his brother Jérôme, the short-lived king of Westphalia (a kingdom made up of Hesse-Cassel, Brunswick, and parts of Hanover and Saxony) in 1807:

> The benefits of the Code Napoléon, the publicity of procedures, the establishment of juries, should be the distinctive characteristics of your monarchy. And, to be honest, I trust more to their effects to extend and strengthen your power to the results of the greatest victories. What people would submit itself again to an arbitrary government after having enjoyed the benefits of a wise and liberal administration?[20]

Wise and liberal it may indeed have been meant to be. And some of the peoples of Europe did indeed look upon the Napoleonic conquests in this light. As one British observer, probably James Mill, the Scottish utilitarian, economist, and historian, and father of John Stuart Mill, remarked contemptuously in 1808, "Bonaparte met no opposition from the people whose countries he overran ... who seem to view the fall of their old governments with the same apathy they would do that of their old houses ... in the certain prospect of having them speedily replaced by new and more commodious ones."[21]

Napoleon's conquests, however, were indubitably *conquests*. And Mill (if it was he) in his bitterness at the reluctance of the other nations of Europe to resist Napoleon as fiercely as Britain, was exaggerating. In fact, the liberating French armies were rarely welcomed with open arms even by the most "oppressed" of peoples; and those who did welcome him more often belonged to the liberal bourgeoisie and enlightened aristocracy, as in Naples in 1799 or the *afrancescados* in Spain in 1808, than to the laboring poor to whom he often appealed or even Emerson's "middle class of modern society." Nor is it very likely, as the great *littérateuse* and longtime companion of Benjamin Constant, Madame de Staël, claimed to believe, that the peoples of the territories Napoleon invaded had looked upon the advancing French armies, for better or for worse, as the future "propagators of the ideas of Montesquieu, Rousseau, or Voltaire," only to discover that while they might find traces of the "opinions of these great men in Bonaparte's instruments of power," these had served "only to stamp out what he called their prejudices and not to establish a single regenerative principle."[22]

Napoleon himself may have genuinely believed, as he complained to the Senate of Bamberg in 1806, that it had been all the "evil in Europe" which had conspired continuously to "undo the plans we have made for the tranquillity of Europe."[23] But he was also seemingly insensitive to the possibility that one person's conception of "liberty" might for another be a form of servitude. In October 1812, as they sat together wrapped in furs on the retreat from Moscow, Napoleon remarked to his general, Armand Augustin Louis de Caulaincourt, that his war on Russia had been waged "in the interests—if those interests are rightly judged—of Old Europe and civilization." Caulaincourt, who was blunt but not generally given to political reflection, replied:

> As a matter of fact, it is Your Majesty they fear. It is Your Majesty who is the cause of everyone's anxiety and prevents them from seeing other dangers. The governments are afraid there is going to be a World State.... All these causes and considerations, which are perhaps partly hidden from Your Majesty, make their hatred of you a national force.[24]

The fear of "universal empire" which had loomed over the European political imagination since the seventeenth century seemed finally to have found concrete form in Napoleon's "true French Empire," the hatred of which would indeed be the source of that "national force" which for the rest of the century would drive all before it.[25]

However, in so far as Napoleon can be said to have had any very clear strategic idea of what this "true French Empire" would one day look like when it was complete, it most closely resembled a greater France in which the states of Europe, rather than being quasi-autonomous, as in the "American Congress," were to be transformed into a series of departments of France, in much the same way as the remnants of the former French Empire—Martinique, Guadeloupe, Mayotte, French Guiana, and Réunion—now are. The Netherlands, the cities of the Hanseatic League, and part of northern Italy, the formerly Venetian Ionian Islands, were all at one time or another divided up in this manner. In 1798, while on his way to Egypt, Napoleon stopped off at Malta, ousted the Knights of St John after a brief skirmish, and transformed the island into a department of France. The occupation lasted only eight days, but Napoleon found the time to organize the native Maltese inhabitants into French administrative districts, arrange for thirty of the most gifted male children to be sent to France for a decent education, divide the city of Valletta into arrondissements, and prepare a new constitution for the island. A small number of French troops were then allotted to guard this latest addition to the republic. (Two years later they were ousted by the British, under whose control Malta remained until 1964.) This, for Napoleon, was the best, indeed the only political future to which any people could reasonably aspire. And he clung to it even as the entire imperial edifice was visibly beginning to crumble. "It is wrong of them to complain," Napoleon remarked peevishly to Caulaincourt of the Poles. "I administer them like Departments of France."

It was, above all, the Napoleonic Code, the *Code Napoléon*—or the "Civil Code of the French People," as it was initially called—on which he ultimately pinned his ambitions for the creation, or recreation, of the European family. Like all the great unifiers and empire builders before him, he looked upon the creation of a single body of law, consistent across all the territories of the empire, as the most powerful instrument of unification available to any ruler. If the "family of Europe" was to be reunited once again through force of arms, coercion, and collusion, it could only be sustained by means of the law. As Madame de Staël, whom Napoleon banished from Paris in 1803, observed acidly, what she described as "that great regularity in Napoleon's despotism" had always consisted in introducing first conscription, then war taxes, then the code.[26]

The code was created, between 1801 and 1804, by four eminent jurists led by Jean-Jacques-Régis de Cambacérès, Duke of Parma, regicide, and former Jacobin, although Napoleon himself is said to have presided over the discussions of its content, sometimes line by line.[27] Its initial objective was to replace the chaotic patchwork of laws which had been passed by the various revolutionary assemblies since 1789 and finally to sweep away all that still remained in some regions of the old pre-revolutionary customary laws, the most famous and most systematic being the *Coutume de Paris*. Napoleon's ambitions for his new code, however, went far beyond merely tidying up the legal disorder within France. Napoleon was a conqueror, but like the emperors of the Roman world with whom he so often compared himself, he also hoped to leave behind him a changed world, a world made modern and efficient, liberal and just. The model he had before him was always the great codification of the Roman law in the sixth century CE under the Roman emperor Justinian. It was intended to be, as Justinian's had been, a means of erasing the differences between the various peoples Napoleon hoped to conquer. It was to be not merely a code for France, but "a European system, a European Code of Laws, a European judiciary," and it alone would ensure that "there would be but one people in Europe."[28] It was the code which would have made possible a "Europe... divided into nationalities, freely formed and free internally," in which, "peace between States would have become easier: the United States of Europe would become a possibility." As such, and despite all attempts to erase it in the former Napoleonic states outside France, it provided the basis for the private law systems of parts of Italy, the Rhineland, the Netherlands, Belgium, Spain (as well as a number of Latin American states), Portugal, and until 1946 Poland. It has also exercised an influence, not always benign, on the legal systems of Egypt, the Lebanon, and Canada, and the state of Louisiana.

IV

The peace, security, and stability which Napoleon wished upon Europe never came. In October 1813, at the battle of Leipzig (dubbed by the Germans the "Battles of the Nations"), Napoleon faced a coalition of the armies of Russia, Prussia, Austria, and Sweden. Some 180,000 French soldiers and Germans from the so-called "Confederation of the Rhine" a collection of client states of the French Empire, fought about 320,000 allies. Over 100,000 men died in the battle, and Napoleon suffered his first major defeat. "A year ago, all Europe marched with us," he told the French Senate on his return to Paris; "today all Europe marches against us." The coalition, strengthened by the defection of the "Confederation of the Rhine," then marched on France. They entered Paris on March 31, 1814, and on April 20, Napoleon, now stripped of all his French titles and replaced by the portly, ineffectual Louis XVIII, left Fontainebleau for exile on the island of Elba off the Tuscan coast—transformed for the occasion into an independent principality. There he was allowed to keep his imperial title, given a meagre allowance by the French government and sovereignty over 94 square miles and some 12,000 people. As he complained later to Las Cases, "When you are on a small island, once you have set in motion the machinery of civilization, there is nothing left to do but perish of boredom."[29]

In September, when Napoleon seemed to be safely out of the way, the representatives of all the greater and many of the lesser powers of Europe began to gather in Vienna. Their initial purpose was to ratify the Peace of Paris signed on May 30 by France itself and the four so-called "Great Powers"—Prussia, Russia, Great Britain, and Austria—joined by Spain, Portugal, and Sweden, which had, or so its signatories then believed, finally put an end to Napoleon.[30] The Congress of Vienna was, superficially at least, a celebration of the end of the French Revolution and the Napoleonic Wars, and of the prospect of a return to the stability of the old order. It was, as one modern historian has described it, "a joyous ritual cleansing" attended by two emperors, four kings, eleven ruling princes, some 200 plenipotentiaries, and a gaggle of uninvited emissaries from bodies as varied as the Jews of Frankfurt and the publishers of Europe.[31] It did not, however, last long.

On March 1, 1815, Napoleon left Elba, accompanied by a handful of troops. He landed at Golfe-Juan, near Cannes in Provence, and made his way north across the foothills of the Alps by a route still known today as the Route Napoléon. He met with very little resistance, and most of the troops sent to oppose him joined him instead, so that by the time he arrived in Paris on March 20, he entered the city at the head of what was, in effect, a conquering army. Louis XVIII had prudently fled the previous day.

Having now realized, however, that even if he were himself to survive his defeat at Leipzig and exile, the First Empire would not, he sought to recast himself as a new "Messiah of Peace" and champion of the rights of all peoples everywhere.[32] Exile on Elba, he declared, however brief, had changed him, although, as he later complained to Las Cases, none of the powers of Europe was prepared to believe him—much, he thought, to their future detriment. "I am not a man for half measures," he protested. Had he been allowed to stay, he "would have been as sincerely the monarch of the constitution and of peace, as I had been of absolute sway and great enterprises." And he added wistfully, in any case, "my resources were no longer the same; and, besides, I had only defeated and conquered in my own defense: this is a truth which time will more fully develop every day."[33]

One person, however, who seems to have at least half believed him was the great liberal political theorist, novelist, and man of letters Benjamin Constant. Constant, who as a member of the Tribunat from 1799 until 1802 had denounced "the regime of servitude and silence" Napoleon had instituted since the creation of the Consulate, had been driven into semivoluntary exile in Switzerland in 1802. In April 1814, with the arrival of the Coalition, he returned to France, now convinced, or at least willing to believe, that although he had once called him "more odious that Attila the Hun and Genghis Khan," a humbled Napoleon might be persuaded to institute a new liberal government along broadly British parliamentary lines. Constant was also, he wrote later, certain that as France was now faced by foreign invasion, abandoning Napoleon at this juncture would have, in effect, meant abandoning the *patrie*.[34] Immediately on his return to Paris Napoleon ordered "An Additional Act to the Constitutions of the Empire" to be drawn up. The real inspiration behind this was Benjamin Constant, for which reason it was referred to mockingly as "*la benjamine*." It is not a markedly liberal document. It retains all the trappings of the empire and confirms Napoleon and his family in their former positions. As Chateaubriand acidly observed, Napoleon had "dressed up the new *democratic* constitution with chambers of peers and a crown."[35] The bicameral system advocated by the Act did however reflect, in part at least, the British constitution, which Constant like Montesquieu so admired, with not only a hereditary upper chamber but also an elective lower one. The Act was adopted by a plebiscite on April 22, 1815, and promulgated at a ceremony held in the Champ de Mars on June 1. In the preamble to the Act, which was clearly written by Napoleon himself, he claimed once again that, ever since the coup of 18 Brumaire—described as his calling "by the will of the French people to the government of the state"—"We have had as an objective the organization of a great European federal system, which we have adopted as conforming to the spirit of the century, and favorable to the progress of civilization."[36]

Had Napoleon in fact succeeded in refurbishing his image as the true heir of the Revolution and in recasting the empire as an international constitutional monarchy, the future of Europe might have been very different. In the end, however, the so-called Hundred Days (they were in fact III) turned out to be little more than an interlude. Within hours of learning of Napoleon's escape from Elba, the Great Powers began preparing to frustrate whatever plans he might have. On March 13 they issued a statement declaring Napoleon to be "the enemy and disturber of the peace of the world," and on March 27 they concluded a formal alliance in which each pledged 15,000 troops to prevent Napoleon from ever occupying the French throne. As the Duke of Wellington assured the British representative Viscount Castlereagh, all the delegates at Vienna were "united in their efforts to support the system established by the Peace of Paris" and to bring "an early conclusion to the business of the Congress in order that the whole and undivided attention and exertion of all may be directed against the common enemy."[37] Napoleon's attempt to persuade the Congress that his return was an internal French matter, that only the French people had the right to choose a French ruler, and that they had clearly chosen him was met with the reply that the demands of international law transcended a nation's right to choose its own rulers. Significantly, this was the first time that a group of states had arrogated to themselves the right to intervene in the affairs of another not in their own particular interests, but in the interests of the greater good of Europe.[38]

Three months later, on June 18, 1815, Napoleon faced the Duke of Wellington and General Gebhard Leberecht von Blücher at Waterloo, and the First Empire finally vanished forever.

V

Napoleon's commitment to some kind of unified Europe was a constant refrain throughout his entire career. The claims he made to Las Cases on November 11, 1816 on St Helena are, however, significantly different from any that preceded them. For unlike them, they contain two references to specific political orders. The "American Congress" was familiar enough. But "the Amphictyonies of Greece" would probably have been obscure to many of Las Cases's readers. During the eighteenth century, they became a useful and, of course, historically uplifting model not only for any possible federal order, but for what was believed to be the only just and binding legal relationship between the settler populations of the British and French overseas colonies and their respective metropolises. It was this which Benjamin Franklin had in mind when he delivered his famous three-hour testimony before the House of Commons in February 1776, denouncing the British Crown for having violated the distinction between "internal" and "external" spheres of legislation—and of taxation.[39] After the Revolution the Amphictyonic Leagues became for some a model, for others a warning of what the government of a new United States might eventually become. "We should consider the Council of the Amphictyons as the Congress of the United States of Greece," declared James Wilson in 1790:

> From the moment of its establishment, the interests of their country became the common concern of all the people of Greece. The different states, of which the union was composed, formed only one and the same republick: and this union it was, which made the Greeks so formidable afterwards to the barbarians.[40]

James Madison, however, who had a firmer grasp on both the forms of government and the actual fate of the Amphictyonies, likened them to the "Confederation of the American States" of 1781 which he was attempting to replace, and warned that "it happened but too often...that the deputies of the strongest cities awed and corrupted those of the weaker; and that judgement went in favour of the most powerful party," resulting in the end in "the weakness, the disorders, and finally the destruction of the confederacy."[41]

We cannot know how much Napoleon or Las Cases knew of this. Most of Napoleon's other scattered claims about his objectives and policies would suggest that anything resembling the United States or the Great Amphictyonic League had been far from his mind. Although he claimed that the "true French Empire" was to be the "federated states" of Europe, his objective, since at least 1803, seems to have been to build an empire with France at its head, himself as emperor, and his extended family as the rulers of its various dependencies. As he told Las Cases in a moment of candor, all he had done had been to work for the day when, "with God's help, a Frenchman traveling through Europe would always think himself at home."[42] In all assemblies of states, he once said, there had always to exist "a superior power which dominates all the other powers, with enough authority to force them to live in harmony with one another," and in the case of the putative European federation France was, of course, the "best place for that purpose."[43] In the end, Nietzsche may well have been right in his assessment of Napoleon's political vision—if it can be so called—that "he wished, as we know, a united Europe so that Europe might be master of the world."[44] But it was always to be a Europe united under France.

Napoleon was not alone in envisaging a unified Europe under the aegis of a single nation. In 1807, in his *Addresses to the German Nation*, the German philosopher Johann Gottlieb Fichte entertained much the same, albeit deeply unpolitical dream of a similar future for Europe, only now with a united Germany as the master nation. Later, in 1943, Hitler, one of Napoleon's most ardent admirers, would repeat the claim that Europe should "seize the leadership of the world," with Germany now as the sole nation able to give to the continent a "coherent structure."[45] As we shall see, some version of the conundrum this created—how to build a federation of pre-existing nations in which no one came to dominate all the others—was to dog the quest for European unity from his day until ours. For all that, Richard Coudenhove-Kalergi was surely right in his claim that the idea of a united Europe which Napoleon had "renewed was no longer to be downed: it persisted in the reactionary, as in the revolutionary camp, under kings as under peoples"[46]

VI

Napoleon's legacy is scattered and uncertain. He remains a symbol of past glories for some, an enduring figure of national loathing for others. He was worshiped as a god by Chinese monks and Madagascan rulers, became an inspiration for the "Liberator" Simón Bolívar, who was in Paris for his coronation (and the proud owner of his copy of Rousseau's *The Social Contract*), was transformed into a legend by Native Americans, and was hailed as an inspiration by Irish republicans and Polish patriots.[47] For others, the British in particular, less persuaded by the self-image and wary of the revolutionary republican personality which was never far beneath the surface, the "upstart Corsican" was and remains nothing but the "opportunist incarnate."[48] For one former French prime minister (of the right), he was the architect of a system to "replace inheritance by merit, and in so doing [he] created an aristocracy open to modernization"; and although that system may have "momentarily failed," it remains nevertheless the place "where the future of the world is to be found."[49] For another (of the left), he was responsible for "Bonapartism," a form of populist authoritarianism which has run like a plague through French politics since the coup of Napoleon III in 1851 to Marshal Pétain and the creation of Vichy in 1940, and possibly now to Marine Le Pen on the right, and Jean-Luc Mélenchon on the left, the malignant stuff of a legend whose nostalgia for past glories has ultimately hampered France's ability to contribute to "the renewal of the vision of Europe."[50]

On any dispassionate historical reckoning, Napoleon's administrative failures outweigh his successes. He failed to liberate Europe entirely from the clutches of kings and priests. He failed to modernize Egypt by transforming it into a happy blend of the Sharia and the rights of man. He failed in the first instance to create a series of "sister republics" across Europe governed according to French Revolutionary principles and failed in the second to build a lasting French Empire ruled over by his extended family. Most of the administrative, structural, and economic reforms he introduced, or tried to introduce, into the areas he overran vanished as soon as he had.

His most enduring legacy was to be found elsewhere, was altogether entirely unintended, and came into being very much *malgré lui*. It was the one that, in his lifetime, had been most responsible for his undoing, and was instrumental in the shaping of modern Europe. For the one thing that Napoleon had no intention of exporting to the peoples of Europe was precisely the French revolutionary project to build the nation into what the historian, biblical scholar, linguist, and philosopher Ernest Renan was to call "a soul, a spiritual principle."[51] Napoleon's actions, however (as opposed to his words), had the effect of generating an ideology which had not previously existed, or at least not self-consciously and certainly not in the form it was finally to take throughout most of Europe. That ideology was nationalism. Napoleon himself was dismissive of what he called "the patriotism of the people," however hard he sometimes tried to harness it to his own purposes. In 1797, in a bid to control the Venetian Senate, he attempted to arouse, or perhaps instill, nationalist sentiments among the inhabitants of the Ionian Islands, which had been under Venetian rule since the fourteenth century, by sending a "distinguished man of letters" whose task was to "manufacture manifestos" to "stir up the shades of Athens and Sparta." When he quarreled with the Austrian emperor in 1809, he issued a proclamation to the Hungarians reminding them that "you have national customs and a national language; you boast of distant and illustrious origins: take up then once again your existence as a nation"; and when he invaded Russia, he attempted to enlist the help of the Poles by appealing to their national past. "Show yourselves worthy of your forefathers," he told a Polish deputation; "they ruled the House of Brandenburg; they were the masters of Moscow... they freed Christianity from the yoke of the Turks."

But although they might have served his purposes, and although he accepted that they had created an "equilibrium of power" between the rulers and the ruled which now made swift victories of the kind enjoyed by Alexander the Great impossible, national loyalties had not, as he pointed out, prevented the division of Poland or the "spoliation of many"; nor would they "prevent the destruction of the Ottoman Empire."[52] He believed strongly in the power of rational choice over sentiment. He was convinced, as he said time and time again, that if asked to choose between a liberal, efficient, and essentially egalitarian regime of the kind he claimed to be offering, even if that regime were introduced and run by a foreign invader, and the dismal, retrograde, tyrannical, national government with which they had always been familiar, a people would always opt for the former. That was, after all, what the peoples of the Roman Empire had chosen to do. Roman arms had secured the empire; but it had been Roman law, Roman administration, Roman roads, Roman engineering, and the *Pax Romana* which these had brought that had ensured its survival. For a man who set such store by loyalty among his officers and his men, he looked upon the loyalty of a people to a nation as merely an obstacle in the path of progress. It was ultimately to prove his most grievous error. As the influential English historian John Robert Seeley—Regius Professor of Modern History at Cambridge—remarked in 1886, "it was not Napoleon, but resistance to Napoleon which had such a bracing effect upon Europe, and which by arming the peoples against tyranny had laid the foundation of European liberty."[53]

By 1814 the fear of a "World State" against which Caulaincourt had warned his master had indeed transformed resentment against Napoleon, the intransigent, imperious conqueror blindly indifferent to the possibility that "freedom" might mean different things to different peoples, into a true "national force." Napoleon's mistake, observed the Swiss jurist Johann Caspar Bluntschli, Professor of Political Science at the University of Heidelberg, in 1895, had been to have "paid too little regard to foreign nationalities"; in so doing, he had gone "back on the course the Romans had adopted. He wished to organize Europe as a vast international State, with individual states as its members," thus hoping to do "in one generation what the Romans had taken centuries to do."[54] But the world had changed since the days of the Caesars. The Romans had overrun tribes; Napoleon had tried to overrun states. The empires of antiquity, as Benjamin Constant observed from exile in 1813, for all their destructive powers, had nevertheless made no attempt to change, much less destroy, "men's strongest attachments: their ways of life, their customs, their gods." They may have deprived their subject peoples of political autonomy, but they had left their beliefs, their ways of life, even to some degree their laws intact, and they had made no attempt to diminish "the feeling of fatherland" in the countries they occupied. Napoleon, by contrast, in his ambition to reunite "the family of Europe" had hoped precisely to sweep away all those things and to replace them with the "same code of law, the same measures, and the same regulations," over the entire continent, so that, in Constant's estimation, "the proud eye of power may travel without meeting any unevenness that could offend or limit its view." Uniformity, Constant concluded, was "the immediate and inseparable consequence of the spirit of conquest."[55] In Constant's vision, such an empire could not last, opposed as it was to what he saw as the diverse and individual private interests of the peoples of the modern nations of which it was composed. It would, he prophesied—accurately, as it turned out—"become the object of universal horror. Every opinion, every desire, every hatred would threaten it and sooner or later those hatreds, those opinions, and those desires would explode and engulf it."[56] Napoleon may indeed have succeeded in usurping power throughout Europe; yet even if this had been, in Constant's words, "sanctioned, recognised as legitimate even by those in whose interests it was never to recognise it," even if it had indeed succeeded in "assembling vast forces to inspire fear, sophism to dazzle people's minds, treaties to reassure their consciences," even if the governments it had overthrown, "be they republican, be they monarchial...were without apparent hope or visible resources"—even if all this had in fact been the case, still the nations to which the vanquished had belonged "survived in the hearts of their peoples." Certainly, most of the peoples of Europe had proved, indeed, to be largely impervious to what Robespierre had called "armed missionaries"; and so powerful had been the attachment of the conquered peoples to their native rulers that it had taken only one battle, the battle of Leipzig in October 1813, and the whole edifice Napoleon had constructed had collapsed so rapidly that now, reflected Constant, barely six months later, in many places "the traveler would be hard put to find any trace of it."[57] In every case, Seeley remarked, all that Napoleon had destroyed was the state. The nation, however, had remained intact and "proceeded to put forth out of its own vitality a new form of state."[58]

But what exactly were those still amorphous nations? What Napoleon had had to face, and inadvertently greatly enhanced, in Spain, in Poland, in Italy, in the Netherlands, in Germany, even indirectly in Britain, was not the kind of attachment to hearth and home, to family and kin, however fierce, that Julius Caesar had faced in Gaul or Trajan in Dacia; that, at least, had existed among all peoples, and among some for centuries. What Napoleon had faced was, instead, the beginnings of something new, what the intellec-tual architect of Italian unity, Giuseppe Mazzini (whom we shall meet again), tellingly called, "the principle of nationality." It was the recognition that all these sentiments of affiliation and attachments to home, religion, kin, place, and institutions might be coalesced into one particular political form separate and independent from—although, in particular for Mazzini, not necessarily hostile to—other forms.[59] The political force Napoleon had helped to bring into being was, furthermore, far more than an isolated, spo-radic, uncoordinated resistance to the alien and unknown. It had, wrote Mazzini, not been the "brute force of kings" which had finally brought down Napoleon, but the very idea of the nation which he had "offended with his arrogance," that idea which now constituted "the soul of a new Era."[60] In so doing, he had, said Friedrich Nietzsche in 1882, created the instrument of his own undoing. The "national movement," Nietzsche con-cluded, was "nothing more than the reaction to Napoleon's efforts and would not exist without Napoleon."[61]

And it was with this "national movement" that a new project to unite the peoples of Europe was to begin.

2

The Birth of the Nation

I

With the final defeat of Napoleon and his dispatch to the fastness of St Helena, the menace of the Revolution seemed to be at an end. The victorious allies celebrated in Vienna with balls, dinners, concerts, operas, and hunting parties, and, on November 29, 1814, with a performance of Beethoven's Seventh Symphony, Rogether with another orchestral piece, *Wellington's Victory*, filled with simulated canon shots and special effects, and the cantata *Der glorreiche Augenblick* ("The Glorious Moment"), specially composed for the occasion, all of which were conducted by the composer himself—aging and now almost totally deaf.[1] On January 21 of the following year, so as to underscore the Congress's dedication to the cause of monarchy, a memorial service was held in the Stephansdom, the great cathedral in the centre of the city, for Louis XVI of France on the anniversary of his execution. A few weeks earlier, during a ball at the Hofburg palace, Castlereagh had leaned forward and whispered in the ear of the Russian tsar Alexander I, "il commence l'âge d'or."[2]

The most lasting consequence of the Hundred Days had been to strengthen what before 1814 had been a somewhat shaky alliance of the European states. As the Russian tsar Alexander I wrote to the now newly re-enthroned Louis XVIII, "the first effect that this event has had on the sovereigns assembled at Vienna is to tighten the bonds to which Europe owes the peace and France the tranquility it was beginning to enjoy under its legitimate king."[3] Napoleon's sudden return and, more startling still, the ease with which he managed to persuade the French people and the French armies to reinstall him, together with the still-smoldering fear that the spirit of "the delirium of revolutionary passions" might "menace anew the security of Europe"—as indeed it was to do in 1848—persuaded the allies to establish what has come to be known as the "Concert of Europe" or "Congress system": the proposal that in the future an open-ended series of conferences should be held at regular intervals to maintain the "balance of power" within Europe, to deal with all possible international crises, and to ensure the continuation of government by "the monarchical principle" throughout the continent.[4] "Twenty-two years of war," wrote Giuseppe Mazzini in 1849, "had worn out Europe." When the "long-cherished peace" finally arrived, "those who had brought it were praised, no matter who they were. Blessed by victory, the old dynasties resumed their interrupted domination."[5]

But if any very clear objective arose out of the congress, it was not, as Mazzini supposed, simply to turn back the clock to where it had stood in 1789. For Napoleon's attempts, inchoate though they finally were, to bring about a federal, united Europe, had had, paradoxically, the effect of persuading many that although nothing resembling the American Congress or the Amphictyonic Leagues was a suitable model for the new post-revolutionary Europe, something more coherent, more likely to endure than the older treaty system established in 1648 by the Peace of Westphalia, was urgently required if the continent was not to slide back once again into intermittent internecine warfare, and if the specter of revolutionary republicanism was finally to be laid to rest. In 1888, the international lawyer Sir Travers Twiss, former Queen's Advocate General and salaried champion of Leopold II's occupation of the Congo in 1856, wrote in rather tortured French:

> Napoleon I brought to its knees the international law of his day; but from the ashes of this ancient system, a community of interests arose, which gave birth to a community of duties. That conscience has contributed powerfully towards the establishment of a new order of things, the greatest expression of which is the European Congress.[6]

In the collective view of the Great Powers, Napoleon had only been responsible for completing a violent, unnatural irruption into a harmonious, balanced world which had begun with the Revolution. Revolutionary France had made war not only on the old order; she had also launched what Edmund Burke had declared to be a civil war across the whole of "the great vicinage of Europe," a "violent breach of the community of Europe."[7] The real victim had been what Friedrich von Gentz, Prussian *littérateur*, Burke's translator, former pupil of Kant, and personal adviser to the Austrian statesman Prince Klemens von Metternich—a man known, half-mockingly, as "Europe's Knight Errant" and "Europe's Presumptive Secretary

General"—referred to variously as the "federal constitution of Europe," the "general union," the "European League," and the "system of public law" which he believed for all its imperfections had, in effect, been initiated by the Treaty of Westphalia of 1648.[8]

Gentz was not inclined to inflate the achievements of the "Westphalian System." Like Kant, he was keenly aware that "among independent nations there is neither executive nor judiciary power," and in his view, despite, as he put it—taking a swipe at his former teacher—the "vain well-meaning efforts" of some, this made any true union of states impossible to attain. Westphalia itself, although it had accomplished far more than any previous agreement between the nations of Europe, was never conceived as, nor was it ever intended to provide, "the basis of a federal system of Europe" or "the solid foundation for a public law of Europe." Yet, despite these limitations, in the years since 1648 Europe had succeeded in obtaining "an extensive social commonwealth" able to "guarantee the rights of all its members."[9] Then, after a century and a half of uncertain peace, the French had launched a revolution which had brought about "the total and hopeless oblivion of all the principles and maxims on which rested not only the stability and greatness but the bare possibility of a federal constitution."[10] After 1815, brought together by its resistance to the universalizing ambitions of Napoleon, Europe had become, once again, a "great political family, united beneath an Areopagus of its own creation." And this, he now insisted, "guaranteed to each of the interested parties the tranquil enjoyment of their respective rights." It had, he admitted, its drawbacks. But if it could be made to last, it was the "best possible combination to ensure the prosperity of peoples and to maintain the peace."[11] Gentz's characterization of the Congress as an "Areopagus" (the supreme court of ancient Athenian democracy) was at best inflated. The Congress, as J. R. Seeley remarked in 1871, was hardly a true law court; and "What would we think," he asked, "of a judicial bench every member of which was closely connected by interest with the litigants and on which in the most important cases the litigants themselves invariably sat?" Every settlement it made, furthermore, was "an adjustment of forces not of rights," and it was doomed finally to fall prey to the old antagonisms which Gentz had so naively believed it might finally eliminate.[12] In his hope that Vienna might result in the resurgence, in a more enlightened and more vigorous form, of the Westphalian system, Gentz had also failed to heed what had been his master's most important message: that no new Amphictyonic League, no new Areopagus of Europe could ever arise so long as the states of which it was composed had not yet made the transition from monarchical despotism to "representative republic."

In 1815, the "monarchical principle" seemed to be unassailable. Mazzini, however, looking back from beyond the democratic revolutions of 1848, believed the "victorious kings" to be "tormented as if by a presentiment" in response to which they had gathered together and "devised new methods to protect themselves against a future storm for which there were hardly any signs at the time." Perhaps the most significant of these new methods was the "Holy Alliance," created on September 25, 1815, at the instigation of the Tsar Alexander I, between Russia, Prussia, and Austria. Its objective was to restore where possible the pre-revolutionary balance of power throughout mainland Europe, based upon the supposedly shared values of conscience, religion, morality, and experience which in their view could only be con-solidated by turning Europe away from secularism and the republicanism which that implied and towards Christianity—Catholic, Protestant, and Orthodox—and monarchism. (Britain would have no part of it. It was, said Castlereagh, "A piece of sublime mysticism and nonsense." The tsar's mind, he added, "is not completely sound."[13]) Significantly, just before the treaty was signed, Metternich, then Austria's foreign minister, altered the original wording, which had evoked a fraternal union *between* monarchs and their peoples, into a call for a patriarchal alliance of monarchs *over* their peoples.[14]

For those smaller nations, in particular the Italians and the Poles, who found themselves under the rule of one of these Great Powers, this was a massive disappointment. To them, the alliance seemed to be anything but holy. It was an attempt, said Mazzini, to undo the centuries-old division between Church and State which the Enlightenment had struggled so hard to reinforce; and it had effectively ushered in a new age in which "dualism [between Church and State] of the Christian age seemed to fade into a pact of mutual love." Henceforth, these new "masters of the world had united against the future," and rather than maintain the peace among otherwise benign Christian states, as they claimed, they had in fact formed themselves into a "league of unlawful powers" determined to crush any kind of "pro-gressive principle." For the Great Powers had indeed seen that the defeat of Napoleon had not been the ultimate destruction of the principles of the Revolution much less of the Enlightenment, and that sooner or later a new threat to their continuing authority would arise. "The powers that signed the Vienna agreement," wrote Mazzini, "foresaw the future. They antici-pated who would be the new adversary to rise up against their dominion, once Europe had recovered from the exhaustion of war: the people"—and not just the people, but the people now "galvanized by the idea of national-ity." Therefore, they had made certain that every time any "oppressed or diminished nation" attempted to assert its own identity or "freely determine its own future," the so-called Holy Alliance would descend upon it "to pre-vent progress and protect the oppressors."[15] The threat which this "spirit of nationality" clearly posed had proved to be so powerful that, as Mazzini noted sarcastically in 1847, "the absolutist governments" have been com-pelled to "overcome all their mutual jealousies and actually form an *alliance* to oppose these developments."[16]

In that, he was not far wrong. It was the Congress system which had restored Louis XVIII to the throne for the second time in 1815. It was the Congress system which succeeded in muzzling any demands for reform that might threaten the existing political order and which had effectively stifled liberal constitutionalism in Germany and succeeded in crushing the consti-tutional monarchies of Naples, Piedmont, and Spain.[17] But for all Mazzini's loathing, for all that the objectives of the alliance, if not quite of the Concert as a whole, were to return to the happier times before 1789, Gentz was also right in claiming that it was responsible for giving some political shape to the vision of a European federation which had been around, in one form or another, since at least the seventeenth century, although hardly ever acted upon. An Areopagus it certainly was not. But it was, as Gentz wrote to Metternich in November 1818, an effective "counterpoise to the disorder which turbulent spirits try to bring into human affairs." "The nucleus of organized strength which this union presents is the barrier which provi-dence itself appears to have raised to preserve the old order of society, or at least to moderate and soften the changes which are indispensable."[18] For if the Napoleonic Wars had taught the rulers of Europe anything, it was that if some future conflagration on a similar scale was to be avoided, then the European states would have to be prepared to act in a far more coherent and cohesive manner than they had in the past. The pre-revolutionary concept of the "balance of powers" to which so many of the post-Napoleonic strategists still clung had proved to be, as Kant had seen even before the rise of Napoleon, "a mere fantasy like Swift's house, that the builder had constructed in such perfect accord with all the laws of equilibrium that it collapsed as soon as a sparrow lighted on it."[19]

As the utopian socialist Claude Henri de Saint-Simon, harking back once again to the abbé de Saint-Pierre, warned the delegates gathering in 1814, the policies of the concert would plunge Europe back into war before very long unless an attempt was made to "create Perpetual Peace," and the only way to achieve that would be to establish a European "confederative society."[20] If European society were to survive, if incessant warfare amongst its nations were to be finally laid to rest, it had to be radically "reorganized." Saint-Simon's *On the Reorganization of European Society* followed the abbé de Saint-Pierre's *A Project for Establishing a Perpetual Everlasting Peace in Europe* in suggesting a realignment of all the European powers and their subjugation to a common authority. But it made a radical break with all its predecessors in that it envisaged a single European parliament and a single European constitutional monarchy after the British model. This, he believed, would "bind all the peoples of Europe together into a single political organization." His model for this—somewhat improbably—was the medieval papacy—infinitely superior in his view to anything dreamed up by Saint-Pierre. Europe, he insisted, should be recreated as a "confederative society united by common institutions subject to a general government which would be for the peoples [of Europe] what national governments are for individuals."[21] Each state should have its own national government, but the federal government should be wholly independent of every one of them. This, he claimed to believe, was how the papacy had been organized, only the "ignorance of those times had prevented these principles from being properly employed."[22] The "general government" would be responsible for what he described vaguely as "general interests" and would be beholden to only one power (*puissance*): "public opinion," which would, in effect, be embodied as a "European Parliament." For Saint-Simon the only peoples who would be capable of building such a society were the English and the French because they were "undeniably superior in force to the rest of Europe" and because, unlike the other European states, theirs were ruled by parliamentary forms of government—hardly, it is true, a very accurate image of France in the immediate aftermath of the collapse of the French Empire and of Napoleon's ignominious departure to take up his new post as "Emperor and Ruler of Elba."[23]

Few of the delegates at Vienna could have shared Saint-Simon's belief that a radically new European superstate could be constructed from the chaos of the post-Napoleonic world, much less that the medieval papacy offered a compelling model for a future united Europe. But many had hopes for the eventual creation of some more loosely conceived federal order. "For the first time Europe appears as a community of states," wrote

Karl Friedrich von dem Knesebeck, Friedrich William III's *Generaladjutant* in a memorandum he prepared for the congress. "May it maintain itself in that form."[24] And for a while at least it did. Ten years later, in 1824, Gentz declared confidently that "Europe through innumerable ties and daily close intercourse between sovereigns and peoples has formed itself into a true federative body, in which no member can be mutilated, wounded or poisoned without the harm penetrating more or less deeply into all the others."[25]

II

Gentz's optimism, however, proved to be short-lived. Anything resembling his "federative body" had little chance of success. By the middle of the nine-teenth century, long before the Great War of 1914–18 had undone the ten-tative balance of the Congress system forever, it was clear that modern nationalism, which, in the nicely calibrated words of the British periodical *The Speaker: The Liberal Review* of 1902, "broke down all the uneasy equilib-riums of Vienna, just as it foiled the panoplied appetites of Napoleon," was to dominate political thinking and state formation well into the foreseeable future.[26] This is why so many of the great novels of the nineteenth century, from Stendhal to Alessandro Manzoni, from Alexandre Dumas and Victor Hugo to the Tolstoy of *War and Peace*, are concerned with what it means to be, and to belong to, a nation. Ultimately, it was nationalism which tore apart the Austro-Hungarian Empire, the Ottoman Empire, and the Spanish Empire in America. "We are still under the influence of the reaction against the Napoleonic world-empire," wrote the neo-Hegelian historian Heinrich von Treitschke (of whom more later) in 1897. "Both Italy and Germany offer the imposing spectacle of two great peoples rising to the attainment of political unity."[27] And not only Italy and Germany. Between 1830 and the outbreak of World War I at least ten new states came into existence in Europe, all in part or wholly the creation of the new nationalism: Greece (1830), Belgium (1830–9), Romania (1856), Italy (1859–71), Germany (1864–71), Serbia (1867–8), Bulgaria (1878), and Norway (1905). Albania followed in 1912, Finland in 1917. (Ireland, after a prolonged war of inde-pendence, followed in 1922.)

The creation of a people, the making of the many into one, was, in every instance, not as it is so often portrayed, a spontaneous voluntarily coming together. It was a self-conscious political act.

It was, as we have seen, the Napoleonic invasions which led to the creation not only of an ideology—"nationalism"—but also, albeit indirectly, to what would eventually become the modern nations of Italy, Spain, Germany, and Italy. None of these, however, for all that their ideologues labored hard to make them so, was the spontaneous expression of long-nourished ethnic sentiments. Italy was the creation of a conquest by the kingdom of Piedmont. "Germany"—although it had long existed in the minds of liberal intellectuals and harked back in some areas of the popular imagination to the Carolingian Empire (as, of course, did Austria)—was a Prussian creation invented by Bismarck and ruled over by a Hohenzollern emperor from a capital in Berlin. In neither case did there exist prior to unification what the German liberal historian Friedrich Meinecke in the early twentieth century called a "cultural nation" which could have provided the newly emergent *state* with a sense of collective identity.[28] And it was not only Italians who had to be "invented"—in Massimo d'Azeglio's famous (and possibly apocryphal) remark—and the Germans, once the state had been created; it was also the Greeks, the Belgians, the Irish. It was a process which was rarely achieved peacefully. There are few, if any, modern nations in Europe or beyond that have not been created by war, either internal or external. And few, if any, that have not come into being in the pursuit of some conception of liberty, either from a foreign colonizing or imperial power or from an internal group that had come to be seen as "foreign." (This, as we shall see in Chapter 6, is the one foundational sense in which the creation of the European Union differs from the creation of any nation state.)

As the German sociologist Claus Offe has pointed out, modern societies are united in a number of different, often, it must also be said, conflicting ways. Their members will "typically communicate in one (or a small number of) idiom(s) and they will presuppose their mutual familiarity with aesthetic and other forms of symbolic expression ranging from pieces of music to national holidays."[29] This in the modern world has been reinforced by shared common cultural preferences and transmitted through schools and celebrated in museums. Little of this was available on the national level before the nineteenth century. If people felt any sense of belonging to anything beyond their immediate families, it was more likely to be the parish, the village, or, at best, the city or town. Their political allegiance was most often to the local overlord or, more remotely, to the king. It was the Revolution and its aftermath—in the sweeping social, political changes effected under Napoleon—which ultimately, and not without struggle, transformed the peoples of Burgundy and Navarre, Gascony, and Provence into Frenchmen. The bloodiest Revolution to the Revolution came, significantly, not from the aristocracy but from the peasantry, Catholic and royalist, of the Vendée, in western France in 1793. They wanted no part of *la Grande Nation.* They were unwaveringly loyal to the kingdom of France and to its king. And they paid a high price for it. "According to your orders," wrote the Republic's trium-phant commander General François Joseph Westermann, "I have trampled their children beneath our horses' hooves; I have massacred their women.... I do not have a single prisoner to reproach me. I have exterminated them all.... Mercy is not a revolutionary sentiment"—nor, he might have added, is it a nationalist one.

III

Nationalism is still the most potent political force within Europe today, and it has done as much to shape and create the present European Union as it has served as the ideological prop for its opponents. But what Émile Durkheim (often referred to as the father of modern sociology, and one of the most influential intellectuals of the twentieth century) in 1895 called that "obscure mystic idea" claims to be and what it is perceived as being have changed markedly over the 200-odd years it has been in existence, and it has come to mean many different things to many different peoples.[30] As a category, "nationalism" may indeed elude adequate definition, but it does have a history, and one which has ultimately been responsible for shaping the ways in which the concept has been employed to determine the course of the shared ways of life of the European peoples—and not only of them.[31]

The term "nation" as we use it today is relatively recent. Its origins are, of course, Latin. (*natio* means "something born"; it was also the name of the goddess of birth.) Initially, it was applied pejoratively to peoples and tribes who were not organized into civil societies, those who were merely "born," not created. In later Roman law it came to describe a race, a stock, a kind, and was also used to designate a group of resident foreigners—usually merchants or students. Thus, as Jürgen Habermas points out, a national origin was often ascribed by others, with the consequence that it was "from the very beginning linked in a conspicuous way with the negative demarcation of foreigners from one's own people."[32] Later, the term came to be applied to social and

political elites, and by the eighteenth century had come to designate a
people—an extended kin group if you will—an "ethnos." This is how
Montesquieu uses the term in discussing those laws which have the
power to shape "the customs, manners, and character of a nation"—and
how David Hume uses it in speaking of "national characters" as those
"peculiar set of manners" and "particular qualities" that distinguish one
people from another.[33] Similarly, when Johann Gottfried Herder spoke of
the *Volk*, it was this that he had in mind; something, that is, which still had
powerful biological connotations. The nation was a people living on a particular patch of earth and speaking a single language (something which has,
of course, subsequently come to be seen as an essential component of a
national identity). Each people—each *Volk*—was the product of a collective
past. It was an indivisible entity created by its unique language and culture
and marked by its own art, its own music, its own poetry, and, crucially for
Herder, its own religion. And all those things had grown up slowly over
time. All his experience, all his studies had persuaded him that "the history
of the world is necessarily a chain of socialness and plastic tradition."[34]

But the idea of the nation which slowly emerged in the early nineteenth
century was significantly different from both these earlier conceptions.
The nation, in Habermas's definition is—or rather should be—the means
by which:

> the inhabitants of a state acquire an awareness of a new form of solidarity
> based upon law [*Recht*] and politics. It is a national consciousness crystalized
> around the perception of a common origin, of a common language and a
> common history which transforms subjects into citizens of one single political
> community, in other words into members capable for feeling responsible for
> each other.

Crucially, the language in which the new nationalism was expressed had
been stripped of all association with the kin group. The *nation* could have
no father. What Habermas called the "intentional democratic community
[*Willensgemeinschaft*] takes the place of the ethnic complex."[35] The nation
was an aggregation of citizens, not a community of descent. This is why the
modern nation which was to become answerable for the idea of "democracy" could only ever be, as the Austrian Hans Kelsen, possibly the most
powerful, most eminent, most lastingly influential jurist of the twentieth
century, insisted in 1955, a "fatherless society."[36] It is why, before 1815, international treaties had been made between sovereigns, lapsed on the death of

one of the signatories, and had to be re-signed (or renegotiated) by his or her successor. Modern treaties, by contrast, are contracted between nation-states by their representatives and considered binding until one or both of the parties abrogates them.[37]

Today, overshadowed by the legacies of Fascism and National Socialism, nationalism appears as a form of tribalism, xenophobic, ignorant, bigoted, sectarian, and usually overtly racist, which the contemporary political theorist John Dunn has called "the starkest political shame of the twentieth century."[38] This, with various shadings and concessions to public sensibilities, is also how it emerges in the rhetoric of the new Right within Europe: the French National Front (now unconvincingly and clumsily rebranded as the *Rassemblement national*—"*The National Rally*"), the Greek Golden Dawn, Italy's League, the Flemish Alliance, the Danish Peoples' Party, the Finns Party, the Alternative for Germany, and their like. Some are more overtly racist than others, but all imagine themselves to be defending what they take to be the true interests of the nation, which they believe to be threatened by any international grouping which claims, as all inevitably do, to exercise some degree of authority, some legal hold over the actions of the supposedly inviolable nation-state. All see any kind of internationalism, and in particular the semi-federalism represented by the European Union, as a threat to national sovereignty—a term which became a shibboleth for nationalists of all hues in the twentieth century, and which most still hold to be, in Thomas Hobbes's definition, "incommunicable and inseparable."[39]

Nationalism has not however always been, as these parties are, as the Fascists and the Nazis were, populist and authoritarian. Nor, although certainly on occasions tinged with mysticism, has nationalism always been so very obscure. Its origins were, in fact, liberal and, paradoxically, internationalist.

The nationalism which emerged out of the collapse of the Napoleonic order, what Giuseppe Mazzini tellingly called not "nationalism" (a term he reserved for a something akin to "patriotism" and which he viewed with intense suspicion) but the "principle of nationality," did not hark back to ancient glories; it did not seek to revive the France of Vercingetorix or the Britain of Boudicca, however fancifully; and it had no need to enhance itself at the expense of others. The liberal nationalism of the nineteenth century, by contrast, was a bid for what after 1919 would come to be hailed as every people's right to "self-determination." It was also, as we shall see, a bid to reinvent the concept of Europe itself.[40]

IV

The modern nation has, of course, many and deep historical roots. It is clearly not improbable to think of Spain after the union of the crowns of Castile and Aragon in 1469 as a single "nation." Similarly, England could be said to have become a "nation" in the tenth, in the thirteenth, and again in the seventeenth centuries. And it has been argued that, despite the claims of the revolutionaries to have created the French nation, there already existed such a thing as early as the fourteenth century, certainly as early as the reign of Louis XIV in the seventeenth. All of these claims hover around conceptions of political, dynastic, cultural, and religious unity.[41] But although those are clearly significant, and although they are also central to the understanding of the nation which appeared in the nineteenth century, none of them was associated with an *ideology* of unification, of cohesion, of a common purpose. Even Louis XIV's ambition to make of France a united nation—*un état unifié*—was only a bid to secure his own royal authority against a powerful and frequently insubordinate nobility. Nations in some shape or form there most certainly were before the nineteenth century; nationalism there was not.

Ever since its emergence as a distinctive and recognizable political type, the nation has been given many different meanings and diverse origins. It has been cast as the political expression of ethnic and linguistic singularity.[42] It has been described as the child of the Industrial Revolution and the creation of a culture of mass communication.[43] It has been seen as the outcome of a centuries-long process of self-awareness. In the aftermath of Woodrow Wilson's famous series of claims that once World War I was over, all peoples, above all colonized peoples, should be granted their right to "self-determination," that "imperative principle of action" as he called it, the nation has been a potent instrument for the dissolution of empires and the ideological buttress of new states across the globe. It was cast as the expression of a collective will, what the French historian, theologian, and polemicist Ernest Renan, in a much quoted essay of 1882, "What is a nation?," described as a "daily plebiscite, just as an individual's existence is a perpetual affirmation of life."[44] Today it has become a ubiquitous phenomenon, to the degree that many, not all of them obvious nationalists, speak of it as if it were somehow a natural political form, what the anthropologist Ernest Gellner described as a "universal necessity."[45]

It is also widely assumed that the modern nation-state is, at present, the only form in which modern liberal democracy can survive. There are many places in the world which claim to be nations but which are very far from being democracies. But there is no properly functioning liberal democracy in the world today which is not also a nation-state. Nor is it coincidental that the term "liberal" was first used in Spain during the Cortes of Cadiz of 1810–14, which abolished the old kingdoms of the peninsula and created what would become, albeit briefly, a constitutional *national*—and "liberal"— monarchy under a national assembly. And just as, for some, the liberal dem- ocratic state marked some kind of end of history, so too, for others, does the nation.

The often unvoiced assumption behind these claims is that for centuries the peoples of the world have been struggling toward political, cultural, and social homogeneity within some order larger than the family or the parish, but smaller than the polyglot, multiethnic associations generally described as "empires" which for most of human history have been the dominant political form in Europe, Asia, large parts of the Americas, and many areas in Africa.

"Nationalism" is, however, often confused or conflated with another per- haps equally elusive term: "patriotism." Initially, this owed its power to the idea that no matter how large nor how diverse the political community is, it remains in essence an extended image of the family. Patriotism derives from the Latin word *patria*, which in turn derives from the word for father (*pater*) and describes the love, attachment, and obligation a person is bound to feel for his or her "fatherland." It is, as Émile Durkheim said in 1905, "a word with a strong element of subjective impressions," and it characterized a "political society felt in a certain way; it is political society seen from an affective point of view."[46] Like Plato's famous "noble lie," it is an attempt to persuade all the members of the ideal city that they are autochthonous— although they clearly are not—so that everyone should look upon his fel- low citizen "as a brother born like him from the mother earth . . . and look upon the other citizens as their brothers and citizens of the same soil."[47] When, following Augustus in the first century CE the Roman emperors attempted to enforce their personal rule over what had hitherto been a republic—a *res publica*, a "public thing"—they adopted the title *pater patriae*, "father of the fatherland," and in so doing transformed the Roman Empire into one vast imaginary ethnic group. Whoever you were, Gaul or Spaniard, Greek or Dacian, you were at some level a member of the emperor's extended family, and the emperor exercised over you the *patria potestas*, the authority which, in Roman law, the father wielded over all his male descendants—and in Roman law the status of children, like that of women, was only a shadow away from the status of slaves. In the process of this transformation the emperor became not, as the rulers of the republic had been, a magistrate—one who enforces the law—but a judge, one who makes it, and one who is, in the celebrated phrase of the second-century Roman jurist Ulpian, *legibus solutus*, "unbound by the law." As the nineteenth-century English jurist Henry Sumner Maine said of it in 1861: "The tenacity of the Romans in maintaining this relic of their most ancient condition is in itself remarkable, but it is less remarkable than the diffusion of the *potestas* over the whole of a civilisation from which it had once disappeared."[48]

This Roman legal conception of patriotism has a great deal in common— as Hitler himself was not slow to point out—with the *Führerprinzip* ("Führer principle"), a term first coined by Herman von Keyserling, a social Darwinist who also held, as Ulpian probably would have, that certain "gifted individuals" were "born to rule"; born, that is, to be *patres*. Patriotism, it should never be forgotten, was primarily a military creed, the governing moral and emotional force within societies which were made up of warrior elites surrounded by their women, their children, and their slaves. For the men, and in that society, they were the only ones who mattered, you did not live for the *patria* so much as defend and die for it. "Dulce et decorum est" ran the Roman poet Horace's celebrated line, "pro patria *mori*." ("It is sweet and fitting to *die* for one's country.") As Durkheim remarked, although a man should be free to choose his own *patria*, he really is not, because "at birth we are incapable of choosing. Later we are not completely free to do so.... A *patria* is not like a religious confession. It demands from us a debt and we cannot leave the *patria* of birth before we have paid that debt and the principal form that debt takes is military service."[49]

After the collapse of the Roman Empire in the west, the European monarchies that grew up amid its ruins adopted the same vision of their authority and of the society over which this was exercised. Each king became "an emperor in his own realm." "Kings are . . . compared to the fathers of families, for a king is truly *parens patriae*, the politic father of his people," James I of England (and VI of Scotland) told the English parliament in 1600.[50] The people were the extension of the monarch's royal person. Hence too, Louis XIV's famous remark to the *parlement* of Paris in April 1655, *L'état c'est moi*

("I am the state"). Like so many such moments in history, this one never actually took place; but it certainly could have, and many similar ones certainly did.

By insisting in this way that the state was a simulacrum of a family, the monarchs of medieval and early modern Europe, like their Roman predecessors, had not only made disobedience and criticism seem improper; they had also ensured that their subjects were dissuaded from any independent judgment. The king agreed to abide by such laws as those for which he was ultimately responsible; but only he was in a position to determine how this compliance was to be judged. He and he alone was the ultimate source of the reason—the *ratio*—of the law, since that law emanated solely from his "frank good will." There was, in other words, no constitution which could restrain him. As John Stuart Mill (in arguing against the subjugation of women) pointed out in 1869, by anchoring their claims to absolute power in a union which was "anterior to society itself" and which was therefore deemed to be natural to the species, possibly to every species, the would-be absolute monarchs—like all patriarchs—could claim that theirs was "the most natural authority of all."[51] Such rulers ruled, as Kant pointed out, over children not adults. In such an understanding of the *patria*, patriotism therefore becomes overwhelmingly a matter of family loyalty. Place, language culture, even religion play at best only secondary roles.

In the eighteenth century, in an attempt to broaden the conception of original allegiance without changing the language in which it was expressed, the idea of a "family" passed from an imaginary patriarchal lineage group into something far more abstract—and uplifting. As the Lord Chancellor, Henri-François d'Arguesseau—said by Voltaire to be "the most learned magistrate France ever possessed"—told the *parlement* of Paris in 1715, "Love of country" should be understood to mean not love of the monarch but love of the common good, which was constituted by the "body of citizens who enjoyed perfect equality" and perfect "fraternity." "Every citizen," he said, "from the earliest age, practically from birth, grows used to serving the state as his own. This perfect equality, and the kind of civil fraternity which makes all citizens like a single family, interests them all equally in the fortunes and misfortunes of the *patrie*."[52] In place of unquestioning obedience, there came instead a reflective and critical love. The idea of the omnipotent father who administered the law as he saw fit was now to be replaced with that of the omnipotent constitution, which created, and in turn was created by, the community. This, as we shall see, was to have a significant impact on

a later, highly influential way of thinking about the ways in which an attachment to a community of different cultures, of different states, such as, in this
case, the European Union, might be created.[53]

This patria thus became a kind of unsituated version of the Greek *polis*
and the Roman (republican) *civitas*, which, although it did not necessarily
imply a republican form of government, relied heavily upon some kind of
loosely conceived republican sentiment. When the Latin term *respublica* was
generally understood in its original meaning as "the public thing" or, as the
English called it, the "commonwealth," it described a society upheld by
what Montesquieu called "political virtue" (of which, for him, the clearest
embodiment was the "moderate monarchy" that existed in Britain). This
was not to be confused with the traditional Aristotelian (and Christian)
moral virtues. It did not determine the relationship of individuals either to
themselves or to one another. It governed only the relationship of individuals to the larger social and political spheres to which they belonged as
citizens. "One can define this virtue"—of republicanism—wrote Montesquieu,
"as love of the laws and of the homeland [*patrie*]. This love requires continuing preference of the public interest over one's own, producing all the individual virtues; they are only that preference."[54] As the eighteenth-century
Anglo-Irish poet and playwright Oliver Goldsmith makes his imaginary
Chinese visitor to England and "Citizen of the World" Lien Chi Altangi
declare, with approval (and surprise), "An Englishman is taught to love his
king as a friend, but to acknowledge no other master than the laws which
[he] himself has contributed to enact."[55] It was this perception of the relationship which should now exist between the ruler and those who were no
longer his subjects, his property, but his fellow citizens, which allowed
Fredrick the Great of Prussia in 1752 to describe himself as the "first servant
of the state" (although, as Kant acidly remarked, he only *said* he was that).

In 1815, however, the idea that the monarch might be a friend or a
"patriot" was largely confined to Britain. Two civil wars, one between 1642
and 1649 and the other, the "Glorious Revolution," in 1688, had all but
beaten down the sense of omnipotence that James I had once assumed. The
monarchs of continental Europe, however, *pace* Fredrick the Great, did not
think of themselves as either servants or patriots; they thought of themselves, as Louis XIV had done, as the embodiment of the state. Patriotism
was still, in Benjamin Constant's dismissive definition, and despite the best
efforts of d'Arguesseau and his heirs, "a factitious passion for an abstract

being, a general idea stripped of all that can engage the imagination and speak to the memory."[56]

No one epitomized this better—though he can hardly have been aware of it—than Louis XVI's brother and heir, the future Louis XVIII. Ineffectual and utterly lacking in anything resembling regal charisma, Louis, who had been in exile since 1792, clung resolutely to the image of kingship as a form of kinship, and the king as the embodiment of *his* people, who huddled together on a patch of land which over the course of the seventeenth century had come to be called "the state" and of which the monarch was the living embodiment. When Louis was installed in 1814 after Napoleon's banishment to Elba, it was as something as close as possible to a constitutional monarch. He was to be "king of the French," not the "king of France," and he was to hold his position not by divine dispensation, but from a constitution drafted for him under the auspices of Prince Charles Maurice de Talleyrand, perhaps the wiliest political operator of the century, who had once served as Napoleon's foreign minister and had presided over the provisional government following his fall in April 1814. Louis, however, dismissed the idea that his was an accession, claiming instead that he had been ruling *in absentia* since 1795 (when the heir presumptive Louis XVII had died) and that he had been doing so "by the Grace of God," not the people. He was only prepared to recognize Talleyrand's constitution if it were redescribed as a "charter" granted by him, Louis, to *his* people (although it finally became the "Constitutional Charter"). He refused to accept the tricolor as the French flag, or the *Légion d'Honneur* which had been instituted by Napoleon, and in 1821 decreed that all the streets, squares, and bridges of Paris would revert to the names they had had in 1790. And he would be "king of France" not "king of the French" and rule by "the Grace of God," as all his ancestors had, and not the will of the people. For Louis, there was no French people, no French nation. These had been mere figments of the Revolution now committed to the bonfires of history. There was only "France," the quasi-mystical extension of his own person.

Half a century later, in 1872, faced by an only slightly different manifestation of what he called "national pride," the staunch Saint-Simonian, and one of the founders of the International League of Peace and Freedom, Charles Lemonier, remarked bitterly that all the nationalist outpouring which had brought on the Franco-Prussian War (among others) was "the dynastic principle simply transported from kings to peoples. The idea, the attributes and the effects of sovereignty conceived as his divine right. . . . The people has become an idol set up in the place of another idol."[57]

But it had not originally been so. The new "nationalism" which Louis struggled so hard (and ultimately ineffectually) to turn back, although it owed much to d'Arguesseau's brand of "civic patriotism," resolutely rejected any idea that the nation might be an extended patriarchal family, no matter who—or what—its *pater* might be. A nation, wrote the abbé Sieyes, in many ways the most lastingly significant political theorist of the French Revolution, in "What is the Third Estate?" of 1789 is "a body of people who join together to live under common laws and be represented by the same legislative assembly." For him this meant that those, the nobility or the monarch, who claimed special privileges were, in effect, seeking to place themselves out-side the nation as "a separate people, a nation within a nation." It meant too that "the Third Estate is the complete nation." This is, in short, what has subsequently come to be called "civic nationalism."[58] It is based not upon a shared past, real or imaginary, nor on a language or a religion, much less on a common descent. It is based upon a broadly agreed set of values and on a shared commitment to a body of laws, a constitution. In Europe at least, the modern nation-state and democracy are, in Jürgen Habermas's words, "twins" created by the French Revolution. And both have "grown up in the shadow of nationalism."[59] For this reason, whatever else any future "European Union" might turn out to be, it could only be a reimagining of "the achievements of the European nation-state beyond its frontiers in a new form."

V

Nationalism also rejected—or at least substantially transformed—that other popular eighteenth-century conception of the ideal mode of human asso-ciation: cosmopolitanism. Cosmopolitanism has a long history. But it seemed particularly attractive in the eighteenth century as the various European—and not only European—nations struggled endlessly with each other over what seemed, at least to the philosophers of the Enlightenment, to be fan-tastical and fanatical forms of tribalism driven on by illusory differences between peoples who had no other reason not to live together in perfect agreement with one another. For them—of whom, as we have seen, Kant was by far the most influential—the only means to bring an end to this perpetual conflict was to dissolve all the differences which distinguished and divided peoples and inevitably set them against each other, to create something like Kant's "universal union of states"—a true cosmopolis.[60]

To many, however, cosmopolitanism, which threatened to dissolve the (supposedly) ancestral differences between peoples and to displace the natural object of love and loyalty from the tribe to humanity at large, seemed to be far too abstract, too ethereal, to be of any real value. "Humanity" is something we can be asked to respect, even perhaps make sacrifices for, but it is hard to see how one can be required to associate with it or work for it or "love" it, much less sacrifice oneself for it, as one is supposed to do for one's *patria* or indeed one's nation. It is also true that the cosmos has neither culture nor custom nor religion to identify it. As the American political philosopher Michael Walzer once said, somewhat facetiously, the "cosmos"—the world—is not something one can very easily be a citizen *of*. "No one has ever offered me citizenship," he protested, "or described the naturalization process... or given me an account of its decision procedures, or provided me with a list of the benefits and obligations of citizenship, or shown me the world's calendar and the common celebrations and commemorations of its citizens."[61] This may seem somewhat literal minded. Calendars and celebrations and commemorations are, one might argue, precisely the stuff of the narrow understanding of patriotism or nationalism that the cosmopolitans most objected to. But he had a point. For although Kant's "cosmopolitan right" was intended to make possible a league of *states*—not individuals—most forms of cosmopolitanism are resolutely individualistic. "I freely admit," wrote Mazzini, "that for Cosmopolitans the end is also humanity; but their pivot or point of support is man, the isolated *individual*." When he was told by "honorable men, motivated by the best intentions" that "we no longer believe in the nation: we believe in humanity; we are Cosmopolitans," Mazzini's reply was that cosmopolitanism, in addition to being a "somewhat outdated idea," was a "much vaguer and [more] difficult [one] to realize than that of Nationality." For this reason, cosmopolitanism, as his "honorable men" understood it, had become a "barren sentiment of reaction against a past which is forever dead in our own hearts." Of course, he said, we are all cosmopolitans, if all that means is approving a general sense of benevolence and obligation toward our fellow beings, and "the destruction of all barriers that separate the Peoples and provide them with opposite interests." But this is hardly enough. In the world in which he lived, the cosmopolitan was powerless.

He stands, said Mazzini, "at the centre of an immense circle that extends itself around him, and whose limits are beyond his grasp."[62] He is not so much wrong, as ineffectual. He does what he can to the best of his abilities, but in the end all that that amounts to is charity and "mere almsgiving," and that was hardly likely to provide an adequate solution to "the social problems that occupy our attention today." The cosmopolitan has "no other aid on which to rely than the consciousness of his unfilled rights." But a person is more than a body of rights; and whenever those rights "remain unfilled," as they inevitably will, the cosmopolitan "just steps back and looks away. He utters the egoist's maxim, *ubi bene, ibi patria* ["where my interest is, there is my country"]."[63] Such rootless individuals lacked that attachment to the soil, to the body of citizens, to all that made each people distinct. "How little worthy of respect," remarked the late eighteenth-century German philosopher and theologian Friedrich Schleiermacher,

> is the man who roams hither and thither without the anchor of a national ideal and love of fatherland; how dull is the friendship which rests merely upon personal similarities in disposition and tendencies and not upon the feeling of a greater unity for whose sake one can offer up one's life.[64]

Little wonder then that "cosmopolitan" became, in the English philosopher Roger Scruton's words, "a term of abuse used by totalitarians of all shades to identify the slippery treacherous enemy within"—Hitler's "rootless cosmopolitan" and Stalin's "cosmopolitan bourgeois."[65]

Cosmopolitanism suffered from another defect. Being a "citizen of the world" was generally taken to mean rejecting the narrow ties of kin and country, the suffocating bigotry of the local, and adopting the cosmos itself as your city. But it could also—and frequently was—taken to mean something rather different: not turning your city into the world, but instead turning the world into your city. If all humanity was to be one, then it made sense to argue that humanity could only belong to one community, one city, and one *polis*. The exemplary cosmopolite was not Diogenes the Cynic—whose is supposed to have been the first to use the word—who lived in a barrel in the marketplace of fourth-century Athens and disdained all forms of human attachment. It was, instead, the second-century Roman emperor Marcus Aurelius, who had declared himself to be "a citizen of the world," but who also believed himself to rule over it.[66] On this understanding, cosmopolitanism and a certain kind of imperialism come out looking like much the same thing. It became what Kant had most feared: the cosmopolitan ideal expressed as universal empire, or what Mazzini tellingly called "Napoleonic" nationalities. These, however, or so Mazzini hoped, were no longer—"thank God"—in a position to impose themselves by force of arms, any more than they are able to do so—as France, Britain, Belgium, and Germany were still trying to do in the world beyond Europe—by "the pretentious coda of permanent exclusive moral and intellectual leadership."[67] Since the new nations of Europe—and subsequently of the non-European world—had all been formed out of a rejection of empire—in particular Napoleon's new French Empire—cosmopolitanism for many was a tainted doctrine.

The new nationalism seemed, therefore, to offer to what have come to be identified as its early "liberal" advocates, a means of combining the virtues of both "civic patriotism" and cosmopolitanism, while overcoming the dangers inherent in both. For the liberal nationalists of the nineteenth century the answer was to be not "cosmopolitanism" but what they called "internationalism." "Ours is not a national project," claimed Mazzini, "but an *international* one."[68]

Mazzini was the most compelling, and the most widely influential, of the liberal nationalists. Although he saw himself as a practical politician, a man of action concerned with the creation of realizable ideals, and in 1849 became, for a few months, one of the triumvirs of the short-lived Roman Republic, his scattered writings in three languages, Italian, English, and French, helped to build an image of the modern nation which was perhaps more broadly congenial and was ultimately to prove more influential than any which had preceded (and most that have succeeded) it. He was known and admired by such dissimilar figures as John Stuart Mill, who met him in 1837 and called him the "most accomplished and in every way superior man among all the foreigners I have known," and the English poet Algernon Swinburne, by whom he was "positively worshipped."[69] The economic historian Arnold Toynbee declared that "not Adam Smith, nor Carlyle, great as he was, but Mazzini is the true teacher of our age."[70] In February 1871, when Mazzini was ill and frail and had only one year left to live, he found himself sharing a horse-drawn sled with Friedrich Nietzsche heading across the treacherous St Gotthard Pass towards Lugano. After a long and animated conversation as the sled lurched over the mountain paths, Nietzsche came away with the impression that he had been conversing with one of the most heroic and noble characters of the age, a veritable *Übermensch*, possessed, he wrote later, of an "absolute concentration on a single idea which burnt like a powerful flame within the individual."[71] He was, said the Russian radical Alexander Herzen, the "shining star" of the democratic revolutions of 1848.[72] Sir Alfred Zimmern called him, in 1922, "the greatest nineteenth-century prophet."[73] His endorsement, said Zimmern, of the "European mission" to bring emancipation, democracy, and the abolition of slavery to the entire world went hand in hand with a denunciation of the "brutal conquest" which had so often been perpetrated in its name. Little wonder, then, that he became a hero also to a succession of liberators, from Gandhi—who said of him that he was "one of the few instances in the world where a single man has brought about the uplift of his country by his strength of mind and his extreme devotion"—to the early Zionists, to Nehru, and to Sun Yat Sen, first president of the Chinese Republic.[74] In 1919, Woodrow Wilson stopped at Genoa, Mazzini's birthplace, on his way to the Paris Peace Conference, and in front of the monument to him in the Via Grenchen, declared that his ambition at the conference would be to realize the ideals of this lonely thinker who "by some gift of God had been lifted above the common level."[75]

Mazzini was not, however, quite as lonely as Wilson supposed. Although he was undoubtedly the most powerful and influential proponent of the new liberal nationalism, he was not the only, or even the first, to see that a more compelling, perhaps more enduring form of cosmopolitanism could be achieved by uniting all the peoples of Europe, first into "nations," and only then into anything larger. The unity of the European peoples, the "United States of Europe," would only be achieved in his time through the union of patriots all working ultimately together for "the progress of all for the advantage of all."[76] Even Johann Gottlieb Fichte—who above all, and in particular after 1914, a century after his death, came to be looked upon as the architect of German nationalism and the champion of a superior German *Kultur*—even he had initially expressed something of what would become Mazzini's view of the "international."[77] In the dialogue *Patriotism and its Opposite*, written in 1806 just before the Battle of Jena, he had described cosmopolitanism as the "will that the purpose of life be reached in all humanity," and nationalism as the will that "this purpose be reached first in all in that nation whereof we are members," the emphasis being quite clearly on the word *first*.[78]

Nor was Mazzini by any means the only major Italian liberal intellectual of the nineteenth century, although he was certainly the most widely read and the best known outside Italy. There was also the Milanese Carlo Cattaneo, who had played an active and decisive role in the Milanese insurrection of

March 18–22, 1848 (known as the "Five Days of Milan") and who subsequently became the most powerful and convinced advocate of a federal Europe. There was, too, Vincenzo Gioberti, who worried that liberalism, although by no means hostile to Christianity—at least not in Mazzini's version—had nevertheless overlooked the crucial role which the Church supposedly played in the life of all Italians, and who therefore advocated the creation of a federal union of states under the sovereignty of the papacy. All shared a common commitment to some form of democracy, to republicanism, and to a vision of what Mazzini insistently called "the principle of nationality," which assumed that the ties that bind peoples were an attachment neither to an imaginary kin group, as in the case of the older notion of "patriotism," nor to a single patriarchal leader. "The old despotic rulers," Mazzini wrote, had "relied on their family, their race and their dynasty as the basis of the nation." In doing so they had generated precisely what he called "a narrow and mean *Nationalism.*"[79] What made a people a "nation," in Mazzini's understanding of the term, was not kin or even an attachment to a body of laws, or a way of governing, although this too was to be an important part of it; nor was it race, language, or climate, the triple pillars on which so much exceptionalism had previously rested.[80] He was not about to fall into the error which Renan would later attribute to most of the new nationalists, that "race is confused with nation, and a sovereignty analogous to that of truly existing peoples is attributed to ethnographic or rather linguistic groups."[81] Race, said Mazzini, counts "for nothing in the constitution of modern nations." What did count was primarily what might be described loosely as a culture: a shared set of customs, habits, desires, and aspirations, a language and a literature, and, in Mazzini's case, a religion. It was this which made the principle of nationality into some kind of common experience which could be shared at once by the members of individual nations *and* by larger groups of nations participating in much the same, although not identical, cultural affinities. It was this which bound together what J. R. Seeley in 1896 called "the European brotherhood of nation states," which had, he believed (unsurprisingly), "produced the vast growth of every kind of power and science which distinguishes modern civilization."[82]

VI

But if a culture was to be transformed into a nation, as a determinate political reality, it required an act of will, the only means by which, in Mazzini's words, man "as the incarnation of the moral law" might achieve his designated ends. We are nothing on our own. Our individual strengths and abilities certainly count, but what they count toward, and are powerless without, is a collective undertaking; a "tradition," that "ever-growing depository of human achievements in time and space" which will finally constitute each people's, each nation's distinctiveness. Oddly, given his general unconcern with economic constraints upon human action, Mazzini likens his new nation to an industry, and industries can only function through the division of labor. "Nationality," he argued, is "exactly a division of labour at the level of Humanity as a whole."[83] Division demanded cooperation and interdependence, and it is through this that each individual people acquires its own distinctive character. It followed, also, that if the nation was based upon a division of labor it could have only one legitimate political form: republican and democratic. Democracy, he wrote in 1847, had now become "a fact, a great European fact."

He was not alone in this conclusion. Even those like the French anarchist, "mutualist," and, after 1848, federalist Pierre Joseph Proudhon, who were no admirers of democracy, or at least of the kinds of democracy which had emerged out of the French Revolution of 1789, had made somewhat similar observations. "Nationality and unity," wrote Proudhon, "in these we have what are today the faith, the law, the reason of state; these are the gods of Democracy."[84] If Europe were to be united at whatever level, it could only possibly be as a body of independent democratic nations.

Mazzini was, of course, writing on the eve of the great revolutions which swept through Europe between 1848 and 1851, from France and Denmark and Switzerland to the German States, to Portugal and Spain, Holland, and Moldavia, to Milan, Rome, and Sicily—where they in fact began—and to the Ionian Islands. Unlike the French Revolution of 1789 which preceded them or the Russian Revolution which followed, the revolutions of 1848 were led by an unsteady and brief alliance between the middle classes—the *bourgeoisie*—and various classes of workers; and most were demands not for revolution as such, but for wide-ranging democratic, liberal reforms.[85]

Mazzini had himself played a significant role the creation of one of the most celebrated, if also ultimately least consequential: the short-lived Roman Republic of February 9, 1849. This was governed by a triumvirate made up of Carlo Armellini, an elderly lawyer, as a representative of the bourgeoisie; a young Roman aristocrat, Aurelio Saffi; and Mazzini himself, as the somewhat incongruous but much respected "representative of the people."

Mazzini had left England after the February Revolution in Paris in 1848 and arrived in Rome on March 5 to a rapturous welcome. He was given honorary Roman citizenship and became, in effect, the executive head of the new government of what had been, until Pope Pius IX fled to Gaeta on November 24, the Papal States. In the brief time he held office Mazzini proved to be an indefatigable and remarkably efficient administrator. Many of the poorest families from the Roman slums were rehoused—with nice irony—in the offices of the Inquisition; lands belonging the some of the religious orders were taken over and rented out to the peasantry; plans were made for the creation of a program of secular and state-funded education for all; the death penalty was abolished; and, while the institutional supremacy of the Catholic Church was preserved, religious toleration was extended to all. (Mazzini also, however, lowered taxes and increased government spending, with the inevitable inflationary consequences.) It was in every respect a liberal, tolerant regime, intended eventually to be extended to the whole of a future united Italy. "No war of classes, no hostility to existing wealth," stated the triumvirate's declaration of April 5, "but a constant disposition to ameliorate the material conditions of the classes least favored by fortune."[86]

The republic lasted a mere ninety-five days. On April 24, Louis Napoleon, president of the French Second Republic (and shortly to transform himself into Emperor Napoleon III of France), in order to appease his fiercely Catholic supporters, sent an army to oust the revolutionaries and to restore the Pope. Resistance was fierce, but despite the presence of Giuseppe Garibaldi and the resolve of the Romans, it did not last long. Mazzini, appalled that one republic should declare war upon another, insisted in treating French prisoners as "guest of war" and sent them home with a document citing Article V of the Constitution of the Second Republic: "France respects foreign nationalities. Her might will never be employed against the liberty of any people." The republic finally fell on July 3; but as Giuseppe Garibaldi, who had led the defense of the city, is supposed to have remarked as he withdrew, "Dovunque saremo, colà sarà Roma"—"Wherever we are, there Rome will be."

The revolutions of 1848 were the first, indeed the only truly European revolutions, and they had widespread repercussions well beyond Europe. Most of them ended swiftly—although few as swiftly as the Roman Republic—often brutally and generally in defeat. The coalition of the bourgeoisie and the workers collapsed as the former, much to Karl Marx's disgust, fell over themselves to make peace with the older monarchial order. The revolution in Denmark, however, resulted in the creation of a constitutional monarchy. The revolution in Hungary led to the freeing of the serfs; the revolution in Switzerland was responsible for the creation of the federal state which survives to this day. The revolution in Piedmont resulted in the promulgation of a liberal constitution (which subsequently became the Constitution of the Kingdom of Italy), as did the revolution in Prussia (although this was significantly curtailed by the markedly less liberal constitution of 1850).

The revolutions themselves may have achieved relatively little, and nothing which was to make any direct contribution to any possible unity of Europe, or even, as Karl Marx complained, to the unity of the working classes. It was clear, however, that in their pan-European scope they had made it possible for many liberals to imagine a way forward toward a shared perception of a common future. For Alexis de Tocqueville, who had served first under the "July Monarchy" of Louis Philippe I and then, after that had been toppled by the February Revolution of 1848, under the French Second Republic of 1849–51, and who was a member of the committee charged with drafting the new republican constitution, they were "the great drama of the European Revolution." There had been, he acknowledged, other revolutions in the past which had involved both the working masses and the bourgeoisie. But this was unlike any which had preceded it in that:

> It was brought about by causes very permanent and of a kind so general that, after stirring up France, it was to be expected that it would excite all the rest of Europe. This time it was not only a question of the triumph of a party; the aim was to establish a social science, a philosophy, I might almost say a religion, fit to be learned and followed by all mankind. This was the really new portion of the old picture.[87]

Over three decades later, Friedrich Nietzsche, who had very little belief in the people, much less in the bourgeoisie as agents of benevolent change, had come to not dissimilar conclusions. True, there was still everywhere across Europe the occasional backsliding into a "robust fatherlandishness" and into "old loves and confines...hours of national outburst, patriotic trepidations and all sorts of other antiquated floods of affect." But what he referred to in 1886 as the "civilization" or "humanization" of the "progress" of Europe was a clear sign that an "immense *physiological* process is taking place and constantly gaining ground—the process of increasing similarity between Europeans." It was nothing less than "the process of the *European in a state of becoming*." Nietzsche, however, was no democrat, and he feared that the "democratic movement" which had made this possible, and in which Mazzini had believed so passionately, would in the end amount to "the creation of a type prepared for slavery.... What I am saying is the democratization of Europe is at the same time an involuntary exercise in the breeding of tyrants."[88] Ultimately, he was to be proved right. The species of tyranny which grew, inevitably, out of the reliance on the kind of direct democracy which had driven the revolutions of 1848 would not arrive until the 1920s, but it created a shadow which has cast itself over the entire process of European Unification from Nietzsche's day until our own.

For Mazzini himself, however, the new concept of nationality was not to be solely an exercise in the national popular will. Its ultimate objective was rejuvenation, and every effort at rejuvenation must, he believed, finally lead to the reconciliation of "country [*patrie*] and humanity."The new principle of nationality was to be "Nationality such as the *Peoples*, free and brotherly associated... conceive it." It aimed not, as the older form of patriotism/ nationalism had done, at "binding" peoples together, but at what Mazzini described as *harmonizing* them.[89]—"cosmopolitan nationalism," the English neo-Hegelian T. H. Green appropriately called it.[90]

In its final form this would result in what Mazzini called the "blending" together of very diverse peoples. For Mazzini and many of his contemporaries, the creation of the nation was always the first step toward something larger, grander, more ecumenical: a league, a union, a community, a federation of all the European peoples united in a shared culture, not beneath a single regime. In Switzerland in April 1834, he founded a revolutionary new society made up of political refugees from Germany, Poland, and Italy and called it "Young Europe." It would, he declared, be "the future of Europe," which would "bring together the two fundamental ideas of the new era: *Patria* and *Humanity*." It was to be a "great association of two levels, one of which represents the national tendency of each individual people, which instructs mankind to love the *Patria*—the other represents the collective tendency [*tendenza commune*] of all peoples which teaches mankind to love *Humanity*."[91] Europe, he believed, was:

> marching towards an *organic* epoch. She stands at the gates of an entirely new career. She is rejuvenating herself. It is necessary that everyone should

understand his own mission and raise himself up to the level of the thinking
of the century.... Old Europe is dying, and as we stand at the beginning of an
organic epoch we must assist with all our might in the European reconstruction,
in the creation of a *young* Europe, a Europe of Peoples.[92]

Mazzini was, of course, an enthusiastic, messianic internationalist who held
firmly to the belief that all the European peoples would be united in "free
and spontaneous unity by a regulated federation [*fédération régulière*] which
would emanate from a European congress in which all peoples would be on
an equal footing."[93] And he was not alone. It is often forgotten that even
Ernest Renan ended his famous lecture "What is a Nation?" by recognizing
that modern nations, although still "something new in history" and now
everywhere dominant, "are not something eternal. They have begun. They
will end. They will be replaced, in all probability by a European confederation." Although more cautious than Mazzini, he added: "That is not the law
of the century in which we are living."[94] Mazzini was not a prophet. But if
the European Union, based as it is upon liberal, democratic, internationalist
principles and not untouched by a form of ecumenical Christianity, has any
single founding father, it is surely he.

Mazzini himself, however, never provided any clear indication of what
political shape his future united Europe would take beyond the by now
obvious fact that it would be a union of democratic states. Although he used
the phrase "the United States of Europe," it is far from clear what exactly he
meant by it. As with Kant's far more expansive "general league of nations,"
any political union between the states of Europe would have, for the time
being, to remain a still remote possibility, and no one, Mazzini warned,
should attempt to "superimpose [on the present] a world whose time has
not yet come." All that humanity could aspire to in the near future was this
"harmonization"; and in the Europe which had emerged, fragmented and
discordant, from the devastation of the Napoleonic Wars, that could only be
undertaken at the national level. To those who would argue that the nation
is a "manifestation of the past, a medieval concept that has caused much
bloodshed and continues to fractionalize God's thinking on earth," Mazzini's
reply was that the new "principle of nationality" was to be no "bitter war on
individualism." It was not intended to foster a new sectarianism. What he
called "Humanity," not the nation itself, was to be the final goal. The nation
was the means without which "you will be able to worship Humanity in
idle contemplation, but you will never be able actually to help it or seriously

attempt to do so." The manner in which this "Humanity" was finally to expresses itself was an "Alliance of Peoples." Yet clearly before there can be an alliance of peoples, the world has first to be divided into peoples.[95]

Mazzini was not the first or the last to insist on the necessary link between the creation of single nations and the ultimate unification of humanity at large. In 1797 Herder had similarly insisted that his conception of the "fatherland" ultimately served to "link the human species in a chain of continuing members who are to each other brothers, sisters, betrothed, friends, children, parents." The members of one fatherland do not, he insisted, fight the members of other fatherlands. "*Fatherlands* do not move against each other in that way: they lie peacefully beside each other, and support each other as families. *Fatherlands against fatherlands* in a combat of blood is the worst barbarism in the human language."[96] A little over a century later, in 1895, Johann Caspar Bluntschli made much the same general point. "*Nationality* and *humanity* are not irreconcilable," he insisted, "for the nations have all within themselves the *common human nature*. Thereby they are united into *one mankind*; and mankind in turn takes manifold forms in nations."[97]

This, of course, meant that "love of country" could not be used to assert the support of one's own kind over all, or indeed any others. It implied an inclination toward a high degree of collaboration between the different nations of the world. The world, however, was simply too large and diverse for any kind of universal cosmopolitan existence to be possible except in the very long term. If the different nations were to unite, they could only do so on the basis of a shared common life made up of shared aspirations, values, assumptions, even legal norms and religious beliefs. And the only place where such a common life, however fraught and fragmented, existed at that time was, of course, Europe. In Europe, Mazzini wrote in 1829, "there exists a concord of needs and of desires, a common thought, a universal soul, which drives nations along pathways that all converge on the same objective— there exists a European tendency."[98]

Many shared his view; many recognized the need for a more general participation by all the states of Europe in what was throughout the nineteenth century widely thought of—at least in some circles—as, if not yet a common project, then at least a shared set of political, cultural, and social concerns. As Bluntschli phrased it, since all the European states now faced a common future, all were "naturally entitled to participate in decisions to do with the general international order and with the management of common

European interests and arrangements."[99] Nietzsche, that "good European," perhaps as a consequence of that conversation he had with Mazzini in the sled across the Alps, agreed. There were, he claimed, "the most unambiguous signs declaring that *Europe wants to be* one." All of those whom he called "the more profound and far-reaching people of this century"—among whom he included Napoleon, Goethe, Beethoven, Stendhal, Heine, Schopenhauer, and (despite his own "self-misunderstanding") Wagner—"had focused all their efforts on preparing the path to this new *synthesis*, and on experimentally anticipating the Europeans of the future." Only when they had grown old and feeble had they become, and then only briefly, "fatherlanders." They had been only "'patriots' when resting from themselves."[100]

VII

The internationalist view of the nature of the new nations and of the potential future of Europe was, however, by no means shared by all. As the various languages of Pan-Europeanism were a reflection of the new nationalism, they were inevitably most prominent in those areas most affected by its rise: in France, in Germany, in Italy, in Poland, and in Greece. In Britain, although there were those such as Thomas Carlyle who were willing to embrace pan-European sentiments, the idea that there might one day exist any kind of pan-European union or a common European *polis* was confined to a very few, most of them international lawyers. Many more would probably have shared the view of Lord Salisbury that what he called "the modern theory of nationality" was "safe from refutation. The blows of argument fall harmlessly upon its unsubstantial forms. Controversy is waste labour in a domain of thought where no term is defined...and no question propounded for investigation."[101]

There were also other strains of nationalism which developed during the nineteenth century and which were to prove to be a great deal less liberal, and very much less in favor of any kind of future community of nations. What Nietzsche in 1886 dismissed as "nationalist nonsense" nevertheless continued. To him, this was most obvious in the new German Reich, that "regime of blood and steel," where it worked tirelessly "to alienate the peoples of Europe from each other." "Is there a single idea," he asked in indignation in the 1880s, behind "this cattle-like nationalism," a version which was so very different from that of Mazzini?

What possible value can there be in encouraging this brutal self-regard when everything today points to larger common interests?...And that obviously takes place under conditions of intellectual interdependence and increasing cosmopolitanism, in which the real value and significance of contemporary culture lie in hybridization and cross-fertilization!...Both the economic unification of Europe—and the response to it, the *party of peace*—are inevitable.[102]

It was, indeed, very hard to keep the idea of the "nation" as a community created through an act of individual will distinct and separate from any kind of tribal longings, distinct from precisely those tribal longings which for Mazzini constituted the basis of the older, now discredited patriotism. For Nietzsche, there were a number of modern "circumstances," driven on by "trade and industry, the post and the book-trade, the possession in common of all the higher culture," and what he saw as a new nomadism among "all those who do not own land" which were all "bringing with them a weakening and finally the abolition of nations, at least the European: so that as a consequence of a continual crossing a mixed race, that of the European man, must come into being out of them." All this had, however, given rise to a new brand of "national hostilities" created by "certain princely dynasties and certain classes of business and society." But once one had been made aware of this, there was an even more pressing reason why "one should not be afraid to declare oneself simply a *good European* and actively to work for the amalgamation of nations."[103]

VIII

In 1933, the year that Adolf Hitler became Chancellor of Germany, the French philosopher and novelist Julien Benda, best known for his condemnation of the meddling of intellectuals in politics—*The Treason of the Intellectuals* of 1927—published *An Address to the European Nation*, a passionate plea for European unity and a bid to do for Europe what, he believed, Fichte's *A Discourse on the German Nation* had done for Germany. Nationalism (or patriotism for that matter), he argued, was composed of two "successive movements." The first was the individual's awareness that he or she shared something in common with all those who look alike, dress alike, speak the same language, and share the same tastes and values or religious beliefs. It is this which leads him to declare that "these are my brothers." This sense of association in turn leads to a lack of egoism and a "surrender of his wish to be a unique individual, distinct from all others." It is, so to speak, the Mazzinian moment.

The second moment is the immediate desire to "draw a circle around himself and all those like him" and declare of all those outside the circle, "these are not my brothers." By this second move he "recovers his individual will," but he does so only "in the name of the group of which he is a member." It is no longer he who is capable of decisiveness and action but his nation, which is something distinct from all the rest of the world. For Benda, true nationalism cannot avoid this dual process.[104] As he told a gathering of the International Institute for Intellectual Cooperation in Geneva in October 1933, the vision cherished by "the most noble elements of nationalism" that it might be possible to bring about a "concert and harmonious accord" between the nations of Europe, while allowing each of them to continue to "enjoy their distinctiveness," was "radically false." No human being could be, as Mazzini had supposed, at once both a "true" nationalist and an antinationalist. Benda had no wish to destroy the "national differences" which existed in Europe. Rather, he wished to "invite all the peoples [of Europe] to feel as if you belonged to a region of your own which we will call 'humanism,' where you can recognise each other as fellow beings [*semblables*], and which is superior to all that makes you feel different from one another." And no matter what form it might take, a European nation was always to be preferred to a single ethnic nation. "Because Europe, even an impious Europe, will necessarily be less impious than the nation, because it will involve the devotion of the man to a more imprecise group, less individualistic and, thereafter, less humanly loved, less carnally embraced." In this way "Europe" would take on the moral and spiritual trappings once claimed by the nation, the *patria*. (Quite how this is to be achieved Benda does not say, and his claim that the model he has in mind was the Christian Church is hardly encouraging.)[105] But no matter what actual form it might take, Europe, as he imagined it, would be "a moment in our return towards God."[106]

For all its evasiveness, Benda's analysis captured succinctly much of what characterized the prevalent sentiments within the Europe of the 1930s which were largely responsible for bringing Mussolini to power in Italy and Hitler in Germany. The ultimate inspiration behind his account of nationalism as a process of association which required both "a wish to unite and a desire for opposition" he owed largely, however, to Georg Wilhelm Friedrich Hegel and his followers. If any were the source, albeit in most instances unwittingly, of Nietzsche's "nationalist nonsense," it was they.

For Hegel, human identity itself is an expression of what he called a *Volksgeist*, a "spirit of the people," which manifests itself in the institutions, the beliefs—in the culture, in the broadest sense of the term—of every nation. His ideal, unsurprisingly, was the ancient Greek *polis*, a community which resembles a living organism, in which the distinction between means and ends is finally transcended in that everything becomes simultaneously both an end and a means.[107] In the post-revolutionary world, this devotion to the nation meant, in effect, becoming a part, an active part, of something larger than oneself. If subjection to a monarch had been a species of subservience, however willingly entered into, the new citizenship was a union of one with the whole. And it was only through this union that true freedom could be achieved. Patriotism, said Hegel, was "in essence that disposition, which in the normal conditions and circumstances of life, habitually knows that the community is the substantial basis and end." It is a disposition, a form of trust that "my substantial and particular interest" as an individual "is preserved and contained in the interests and end of another (in this case the state), and in the latter's relation to me as an individual. As a result, this 'other' immediately ceases to be an 'other' for me, and in my consciousness of this, I am free."[108] Freedom was always the final objective, and freedom could only ever have been achieved not, as the misguided advocates of cosmopolitanism had supposed, by individuals struggling alone in a world shorn of all meaningful local attachments, but as part of something larger, grander, more imposing, and more enduring than the self.

In the process of shedding its identity as an overextended kin group, the nation for Hegel acquired not only a territory and supposedly a culture. It also acquired what came to be called a state. Originally the term state—*status, stato, état, Staat, stat, estado*, etc.—had been used to describe little more than the region inhabited by the people over whom the ruler exercised his power. During the course of the sixteenth and seventeenth centuries, however, it came to describe something more like the body of laws and institutions which prevailed over that territory and its inhabitants, and from then onward was endowed with a relatively new concept: "sovereignty."[109] For the state theorists of the seventeenth and eighteenth centuries, from Hobbes to Locke to Rousseau to Kant, as for the French and British and Italian liberals of the nineteenth, the state was a contractual apparatus whose sole function was to provide the people, or the nation, with its political coherence and security. The people entered into a contract—or, in Hobbes's case, a covenant—with their sovereign, who, in exchange for the voluntary surrender of the sovereign power that each man (and in these accounts they were always "men") had possessed in the state of nature, undertook to provide, in Hobbes's words, "Peace at home and mutual aid against their enemies abroad."[110] This with significant modifications and adjustments is, of course, the theoretical basis upon which all modern liberal democracies now rest.

Hegel's notion of the state entirely reversed this idea. To his mind, the social contract theory of the origin of the state was the consequence of "superficial thinking." (His prime targets were Rousseau and Fichte.) Worse, it resembled nothing so much as Kant's account of marriage. Kant had a horror of sex, which he believed could only be rendered acceptable for the unfortunately indispensable purpose of procreation if it were confined by a legal agreement.[111] For Hegel, any such conception of what he regarded as not merely humanly necessary, but also as "essentially an ethical relationship," could "only be described as disgraceful." By analogy a "social" contract was nothing other than a wholly unwarranted and damaging transfer of "the determination of private property to a sphere of a totally different and higher nature."[112] Worse, in an effort to provide the origins of the state with what was "supposed to be a purely *rational* basis," it had committed what was for Hegel the ultimate folly of "taking the externality of appearance and the contingencies of want, need of protection, strength, wealth, etc. not as moments of historical development but as the *substance* of the state."[113] For Hegel the people, the nation—the term he uses is, of course, *Volk*—is an instrument that transforms isolated individuals and families—and for Hegel the family *is* an individual—of which primitive mankind was composed into a coherent whole.[114] This transformation creates, however, not a "state" or a "sovereign," but what Hegel called "civil society"—*bürgerliche Gesellschaft*—an entity which Hegel is often credited with having invented (although there are earlier intimations of something similar in Locke).[115] This he called "the [stage of] difference which intervenes between the family and the state."[116] It is a "universal family" which makes the individual "a son of civil society which has as many claims upon him as he has rights in relationship to it." Since it operates as a family, it is also responsible for such things as education, if the parents are unable or unwilling to provide adequately for their own children, and, most strikingly perhaps, the care of the poor; for "just as every human being has a right to demand a livelihood from society, so also must society protect him against himself."[117] It remains, however, predominantly a realm of private activity, the realm above all of the market economy, of "subjective selfishness," in which, in Hegel's view of how the modern market operates (which he derived largely from Adam Smith), each individual, by working for himself also "earns and produces for the enjoyment of others."[118] Since, however, these individuals *are* only working for themselves, and since Hegel does not share Smith's "trickle-down" theory of the mode of production, it also "affords a spectacle for extravagance and misery as well as the physical and ethical corruption common to both."[119]

It is the state which constitutes the "formal *realization* of the Idea in general within [the nation]"—and in so doing provides its members with their ethical being through its institutions, without which the *Volk* "lacks the Objectivity of possessing universal, and universally valid, existence [*Dasein*]."[120] Hegel's nation-state (*das Volk als Staat*) is no "Artificial Man." Instead, it is a "wholly spiritual entity.... Spirit in its substantial rationality, and immediate actuality, and is therefore the immediate power on *earth*."[121] In making this move, Hegel went far beyond anything earlier European state theorists had envisaged for any human community—with the possible exception of Rousseau. (Hegel, however, dismissed Rousseau's idea of the contract, since, although it was supposedly based upon a will that was "capable of thinking for itself," it was still a contract, and like all contracts, inherently destructive of the "divine [element] which has being in and for itself and its absolute authority and majesty."[122])

For all European contractarians, and for their liberal heirs, the moral qualities of the state and the nation could only be conferred on it by its individual members. On the Hegelian account, by contrast, the *Staat* is a self-sufficient spiritual entity which, although it somehow emerged *from* its members, nevertheless confers ethical being *on* them. If Hegel looked back, like everyone else in Europe in the eighteenth and nineteenth centuries, to ancient Greece, it was not the Amphictyonic Leagues he noticed: it was the cohesion, the power, and the singularity—or what he imagined to be the cohesion, power, and singularity—of the Greek *polis*, that "political work of art," that "living universal Spirit which is at the same time the self-conscious Spirit of the individuals composing the community."[123]

The Hegelian nation-state stood as a completely independent totality in itself and in opposition to all others. It was "the spirit in its substantial rationality, and immediate actuality and is therefore the absolute power on earth."[124] More importantly still, for Hegel, unlike any of his predecessors, it stood potentially at least in *opposition* to all others. As the bearer of the ethical being of its citizens, the state could only be an individual. But Hegel's idea of individual self-recognition and self-consciousness always required the presence of an "other" for the full realization of the self. In precisely the same manner, the state, if it is to reach the full realization of itself, must also have an "other." And that "other" can only be other states. "Without relations [*Verhältnis*] with other states," he wrote, "the state can no more be an actual individual [*Individuum*] than the individual [*der Einzelne*] can be an actual person without a relationship with other persons."[125] Hegel, in common with all the theorists of the "law of nations" from Hobbes to Kant, believed states existed "in a state of nature with relation to one another."[126] The implications of this for any possible federation of states were overwhelming. If the individual is dependent upon the state in this way for his or her very ethical existence, he or she is in no position to risk jeopardizing that by merging it in any way with other states and hence other ethical beings, other "spiritual entities." Clearly, then, no state could consent to be bound by anything outside itself. The only possible form of "international law" would have to be nothing more demanding than a mutually agreed set of conventions, "institutionalized not in a universal will with constitutional powers over them, but in their own particular wills," which could be overturned whenever any single state saw fit.[127] This, in effect, meant that the true "international law" ended up being merely the law of the most powerful. Napoleon, Hegel once remarked, was "the only true professor of International Law."[128]

The same logic applied to any species of federation. So long as it was limited to the kind of cooperative venture which the Concert of Vienna had been, then some good might come of it; and it would survive, as indeed the Concert had, so long as it served the interests of all the parties concerned. For every state requires "recognition on the part of other states" as a condition of its legitimacy; but it also has "a primary and absolute entitlement to be a sovereign and independent power *in the eyes of others*, i.e. *to be recognized by them*."[129] Any true federation, therefore, would ultimately run up against the question of how the wills of the various states were to be reconciled, and what would happen to them in the process. In other words, who was to govern, and how? The simple, hopeful answer was, of course, that the federation itself would share sovereignty and executive power equally among its members. In practice, however, federations tended to fall, either directly or indirectly, under the influence of the most powerful state. Any federation of any kind is doomed, in Hegel's view, for "even if a number of states join together as a family, this league in its individuality must generate opposition and create an enemy." Kant's *Völkerbund* and the "Holy Alliance" of Prussia, Russia, and Austria (which Hegel regarded as much the same thing) are a denial of the fact that the "state is an individual, and negation is an essential component of its individuality." "Perpetual Peace" was a delusion, an impossible outcome for the human race: "talk," he concluded ominously, "falls silent in the face of the solemn recurrence of history."[130]

For the state, the ultimate "negation" could only take the form of warfare; and what Hegel calls "the ethical moment of war" is that moment when the citizens, in defense of the "substantial individuality of the state," are prepared to surrender all that belongs to them as individuals, "their own life and property, as well as their opinions, as well as all that falls within the province of life."[131] Not that Hegel looked upon war as a good in itself, nor did he actively condone acts of aggression in order to strengthen the ethical fibers of the state. But neither did he see it as an "absolute evil," as he supposed (wrongly) that Kant had done; and when it does occur, when a state is faced with no other alternative, then war should be embraced as the "moment in which the ethical health of nations is preserved in their indifference towards the permanence of finite determinacies." Kant's "perpetual peace," by contrast, could only result in a "stagnation . . . among nations," which, in the minds of most Europeans, was what had befallen the once great empire of China.[132]

Hegel was prepared to recognize that "the European nations [*Nationen*] form a family with respect to the universal principles of their legislation, custom, and culture [*Bildung*]."[133] He even believed in the existence of a "European mind," and he was, of course, as convinced as any other nineteenth-century European of the inherent superiority of the European peoples over all others. They all, he believed, possessed a "preponderant inwardness, a self-possessed subjectivity" lacking elsewhere in the world, and it was in the Europeans that "mind or spirit first emerges from its abstract universality to display the wealth of its particular forms." The European is also "interested in the world, he wants to know it, to make this Other confronting him his own," something he does not only on the intellectual (theoretical) level but also in "the practical sphere" by subduing this "outer world" to his will with force. It is this which has ensured for him "the mastery of the world."[134] In itself, this might be thought to provide the basis for some kind of family resemblance between the various European nations and, therefore, the possibility of some future European union. But Hegel was also convinced that Europe's superiority had been acquired precisely because of the "immanently varied character" of its peoples, above all because of the tension which he believed to exist between the characters of the northern and the southern nations.[135]

How, he asked, could any kind of lasting union be forged between the Italians, who he believed were so marked by naivety and so "undisturbed by universal aims" that the "general interest of the State" has been "unable to prevail over the predominant party spirit," and the overbearing Spaniards with their fanatical Catholicism, their obsession with personal honor, and passion for long strings of names? How could the French, filled with *esprit*, rather superficial and amusing, although capable of achieving great things in "talented persons like Montesquieu and Voltaire," be expected to make common cause with the English, "the people of intellectual institutions" whose worthy parliamentary forms are, however, derived only from tradition and not "general ideas" (that is, theoretical suppositions), and who, "though pursuing the universal ... always clings to [their] own particularity"; and how could any of these hope to reach an agreement with the Germans, who he said (with perhaps unintended self-irony) "have the reputation of being profound but frequently obscure thinkers" and, perhaps surprisingly, are the people who have "always liked to speak of their loyalty and integrity" but whose "patriotism was not very lively."[136] How could all of these divergent and discordant national characteristics hope to form a common political unity invested with any degree of the *Geist* it would require to survive the first conflict of interests? Any European federal union could only ever be a denial both of the state itself and of the very qualities which had driven the Europeans to create it in the first place.

There was, for Hegel, one further reason why there could be no union of European states, much less anything remotely resembling a "United States." For all the projects, however vague, for any association larger than the nation-state had at least since 1795 rested, as had Kant's "cosmopolitan right," on broadly republican and democratic principles. For Hegel, however, the only political form in which the state could find its true expression was some kind of constitutional monarchy. Republics, whether democratic or aristocratic, were, for him, only an incomplete transition, an "undeveloped condition" on the road from the "patriarchal tribe" to true monarchy. "Popular sovereignty" was, he wrote, only "one of those confused thoughts which are based on a *garbled* notion [*Vorstellung*] of the people. Without its

monarch and that articulation of the whole which is necessarily and immediately associated with monarchy, the people is nothing other than a form-
less mass."[137]

What in the end was to have the most lasting impact on all subsequent
nationalist sentiments, what lingered, despite the thickets of language in
which it was expressed, as an argument in favor of the necessary hostility
between states was Hegel's central belief that any state required for the creation of the ethical self, and therefore for its very existence, an "other" with
which to confront itself. In however vulgarized a form, this argument has
had a long and enduring afterlife, from Treitschke to the German legal, constitutional, and political theorist Carl Schmitt and their innumerable followers. It assumes that people and nations can only acquire their true identities,
can only become their true selves, in opposition to others. We need to distrust, even to hate, our neighbors in order to be ourselves. And, of course, in
this relationship there had also to be winners and losers, or in Hegel's famous
metaphor "slaves" and "masters." So long as one is committed to thinking in
this way, there can be very little room for anything like the mingling of
identities, much less for the belief that an "identity" might not, after all, be
so very important for the creation of the "internationalism" required for the
realization of any kind of cosmopolitanism. So long as those "others" remain
where they should be, fulfilling their allotted roles as "others," they are vital
to our being. But once we let them inside, once they cease to be the object
of our "negation," they become, in their continual flaunting of their "otherness," a threat to our being. As one anti-European in Britain phrased it
during the days leading up to the referendum in June 2016 on continued
membership of the European Union, British identity was being "drained
away" by the constant presence of foreigners on British soil. Hegel might
well have agreed.

I am not, of course, suggesting that in order to harbor such feelings one
has to be a Hegelian. Most of those who resent those who look or act in
ways which do not conform to their accepted notions of decorum, who
build mosques or synagogues or churches in their midst, who wear, or
force others to wear, headscarves in public have also surely, like the anon-
ymous British voter, never ever heard of Hegel. For centuries, as long at
least as there has been anything resembling the idea of a people, of a
nation, those peoples, those nations have sought their sense of collective
identity not merely in the celebration of themselves or what they believe
to be most distinctive about themselves, but in the rejection of all others

and in particular those geographically closest to them. "But now practically every Angle hates the Gaul, and every Gaul the Angle, for no other
reason than that he is an Angle," lamented the great Dutch humanist—and
therefore committed cosmopolitan—Desiderius Erasmus in 1516. "The
Irishman, just because he is an Irishman, hates the Briton; the Italian hates
the German; the Swabian, the Swiss; and so on throughout the list. District
hates district, and city [*civitas*] hates city.""Why," he asked despairingly, "do
these stupid names do more to divide us than the common name of Christ
does to unite us?"[138] This was the kind of motive for patriotism which in
the late eighteenth century the German poet Heinrich Heine had seen
lurking in in his native land. The patriotism of the Frenchman, he claimed
to believe, "means that his heart is warmed and with that warmth it
stretches and expands, so that his love no longer embraces merely his close
relatives, but all of France, the whole of the civilized world." But "a
German's patriotism," he wrote despairingly of his fellow countrymen,
meant only "that his heart contracts and shrinks like leather in the cold,
and a German then hates everything foreign, no longer wants to become
a citizen of the world, a European, but only a provincial German."[139]

But it was Hegel who built the sense of unease and hostility which
humans, like all territorial animals, feel, at least initially, when confronted
with others into an argument which could be used not merely to elevate it
to a principle of existence, but to glorify the conflict which has so often
flowed from it. It was Hegel's concept of the state that had the effect not
only of asserting the political autonomy of one's own state, but also of
sacralizing it. Like the Greek *polis* to which he was so attached, political
autonomy, for Hegel, was dependent upon self-praise, on the endlessly reiterated claim that "We are the best." This independent, self-determined "we"
of which the state is the highest manifestation is not only the best for us,
one among many; but precisely because it is *that*, it must also be the absolute
best.[140]

For all his glorification of the state and of the German people, Hegel
himself, however, was not quite the sectarian nationalist which subsequent
generations have often made of him. He believed in the destiny of the
German people as the "bearers of the Christian principle ... of Spiritual
freedom." And "that freedom ... has its own absolute form as its purport."[141]
He believed too, like Fichte, that as the Germanic tribes had been responsible for the collapse and subsequent rebirth, under Charlemagne, of the
Roman Empire, and because the Reformation—the expression of "Man in

his very nature destined to be free"—had taken place in Germany, the Germans were the true creators of the modern world.[142] But he was hardly uncritical of his fellow citizens. They could be indecisive, slow to act, inward-looking, and, he remarked sardonically, clung resolutely to the belief that "the importance of person and the respect due to them could, in almost every case, be measured with perfect certainty by the difference of title."[143] His writings, in particular his endorsement of constitutional monarchy, were all broadly in accord with the reform movements of the 1820s. He harbored no longings for the creation of a new German Reich—particularly not one created by Prussia—and would ideally have liked Germany to have formed part of—and ultimately to have led—Napoleon's liberalizing empire.

It was his followers, in particular after the creation of the new German Reich in 1871, who succeeded in identifying Hegelianism with the Prussian *Machtstaat* and were largely responsible for the subsequent reputation of his political philosophy as a forerunner of German imperialism and ultimately Fascism and National Socialism. Perhaps the most symptomatic of these (if hardly the most profound) was the pan-Germanic historian and member of the Reichstag Heinrich von Treitschke. Treitschke had been a friend of Bismarck, and was highly influential in his day. He was a racist—"We must," he urged the new Germans, "and will take our share in the domination of the world by the white races"—and an anti-Semite who coined the phrase *Die Juden sind unser Unglück!* ("The Jews are our misfortune!"), which was later adopted as its motto by the Nazi weekly tabloid *Der Stürmer*.[144] He belonged to a group of historians which included Johann Gustav Droysen, chief architect of the German hermeneutical school of history, who, in the judgment of the militant nationalist Friedrich Naumann in 1915, had "helped themselves and many others to an understanding of the coming National State."[145] Treitschke's *History of Germany in the Nineteenth Century* continued to be influential throughout World War I. As the philosopher, sociologist, and first president of the independent Republic of Czechoslovakia, Tomáš Garrigue Masaryk observed in 1918, "today pan-Germanism is mainly a philosophy of history, the history of the German nation and all of mankind.... Treitschke is its historian, and Kaiser William is its statesman."[146]

For Treitschke the "moralizing conception" of the modern state offered by German liberals had been an aberration. They had made of it "a good little boy to be washed, brushed and sent to school... to be thankful, just-minded and God knows what else."[147] Whereas the true state had to be something quite other, something whose power "had to be exerted fiercely and in full view"—which meant inevitably in competition and conflict with other nations. "Without war," wrote Treitschke, "no state could be."[148] It was war which gathered the forces and stimulated the need for sacrifice and the sense of brotherhood which every state requires if it is to fulfill itself as a state. War is the only agent of true progress. Peace is its negation. For all his occasional admiration for Kant, Treitschke looked upon any ideal of perpetual peace as nothing other than a sign of degeneracy, constantly thwarted by "the feeling of patriotism [that] breaks involuntarily through the cosmopolitan phrases of even the apostles of perpetual peace."[149] It was "patriotism," not "nationality," which constituted "the high moral ideal of national honor" and which will always find its highest expression in war. "The historian who moves in the world of the real Will," he wrote, "sees at once that the demand for eternal peace is purely reactionary. He sees that all movement and all growth would disappear without war."[150]

A measure of the impact of this "cattle-like nationalism," this bowdlerized version of the Hegelian theory of the state, can be gauged from a brief pamphlet entitled "Germany above All Others," published in 1915 by Émile Durkheim as part of a series intended to provide the French people with an ideological explanation for the conduct of Germany during the First World War.[151] The Germans, wrote Durkheim, who "until yesterday formed part of the great family of the civilized peoples" and who so obviously "belong to the same moral community as ourselves," have suddenly become "barbarous, aggressive and unscrupulous beings." How had this come about? The answer he believed lay buried deep in the German psyche, in what he dubbed "the German soul," and the clearest manifestation of that was Hegel's conception of the state. "The [Hegelian] state is *autarkes*," he explained, "in the sense the Greek philosophers gave to that word. It is an absolute. Made only to command, its will should never have to obey anything other than itself." And its "true expression," as Hegel had said, was a "powerful striving for the possession of importance and splendor." The man who "had set out this system with a plain and clear understanding of the principles on which it rests" was not, however, Hegel himself, but Treitschke.[152]

For Durkheim, the French—and more broadly European—understanding of the nation, the understanding which had emerged out of the collapse of the Napoleonic order, was essentially one in which civil society, as constituted by "the people" and the state, constituted "two aspects of the same reality." The state for Durkheim is, in fact, not a separate self-generating

THE BIRTH OF THE NATION

entity, but "the people seizing their awareness of themselves." The Hegelian distinction between the state and "civil society," in contrast, had made any such self-awareness untenable. Civil society without the state could possess no common unity, no coherence, no endurance. It was merely a random collection of customs, beliefs, and shared and ephemeral memories "destined" in Treitschke's words "to vanish like the winter snows."[153] Only the state had the power to provide this with cohesion and endurance; only the state could give lasting meaning to the histories, beliefs, myths, even the language of which civil society is so randomly and haphazardly composed. But for it to succeed in doing this, the people have to follow its demands unquestioningly. Clearly, that is hardly possible if the state is placed directly under the control of the very beings which make up civil society. For Treitschke, then, as for Hegel, the true state can only be a monarchy. But Treitschke's sovereign is not, as he was for Hegel, one whose role is to provide the final and necessary "I Will" to any form of legislation; he is the one whose role is to "dominate, to control both citizens and foreign states." He is, in short, the most recent incarnation of the archetypical Roman *pater patriae*; and, unsurprisingly, Treitschke's own model was Bismarck, "the Iron Chancellor."[154] Once one had read Treitschke, Durkheim concluded, it was easy enough to see "how Germany could be capable of the acts of which it is accused." For the true international role of the state constituted in this way was not, as Mazzini had insisted, international "harmonization"; it was for all great states to absorb all lesser ones, because, for Treitschke, all those states which had not achieved a certain size and level of historical grandeur did not count as states at all. They were nothing more than "veritable historical anachronisms destined to be absorbed by greater states, and the greater state which absorbs them is, in effect, doing nothing more than realizing their true nature."[155] This, which Durkheim saw as the intellectual and moral roots of what he characterized as the German "taste for conquest and annexation," had been, in effect, the real reason for Germany's invasion of neutral Belgium in August 1914.[156] The ultimate fulfillment of the neo-Hegelian vision of the all-powerful state lay not, as the liberal Mazzinian version had, in peaceable internationalism, but in a new form of universal monarchy.

The conflict between Durkheim's two contrasting views of the relationships between the state and civil society was to determine the course of European politics until 1945. In one direction lay a series of ambitious and often fantastic projects for an all-embracing European—sometimes even global—federation of free peoples bound together by shared interests and a common purpose, happily sharing sovereign powers equally among their members. In the other, quite another kind of union, one which would result in the attempt to create Kant's worst nightmare, that "graveyard of freedom," the "universal monarchy," in which one great power—Germany—would dominate all others.

But although the celebration of the state as an omnipotent, quasi-mystic being was the creature of Hegelianism, and in Durkheim's language lay buried deep in the German psyche, the desire for "conquest and annexation" among the peoples of Europe was certainly not unique to Germans.

3

The Scramble for the World

I

The claims that the Congress of Vienna had ushered in a century of peace not to be broken until World War I are, in many respects, illusory. The "Century of Vienna," as it has been called, was punctuated by more than forty internal wars, not to mention an equal number of revolts, revolutions, and civil disorders involving one or another of the "Great Powers." It is true, however, that most of these were either, like the Italian and Greek Wars of Independence, uprisings in pursuit of national sovereignty, or internal, civil wars, like the Carlist Wars in Spain between 1833 and 1876 or the great democratic and liberal revolutions which swept through Europe between 1848 and 1851.

The longest-lasting and bloodiest of all the interstate wars of the century, the Crimean War of 1853–6, although it involved two major European powers (France and Britain—and one minor one, Sardinia), was not a conflict between them, but rather a joint attempt by them to prevent Russia from absorbing the Ottoman Empire. Even the most lastingly significant conflict to be fought on (western) European soil, the Franco-Prussian War of 1870-1, was not aimed at the annihilation or assimilation of states. And there certainly were none which could compare with the range or destructive force of the Napoleonic Wars or the ravages of the Thirty Years War. To be sure, the "Century of Vienna" was peaceful enough to allow the liberal jurist, sociologist, and anthropologist Henry Sumner Maine to reflect in 1888 that "War appears to be as old as mankind, but peace is a modern invention."[1]

Maine's modern invention had however come, in part at least, at the expense of someone else. Increasingly, after 1815, the large-scale internal wars between the various European states had been mitigated, if not entirely replaced, by the quest for imperial expansion overseas. Already, in 1814,

Saint-Simon had urged upon his future "federative society" that "the surest way to maintain peace" would be for Europe to carry itself "ceaselessly beyond its own borders" and thus to "people the globe with the European race, which is superior to all the other races of mankind."[2] By the last decades of the century, it would seem that, even without the assistance of Saint-Simon's European parliament, the major European nations had taken his message only too abundantly to heart. Indeed, as Hegel remarked astutely, nations, "as a result of a long period of internal peace," were more likely to "seek and create an occasion [*Stoff*] for action abroad,"[3] so much so, indeed, that the continuation of peace was likely to become dependent precisely upon some external action. "For ten years," observed the highly influential political economist Paul Leroy-Beaulieu in 1874, "colonization has become the condition of peace within Europe....It has quenched the desire for conquest and the restlessness of peoples: their eyes fixed on the immense spoils to be had in distant lands, they have forgotten their mean quarrels with their neighbours."[4] As the German jurist Carl Schmitt (of whom more later) noted, since at least 1815, "the colony was the basis of hitherto existing European international law." It was, he argued, only the existence of her colonies which had allowed France, who had been "totally defeated" twice in the course of the century—once in 1815 and then again in 1870—to survive. It was the colonies which had prevented the "bloody wars of this era" from ever becoming "total in the sense of a struggle for final existence, since the upholders of this international law had available sufficient free space in the colonies in order to rob their mutual confrontations in Europe of a genuine existential severity."[5]

There was, however, more to this new thirst for overseas expansion than a bid to establish a terrain of conflict for Europeans beyond Europe. The new nation-state, as Mazzini had claimed, had made possible the creation of a new, more encompassing form of universalism than had been possible under the older "patriotism," and one now possessed of a seemingly insatiable desire to expand beyond the limits which the older ethnicities had created for it.[6] This might continue to divide Europeans while keeping their most rapacious instincts safely confined to territories beyond Europe. It might also, however, serve to unite them. The overseas colonies, Richard Coudenhove-Kalergi argued in 1926, constituted a vital part of what he called the "power-complex" of the states which would make up his "Pan-Europe." (He seems to have measured power by population size and territorial expanse.) "In order rightly to estimate the possibilities of Pan-Europe," he argued, "its colonies must also be taken into account." Africa, the "garden of Europe," could, he believed, be "opened up" if the European powers would only "cooperate in the continent, instead of transferring to it [their] rivalry, disunity and divisions." Africa might then, he concluded, "compensate Europe for the loss of America."[7] This *Eurafrique*, as he later called it, would then bring wealth to the European nations by developing vast tracts of largely underused arable land and benefit to the Africans themselves by committing the European powers to a policy of development and healthcare. Something of this vision survived even after most of the European overseas possessions were no more. The Treaty of Rome of 1957—the foundational document of the European Economic Community—extended access to the single European market to the "Association of Overseas Countries and Territories" of Belgium, France, Italy, and the Netherlands, with the declared intent, broadly in keeping with the new economic version of the "civilizing mission," of "the furthering of the interests and prosperity of the inhabitants of these countries and territories in such a manner as to lead them to the economic, social and cultural development which they expect"—which, with nice irony, meant that in effect nearly 90 percent of the territorial space of the new single market lay outside Europe.[8] Indeed, some version of *Eurafrique* survived, particularly in France, until the process of decolonization of the 1960s finally severed the African states, at least politically, from their former European masters.[9] This was, however, by no means, despite Coudenhove-Kalergi's somewhat offhand manner of referring to "the garden of Europe," intended only as a cynical means of preserving what remained of the European empires in a now rapidly decolonizing world. It was a way of reimagining and restructuring the relationship between Europe and Africa so as to bring the African colonies into Europe as what the French had indeed long claimed them to be—parts of France and now therefore of Europe, overseas. For this reason, Léopold Senghor, who would go on to become the first president of an independent Senegal, initially supported *Eurafrique* as a means of extending social democracy to Africa through new forms of "cultural reciprocity."[10]

In Coudenhove-Kalergi's opinion, only the British Empire—the largest, geographically the most dispersed, administratively and ethnically the most diverse of all the European empires—stood in the way of his grandiose conception of transcontinental transformation. For this, however, Coudenhove-Kalergi believed that he had a solution, although it was one which, as H. G. Wells, who referred to him dismissively as a "pro-Japanese propagandist" remarked in 1940, "might embarrass anyone but our author."[11] In Coudenhove-Kalergi's plan, India and the dominions would have to be allowed to go their own way. Canada should become part of "Pan-America" and so too would both Australia and New Zealand, since they were "more closely related by speech, culture, and interests to the United States of America than to the continental states of Europe." Once the British "Commonwealth of Nations" had been dismembered in this manner, a Europe united at home and overseas would be able to "become one of the strongest, perhaps the strongest, power-group on earth." By "unifying its organisation and rationally opening up its African colonial empire," Europe would be in a position to "produce all the foodstuffs it requires, and thus also become independent in a material way."[12] He also envisaged the possibility that one day Egypt and South Africa might join the "European League" to form something called the "European–African world empire." There was indeed some truth in Lenin's sarcastic remark of 1915—although that was not quite what he had in mind—that "A United States of Europe under capitalism is tantamount to an agreement on the partition of colonies."[13]

The assumption that the states which would make up the future united Europe might not only be able to hang onto their colonies, but that those colonies might even become a source of potential growth for whatever form the new federation or confederation might take, survived well into the 1940s. As late as 1945, when the former British colonial empire seemed, at least to those on the left, to be well on its way to extinction, Ernest Bevin, British foreign secretary and Labour Party politician, fearful, as were so many, of the possible outcome of the emergence of the Soviet Union as a new "Great Power," could still speak of the need for Britain to "mobilize the resources of Africa in support of a western European Union...[to] form a bloc which, both in populations and productive capacity, would stand on an equality with the western hemisphere and the Soviet blocs."[14] Britain would, of course, take no part in it; but it would serve to protect her and her empire from any new threat from the European mainland.

The belief that imperial expansion was both the product of, and a necessary condition for, the economic and cultural development of Europe was, of course, hardly new. "There needs be no hesitation," wrote John Stuart Mill (who had been Leroy-Beaulieu's prime inspiration) in 1848, "in affirming that Colonization, in the present state of the world, is the best affair of business, in which the capital of an old and wealthy country can engage."[15] Mill was commenting on a process which was already underway. The new Europe which had emerged from the Congress of Vienna would, by the

1860s, develop into a coalition of expansionist or would-be expansionist nationalist states, dependent increasingly upon loosely liberal democratic modes of government, however reluctantly accepted by their ruling elites. "Colonization on a large scale," wrote Ernest Renan, himself a staunch, if often conflicted liberal in 1871, "is an absolutely first-order political necessity. A nation that does not colonize is irrevocably reduced to socialism, in the war of the rich against the poor."[16]

And the rate of expansion was prodigious. It has been estimated that in 1500 the future imperial powers of Europe—Spain, Portugal, France, Britain, and Holland—occupied or controlled in one way or another about 10 percent of the land surface of the planet. Over the following two centuries this had perhaps doubled, so that by 1800 the major western powers—Britain, France, Germany, Austria, Russia, and the United States—plus what still remained of Spain and Portugal's overseas dependencies—between them occupied or controlled some 35 percent. By 1878, however, they had taken 67 percent. Even if we allow for the fact that all of these figures can only be approximate, that "controlled" can be made to mean many things, and that the rate of expansion was by no means steady or unchecked, this is nevertheless a remarkable rate of growth.[17] "The European sprit," wrote Johann Caspar Bluntschli in 1895, is already turning its gaze towards the globe, and the Aryan race feels itself called upon to order the world."[18] Less than a decade later, by which time all the great European empires had begun to devour themselves, the figure was closer to 84 percent. "E. is for Empire...," wrote the aptly named Mrs. Ernest Ames in her primer for infant imperialists, *ABC for Baby Patriots*, in 1898:

> Where sun never sets
> The larger we make it
> The bigger it gets.

Most obviously Empire provided (or at least was widely believed to provide by those who benefited from it) some of the vast resources which would fuel the Industrial Revolution of the later part of the nineteenth century. "Colonial politics," as Jules Ferry, prime minster of France (and one of the most influential and vocal proponents of a new French overseas empire) once observed, "is the daughter of industrial politics."[19] It was also believed to hold out, to those daring enough to seize it, an opportunity to prove themselves in ways which Europe itself seemed to deny. Nietzsche took a similar, if rather more sardonic view of the benefits Europeans were supposed to derive from expanding—or at least migrating—overseas. "Only in distant lands," he wrote in 1881:

> and in the undertakings of swarming trains of colonists will it be really clear how much reason and firmness, how much healthy mistrust, mother Europe has embodied in her sons—sons who could no longer endure it with the dull old woman and were in danger of becoming querulous, irritable and pleasure-seeking as she herself was.

Only beyond Europe would the true virtues of Europe flourish once again. (He also hoped that, in compensation for the loss of a substantial part of its population in this way, Europe would import "numerous Chinese," who would bring with them "the modes of life and thought suitable to industrious ants... and something of Asiatic calm and contemplativeness and—what is needed most—Asiatic *perseverance*.")[20]

II

From a historical perspective, however, the nineteenth-century mania for colonization, new or renewed, was by no means obvious. The Seven Years War of 1756–63, which was fought all the way from Pomerania to Pondicherry, had deprived France of most of its overseas possessions, and had made Britain Europe's leading imperial power, had also precipitated the American Revolutionary War, which, by the time it began (let alone ended) had persuaded many, Adam Smith among them, that in the modern interlocked, "globalized" world economy colonial empires were a thing of the past. Settler populations would always, sooner or later, seek independence and drag their mother countries, emotionally and politically unable to let them go peaceably, into costly and inevitably futile civil wars. Colonists, as Smith noted wryly, would always be more profitable as "brothers"—and willing trading partners—than they would ever be as subjects. In the long run "commerce"— which meant not merely international trade, but the culture of peaceful, cooperative interactions between nations that made it possible, and which, as Montesquieu had famously believed, "softens and polishes barbarous customs as we see every day"—would eventually replace conquest, and trading partnerships among free peoples would replace empires.[21]

After the final independence of all the colonial settlements in the Americas (with the sole and partial exception of Canada), it seemed to many that the age of empires had now, indeed, finally come to an end. What had once been sought through conquest would now be gained, peacefully and to the benefit of all, through commerce. And if the American War of Independence had not been sufficient to persuade Europeans that empire was an archaic, debased form of human association, Napoleon's attempt to create an empire in Europe itself certainly had. The modern transition from warfare to commerce, argued Benjamin Constant in 1813, had not so much "made men gentle," as Montesquieu claimed, but, by altering the ways in which goods were acquired, it had changed the very nature of the goods desired. In antiquity men had sought glory and despised luxury. Now the positions were reversed. In the ancient world, the tribal leader had only to point to the region of the world he wished to conquer and his warriors would follow him there unquestioningly. The objective was unimportant. Conquest of any kind and for any ostensible reason inevitably brought glory, and glory was the preeminent social good. In the modern world, calculating and concerned to protect individual rather than collective interests, glory had generally become of only secondary importance. The only response a modern people would give to a leader who urged them to follow him and conquer the world would, claimed Constant, be "to reply with one voice: 'We have no wish to conquer the world.'"[22] As Constant was one of the first to see, modern Europe, if not yet quite democratic Europe, was dependent to an unprecedented degree upon a new political force: "public opinion." In the monarchical, illiberal past, men might still be coerced or paid to fight, but the modern conqueror could never be able to mobilize what for Constant was the source of lasting political power in the modern world, without the support of which, as he had seen, no future, post-revolutionary society could hope to survive for long. Representative government—if not yet "democracy"—could not be persuaded to act against its own interests. "The force that a people needs to keep all others in subjection," he wrote, thinking largely of Napoleon,

is today, more than ever, a privilege that cannot last. The nation that aimed at such an empire would place itself in a more dangerous position than the weakest of tribes. It would become the object of universal horror. Every opinion, every desire, every hatred, would threaten it, and sooner or later those hatreds, those opinions, and those desires would explode and engulf it.[23]

For Constant, empires of the kind which Napoleon had hoped to create in Europe were mere anachronisms doomed to wither away in the fierce light of focused self-interested calculation. Napoleon, wrote Constant, had attempted "to make Europe go backwards." But he was now confident that, unless a new race of barbarians were suddenly to present themselves on Europe's frontiers, progress toward a more civilized, rational, more "liberal" future could no longer be reversed. The older imperialism of which Napoleon had been the last manifestation could, therefore, be safely relegated to an earlier age of human history.

These bright hopes for a new post-imperial, peaceful utilitarian world turned out, however, to be short-lived. For if the nation-state was ultimately responsible for the undoing of one kind of imperial project, it was also largely responsible for creating another, yet grander and more extensive one. The European empires of the nineteenth and twentieth centuries, so very different from their early modern predecessors, were not a denial of the impulse to nation building, but an expression of it. Few had seen this more clearly and witnessed its withering consequences more directly, or written about them so lucidly, as the great Bengali poet, musician, painter, and cultural reformer, Rabindranath Tagore. India, he wrote in 1917, had been overrun for centuries by hordes of Moguls and Pathans. The Indians had known them "as human races" whom they "loved and hated...as the occasion arose." With the coming of the "British Nation," however, they had found themselves forced to deal, "not with kings, not with human races, but with a nation—we who are no nation ourselves." And that "abstract being," that "ghastly abstraction of organizing man," the nation-state, had utterly obliterated them. "Have you not seen" he asked, "since the commencement of the existence of the Nation that the dread of it has been the one goblin dread with which the whole world has been trembling?"[24]

Modern man might indeed, as Constant had hoped, have no wish to conquer the world if he were asked to participate directly in the conquest himself, but he had little objection to the benefits which conquest and imperial expansion could bring. In this way empire became a source of national cohesion, or what the formidable Lord Nathaniel Curzon, Viceroy of India, referred to in 1898 as "more and more the faith of a nation."[25] In this new nationalist calculus, the more of this earth you could take away from those who, in the words of the novelist Joseph Conrad, "have a different complexion or who have slightly flatter noses than ourselves," the greater you became.

"C is for colonies," Mrs. Ames informed her baby patriots:

> Rightly we boast,
> That of all the great nations
> Great Britain has most.

The new imperialism of the nineteenth century had seemingly brought a measure of peace to the continent of Europe; it had indubitably brought immense wealth to those who had benefited from it; and it had, seemingly at least, allowed Europeans to perfect Nietzsche's "European virtues" in a climate which the "dull old woman" herself could no longer offer. But that was not all. Expansion was also a means of acquiring political status within Europe itself. In 1830, after the French consul Pierre Deval had been attacked by the Algerian ruler Husayn Dey with a fly whisk, the French occupied Algiers, then a vassal state of the Ottoman Empire. Few at the time doubted that the enthusiasm for the invasion was motivated less by the humiliation inflicted on an obscure French diplomat, and more by an attempt to re-establish the image of a France still tarnished by the defeat of Napoleon. Over a decade later, in 1841 when, despite continual fighting, France was still only in control of the coastal regions, Alexis de Tocqueville warned that, no matter what the cost, France could not afford to abandon its new colony. It had become "the greatest undertaking of this country," and if she were to surrender it, France "would seem in the eyes of the world to be yielding to her own impotence and succumbing to her own lack of courage," something which would have disastrous consequences "at a time such as our own when she appears to be falling to the second rank and seems resigned to let the control of European affairs pass into other hands."[26] To have given up the struggle, although he admitted that "we will never do all the great things we set out to do in Algeria," could only appear "in the eyes of the world...a certain declaration of the decadence [of France]." And not only would defeat in Algeria have threatened her still precarious position as one of the great powers of Europe. A decadent France could not have hoped to resist for long the revolutionary undertow which threatened constantly to tear the fragile new constitution apart, as indeed it would do just seven years later.

The same sentiment and the same fear of possible international humiliation were echoed by Charles de Saint-Vallier, the French ambassador in Berlin. On January 26, 1881, he wrote urging the government in Paris to seize immediate control of Tunisia, which had been ceded to France by the

Berlin Conference of 1878, adding, "If we give one more sign of weakness, we will succeed in relegating ourselves to the level of Spain."[27] The conquest of Tunisia began three months later, on April 28.

Nor was France alone in believing that a nation's standing within Europe relied heavily upon its capacities to sustain an empire overseas. For Britain in particular, the ability to preserve and expand had, by the mid-nineteenth century, become the only kind of international prestige that now mattered, the only kind, indeed, that now seemed accessible. "As long as we rule India," wrote Lord Curzon, "we are the greatest power in the world. If we lose it, we shall drop straight away to a third-rate power."

It was this belief that to be great a nation had to be imperial which persuaded France in 1852 and Germany in 1871 to declare themselves to be, once again, "empires." It also led the Ottoman Sultans to revive the title of "*Kayser i Rum*" (Caesar of Rome) first assumed by Mehmed II, the conquer of Constantinople in 1453, and Meiji Japan, after seizing Taiwan in 1895 and Korea in 1910, to reinvent itself as a European-style empire with a semi-sacred emperor. Even the United States, despite the generally hostile view of empire taken by most Americans, tried to cobble together something resembling an overseas empire—even if few ever called it that—in the Caribbean and the Pacific in the 1890s.

Even Spain, Europe's first great overseas imperial power, which by the late nineteenth century had seen itself reduced to one of the poorest nations on the continent and had only a handful of overseas possession left to lose, could make at least rhetorical gestures to what, in the view of so many, had been its glorious colonial past. In a lecture delivered at the Ateneo de Madrid on November 6, 1882, Antonio Cánovas del Castillo, then Spanish prime minister, speaking in the name of "the honour that we inherited from our forefathers, an honour that is still alive today," extolled Spain to take up once again its proper role as "part of the group of expansive, assimilative nations that have burdened themselves with the arduous task of civilizing the whole world."[28] And as Schmitt complained bitterly, in 1939 it had been precisely the exclusion of Germany "from extra-European colonial possession" after 1919 that had been the cause of "her real defamation and disqualification as a European power."[29]

The association of empire with great-power status survived even World Wars I and II. As late as May 1945, on the day after the German surrender, Charles de Gaulle was still able to insist amidst the construction site which was the French Fourth Republic that one of the most urgent needs for the new French state had to be the recovery of "our Indochina"; since, he declared, "It is in union with the overseas territories that France is a great power; without these territories she would no longer be one."[30] It was not until the 1950s at the earliest that the European leaders came grudgingly to recognize the force of the argument of two generations of critics—from Victor Riqueti, marquis de Mirabeau, Diderot, the abbé Raynal, Adam Smith, and Benjamin Constant all the way to the great Austrian economist Joseph Schumpeter in 1918—that, in Schumpeter's words, "Imperialism . . . falls into that large group of surviving features from an earlier age. . . . In other words it is an element that stems from the living conditions not of the present but of the past."[31]

III

It was not, however, only the political standing and the wealth of every individual nation that the acquisition of an overseas empire was believed to enhance. It was also seen as something intrinsic to the collective identity of Europe itself. The ability to create an empire was not simply a proof of great power. It was a mark of that shady, shifting, but always central concept, "civilization." Not for nothing had the Romans, who more than any other ancient people defined the cultural, political, and, perhaps most important of all, legal identity of the continent, been the imperial people par excellence. "Savages and barbarous peoples emigrate," remarked Leroy-Beaulieu, laconically; "only civilized peoples colonize." True Europeans were by no means the world's only imperialists; they were not even the first (that honor, it was generally agreed, belonged to the peoples of Asia). But by the mid-nineteenth century it had become obvious that they were by far the most successful. As we have seen, expansion was, in Hegel's eyes, a determining feature of the continent, not because of any innate property of geography (although, in his view, it helped that Europe was located in the "temperate zone; or rather its northern half," which is the "true theatre of History"[32]), but because only the Europeans had fully developed what he called "the formal realization of the Idea in general of the State . . . which, although it is inherent in all peoples as tribes, kinship groups or masses . . . it is only in Europe that the State displays the development and realization of freedom by means of rational institutions."[33] It is this development which "entitles civilized nations to regard and treat as barbarians other nations which are less advanced than they are in the substantial moments of the state"; and it does this because—and this for Hegel was the crucial point—"their independence is merely formal."[34] This gave to Europe a special capacity for imperialism, for carrying the World Sprit to those, the Africans, the Native Americans, and their like, whose "culture is purely national," by which he meant that they lacked the state-creating capabilities of the civilized peoples of the world. "The expansive force of a people," wrote Leroy-Beaulieu in his most Hegelian mood, "is the power of reproduction; it is dilatation through space. The people who colonizes the most is the first among peoples; if they are not today, then they will be tomorrow."[35]

The new post-Napoleonic empires were, however, far from being replicas of the old. They had two broad objectives. The first was purely instrumental: to rely as little as possible on overseas settler populations. The wars of independence in both North and South America had taught the European imperial powers that dependence upon European settler populations would ultimately be wasteful and damaging to all those caught up in it. For they had been wars not only of self-determination. The had also been wars of national creation. This and the subsequent rise of nationalism within Europe itself had alerted many to the possibility that any new empire was, before it had even really begun, already sowing the seeds of its own destruction. As Lord Selbourne said in 1813, "It appeared a madness to think of [acquiring new] colonies after what had passed in North America."

To avoid what seemed to have been the fate of all previous overseas empires, the new settlements in Asia and Africa between the 1830s and the end of the century were governed predominantly by some version of what the French general Joseph Simon Gallieni in Madagascar in the 1890s called the "politiques des races," and what F. D. Lugard, governor and governor-general of Nigeria between 1912 and 1919, described as "indirect rule."[36] This, although Gallieni's version was, in theory at least, a great deal more brutal than Lugard's, crucially involved dividing effective sovereignty with indigenous rulers so as to reduce the need for European settlers, European administrators, and in many cases European armies. To survive as their creators hoped they would, these new post-Atlantic empires had to be ruled, in part or, apparently, more directly, with the cooperation and in the interests of at least the most powerful of those involved in the imperial process. The "Orientals," as Christiaan Snouck Hurgronje (adviser to the colonial government of the Netherlands East Indies) pointed out in 1908, were, after all, no different from the Irish, the Finns, or the Poles: they much preferred to be ruled by their own people, for all their faults, than by foreigners.[37] If yet further struggles for self-determination by upstart colonists were to be avoided in the future, it would be wise to allow the colonized some kind of control over their own affairs.

These were the brutally realistic objectives. They were also, however, believed to be not without their ideological benefits. "Civilizing" now took on a rather different meaning than it had for previous generations of empire-builders. The Europeans were no longer faced with the obligation of incorporating the natives into a new kind of multiethnic European society. Now the chaotic tribalized societies would gradually transform themselves into something resembling European states, which would be of their own making through the imitation of what they recognized to be the obvious superiority of the European model; and crucially they would be racially, if not always ethnically, heterogeneous. As the historian, ardent federalist, and evangelical Christian Lionel Curtis wrote in 1907, Britain at least had increasingly abandoned what he called the "Cape idea" of "mixing up white, brown and black" and of "developing the grades of culture strictly on the lines of European civilization" in favor of "the very opposite of encouraging the black man to separate from the white and to develop a civilization...on his own lines."[38] In this manner, what Edmund Burke had called the "sacred trust" of empire, a phrase subsequently repackaged as "the sacred trust of civilization" and repeated time and again until at least the twentieth century, was cast as a body of goods whose ultimate benefits would be shared by all of those whom Burke had tellingly called the "fellow citizens" of the empire.[39]

In December 1917 Lord Robert Cecil, then assistant foreign secretary, explained to a Zionist meeting at the London Opera house what he understood to be the objectives of the new British imperium. There was, he insisted, nothing new in the current talk of "self-determination." The British Empire, he insisted, had "always striven to give to all the peoples that make it up the fullest measure of self-government of which they are capable. We have always striven to give to all peoples within our bounds complete liberty and equality before the law."[40] The key phrase here, however, was "of which they are capable." All previous European empires, perhaps all previous empires anywhere, had seen integration and "civilization" as a central part of their objectives, if only to make subject peoples less troublesome to rule. As the Roman historian Livy famously remarked of the Rome of Augustus, at the end of the first century BCE, "An empire remains powerful so long as its subjects rejoice in it."[41] But in order to rejoice in it they had also to become integral parts of it. "Civilizing," at which the Romans were believed to excel, was always a process of legal, political, and eventually cultural assimilation. The new empires, of which, in Cecil's view, the British Empire "was the first organisation to teach that principle [of self-determination] to the world," were committed, at least in principle, to something quite different: the duty of preparing their colonial subjects to take their place among the "civilized nations" of the world as members of independent states.

True, this process would inevitably be a long, complex, and difficult one. "The era of complete independence is not as yet visible on the horizon of time," wrote Lugard in 1923. "The danger of going too fast with native races is even more likely to lead to disappointment, if not to disaster, than the danger of not going fast enough."[42] But it was clear that it could not be postponed forever. And when the moment of emancipation finally arrived, when what the "Poet of Empire," Rudyard Kipling, had infamously called those "lesser breeds without the law" had taken their place among the civilized ones as nations, they could hope for no better future than to join the Europeans in one vast world order, peaceful and prosperous.[43]

There was, however, considerable disagreement among the imperial nations as to just how this goal was to be achieved. Even after the end of World War I, when the doctrine of "self-determination" was first insinuated into an international treaty by the American president Woodrow Wilson in 1919 and had been widely, if grudgingly, adopted as a guiding principle for the new League of Nations, former German and Ottoman territories in Africa and the Middle East were not, as some of their inhabitants had hoped, given their independence. Instead they were parceled out among the victorious allied powers under the mandate system, for, it was argued, their own future wellbeing. "To those colonies and territories which... are inhabited by peoples not able to stand by themselves under the strenuous conditions of the modern world," ran Article 22 of the Covenant of the League of Nations of 1924:

> there should be applied the principle that the well-being and development of such peoples form a sacred trust of civilization... The best method of giving practical effect to this principle is that the tutelage of such peoples should be entrusted to advanced nations who by reason of their resources, their experience or their geographical position can best undertake this responsibility.[44]

The "civilizing mission," as it came to be called, has of course been denounced for as long as the term has been in use as a thinly veiled justification couched in unctuous, self-serving terms for rendering the ruthless exploitation of mostly defenseless peoples across the globe acceptable, if not to its victims, then at least to the more squeamish citizens back home. And so in a great many respects it most certainly was.[45] But the insistence that the role of the new European empires was to encourage, cajole, and if necessary force the "barbarous" peoples of the world to adopt the legal, political, and broadly ethical standards of the "civilized" one had more to it than this. For it was not only, not even primarily, a justification; it was also an ideology.

Even Mazzini, contemptuous though he was of what he denounced as the imperial powers' "pretentious coda of permanent exclusive moral and intellectual leadership," firmly believed that Europe had a "moral mission" to bring—or, as he understood it, bring back—to Asia a world which in Europe had grown from the "first seeds of civilization and the first national tendencies" that the Asian immigrants themselves had first brought to Europe, many centuries earlier. (Like many of his contemporaries, Mazzini firmly believed in the Indo-European or, as he calls it, "Vedic" origins of the peoples of Europe.)[46]

IV

Behind Mazzini's assertion there lies also the long, tortured, muddled history of race. In the 1780s the great orientalist Sir William Jones had developed the idea that certain linguistic affinities between Sanskrit and most of what are now called the "Indo-European" languages implied that all the peoples who spoke those languages must have had a common ancestry. These peoples, the European *Urvolk*, he called "Aryans," borrowing a Vedic term. Jones, who ranked the sages of ancient India, Valmiki, Vyasa, and Kailas, as equal to "Plato and Pindar," believed that he had established an association between two great but otherwise distinct cultures. Later scholars, and in particular the German philologist Friedrich Max Müller, who became Professor of Sanskrit at Oxford in the 1860s and '70s, developed Jones's ideas into a theory which provided the "Aryans" with a common heritage, a complex migratory history, and an ancestral home in southern Russia. From there they had supposedly spread out and colonized a vast area of land reaching all the way from northern India to western Europe, carrying with them that distinctive way of life, urban and law-governed, which by the late eighteenth century had come to be called "civilized." Müller's account became so widely accepted that by the time Henry Maine—who, among his other roles, was Law Member of the Council of the Viceroy of British India—came to write his immensely influential *Ancient Law* in 1861, he could declare categorically that civilization was "nothing more than the name for the old order of the Aryan world."[47] None of this was explicitly racist. The link was solely a linguistic one; but the implications of the belief that a common language use supposed a common ethnic identity were not hard to find. In 1888, Müller, alarmed to learn that he was being hailed as the discoverer of a new brand of "scientific" racism, protested that his claims had never been racial. Aryans, he said, were only those "who speak an Aryan language, whatever their colour, whatever their blood. In calling them Aryans we predict nothing of them except that the grammar of their language is Aryan."[48] By then, however, no one was listening.

During the course of the nineteenth century various kinds of racism, driven by new brands of dubious biological and medical sciences, made a bid to establish a distinction between races based primarily upon physical appearance. The not-so-hidden purpose behind this was, unsurprisingly, to demonstrate the superiority of the European peoples over all others. As Johann Caspar Bluntschli summarized it succinctly in 1895, borrowing again from Müller, the "highest [races] in the scale" were what he called the "Caucasian or Iranian nations," for these are "pre-eminently the nations which determine the history of the world. But they are divided into two: the Semitic and the Aryan. The function of the Semites in the world is above all a religious one." "The Aryan family of nations," he went on, "whose language is the richest in forms and in thought, holds the first place in the history of States and the development of Rights: they have found their true home in Europe, and it is here that their manly genius for politics has unfolded and matured."[49] Aryans were state builders, lawmakers, and civilizers. This did not mean that other less fortunate peoples of the planet, in particular those of the "Orient"—especially Turkey—and Africa, could not also create states and devise laws by which to live their lives. It did mean, however, that they were very unlikely to be able to do so without some assistance from one or another kind of Aryan. And this superiority carried with it a historical and moral obligation "to develop and complete the domination of the world . . . in a consciously humanistic and noble way so as to teach civilization for the whole of mankind."[50] The ultimate goal of the "civilizing mission" could hardly have been stated more starkly.

One of the problems with racism, apart from the very shaky pseudo-scientific principles on which so much of it was based, was that it could not easily be confined to simple demarcations between Europeans and non-Europeans. All Europeans might share the same remote ancestry. But in their prolonged wanderings they had clearly been divided up into very distinct peoples. During the nineteenth century, the Germanic peoples, the British, as "Anglo-Saxons," and even sometimes the French—those European nations, that is, which had emerged politically and economically triumphant during the seventeenth and eighteenth centuries—came to look upon themselves as superior to the "Latin races" of the south—who had dominated the continent for much of the period from the collapse of the Roman Empire in the sixth century until the end of the Wars of Religion in 1648. The self-styled Count Arthur de Gobineau, often referred to as the "father of racist ideology" and another attentive reader of Müller, tried in *On the Inequality of the Human Races* (1853–5) to demonstrate that the Germans, the French aristocracy (whom he assumed to be pure "Gothic" and thus of Germanic stock), and possibly the "Anglo-Saxons" had retained the original virtues of the Aryan peoples. All the rest, mongrelized and bastardized by centuries of interbreeding, had long since abandoned the civilized ways of their remote ancestors.[51] Clearly, in the mind of someone like Gobineau, there was a more marked distinction between any European "race" and any African or Asian one than there was between, say, a German and a Portuguese.[52] But those differences were, nonetheless, significant. This, as we have seen, was one of the reasons why Hegel—although he does not employ the language of race—believed that no union of the European peoples was either possible or desirable. Hegelian nationalism (if not exactly Hegel's nationalism) could all too easily slide, as it did with Treitschke, into a species of racism.

For many, however, race was seen as at best an intellectually disreputable and unreliable indication of difference, at worst a threat to the necessary unity of the human species. Races were fixed and immutable. The "lesser races" might be able to imitate the behavior of the higher races; but they could never replicate it. And this ran directly counter to the idea that human characteristics, abilities, and dispositions owe more to habit, training, and upbringing—what the Greeks called *ethismos*—than they do to any innate disposition. The entire concept of "civilization" rested upon this assumption.

For this reason, if no other, most of the liberal thinkers of the nineteenth century poured scorn on the obvious incoherencies and inconsistences in what purported to be a natural science. They might, like John Stuart Mill and Alexis de Tocqueville, have been fully prepared to accept that there existed different human groups—or "races"—all of whom had attained different levels of achievement at different periods in their histories. They were certainly willing to concede that the Europeans had advanced farther along the road to civilization than the slothful Africans, indolent Arabs, and stagnant Chinese. But they were highly skeptical of the claim that there was anything biological and thus invariable and determinate to which these features could be attributed. If, said Mill, the "European family of nations" was the "improving, instead of stationary, portion of mankind," this could not be attributed to any "superior excellence in them, which when it exists, exists as the effect not the cause."[53] Race was in essence a fiction dreamed up to justify not the process of civilizing, much less the idea of any species of international legal order of the "civilized"; it was merely a justification for conquest and expropriation. As Ernest Renan wrote to the German Protestant theologian David Friedrich Strauss (who, like him, had written a life of Jesus) in 1871:

> Our policy is the policy of the law of nations (*droit des nations*); yours is the policy of races: we believe ours has greater worth. The excessively accentuated division of humanity into races, in addition to resting on a scientific error—since very few countries possess a truly pure race—can only lead to wars of extermination. These "zoological" wars, allow me to say so, are analogous to those the different species of rodents or carnivores wage for life.[54]

Human history, as he said emphatically elsewhere, "differs essentially from zoology."[55]

An empire based upon a conception of race could also, of course, only ever be static. An empire as "civilization," by contrast, was necessarily progressive and generally cast as a system of exchange. The Europeans would bring to the barbarous peoples of the world the laws, the understanding, the order, and the education they so badly needed. In return, these barbarians would deliver to the Europeans their natural resources (which, in any case, they had neither the understanding nor the technologies to develop to the full: science was the sole prerogative of the civilized). And although this meant that these "barbarians" would have to be helped to climb, very largely against their will, up the steep slope of progress, the long-term consequences would be beneficial to all. This, after all, as Mill argued, was how the Europeans themselves and the peoples of India—their nearest equivalents—had first been persuaded to abandon their primitive destructive ways. Before then, "the race itself may be considered as in its nonage." All mankind, "until they have become capable of being improved by free and equal discussion," had no choice but "implicit obedience to an Akbar or a Charlemagne, if they are so fortunate as to find one."[56]

This "civilization" was, however, an ever-shifting, ever-expanding ideal. Beyond the ability to subdue and to command, it implied above all else the capacity for self-government according to a body of universally accepted laws. But it supposed the existence of heterogeneous groups who had ties to each other which relied not upon those simple, atavistic obligations to kin which characterized the "tribe" but on perceptions of who they were rather than to whom they were affiliated. It also implied an attachment to, or at least a recognition of, the importance in the life of any society of place: it implied, that is, the existence of nations.

V

The creation of nations—of the kind of liberal nations which Mill, like Mazzini, had in mind—was a collective, rationalizing enterprise. It demanded that liberty made possible by Mill's "free and equal discussion." It described what was believed to be a set of shared values, aspirations, beliefs, cultural preferences, and their like which had been reached through the collective action of collaborative, reflective, reasoning individuals. Unlike brute custom, prejudice, and unreflective passion, civilization was in essence something artificial, created, thought, willed. It was, for the nineteenth-century French historian Jules Michelet, the final victory in the war which had begun with the creation of the world, the "war of man against nature, of mind against matter, of liberty against fatalism." The "barbarians," by contrast, still lived very largely as Hobbes had imagined pre-civil man to live: still immersed in the struggle against "matter" and fatalism. Unlike civilized mankind, they were not organized into nations but instead grouped by kin into what were called, in an allusion to the pre-Roman peoples of Europe, "tribes," and were generally held in Maine's words to have based "no claim of right upon the act of territorial possession, and indeed attached no importance to it whatsoever."[57] What had been true in the ancient world was true in much of the modern world beyond Europe. As with the Belgae, so with the Matabele.

Although there were quite obvious differences between the various peoples of which "Europe" was composed, they all somehow shared in a collective vision of a world in the making, of the triumph of the human over the brute incoherence of nature—features which clearly, in their own estimation of themselves, set them apart collectively from all the other peoples of the world. Europe, wrote Renan in 1871, "is a confederation of states united by the common idea of civilization."[58]

The person who had perhaps best explained just what this "civilization" meant was the historian Francois Guizot, who between 1840 and 1847 had been foreign minister, and then from September 19, 1847 to February 23, 1848 prime minister of France. In 1828, he delivered, in a politically volatile Paris, a highly influential series of lectures later published as *The History of Civilization in Europe*, which, in the opinion of John Stuart Mill, had ushered in a new era of historical writing. "It is evident," Guizot wrote,

> that there is a European civilization; that a certain unity pervades the civilization of the various European states; that notwithstanding infinities of time, place and circumstances, this civilization takes its rise in facts that are almost wholly similar, proceeds everywhere upon the same principles and tends to produce well-nigh everywhere analogous results.[59]

The European tendency to achieve progress through conflict—most obviously in Guizot's day class conflict—was, he said, "the fact of progress, of development; it presents at once the idea of a people marching onwards, not to change its place but to change its condition." Since there can be no end to progress, the Europeans can make no claim to have arrived at a perfect civilization, if only because no such thing can possibly exist. What they had achieved, however, was a remarkable balancing act. They had successfully shed the crude and barbarous condition of their ancestors, in which "there is a great display of individual liberties, but where disorder and inequality are excessive," a condition which is the "empire of force." But having got this far, they had resisted the temptation to decline into laxity, effeminacy, and the "state of immobility" to which so many other civilized peoples had succumbed and which was now the sad fate of "most of the populations of Asia."[60]

Guizot was not the first to make this argument, or something very like it. The vision of true human potential lying somewhere between extreme ferocity and indolence and submission is as old as Aristotle.[61] But Guizot's account of just how this had supposedly operated throughout the course of European (although, admittedly, predominantly French) history was to make a lasting impact on his contemporaries, in particular Mill, who defined civilization as "the best characteristics of Man and Society; further advanced in the road to perfection, happier, nobler, wiser."[62] It was not a condition, but a process. It was, said the English historian, philosopher, and archaeologist R. G. Collingwood in 1940, at a moment when "civilization," however understood, seemed to be rapidly vanishing from Europe altogether, "a process of approximation to an ideal state."[63]

This progress was expressed in social, personal, and, above all, legal terms. If, as Collingwood insisted, the term civilization meant "living as far as possible dialectically, that is, in a constant endeavour to convert every occasion of non-agreement into an occasion of agreement," it was evident that such agreements could only ever be reached in any lasting way by means of the law. All societies, however barbarous, have, of course, been recognized as possessing some kind of law, or what Maine called "Ancient Law." It was this which distinguished societies from simple kin groups. As John Westlake, Professor of International Law at Cambridge, nicely put it—adapting an ancient phrase—*ubi societas, ibi jus est*—"where there is society, there is law."[64] But Maine's ancient law, although it marked the first step out of simple barbarism, was, for the most part, made up of unexamined customs imposed by priestly or aristocratic castes who had manipulated it to their own ends, and consequently it "knows next to nothing of Individuals. It is concerned not with Individuals, but with Families, not with single human beings, but groups."[65] The move from societies such as these to what Maine called "progressive societies" was established by what in one of his best-known, most sweeping declarations, he described as the "movement from Status to Contract."[66]

True civil societies were, axiomatically and obviously, subject only to those laws which their members had agreed upon among themselves and which were binding upon and equal for all. This, it was widely assumed, was the basis upon which all European law rested. It was also the case that although the legal codes of the separate European nations were in many respects widely divergent—in particular after the implementation of the Napoleonic Code through so much of the continent—the same basic system of law, the same conception of justice, the same jurisprudence sustained them all.

And as with the law itself, so with the values, suppositions, and beliefs that had made it possible in the first place. "We are free, we are civilised to little purpose," Thomas Babington Macaulay had told the House of Commons in 1833, in support of the renewal of the charter of the British East India Company, "if we grudge to any portion of the human race an equal measure of freedom and civilisation." The true goal of the British mission in India lay in granting to the peoples of India, "sunk in the lowest depths of slavery and superstition," their due measure of freedom and civilization so that "by good government we may educate our subjects into a capacity for better government; that having become instructed in European knowledge they may, in some future age, demand European institutions." He did not know when this would come about, but he was certain that when it did, "it will be the proudest day in English history." There was he declared, in a great rolling Victorian peroration, only one "empire exempt from all natural causes of decay . . . that empire is the imperishable empire of our arts and our morals, our literature and our laws."[67]

Half a century later, in 1883, James Fitzjames Stephens, judge and legal scholar, who from 1868 to 1872 had served as Law Member of the Viceroy's Council in India, insisted that the British Raj in India was meant to enact what he termed a "true Liberalism." And what this meant, he declared, was that all the laws of India were to be based upon

> European secular morality, on European views of political economy, and on the principle that men ought to be enabled by law, irrespective of religion, race, caste, and similar considerations, to enjoy whatever property they have, to get rich if they can by legal means, and to be protected in doing as they please, so long as they do not hurt others.[68]

No one could have phrased the utilitarian view of the civilizing mission imbued with what he called "the liberal imperial spirit" more succinctly. But what is striking about both Stephens's claims and Macaulay's is that, despite both men's obvious commitment to what Stephens called the "patriotic sense of English pre-eminence," the values and the goods which civilization supposedly embodies and which the British Empire would confer upon the Indians are described consistently by both as not British, or English, but *European*.[69]

It was with this vision of an ever-expanding European civilization before him that in 1849 Victor Hugo—poet, playwright, novelist, biographer, the most celebrated literary figure in France in the nineteenth century, and a member of the French parliament—urged the governments of Europe to give up the persistent and fruitless struggles with each other and instead direct the vast sums they spent on warfare to overseas expansion. "Instead of making revolutions, we will found colonies," he enthused. "Instead of bring-ing barbarism to civilization, we will bring civilization to barbarism." All of this, he assured his audience, would result in a new kind of cosmopolitanism and "internationality"—to borrow Mazzini's term—that would bring about "the elimination of frontiers on maps and of prejudices in men's hearts."[70] This alone, he went on, would be the "true politics" which would

> make sure that all nationalities are recognized, all the historical unity of peoples is restored; and by rallying this unity to civilization through peace, it would continuously enlarge the civilized peoples, thus setting a good exam-ple for the still barbarous ones, by substituting arbitration for warfare; and finally, and this summarizes everything, to make certain that the last word should be declared through justice which the old world had pronounced by force.[71]

In 1949 the Swiss cultural and political theorist Denis de Rougemont, mak-ing what by then had perhaps become an obvious point, remarked that Europe had "always conceived of its civilization as a collection of universal values" and that this had been "rightly or wrongly, by virtue of its faith or because of its imperialist views."[72]

By the late nineteenth century, one of the clearest indications of having arrived at a state of "civilization" was the willingness to be bound by a new code of transnational law, known since Jeremy Bentham first coined the term in 1783 as "international law."[73] It has a long and troubled history, closely associated, as so many of its critics have insisted tirelessly and repet-itively, with the history of European empire-building. Its origins lie in the "law of nature and nations," a complex, sometimes overburdened intellec-tual edifice created in the course of the period from the sixteenth through to the eighteenth centuries which rested upon an underlying Stoic belief in the existence of a "natural law" supposedly shared by all and thus one upon which all peoples could, hypothetically, be assumed to agree, were it possible to assess what their collective judgment might be.[74] In time, however, it was shrunk by the great seventeenth-century Dutch jurist—the "Father of International Law"—Hugo Grotius and his successors to those laws to which not *all* peoples, but only all "civilized peoples" could *ex hypothesi* be supposed to have given their consent. (Even today, although the word "barbarian" has dropped out of respectable use, the International Court of Justice still lists among those principles it seeks to apply to "such disputes as are submitted to it" "the general principles of law recognized by civilized nations."[75])

By the middle of the nineteenth century this broadly ecumenical view of the possibility of a law between states derived from a presumed "consensus of all peoples," however restricted, had been largely, although by no means exclusively, replaced by a new form of positivism.[76] What this amounted to was not a law for all mankind, as the earlier "law of nature and nations" had aspired to be, but rather something akin to a domestic or civil law observed by all those nations which agreed to be bound by it. Its content was, therefore, clearly based upon the legal norms shared only by those nations who were party to it. What this meant, as the American jurist Henry Wheaton, author of the *Elements of International Law* of 1836 (one of the most widely used textbooks of the day), explained, was that "the subjects of international law are separate political societies of men living independently of each other and especially those called Sovereign States."[77] Wheaton accepted that there existed "Sovereign States" other than those in Europe. But this did not mean that some universal law based upon universal principles could be found that would embrace them all. It meant, instead, that true international law could be "only a particular law, applicable to a distinct set or family of nations, varying at different times with the change of religion, manner, government and other institutions among every class of nations."[78]

There might, in principle, and indeed in fact, exist a number of such "families of nations," the most obvious being what he called "the international law of the civilized Christian nations of Europe and America" and that "of the Mohammedan nations of the East." However, for all this seeming ecumenism, Wheaton had no doubt that of all these systems, actual and possible, "the international law of the civilized, Christian nations of Europe and America" was far superior to any other. It alone possessed robust theoretical foundations of long duration; and because "the international intercourse of Europe, and the nations of European descent, has since [the seventeenth century] been marked by superior humanity, justice and liberality in comparison with the usages of other members of the human family," it clearly offered the standard by which all other peoples should attempt to govern their relationships with one another. International law, wrote the positivist (and indefatigable traveler) William E. Hall in 1884 in much the same vein, "[i]s a product of the special civilisation of modern Europe" and constituted a "highly artificial system" which was firmly grounded upon "fundamental rights" and a "duty of sociability."[79] Crucially for Hall and many other jurists of the period, international law, although no longer (for the positivist at least) based upon a universal natural law, was still grounded upon a common moral understanding which was "essential under the conditions of modern state life" and as such could only be the creature of "a society and the moral principles to which that society felt itself obliged to give legal effect."[80] It was evidence, too, of the steady and, in his view, inevitable if still remote emergence of what Émile Durkheim in 1893 called a "European Society." "If today," wrote Durkheim

> that part of international law which regulates what we might call the real rights of European societies has more authority than heretofore, it is because the different nations of Europe are much less independent of one another, because, in certain respects, they are all part of the same society, still incoherent, it is true, but becoming more and more self-conscious. What we call the equilibrium of Europe is a beginning of the organization of this society.[81]

But no matter how curtailed the conception of its origins might be, no matter how crucial it was seen to be as both an instrument and an indication of an ever-increasing shared European civilization, international law was always intended to be more than the expression of a common European legal personality. In September 1873, in recognition of the increasing significance of the new law, a group of prominent international jurists from all over Europe, on the initiative of the Belgian jurist and government minister Gustave Rolin-Jaequemyns, met in Ghent to create an *Institut de droit international*, which was to become immensely influential in the years leading up to World War I, so much so that in 1904 it was awarded the Nobel Peace Prize. Its objective was to "facilitate [*favoriser*] the advancement of international law so that it might become the juridical conscience of the civilized world."[82] This "civilized world" may have been largely confined to Europe, but in the vision of Rolin-Jaequemyns and his colleagues it was also, as the Roman Empire had been, open to all those who would—and could—accept to live by its laws; and it was not bound by anything resembling kin, race, or ethnicity. Any people who, in the words of the German positivist Lassa Oppenheim in 1905, "expressly or tacitly consent to be bound for [their] future international conduct by the rules of International Law" could, by the grace and favor of its members, be admitted.[83] If they did, then they would be rewarded for their efforts by being granted what amounted, in the words of another international lawyer, T. J. Lawrence, in 1895, to "a kind of international testimonial of good conduct and respectability."[84] What all this could mean in practice had been sharply underlined in 1856, by the Treaty of Paris, which brought the Crimean War formally to an end. In the hope of halting or at least hindering the steady encroachment of the Russians, the signatories for the "Great Powers" had formally welcomed the crumbling Ottoman Empire into the "Family" by declaring briskly that "the Sublime Porte [be] admitted to participate in the advantages of the Public Law and System (Concert) of Europe."

The new "International Law" rapidly became a means by which the European powers (and the United States) sought to regulate their relationships with each other and with those powers which still remained beyond their political reach. It became a powerful force in international relations in the post-Napoleonic era and the central component of the juridical formulations of the new imperialism. This "new law of nations" was, said the British Liberal prime minister William Gladstone in 1879, "taking hold of the mind…which above all recognizes, as the tribunal of paramount authority, the general judgment of civilized mankind," proof in his opinion that history was bringing "the nations of the civilized world, as well as the uncivilized, morally as well as physically nearer to one another, and making them more responsible before God for one another's welfare."[85]

All of this, however, could be, and with hindsight frequently has been, dismissed as at best wishful thinking, at worst a high-minded legal gloss on what was, in fact, a ruthless systematic quest by one part of the world to seize the resources of much of the rest; a thinly garbed "ethical rationalization of the will to global power."[86] Unsurprisingly, not everyone, and indeed very few of the international lawyers themselves, saw it in quite that way. No matter how beneficial the despotism of the modern European Akbars and Charlemagnes might ultimately be for their hapless subjects, there was no law which could render it legitimate. Any law of nations had to be applicable to all. "The civilized powers have no more right to seize the territories of savages, than savages have to occupy the European continent," wrote the French jurist Gaston Jéze in the aftermath of the Berlin Conference of 1885 which had attempted to regulate the relationships between the competing European colonial powers in Africa. "The law of nations," he went on, "does not admit any distinction between the barbarian and the so-called civilized: men of all races, white or black, yellow or red, however unequal they may be, in fact have to be considered equal in the law."[87]

For all that, Jéze and his colleagues were convinced that the new law was a truly universal code based, just as the older natural law had been, upon principles no reasonable, rational person could deny, and that those principles were ones that had first arisen in Europe and only in Europe. However questionable the assumption might be that outside Europe there could be no, or at least only a very ramshackle, understanding of universal jurisprudence, its very existence helped to reinforce the idea that, in this at least, the peoples of Europe shared a collective identity and common purpose for the future. "Modern nations of our family have come to agree in much, and the agreement is growing" wrote the German–American jurist Francis Lieber (best known as the author of the "Lieber Code" for the government of armies) in somewhat Germanized English in 1868:

> We have one alphabet; the same systems of notation, arithmetical and musical; one division of the circle and of time; the same sea-league; the same barometer; one mathematical language; one music and the same fine arts; one system of education, high and low; one science; one division of government; one domestic economy; one dress and fashion; the same manners, and the same toys for our children (Asia and Africa have no toys): we have a united mail system, and uniting telegraphs; we have an extending agreement in measures, weights, coinage, and signals at sea, and one financial conception, so that all merchants' exchanges have become meetings of international import, at least of equal effect with that of international diplomacy; we have a rapidly extending international copyright; perfectly acknowledged foreign individual property; we have a common international law, even during war.

"Add to this," he went on, echoing Herder and Goethe, "that we really have what has been, not inaptly, called an international literature, in which a Shakespeare and a Kepler, a Franklin, Humboldt, Grotius, and Voltaire are belonging to the whole Cis-Caucasian race; we have a common history of Civilization; and Columbus and Frederic, Napoleon and Washington, belong to all." What held all this together, however, what ultimately allowed "the civilized nations... to constitute a community" and "a commonwealth of nations" was precisely "the restraint and protection of the law of nations."[88]

International law was manifestly a European creation. In this respect it was, as Rolin-Jaequemyns and his colleagues and successors believed, the most significant cultural and ultimately moral achievement, not of individual European nations but of "Europe." And because it was that, it was also the one thing that promised to unite the scattered nations of the continent. What it could not provide, however, was anything by way of a political form capable of enforcing it. In this respect, at least, it was not much of an advance on the older "law of nations." Kant's vision of the future, not only of a European but of a world cosmopolitan order, a "league of peoples," a "state of nations," etc., had been swept brutally away by the Napoleonic Wars. But as many had insisted at the time, there already existed several possible alternatives to the French Revolutionary model: the Swiss Federation, the United Netherlands, and, most compelling of them all, the new United States of America.[89]

VI

As early as 1786 the marquis de Condorcet reflected that had Saint-Pierre cast his "European Union" not as a coalition of existing powers, but as a true federation, much as the newly independent British colonies in North America were in the process of becoming, it might have had more chance of success. Like so many of his kind—the liberal enlightened champions of the early stages of the Revolution—Condorcet greatly admired what he thought he saw unfolding across the Atlantic. It was not enough, he wrote, that the principles of good government "should be written down in books of philosophy and in the hearts of men of virtue"; it was also vital that the ignorant or the weak man might be allowed to read them "in the example of a great people." That people he believed were the new Americans. "The act by which they declared their independence is an exposition, both simple and sublime, of those rights [of Man] so sacred and so long forgotten. Among no other nation are they so well known or preserved with such perfect integrity." True, slavery still persisted in some of the states, but he was convinced that "all enlightened men are ashamed" by that fact, and he was confident that "this stain would not for long sully the laws of America."[90] Although Condorcet stopped short of calling for a "United States of Europe," in his analysis of the Articles of Confederation of 1781, he remarked that "the considerable advance of philosophy" which he saw reflected in the document "gives one hope that one might one day [see in Europe] a confederation which would greatly diminish the evils of humanity."[91]

In the years following the Congress of Vienna, as any hope of anything faintly resembling Gentz's "federal system of Europe" swiftly faded, the only possible future for the European continent, if it were to avoid yet another conflict between democratic nationalism and recidivist monarchism, seemed increasingly to lie in some European analogue of the United States. "We do not strive simply to create Europe," wrote Mazzini in 1850; "our goal is to create the United States of Europe." But while for Mazzini this remained something of a distant possibility "whose time has not yet come," for his contemporary and admirer, the Milanese philosopher, historian, and staunch republican Carlo Cattaneo, it could only be a present and urgent necessity. In the years following 1848, which saw democratic revolutions of one kind or another break out across Europe, Cattaneo pressed the claim that for Europe there could now be only two future options: either what he called the "European Autocrat"—monarchical and imperial—or the "United States of Europe."[92] The former was the path that Napoleon had chosen, and although Cattaneo was prepared to grant that Napoleon's attempts to bring, as he saw it, the values of the Revolution to the rest of Europe had had the benefit of shaking the foundations of the old order all the way across the continent in ways from which it could never now recover, any form of autocracy could, nevertheless, only lead to future disasters. Like Mazzini, Cattaneo hoped and believed that only once the "principle of nationality" had united all the peoples of Europe would it be possible to rebuild "the edifice built by kings and emperors" after the "pure American model," and only when "we have a United States of Europe" would peace finally be achieved.[93]

Cattaneo's contribution to the ensuing debates over the future of Europe is not widely known outside Italy, but his conviction that Europe faced a choice between accepting autocratic imperial rule under some future Napoleon and reconstituting itself as a democratic confederation haunted the political imagination of much of the continent from his day until 1945. A conviction that that federation should take the form of a "United States of Europe" has had an even longer life. It was evoked by Pierre-Joseph Proudhon, by the Welsh utopian socialist Robert Owen, by August Comte (although Comte's "Occidental Positive Committee" only began with Europe and ended with the entire globe) and his disciple Émile Littré, by the German Arnold Ruge (another associate of Mazzini), by the international jurist and "minister plenipotentiary" to the United States in the 1860s Giuseppe Bertinatti, and by the Polish scientist and pioneer of ergonomics Wojciech Jastrzebowski, among many lesser others, and it was dismissed by Lenin as a mere "political slogan."[94] From 1867 all the way through the dark days of 1914–18, until its final demise in the still darker days of 1939, the "International League of Peace and Freedom" published (with one short interruption) a journal entitled *Les États-Unis d'Europe*. In a session held in 1929 the League of Nations adopted the "Briand Plan" (about which, more later), described as "a motion favorable to the idea of a United States of Europe."[95] The project was championed by Gaston Riou (whom we shall meet again), radical socialist and founder and president of the "International League for the United States of Europe." The phrase was used by Altiero Spinelli and Ernesto Rossi in the *Ventotene Manifesto* of 1941 (often considered to be one of the founding documents of the future EU) and again by Winston Churchill, who might be supposed to have known a great deal about the history of the USA and just how its federal system functioned, in his celebrated speech to the University of Zurich in September 1946 (although he did call it "a *kind* of United States of Europe" and repeated Napoleon's wish to "re-create the European Family"). "The United States of Europe has begun" was the title Jean Monnet, the "Father of Europe," gave to the speeches he made between 1952 and 1954 on the launching of the European Coal and Steel Federation.[96] In 2017, the former Belgian prime minister Guy Verhofstadt described the creation of a United States of Europe (although one that would look quite unlike the USA) as "Europe's last chance," and the same year Martin Schulz, former President of the European Parliament and then leader of the German Social Democrat party, called provocatively for the creation of a constitution for a United States of Europe by 2025.[97]

Of all the early advocates of a "United States of Europe," perhaps the most prominent, if not always the most consistent, however, was Victor Hugo. Throughout most of his long career Hugo spoke repeatedly of Europe as a common homeland, as the "Republic of Europe," the "United Peoples of Europe," and the "European Community."[98]

"Today," he wrote in 1843 in the preface to his play *Les Burgraves*, "there is, in effect, a European nationality, just as in the days of Aeschylus, Sophocles, and Euripides there was a Greek nationality." All the "civilized nations" of Europe, he insisted, despite the "momentary antipathies, the jealousies of frontiers," are "indissolubly linked by a secret and profound unity. Civilization has given to all of us the same guts (*entrailles*), the same spirit, the same goal, and the same future." But for all that the nations of Europe share in common, each is also, at the same time, a member of an individual and distinct nation. "France," he concluded is our "first nationality, as Athens was the first *patrie* of Aeschylus and Sophocles. They were Athenians as we are French, and we are Europeans as they were Greeks."[99]

Six years later, however, he seems to have embraced a far stronger notion of what this "European nationality" might be. No longer confined to the general awareness of a common culture, a common "civilization" analogous to the ancient belief in "Greekness," it now acquired a specific, if still largely indeterminate, political form as, once again, the "United States of Europe."

At the first International Peace Conference held in Paris on August 21, 1849, Victor Hugo, the nominal president of the congress, was called upon to make the opening speech.[100] The conference had attracted a remarkable gathering of delegates from across Europe and beyond, including one Canadian, one Guatemalan, and twenty-one from the United States. The most remarkable of these, who also wrote a vivid account of the event, was the black abolitionist, novelist, historian, and on his own self-description, "Fugitive Slave" from Kentucky, William Wells Brown. The conference was sponsored, although evidently with some misgivings, by Alexis de Tocqueville, at the time French minister for foreign affairs, who, despite the highly charged political atmosphere of the meetings, asked that no political issues should be addressed directly ("padlocks that the government put upon our lips," remarked Wells Brown).[101]

"A day will come," Hugo told his enraptured audience, "when all the nations on our continent will form a European brotherhood... A day will come when we shall see... the United States of America and the United States of Europe face to face, reaching out for each other across the seas." Echoing the now familiar belief in the curative powers of international trade, he evoked the image of "new markets opening themselves to commerce" as an alternative to new battlefields. Soon, he promised, the new technologies of communication, the steam train, the steamship, and the telegraph will have shrunk Europe to the size which France had been in the Middle Ages.

"The day will come," he continued, to loud applause:

> When you France, you Russia, you England, and you Germany, when all you nations of the continent, without losing the distinctive qualities or your individual glories, will bind yourself tightly together into a single superior entity, and you will come to constitute a European fraternity, as absolutely as Brittany, Burgundy, and Alsace are now bound together with France... A day will come when bullets and bombs will be replaced by votes, by the universal suffrage of peoples, by the venerable judgments of a great sovereign body (*sénat*) which will be for Europe what the Parliament is for England, the Diet for Germany and the Legislative Assembly is for France.[102]

It was, concluded Wells Brown, "one of the most impressive and eloquent pleas in favour of peace that could possibly be imagined."[103] In a tribute to Hugo's enrapturing eloquence, Coudenhove-Kalergi's wife, the Austrian actress Ida Roland, read out Hugo's speech at the opening of the first Pan-European Congress in 1924 "in service of propagating the Paneuropean idea."[104]

Hugo was, of course, preaching to the converted. Two years later, however, on July 17, 1851, he evoked the same vision of the future, this time before the more raucously skeptical audience of the French Legislative Assembly. He spoke vehemently and at length against the attempts by Louis Napoleon Bonaparte—*Napoléon le petit*, as he famously described him—to change the French constitution so as to allow him to extend his presidency by another four years. Any Attempt to change the constitution, Hugo declared, could only be an attack on the republic, and an attack on the Republic was an attack upon the Revolution for "the Republic and the Revolution are indivisible." It was, he declared—to general approval at least from the left of the chamber—the Revolution which had made France, and "The French people," he went on to mounting agitation from all his listeners, "have carved in indestructible granite and set down in the midst of the old monarchical continent the first building block of that immense edifice of the future which one day will be called the 'United States of Europe.'" This was greeted with howls of derisive laughter and by a "torrent of interruptions, an avalanche of invective, and hail of sarcasms" from the right wing of the chamber and stunned silence from the left.[105]

Hugo never once specified what form this new political entity would take, but at its core were always—at least before the Prussian invasion of France in 1870—France and Germany. They had been the true makers of Europe, the old heirs, as he (and many others) saw it, of the Roman Empire in the West and, perhaps more significantly for modern Europe, of the Carolingian Empire of 800. After that empire had collapsed at the end of the ninth century, it had been the French and the peoples of the German-speaking lands who had gone on to create or recreate the "old citadel" of Europe. Neither Russia—that "savage menace from the shadows to the light, from the North to the South"—nor frequently Great Britain was a part of it. All that constituted Europe and "Europeanness" could be summed up by the word "civilization" and of this, wrote Hugo in 1842, "France is the head...Germany is the heart." "Civilization," he went on, "is, in essence, France and Germany. Germany feels; France thinks. Feeling and thinking are the sum of civilized man." In Hugo's vividly schematic historical imagination, it was Charlemagne the "feeling" German, and then, centuries later, Napoleon the "thinking" Frenchman, who had been the only ones to attempt to fashion a new unified Europe. Both had failed because they had tried too hard to make the idea of Europe a reflection of their own personalities and had allowed themselves to be led astray by the "jealousy of nationalities." In future, it would be neither a new Charlemagne nor a new Napoleon who would defend Europe against its enemies from the orient (Russia) and from the west (Great Britain). Instead, it would be "Europe" itself.[106] France and Germany have, of course, remained—as many Euroskeptics bitterly complain—at the heart of the new Europe.

The fear expressed by both sides of the aisle of the National Assembly and repeated by Euroskeptics of all political persuasions ever since—that any such thing as a "United States of Europe," however fanciful, constituted a menace to national sovereignty—was, in Hugo's case, largely unfounded. He spoke repeatedly of the abolition of frontiers and customs tariffs, of a single European currency, of one civil service, one army, even—although Britain was frequently excluded from his vision of Europe—of a cross-Channel tunnel—a "far better treaty of union," he added, "between two peoples than a handshake between Lord Palmerston and Mr Bonaparte." Sometimes, these highly unspecific projects could vanish into a futurist fantasy in which "all laws would disappear, leaving only the laws of nature." In time, the government of the USE would, like the Marxist state itself, wither away, leaving in its place only *"L'Institut* [the scientific and literary body created in 1795], an "assembly of creators and inventors discovering and promulgating, not creating laws."[107] It was the most fully articulate vision of an entirely "technocratic" society. But for all that, Hugo was never in any doubt that whatever future shape and scope these new United States might acquire, they could only be brought about through "the education of all nations by the example of France." The head of this new Europe was to be France. Paris, "the center of the world, a volcano of light," was to be its future capital and French its "universal language."[108] France was to lead all the other nations of Europe into the ultimate fulfillment of the Revolution the fulfillment ultimately, indeed, of *Napoléon le Grand*'s design for the "family of Europe."[109] For it had been Napoleon, he told the *Académie française* in 1841, who "allowed France to grow so great that she had filled Europe."

Like Napoleon before him and many of the future advocates of a united Europe (including, most notoriously, Hitler) after him, Hugo could not conceive of a federation of European states which would not, in fact, be dominated, at least culturally, linguistically, and ultimately politically, by one of them. It was this too which John Stuart Mill in 1861 had warned against.

Although he firmly believed that "whatever really tends to the admixture of nationalities, and the blending of their attributes and peculiarities in a common union, is a benefit to the human race," he was also convinced that this should always be done, not "by extinguishing types... but by softening their extreme forms and filling up the intervals between them." For there was always the danger that uniting different nationalities under a single government might very well lead to one of them indeed growing so great as to fill all the others. If this were to occur because the dominant nation was "superior in civilization," then, in Mill's view, the "inferior" nations could only rejoice. He had little taste for minorities. "What Breton, or Basque of French Navarre," he asked, would not prefer to be "brought into the current of the ideas and feelings of a highly civilized and cultivated people... than to sulk on his own rocks, the half-savage relic of past times, revolving in his own little mental orbit, without participation or interest in the general movement of the world?" The same, he added, went for the Scots and the Welsh. But if the union was achieved solely through force, it would be "a sheer mischief to the human race, and one which civilized humanity with one accord should rise in arms to prevent." The destruction of the democratic city states of ancient Greece by Alexander the Great had been "one of the greatest misfortunes which ever happened to the world," and, he went on darkly, so would "that of any of the principal countries of Europe by Russia."[110] For this reason a true federation could in his view only exist when "there be not a very marked inequality of strength among the several contracting states."[111] And this in mid-nineteenth-century Europe was clearly not the case.

It was, that is, often hard to determine what really distinguished a "federation" from an "empire." This anxiety, of course, was to overshadow most of the projects for European integration from that day to this, and it has fed innumerable conspiracy theories, in particular from the British side of the Channel, that all this talk of a united Europe has only ever been but another means of pursuing a quest for European domination, which, in the French case, went back at least to the reign of Louis XIV.

Hugo's vision of a Franco-German alliance between head and heart was shattered in July 1870 with the outbreak of the Franco-Prussian War, the most far-reaching, the most lastingly significant of all the wars which punctuated the "Century of Vienna," in particular for those who held out any belief in the possibility of future European unification. Although it had begun as a squabble over the succession to the Spanish throne, this was in effect a struggle between the Prussian chancellor Otto von Bismarck—known appropriately as the "Iron Chancellor"—to unify Germany under Prussian leadership and the determination of Napoleon III to stop him. The French suffered one defeat after another until, on September 1, 1870, barely more than two months after the war had begun, Napoleon III was himself captured at the Battle of Sedan. The Germans then went on to besiege Paris, which finally capitulated on January 19, 1871. One day earlier, and as a further act of humiliation, Bismarck chose the Hall of Mirrors at Versailles as the place to declare King Wilhelm I of Prussia "Kaiser," thus creating what would subsequently be known as the "Second German Empire" (the first being the "Holy Roman Empire of the German Nation" of 1512–1806). The new German Empire was still in effect a federation of semi-independent principalities, as it had been under the first Reich, and the three largest of them, Baden, Bavaria, and Württemberg, even kept their own armies. But in reviving the grandeur of the empire of Charlemagne, and by doing so in the very palace which was always seen as the most flamboyant symbol of the French attempt to dominate Europe, Bismarck, it was said, had finally secured revenge for the Battle of Jena of 1806 in which Napoleon had annihilated the armies of King Frederick William III, and reduced Prussia to a satrapy of the French Empire.

The Treaty of Frankfurt of May 10, 1871, which brought the war finally to an end, stripped France of most of what it had gained under Napoleon, most importantly Alsace-Lorraine. But this was a war of attrition, not one of conquest, and the Germans renounced any claims to further territorial ambitions, and on January 28 withdrew. For months afterwards, however, the war filled the rest of Europe, even Britain, with wild rumors that a new war of Napoleonic dimensions, with Germany now as the new conqueror of Europe, was imminent.[112] The subsequent impact of the struggle on the "European System" was cataclysmic and contributed to the final confrontation between the two powers in 1914. A relatively weak and divided Germany had now been replaced by a vastly stronger, more resolute, more determined Reich—gone now was any trace of Hegel's Germans whose "patriotism was not very lively"—and the loss of Alsace-Lorraine was to remain a source of persistent conflict and anti-German sentiment within France until the end of World War I.

On March 1, Hugo made another impassioned address—tellingly entitled "For the War of the Present and for the Peace of the Future"—to the National Assembly, which now ruled over a newly created Third Republic. France, he insisted, even in bloody defeat, was still the home of freedom and enlightenment, of "not divine rights but human rights." Now, however, she also stood for the whole of civilization, while Germany, that "empire of servitude," represented only barbarity. This would, he was convinced, however, be only a transitory moment. By her actions in the war, Germany had brutally forsaken her role as the feeling part of Europe, but he was confident that one day France and Germany would resolve their differences, and the two would be reunited as a "single family, and single republic." We will, he concluded—to loud applause, this time, from the left—be "the United States of Europe, the continental federation; we will be the liberty of Europe, the peace of the world."[113] On July 14 he planted an oak tree in the grounds of his house in St Peter Port on the island of Guernsey, predicting that when it came to maturity, "the United States of Europe" would have become a reality. It is still there.

The following year, at the peace congress in Lugano, Hugo assured his listeners that although the Franco-Prussian War, more than any other previous conflict between European states, had "thrown civilization into question" and filled the future with "an immense hatred," Europe itself would survive. Politically, however, the outcome of the war now presented the continent with a hitherto unforeseen political dilemma. It was, he argued, now faced with only two choices: "to become Germany or to become France; I mean to say, become an empire or become a republic." In truth, however, the choice was an illusion. Empires were now things of the past. The *Deutsches Reich* inaugurated in 1871 was already an anachronism. No one could choose, as Bismarck had, to move backward for long. No matter what form of government Germany might now have, one day, Hugo assured the delegates, it would become, like France, a republic. And when that day arrived, when his oak tree had grown to maturity:

> We will have those great United States of Europe, which will crown the old world as the United States of America crowns the new. We will see the spirit of conquest transformed into the spirit of discovery. We will have the generous fraternity of nations, in place of the ferocious fraternity of emperors. We will have a patria without frontiers...trade without customs, circulation without barriers.[114]

VII

The United States of America—Cattaneo's "pure American model"—was the most obviously successful, fully functioning, and flourishing federal state then in existence. It was also, of course, a democratic republic, and most of the proponents of European unification from the mid-nineteenth century until today have been convinced, as Hugo was, that if Europe were to be unified, it could only be as some form of federation or confederation of democratic republics. In the mid-nineteenth century, of the only possible home-grown models, the United Netherlands and the Hanseatic League had long since ceased to exist. The only other, Switzerland, although frequently cited as evidence that Europeans from different language groups and cultural and political backgrounds were capable of uniting to create a genuine confederation, was too small and too anomalous to count. As the great jurist Hans Kelsen noted in 1944, Switzerland is made up of "insignificantly small portions of the German, French and Italian nations separated from these nations by historical and political circumstances" rather than of the "mighty nations" themselves. It was also, he pointed out, significant that both the United States and Switzerland were "geographically contiguous territories [which had] united to form a single state," something which was not the case for most of the states of Europe, let alone the world.[115]

But for all the many evocations of the USA as an example, few of those who called for a European federation or confederation ever said very much about how the new European version would actually be governed. Many, as far back as the abbé de Saint-Pierre (as far back even as the Duc de Sully's "Grand Design" of 1600[116]), had spoken in very general terms of a European assembly, a diet, a general council, even a European parliament. But none of those who claimed the United States of Europe as their goal, not Mazzini, not Cattaneo, not the organizers of the "International League of Peace and Freedom," not Hugo himself, had apparently given much serious thought as to how the North American structure of government, with a House of Representatives and a Senate, much less an executive presidency with virtually monarchical powers, might be replicated in Europe, in particular in a Europe which was itself going through a very painful transition from autocratic monarchy to representative democracy.

For one thing, as many of those who endorsed the idea of a future USE, as well as those who opposed it, often pointed out, the populations of the Thirteen Colonies which had become the "states" were largely homogeneous both culturally and politically; they all spoke one language, observed the same overall system of laws, shared more or less the same political assumptions, followed more or less the same religion, with few exceptions all came from the same region of Europe, and all shared a common history as

British overseas settlements. They possessed, that is, none of the variety, the cultural, legal, political, linguistic, or religious divisions, of the European states. The differences that did exist between say Massachusetts and the Carolinas shrink to vanishing point when compared with those between Catholic Spain and Lutheran Prussia. Then there was the inconvenient fact that the USA had been created out of a war in which the vast majority of its future citizens had fought on the same side, for the same objectives. The Founders themselves had recognized that this was indispensable to their continuing survival. "Independent America," wrote John Jay, "was not composed of detached and distant territories." Providence, he believed,

> has been pleased to give this one connected country to one united people—a people descended from the same ancestors, speaking the same language, profess-ing the same religion, attached to the same principles of government…and who by their joint counsels, arms and efforts, fighting side by side through a long and bloody war have nobly established general liberty and independence.[117]

In 1873, in his impassioned plea for what would become the *Institut de Droit International*, Gustave Rolin-Jaequemyns similarly reflected that those "oth-erwise serious men" who believed that it would be enough to replicate the conditions which had led to "the formation and existence of the American union" to render all mankind "peaceful and happy" had failed to take into account that in Europe, each of whose varied peoples "glories in its historical past, its language, its literature and everything which constitutes its individuality," no such proposal could ever be made to work. "We favour the Italian school," he concluded (by which he meant the successors of Mazzini and Cattaneo, and his fellow founders of the *Institut de Droit International*, Pasquale Stanislao Mancini and the constitutionalist Augusto Pierantoni), "which tends in general to develop and strengthen the national element…and to represent the future progress of humanity as destined not to absorb, but on the contrary to guarantee, the existence of the rights, and the autonomous development of each of the collective members of the human family."[118]

The model which most of the advocates of a United States of Europe had in mind—although few of them were quite so precise in their analogies—was something similar to the union of separate fully independent confederated states favored by the "Articles of Confederation and Perpetual Union" of 1781. This—a "sovereignty over sovereigns, a gov-ernment over governments," in James Madison's disparaging words, had preserved the sovereignty and independence of the individual states, and granted the new central, "confederal" government only those powers which, in the view of the colonists, had once belonged to the king and parliament.[119] But had the former Thirteen Colonies finally adopted that proposal, they would hardly have been in a better position to achieve the kind of unity and stability the European federalists so admired than the independent, squabbling republics of the Spanish south were to be. What had sustained the new United States through its initial period of consolidation and through the Civil War had been the federal Constitution of 1789, in which, in Tocqueville's words, "the principle of the sovereignty of the people is...a legal and omnipotent fact that rules the entire society."[120] And anything like that would have been utterly unworkable in the Europe of the nineteenth century.

Much the same point was made by J. R. Seeley in a lecture he delivered to the Peace Society in 1871, in the midst of the Franco-Prussian War (and praised by Charles Lemonnier as a *fort bon discours*).[121] Had "the American Confederation" remained as it was, Seeley argued, it would eventually have gone the way of all the other failed confederations with which European history was littered, the "helpless Amphictyonic Leagues of ancient Greece," the Holy Roman Empire, and the "German Bund which fell to pieces in 1866." Instead, the "American Confederation...gave way in 1789 to the American Union" to establish "the one pre-eminently successful federation of history." Seeley seems to have had a generally low regard for American political culture, but in the system itself he believed that the Americans "have found a higher political unit for mankind; they have found a name greater than that of State; they have created a virtue beyond patriotism."

Unlike so many who followed him, however, unlike even Altiero Spinelli, Jean Monnet, Robert Schuman, and the other "founders of the EU," Seeley had seen that it would not be so easy to detach political alliance from cultural and social identity. It was one thing to weld together a "population homogenous, and united by language, institutions and religion," quite another to "yoke together indissolubly so many rival races and rival states and rival religions, the Englishman and the Frenchman, the German and the Slave [*sic*], the German and Italian!" It would be hard, he went on, even to imagine

> [a] federal name which should fall like a covering upon so many secular discords, and hide at once so many inveterate wounds; to reconcile in one act all

the most rooted antipathies, to unite in common political action the subjects of a Czar, of a Kaiser, of a Constitutional Queen, and of a Swiss Republic; to accustom to familiar intercourse those whom difference of speech has so long made barbarians to each other.

And then, of course, the United States of America had not, in reality, become a true nation even after 1789.[122] Toward the end of his study of American democracy Alexis de Tocqueville made the dispiriting observation that:

> I would like to contribute to the faith in human perfectibility, but until men have changed their nature and are completely transformed, I will refuse to believe in the duration of a government whose task is to hold together forty diverse peoples spread over a surface equal to half of Europe, to avoid rivalries, ambition and struggles among them and to bring the action of their independent will together toward the accomplishment of the same projects.[123]

His skepticism was well founded. Less than thirty years later, although not quite for the reasons he had imagined, the United States collapsed into one of the most ferocious civil wars in western history. And it was, as Abraham Lincoln himself declared, in perhaps the best-known speech in American history on November 19, 1863, a war "testing whether that nation or any nation so conceived and so dedicated can long endure."[124]

The American colonists, unlike the Europeans, unlike even the members of the National Assembly in France in 1791, also did not have behind them, as the founders of the European Union did in 1945, in Habermas's words, "200 years of constitutional practice."[125] They invented as they went along. And what they finally ended up with, as their critics have frequently and bitterly pointed out, was a Romanized, "mixed" version of the British constitution created out of the so-called Glorious Revolution of 1688, which in the minds of the American revolutionaries King George III had violated, not they.[126] What became the USA survived the early constitutional crises and one of the bloodiest civil wars in history largely on account of the fierce, if ill-defined, "patriotism" which had animated the Revolutionary War; the fetishization of the constitution; the relentless incantation of a set of simply unitary values based upon a hazy notion of "freedom" and "liberty"; and the repeated insistence from politicians of all persuasions that there really does exist such a thing as "the American people," from Alaska to California, *e pluribus unum*, capable of sustaining the image, despite an unchecked stream of (legal) immigrants, of "one Nation under God, indivisible, with liberty and justice for all." What the

Northern States managed to do in 1867 was to make possible a compelling sense of both citizenship and identity, however shabby it might sometimes seem. Were it not for that, the United States might well have gone the way of Simón Bolívar's union of "Gran Colombia" of 1819–31.

In Seeley's view, the lesson to be learnt from the initial failure of the American *con*federation was that "the decrees of federation must not be handed over to the officials of the separate States, but that the federation must have an independent and separate executive through which its authority must be brought to bear upon individuals." For the same reason, any European federation would fail if it were to be nothing more than a mere aggregate of existing states. "The individual and not merely the State," he wrote, "must enter into a distinct relation to the Federation" and must be conscious of his or her obligations and loyalties to it. All federations, he warned, "are mockeries that are mere understandings between governments." Any future "United States of Europe" must, therefore, have a constitution and a legislature and an executive. And not merely must it have them, but they must constitute the foundations of a new form of citizenship. It would never be possible to abolish warfare within Europe until all Europeans are prepared to "take up a complete new citizenship. We must cease to be Englishmen, Frenchmen, Germans and must begin to take as much pride in calling ourselves Europeans." Nor, he warned, would they succeed unless these new Europeans were prepared to "overcome discrepancies of language race, culture and religion." The new Europeans would have to learn to value their new citizenship over the old, so that should a conflict arise between the federation and the state, as it had in the US in 1861, they would, as the citizens of the Confederacy had not, unhesitatingly and consistently "prefer the Union to the State."

The only means by which any kind of lasting unity could be brought to all these would be "to spread a new conviction over Europe." If a "real union of peoples" is to be created in Europe it would never, he believed, "be attained by mere diplomatic methods, or by the mere action of governments, but only by a universal popular movement. Now a hundred years ago such a popular movement, extending over Europe, was barely conceivable, but in the present day nothing is more easy to conceive."

Similar movements had, after all, happened before. The Reformation and the seizure of the political imagination by "popular principles of government" after 1789 had all been unimaginable before they had happened. If "an opinion rising in the people and slowly gathering strength under the influence of rational argument" was able to impose the abolition of slavery upon "cold or reluctant legislatures," then who could seriously doubt that "federation, too, will have its day?" It was, he warned, likely to be a long journey, but it would be carried inexorably along by "the steady wind and irresistible tide of manifest destiny." The difficulties, he concluded, triumphantly,

> are unprecedented only in number and degree; they would certainly be insurmountable if the advantages of union were only moderate; it remains to be seen whether they would be insurmountable to a European public opinion gradually educated to see before it a new Federation rising like a majestic temple over the tomb of war, emulating the transatlantic Federation in prosperity and unity, but surpassing it far in all the riches of culture, manners, and science, and consecrated with all the traditions and reliques of the ancient world.[127]

Seeley's vision of what would be needed to create a true European federation goes far further than any subsequent European project. But for all that the United States of Europe was and has remained an ideal, no such proposal has ever tried to link the benefits to be gained from peace—which was, of course, always the first incentive for unification—to international trade or attempted to associate that with the preservation of the far more elusive ties of language and culture which create human communities. And it is this which, for all its stumbling uncertainties, the EU has always tried to achieve.

VIII

For even its most impassioned advocates, however, the "United States of Europe" remained, if rather more than Lenin's "slogan," then more a rallying cry than a project for a future government. Most tended to agree with Seeley that something which rose above the mundane business of actual government was needed if the USE were to become—and to remain—a reality: a common culture, an ideal, and a new form of citizenship. But just what exact *political* shape any future European federation might take remained, and many would argue still remains, curiously imprecise.

The two writers, both jurists by training and profession, who in the course of the second half of the nineteenth century did most perhaps to flesh out a project for a new united Europe which might have had some chance of overcoming the obvious difficulties posed by any attempt to import aspects of North American federalism into Europe were Johann Caspar Bluntschli (whom we have already met) and James Lorimer, Regius Professor of Public Law and the Law of Nature and Nations at the University of Edinburgh and one of the founders of the *Institut de Droit International*. Although Bluntschli and Lorimer are rarely mentioned today, least of all by the drafters of the successive treaties which have created the European Union, nevertheless, if any single person or group of people could be said to have foreseen the difficulties that any future European Union would have to face and the kind of aspirations it would have to embody, it was they.

There are, it must be admitted, a number of reasons today for not taking Lorimer very seriously (although most of his contemporaries clearly did); for one thing, he was a natural-law theorist. He believed, like the great jurists of the seventeenth and eighteenth centuries, that the world was governed by a form of law—known most commonly as the "law of nature"— which was inscribed in nature, to which all human beings could have access through reason, and which was, therefore, applicable to all peoples everywhere. He lived, however, in a professional world made up largely, if by no means exclusively, of positivists, for whom all law was a matter of purely human convention. He was also, more damningly, a diehard racist (and an anti-Semite) who believed that no "modern contribution to science seems destined to influence international politics and jurisprudence to so great an extent as that which is known as 'ethnology or the science of races'"—by which he meant the physiology of Johan Friedrich Blumenbach and social Darwinism, not modern anthropology.[128] For all that, Lorimer's approach to the possible future of a united Europe is entirely free from any racial shading. Both he and Bluntschli insisted that what held Europe together was not race, but the assumption of the existence of a common cultural heritage, a common history, and, above all, for both, a common understanding of the role—if not always of the nature—of the law.

Lorimer's understanding of the law of nature could also, at times, be highly eccentric, but of all his contemporaries he was perhaps also the one who was most concerned with the creation of a broad theory of international law. This made him a convinced cosmopolitan, and thus (if for no other reason) something of a Kantian. Like Kant, he believed that jurisprudence, once "elevated to the clearer atmosphere of cosmopolitan conceptions," might be able to demonstrate "that as national order is the condition of personal freedom and international order the condition of national freedom, so it is in cosmopolitan order that international freedom of action must be sought."[129] Like Kant, he was certain that no system of law among states could possibly have any meaning in the absence of what he characterized as "a system of mutual responsibility."[130] In the fateful year of 1871 he published, in French, a "Proposition for an International Congress Based on the *de facto* Principle" which set out in broad outline his proposal for a future "International Government."[131] Seven years later Bluntschli published his own account of "The Organization of the European States" (*Die Organisation des europäischen Staatenvereines*), which was both a critique of Lorimer's scheme and, as he saw it, a far more plausible alternative. In 1884, Lorimer published an extended version of his original article and a series of responses to Bluntschli's objections under the resounding title, "The Ultimate Problem of International Jurisprudence" as the final book of his magnum opus, *The Institutes of the Law of Nations: A Treatise of the Jural Relations of Separate Political Communities.*[132]

Lorimer speaks throughout of an "international" government, but despite the fact that he left open the possibility that one remote day such a government might be extended to the entire globe, he had, as he said, approached the problem of how to create peace, stability, and the rule of law between states "as a general European question, and mainly from a Continental point of view."[133] Like his predecessors, and most especially Kant, Lorimer fully recognized that if it was to be realized, his proposal would require "a period of time, and a degree of advancement in the civilisation of individual States, to which I venture to assign no limits." Unlike his predecessors, however, at least as he had read them, his was, as the title of his original article had made clear, based on *de facto* reasoning and was thus precisely not to be classed with "such conceptions as the Utopia of Sir Thomas More, the Republic of Victor Hugo, or even Plato's Republic and Kant's Perpetual Peace."[134] In his own eyes, if not Bluntschli's, Lorimer was nothing if not a realist.

Despite his belief in the existence of a guiding set of principles for all humanity, and not infrequent evocations of Providence, Lorimer believed, as he said, "in the reasonableness of omnipotence and in the omnipotence of reason; and, from an absolute point of view, I venture to set no limits either to the scheme of Providence or to the perfectibility of human society."[135] He was as persuaded as his positivist colleagues that if law were to be anything more than a vague moral injunction, it had to be capable of enforcement. And this meant, as it had for Kant, that international law, like all law, could only be *law* within a given political order, which meant in the case of Europe, as it had done for Kant, a form of federalism. Any such order had, however, first to be built. It would not, as Hugo and others seemed to have believed, arise naturally out of common affinities, driven onward by increasing economic prosperity, the "civilizing" power of commerce, and "public opinion." Furthermore, not only would it not evolve naturally from the inevitable progress of all the European peoples, but it was in reality only ever likely to be built in response to a crisis. "It is inevitable," Lorimer wrote in 1871, shortly after the Germans had left Paris, "that the problem of a European or cosmopolitan order should arise at the beginning or more often at the end of a great war."[136] Nor could the doctrine of the "balance of powers," which had supposedly emerged triumphant from Vienna, provide any long-term solution. It was, at best, in Lorimer's words impossible "[t]o define...with any approach to precision...and it has accordingly received as many interpretations as different States have entertained different opinions, or been swayed by different interests, at different times."[137] For it to work for any period of time, furthermore, it had logically to eliminate any future development of the states involved: to strengthen one or weaken another would be to destroy the balance. And as Bluntschli remarked, it was not the task of international law "to protect the status quo" but rather to "recognize and to promote the development of states"; and developing states could not be expected to remain in balance for very long.[138] Now, wrote Lorimer, that "all the great powers know from their own painful experience that none of them are powerful enough to subordinate all others, nor are they strong enough in the long run to resist a united Europe," the time had come to build a political community of states rather than to rely upon a forever unsteady equilibrium between peoples in permanent condition of flux. The effect of this would be to transform international law, or "European Public Law," into a species of domestic law.[139]

The problem, however, as Kant had clearly seen, was how to do this without falling prey to the kind of "universal monarchy" represented by Louis XIV and subsequently Napoleon. The solution, in Lorimer's opinion, and again in this respect it is not unlike Kant's, was to ensure that all the states of which the "international government" is to be composed retain their individual sovereignty as states, for an "an international nation...is a contradiction in terms."[140] The government which bound them all would, therefore, "for international purposes exclusively, consist of a legislature, judicature, executive, and exchequer."[141] Lorimer's proposal is, as Bluntschli unkindly pointed out, unwieldy and not infrequently eccentric. The legislature would be bicameral, made up of a Senate (which seems to have been modeled on the British House of Lords) and a Chamber of Deputies, not unlike the House of Commons. In addition, there was to something Lorimer called a "Bureau or Ministry" composed of members drawn from the two branches of the legislature.[142] This would be responsible for electing a president of "the international state" from among its members for managing economic affairs; it would also be responsible for what he called a "standing force"— somewhat like the ill-fated European Defense Force—which would allow individual states to reduce the size of their standing armies. The "Judicial Department" would be made up of two separate courts, one civil, one criminal. The civil would be responsible for "all questions of public international law, involving pecuniary or territorial claims, rectification of boundaries, and the like, in so far as their solution depends on the construction of subsisting treaties, or of the legislative enactments of the International Government."[143] The criminal branch would act very much as the European Court of Justice does today. The details of the Executive Branch are left somewhat vague; but it would be made up of members chosen by the bureau and would have some kind of regulatory force (quite what, he does not say) at its disposal "for the enforcement of the enactments of the International Legislature, and of the decrees of the international courts."[144]

In Lorimer's view this somewhat cumbersome administrative apparatus could not be peripatetic, as Bluntschli had suggested should be the case for any truly international authority, because the transfer of administrative institutions from one place to another would be so impossibly clumsy as to make their functioning virtually impossible. (It would be hard to imagine all those horses and carts dragging themselves over rain-soaked roads and mountain passes. Even with modern means of transportation the workings of the European Parliament are regularly interrupted as it shuttles back and forth between Brussels and Strasbourg.) Since, however, "an international nation" with a single administrative geographical center was, in his view, "a contradiction in terms," "international life in a material world must diffuse itself from an international centre, where, without disturbance from national elements, it is permitted to breathe an international atmosphere." The capital of the new Europe would have to be, like Washington, a place with no geopolitical ties to any of the states of which the greater union was composed. The best place for this in Lorimer's view would be a "denationalised" Constantinople, "which, in consequence of the political incapacity of the Turks and other historical causes, had become *res nullius gentis* [a thing belonging to no people], and should therefore be declared to be *res omnium gentium* [a thing belonging to all people]—the common forum of nations, and the centre of international life." If that could not be made available, then he believed that the canton of Geneva should be declared an "international territory" and thus be transformed into the "centre of European life" and the "centre of decentralization."[145]

But no matter where it was finally located, it was crucial that the laws passed by this international government should not impinge in any way upon the internal affairs of the states concerned. Lorimer was not, he insisted, attempting, as his predecessors had been, to create a single state out of many—even so amorphous a state as the Holy Roman Empire—but to build a true confederation which would resolve the seemingly intractable problem of how to create a system of legislation for the European states which regulated only those affairs that were of common concern to them all, while leaving all other matters entirely in the hands of the individual states themselves. In this his project has affinities with the "principle of subsidiarity"—to which I shall return—introduced by the Maastricht Treaty (the Treaty on European Union) of 1992, now one of the general principles of European law, which similarly insists that all decisions should be made at the most immediate (or local) level that is consistent with their resolution.[146]

For all his warnings about the possibly deleterious consequences of a too intrusive supranational legislature, Lorimer was also aware, as the successive generations who have struggled with the shaping of the EU have been, that "in order that the international government may act as the guardian of the freedom of all national governments, and of all national governments equally, it must enjoy a separate freedom of its own; and this, as it seems to me, it can do only by means of a separate executive."[147]

Bluntschli's main objection to Lorimer's "International Government" was that it drew too heavily upon what Bluntschli called "the Hamilton model" (*Gedanken Hamiltons*)—that is, the US Constitution of 1789 (although Lorimer in fact makes no direct allusion to the USA or to any future "United States" of Europe). This, he insisted, could never be imposed upon Europe for the by now familiar reason that whereas there existed, in however ramshackle a form, an American "people," Europe, by contrast, was made up of many peoples. "The Union of the United States," Bluntschli wrote, "although composed of relatively independent states, is a sovereign society in which the people of North America, united by a common fatherland, common language, culture and law and interests, share a common national identity." The opening words of the US Constitution, "We the

People," presupposed there already existed an American *people* before any attempt was made to create a federation of American *states* on the basis of it. This alone had made possible what Bluntschli described elsewhere as a "new independent state personality endowed with its own will and its own organs," which in turn was capable of creating a political society in which "the unity and freedom of the whole was no less certain than the unity and freedom of the parts, and both, the whole and its members, were organized as states. The thought was completely new. No such state formation had ever existed before in world history."[148]

Even under such favorable conditions as these, the new United States had failed in the short run, as Tocqueville had predicted it would, "to hold together forty diverse peoples...to keep them from falling into rivalries, plots and struggles and to bring together their independent wills into action for common plans." If the USA had required a prolonged and bitter civil war finally to cement its unity, asked Bluntschli, what chance had Europe, where there is not, nor has there ever been, a single people? Instead, Europeans are as "divided politically as they are by their location, race (*Rasse*), their history, their culture, their interests, and their rights." "A political unit without a people," he insisted,

> is a contradiction in terms. Since there is no European people there can exist no state called "Europe." Any bid to create a new constitution for Europe which would absorb all the existing sovereign states would be doomed to failure. Neither the Union of the United States nor the German Reich nor the Swiss Confederation could, therefore, serve as models for any possible future constitution of Europe.[149]

Just as the Bourbon and Napoleonic bids to unify Europe under a universal monarchy had failed "because of the resistance of the European princes and peoples," so too would any attempt to create a "European Commonwealth" (*eine europäische Gesammtrepublik*) along the lines which Lorimer had suggested.[150] Although Bluntschli broadly shared the prevailing confidence in an ever-increasing assimilation of the peoples of Europe and claimed that "an examination of the European community today reveals a natural growth in the desire for an improvement in the organization of Europe capable of securing and strengthening peace and of protecting effectively European interests," he, like Lorimer, was skeptical about the possibility of any gradual spontaneous political merger of the peoples of Europe. The kind of treaty-building between the "Great Powers" and the (somewhat generalized, over-optimistic) talk of European federalism that had followed the Congress of

Vienna, rather than serving to unite the European nations, had, in his view, led instead to an insistence on the part of the individual states of Europe that they "feel themselves to be sovereign persons, and all are determined to assert this sovereignty and to avoid the supremacy of all other states."[151]

Lorimer rightly protested that he had never suggested anything resembling a federal order for Europe. What he called "denationalised internationality" was, he insisted, "as much a contradiction in terms as denationalised nationality. An international government, as such, can consequently be in no other hands than those of the representatives of separate nations." Nor had he proposed, as Kant had, that all the states which participated in his international government should be "representative republics." As a subject (even as a Scot) of His Britannic Majesty, he was convinced that what Bluntschli called the "republicanization" of Europe, which was such a marked feature of the new nationalism, in fact ran contrary to the "historical development of the European states." Nothing, protested Lorimer, could be further from his intention than requiring that the states that joined his "international government" change their "internal government." It did not follow, he claimed optimistically, as Kant had supposed, that an assembly of nations with different constitutions, even if "not one of [them] is itself, or is willing to become, a republic," would therefore necessarily be unwilling to collaborate in "the establishment of an international republic for purely international purposes."[152] As for the claim that there could not exist a union of European states so long as there was no European people, Lorimer replied that since there was no "international man," there was, implicitly, no "national" one either. So long as there were, "two nations in the world, every citizen of each of them must *eo ipso* be an international man, and cannot *eo ipso* be only an international man. In order that he may be either national or international, he must be both; and must be governed, or must govern himself, in both capacities."[153] The somewhat tortured logic behind this claim would seem to be that in order to be, say, French in a world which also contains Germans, one not only could but had to belong to something larger than France, something which included *both* France *and* Germany. That something was most obviously "Europe." While Germans and French may never cease to be German and French, nor should they, there was at the same time nothing to prevent them from also becoming, if only as a secondary identity, Europeans. As with the shakily imprecise notion of EU citizenship, this did little, however, to set any limits to the "international," and nothing to address the troubling notion of a national identity, much less the

Hegelian claim that it was precisely the existence of "other" nations that was necessary for the creation of the "national" man in the first place.

Bluntschli's own proposal was for a confederation rather than a federation, or what he called a "union of states" (*Staatenbund*). This—which he casts as a successor to Sully's "Grand Design" and which he believed to be quite unlike "the utopias of both the abbé Saint-Pierre and my friend Lorimer"—was for the creation of a union of what he identified as the seventeen "sovereign" states of Europe, together with Turkey. [154] Legislation would be entrusted to a bicameral parliament made up of representatives drawn from each of these countries, who would all be expected to vote in accordance with their individual political convictions and in the interests *not* of the nation from which they came, but of Europe as whole. The distribution of seats in this assembly would, however, give a far greater power to the six leading states—corresponding to the "Great Powers" Germany, Italy, France, Austria, Britain, and Russia—than to the other twelve. In addition, Bluntschli envisaged a body something like the European Council made up of delegates from the eighteen states, whose task was to safeguard the national interests of those states. The laws agreed upon by a majority of the two houses of the parliament would become European law and thus binding on all the member states. But the upper chamber—a Federal Council—would also be in sole charge of what he called "the greater politics" of Europe," presumably its relationship with those states which did not form part of the confederation. [155] Furthermore, for Bluntschli, the execution of policy had to be the responsibility of the individual states, not the confederation. There was to be no federal army of the kind Lorimer insisted on (although there would be a "college of the Great Powers" which would decide collectively on military matters) nor even—something which distinguished this from any subsequent European project—any common "tax-law or financial sovereignty" or even shared financial resources. [156]

Bluntschli admitted that what he called his "sober and modest" proposal for a European constitution could not rule out warfare altogether, since no constitution, although it might prevent the members of one state from waging war upon other states, could eliminate the possibility of civil war. But he was convinced that it would greatly reduce the possibility of future conflicts by offering real channels of arbitration without in any way threatening state sovereignty, while at the same time providing to a far higher degree for the "development of European international law and for European welfare" than was currently available. [157]

Casting a shadow over both Lorimer's and Bluntschli's projects, however, was once again the inescapable fact that the major states of Europe were not merely sovereign; they were also imperial. Indeed, it is no small irony, seemingly unnoticed by so many of the European federalists, that the model which most of them had chosen was precisely a state which saw itself as having been conceived in opposition to a Europe which had, in Hamilton's words, plumed herself "to be Mistress of the World and to consider the rest of mankind as created for her benefit." And that the role of the new United States of America would be to "vindicate the honour of the human race" against the "arrogant pretensions of the Europeans."[158] Given these differences, would it indeed ever be possible, asked the historian Anatole Leroy-Beaulieu (brother of Paul) in his concluding remarks to a conference organized by the *Congrès des Sciences Politiques* in 1900, to imagine a European union as anything resembling the "United States of America"? Quite apart from the now familiar objection that at the moment of its creation the USA had possessed a single and, in his view, uniform (although also clearly inferior) culture to those of the peoples of Europe, whose differences were the product of centuries of history, would it, he asked, ever be possible "for all of Europe to enter into the same federation, together with all of their dependencies and colonies in other parts of the world?" And while a federation which encompassed "the continental states of Central and Western Europe" might be realizable at least in the long run, where would this leave Great Britain, Russia, and Turkey? Could "Europe" possibly be made to encompass "three states, three empires, all three of which, in diverse ways, differ so markedly from the old continent of Europe"?[159] The answer clearly was no.

If it was hard in 1900 to conceive of a European federation, however loose, of imperial states, it was to become unimaginable after the end of World War II. In part, at least, this was a question of sovereignty. It was clear that no matter what form it eventually took, in any future European union the external relationships between the states of which it was composed would necessarily have to be controlled to a very high degree (as they are today) by the laws and institutions of the union itself rather than by each individual state. And this, of course, posed a far greater threat to those states with extensive overseas empires than to the others, far greater to Britain and France than to Italy or Sweden. For being asked to surrender control over foreign trade was one thing; being asked to surrender sovereign political authority over colonial populations was quite another. How, asked the one-time socialist Charles Albert in 1941, could Britain be expected to "participate in the creation of a European Union which would deprive her of her right... to deal freely with her dominions" when without her dominions she would be nothing?[160]

There were also more broadly cultural reasons for assuming that a federation of imperial powers, even if imaginable, would find itself sharply at odds with a core set of cultural and political values which opposed the willingness to deprive other peoples of their capacity for self-fulfillment, as peoples. Since the beginnings of the first European overseas empires in the sixteenth century, Europeans themselves have been divided between the empire-builders and those who, until recently most often in the minority, looked upon any policy, any form of life, in which the individual was effectively robbed of his or her autonomy as illegitimate at best, at worst a violation of a fundamental human right. Over the centuries, the clamor has risen steadily against what Michel de Montaigne in 1580 had described despairingly as "so many cities razed to the ground, so many nations wiped out, so many millions of individuals put to the sword, and the richest and most beautiful part of the world shattered on behalf of the pearls and pepper business."[161]

Few, however, of the earlier advocates of some idea of European unity seem to have shared Anatole Leroy-Beaulieu's awareness that empire might in itself constitute a threat to their ambitions. Jeremy Bentham had seen that the older European empires which, in 1789, he dismissed as "violations of common sense" and nothing more than "bungling imitations of miserable [Greco-Roman] originals" should now be discarded in order to make the advance of true cooperative and thus ultimately peaceful international order possible.[162] But his concern was with international peace and the possibility of an international law, not European union. Kant, as we have seen, in addition to his generally dismissive view of empires as graveyards of freedom, had recognized that if the world were moving toward the "cosmopolitan condition" of an international federation, all the members of that federation had to be self-governing as representative republics. For Lorimer (who dismissed Bentham's project on the grounds that it called for Britain to shed its colonies), as for Victor Hugo, by contrast, colonization was a major instrument of civilization and as such the only means by which his international government might one day expand beyond Europe. As late as 1924, after the greatest war between

European empires in the history of the continent had left two of them in ruins, Richard Coudenhove-Kalergi, in the name of his quixotic "Pan-Europa Program" envisaged a merger of the French and the former German colonies in Africa into one great European colony, and its "systematic exploration...as a European resource."

Few, before the final unraveling of the European imperial system in World War II, seemed to have considered the possibility that the very existence of overseas settlements might in some way render the metropolitan powers unsuitable for entry into a federal union, however loose, which involved the necessary surrender of some degree of their sovereign authority. Neither, it would seem, had anyone in this context taken to heart the successive warnings made by Montesquieu, Diderot, Edmund Burke, and Alexis de Tocqueville that metropolis and colony, however remote they might be from one another, were never wholly separate realms, and that whatever abuses took place in the one would eventually seep back to corrupt the other. Colonization had, as Diderot phrased it in 1783, "reduced all things to chaos, and mixed in among us the vices and the corruptions of every climate." Even Coudenhove-Kalergi, who all too often spoke as if he looked upon the colonies as little more than repositories of foodstuffs and cannon fodder, wondered how the same people could possibly create a community based on "the lifestyle of a true gentleman and the declaration of human rights" necessary for the creation of Pan-Europe while simultaneously transforming the lands and the peoples of West Africa into a "European resource."[163]

It was only the long process of decolonization after the end of World War II which made possible, and compelling, the idea of a European community which was whole unto itself and now wholly innocent of any further desire to subjugate others. As the French sociologist Edgar Morin remarked in 1987, "the process of decolonization...has purged the notion of Europe of its worst aspects; and it has unknowingly resulted in the purification of the idea of Europe, in reducing the tragic ambiguity of a term which implied *intra muros* liberty, human rights, democracy, and *extra muros* domination, exploitation, enslavement." Admittedly, the process was not entirely complete; some still held that "neocolonialism has been a substitute for colonization." But for all that, "the opprobrium that was once attached to the idea of Europe has diminished, and the repulsion attached to the feeling of belonging erased."[164]

This is not, of course, to claim that the legacy of empire, much of it deleterious for the former colonized peoples, particularly of Africa, has been erased by the process of Europeanization. It is also true that the economic relations between the EU and those parts of Africa once under European domination have been and continue to be determined to a significant degree by their former colonial histories. As the Schuman Declaration of 1950 which would lead to the creation of the European Coal and Steel Community (the first post-war attempt at European integration) stated unequivocally, not only would the creation of the community lead to "raising living standards and to promoting peaceful achievements," but "[w]ith increased resources Europe will be able to pursue the achievement of one of its essential tasks, namely, the development of the African continent."[165] Alas, however, very little was subsequently done to reach these goals; and it has been widely and bitterly argued that the EU's Common Agricultural Policy, introduced in 1962, has been generally devastating for emerging countries, particularly in Africa.

The former colonial powers in the EU still take a singular interest in the affairs of their former colonies (the French intervention in Mali—formerly part of French West Africa—at the request of the Malian government and with the backing of a United Nations resolution in 2014 is perhaps the most recent example).[166] But while the EU may still live in the lengthened shadow of empire and, as the refugee crisis has demonstrated, while it may often find itself unable to meet the challenges which that has thrown at it, nevertheless it is today, as the political theorist Jan-Werner Müller has argued, best understood as a "sophisticated institutional expression of anti-imperialism."[167]

The nineteenth-century quest for empire had served, as Paul Leroy-Beaulieu had argued, to shift at least a part of the theater of international conflict away from Europe itself. It had also fueled the growth of a new species of international law and created a revised and durable conception of "civilization," both of which had enhanced the sense that there did indeed exist a collective European identity on which men like Lorimer were convinced that it might one day be possible to build a lasting political union. At the same time, however, the vertiginous growth of empire driven by national self-aggrandizement and a new brand of international competition had also contributed massively to undermine the older liberal nationalism on which Mazzini and Mill's aspirations for the future of Europe had originally lain.

Few had seen this so clearly as the English economist, socialist, and one of the fiercest and most influential critics of empire, J. A. Hobson. In 1902 Hobson, like Mazzini, believed that nationalism should have been "the plain highway to internationalism" and that "a strong internationalism in form or spirit" could not arise out of "anarchic cosmopolitanism from individual units amid the decadence of national life" but only from "the existence of powerful self-respecting nationalities." What he called the "older national-ism of the earlier nineteenth century"—Mazzini's nationalism, that is—had been primarily "an inclusive sentiment whose natural relation to the same sentiment in another people was lack of sympathy not open hostility"; and under such conditions there had been "no inherent antagonism to prevent nationalities from growing and thriving side by side."

The new nationalism, by contrast, "bristles with resentment and is all astrain with the passion of self-defence." The transformation from one to the other "could have only been brought about by a perversion of its nature and purposes [and] such a perversion is Imperialism." Imperialism had put an end to any possibility that the new nationalities might, in Herder's met-aphor, lie peacefully beside each other and support each other as families. For, said Hobson, while "coexistent nationalities" pose no threat to each other, "coexistent empires following each its own imperial career of terri-torial and industrial aggrandisement are natural necessary enemies."

"The scramble for Africa and Asia" may have quietened the hostilities and rivalries between the European nations, but only in the short term: in the long term it had, in fact, created a "constant agent of menace and per-turbation to the peace and progress of mankind."[168] For it was in the end imperialism which Hobson rightly saw as having led ineluctably to "a debasement of . . . genuine nationalism, by attempts to overflow its natural banks and absorb the near or distant territory of reluctant and unassimila-ble peoples."[169]

Hobson might indeed have reflected that Europe had found itself in a very similar place a century and a half earlier. It had been precisely the rivalry between the European imperial powers, bent upon their own aggran-dizement, that in 1754 had led finally to the outbreak of the Seven Years War, which would eventually bring in its train the final collapse of the British and the Spanish empires in the Americas. In 1902 Hobson could see no new Seven Years War on the horizon. But for all that, it would not be long in coming.

When, fifteen years later in 1917, that war was at its height, the African American political theorist, sociologist, classicist, and activist W. E. B. Du Bois wrote in indignation, "This is not Europe gone mad; this is not aberration nor insanity; this *is* Europe." "Manifestly," he concluded, "it is expansion over-seas—it is colonial aggrandisement which explains, and alone adequately explains, the present war."[170]

4

The War That Will End War

I

On June 28, 1914, a Serbian nationalist student named Gavrilo Princip assassinated the Archduke Franz Ferdinand of Austria, heir apparent to the Austro-Hungarian throne, and his wife Sophie in the city of Sarajevo. A month later Austria declared war on Serbia. The news filled a usually phlegmatic Sigmund Freud with unexpected patriotic joy. "For the first time in thirty years I feel myself to be an Austrian," he wrote, "and feel like giving this not very hopeful empire another chance."[1] Untypically for Freud, he could hardly have been more mistaken. One by one, until May 1915, most of the powers of Europe were drawn into what, as late as July 1914, the British foreign secretary Sir Edward Grey had called dismissively "a Balkan question"; and since all the major combatants had extensive overseas empires, so too was much of the rest of the world.[2]

On one side were the German Reich, the Austro-Hungarian Empire, and Bulgaria. On the other, an alliance between Russia, France, Great Britain, and Italy. On August 13, 1914, Japan entered the war on the side of the Allies and on October 29, the Ottoman Empire joined on the side of the Germans. On April 6, 1917 the United States declared war on Germany, and in December on Austria-Hungary. The "Great War," as it came to be known, did not, in fact, last very long, at least not by comparison with many of its predecessors (and some of its successors). But when it was finally over on November 11, 1918, it left in its wake more people dead and more devastation than any previous single conflict in European history.

To this day there is still some confusion, and much disagreement, as to why half the world went to war because of the assassination of a Crown prince—however powerful—in a relatively obscure Central European state. To many contemporaries, however, what made it possible and what kept it going—apart, that is, from an unbridled military competition between the nations of Europe which had been building steadily since, at least, the Franco-Prussian War of 1870–1—was the newly minted brand of nationalism, jingoism, xenophobia, and outright racism pioneered by the neo-Hegelians which had now spread far from the borders of the German Reich. Ever since the very beginning of the conflict, Richard Coudenhove-Kalergi later recalled, "chauvinist ideas began to colour all the issues of the day." He did not, he wrote to his wife Ida Roland, in the fateful month of August 1914, consider "the terrible murders and cruelties now raging in all the parts of the world the most tragic elements of the World War." No war had ever been fought without them. They were appalling, but they were not new. What for him was "more terrifying than anything, perhaps for centuries to come, is the awakening of the aggressive tendency of nationalism which is nothing but the apparently vanishing religious fanaticism reappearing under a new form."

This was a nationalism quite unlike its nineteenth-century predecessor in its violence, its blindness, and above all in its racism. The "Aryanism" and the ever-burgeoning anti-Semitism which, in Germany at least, had taken the place of the kind of ecumenical and broadly internationalist struggle for liberty which had characterized, above all, the Italian Risorgimento were now seeping out into the rest of Europe. What had once been "defensive" had now turned blatantly aggressive, and had become suffused with a growing hatred, "just as religious hatred did in the past thousand years." It had now, Coudenhove-Kalergi insisted, become "the duty of all objective-minded people of all countries to fight this hatred, this lie and this blindness with full force . . . else this war is not an end but only a beginning of more slaughters."[3]

The much-vaunted "balance of powers" which the great Swiss international jurist and diplomat Emer de Vattel in 1757 believed to have been responsible for transforming Europe into "a kind of republic of which the members—each independent, but all linked together by the ties of common interest—unite for the maintenance of order and liberty" had turned into an arms race.[4] Faced with an ever-escalating bid for supremacy on the part of Russia, Germany, and Britain, most illusions about the mediatory power of the "Congress System" had, by the first decade of the twentieth century, all but evaporated. Along with them, at least temporarily, went any further belief in the restraining power of "sweet commerce" and Benjamin Constant's conviction that the "sole aim of modern nations" was "repose and with repose, comfort and as the source of comfort, industry." War, Constant had predicted with nice irony in 1814, after what he believed to be the last attempt by one European power to seize control of the entire continent, "[h]as lost its charm as well as its utility. Man is no longer driven to it either by interest or by passion."[5] As late as 1913 such sentiments still had enough credibility to persuade the Nobel peace laureate Norman Angell that "The warlike nations do not inherit the earth; they represent the decaying human element," and that what he called "the delicate inter-dependence of international finance" would prevent any global conflict from occurring in the future.[6] One year later all such hopes appeared to have evaporated forever. As René Brunet, the jurist, politician, and legal adviser to the first French chargé d'affaires appointed to Germany after the war, remarked poignantly in 1921, "In truth it is Europe that has lost the war."[7]

This, it seemed, was a war as no other had ever been. But it was also one which for some, at least in the early days, seemed to hold out a hope that, when it was all over, a new Europe might arise from the rubble and put an end to the ever-growing, massively divisive rivalries between the European "Great Powers." In October 1914, when the hostilities were still only few months old, and it was widely rumored that the war would "be over by Christmas," the English novelist and essayist H. G. Wells published a pam-phlet entitled *The War That Will End War*.[8] Wells had no doubt about the possible magnitude of the conflict. This war, he declared, "is already the vastest war in history. It is war not of nations, but of mankind. It is a war to exorcise a world-madness and end an age." It was also, however, a war which would allow the Allies—Wells had little doubt which side would win—finally to draw up a "new map of Europe." Wells had no interest in a unified Europe, merely in a more just and, on his understanding of the term, a more liberal one. His new map was, therefore, to be drawn by the "liberal English" with some assistance from "the intelligence and consciences of the United States and France and Scandinavia," and its purpose would be finally to free the continent from the menace not so much of Germany, much less of the German people—Wells was true to his distrust of nationalism of any hue—but of what he called "the Prussia War-Lordship."[9] Then, and only then, would the other states of Europe, and even Germany itself, be able to return to the conditions of stable entente they had enjoyed throughout much of the nineteenth century.

There were others, too, in these early months who looked upon the war, catastrophic as it increasingly promised to be, as the opportunity to draw up a far more ambitious new map for a new Europe. On August 6, three days after Germany declared war on France, the novelist André Gide wrote in his *Journal*:

> One foresees the beginning of a new era: the United States of Europe bound
> by a treaty limiting their armaments; Germany subjugated or dissolved; Trieste
> given back to the Italians, Schleswig to Denmark; and especially Alsace to
> France. Everyone talks of this remaking of the map as of the forthcoming issue
> of a serial.[10]

In the Netherlands (which remained neutral during the war), and even in Germany itself (although they were soon banned as unpatriotic), groups were formed in opposition to the war which also argued that a greater European union was the sole means of preventing any similar conflagration in the future. (One of these, the Austro-German *League for a New Fatherland*, included Albert Einstein among its members.) Even in Britain, which had shown scant interest in any previous proposal for a united Europe, there were those on the left who argued vigorously in the early months of the war for a post-war European federation. The widely read *Review of Reviews* opened its issue of September 1914, when the war was barely a month old, with an article entitled "The United States of Europe: The Only Way Out."[11]

These aspirations did not, however, last very long. As the war dragged on the possibility of, once it was over, reuniting the belligerents in any kind of union of European nations came to appear increasingly remote. The neo-Hegelian Italian philosopher and historian Benedetto Croce, among others, was prepared to believe, even as late as 1916, that he could see "in every part of Europe, the emergence of a new consciousness and a new nationality."[12] But by the time the fighting came to an end in November 1918, most had come to the realization that if a real and lasting peace were ever to be restored, then something far more ambitious than a European federation would be required: a league not merely of the European nations, but of all of the nations of the entire world, what the American president Woodrow Wilson described as an "international concert of peace."[13] Some, like Sir Alfred Zimmern, had come to understand by June 1915 that the nation-state was "only an outworn stage in the political evolution of mankind." He had arrived at this conclusion, he wrote, partly because of his recognition that he was not "an Englishman in the deeper side of my nature," and partly because

Mazzini had taught him that "nationality" was not a matter of politics of "sovereign governments, armies, frontiers and foreign policy," but was instead "primarily and essentially a spiritual question, and in particular an educational question." What he concluded from this was that "all forward-looking men who desire better international relations and a better political organisation of the world" should now be looking to something like "the great governing religious systems of the past, like mediaeval Christendom and Islam [which] find room for all sorts of conditions and communities and nations."[14]

II

By the time it came to it an end, the war had utterly transformed the political landscape of Europe, and much of the world along with it. The German Reich was no more and its emperor, the first national leader to be seriously threatened with prosecution for a "supreme offense against international morality and the sanctity of treaties," had fled into exile in the Netherlands. The Austro-Hungarian Empire had been dissolved and lost almost nine-tenths of its previous territory, and the Russian Empire had been replaced (briefly) by the Russian Soviet Federative Socialist Republic. The Ottoman Empire was in ruins, its capital city occupied by British, French, and Italian troops. All that survived of its Anatolian heartlands would be reborn in 1923 as the modern Turkish nation. The rest would be carved up and reconstituted as new states directly or indirectly under the aegis of the victorious allies.

The end of the war seemed to have left two of the old imperial powers, Britain and France, stronger than they had been before. But the entry of the United States into the war and Woodrow Wilson's insistence in his famous "Fourteen Points" speech of January 8, 1918 to the American Congress that in all subsequent discussions over the future of formerly colonized peoples, no matter by whom they had been colonized, "the interest of the populations concerned should be paramount" seemed to have undone for good all the premises on which the older international hegemonies of power had rested.[15] In large measure this would turn out to be an illusion, but it was certainly the case that the old regime born in 1815 and dedicated to sustaining—and where possible extending—the ancient monarchical order of the most powerful European states had now passed away. Whatever the new generation which had emerged from the sufferings of the war might now create, it could surely only be a new European—possibly even a new world—order. "We all felt," wrote Richard Coudenhove-Kalergi, of Wilson's initiative,

> that the crumbling world of imperialism and semi-feudalism was linked to the old generation responsible for the terrible war and that it was now up to our generation to build a new and brighter world on sounder and more moral principles.... That it was up to us to build a new and better Europe on the ruins of the old.[16]

Before very long, however, the hopes which Wilson's initiative had inspired began themselves to disintegrate. On January 18, 1919 the victorious allies gathered in the great Hall of Mirrors in the Palace of Versailles outside Paris for the opening of the Paris Peace Conference in order to establish a settlement with Germany. It was held, not coincidentally, in the very same hall and forty-eight years later to the day that Bismarck had declared King Wilhelm I of Prussia "Kaiser," thus inaugurating the second German Reich, over whose ignominious dissolution the conference was now presiding. The French president Raymond Poincaré opened the conference with a speech which could have left no one on either side in any doubt that while this might be a peace, it was not to be a reconciliation. It began:

> This very day forty-eight years ago, on January 18, 1871, the German Empire was proclaimed by an army of invasion in the Palace of Versailles. It was consecrated by the theft of two French provinces. It was vitiated from its origins and by the fault of its founders; born of injustice, it has ended in opprobrium. You are assembled in order to repair the evil that it has done and to prevent a recurrence. You hold in your hands the future of the world.[17]

On June 28, their work done, the delegates signed what has subsequently come to be known as the Versailles Treaty—although in the end there were five of them. Despite all the pomp and self-congratulation which surrounded the events, few of the delegates were happy with the outcome. "After the 'war to end war'," Brigadier General, later Field Marshal, Earl Wavell, who had served on the Supreme War Council in the closing years of the war, is supposed to have remarked, "they seem to have been pretty successful in Paris at making the 'peace to end peace.'"[18]

Under the terms of what came to be known in Germany as the "Versailles Diktat," Germany was forced to hand back Alsace-Lorraine, which she had seized from France in 1870, and to cede part of western Prussia to Poland, which thus gained access to the sea through the "Polish Corridor." Her overseas colonies were confiscated, her military was all but annihilated (the army was capped at 100,000 men and rearmament was forbidden), and the Rhineland was demilitarized. On top of that she was required to pay a crushing twenty billion gold marks in reparations. And then there was the notorious "War Guilt Clause" (Article 231) of the treaty, which required that Germany accept "the responsibility of Germany and her allies for causing all the loss and damage to which the Allied and Associated Governments and their nationals have been subjected as a consequence of the war imposed upon them by the aggression of Germany and her allies." As Carl Schmitt (whom we shall meet again) argued in a paper given to the Association of German Jurists in 1937, these actions determined that the war had been undertaken by the Allies not as all true wars had, in his view, hitherto been conducted, as a "duel" between states, but as a total war of annihilation against Germany, which was held to have become by her actions a "rogue state" (*Räuberstaat*) deprived of sovereignty and against whom any action was, therefore, held to be permissible within the limits of human morality.[19]

Since this was a position which Germany could not possibly accept for long, a new war seemed inevitable. The great German sociologist Max Weber, who had been called in to advise on the negotiations at Versailles, believed the attempt to blame Germany for the hostilities was "dishonourable" (in his view, if any single power was to blame, it was tsarist Russia), and the economic terms of the treaty were potentially so crippling that "we would see before us only a dark hole without even the most distant beam of light." It would be best, he argued, to reject such a "rotten peace," although he knew full well that Germany was in no position to resume the war.[20] The hope that a new, vibrant post-war European order might arise out of the debris and the carnage of the war seemed to have been shattered once and for all. As Coudenhove-Kalergi remarked bitterly, "After the future had vanquished the past on the battlefields of Europe, this past now took its revenge by defeating the future at the peace table." Far from being united, Europe seemed now to be "more torn, more dismembered, more divided by hate than ever before."

One of those who attended the conference as a member of the Supreme Economic Council of the Allied Powers was the English economist John Maynard Keynes. He observed most of the proceedings with some dismay. Amid all the grandeur and "the theatrical trappings of the French Saloons of State," he wrote, "the Four [Britain, France, the United States, and Italy] fulfilled their destinies in empty and arid intrigue," and all the while "a sense of impending catastrophe overhung the frivolous scene; the futility and smallness of man before the great events confronting him; the mingled significance and unreality of the decisions." Keynes wrote, he said, as an Englishman, as one who saw England as standing outside continental Europe. Yet during the months he spent in Paris, he was, he confessed, "bound to become...a European in his cares and outlook." Europe, he warned, was "solid with herself." "France, Germany, Italy, Austria and Holland, Russia and Rumania and Poland, throb together, and their structure and civiization are essentially one." And he went on to warn the peacemakers:

> They flourished together, they have rocked together in a war...[but] they may fall together. In this lies the significance of the Peace of Paris. If the European Civil War is to end with France and Italy abusing their momentary victorious power to destroy Germany and Austria-Hungary now prostrate, they invite their own destruction also, being so deeply and inextricably inter-twined with their victims by hidden psychic and economic bonds.[21]

Keynes later resigned from the Supreme Economic Council in despair at what he described as the treaty's failure to make any "provisions for the economic rehabilitation of Europe" or to attempt anything to transform the "defeated Central Empires into good neighbours" or to stabilize the "new States of Europe" or to "reclaim Russia."[22] He warned that what he called "the great historic drama of these days" could lead only to a tragedy "which will destroy great institutions." But, he added almost as an afterthought, they "may also create a new world." In the end, both predictions turned out to be true.[23]

In fact, however, much of the dire foreboding as to the immediate fate of Germany proved to be illusory. Post-war Germany was not, in reality, anni-hilated. As the French journalist and historian Jacques Bainville pointed out in what was—although he claimed it was not—a pointed response to Keynes's condemnation of the treaty, Bismarckian Germany had been left substantially unaltered, even if some of the injustices imposed upon France in 1871 had now been reversed. The Allies had not only upheld German unification, but had in effect greatly strengthened it, making possible what would, under the constitution of the Weimar Republic of 1919, be a far more unified and potentially far more powerful state than the loose coalition that went under the name of the German Reich had ever been. Germany remained Europe's most populous nation, and Europe's "industrial powerhouse" despite the loss of Saar coal and the iron ore from Lorraine; and within a remarkably short time she had come to dominate trade in central and eastern Europe.[24] The real sufferings imposed by the treaty were psychological and political, and they derived largely from the "War Guilt Clause" whose long-term impact would eventually prove to be catastrophic not only for Germany, but for much of the globe. As Bainville remarked even as it was being signed, "The Treaty of Versailles set in motion forces which had already escaped from the will of its creators."[25]

III

The Versailles Treaty was not, however, only an attempt, however misguided, to end the most calamitous and costly war in European history. It was also, like Kant's imaginary treaty "for perpetual peace among nations," an attempt to eliminate all future warfare by creating what some at least, most emphatically Woodrow Wilson, saw as a modern analogue to Kant's "pacific league"—for written into the first twenty-six articles of the Versailles Treaty was the initial draft of the Covenant for the League of Nations.

The Covenant as it finally emerged after months of negotiations was in most respects, however, a very un-Kantian document. The League it created was less a world federation than a coalition of the victorious presuming to act in the name of all mankind. Many of those who worked on drafting the document, such as the South African former Boer guerrilla commander, General Jan Smuts—who, among his other achievements, coined the term "holistic"—saw it as a way of perpetuating the older imperial order. Similarly, France and Britain, the chief beneficiaries of the mandate system which allowed much of the former Ottoman territories and the German colonies to be handed over to the victors, looked upon it as a device for extending their empires by other means. Its ambitions, however, reached far beyond these simple immediate goals. It was intended to regulate behavior not merely between states but also within them. It set up a committee for refugees, a health organization, a slavery commission, and a commission for the study of the legal status of women, and guaranteed a series of "Minorities Treaties" to secure the rights, religious, civil, and cultural, of all peoples; and it made a provision—forced upon a reluctant President Wilson—for a Permanent Court of International Justice. In effect, it established the principle that a lasting peace could not be achieved merely by limiting or even eliminating the conditions of conflict. It could only be sustained through union, without which, declared Smuts, Europe "would continue to writhe in her convulsions into the blackness of final anarchy."[26]

The creation of the League was initially greeted with widespread, if sometimes cautious enthusiasm. In the eyes of many it simply had to work. Neither Europe nor the world could suffer anything like the aptly named "Great War" again. "The present war," wrote the international jurist Georges Scelle in 1919 shortly after the signing of the Versailles Treaty, "has already been the cause of infinite misery, and all misery is a regression. It is unlikely that European civilization could survive another so devastating a cataclysm."[27] Civilization, Scelle argued, simply could not afford to go on retreating forever. And the only way to prevent mankind from sliding back into a Hobbesian state of nature was, in his opinion, the creation of a federal union. For all his enthusiasm for what the League seemed to promise, Scelle was by no means certain that this was, in fact, the direction in which it was ultimately heading. The powers which had created it had been careful to avoid empowering it with any real political or legal authority of its own. Its charter had granted, but also proscribed, a large number of measures. It had a court of law, but no instrument with which to enforce its decisions. As Sir Alfred Zimmern remarked in 1936, when its credibility was all but spent, what the League most closely resembled was, in fact, a constitutional monarchy in that "it cannot command. But it can wield an ever-present influence"—a somewhat pallid objective for a once so ambitious project.[28] E. H. Carr, who had been a member of the British Delegation at the Conference of Versailles and had been involved in drafting the Covenant, wryly observed two years later that any post-war attempt to raise what he called "such elegant superstructures" as the League or a world federation "must wait until some progress has been made in digging the foundations."[29]

Furthermore, despite the aspirations of Wilson and others, the true objective of the Covenant was less the creation of a new "commonwealth of nations" than the recreation of the old balance of powers between the European states, now extended to include the United States (although in the end the USA refused to join the League). What it clearly failed to do was to lay the foundation for a world peace federation along Kantian lines. "It will not," complained the historian and militant French pacifist Théodore Ruyssen, "amount to so much as a confederation of states, much less a federal state of the type of Switzerland or the United States."[30]

The main objection that was raised against the League, the objection which the anti-Federalists had raised against the US Constitution and which Euroskeptics continue to raise against the European Union, was the very simple fact that, however little actual coercive power it might have, any federation necessarily involves the surrender, in part at least, of the sovereignty of the individual states of which it is composed. As Carl Schmitt noted in 1932, when the limitations of the League had become all too apparent, it did not represent the "ideal of a global organization," which for "many people" (although he seems to have been thinking primarily of Kant) meant "nothing else than the utopian ideal of total depoliticization . . . and with it particularly, the nonexistence of states," for that would necessarily mean that the entire world would become "a unified entity based exclusively upon economics and on technically regulating traffic." And if *that* were to come to pass, "Upon whom will fall the frightening power implied in a world-embracing economic and technical organization?" What, however, had in fact emerged from the Treaty of Paris was no such thing. It was rather an international alliance of the kind that not only does not abolish wars, but "introduces new possibilities for future wars, permits wars to take place, sanctions coalition wars, and by legitimating and sanctioning certain wars it sweeps away many obstacles to war." This, in Schmitt's view however, was in itself no bad thing. The so-called League could be seen as "a very useful meeting place under certain circumstances," in which the necessary protective sovereignty of the individual states remains undiminished.[31]

IV

The sovereignty issue was also the reason why the USA refused to join the League, despite the fact that it had been in great measure Wilson's brainchild. When presented, in particular, with Article 10 of the Covenant, which required all signatories "to respect and preserve as against external aggression the territorial integrity and existing political independence of all Members of the League," many, like the Senator for Idaho, William E. Borah, worried that this would amount to handing over to the League the nation's power to decide whether to go to war or not, something which, in the terms of the US Constitution, could only be done with the approval of Congress. And it is significant that the founding document of the League described itself as a "Covenant," not, like the less assertive founding document of the United Nations, a "Charter." For a covenant was, as Hobbes had said of it, the "mutual transferring of right."[32] Once transferred, it could not be reclaimed. The Americans might, or feared that they might, therefore find themselves engaged in conflicts in which not only did they have no immediate interest, but which they might even find morally offensive. Beyond the anxiety over what George Washington had famously denounced as "foreign entanglements," there was also the belief that membership in any international body with legal authority might ultimately weaken the ability of the USA to control its own domestic affairs, and thus to protect its own borders. By joining the League, Borah told the Senate, "We may become one of the four dictators of the world" but, he warned, "we shall no longer be masters of our own spirit."[33] (It is not insignificant that Borah had assumed that the purpose of the League was, indeed, to create a "dictator-ship of the world.") In the early twentieth century the threat of the "Yellow Peril"—migrant labor from Asia—incensed and fascinated the American public, much as the supposed threat of immigrant labor from Latin America does today. "Is it possible," Henry Cabot Lodge, leader of the Senate, asked Congress on February 28, 1919, "that anyone who wishes to preserve our standards of life and labor can be drawn into a scheme ... which would take from us the sovereign right to decide alone and for ourselves the vital ques-tion of the exclusion of Mongolian and Asiatic labor?" Lodge had, in fact, initially been a cautious supporter of the League, but of a League which would have constituted a strong legal body with little or no sovereign powers, certainly none so sweeping as those which he thought he saw in the Covenant. He was prepared to endorse the League but only with twelve "reservations." He did not get them, and on November 19, 1919, Congress voted to reject the Versailles Treaty and the League along with it.[34] The Americans were not, however, the only ones to be troubled by the possible implications of what the jurist Georges Scelle called con-temptuously the "dogma of sovereignty." The treaty set in motion a repeated and a seemingly all-encompassing debate which has remained largely unresolved to this day.

The very concept of sovereignty has a long and troubled history. The term itself was coined by the sixteenth-century French jurist Jean Bodin as the ruler's "absolute and perpetual power." He defined it in terms of seven "marks" or rights, all of which, however, could be reduced to one overrid-ing legislative principle: "the power to give laws unto all and every one of the subjects, and to receive none from them."[35] Bodin's *Six Books of the*

Commonwealth of 1576, fittingly described by Carl Schmitt as the "first depiction of modern public law," was written in the context, and in the hope, of bringing to an end the prolonged Wars of Religion, the bitter conflict between Catholics and Protestants, and between the Crown and the French nobility in France, which lasted on and off from 1562 until 1598.[36] In order to eliminate the possibility of civil war, the power of the state had to be superior to that of all local, regional, and religious powers. Henceforth, no duke or baron, no religious community, no church or guild could be allowed to exercise any independent political authority, and only the sovereign would have the authority to make laws, mint money, and wage war. Sovereignty could therefore only be, as Thomas Hobbes phrased it, "incommunicable and inseparable."[37] Some version of this conception of "absolute and perpetual" but also and crucially *indivisible* power has continued to define not only the power of the state, but what the state was, the functions it was supposed to perform, and the good it was bound to deliver. What this actually means in practice has of course varied greatly over time, but the notion of indivisibility has remained central and incontestable. It eliminated internal domestic competition. But it also determined the relationship which all states would have with each other, in that whatever agreement they might come to between themselves could not, to any degree, be allowed to infringe upon the sovereign power of each one of them.

It was this hallowed notion of sovereign authority which Napoleon, with his claim that an enlightened nation might "liberate" a people from its legitimate but unjust rulers (even against their will), had tried, successfully for a while, to overthrow. It was this conception of sovereignty, now reinforced with appeals to the unique character of each nation's identity, its history, its Hegelian *Geist*, that the nationalists of the nineteenth century had succeeded so forcefully in re-establishing. And it was this understanding of sovereignty on which the "Congress System" had been based.[38]

It was not, however, universally recognized. There were many during and after World War I, and there have been many since, who saw the whole notion of sovereignty as the prime impediment to achieving a universal and lasting peace. One of the most influential at the time, although he is little known today, was the Milanese journalist, economist, and subsequently president of the Italian Republic, Luigi Einaudi. In January 1918, Einaudi published a series of articles in the Milanese newspaper *Corriere della Sera* under the pen name "Junius" (the founder of the first Roman Republic), with the title: "Is a Society of Nations a Realizable Ideal?"[39] From all sides,

he wrote, he could discern what amounted to a single claim, that the outcome of the war "must be the birth of a 'society of nations.'" But what, he
asked, would this look like? A union between the United States of America
with an as yet to be created "United States of Europe" in the hope that "at
some future moment this might result in the birth of a 'United States of the
World' so as to put an end to human brutality"? Any such proposal seemed
to fly inexorably in the face of history. If a "league of nations" of the kind
then being widely discussed was to be "a confederation of sovereign states,"
then it was doomed to failure. Compare that with what he called "the magnificent success of that other type of league of nations," which demanded
the surrender of a large part at least of the sovereignty of each individual
state to some kind of federal government. This, he pointed out, had clearly
been the message of the troubled years between 1781 and 1789 in the United
States. The first constitution (the Articles of Confederation of 1781) had
attempted to create something very like the League, as a "confederation and
a union" in which the sovereignty, liberty, and independence of the individual states had been preserved; yet this had immediately threatened to collapse. The constitution of 1789, however, had effectively transformed the
Thirteen Colonies into what was in fact "provinces of one single larger
sovereign state," and the United States had survived (despite the Civil War)
to become what was by 1918 clearly the greatest power on earth.

But the dismal history of attempted confederation was far older than that.
One only had to look at the Greek leagues so beloved of Kant (and
Napoleon). Even the most powerful of them, the Delian League, had been
merely the "shadow of a state," unable to prevent the struggle between
Sparta and Athens or to prevent the final dissolution of the whole of the
Greek world into the empire of Alexander the Great. Then there was the
Holy Roman Empire, to which, after 1815, some had looked back wistfully
for inspiration (as many have done subsequently), but which, in reality, had
"for a thousand years been a sterile attempt to build under the aegis of a
single emperor a true society of nations" and which had failed precisely
because none of the petty principalities of which it had been composed had
been prepared to share sovereignty with any of the others, much less concede it to the emperor, who remained, until the whole charade was dissolved by Napoleon in 1806, merely an arbitrator, a "first among equals."
The "Holy Alliance" of Austria, Prussia, and Russia of 1815, which had aimed
at another kind of league of nations in which all would live in harmony "as
members of a single Christian nation," had very rapidly shown itself to be

both "hypocritical" and utterly ineffective. All the other attempts to create unions with which the history of Europe was littered had, as with Louis XIV's "unified state" of France, or Germany under Bismarck, or Italy in 1871, resulted in the transformation of what had once been independent states into provinces of a "single more powerful sovereign state." The sole exception, in Einaudi's opinion, would seem to have been the (ancient) Roman Empire: an all-encompassing state which absorbed and embraced all the peoples whom it conquered into a citizen body. "It might be said that the Romans did not spread themselves over the globe," as Francis Bacon, whom Einaudi quoted admiringly more than once, had written in 1605, "but that the globe spread itself over the Romans."[40] Since, however, although Einaudi never quite said so, the conditions for the Roman model seemed in 1918 to have long since passed, it was clear that "We must destroy and banish forever the dogma of perfect sovereignty. The truth of the matter is not the sovereignty of states. The truth is the interdependence of free peoples, not their absolute independence."[41]

In the years following the end of the war, the "dogma of sovereignty" became something of a political and legal battleground. For many it was obvious, as it had been for Einaudi, that only once the entire concept had been effectively eliminated could some kind of lasting peace be restored to the world. As the American jurist James W. Garner claimed optimistically in 1925, the world had always had the character "of a federation endowed with corporative juridical personality." Sovereignty had been created in the sixteenth century to meet a very specific kind of threat and had then been allowed to grow into a monstrous piece of state machinery, ultimately responsible for encouraging and enlarging precisely the kind of internecine warfare it had been invented to prevent. It now stood as "the principal obstacle to a world organization" and "an obstacle to the maintenance of peace and to the progress of the common interests of states."[42]

There were many who agreed. The conflict over sovereignty had been the main reason for the ultimate failure of the League of Nations, as Hans Kelsen pointed out in 1944, when the final demise of the League was all too evident. Any attempt to conjure up the possibility of what Kelsen called a "World Federal State" with a "democratic character"—that is, one which was not merely an empire—required adherence to the Wilsonian "principle of self-determination," and that made it impossible to imagine anything resembling a "world parliament," if only because the numerical strength of the nations of which it would be composed was one in which China and

India would have approximately three times the number of deputies as Britain and the USA combined. Kelsen was in no doubt that the victors of any major conflict, buoyed up by the "nationalistic feelings" which victory would inevitably bring, would hardly be likely to surrender willingly to what he called "State suicide," no matter what the long-term advantages might seem to be. "Opinion may differ as to the value and justification of nationalism," he remarked, but it could not be wished away.[43] Kelsen's solution was to replace any kind of administrative or legislative power—any kind of international government—by an international court. The League had "failed completely" because the Covenant had placed at its center the Council, which constituted a form of "international government," and the Assembly, which "gives the impression of an international legislature" rather than the Permanent Court of International Justice.[44] The problem remained, however, as to how this court was to enforce its decisions in the absence of some version of Kant's "external constraint." This could surely only be provided by a political union of some kind, with, as Kelsen himself recognized, the military capacity to enforce its rulings. And that union could only be in effect a federal state which would exercise the same kind of sovereign powers—although clearly in different ways—as individual states had hitherto.

For Kelsen the concept of sovereign authority of the kind advocated by Bodin and Hobbes was an existential threat that should be eliminated altogether. For what was truly sovereign in any state could only be the law itself. There existed nothing beyond or above this—no "unbound legislator," no "sovereign." The state was a legal entity governed only by a hierarchy of legal norms which culminated not in a sovereign above and beyond it, but in a final "Fundamental Norm" (*Grundnorm*) whose authority derives from the historical founding of the legal order itself and which is enacted by the constitution of the state. On this account, what distinguishes a federal state from a nation-state was a question of what he calls "the degree of decentralization," not the kind. A federal state is distinguished by the fact that it has a higher degree of decentralization than that of a national state. "The legal order of a federal State is composed of central norms valid for its entire territory, and local norms are valid only for portions of this territory." Similarly, what distinguishes the "international confederacy of states"—such as the League—is a yet higher degree of decentralization. But since decentralization is basically a "principle restricted to administration," it does not alter the legal or, one might suppose, the political identity of the whole. This means, in effect, that the "international union of States, as, for instance, the

League of Nations can resemble a federal state in many respects." The "constitution" of the League—that is the Covenant—is obviously a legal order "valid throughout the territory of all the States." It has, therefore "the character of a central order and constitutes a partial community, the 'confederation,' of which all the other member states are themselves 'partial'—but lesser—communities." "Ordinarily," he admitted, federal constitutions contain no provisions "in regard to the constitutions of the member states." But there was also nothing "to prevent them in law from introducing such provisions." In that case, Kelsen concluded, there would be nothing "to prevent the agreement comprising the constitution of a confederacy from obliging the member States to have democratic-republican constitutions"—just as Kant had assumed the members of his "union of states" did, and just as the treaties which collectively make up the "constitution of the European Union" do.[45]

Kelsen's understanding of legal federalism has had considerable influence on the subsequent evolution of EU law. Kelsen himself, however, seems to have had relatively little interest in the possibility of a post-war *European* union. His concern was with the international order more broadly and the possibility of a "Permanent League for the Maintenance of Peace" which would allow all states, and not merely those within Europe, to arrive at a condition of peaceful cooperation without the need for a sovereign authority to compel them to do so.[46]

"Now the machine runs itself," was Carl Schmitt's sarcastic reply to all this. Schmitt, Kelsen's arch-enemy and the most ferocious opponent of the modern liberal democratic state, took the exact opposite position to that of Kelsen.[47] Law did not create, but was the creation of, the state, and its force depended entirely upon the will of the sovereign. Schmitt's conception of what he calls "the political" is broadly based upon the neo-Hegelian idea that that all political bodies are created in response to a friend/enemy distinction, and that the role of the "sovereign," whether a person or a group of persons, is to decide who is friend and who is foe, and whether an "exception" has arisen which might require the suspension of the rule of the law. Sovereigns are they who make those decisions. The sovereign, in what is probably Schmitt's most quoted phrase, is "he who decides on the exception." Schmitt, as we shall see, did have his own theory of how states could cooperate with one another without compromising their individual sovereignty. But he could not, of course, tolerate Kelsen's claim that states could somehow exist in harmony and equality with one another without being

constrained to do so any more than he could accept that any state might be
prepared to surrender, or even share, its sovereignty with another; much less
could he conceive of any federation which was, in effect, anything more
than a contract between states whose purpose is, as it was for Hobbes, self-
protection. Anything resembling a "European Union" would be unimaginable. If the "United States of Europe" should come to pass, then it would
be—as was, in Schmitt's view, the United States of America since the end of
the Civil War effectively annihilated all possible right of seccession—merely
another single sovereign state divided into semiautonomous regions.[48]

Kelsen and Schmitt represent the polar opposites of the sovereignty
debate. There were, however, others who took less extreme positions, from
which they believed—or hoped—that some federal or quasi-federal solu-
tion might be found to the current round of interstate conflict and civil war.
One of these was Georges Scelle. Scelle was a professor of International
Public Law, first at Dijon and then at Paris, a prominent member of the
Institut de droit international, a member of the International Law Commission,
and president of the French section of the New Commonwealth Society.
Together with the Austrian emigré Hersch Lauterpacht, Professor of
International Law at Cambridge, he was probably the most influential international lawyer of his generation. Like Lauterpacht, he was also an ardent
federalist who exercised a considerable influence on French public life
throughout his long career. Ironically perhaps, in view of his skeptical views
of its possibilities, he was not only the technical adviser to the French delegation at the fifth session of the Assembly of the League of Nations in 1924,
but also the French delegate at the final session held in 1946.[49]

Like many others, Scelle looked upon the perennial struggle over the
"dogma of sovereignty" as the main obstacle in the way of any future
international cooperation and development. Unlike Kelsen, he was perfectly prepared to accept that there had to exist some conception of a
"sovereign"—other than the law itself—within the state. But any conception of sovereignty which sought to bind together control over both
the internal and the external actions of states was in Scelle's opinion both
legally and philosophically incoherent. It derived from the notion that
the territory of the state could be identified with the person of the sovereign, who, in feudal law, had retained what was called "eminent domain,"
ceding to his subjects only effective use rights—*dominium utile*—over
their lives and property. (This is, indeed, more or less how Bodin uses
the term.)

In other words, sovereignty could be seen, once again, as a lingering remnant of the Roman *patria potestas*. Although the last vestiges of feudal law had vanished from France in the Revolution, the conception of "patrimonial sovereignty" had, Scelle claimed, been "perpetuated to the advantage of the modern state but to the detriment of the law and above all of peace." "One should, therefore," he urged the rulers of Europe, "abandon once and for all this term which is so unscientific, so contrary to reality that it constitutes not merely an error but a danger." This, he added sharply, would be the most uplifting "conquest" which international law could carry out in the name of "civilization." Instead of "sovereignty" we should think only in terms of "interdependence." This, he explained, was more fitting because it was to be understood as a relative notion "in which the freedom of each individual is limited by the freedom of all."

Legally, what this meant was that "the dogma of sovereignty," which was nothing other than "an incomprehensible equality of facts," was to be replaced by "a logical equality of law."[50] A world made up of states which saw themselves as "independent," but non-sovereign as far as their external relationships were concerned, would always prefer to reach some common accord rather than go to war when some conflict between them arose. Now he believed was the time for all states to "search for a democratic system for an international society, or rather to adopt the one that already exists, for that system has already been found: it is the Federation." There already existed examples of independent sovereign states which had

> discovered that their supposed sovereignty constituted a danger rather than a protection. They then willingly subjected themselves to a common authority. This is what the Swiss cantons did, and the Germans and English colonies in America which then became Switzerland, the German Empire and the United States. They saw clearly that they had gained, and did not imagine that they had lost something precious nor even real in renouncing their theoretical sovereignty. That is the example, that the remedy.[51]

The League might, therefore, become a "vast federal state" which would guarantee "freedom for all in power and security." Enticing, ecumenical, and liberal though all this clearly was, Scelle knew full well that in practice, and at present, the states of Europe clung blindly to their supposed sovereign powers. His federal state might, he admitted, become reality in some "remote future. But we do not think that it can be at the present."[52]

The problem, however, with Scelle's proposal, as with so many of its kind, was in the detail—or rather lack of it. The Swiss Federation, the German

Empire, and the United States were, in fact, three very different kinds of polities, with very different histories, each allocating sovereign authority to the individual states of which they were composed in very different ways. What they all shared in common, however, was that they were all sovereign states at the federal level. As the Austrian jurist, and another opponent of Schmitt, Herman Heller pointed out, the states of which any true federation is composed can only, in effect, be regional bodies. "Thus, the member state, by its nature is a particular territorial decision-making unit, just like every province and municipality, while the federal state is, like all unified states, by its nature a universal decision-making institution." And in the case of the United States, "the federal state as a whole constitutes a sovereign state that decides universally on its territory." This is, in effect, what occurs in the other most cited federal model—Switzerland—and would necessarily be the case for any future "United States of Europe."[53] It is, of course, precisely this that the national governments of the European Union—not to mention Euroskeptics of all hues—have objected to the most.

For all the best efforts of Kelsen, Heller, Scelle, and numerous others (among them the Greek diplomat Nikolaos Politis; his colleague, the jurist Albert de Lapradelle; the arch-Catholic Monarchist theologian and just-war theorist Yves de La Brière; and Scelle's nemesis the ultraconservative— and Catholic—federalist Louis Le Fur) to find some workable solution, the sovereignty issue remained to dog the fortunes of the League and the advocates of a European federation until the entire edifice, and all the hopes that it had inspired, collapsed in the 1930s.[54] Léon Bourgeois, one-time French minster of justice and foreign affairs of the French Third Republic, and first president of the Council of the League, in his letter of acceptance of the Nobel Peace Prize in December 1922, made an impassioned plea to all the members of the League. "What was and is necessary and at the same time sufficient," he wrote,

> is that each nation understands that mutual consent to certain principles of law and to certain agreements, acknowledged to be equally profitable to the contracting parties, no more implies a surrender of sovereignty than a contract in private business implies a renunciation of personal liberty. It is, rather, the deliberate use of this very liberty itself and an acknowledged advantage for both parties.[55]

Bourgeois was, in effect, echoing a claim which Henry Maine had made forty years earlier that "indivisibility of Sovereignty . . . does not belong in

International Law." The sovereignty exercised by individual states within their own borders—what Maine called "tribe-sovereignty"—did not need to be surrendered. It needed to be *shared*.[56]

The covenanting nations of the League did not, however, on the whole, see things that way. In the end, Borah and Lodge need not have worried. They had taken their president and the claims outlined in the Covenant too much at their word. In effect, the signatories of the Covenant, as Bourgeois feared, had no intention of allowing their political authority to be modified in any really significant way by their allies, much less by any independent international body of law. "Did the Great Powers ever really look upon the League as a world organisation which could be used to curb the excesses of their own national sovereignty?," asked the socialist British Labour MP and European federalist R. W. G. ("Kim") Mackay in 1940.[57] The answer, as he knew, was a resounding no. But without the willingness of its members to share their sovereign authority, the League could only ever be something like a substitute for the old Concert of Europe, and that, observed Alfred Zimmern in 1922, had already "proved a disappointment." Any such "standing organ of European and still more of world policy," he added, would surely turn out to be "as impracticable today as it proved to be after 1815."[58]

V

Zimmern was not the only one to be skeptical. The question of sovereignty, although it was and has remained to this day the most impassioned and intractable legal problem facing any attempt to replace the nation-state by some kind on interstate, international organization, was by no means the only one. In the immediate post-war years, the sensation experienced by many of those who gave the future more than passing thought was one of fragility and impending chaos. The war itself might have come to an end, but so too, it often seemed, had any hope for a brighter European future. And the struggle over the possible role of the League did nothing to improve the situation. Europe, as Zimmern put it, was "in convalescence," and the patient was not responding as well as many had anticipated. "Civilization," if it still retained any coherent meaning, had all but vanished in the trenches of the Western Front. The horrors which the European great powers had blithely inflicted on the peoples of Africa and Asia, they had now inflicted, in far greater measure, upon themselves. "*Edam, Nineveh, Babylon* were

vague and splendid names," wrote the French poet Paul Valéry in a celebrated essay in April 1919:

> the total ruin of these worlds, for us, meant as little as did their existence. But
> France, England, Russia, these names too are splendid. And now we see that
> the abyss of history is deep enough to bury all the world. *Lusitania* was also a
> splendid name. We feel that a civilization is as fragile as a life.[59]

Geographically, Europe is a small place, little more than—to use a phrase he
repeated more than once—"a small peninsula of the continent of Asia." Yet
"in spite of her limited extent, and although the richness of her soil is not
out of the ordinary, she dominates the picture"; over the centuries she has
made herself into "the elect portion of the terrestrial globe, the pearl of the
sphere, the brain of a vast body." There was, he believed, no significant difference between European man ("*Homo europeus*") and the rest of the species; nothing set him apart, "neither race nor language nor customs," but
only "a driving thirst, an ardent and disinterested curiosity, a happy mixture
of imagination and rigorous logic, a certain unpessimistic scepticism, an
unresigned mysticism." The question now was whether this diminutive continent, this subcontinent, would continue to exercise her influence or shrivel
up to little more than what she actually represents geographically. For Valéry,
this was the choice. For all of Europe's past achievements, or perhaps indeed
because of them, Valéry was convinced that "the imbalance maintained for
so long in Europe's favor was, by its own reaction, bound to change by
degrees into an imbalance in the opposite direction."[60] Many shared his
view, few his final optimism.

The apparent chaos that had followed in the wake of the war was, for
many in Europe, deepened by a sense that the decisive role in the final victory played by the United States and Japan now threatened what they saw
as Europe's hitherto uncontested hegemony over world affairs, the supremacy of what was often hazily understood to be a collective "European"
culture, and in particular the liberal values so many had fought so hard for.
One of those who took up Valéry's contrast between the size of Europe, its
natural resources, and the disproportionate intellectual and cultural achievements of its peoples was the French social geographer Albert Demangeon.
For him, the war had been more than yet another crisis, however deep, in
Europe's protracted history of crises. It had been a decisive turning point in
her history and in the history, more significantly, of her relationship with the

world. The task of defeating Germany and Turkey, he argued in the *Decline of Europe* (*Le Déclin de l'Europe*) in 1920, had been shared

> between Europe, North America, and the Japanese archipelago, between two groups from the white race and one from the yellow. There now exist several homes of the higher forms of humanity [*haute humanité*] in place of one. A new classification of the regions of the globe is in motion, in which Europe will no longer be at the head.

Did this mean, he went on to ask, that Europe was now doomed to become in reality nothing more than Valéry's "small peninsula of the continent of Asia"? Perhaps not, since greatness (*grandeur*) depends not on space and size but on "the level of civilization, on mental progress, on the ability to control nature; it depends more on value than on size." But one thing now was clear: If Europe could no longer maintain the place she had once occupied unchallenged in the political, economic, and military "scale of greatness," she still "owed it to her powerful originality to maintain a very personal place in the scale of values."[61]

It was by no means clear, however, that those values were either as obvious or as robust as Demangeon seems to have supposed. For a great many, what most threatened European hegemony, and even Europe itself, was not—or not only—the rise of other powers, least of all the United States, which, in the early twentieth century was still a progeny of Europe, still bound by much the same universal civilizing vision of the world. The real problem was "civilization" itself. For some, like the habitually gloomy Spanish philosopher, poet, novelist, and playwright Miguel de Unamuno, and others more broadly on the right of the political spectrum such as the social Darwinist Hermann von Keyserling, the war had been the culmination of a long period of betrayal of the values, in particular those Christian moral values, on which the Roman and subsequently Germanic European civilization of Europe had supposedly been built. Many, also mostly on the right, now looked to a revival of Europe's Christian past as the continent's only salvation. "Everything proceeds," wrote the arch-conservative, ultra-nationalist Henri Massis in 1925, "in what we think and what we are, from that Western theology, from that Judeo-Christian monotheism, 'garbed in the heritage of Graeco-Latin culture.'" The current situation was one in which European—Western—culture was, in his imagination, assaulted from all sides by Bolshevism, materialism, and Asiatic mysticism.

"A well-balanced mind would conclude from this: Europe and the world must be re-Christianised."[62]

For others, however, it was not that the value systems on which the concept of European or Western civilization had always rested was now under threat from wily Asians, brash Americans, or atheistic Bolsheviks; it was rather that those very value systems had now been revealed for what they had always been: miserable illusions at best, elaborate deceptions at worst. "Europe's pride," wrote the German playwright, Nobel laureate, eugenicist, and subsequently ardent Nazi sympathizer Gerhard Hauptmann, had now become "Europe's shamelessness." And the most shameless of its lies, he said, were those old beloved gods:

> Christianity, love of mankind, the rule of reason, international law, the League of Nations, humanity, culture. Instead of this they must be called bestiality, hatred of mankind, the rule of unreason, international lawlessness, the persecution of nations, inhumanity; and instead of the word "Culture," theft, robbery, arson, murder, and plunder must stand.[63]

The older European values—Christianity most preeminently among them—had now revealed themselves to be essentially empty of meaning and devoid of promise. (That meaning and the promise he would later find in National Socialism, in a new Europe based upon a new set of values, also uniquely European, but now supposedly enshrined in the "Aryan race," not in an originally "Semitic" religious system.)

For nearly all of these, modern Europe had been brought down not by an arms race, much less by the collapse of the old Congress System; it had been undermined from within, its values and objectives destroyed. All the sources of this decay were believed to be deep, and some were ancient.

The peoples of which this "Europe" was made up might, however, yet survive, because even if their much-vaunted values had proven to be self-destructive at best, no matter how diverse their cultures, languages, laws, and beliefs might be, they nevertheless, at some level, all possessed what the great German phenomenologist Edmund Husserl called "a special inner affinity of spirit that permeates all of them and transcends their national differences. It is a sort of fraternal relationship that gives us the consciousness of being at home in this circle."[64] For Husserl "Europe" designated the "unity of a spiritual life and a creative activity." The crisis of "European man" was for him, therefore, a "problem belonging purely to a science of the spirit" which did not have a political or even geographical component to it. If the

"European nations are sick"—and he was in little doubt that they were—this was because, although philosophy, and the human sciences more broadly, had been the creation of European and, more specifically, Greek civilization, there was now no human science capable of doing for mankind what the natural sciences had done for nature, which was to create a "purposeful way of living, manifesting spiritual creativity in the broadest sense, creating culture within historical continuity."[65]

Husserl gave his lecture on the *Crisis of European Man* in 1935, two years after Hitler's seizure of power, when he, the son of orthodox Jewish parents—although a convert to Lutheranism—might well have had cause to believe that "the lack of genuine rationality on all sides is the source of what has become for man an unbearable unclarity regarding his own existence"[66] He might also perhaps have reflected that what Europe most needed was not so much a new human science capable of creating a new culture of a "purposeful way of living" as a new science of politics to combat the onslaught of National Socialism. Husserl, however, was still bound by an older literary concern with what, even before the outbreak of war in 1914, had been looked upon as the inescapable, impending decline or decay of European civilization.

The arch-prophet of doom was the German philosopher and historian Oswald Spengler. Between 1918 and 1922, Spengler published a great sprawling work entitled *The Decline of the West*. Unlike most of the other pessimists of his day, Spengler was prepared to offer his readers a grand and unflinchingly deterministic account of why Europe was now irrevocably in decline. For him, an examination of the historical record had demonstrated that humanity was naturally divided, not into nations but into "cultures," and that all cultures had a limited life span of about a thousand years, after which they were doomed to decay and final extinction. On his reckoning, the "Faustian" culture of the "West"—or what he called "the West-European-American"—whose tendency was "overpoweringly towards extension, political, economic or spiritual," was now entering its final "civilizational" phase.[67] What Spengler understood by this was predicated upon the nineteenth-century German antinomy between *Zivilisation* and *Kultur*. Culture was good. It was soft, human, and warm. It was all that constituted the inner being of a nation; its arts, its customs, its religion. Civilization, by contrast, in Nietzsche's words, "means something else than culture, something which is perhaps the reverse of culture." It was a form of enforced domestication which was "intolerant of the most audacious and brilliant minds."[68] For Spengler, all mankind was doomed sooner or later to pass from one to the other. This was the meaning of progress. "Civilizations," he wrote, "are the most external and artificial states of which a species of developed humanity is capable." They are "the inevitable destiny of culture," and its inevitable death.[69]

Although written in an opaque or, as he saw it, inspired, impressionistic style which attracted a great deal of professional contempt, *The Decline of the West* was, as the eminent American critic Northrop Frye noted in 1974, "a work of historical popularization" (although, he added, "historians are the last people who should be influenced by it"), and as such it was one of the most widely discussed, if perhaps less widely read books in Europe in the interwar years.[70] Partly this was because it seemed simply to confirm what many believed they could observe around them, that "everything that does not belong to the matter-of-fact side of life—to politics, technics or economics—is . . . in the grip of decay."[71] Partly it was because, although Spengler himself insisted that he had conceived the work before 1914 and completed it before 1917, his thousand-year cycle could be interpreted to mean that the destruction of the German Empire and of Austria-Hungary was not so much a work of hostile allied powers as a moment in an inescapable historical evolution, of which the Allies had simply been the instrument. The war, Spengler declared, was not

> a momentary constellation of casual facts due to national sentiments, personal influences, or economic tendencies endowed with an appearance of unity and necessity . . . but the type of a historical change of phase occurring within a great historical organism of definable compass at the point preordained for it hundreds of years ago.[72]

Faced with the inevitability of its decline, the West would eventually be engulfed by what Spengler called "Caesarism," the politics of brute military power, and in this final phase Germany might yet come to resume her former position of might. As Frye remarked, "Although the theme is very muted . . . Spengler seems to have a hope—he regards it as a hope—that Germany may yet become the Rome of the future." (This initially endeared him to the Nazis, although he himself rejected their anti-Semitism, and after meeting Hitler in 1933 came to the conclusion that he was a vulgar little man and certainly not the "hero" that the West now needed.)

The Decline of the West captured a prevailing mood of the interwar years, pessimistic, vacillating, and uncertain. It was, however, largely thanks to the title of the book that Spengler "owed most of his celebrity with an immense public who know only that [he] was famous and that he had prophesied our decline," the Swiss cultural theorist Denis de Rougemont dryly observed.[73] Today, wrote Miguel de Unamuno in 1922, "it is possible to see throughout the whole of Europe a state of pessimism and despair. It is a matter, as Spengler and others have seen, of the twilight of western civilization." To Unamuno, it seemed as if a mood of collective hysteria had gripped the peoples of Europe, and "there is barely anyone who does not believe himself to be the victim of another."[74] And no one had understood that better than Spengler, even if no one, not even Unamuno, was quite certain what he was predicting.[75]

Yet amid all the gloom, there also existed a cautious optimism that the crisis, rather than being the sepulcher of Western civilization, might in the end offer an opportunity for its renewal. In January 1923, André Gide— who had remained cautiously optimistic throughout the war, to the point of believing that when it was over, the entire continent, even Britain, might emerge as a republic—contributed a brief essay on the future of Europe (tellingly subtitled "A Review of the European Elite") to the *Revue de Genève*, a journal created by the Swiss novelist and essayist Robert de Traz as an intellectual and literary contribution to what he envisaged as the guiding spirit behind the League of Nations.[76] Like Hauptmann, Gide believed that the war had "made of Europe a place of lies and compromise." "I believe that we are participating in the end of a world," he continued, "of a culture, of a civilization; that everything must be thrown into doubt." "The question of Europe" was also, he complained, something with which very few people now concerned themselves. A feeling of common interest was, he believed, something which is only ever created out of a feeling of common danger; but "until now the feeling of danger has done nothing but pit the peoples of Europe against each other." Yet for all that, he was not entirely prepared to give up on "Western civilization." He had no remedy, no panacea for the future to offer. Of one thing, however, he was certain:

> That no country can henceforth hope for any real progress of its own culture in isolation, nor without the direct collaboration of other countries. The same is true from the political, economic, and industrial points of view—in fact, from any point of view whatsoever—the whole of Europe courts eventual ruin, if every country of Europe is prepared to consider only its individual wellbeing.

What form the Europe that was slowly emerging from the ruins of the war would finally assume he was no longer prepared to say. It was unlikely to be the union of like-minded republics he had seen in 1917. Of one thing, however, he was confident: while "the true spirit of Europe reject[ed] the isolating infatuation of nationalism," it was also as firmly opposed to what he called "the depersonalization of internationalism."[77]

But if that were the case, then where was the middle way? What would be capable of undoing the pernicious lingering effects of the nationalist hysteria the war had so carefully fostered, while at the same time avoiding the anomalous, icy, formalized, and ineffective institutionalism which was all that the League seemed to offer? The most obvious answer would appear to be, once again, some kind of union of the European states. Europe clearly could not look to the League to solve what was in effect its own internal cultural and moral problems, much less could it rely upon the United States. If anything, the only way forward for the League itself was, as Scelle argued later, a process of "decentralization," of which the creation of a European federation would be the first, most necessary step.[78]

This was echoed by the Spanish philosopher, social theorist, cultural critic, and politician José Ortega y Gasset: the time had come, he reflected in 1929, in *The Revolt of the Masses* (*La rebelión de las masas*)—a book which offers the earliest and still one of the most acute attempts to account for the phenomenon now called "populism"—for the continent of Europe to convert itself into a "national ideal." Nationalism, he argued, or at least the "nationalisms" which had emerged after the war were so many "blind alleys." "Nationalism...is always an effort in a direction opposite to that principle which creates nations. The former is exclusive in tendency, the latter inclusive." Once the nation has been established, as was now the case throughout Europe, nationalism becomes a mere "mania...a pretext to escape from the necessity of inventing something new, some great enterprise." (Ortega, a good liberal throughout his life, despite his later uneasy accommodation with the Franco regime, did not consider either National Socialism or Fascism to be in any significant sense "new.") The "great enterprise" of which Europe was now in such urgent need he called "the national state of the West." It had, he believed, despite constant failures, of which the Great War was only the most recent, always been in a "condition of becoming," and if it were to remain true to its "genuine inspiration," then it could only one day evolve into a "gigantic continental state." For "[o]nly the determination to construct a great nation from the group of peoples of the Continent would give new life to the pulses of Europe. She would start to believe in herself again and automatically start to make demands on and to discipline herself." But, he warned,

> the situation is much more difficult than is generally realised. The years are passing, and there is the risk that the European will grow accustomed to the lower tone of the existence he is at present living, will get used neither to rule others nor to rule himself. In such a case all his virtues and higher capacities would vanish into air.[79]

If this dismal future were to be avoided, if anything resembling the "national state of the West" was to become a reality, no faith in some neo-Hegelian historical process was going to bring it about. Europe was now on her own. As Zimmern warned, Europe would "be wise to adopt the old Italian motto *Europa farà da sé*. She must look to her own healing"[80] "Taking care of herself" was, of course, precisely what the new European federalists had in mind.

VI

One of the most persuasive, certainly the most colorful of these was Count Richard von Coudenhove-Kalergi.[81] Coudenhove-Kalergi was an exotic figure, not least because, in the world of carefully orchestrated marriages among the upper echelons of the diminishing Central European aristocracy, his mother was Japanese and his father an Austro-Hungarian diplomat with Flemish, Polish, Greek (the Kalergis were from Crete), and even Norwegian origins. Unsurprisingly, he was cursed by Hitler as a "rootless cosmopolitan and elitist half-breed." He has been identified as the source of the Resistance hero Victor Laszlo in the film *Casablanca*, more recently has been targeted by a variety of anti-Semitic conspiracy theorists because of the support his "Paneuropa" movement received from the Rothschilds and the Warburgs, and has been excoriated by various species of white supremacists because of his belief that racial intermixing would one day produce a new kind of western man, what he called "the Eurasian-Negroid race of the future externally similar to the ancient Egyptian."[82] (A brief survey of Internet sites with titles such as "Western Spring," "Fighting for a White Revival," and "Dutch Anarchy" reveals claims that this project is even now being furtively pursued by the various leaders of the EU and the United Nations, which apparently explains their support for the continuing migration of refugees from Africa and the Middle East into Europe.) In fact, his inspirations were largely and unsurprisingly conservative, aristocratic, and Christian, and his "philosophy of life," in so far as he had one beyond his passionate and relentless belief in a unified Europe, rested solely on what he identified as "the three foundations of Western civilization"—a classical education, a Christian philosophy of life, and a "chivalrous outlook."[83]

In 1923 Coudenhove-Kalergi founded the International Pan-European Union, and created a journal *Paneuropa* (which lasted until 1938) to go with it. It was named, he said, after the Pan-American Union of 1890 (now the Organization of American States), which he seems, at least in the pre-war years, to have imagined as the ideological successor to Simón Bolívar's "Gran Colombia," a short-lived project for a federal union of all the states of Spanish America, which had now—at least in Coudenhove-Kalergi's estimation—become "a cornerstone of world evolution."[84]

The union attracted a considerable following (even in Britain). Einstein, Heinrich and Thomas Mann, Rainer-Maria Rilke, and the Austrian novelist Franz Werfel, to name but a few of the most prominent, were members, as were at one time or another Sigmund Freud, Benedetto Croce, the Austrian chancellor Bruno Kreisky, and the French prime minister Georges Pompidou. Aristide Briand (of whom more later), then foreign minister and subsequently prime minister of France, was a founding member and became honorary president in 1927. Although it was closed down during World War II, when Coudenhove-Kalergi himself fled first to France and then to the United States, it was re-established after 1945 and survives to this day. Coudenhove-Kalergi was also responsible for suggesting the final moment of Beethoven's Ninth Symphony, the "Ode to Joy" (but without Schiller's words), as the European anthem.

Coudenhove-Kalergi's own personal vision of the possible future of Europe (and of the world) was, however, as Winston Churchill said of it, "premature, erroneous and impracticable": too vague, too eccentric to have been more than an uplifting call to arms for those already convinced of the need for a unified Europe. In addition to Coudenhove-Kalergi's belief that the future "Eurasian-Negroid" would be more capable of peaceful cooperation with his fellow human beings than his "Aryan" ancestors had been, he also believed that "Europe" could be persuasively compared to India or China (or to what he imagined India and China to be): a single nation and a "great motherland." "Ask anyone from Hyderabad to what nation he belongs," he wrote, "he will tell you that he is an Indian; ask a man from

Shantung, he will reply China, ask a man from Texas, he will reply 'I am an American.'"[85] But the Hungarian will only ever reply "I am from Hungary," and so on. At present there simply did not exist any persuasive sense of a common European identity. Yet Coudenhove-Kalergi was also convinced that just as for centuries the Indians and the Chinese had had no "sense of nationality," but "both have today been reawakened," so would the Europeans—"tomorrow." Despite his partly Asian origins and his belief that culturally the world was divided into China, India, and Europe (the Americas being a merely cultural appendages to Europe), Coudenhove-Kalergi seems to have known nothing very specific about the political situation in either China or India in the first decades of the twentieth century. All he knew was that they were vast territories with highly diverse populations speaking many different languages and sharing different religions and different customs. In that, at least, they were both similar to Europe. He appears, however, to have been unaware—or to have simply ignored the fact—that if China and India were, in any plausible sense, "nations," it was because a succession of external imperial powers had made them so. The same, of course, was largely true even of the United States, which, for all his lack of precision about what any kind of federal system the future United States of Europe would adopt, was his main model. Like so many others, Coudenhove-Kalergi also looked wistfully back to the Roman Empire as the last period in history in which Europe had been—supposedly—at peace and "united through the *Pax Romana*."[86] Julius Caesar, he declared unambiguously, became "the founder of European unity" by transforming through conquest what had hitherto been only a Mediterranean power into a "Pan-European Empire."[87] (At times he even spoke of the possibility of a future "European empire," without saying quite what that might consist of.[88]) Europe, he recognized, was "not a natural but an artificial Continent" (as were both India and China).[89] It was, however, one that had been created through a prolonged historical process which on his account (and it was, of course, not only his) ran from ancient Greece, the creator of "the European idea," through ancient Rome, through the Carolingian Empire to the Crusades— the "liveliest expression of European feeling"—through the Napoleonic Wars, through the efforts of the Holy Alliance to build a new European state system, until it had finally collapsed in 1914.[90] Throughout this long period, a succession of writers, prophets, and pamphleteers, starting, in his version, with Dante and going through the duc de Sully to the abbé de Saint-Pierre, to Rousseau and Kant, and ending with, *inter alios*, Victor Hugo, Nietzsche, and "the great Italian philosopher Giuseppe Mazzini," who, along with Garibaldi and the sometime Italian prime minister Francesco Crispi—later praised by Mussolini for having initiated a form of "Italian" as opposed to "Western" imperialism by his invasion of Ethiopia in 1893—had been "the forerunners of Paneuropa." They had in varying guises been the "living links in the spiritual chain which led from the Pan-European age of the Crusades to the present Paneuropa movement, from the Christian Western world of yesterday to the United States of Europe of tomorrow." The chain, however, had been broken in the second half of the nineteenth century, and instead there had arisen "a fierce wave of nationalism, leading Europe steadily towards the First World War."[91] But for all that, he was convinced that the desire for union was still there; the vision was still there; all that was lacking was the will.

What now, in 1938, faced Europe were the two threats of "nationalism and extreme internationalism"—by which Coudenhove-Kalergi meant international communism. "Paneuropa" could only work, he knew, if all the states of which it was composed were more or less democratic. And both the kind of nationalism which had seized control of Italy and Germany and communism threatened this in different ways. Communism did so because its objective was to eliminate Europe altogether and to dissolve European culture, European religious traditions, and European customs and habits into a universal order dominated by "collectivism," "materialism," "atheism," the "spirit of Machiavelli," and "the principle of equality." It was "not merely un-European but anti-European." In Coudenhove-Kalergi's opinion, while you could be both a good European and a socialist "of European coinage," because socialism had already been incorporated into social democracy, it was impossible to be a "Bolshevik," because Bolshevik internationalism sought to erase all the differences which existed between the Europeans and the rest of the world.[92] It was also clearly a violation of all three of Coudenhove-Kalergi's "three foundations of Western civilization."

Fascism, by contrast, as distinct from National Socialism, was, he believed, limited to politics, leaving "extensive liberty...in questions of conscience and economics." Coudenhove-Kalergi had a weakness for Fascist "corporatism," and in the early years of the Fascist regime did his best to persuade Mussolini to support the "Pan-Europe" movement. In 1923, he even published an open letter to the Italian dictator in the Austrian *Neue Freie Presse* appealing to him in the "name of Europe's youth" to "save Europe!" The now united Italy, as one of the "three great nations that have emerged from Charlemagne's Empire," was, he claimed to believe, now ideally suited to act as the arbiter between the other two—France and Germany—who "have been fighting each other for ten centuries." Both Great Britain and Russia had now outgrown Europe, geographically at least, and "could survive its fall." Not so the other nations of the continent, which have now become, he declared—using a phrase later recycled by the Nazis—"a community of fate, facing the alternatives of union or death." Now, he wrote, unwittingly anticipating Carl Schmitt, "Europe ought to proclaim its Monroe Doctrine: Europe for the Europeans." And who better to do that than Mussolini, the new Marius—sometimes known as the "Third Founder of Rome"—and the new Caesar, by laying the "foundations for the United States of Europe."[93]

Unsurprisingly perhaps, his letter went unanswered. Undaunted, in 1933 Coudenhove-Kalergi asked for, and was granted, an audience with Mussolini. On meeting him, he found the "upper part of the Duce's face to be noble and fine," his "forehead beautifully shaped," his "coal-black eyes . . . very expressive." He noted, however, that they "lacked the bright spark of ideal- ism," and that his "mouth and jaw expressed cynicism and brutality, which grew more obvious when he smiled." The two men seem to have had a lengthy and animated discussion on a variety of topics ranging from Nietzsche to Gobineau, and Coudenhove-Kalergi came away with the impression that Mussolini, while he thought Nazi anti-Semitism, which Coudenhove-Kalergi insisted was in effect "directed against all Mediterraneans" and not just Jews, to be "pure nonsense," had some only slightly less distasteful racial theories of his own "which advocated the supe- riority of the Latin races over the Germanic ones. It was still racism, but it reversed the values." Coudenhove-Kalergi singularly failed, however, to get any commitment out of Mussolini for any kind of Pan-European union, although he remarked somewhat wistfully that Mussolini seemed "willing to follow its further development from a neutral and not unsympathetic vantage point."[94]

Nationalism was another beast altogether. Having started in the nine- teenth century as a challenge to oppression, it had, in the post-war years, degenerated from what had been for the Italians of the Risorgimento a force for what Coudenhove-Kalergi called "national toleration," and thus one of the possible sources for European unification, into little more than "national megalomania," now enhanced by "racial theories which detected blood-groups in speech or faith groups," and which had led inexorably to the rise of dictatorship.[95] Narrow sectarianism had replaced the "European nationality" which Mazzini had fought for—that narrow sense of belonging to different national states, all of which, however, were members of the same "great cultural community in the same sense as China or India."

Despite the deplorable condition of tribalism into which many of the nations of Europe had now sunk, Coudenhove-Kalergi remained convinced that soon all "Englishmen and Frenchmen, Germans and Italians, Poles and Spaniards" would awaken to the realization that they were all "children of a common civilization, a common race, a common continent, heirs of a common tradition, bearers of a common mission, bound together forever in a community of destiny and life."[96] Then, Coudenhove-Kalergi hoped, in good Mazzinian tones, the day would come when "national toleration will not destroy but ennoble the conception of nationality, and open out the way to the United States of Europe, a community of free nations in our part of the globe." It would, he believed, "open a new chapter in world history" as momentous as the discovery of America.[97]

Coudenhove-Kalergi's "Paneuropa" was a grandiose, overinflated, and inherently unrealizable project to reinvigorate European "civilization"— Churchill was certainly right about that—which would, he fervently hoped, bring what he always understood to be the "destiny" of Europe to its natural, final, and triumphant fulfillment. For Coudenhove-Kalergi and a great many of his co-federalists, the quest for a unified Europe was not merely a bid (as most of the projects for European union, from Sully's "Grand design" of 1600 to the "Areopagus" of Europe of 1815 had been) to secure a perpetual and lasting peace within Europe and to bring finally to an end what Napoleon in 1802 might have been the first to call a European civil war.[98] For Coudenhove-Kalergi, as for so many of those who survived the Great War, the more immediate threat was not so much civil war, or even impending Spenglerian decadence. It was the fear, real or imagined, that Europe— and more precisely European civilization and all it represented—was facing the prospect of being swept aside, either by the bastardized, culturally diminished version of its own self represented by the United States of America or—more menacing still—by an as yet largely impoverished and impotent, but threatening Soviet Union.

Coudenhove-Kalergi's anxiety was not entirely new. In 1840, when the Russian Empire had already replaced the Ottoman as the predominant imperial power east of the Urals and was expanding at an unprecedented rate, Alexis de Tocqueville had warned that, while Europeans were looking the other way, a bipolar world was steadily emerging in which America and Russia seemed to be "striding with a swift and easy step towards a destiny, the limits of which no human eye can behold." In the aftermath of World War I, however, with the decaying tsarist empire now replaced by a newly invigorated Bolshevik one, and the unquestionable emergence of the United States as a new "Great Power" to rival and exceed all the others, this sense of being caught between a politically hostile state on one side and a friendly but increasingly alien one on the other seemed to some to have reached potentially overwhelming, apocalyptic proportions.

If, however, Europe were only to unite, if it were to pool all the resources of the continent and those of its overseas colonies by "unifying its organization and rationally opening up its African colonial empire," it would, Coudenhove-Kalergi hoped, finally be able to become self-sufficient in both food and raw materials. Thanks, then, to the geographical position it occupies midway been Russia to the east and America to the west, "and thanks also to the tradition and native gifts of its inhabitants, it would be both able and fitted to be the cultural center of the world for a long time to come."[99]

Coudenhove-Kalergi's blend of authoritarianism and yearning for the Austro-Hungarian past was unique among European federalists. But the appeal to a set of suitably imprecise universal Christian ideals, coupled with an explicit racism—even if Coudenhove-Kalergi's was certainly original—was not. In 1928 the *littérateur* and radical socialist parliamentarian Gaston Riou published a short polemical book *Europe, My Country (Europe, ma patrie)*, followed one year later by a sequel, *Unite or Die (S'unir ou mourir)*. Riou had spent eleven months as a prisoner in Germany at the start of the war. It was an experience which had turned him into a convinced pacifist. "When will it end," he asked from captivity, "this sinister interlude in the book of peace, our book, our true book, the book of humanity?"[100] It had also made him an ardent Europeanist. Unlike Paul Valéry, whom he so obviously admired and to whom his bleak alarmist view of Europe's possible future was clearly indebted, Riou saw the cleavages and conflicts emerging within the modern world initially in terms of race. There was for him a world "of colour"—Africa but also and most importantly Asia—and there was "the white world". This was made up of Europe, which constituted its "heart and the head," the USSR, the United States, and (for the time being at least) Britain and its dominions. Of all these, only Europe, although no longer at war, had so far failed to achieve any degree of real unity and because of this was in danger of losing what he called persistently her "primacy"—economic, cultural, spiritual—over all the other places on the globe.

Riou was not wrong about the lack of unity among the peoples of Europe. Even at a national level the instability of the post-war democratic order was remarkable. Hardly any of the post-war cabinets in any of the major nations lasted more than a year. No French government in the years that Riou was writing his books lasted more than eight months (in the period 1932–40 this had dropped to a mere four).[101] What José Ortega y Gasset in the *Revolt of the Masses* called "hyper-democracy," or what today would be called "populism," had turned the orders of society increasingly against each other. True democracy, or as Ortega called it "the old democracy," was "tempered by a generous dose of liberalism and of enthusiasm for law." In this version, the mass was fully prepared to surrender control of the state to what today are referred to as "elites" (or what he calls "minorities" and "specialized persons"), since they "took it for granted that after all, in spite of their defects and weaknesses, the minorities understood a little more of public problems than it did itself." Now, however, "the mass believes that it has the right to impose and to give force of law to notions born in the café. I doubt whether there have been other periods of history in which the multitude has come to govern more directly than in our own."[102]

Riou saw the rise of mass culture and mass power in much the same light. It was not, however, the populism of the masses (Riou was after all something of a populist himself) or the brand of nationalism they had embraced which he identified as the real source of Europe's encroaching decadence. Like many of his generation, Riou was acutely aware that the true challenge to European civilization, European success, and European dominance now came not only from within. It came also, and predominantly, from without. The emergence of the United States as a world power after the Spanish–American War of 1898, and of Japan after her crushing defeat of China in 1894–5, made it obvious that the "Great Powers" of the world were no longer confined to Europe. What Riou called the continents of "colour," above all Japan and "Indochina," were now looking toward the "white world" for inspiration and rapidly modernizing—and, he warned, it "would be naive to suppose that this was not a threat to us!" There was also India, which he describes—he was an unapologetic believer in the Aryan myth—as "a reservoir of four hundred million men of our race," now awakening, urged on by Mohandas Gandhi and Rabindranath Tagore, from a long "metaphysical sleep." Someday these masses might well overwhelm Europe. That day, however, still lay sometime in the future. "The Hindu," he wrote dismissively, "is not in a hurry."[103] But the Europeans would, nevertheless, be unwise not to take precautionary measures.

The greatest menace of all, because they were openly friendly and insidious, came from "the less civilised" portions of the "white race" itself, by which he meant Britain, the USSR, and the United States. Britain, or what he called the "Britannic block" (which included the Commonwealth of Nations), was a species of pseudo-Europe which "de-Europeanizes further each day" and whose "destiny lies elsewhere (so she believes)," but who had chosen for narrowly strategic reasons to remain on her own in "splendid isolation." For Riou, Britain was always the traitor within, the "impure European," the nation that could have prevented the war, had she told Berlin that she sided with the French immediately after the Treaty of London in 1914. Britain, he believed, needed a "feeble Europe" because Britain knew that a united Europe "will not only be stronger than she, but would become the major power in the world." The future European Union, he concluded—prophetically as it now seems—"would be continental or it would not be at all."[104] The "atheist" USSR was an, as yet, relatively impoverished nation on the fringes of Europe against which Britain and America stood together with Europe in a "holy war." Yet, he added—also prophetically as it turned out—Russia would "always remain imperialist. The work of Peter the Great continues.... Russia has only arrived at the dawn of her day."[105]

The greatest single threat, however, to what he called repeatedly the intellectual, spiritual, and cultural "primacy" of Europe came from the USA. What had given the Americans their increasing ascendancy in the world was not their unquestionable military might, much less "virtue"; it was an emphasis on "quantity" rather than "quality." The American system of values was wholly antithetical to everything shared by all the peoples of Europe—what he describes broadly as "humanism." For Europe's primacy, is, or was, based neither on economics nor on technology, in which fields the United States had come to excel over all others. It was based, instead, on what he called airily "the feeling that she [Europe]—or at least her most noble representatives—have of the sacred character of the human person."[106]

The USA, dedicated as it was to the single-minded pursuit of wealth (what he calls "mercantilism"), had little or no regard for the sacredness of the purely human. Like Valéry (and a great many others), Riou was excessively worried by the encroachment of what he saw as a set of alien aspirations

embodied above all in the threat of "Americanization," a concern which has
grown over the past century, although, contrary to what Riou anticipated,
its effects have been limited largely to popular culture.

Yet for all that modern America had evolved into a threat to Europe's
"primacy," the United States was for Riou, no less than it had been for
Hugo, precisely the political model to which the current Europeans should
now look. For Riou, as for so many others, the true American was Alexander
Hamilton (significantly, he pointed out, the son of a French mother from
Louisiana), a "Genius who was strictly civil, having no other means of action
other than his human logic and popular persuasion" and without whom
America today would be nothing other than a "bundle of nations in the
image of Europe." It was Hamilton who had created, out of a post-
revolutionary world of thirteen squabbling former colonies, a great nation—
who had brought forth a "wise daughter" from a "mad mother." And it was
of a new Hamilton that "Europe now stands in need."

For Riou, the modern Americans who had emerged from Hamilton's
initiative were the new Persians as portrayed by the Greek historian
Herodotus: wealthy, often courteous, even cultivated, at least in their willingness to accumulate European art, but lacking subtlety and originality.
The modern Europeans, for their part, now occupied a place analogous to
that held in the fifth century BCE by the ancient Greeks, by "Socrates and
the immortal Pleiades of his friends," poor in material goods, yet rich in
spirit, courage, and intellect.[107] And just as the ancient Greek states were
dispersed and constantly at war with one another, so are the modern
European nations, while the great Persian Empire, like the modern USA,
was united, stable, prosperous, and at peace. The lesson to be learnt from this
analogy was, of course, that if Europe wished to resist the lure of this new
"barbarism," if it did not want to go the way of ancient Greece when it
finally fell prey to the "Persianizing" tendencies of Alexander the Great,
then it too had to become united. "As for us," he concluded "we say to all
the young forces of the West: the moment has come to make Europe. Unite
or die."[108]

That unity could only come by way of a federalized Europe. Riou does
not, it must be said, offer any very precise indications as to how this would
be brought about or as to what form it would eventually take, other than
that it would probably be something like the Swiss Federation because of
the diversity of its languages. He seems to have believed that it could be
made to accommodate various political forms (as he claims the Holy Roman

Empire had once done), including even Fascism; but he was also convinced that the only true political system, the only one which would reflect the true "humanist" values of European civilization, was democracy. This he describes as "a collective lyrical state" and "the political form of humanism" born out of a "truly religious" feeling for the individual. For Riou, however, democracy can only flourish when considerations of interests, and above all of profit, crucial though those might be for the survival of the state, take second place to the "ardent sentiment of fraternity."[109]

The future "Federative European Democracy" was to have a European president elected for four years. There would be a council of state made up of two representatives from each European nation, and the legislative power would lie with a chamber of representatives. There would also be a supreme court which would act both as the guardian of the constitution and as the arbitrator both between the confederated states and between the individual citizens of the confederation and the confederation itself (much indeed as the European Court of Justice does). What, however, was crucial was that there should be only one European armed force, a single currency, and a customs union which would allow either for the total suppression of dues within the union (as he imagined to be the case within the United States) or that members of the federation should benefit from preferential tariffs, "as is the case in the British Empire."[110]

If Europe were to fail to unite economically, he warned, she would become so impoverished that she would very soon "fall to the level of a colonized land." If she were to fail to unite in a federal union, she was doomed to become, in a very short space of time, the vassal of one of the "three unified white blocks." And once thus poor and in thrall, she "will have lost her civilizing primacy, and the entire white race with her." In short, he concluded, there were "three imminent dangers" now facing post-war Europe, and indirectly, it would seem, the whole of Western civilization: "poverty, vassaldom, and barbarism." And there was but "one sole road to renewal: the United States of Europe."[111]

To the British on the far side of the channel, ever suspicious of anything that sounded too much like high-flying "continental" rhetoric, observations such as these appeared all too clearly to be manifestations of a French and more broadly continental European bid to reassert the Great Power status of the pre-war years. As one British Foreign Office official commented in 1930, the idea of the "United States of Europe," and of Coudenhove-Kalergi's Pan-Europe, had always been intended "to assure France and the rest of

Europe against the ever growing strength of non-European and especially American competition. Without this it is hard to see that the word 'Pan-Europe' can mean anything at all." It was, perhaps, a characteristically overly reductionist judgment born of an ignorance of the nature and influence of the Pan-Europe movement, which the British minster in Vienna, Viscount Chilston, had dismissed in 1926 as simply "fantastic," a view shared at the time by most of his colleagues.[112] But there can be no doubt that both Riou and Coudenhove-Kalergi, like most of the European federalists of the inter-war years, if they did not quite share the degree of apprehension about Europe's economic and military collapse that the British attributed to them, certainly feared the demise of what they perceived to be Europe's cultural, political, and "moral" ascendancy. As the English federalist and subsequent colleague of Jean Monnet Sir Arthur Salter observed sadly, although the main objective of the International Economic Conference which met in Geneva in May 1927 under the auspices of the League had been "how to increase world prosperity,"

> it had been gradually, in the public mind, taking another form, viz. "how can Europe compete against America?" As to the strength of this develop-ment there can be no question. In France, in Germany, in Spain, in Czechoslovakia, the evidence as regards not only public opinion, but also official opinion, is overwhelming for something that is usually called the "United States of Europe." Strong, however, as is the feeling behind such a conception, it is difficult to obtain any clear and precise definition of it. What emerges clearly is, however, that the conception usually assumes an anti-American form.[113]

For so many like Riou there was, however, far more at stake than simple economic mastery; there was the place of Europe at the core of all that the new emerging global civilization might come to represent. None of the nations of Europe could hope to face alone the might of a future vastly expanded Soviet Union, or a Japan, or what Riou saw as a new China, whose prolonged civil wars had transformed a once "tranquil empire" into a "bellicose empire"; nor could it hope to compete on the world stage, eco-nomically, morally, or culturally, with either the United States or the British Empire.[114] There was, in short, the perennial fear that European "primacy," which had for so long been simply taken for granted, might now soon be eclipsed for good, unless something urgent and immediate was done to reassert it.

"Europe is at a crossroads," Riou concluded *Europe, ma patrie*:

> To be or not to be. The yes and the no. Will our descendants still be the master
> race ["*peuple-maître*"] or will they live the mediocre life of a people forever
> trailing behind, poor, semi-enslaved, without a mission? Are we a generation
> of strays incapable of either decision or of action? Will we abdicate without
> shame our millennial primacy? Will we write with our own hands *Finis
> Europae*?[115]

Riou's two books are thin on detail, weak on analysis, and rich in epideictic
rhetoric. His account of the future of the power struggles he envisaged
between Europe and the rest of the globe is also driven unapologetically
(but then, like most of his generation, he would have seen no reason to
apologize) by a racism which in France, as in most of Europe, became in the
1930s a source of violent and bitter conflict, mostly, but by no mean exclusively, between those on the right and those on the left. Riou, although he
remained a radical socialist throughout his life, speaks persistently of the
"white race," of "white civilization," of the "world of colour," of the "white
world." He admits to being a "white imperialist," although only because he
believes that "the destiny of the white man ['*le destin blanc*]" lies in universalism.[116] He believed that "the most recent ethnological studies" had
demonstrated that "the yellow race" is nothing other than a mixture of
white and black, and that "the superior peoples of Asia are the ones in
whom the white predominates."[117]

   Like many who shared such views, like the journalist, economist, and
ardent pan-Europeanist Francis Delaisi; the journalist Georges Suarez—
executed by firing squad in 1944—and the novelist, essayist, dandy, and
notorious philanderer Drieu de la Rochelle, Riou found himself looking
with some sympathy on the exclusivist ideologies of Fascism and National
Socialism, which offered the strong centralizing arguments—and the
racism—which the liberal democracies of Europe clearly did not. It is
little wonder, perhaps, that Riou, despite his socialistic affiliations, was one of
the 568 members of the French parliament who in July 1940 voted to give
Marshal Pétain full powers over the Free French Zone of Vichy, thus effectively transforming much of France into a client state of Germany.[118] (My
copy of *Europe, ma patrie* once belonged to a French soldier named Gilbert
Bonnefoy who was held in the notorious Stalag III B prisoner-of-war
camp near the border with Poland. On the title page he had written
laconically, "In Captivity (Germany) June 20, 1942." The next page carries

the camp censor's seal of approval: *Geprüft* ("checked"). There was, indeed, nothing in Riou's book to which the Nazi regime could take much exception.)

Yet if we strip away the racism, the sectarianism, the drumming insistence on an always shifting set of European "values," the fear of falling under the weight of either Communist tyranny or insidious American materialism, Riou had seen perhaps more clearly than many that the nations of Europe were moving inexorably away from a once dominant past, one sustained by militarism and persistent overseas expansion which, although for some European states, Germany most obviously, it still hung precariously in the balance, was now poised to vanish for good. He could see too that in the new globalized cosmos the only way forward was not now by means of interstate rivalry, which had previously been Europe's strength, but through unity. Like Coudenhove-Kalergi, Riou was keenly, painfully, aware that the USSR and the USA were not only a threat to a now dwindling European cultural and political hegemony, but also examples to be emulated.

VII

One of those on whom Riou's writing appears to have left a deep impression—although he passed over in silence all the prattle in favor of the "destiny of the white man"—and who wrote a glowing preface—a "declaration," he called it—to a combined and revised edition of both his books, was Aristide Briand. Briand served eleven terms as prime minister of the French Third Republic from 1909 until 1929, and was one of the authors of, and the chief inspiration behind, the optimistically named "General Treaty for the Renunciation of War as an Instrument of National Policy" of 1928, which he hatched jointly with the US Secretary of State Frank B. Kellogg, and which has been known since as the "Kellogg–Briand Pact" or the "Paris Peace Pact."[119] Parts of this were subsequently incorporated into the Charter of the United Nations, and technically it remains in effect to this day. The most significant clause of the pact, however, was indubitably Article I, which declared that the "High Contracting Parties ... condemn recourse to war for the solution of international controversies, and renounce it as an instrument of national policy in their relations with one another."[120] The pact provided the legal grounds for all subsequent attempts to hold governments, not individuals, liable for all future acts of war and their consequences.[121]

But Briand knew full well that acts of legislation, in particular one of such sweeping condemnation, would hardly be sufficient in practice. The Article might provide an instrument for future legal redress, it might possibly give potential antagonists a reason to pause before declaring war, but peace— Kantian perpetual peace—could only really be achieved, as Kant himself had seen, through a closer union between those who might in any other circumstance be tempted precisely to use war as "an instrument of national policy in their relations with one another."

As a tentative first step in this direction, Briand, at that time French foreign minister, together with the German chancellor Gustav Stresemann— for which both men were jointly awarded the Nobel Peace Prize—and the British foreign secretary Austen Chamberlain, drew up a nonaggression pact between Paris, Berlin, and Brussels, by the terms of which at a meeting held in Locarno in October 1925 Germany was admitted to the League of Nations. Although only a treaty agreement, and one which only applied to Western Europe, the Locarno Treaties (there were in fact seven of them) were hailed as the beginning of a new entente between the major European powers. They were, said Briand, the "draft of a European family within the League of Nations ... the beginning of a magnificent work, the renewal of Europe."[122] When the conference was finally over, he emerged triumphant from the great hall of Locarno, a small Swiss town on the shores of Lake Maggiore, and declared that "we spoke European, a new language which we shall all have to learn." For Briand, the idea of a united Europe which, he claimed, had for so many years "haunted the imagination of philosophers and poets" had now become "a response to a necessity."[123]

One year later, on September 5, 1929, Briand set before the assembly of the League of Nations at Geneva a plan for a "European Federal Union." "He stood there," wrote Coudenhove-Kalergi, who was watching from the diplomatic gallery, "like another Columbus on his way to discover a new continent." When he had finished, the "audience cheered and rose." It was now, added, Coudenhove-Kalergi, "for the other European representatives to take up the challenge."[124] (Later, in 1948, his enthusiasm apparently unabated, despite all that had occurred in the intervening years, he likened it to the creation in 1890 of the Pan-American Union, which he saw as a precursor of his own Paneuropa movement.[125])

On closer examination, however, and when the fervour of the moment had largely evaporated, the "European Federal Union" turned out to be little more than a limited project for economic cooperation. Yet Briand, although he was nothing if not a realist, recognized that although in the current circumstances "the most pressing need" was an economic union, he hoped that this would ultimately lead to what he famously called a "sort of federal bond" (*une sorte de lien fédéral*) between peoples "geographically grouped as the peoples of Europe are." Between them, he insisted,

> there should exist at every moment, the possibility of entering into contact with one another to discuss their common interests, to take common deci-sions. They should, in a word, establish between themselves a line of solidarity which would allow them to confront, at any moment, dangerous circum-stances, should they arise.

"I am certain," he went on, "that from the political point of view, or from the social point of view, this federal bond, without touching upon the sov-ereignty of any of the nations which might form part of such an association, can be beneficial."[126] This, he claimed, would allow for any one of the European states to enter into contact with any or all of the others with the purpose of reaching "common resolutions" and of taking "collective respon-sibility in the face of a danger threatening European peace." Briand had attempted, as Chamberlain said later, to "raise a new temple of peace" from the "blood-soaked ruins of the past."[127] Gustav Stresemann, with whom Briand had a close working relationship, welcomed it as a "great idea," albeit one which might seem, as it clearly did to many, "crazy at first." As he had told *The Times* on December 2, 1921, "The war has taught us . . . that a com-mon fate binds us together. If we go under, we go under together. If we wish to recover, we cannot do so in conflict with each other, but only by working together."[128] The conception of a "sort of federal bond" was, how-ever, a long way from the "United States of Europe." The "Briand plan," as it came to be known, although it was subsequently hailed as a precursor of the European Economic Community, was, like most of its predecessors, thin on precise details. It was, however, clear on two things, which would be taken up again after 1945: first, that any future union of the European states would have to be a union of sovereign national states and not, as some had imagined it should be, an eventual superstate, what Ortega y Gasset had called "a gigantic continental state";[129] and second, that the way to achieve political union must lie initially through economic cooperation. As Jean Monnet remarked later of the Schuman Plan, "This was a homage to Aristide Briand." But, he concluded, it was "also a farewell to rhetoric."[130]

On May 17 the following year a somewhat more precise and robust ver-sion of Briand's "plan," drafted by his assistant Alexis Léger (better known as the poet and Nobel laureate Saint-Jean Perse), was formally presented to the twenty-six European member states of the League of Nations. Léger's *Memorandum for the Organization of a European Federal Order* (*Mémorandum sur l'organisation d'un régime d'union fédérale européenne*) speaks repeatedly, and often confusingly, of a "European Union," of a "European Federal Union," of a "European Pact," of a "Moral Union of Europe," and of a "European Community." Initially the *Memorandum* laid out, in very general terms, a proposal for the creation of a "European Conference ... composed of representatives of all the European governments," with an annual rotating presidency and an executive branch in the form of a "permanent political committee." This was also to have a rotating presidency, but one drawn only from the members of certain, but not all, the European states (which states, however, was left unsaid), and a secretariat. Léger insisted that all matters concerning any possible future economic union (including any customs union) had to be subordinate to the political order, and that this crucially would take the form of "a federation founded on the principle of union not unity." This, he claimed, would respect the independence and sovereignty of every member state, "while assuring them all of the benefit of collective solidarity for the regulation of political questions concerning the future of the European community or that of each of its members," something which he believed could be extended to a single system of arbitration and security for the whole of Europe.[131] The new union would constitute a "field of European cooperation" in "general economic life," communication, transport, finance, hygiene, cultural and intellectual life, "interparliamentary relations," and administration. "To unite in order to survive and prosper," he concluded, "that is the strictest necessity which now faces the Nations of Europe."[132]

Both Briand and Léger, however, insisted that their proposal had to be seen in the context of, and in collaboration with, the larger union of states represented by the League. It was, indeed, very much as Briand had conceived it in 1925, a proposal for "a European family within the League of Nations." As Georges Scelle pointed out, the *Memorandum* made no real distinction between the terms "Union," "Federal Union," and "Federation," and it "denied the European Union any jurisdiction [*'compétence'*] in matters of conflict resolution."[133] Nor had the plan resolved or even adequately addressed the central problem of the possible relationship between national and federal sovereignty, for there was clearly a stark contradiction in the claim that this was to be a "sort of federal bond" and that it would, nonetheless, in no way affect "any of the sovereign rights of the member states, since there could be no federalism which is not a juridical phenomenon." In the end, Scelle concluded, these two documents (the pact and the *Memorandum*) left him with the general impression that for its authors their new idea seem filled with hazards and dangers "which inspired in them more apprehension than sympathy."[134] Briand's plan, as the American political scientist Francis Deák pointed out in 1931, was still working with "the conception of sacrosanct sovereignty and political independence which we have inherited from Bodin," but this was clearly unworkable in the context of "the realities of a steadily moving civilization" which now "requires a completely different method of dealing with the intricate relations between nations." And if that method were not found, and found soon, then "there can be little doubt that this European union will bring just as much disappointment as did the League of Nations."[135] Coudenhove-Kalergi, despite his outward display of enthusiasm in 1929, largely agreed. The Briand proposal was, he remarked bitterly in 1943, "couched in vague and over-careful terms." It rejected the idea of a European Customs Union and insisted on the primacy of national sovereignty and on the authority of the League. "It aimed," he concluded, "at no European federation, but at an ineffective European League of Nations. It was a substitute, not the real thing."[136]

Briand's new "European Pact" was, in reality, intended to constitute (initially at least) a "regional entity" as set out in Article 2 of the Covenant of the League and even in "its own domain as the organisation of Europe" to coordinate all its activities with those of the League.[137] So closely bound were the two meant to be, indeed, that it stipulated that every meeting of the European nations which had any bearing on subjects other than those of a strictly internal nature should be conducted in collaboration with both the European and the non-European members of the league. This, as Scelle objected, would mean not only including in the decision-making processes carried out by the "sort of federal bond" a number of states which could not, in any sense, be understood as belonging to "Europe," however one chose to define it, but also excluding many which equally clearly were. And if the idea of a European Union were to be based, as Scelle was certain it had to be, on the existence of a shared "European solidarity," it could only be one which encompassed nations that were not part of what he called the "Wilson Pact." In which case it would be necessary "to abandon the idea of a regional agreement [*entente*] ... and constitute a European Union after the model of the Pan-American Union, that is to say, one that is *parallel* or

lateral to the League of Nations, and not integral to it." This "imbrication," as
he called it, "[a] complementation of diverse federal systems, would constitute one of the most precious, most effective indications of peace." But
the adoption of such a system would also mean that the European "federal
union would belong to the international universal Society [*sic*], and no
longer belong at the heart of the League of Nations." And this, from the
point of view of the League, would entirely defeat its purpose, which, he
believed, was "far from being without merit, and which had always been to
ensure that no future European union become a threat to the League
itself."[138]

Casting any possible European federation as a dependency of the League
clearly meant, although Léger does not say so explicitly, that while it limited
the danger that the new "European federation" would eventually collapse
into a single national state, it also restricted its ability to form an independent foreign policy.[139] As R. W. G. Mackay remarked bitterly of the whole
enterprise, "Closer examination shows that the scheme bore no resemblance to a Federation, and that it was merely a regional League of sovereign
states within the framework of the League."[140]

In the months that separated Briand's original speech from Léger's proposal, much had occurred, not least the Wall Street Crash on October 29,
1929 and the death of Stresemann, which explains, in part, the generally
unfavorable response the plan received from most of the representatives of
the twenty-six nations which heard it. The Germans, in particular, now saw
in it a ruse to perpetuate French supremacy within Europe, not perhaps
unreasonably in view of the French tendency to view, as Scelle clearly did,
any larger international project as ultimately the product of that French
"humanism" to which the Revolution had given birth. The League itself,
declared René Brunet, had essentially been a French political idea, or at least
its true origins lay in the duc de Sully's "Grand Design of 1600."[141] Given
the crucial role played by both Briand and Léger in its articulation, this,
although surely hyperbolic, was not an utterly unreasonable claim. It was
not, however, one that was calculated to calm the apprehensions of a
Germany still suffering from the humiliations, real and supposed, inflicted
by the Treaty of Versailles. Stresemann's successor as chancellor, Heinrich
Brüning, denounced the plan as an attempt to rob Germany of—in a phrase
which sounded all too like an anticipation of the Nazi doctrine of
Lebensraum—"sufficient natural living space" (although quite how it did
that he did not explain), and the German cabinet urged the new minster of

foreign affairs, Robert Curtius, to give it a "first-class burial."[142] The British, for their part, despite Léger's strenuous attempts to bind his "European Union" to the League, looked upon it as a threat to the latter within which they played the dominant role.[143] The only positive outcome was the creation on September 7 of a "Commission for the Study of a European Union," to examine ways of further enhancing European cooperation, whose presidency was, unsurprisingly, entrusted to Aristide Briand. It lasted until 1932, the year of Briand's death, by which time he was too exhausted and ill to have much influence over the proceedings.[144]

One year before Briand had put forward his original plan, Léger, as Saint-Jean Perse, had written tellingly in what is perhaps the greatest of this poems, *Anabase*:

> Not that this stage was in vain: to the pace of the eremite beasts (our horses with pure eyes of elders) many things undertaken on the darkness of the spirit—infinity of things at leisure on the marches of the spirit—great Seleucid histories to the whistling of slings and the earth given over to explanations . . . [145]

It was not intended to capture the hopes and despairs of the moment. (The poem was begun in 1917, and part of it was written in China.) But it echoed the futility of so much of what was to follow.

The suspicions which the British and the Germans harbored toward Briand and Léger's proposal were, however, ill-founded. Briand might have read Riou's two books with approval (although his declaration, in fact, makes no explicit reference to the content of either), and he certainly shared Riou's anxiety over Europe's confusion and political and economic disintegration in the interwar years; but he clearly had no sympathy with Riou's ambitions for a new European block intended to overawe both the USA and the Soviet Union and to keep the menacing peoples of the "world of colour" firmly in their place. Briand's "Plan" may ultimately have come to nothing. But in the ever-tumultuous struggle to find some compellingly intelligible vision of a new unified Europe, it marked a move away from the kind of quasi-imperialism which the British suspected Briand of secretly harboring, and which Riou's two books were unashamedly intended to promote, toward a vision of a unified Europe which would finally be able to take its place in a larger, more interconnected world of independent, post-imperial states.

Briand and Léger's plans for a unified Europe under the crumbling aegis of the League were as doomed to ultimate failure in an "earth given over to explanations" as was the League itself. What might, however, be a present or at least a not-so-distant possibility was a wholly distinct, independent, regional federation of some kind. In 1931, Scelle published an article laying out a plan for the creation of a "continental or European union." The League had, he said, been "the first official attempt to create a universal federation," but precisely because it was universal, all it had ever become in reality was a superimposition of several "regional federal systems."[146] Nothing on that scale was ever likely to work. It might have—indeed it had—helped to restore order after the end of the first truly global war, but it could not provide a model for a lasting post-war order. Scelle was heavily influenced by Durkheim's argument that "social solidarity" in modern societies such as Europe was "organic" in that social cohesion was achieved through the interdependence of its various and diverse parts. And as Durkheim had argued long before the war, the ideal that "all men form one society, subject to the same laws" was still a long way from being realizable. There were, Durkheim believed, at present "too many intellectual and moral diversities between different social types existing together on the earth to admit of fraternalization in the same society." But what was possible was that societies of the same type might come together, and it is, indeed, "in this direction that evolution appears to move." He was convinced that "by spontaneous movement, a European society which has, at present, some idea of itself and the beginning of organization" was already beginning to take shape and that if "the formation of a single human society is forever impossible, a fact which has not been proved, at least the formation of continually larger societies brings us vaguely near the goal."[147] Not only *could* what Scelle called a "European Union" be made to work; it *had* to, and not merely because it was the only way out of the situation in which the European states now found themselves, but because it was the inevitable conclusion of a long historical process of "organic" growth. It was, he argued, nothing less than "the constant law of evolution in human societies."[148]

Durkheim himself, however, was skeptical of anything less than imagining "humanity in its entirety organized as a society," and this could only ever be "set in so distant a future that we can leave it out of our present reckoning." A European confederacy would only be a "half-way course to achieving societies on a bigger scale than those we know today. This greater federation would be like an individual state, having its own identity, and its own interests and features. It would not be humanity."[149]

Scelle disagreed. He saw a continuous human history, "organic" and to some degree inevitable, although different peoples were bound to proceed through it at different rates of development, which ran from the disintegration of tribes, clans, phratries, and their like to the rise of the "earliest political aggregates from the city to the empire." Similarly, "the aggregation of collectivities which have hitherto been autonomous" would eventually coalesce into federal systems. And federalism, he believed, was alone capable of satisfying two apparently contradictory human needs; the innate human desire for autonomy and "self-government" (a term for which he could apparently find no satisfactory French equivalent) on one hand, and, on the other, the need for order and security. This was a "continuing extension of the phenomenon of inter-social solidarity," and it implied "a juridical and institutional hierarchy" which would, of necessity, exclude any narrow conception of sovereignty. It was toward this end that "all the political and social vicissitudes of humanity have been converging, more or less consciously for more than twenty centuries." In the past this had been the "law by which Empires were formed"; today it was the law by which "democratic federalism" would be created, not, that is, by conquest or exploitation, but through an "agreement of interests."[150] Only such a union would be capable of extinguishing the older "political aggregates" and thereby of finally solving the problems of Europe, finally bringing to an end what Keynes, among others, had called the "European civil war" which had begun in 1914, and of erasing the nationalist antagonisms fueled so abundantly by the outpourings of xenophobia which made up most of the propaganda issued by both sides during the war.[151]

In Scelle's mind, the necessary condition for this European federation already existed, and had, indeed, existed for centuries. This "European solidarity," as Scelle called it, was an integral part of European history. It had been created during the Roman Empire and thereafter had taken many and sometimes potentially antagonistic forms, from the Christian Europe of the Middle Ages through the Europe of what he dubbed "legitimate Monarchy" to the Europe of the Enlightenment and the French Revolution, to that of the Holy Alliance, and subsequently to contemporary Europe, the Europe of "industrial democracy" and, of course, of nationalism. In 1931 this Europe was now, he believed, in the grips of "a chaos of contradictory aspirations" in which what he called—borrowing once again from Durkheim—a "mystic" mode of nationalism struggled with the peoples' demand for self-determination—something which, because it could result in destructive demands for secession, constituted a threat to the very notion of the state on which it was itself grounded. The movement toward internationalism, on the other hand, the movement of capital and of labor, all of which was bound up with an overarching need for order, could all too easily result, as it had already done in Italy and was clearly about to in Germany, in "the false remedy of dictatorship." It was, however, precisely the fact that all of these contradictions were common to a greater or lesser degree in all the nations of Europe that demonstrated the existence of "European solidarity." For solidarity, he concluded, "reveals itself better in the sufferings of anarchy than it does in prosperity."[152] The solutions to each of the varied difficulties— economic, psychological, political, and geographical—with which the Europeans had to struggle, were for the respective experts to sort out. One thing, however, was certain, "that solidarity, in common with every social phenomenon has its laws." It would, therefore, be sufficient for the peoples of Europe "to be made aware of them and to proclaim them for them to produce in this social milieu the reactions necessary to transform these laws into rules of normative and constructive law [*droit*], that is to say, into judicial institutions."

What this meant, in essence, was that if there was ever to be a future European Union, it would have to be, at bottom, a legal one. "The problem of federalism," he wrote, "is itself a federalism of problems; but in social matters the juridical solution must necessarily take precedence over all others."[153] Not, perhaps, a surprising conclusion for a jurist. But Scelle was not merely insisting upon the importance of his own discipline. He was insisting, as Durkheim had done, that only a judicial federalism would be able to solve the seemingly insoluble problem of sovereignty, since on his account every governing agent within each of the individual states of which any federation is made up is also a "governor"—or in contemporary terms "lawmaker"—of the federation. This means, of course, that within a federation sovereignty has to be looked upon as something which can and must be shared; and this, of course, runs directly counter to the hallowed Hobbesian notion of the "immortal...incommunicable and inseparable" sovereignty on which the post-Westphalian states were founded. In Scelle's opinion, however, federalism, as he understood it, did not suffer from the problem of overlapping and potentially conflicting sovereignties which Hobbes had struggled with, since the sovereign power of a federation, unlike that of a single nation-state, derives precisely from the parts of which it is itself composed. That, he believed, was how the United States and the Swiss

Federation operated. The problem, of course, as Scelle fully recognized, was how to decide on "the degree of jurisdiction or 'self-government' to be allocated to local governments." One thing, however, was clear: the more the "local collectivities" coalesce, the more the social cohesion between them increases, and the more the autonomy of local lawmakers decreases, then the more it becomes possible to relocate the solving of international problems to international institutions and international courts, and the easier and more efficient and smoother the process becomes. As a consequence, however, those who are accustomed to exercising power at the local level will find themselves increasingly marginalized. (For Scelle, the counterexample was the British Empire, in which, although it chose to designate itself a "commonwealth," very little, if any "solidarity" existed between local "communities" and the executive, and in most cases even judicial power remained very largely in local hands, the central governing power limited to little more than an agency for collecting revenue and enforcing order.) Many of the opponents of the EU policy of "ever greater union" have made the same complaint. In an ideal federal system, Scelle argued, there would exist what he called "a neutral or common zone" in which the jurisdiction belongs both to "the federal governors and to the local governors."[154]

What then emerges is a vision not so much of a "United States of Europe" in which all the member states preserve at least a substantial degree of sovereignty and the entirety of their cultural, religious, and political identity, much less the kind of federation conjured up by Victor Hugo and Julien Benda (among many others) in which, although the member states would preserve something of their former selves, they would nevertheless be slowly absorbed by one culturally and intellectually dominant state—which in Hugo and Benda's case was, of course, to be France. (This is what Benda seems to have meant by describing a future united Europe in the fateful year 1933 as "a region of your own which we will call 'humanism,' where you can recognise each other as fellow beings ['semblables'], and which is superior to all that makes you feel different from one another.")[155] What emerge instead are the lineages of a polity which will eventually replace the nation-state. In its place would come a complex of technical forms of government, institutions organized to promote strictly utilitarian concerns; the welfare and prosperity of all individuals; the lives of all citizens; and, of course, a guarantee of perpetual peace. Since this vision is grounded upon the assumption that all the peoples of Europe share broadly the same cultural affinities and moral and cultural values, there is no need to seek any over-arching "European" identity, or at least not one which would one day replace the cultures of France, Germany, Denmark, Italy, and Spain in the same way that Coudenhove-Kalergi had imagined an "Indian" identity to have replaced the "Bengali" one or a "Chinese" identity to have replaced that of Jiangsu. It is a conception of the federation (or confederation) which would in large measure provide the model for some at least of the future founders of the European Union. In 1931, however, or so it seemed to Scelle, it could only be what he called an "ideological type" to which the facts would only ever "correspond imperfectly or by chance."[156]

5

A New Order for Europe

I

"For all the men of my generation," the French poet Georges Duhamel told the League of Nations' "International Institute for Intellectual Cooperation" in October 1933, "the European spirit was easily confused with the idea of civilization, and since we never imagined that such an idea could find itself in any danger we were entirely unconcerned by it and had no real opinions about it." It had been the experience of the Great War, in which he had served as a doctor on the Western Front, that had made him and all those like him "fully conscious of Europe and of what it meant in the world." After the war he and his companions, buoyed up by the sense of friendship and hope which the allied victory had given them, had done their best to create "lines of friendship" among Europeans and to fortify and "clarify what we understood to be the European spirit." For fifteen years, he declared,

> we have been celebrating Europe, and we have long had the sense that this Europe, our Europe, indeed existed . . . and that the health of Europe had every reason to be of interest to the entire world, because it was identical with the cause of peace. We were all during those years borne up by a great hope.
>
> That, however was yesterday.

"Today," he went on, "an enormous, and terrifying silence has fallen on the genius of Europe. We have all had the startling impression that the European spirit has been struck dumb, that an infinite discouragement has overtaken the workers for the future of Europe." If, he lamented, one were to examine the inhabitants of any great European city such as Paris or Berlin, one would be forced to admit that only a very small number would feel with any real conviction what they had so strongly felt before, that "a new war among

Europeans would be a civil war and that the genius of Europe cannot survive and prosper unless a harmony is established among all the members of the society of Europe."[1]

Like many of his contemporaries, Duhamel had come to look upon 1919 not as the end of an old war and the beginning of a new age of peaceful cooperation and prosperity, but merely as a truce in Europe's great civil war, a war which was to last until 1945. The period from 1914 until 1945, said the great French liberal political philosopher Raymond Aron in 1960, had been a new Peloponnesian War, the war that in 431–404 BCE had finally destroyed the shaky stability of the leagues of the ancient Greek city states, to which so many had appealed with misplaced nostalgia. Like both world wars, the Peloponnesian War, wrote Aron, had erupted "when all of the cities which made up the Hellenic system—just as the states of the Old Continent made up the international system of Europe—[collapsed]. A system of equilibrium slid by itself toward an inexplicable war when . . . one of the two coalitions into which it was divided seemed to be at the point of establishing a hegemony over the whole."[2] As E. H. Carr wrote in 1939, looking back upon what he believed to be the "end of the old world order," the interwar period had been a precipitous descent from "the visionary hopes of the first post-War decade to the grim despair of the second, from a utopia which took too little account of reality to a reality from which every element of utopia seems rigorously excluded."[3]

In the years between 1919 and 1939, however, something quite new had entered the scene. The war of 1939–45 was not only a struggle for control of the continent; it was also the culmination of a conflict between three divergent political ideologies: democracy, communism, and the combined forces of Fascism and National Socialism.[4] All had been nurtured by the Great War, and both Fascism and National Socialism had been shaped, and to some degree made possible, by the terms of the Treaty of Versailles. For whereas a Frenchman such as Duhamel could emerge from the war with a new awareness of what it might mean to be not merely French but also European and with new hopes for the future of a truly "European spirit," the Germans and the Italians were left only with a sense, real and imagined, of having lost the peace, of inhabiting a Europe now divided between two victors, France and Great Britain, aided by an ever-intrusive United States eager to put its own stamp irrevocably upon the continent.

The Treaty of Versailles had imposed upon Germany what the government of the New Weimar Republic in 1919 called an "unheard of injustice";

and it had forced her into a position of humiliation which throughout the brief life of the republic remained, in the political imagination, whatever the realities of the political and economic situation of the post-war world, the one certain tie binding a divided nation.[5] What Carl Schmitt called "the liberal democratic Holy Alliance of the Western Powers" had gathered together in Paris in order to "suppress both new political ideas as well as new growing nations."[6] They had, in effect, declared a limitless, interminable war against Germany.[7] Viewed like this, the treaty was easily mobilized as an instrument of mass persuasion and would ultimately help to make possible the nomination of Adolf Hitler as chancellor in January 1933. It had been, said Friedrich Ebert, the first chancellor of the Weimar Republic, "the greatest enemy of German democracy and the strongest impetus for communism and nationalism."[8]

Undoing Versailles became the Nazi rallying cry. But in many respects it was an easily identifiable target of dissatisfaction. The real objective of National Socialism was not merely to right the wrongs inflicted upon Germany by the allies. It was to build a new Third Reich to replace the old and thereby to create a "New Order of Europe" (*Neuordnung Europas*) in which Germany would control the future of the continent.[9] Initially, the only intellectual and ideological content this "New Order" possessed (other than crudely conceived "racial distinctions" between Germanic and Anglo-Saxon northern Europeans, the overrated "Latins," and the Slavs of the south and east) was largely informed by a somewhat muddled and highly selective understanding of the idea of *Raumtheorie* ("space theory") which had been widely discussed by German academics from several disciplines in the 1920s. The most prominent exponent of the idea was the political geographer Karl Haushofer, from whom the Nazis took the idea of *Lebensraum*, or "living space": the claim that a population—by which was meant initially a politico-ethnic and subsequently a racial group—had the right to occupy the territory necessary for its needs. This became the ideological force behind the Third Reich's *Anschluss* with Austria, and the occupation of first the Sudetenland and subsequently of Bohemia and Moravia.[10] Closely tied to this was the conception of "Central Europe" (*Mitteleuropa*).[11] The idea, first suggested in the 1820s by the liberal German economist Friedrich List, an early immigrant to the United States, a staunch critic of Adam Smith and Smithian free trade, and a fierce advocate of protectionism, was for the creation of a single economic union made up of states of Central and Eastern Europe, which would then be powerful enough to resist the economic power of Great Britain. Although List's *Mitelleuropa* was never intended to develop into a political union, he was insistent that "Germany," which, in his view, included, or would one day include, Belgium, the Netherlands, Denmark, and Switzerland, should take priority over all the other nations in the union. In 1915, the scheme was recast as a political objective by the liberal—albeit militant nationalist—Friedrich Naumann, a friend of Max Weber and one of the founders and subsequently the first president of the German Democratic Party. Naumann's immensely influential treatise *Mitteleuropa* of 1915 envisaged an ultimate destiny of mankind as a coalition of all the peoples of the world into "one immense organisation," a "United States of the World." Before that moment arrived, however, there would, he believed, "probably be a very long period, during which groups of human-ity, reaching beyond the dimension of the nation, will struggle to direct the fates of mankind and so secure the product of its labour." If Germany were to prosper and survive during this period, in a world increasingly dominated by political units larger than the traditional nation-state—by which he meant Russia, Great Britain, and the United States—she would have to control the economic and demographic resources of Central and Eastern Europe. Compared to the other three great powers *Mitteleuropa* might be small, but she would be "vigorous but lean!"[12] Naumann's proposal is thin on political details; but it was clear that what he had in mind was some kind of confederation rather than either an empire or a true federation. It would have granted extensive sovereignty to its member states, and although Germany would obviously be the dominant one, and the common language would be German, Naumann resisted any suggestion of "Germanification" and the racism, in particular anti-Semitism, which generally went with it.[13]

Mitteleuropa has at least some affinities with the attempt by Naumann's contemporary, the historian Karl Lamprecht, a member of the nationalist and markedly racist "Pan-German League," to revive what in National Socialist historiography came to be called the "First German Reich." This referred to the "Holy Roman Empire of the German Nation" (as, in a wild mixture of contradictions, it came to be called after 1512). In theory it was the successor state to the Roman Empire in the west. Superficially at least, it could be said to bear some resemblance to Naumann's Mitteleuropa (although it must be said that Naumann himself did not see it like that). The entire area had been divided into a number of different political communities— free towns, principalities, prince bishoprics—all of which, together with the "Free Imperial Knights," exercised some kind of autonomous political, economic, and legislative authority. Presiding over all of these political factions was the Holy Roman Emperor, who was not, except in name, absolute overlord of his realm, but only what in nice terms of compromise was called the "first amongst equals" (*primus inter pares*). For centuries the emperors had been content to act in this way as judges among their persistently quarrelsome subjects, calling regular assemblies—or "diets"—to adjudicate between warring factions in a region which, throughout most of its history, was in a state of near-permanent conflict. In keeping with ancient Germanic traditions of kingship, the emperor was, technically, elected from among any one of the crowned heads of Europe by a group of six "electors" composed of the rulers of Brandenburg, Cologne, Mainz, the Palatinate, Saxony, and Trier. After 1438, however, the empire in effect passed into the hands of the Austrian Habsburgs, where it remained more or less until it was brought to an ignominious end by Napoleon in 1806. Throughout much of its history it was, as Voltaire famously said, neither "Holy, nor Roman, nor an Empire." (Nor, it should be added, was it ever in any meaningful sense "German.") The imperial title, however, descending from the Caesars and Charlemagne, carried with it immense prestige, if very little else, and continued to be squabbled and fought over until the Treaty of Westphalia of 1648. Many have subsequently come to look upon it as some kind of model of toleration and international cooperation: a cosmopolitan empire made up of independent states that consented to be governed, as far their external relationships with one another were concerned, by a common sovereign.

For Naumann, the empire had been, for much of its history, nothing more than "a country full of splendid cities and cathedrals, with golden crops and precious vineyards but without military strength of its own and without political feeling."[14] For Lamprecht, however, as for the National Socialists more broadly, it offered not a model of political organization but a source of inspiration, a period in which something labeled the "German Nation" and some kind of "Germanness" had dominated most of Central and Eastern Europe. Although Hitler professed to abhor the Holy Roman Empire with its horrific "Babylonian" mixture of different peoples, languages, cultures, and races—precisely what has so often made it seem so attractive to others—it was still the First Reich, and at its core there had lain the original German Nation. He therefore named his imperial project for Central and Eastern Europe the "Greater Germanic Reich of the German Nation." In April 1938, a month after the occupation of Austria, he staged a symbolic *translatio imperii* by removing the traditional imperial insignia from

Vienna to the National Socialist Party headquarters in Nuremburg, and a year later, when German troops occupied Bohemia, he declared the "Holy Roman Empire has been resurrected." The Third Reich, however was to be evidently superior to the old heterogeneous Catholic "Roman" one in that it would be racially pure and nationally whole, and it would, of course, last a thousand years. It was to be defined by "racial blood" (*Volksblut*). "One blood," as Hitler had declared in the very first page of *Mein Kampf* "demands one *Reich*." Europe, he insisted, was a "blood-determined concept."[15] "Because of our organizational brilliance and racial selectivity," declared the propaganda minister Joseph Goebbels, "world domination will automatically fall to us."[16]

Much of this was consolatory and declamatory. It served to shore up Nazi claims to legitimacy through continuity, coupled to the projection into the remote future of what they imagined to be an utterly new kind of society. It did not, however, come with anything much by way of political or legal substance. The person who transformed *Raumtheorie* into what was intended to be an entirely new way of conceiving both international relations and international law was Carl Schmitt. Schmitt, once called "the Crown Jurist of the Third Reich,"[17] was, together with his polar opposite and arch opponent Hans Kelsen, perhaps the greatest of the interwar German jurists. Like many, but perhaps with greater clarity, he had seen that the world which had emerged out of World War I was best understood not in terms of individual sovereign nation-states, whose moment in the nineteenth century had now all but passed, but rather as the grouping of what he called *Grossraüme* ("Great Spaces"). Schmitt did not invent the term. Indeed, it had, by the mid-1930s become, in his own phrase, a "beloved buzzword." But Schmitt's conception of the "Great Space" was far grander, far more coherent than that of any of his predecessors. It was also, unlike most of the more extreme fantasies of the Third Reich, an attempt to confront what he rightly saw as a problem which would eventually disrupt the entire course of European— indeed, on his reckoning, world—history. Ever since the early 1930s Schmitt had become increasingly convinced that the current state system as it existed in Europe was bankrupt and in a process of rapid disintegration, and that the emergence at the end of the nineteenth century of what he called the "technical-industrial-economic order" demanded the creation of an entirely new system of international law and politics.

In Schmitt's view the Great War had effectively dissolved all the older established "notions and spatial measures of the earth" in a conflict which had now become "planetary." The old *ius publicum Europaeum*, or what he referred to dismissively, but not entirely inaccurately, as the "Christian-European international law," had crumbled away, having been diluted first by the Monroe Doctrine in 1823 and then by the formal admission in 1856 of the Ottoman Empire into the "family of nations." The Versailles Treaty—what he calls contemptuously "the Paris *Diktats* of 1919" (no one excoriated and vilified the treaty and the League more often and more consistently than Schmitt)—had finally erased it altogether.[18] Now the victors used international law merely as an instrument to impose an unjust, dishonest peace upon the vanquished. Looking back from the vantage point of the 1950s, it seemed to Schmitt that what the League had created was not the new world of Woodrow Wilson's imagination, but instead what he called a "spatial chaos." The consequences for Europe had been catastrophic. Since the League was intended to be a "universal organization," not a European one, its creation had meant that "a completely disorganized world attempted to create a new order for Europe," rather than, as should have been the case, the other way around. Furthermore, an institution that should have "functioned as the arbiter of fundamental European problems" dictated by the major European states had instead fallen under the sway of the United States as the "leading Western Hemisphere power." Yet not only was the United States not itself a member of the League; it exercised—or so Schmitt believed—a hidden and indirect influence through a number of Latin American states that were.[19] This alone had been "sufficient to transform all plans for a European Union into empty discourse."[20]

On April 1 of the same year, two weeks after Germany had completed the annexation of Czechoslovakia, and four months before the outbreak of war, Schmitt gave a now famous—or infamous—lecture to the Christian Albrecht University in Kiel on the "*Grossraum* Principle of International Law." His concept of *Grossraum* differed markedly both from much of the previous scholarship on *Raumtheorie* and from simple *Lebensraum*, which, in Schmitt's view, constituted merely a "demographic right" and was not one that could be translated into international legal principles with "recognizable limitations and standards in itself."[21] It also, unsurprisingly, bore no resemblance to any of the "so-called regional pacts" created by the League of Nations, which he looked upon as nothing more than a now obsolete expression of French security needs and thus of no use as the "basis for a new concrete conception of a spatial order."

The *Grossraum*, by contrast, was a territorial space made up not of "states" but of "nations," a state being an "organisation," while a nation was an "organism."[22] Unlike the term "people," which designated only "something that belongs together ethnically or culturally," the "nation," as he defined it in his *Constitutional Theory* of 1928, was a people in its capacity as a "unity capable of political action" or "a people brought to political consciousness and capable of acting."[23] Each of the nations which make up a *Grossraum* is (or is possessed by) a certain indeterminable "political idea," an idea which, he stresses time and again, is inseparable from the space it occupies, so "there are neither spaceless political ideas nor, reciprocally, spaces without ideas or principles of space without ideas." However, the political idea which determines each space does not, of necessity, possess any given ideological content. It can just as well be a "liberal-democratic" one (as is the United States) as it can be what he calls elsewhere "our National Socialist idea."[24] But no matter what form it takes, it has always to be created in accordance with the Hegelian principle of "otherness" with "a certain enemy in mind." It is clear, however, that if it is to be the embodiment of a political idea and not a mere accident of geography (like, say, Germany or Italy before unification), a *Grossraum* must be dominated by one hegemonic "leading and bearing" nation. To describe this nation, Schmitt uses the term *Reich*, which, he claims, curiously, is the only one not contaminated by "universalistic–imperialistic" overtones, and which alone would be capable of providing the *Grossraum* with its "political idea." *Reich* also supposedly bears none of the conceptual freight carried by the "once absolute" concept of the state, nor does it attempt to challenge the unique status of each and every one of the nations of which it is composed. In this, he claims, it is unlike such terms as "great power sphere," "commonwealth," and, worst of all, that "totally meaningless spatial designation "zone."[25] *Reich* alone is always used to designate a "concrete order" which has arisen in contrast to and in conflict with other *Reiche*.

Schmitt carefully avoids saying how a nation acquires the status of a *Reich*, but it would seem clear that it cannot be achieved by the use of force, as in all of the "universalistic–imperialistic" methods employed by Teddy Roosevelt and Woodrow Wilson which he denounced as a "corruption of the genuine *Grossraum* principle." There is also more than a little obfuscation of the degree to which the Reich operates as a kind of benign overseer of the nations of the *Grossraum*, or whether it is in fact, or will in time become, identical with them, and they with it. It is not, he insists, "simply an expanded state," but then neither can any state exist, nor has it ever done, without a *Grossraum*.[26] And while the *Grossraum* is described as a "connected *achievement space*," it is also said to belong "to the historically fulfilled and historically appropriate *Reich*, which brings and bears in itself its own space, inner measures, and borders."[27] The main role of this hegemon, however, as he stresses again and again, is not to dominate the other nations in the region, but to prevent all foreign intervention, something which he claims would, when it is properly understood, and presumably properly implemented, "unfold its developing effect into a new international law."[28] This "core," as he called it, of the doctrine could be summarized as "the connection of a politically awakened nation, political idea, and a *Grossraum* ruled by this idea, a *Grossraum*, excluding foreign intervention."[29]

For Schmitt, Eastern and Central Europe—or possible simply Europe—in 1939 was in the process of becoming the kind of *Grossraum* he imagined the Americas to be, and one that was soon to be dominated by the "political idea" of the German Reich. The new legal order, which the League had so lamentably failed to provide, the true *Völkerrecht* and "the new ordering principle of the new international law," was to be "our concept of *Reich*." A "new Europe" had come into being which would now replace the old decadent Europe, which he described in a lecture delivered to the *Instituto de estudios políticos* in Madrid in 1943 as "so corrupt that every man, however honest by nature and character, cannot fail to be transformed into a criminal and a delinquent."[30]

Schmitt's prime example of what he understood by *Grossraum*, which had indeed created "a precedent for an international legal principle of large spaces" by seeking to cordon off the Americas, both North and South, as a single geopolitical area, was the Monroe Doctrine of 1823, the first of several attempts by the United States to prevent any further encroachment by the European powers into the western hemisphere. The doctrine asserted that while the United States was prepared to recognize the remaining European colonies in the Americas, it would regard any attempt on the part of the European monarchies "to extend their system to any portion of this hemisphere as dangerous to our peace and safety," and it would look upon any move to reclaim the newly emergent states of Spanish America, "whose independence we have, on great consideration and on just principles, acknowledged," as nothing other than "the manifestation of an unfriendly disposition toward the United States." What this in fact meant, as Schmitt understood it, was that while each of the individual states of the American continent would remain free, independent, and republican, all would, nonetheless, be placed under the de facto suzerainty of the

United States, which had thereby assumed the role of defending and controlling a geographical space defined in terms of the "political principle" of liberal democracy against an "other," a "certain enemy," defined by the "monarchical dynastic principle of legitimacy."[31]

Schmitt explicitly denied that what he was advocating was the creation of a "German Monroe Doctrine" in Europe. But it is hard to believe him entirely, and that indeed was precisely how his claims were understood, not least of all by Hitler himself. Hitler was so taken by the idea that he appropriated it for himself (he was a consummate plagiarist) and used it in a speech to the Reichstag on April 28, 1939, in reply to a request from Roosevelt that Germany cease all further aggression against its neighbors. (Schmitt was warned bluntly that he should remain silent as to who had been the true author of the idea. The Führer, he was told, was proud of the originality of his ideas—and none too choosy about where they actually came from.) It seems clear that, at this stage, the main attraction of the notion, as far as the Hitler was concerned, was to provide a justification for his expansionist policies which might be sufficiently persuasive to prevent the United States from imposing sanctions on Germany. The wider implications of Schmitt's observations, however, were striking enough for them to be taken up the following year by The Times of London and by the Daily Mail. The Mail described Schmitt warmly as "middle-aged and handsome" and as "Herr Hitler's key man," and it reported that the Führer would soon give the "German Monroe Doctrine" to the world as his justification for Germany's relentless expansion.[32] The Americans themselves, however, took an understandably hostile view of the appropriation of the doctrine to justify what were, in fact, acts of unwarranted aggression. In March 1940 the American undersecretary of state Sumner Wells told the Reich's foreign minister Joachim von Ribbentrop that he and his leader were "labouring under a misapprehension as to the nature of the policy," which the United States now looked upon as a relic of the past. "At this moment," Wells recalled later, "I was glad to say, a new relationship existed in the Western Hemisphere."[33] The rebuttal was repeated some months later by the Secretary of State Cordell Hull, who stated unambiguously that the Monroe Doctrine "contains within it not the slightest vestige or any implication . . . of hegemony on the part of the United States."[34]

Schmitt himself fully recognized that the doctrine had had a checkered history, during the course of which it had been interpreted in a number of different ways, and that it had been subject to "imperialistic corruptions."

None of this, however, in his view in any way diminished its validity as the sole "point of departure" for the introduction of the "*Grossraum* principle into international law."[35] Nor was he suggesting that the doctrine should simply be translated to "other countries and times." His objective was to extract from it what he called its "core thought" so as to make it usable as a model for his own conception of how the post-war world should now be ordered in law. He also recognized that it possessed such an "indeterminacy of normative content" as to leave the legal positivists reeling. As the US Secretary of State Charles Evans Hughes had said in 1923, the doctrine means only and precisely what the United States "defines, interprets, and sanctions" it shall mean. This, Schmitt remarked with approval, was an instance of the "purest decisionism."

For Schmitt this was the first time that the international sphere had been conceived, not as Talleyrand and Gentz had conceived the "Congress System" as a series of relationships between states, but instead in spatial terms, what Schmitt considered to be a "modern sense." This, then, made the idea of the *Grossraum* easily translatable to other regions of the world, other states, and, crucially, other situations in which there existed "other friend–enemy groupings."[36] One of these was to be not Europe as whole, but Central and Eastern Europe; the lands, that is, of *Mitteleuropa*. Eastern and Central Europe now constituted, Schmitt claimed, a genuine *Grossraum* made up of numerous peoples, who although they may be culturally distinct from one another are not "racially alien" (except that is, he added darkly, the Jews). Over all of these there hung the controlling, protective presence of the National Socialist Third Reich, "untranslatable in its uniqueness and magnificence."[37]

What Schmitt had in mind, however, was very different from the crudely expansionist visions shared by most members of the Nazi high command, who saw the world rather more simply in terms of a German master race (*Herrenvolk*) which would eventually come to exercise absolute sovereign authority over, if not the entire world, then certainly over the whole of Europe. For Schmitt, the *Grossraum* was not to be an *imperium* like the Roman Empire, whose ambitions, he believed, had been the creation of a single universal state, nor a colonial empire like the "British world *Reich*."[38] It was, instead, to be a new kind of polity based on "a fundamentally non-universalistic legal order built on the foundation of respect for every national identity." What Schmitt called the "Versailles system" had, he claimed, responded to the post-war collapse of the conception of the state "as the central concept of an international law" by "assaulting the concept of sovereignty." In its place it had erected a "universalistic global law" whose objective, although it had been consistently represented as "pacifistic and humanitarian"—not that these were for Schmitt particularly desirable virtues—had only ever operated in the political interests of the Allied powers, which, by seeking to grant "self-determination" to every minority nation on the planet, were attempting to "integrate" every one of them into a single political, economic, and cultural ideal, under their own political and economic control. It was empire not by conquest but by assimilation. It crushed the genuine freedom which alone truly determines what a nation is, and by so doing it removed the possibility of the friend/enemy distinction, which alone made viable nations possible.

Now, however, the "victory of the National Socialist movement," which, or so Schmitt claimed to believe, was based upon "totally different goals from the pacifist–universalistic dethroning" of the state, had made a new ordering of the world possible. Caught between the "nation-assimilating" Western powers on one hand, and the universalistic and nation-annihilating communist east on the other, the sole future for Europe now lay with the German Reich, which alone was able to defend "a non-universalistic *völkisch* order of life with respect for the nation."[39] With the triumph of National Socialism "a powerful German *Reich* has arisen" at the center of Europe, one which was capable of refashioning the eastern and central parts of the continent into a true *Grossraum*, and of protecting it from all interference by "spatially alien and *unvölkisch*"—that is, by "globalist," "internationalist"—powers. "The action of the Führer," he concluded, "has lent the concept of our *Reich* political reality, historical truth and a great future in international law."[40] Yet despite these frequent tributes to National Socialism—about whose political and juridical content he has nothing whatsoever to say—and the occasional deferential reference to Hitler and his ministers, the image Schmitt seems to have had in mind as the inspiration for the new European *Grossraum* is not so much the Third Reich as the First.[41]

German Europe, however, could clearly be only one *Grossraum* among several. There were, by implication at least—Schmitt was never very precise as to the geographical limits of the world's "Great Places"—five others: Italy, Japan, Great Britain or the "British Commonwealth of Nations," the Soviet Union, and of course the United States. On September 27, 1940, three of these—Germany, Italy, and Japan—signed the "Tripartite Pact," a self-described bid to "create a world order in which the really vigorous nations can live together" and hailed significantly by the *Kölnische Zeitung* as the

"Magna Carta of the New Order." Now, or so it seemed, the "Rome–Berlin Axis" (although now with the addition of Tokyo) first announced by Mussolini in 1936, along which the world would henceforth be distributed, had become a reality. By the terms of the pact, Japan recognized "the leadership of Germany and Italy in the establishment of a new order in Europe," while Germany and Italy recognized "the leadership of Japan in the establishment of a new order in Greater East Asia." Although the big three were later joined by smaller states—Hungary, Romania, Slovakia, Bulgaria, Yugoslavia, and Croatia—which could certainly not be considered *Grossraüme* in their own right and most of which were regarded by the Nazis as simply parts of the German Reich, the pact was, in the words of the historian Mark Mazower, "nothing less than the international diplomatic expression of Schmitt's *Grossraum* concept."[42] Here, then, were the two supposed "victims" of the Versailles Treaty united against the victors, and in particular those other *Grossraüme*, the United States, Great Britain, and the Soviet Union.

Because of Schmitt's persistent if ultimately ineffectual attempts to curry favor with the Nazis, and the partial if largely uncomprehending early endorsement of the concept of the *Grossraum* by the regime, the idea has been largely condemned or ignored even in the form in which it appears in possibly the most eccentric but also the most significant of Schmitt's postwar works, the *Nomos of the Earth*, which, in so far as it was possible, was carefully stripped of any associations with the Reich. Yet while certain aspects of Schmitt's political thinking—in particular his conception of the "state of exception"—have been eagerly adopted, mostly by the left in recent years, as an instrument with which to demolish the claims of liberal parliamentary democracy, the *Grossraum* is, in effect, perfectly compatible with an international order of liberal democracies—as he himself, of course, fully recognized—and offers, at least in broad outline, one of the more persuasive conceptions of the modern world order. It is certainly more illuminating than the historically misleading and politically contentious use of the term "empire" to describe any large state or federation of states, from the United States to the European Union. Schmitt's basic contention—that in the modern world most nation-states are simply too small to survive on their own; that they can, therefore, only remain sovereign within certain limits; and that all the nations of the world are, for the most part, gathered into larger interstate groupings, in which one or possibly two states tend to predominate—has become the reality of most international relations in the

Cold War and post-Cold War era. The image of a "Great Space" was even latched on to, perhaps unwittingly, by Vladimir Putin in 2012 to describe and vindicate his vision of a "Eurasia"—not unlike Mitteleuropa, only with Russia at its core—dedicated to the eradication of liberalism, the return of "Christian Russian values"—"civilization," in his language—and the ultimate destruction of the EU.[43]

II

For the Nazis themselves, however, the idea of a German-dominated *Grossraum*, appealing though it was, in particular in the years before the destruction of France in 1940, was also only one of the many, often fleeting suggestions for a Europe united under German domination. Throughout the war, members of the Nazi high command came up with a number of generally contradictory suggestions as to what the Nazi "New Order of Europe" might look like. Quite what these were intended to achieve was never precise or consistent. Some envisaged an extended alliance of states which, once the war was over (and won), would protect a Germany now extended—depending on whose plan it was—to all of Northern and Eastern Europe. But it was never clear what form these new states would eventually take or what political purposes they were intended to serve. Ultimately, for all the grandiloquence, what was clearly uppermost in the minds of the leading members of the regime was not so much a new Europe, whether federal or otherwise, as a German Europe.

In July 1940, buoyed up by the euphoria over the crushing defeat of France the previous month, Leopold Gutterer, Joseph Goebbels's close associate, announced at a secret meeting in Berlin that Germany would now "take over the ordering of Europe, especially its political leadership."[44] This, however, was to be much more than the guiding, controlling presence of the "political principle" Schmitt had imagined. Germany and Italy were to take responsibility for the "establishment of a new order in Europe," although no specifications were given as to what shape that might take, how it would be achieved, or what political form it would ultimately acquire. A year later, the Nazis hosted representatives of the Axis powers in the new Chancellery in Berlin for what was described as the first "European Congress." German radio broadcast a new "Song of Europe," and the Berlin post office issued a commemorative rubber stamp with a map of Europe emblazoned with a sword and swastika and the legend "European United Front against Bolshevism." And in November the *Deutsche Allgemeine Zeitung* proclaimed that "born out of discord and struggle and misery, the United States of Europe has at last become a reality."[45]

There were many across occupied Europe, particularly among intellectuals in France—some of whom were conservative liberals such as Bertrand de Jouvenel and Drieu de La Rochelle, others socialists or former socialists such as Charles Albert—who, after 1940, were ready to agree that a post-war union of the European nations could only be achieved under the hegemonic rule of Nazi Germany. Even before the outbreak of the war, Jouvenel, who had conducted a sympathetic interview with Hitler in the daily newspaper *Paris Midi* as early as 1936, had come, somewhat reluctantly, to believe that Germany was now the sole nation in Europe capable of unifying it. It was, he wrote in 1941, not a matter of economic performance or military preparedness. It was rather the sense that Germany was possessed of a deeprooted national mission. It possessed, as he put it, a "spiritual order," a "drive engrained in the minds of the national elite of generations." It was this which had made the victory of the previous year possible. The Germans, unlike the French, had always had a single national objective, "to reconstitute the universal monarchy of Rome"—by which he meant the Holy Roman Empire. They were compelled by a single-minded intensity of purpose no other Europeans could match. It was as if they possessed "an immortal brain which, while constantly nurturing itself on new impressions, never ceased to watch over the destiny of the German homeland." They were a species of nationalist Jesuit Order, always working "for the greater glory of the Homeland." By comparison the French were a fickle and divided bunch, always at each other's throats. Among us, he wrote despairingly, "every intellectual prides himself on taking a position which distinguishes him from all the others. We have the pretension of offering to the world the broadest possible range of ideas and arguments. Chateaubriand ruins Voltaire; Gobineau destroys Rousseau."[46]

Four years later, when the regime whose "spirit" he had so admired was in the final stages of disintegration, he asked despairingly "What Europe do we want?" Liberalism on the English model or totalitarianism as in Soviet Russia? Neither, it seemed, could bring the continent back to those "days of sweetness and liberty" which he supposed to have existed before 1914.[47] In place of the new Carolingian Empire, which he fancied he had seen emerging under the Third Reich, Europe had been given over once again to an unbridled belief in national sovereignty, which, as he saw it, had been increasing steadily since the Middle Ages. Everything, from culture to the economy, was now being "nationalized." Even "[t]he moral law itself has become nationalized: duty and the good now consist in obedience to the state... for it is the sovereign authority which now decides what is licit or illicit, just or unjust."[48] For a staunch Catholic a universal state, something such as the Church had once been, or imagined itself to have been, could be the only acceptable alternative to a world in which a liberal democratic Europe, inevitably harnessed to the United States, stood in opposition to the USSR. As for the Europeans themselves, they had now been so ground down by decades of internecine conflict that they had lost "all confidence in themselves." All Jouvenel could see was evidence of the collapse of what he believed had once been the spirt of progress and individualism which had hitherto characterized all the peoples of the continent. Now "her individual energies are being extinguished as in a nightmare by sluggish inertia."[49]

Jouvenel, who fled to Switzerland shortly before the liberation, was not alone in his admiration of the purposefulness, if nothing else, of Nazi Germany. Even the journalist Hubert Beuve-Méry, who in 1942 joined the Resistance and then two years later, at the request of Charles de Gaulle, founded Le Monde, still probably the most significant newspaper of the European left, had been prepared to argue in 1939 that National Socialism was "an excessive but necessary reaction against the depravations of intellectualism, individualism, liberalism and capitalism." Although, unlike Jouvenel, he had no illusions about the savagery of the Nazi regime and its propensity for descent into "lies, corruption, and cruelty," he nevertheless hoped that a "new synthesis" might come out of it which would lead eventually to a "more unified and a juster Europe."[50]

The Nazis themselves, however, viewed such ecumenical aspirations for a final accord and cooperation between France and Germany which would lead to the creation of a new Carolingian Empire at the heart of Europe as more of a subterfuge than a political ideal. In February 1943, by which time it was becoming increasingly obvious that the great "Liberation" of the Soviet Union was not going as planned, much of the confidence that had followed the rapid defeat of France had begun perceptibly to wane. Goebbels warned that it was "undesirable to present the future new order in Europe in such way that foreigners gain the impression that German leaders intend to keep them in permanent subjection."[51] One month later, when news of the calamitous defeat of the Wehrmacht at Stalingrad had reached Berlin,

Ribbentrop suggested that the time had come for the immediate proclamation of a "European Confederation" (*Europäischer Staatenbund*), in "quite a specific form." The main purpose of this, however, was not to offer to the world the vision of a great unified post-war Europe living in peaceful and harmonious order under the benign aegis of National Socialism so much as to meet what Ribbentrop perceived to be the immediate need to "dispel the fear of our friends and allies" that once the war was over, they would find themselves "under German Gauleiters [regional Nazi Party leaders]," and to reassure Italy, in particular, that Germany had no wish to "drive her into a corner." More important still, it was vital for the Russians to be given the impression that "all Europe was against them." It would also, he hoped, disarm the "fighting spirit" of the Allies "if they found that they were not liberating European states, but attacking a Europe which stood solidly against them."[52]

Throughout, however, no matter what form this "New Order of Europe" was finally intended to take, it was always to be an *Order* controlled by and in the interests of the German Reich. As Hitler himself told the Gauleiter, "The objective of our struggle is to create a unified Europe, but Europe can only be given a coherent structure through Germany."[53] Self-consciously or not, this sounds like an allusion to Napoleon's vision of the "true French Empire" of Europe, with Germany now in the leading role in place of France. And for Hitler, Napoleon seems always to have been something of a hero. His visit to Napoleon's tomb on June 23, 1940, was, he said, "the greatest and finest moment of my life," and he took elaborate precautions to protect Les Invalides from Allied bombing (and the floor of the building from Nazi jackboots). But although Nazi propaganda portrayed the invasion of the Soviet Union in 1941 as a "liberation" and a "crusade for Europe" against the "Asiatic–Jewish–Bolshevik" menace in the name of a "common European identity," Hitler, unlike Napoleon, had no wish to offer "liberty" to his conquered peoples, only subjection to what the radio commentator Hans Fritzsche in 1941 called the "imperial European idea."

For all these stillborn, last-minute attempts to come up with something closer to Schmitt's *Grossraum*, or indeed a confederation, with Germany as the hegemonic power, it was clear that until the end, for Hitler himself, and most of the Nazi high command, whatever else the "New Order of Europe" over which this Reich was to rule was ultimately intended to be, it was neither a federation nor a hierarchical organization of semi-independent peoples—as Mussolini's "Imperial community" had been intended to be.

It was, instead, to be a Reich—a kingdom, an empire—a single unitary state. For Hitler, the model was not the Amphictyonic Leagues, nor even Napoleonic Europe, much less the Monroe Doctrine (despite his unsuccessful attempt to peddle this analogy to the Americas) so much as the British Empire in India, for which he had an inordinate admiration, if only an approximate understanding.[54] Despite initiatives by members of the Nazi inner circle, Goebbels among them, to promote a Nazi "European mission," Hitler himself had no interest in a united Europe except as a conglomerate of unequal states all under German rule, all working in German interests. Inevitably, both the tone and the ambition of all these projects were less inspired by the ideological concern to offer the peoples of Europe a brighter future under the aegis of National Socialism than they were responses to the success and failure of the Nazi war machine. "We are fighting primarily not for a New Order in Europe," declared the Propaganda Ministry bluntly and revealingly in 1940, "but for the defense and security of our life interests."[55]

In 1945, the brilliant, quixotic, and immensely influential Russian-born French philosopher Alexandre Kojève, a former pupil of Karl Jaspers, wrote an "Outline" for the French government of the policy he believed it should pursue in the post-war years if France were to avoid "reduction to the rank of a secondary power within continental Europe." Kojève, who from 1945 until his death in 1968 worked in the French Ministry of Economic Affairs, because, according to Raymond Aron, who knew him well, he "wanted to know how it [history] happened," was at once a Hegelian, a highly unorthodox Marxist, and a Heideggerian. The lectures he delivered on Hegel's *Phenomenology of Spirit* in the years immediately after the war (although he never held a university position of any kind) exercised a lasting, if eclectic, influence over a wide range of French intellectuals from both the left and the right.

Kojève believed that humanity was making steady progress through clearly marked stages toward what would be the final emergence of a universal legal order. Every state, he believed, tended to propagate itself. It either did as a "political entity," in which case it operated through conquest and presumably became in time an empire, or it operated as a "juridical entity," in which case "it limits itself to imposing abroad its domestic *droit*. In other words, it tends to create a Federation of States or federal state by becoming itself one of the federated states." At this point, however, it does not, on Kojève's account, necessarily come to a halt at whatever is perceived to be the convenient political frontiers of the federation (as, say, the United Sates has done). But because "it will always have common enemies and will only be able to be reconciled with them in common," it will grow until finally it becomes a simple world-wide juridical Union."[56]

Germany, however, because of its pursuit in the course of the Middle Ages of "an imperial project [the Holy Roman Empire], at once anachronistic and premature, and thus utopian," had skipped the stages of modernization through which, in their different ways, the other nations of Europe had gone, only to emerge again in 1939 in much the position where, more or less, France had been in 1789. It was for this reason that Hitler had "created his Third Reich as a State strictly in keeping with the national ideal," which had "already reached its perfect form and realization in the revolutionary ideology, signed with the names of Robespierre and Napoleon." This explained Hitler's admiration for Napoleon, despite his contempt for the egalitarian principles of the French Revolution itself. What he saw in revolutionary France was, rightly, the triumph of the nation and the kind of "socialism" incarnated by Robespierre. The Führer was, on Kojève's analysis, "but a German Robespierre, which is to say, an anachronistic one, who—having known how to master his Thermidor—was able to undertake the execution of the Napoleonic plan himself." The Hitlerian slogan "*Ein Reich, ein Volk, ein Führer,*" Kojève claimed, was a perhaps unconscious (and poor) German translation

> of the watchword of the French Revolution: "The Republic, one and indivisible".... Moreover, Hitler expressed the essence and the motive of his political thought very well by putting himself at the head of a movement which calls itself "national socialism," and which consciously contrasts itself with Soviet "imperial socialism" as much as with Anglo-Saxon "imperial capitalism."

What Kojève had seen most clearly was that, for all the analogies of an interstate formation with a German hegemonic state at its center offered up by Hitler's apologists (Schmitt among them), the "Third Reich" was undoubtedly "a national State, in the particular and precise sense of the term." This, and the commitment to the idea of "*ein Volk*" and to the racism which, in this case, accompanied it, meant that it was unable to assimilate "non-nationals." It could only, as the Third Reich had indeed done, "treat them politically as slaves." For this reason, if for none other, "Hitler's 'nationalist' ideology would have been enough by itself to ruin the imperial project of the 'New Europe', without which Germany could not, however, win the war." Despite the Hegelian twist which Kojève gave to his account of Hitler's place in the singular evolution of the German "nation," this was the most perceptive

analysis of the ultimate failure of the Third Reich to emerge in the immediate aftermath of the war. And the lesson which Kojève had taken away
from it and which he now wanted to impress upon the new post-war French
government was that if Hitler's "sin" (and also in his view that of liberalism)
had been his inability to conceive of a world without nations, one of which
would invariably come to dominate all others, it was "internationalism's sin"
to be unable to see "nothing politically viable short of Humanity." This,
although he does not say so, had clearly been the major failing of the League.
What the new European nations—France in particular—now needed to do
was to discover what he described as "the intermediary political reality," that
is, empires, by which he meant not Nazi or even Schmittian *Reiche* so much
as "unions, or even international amalgamations of affiliated nations," which
he claimed to be "exactly the political reality today." That "empire," although
it was not what he had in mind in 1940, would eventually come to look
very much like the European Economic Community which, two decades
later, he helped to create.[57] It was an immensely potent analogy, and we shall
come back to it again.

III

Italy, for her part, looked upon the Treaty of Versailles as a different kind of
betrayal. Italy had been one of the victors—sometimes portrayed in the
Italian popular imagination as the only true victor—of World War I. Yet in
the eyes of many, she had been cynically deceived and marginalized by the
peace. Once the war was over, complained the fascist ideologue Giovanni
Gentile in 1929, the Allies had simply turned their backs on the Italians,
"forgetting and ignoring all our sacrifices and the value of the contributions
we had made to the victory." In so doing, what for Italy should have been
a victory "was transformed into a defeat, and it helped to diffuse among
the people of Italy the spirit of the vanquished."[58] What rankled most was
that, although Italy had gained the South Tyrol and had been given her
due share of the reparations, the treaty had denied her the north Dalmatian
coast which she had been promised by the (secret) Treaty of London of
1915. In September 1919, in an attempt to recover the honor of the nation,
Gabriele D'Annunzio,—poet, playwright novelist, parliamentarian, sometime collaborator of Claude Debussy, and one of the great literary figures of
turn-of-the-century Europe—enraged and histrionic, at the head of a band

of Italian irregulars, seized the Istrian port of Fiume (now Rijeka in Croatia), which by the terms of Versailles had been given to Yugoslavia, although its population was largely Italian. There he set up the short-lived *Reggenza italiana del Carnaro*, or the *Impresa di Fiume*, with himself as "Duce," and drafted a constitution—the *Carta del Canaro*—which, despite making music a fundamental principle of the state, offered a populist amalgam of right and left-wing policies, declared Canaro to be a "direct democracy," granted equal rights to men and women "in all public and private roles," and went on to exercise a considerable, if largely symbolic influence on the later development of Italian Fascism.[59] "Il Duce" was finally ousted by the Italian army itself in December 1920. Four years later Italy fell under the control of Benito Mussolini's Fascist Party, and another self-styled Duce, who pressed much the same grievances against the terms of the treaty and adopted much of D'Annunzio's theatrical trappings as his own, most effectively the strategy of the "balcony speech." (D'Annunzio, however, although courted assiduously by Mussolini, who paid for the transformation of *il Vittoriale degli Italiani*, the villa on the shores of Lake Garda where he passed the final years of his life, into the delirious monument it is today, was never himself a consistent or uncritical Fascist, and he deplored and even tried to sabotage Mussolini's "Pact of Steel" with Hitler, which he saw as not merely detrimental to Italian interests but a betrayal of the true Fascist faith.)

In May 1936, Italian troops invaded Ethiopia, supposedly in retaliation for the Italian defeat at the battle of Adowa in 1896, an earlier failed attempt to establish an Italian empire in North Africa, and also to avenge the Italian troops killed in a subsequent border skirmish between Ethiopia and Somalia. Cast, as with so many other colonizing ventures, in terms of a "civilizing mission" which would bring modernity, civilization, and peace to the peoples of Ethiopia, it was hailed as "the first autonomous act of the Nation" and declared by Mussolini to be "the most gigantic spectacle in the history of humanity." Its objective, however, was intended less as the bearing of goodwill and "liberation" to the peoples of North Africa, than it was to transform the Italians, dispirited and suffering since 1919, from a crippling "national inferiority complex" (at least in Mussolini's eyes) into a "new kind of humanity" fitted for conquest and expansion, and to be the bearer of the new political order which would finally set Italy free from the "prison" of Versailles.[60] Italy had now acquired an empire, albeit a rather skimpy one, and by so doing had joined the "Great Powers." It was the first step in a process which would lead inexorably the following year to the Italian departure from the League of Nations in response to the imposition of sanctions during the invasion of Ethiopia—which Mussolini, from his balcony in the Piazza Venezia in Rome denounced to cheering crowds as a "shameful strangulation of the Italian people"—and thence to the "Pact of Steel" with Nazi Germany in 1940.

The new Fascist Italy was not, however, merely an attempt to redress the evils of Versailles, or even a bid to shrug off the debilitating influence of liberalism—that sad "debacle of individualism," as Mussolini called it—in whose name Italy had been largely created and governed since unification. Like National Socialism, Fascism was the expression of an extreme form of nationalism. It was a bid to give—or give back—to the Italians the dignity and self-respect which, in the opinion of many, had been taken from them not merely by the victorious allies in 1919, but by successive waves of invaders and usurpers—not to mention supercilious foreign visitors—since at least the fifteenth century. World War II was the war that Mussolini had called for in 1914–15—when he was still some kind of socialist—which would be a "*great* war," a war which would eradicate forever the image of Italy as a land "of travelling storytellers, of peddlers of statuettes, or Calabrian *banditi*."[61] The Risorgimento and the Unification of Italy in 1871, through which Italy had broken free from Austria and created, for the first time in the history of the peninsula, a single nation, had been only the first step, for, in the end, the nation which unification had created had turned out to be monarchist, bourgeois, liberal, and weak. Fascism would complete the true Risorgimento and carry it out into the world. It was to be the final, authentic expression of the nationalism of the nineteenth century; but it would also be its nemesis. For Fascism, although rooted both historically and, as its ideologues rarely tired of repeating, "spiritually" in Italy, was also looked upon as a universal creed, an ideology for export. It was not, explained the historian Delio Cantimori in 1931, in the traditional and, in his view, reactionary sense of the term, "nationalist," because its true vocation was to bring about what he described as "a modern revolution, a revolution of the people, a true revolution, which means a revolution with a European and universal nature."[62] From this emerged the conception of the "European New Order."

The name bore more than a passing resemblance to Hitler's *Neuordnung Europas*, and the theory on which it was based, chaotic and inconsistent though it was, was also heavily indebted to Schmitt. Politically, it was intended to be a hierarchy of European states under Italian and, in Northern

and Eastern Europe, German leadership. Each would have its own sovereignty preserved, as far as its internal affairs were concerned; but each would
be governed in accordance with Fascist (and National Socialist) principles,
totalitarian, and corporatist. For the Fascists, the initial appeal of this greater
European community seems to have been more often cultural than political.
It was based upon a distinctly Fascist and distorted image of ancient Rome,
derived from Mussolini, who in turn had taken it from the amateur
historian-philosopher and "bloodthirsty recluse" Alfredo Oriani, who
insisted that the Risorgimento would never be complete until the new Italy
had assumed Ancient Rome's mission in Africa and the Mediterranean.[63]
The objective was not to create a unitary superstate, much less a "United
States of Europe," dismissed in July 1929 by Benito Mussolini's brother
Arnaldo as "founded on cartels for steel and potash," so much as one
immense political, legal, and cultural community whose different peoples,
while they would have been allowed to preserve much of their original
identity, would, supposedly, have also been vastly enriched by incorporation
into the "modern"—that is, Fascist—"civilization" which the Italians would
have spread across Europe, much as their Roman ancestors had done.[64] All
of this was influenced not only by Schmitt's geopolitical vision, but by
Spenglerian and neo-Darwinian notions of the decline—and subsequent
need for renovation—of peoples. It was heavily reliant too on distorted
readings of Mazzini and the other great intellectual architect of the
Risorgimento, Vincenzo Gioberti.

    Much of the real thinking behind this vision of the new Roman Empire,
however, can be attributed to Giovani Gentile, the neo-Hegelian, self-styled
"philosopher of Fascism" who was minister of education from 1922 until
1924 and a member of the Fascist Grand Council from 1925 until 1929. In
Gentile's hands Mazzini ceased to be the liberal who, in Gentile's perpetu-
ally sneering tone, provided the "creed for the new Americanized democracy." On Gentile's reading, he had conceived the nation in terms of "neither
territory nor race nor language nor a tradition nor even a common
history"—as the despised liberal democrats persisted in believing—not that
these were entirely irrelevant. But for the true Mazzini, the Mazzini who
was destined to become the intellectual and spiritual (Gentile dwells at
length on Mazzini's unquestionable Catholicism) prophet of the new Fascist
order, the true nation could not be defined by ideas but only by actions, so
the true nation had to "place its emphasis on a common intent, an objective,
a mission organized in a positive manner and which would provide the

collectivity with unity and effective and dynamic force."[65] The widespread
belief that Mazzini had himself helped to propagate, that the Risorgimento
had been "an incomplete national revolution" because it had failed to create
a strong national sentiment among the Italians, helped to sustain the claim
that it was Fascism which would provide that religion, that it was Fascism
that would, in Gentile's words, "step by step gather into itself effectively and
not merely nominally, in history and in the civil state, all Italians and educate
all of them, and bind them all together in the new faith."[66] In so doing
Fascism would also provide Italy with a national mission that she was now
bound to carry beyond the borders of the state.[67]

The vision of the future shape of the international sphere which emerged
was one of what the Fascists called the "vital space" (spazio vitale). The idea
was to create a world of large nations or empires, of which the Italian
would, of course, be dominant. In this way it was, or believed itself to
be, distinguished from all previous conceptions of the primitive nationalism that had preceded it, and from the nationalism of other lesser nations.
The Fascist "nation," explained the biweekly periodical Critica fascista in
1931, "was not bound within the narrow confines of the nation itself. For us
the nation is the necessary premise, the point of departure, for expansion,
and expansion means not only territorial conquest, but above all spiritual and
political conquest."[68] Woodrow Wilson's conception of "self-determination"
was rejected as nothing more than an indication of weakness, a pandering
to the claims of inferior peoples that they be allowed to determine their
own futures, which would, in any case, merely be abandoning them to
eventually become the prey of other peoples—such as the French and the
British—more powerful than they, but far less benevolent and civilized than
Fascist Italy. Such peoples would instead be "integrated" into the larger
"vital space" following what Critica fascista in July 1941 described as the
"Imperial Roman and Fascist organizing principle, which does not intend
to deny, but to safeguard, the other ethnic and cultural entities by integrating them, in this way, into the Mazzinian experience."[69] This was to be the
"new imperial civilization." In this manner, Fascist Italy was to dominate an
area somewhat vaguely characterized as the "Mediterranean." In addition to
large parts of North Africa this was to include variously the Alpes-Maritimes,
Savoy, Corsica, the Balearic Islands, Malta, the Ionian Islands, Epirus, Aetolia-
Acarnania, Bosnia-Herzegovina, Slovenia, the Dalmatian littoral, and the
Swiss Cantons of Ticino, Vaud, and Valais. All the lands to the north the Fascists
ceded to Germany. As for the "decadent" French and British, they would soon

be swept away, militarily, spiritually, and economically, by the combined forces of the Axis. All of this was to constitute what the journalist Giuseppe Bottai in 1941 called—ironically, in a distinct allusion to the British Commonwealth— the "Imperial Community."

IV

All of these projects perished with the collapse of Fascist Italy in 1943 and of Nazi Germany in 1945. But the dream of a new united Europe resting upon a set of presumptive values able to defeat the newly emergent scourge of communism, now seen as the prime threat to the future of Western civilization, did not entirely die with them. In 1936, Oswald Mosley, founder and leader of the British Union of Fascists, had called for Britain and France to "synthesize" their policies to create a united "Fascist Europe" based upon "the basic fact of an established community of interests, the universalism of Fascism and National Socialism," which would erect "the majestic edifice of a new world idea which commands the mind and spirit of man with the fiery force of a new religion."[70] As late as 1958, Mosley, now living in self-imposed exile in Paris, wrote a short book (self-published by the aptly named "Euphorion Books") which, although it scrupulously avoided any direct allusion to the Axis, called for the creation of a "European Nation" governed by a "party" which was to be far more than a mere "social organization" limping from election to election. It was to be a movement "more akin to a religious order than a social organization." Such a vision of the true political force within society had been, he added darkly, "discarded in very recent times," but was certain to return "when serious ideas and serious people are in demand." Nothing but a "failure of will and spirit" now stood in the way of the creation of his vision of a new Europe, which, in its inspiration if not in the details, differed little from that of Goebbels and Mussolini and would result in "the rapid development of the highest civilization the world has ever seen."[71] Mosley's idea understandably failed to gather much support even from the remnants of the far right, most of whom by the 1950s had abandoned any dreams they might have had of world (or European) domination for a narrower more sectarian nationalism.

Mosley was not, however, an isolated case, although he was certainly the most prominent. Little wonder that for many on the left in the immediate aftermath of the war the entire "European project," however defined, or refined, had become irreparably tainted by its exploitation at the hands of the Fascists and the Nazis. The very word "Europe," wrote Jean-Paul Sartre with disgust in 1948, had "formerly referred to the geographical economic and political unity of the old continent. Today ... [it] preserves the stench of Germanism and servitude."[72] Even those who were not either true Nazis or Fascists or even, like Riou and Jouvenel, collaborators or fellow travelers with one or another regime seemed to come perilously close. Whatever else the ideal of a united Europe might once have been, by 1945 it appeared to be, if not a relic of an extremist, reactionary past, at least treacherously mired in Christian universalism, anticommunism, and fawning pro-Americanism.

Subsequently, the European Union has itself been cast as a plan (even a conspiracy) on the part of the French and Germans, who, in 1950, had come to understand that since neither could any longer dominate the continent individually, their only salvation would be to unite together to create a European superpower capable, both economically and politically, of confronting the United States and Soviet Russia, an amalgam, in the words of Peter Jay, a former British ambassador to Washington, of a "Napoleonic Third French Empire and a Carolingian Fourth Reich."[73] In 2016, in the run-up to the Brexit referendum, Boris Johnson, who later became prime minister, repeated—less elegantly—the same claim. The EU, he told the British conservative newspaper the *Daily Telegraph*, was only an attempt to resurrect a German or French empire in Europe "by different methods." "Napoleon, Hitler, various people tried this out," he warned, "and it ends tragically."

There may have been very little substance to such conspiratorial claims. But they did offer a narrative which the anti-federalists could easily understand; they also had one small grain of truth in them. For it was certainly the case that the experience of the rise of National Socialism and Fascism had persuaded many throughout Europe, across the entire political spectrum, that, while they had no desire to see a democratic revival of either the *Neuordnung Europas* or the Fascist "Imperial Community" (much less a "Third French Empire or a Carolingian Fourth Reich"), the war had finally confirmed what many had claimed in 1919, that the reign of the modern nation-state, brief and furious, was now at an end. In 1940, shortly after the signing of the "Pact of Steel" between Germany and Italy, a meeting was held in Central Hall, Westminster to discuss "the New World Order—Its Basic Principles" before an audience of 3,600, under the aegis of the National Peace Council presided over by the popularizing philosopher C. E. M. Joad. The speakers were H. G. Wells, Salvador de Madariaga, and the writer John Middleton Murry. "What are we fighting for?," asked Joad. After examining a number of things which the war was clearly not about (including the English public school system and the sanctity of foxhunting), he concluded that the New World Order had to have three, as he put it, "essentials"—"Democracy, peace and federalism." Madariaga, who had been calling for some kind of European federation ever since the Spanish Civil War, which had impressed on him the horrors that seemingly decent people were prepared to inflict upon their neighbors in the name of "the nation," was even more emphatic. "If you want peace in Europe," he told the audience, "the first thing you must want is the existence of Europe. If you don't want a European community to exist, you don't want peace in Europe.... We cannot have peace unless we create the world community and the European community."[74]

Not everyone would have gone so far. Madariaga was a Christian idealist whose gaze was always fixed on the wider ambitions of the League and subsequently of the United Nations. But there was a general consensus that the war between Fascism, National Socialism, and Democracy had been won by democracy, and not only by democracy, but by a liberal democracy which could only survive in a world dominated by transnational political groupings, not national ones. Kojève, as we have seen, strongly believed that the arc of European history would carry the continent from a world of nation-states to a world of transnational groupings—what he called "empires"—and finally, at some distant point in the future, to what he called simply "humanity." The war had marked a crucial moment in that trajectory. "There is no doubt," he wrote in 1945,

> that we are currently witnessing a decisive turning point in history. Nation-States... irresistibly, are gradually giving way to political formations which transgress national borders and which could be designated with the term "Empires." Nation-States, still powerful in the nineteenth century, are ceasing to be political realities.... The modern State, the current political reality, requires a larger foundation than that represented by Nations in the strict sense. To be politically viable, the modern State must rest on a vast "imperial" union of affiliated Nations.

Although he believed that the "era where all of humanity together will be a political reality" still lay "in the distant future," it was now evident that the old world order which had somehow survived the Great War—that "period of national political realities"—was also at an end. "This," he concluded, "is the epoch of Empires, which is to say of transnational political unities, but formed by affiliated nations," by which he meant only large "political formations which transgress national borders," not ones based upon colonization and the export of populations.

France, Kojève warned, if she were to attempt to establish herself, together with her former colonies (as de Gaulle seemed to think might be possible) as the unitary nation-state she had been before 1940, would condemn herself to ending "fatally, by being politically absorbed by the Anglo-Saxon Empire, which stands to become a Germano-Anglo-Saxon Empire." But given the differences of race, of culture, of language, of religion, of traditions, and of lifestyle, there can be no question of a "true fusion between this Empire and France." In the end, France would inevitably be eclipsed by the other European "empires" and reduced to the status of, at best, a second-rate power.

To escape this dismal fate, he believed that France should now create a new "Latin Empire" based upon what he called the "kinship of nations," a kinship which expressed itself in terms of "language, of civilization, of general 'mentality', or—as is sometimes also said—of 'climate,' and crucially of religion." (Kojève was not himself a believer, but he was convinced of the socially cohesive and culturally transformative power of what, ever since antiquity, has been called a "civil religion.") This combination of factors had produced what he called a *mentalité*—a term that was to become a buzz-word during the 1960s and '70s—which "is specifically characterized by that art of leisure which is the source of art in general, by the aptitude for creating this 'sweetness of living'... and entails a profound sense of beauty generally." It is this which "not only assures the Latin people of their real— that is to say, political and economic—union. It also, in a way, justifies this union in the eyes of the world and of History." He accepted that this empire would inevitably be a liberal democratic one—for all his *marxisant* sympathies, Kojève had little time for the realities of Soviet communism. Furthermore, "The spiritual and mental kinship which unites the Latin Nations seems to guarantee the character of liberty, equality, and fraternity, without which there is no true democracy, to their relations within the Empire." All the nations which would have made up his "Latin Empire" were, therefore, Catholic: France, of course, which would be the guiding power in this new political order—indeed, it was to ensure her ascendancy that it was to be created in the first place—Italy, Spain (once rid of Franco), and ultimately, perhaps, a Portugal freed both of the clutches of Salazar (whom oddly he does not mention) and of the undue economic influence exercised by Great Britain ever since the Methuen Treaty of 1703.

No matter what form the future "empire"—or "empires"—of Europe might eventually take, it was already obvious by the end of the war that it could only be built, as all past conception of European unification had been, with a united or at the very least strongly allied France and Germany at its core, and that it would largely disregard the differences in culture, language, or religion that supposedly existed between the "Latin" peoples and the "Germano-Anglo-Saxon."[75]

V

Kojève's "Latin Empire" died at conception. (Presumably he said little about it during his subsequent life at the Ministry of Economic Affairs.) But it was, of course, far from being the only liberal democratic project for a future European union to emerge from the experience of the war. The resistance movements within occupied Europe also looked to a post-war unification as the only possible means of bringing to an end the civil war which had ravaged the continent since 1914. And all, whether they belonged to the communist–socialist left or the broadly Catholic right, were in agreement that if any union were to be achieved it could only be done by finally abandoning the old Westphalian conception of national sovereignty. Even as early 1942, when the Axis was still confident of ultimate victory, the "Kreisau Circle," a German resistance group around the international jurist Helmuth James Graf von Moltke, although firmly committed to the creation of a united post-war Christian Europe "through the determined energetic exploitation of the Christian heritage," came to the conclusion that although a reconstituted German Reich would be the legitimate government of the German people, it must also be one that would "enable it to be integrated into the community of European nations." Moltke also believed that "while the intellectual and historical tradition of [a] people must be respected and protected," nothing should be allowed to impede the transition to a unified federal Europe. "The free and peaceful development of national culture is incompatible," he wrote, "with the retention of absolute sovereignty by each individual state. Peace demands the creation of an order that spans the separate states."[76]

Some of the members of the resistance were, like the members of the "Kreisau Circle," primarily Christian, often staunchly Catholic, in their inspiration. Others belonged to the fledgling European communist parties and inevitably looked less to a "United States of Europe" than to the Communist International as the ultimate solution. Others, although they held unwaveringly to the conviction that any post-war Europe had to be founded on welfare and social solidarity, rejected both communism and the church—and subsequently Christian democracy—as a possible solution for Europe's ills. For all of them, left and center-right, the true enemy was now the nation-state itself.

Altiero Spinelli, who would go on to become one of the eleven "Founding Fathers" of the European Union (the parliament building in Brussels is named after him), began his political career as a somewhat maverick member of the Italian Communist Party, from which he was expelled in 1937 for his outspoken opposition to Stalin and his Trotskyist sympathies. Four years later "in the middle of the journey of our life"—*nel mezzo del camin di nostra vita*—"in the most precise Dantesque meaning of this phrase," he later recalled, he set himself "to work for a European federation [which] seemed to me the only possible way to create a political power, capable of overcoming the illiberal features of the national State, which, with its demands and its logic, was the fundamental enemy of liberty in Europe."[77] At the time, Spinelli was confined, along with some 800 other opponents of Mussolini's regime, on the island of Santo Stefano, a volcanic outcrop in the Gulf of Gaeta in southern Italy, and part of the archipelago of Ventotene. For centuries the islands had had a grim reputation. In the second century BCE, the Roman emperor Augustus had banished his daughter Julia there for "excessive adultery," and in 41 CE the Emperor Claudius sent his troublesome niece Julia Livilla to the island, where she was "discreetly" starved to death. Twenty years later, the first wife of the Emperor Nero, Claudia Octavia, suffered a similar fate. It was largely abandoned thereafter, until its transformation into a prison under the Bourbons at the end of the eighteenth century, and its later recommissioning by Mussolini as an internment center for political dissidents who could not, for one reason or another, be quietly disposed of.[78]

There, in the summer of 1941, during what he called the "long days of confinement broken only by the need to find ways to supplement our meals or improve our accommodation," Spinelli, together with the antifascist journalist and economist Ernesto Rossi, wrote on innumerable cigarette papers which were then smuggled out in the false bottom of a tin box what came to be called the "Ventotene Manifesto" (*Il manifesto di Ventotene*), later

published as "For a Free and United Europe." Spinelli's objective was nothing less than to find a way out of the "crisis of modern civilization." That
civilization, he claimed unremarkably, is characterized by a desire for liberty
understood in Kantian terms as the right of every being to be considered
not as an instrument in the hands of another, but as an "autonomous center
of life." In the nineteenth century the struggle for national recognition, the
"ideology of national independence," had helped to make this a possibility.
It had contributed to the destruction of "the most miserable tribalism" by
uniting diverse communities in a struggle against a common foreign oppres-
sor. (He was, of course, thinking primarily of Italy.)[79] This early nationalism
had broadened horizons. It had also, however—Spinelli never quite shed his
Marxist past—"carried with it the germs of imperialist capitalism," which
in their turn had given rise to totalitarian regimes and thence to global
conflict. Now nations, as Mazzini had imagined them, could no longer be
considered as "the historical outcome of human cohabitation" and as a
political, social, and cultural solution to the problem of how to find "the
most efficient way to organize collective life within the context of the
entirety of human society." Instead, in the course of the ideological turmoil
of the 1930s, they had been transformed from a historical solution to a universal human problem into nothing less than "a divine being, an organism
which thinks only of its own existence and development."

In the aftermath of the present war, Spinelli warned, we should not
expect a simple "reordering of Europe according to our ideal of civilization." The victors would certainly attempt to return to the status quo ante
and to "crush the wave of internationalist passions and sentiments" which
he believed the experience of conflict had generated in the hearts of all free
men and women. In its place they would attempt to resurrect the nation-
state much as it had existed before the rise of Fascism and National Socialism.
It would, in other words leave in place the same institutions, the same structures, the same "reactionary forces" of monopoly capitalism which had
"harnessed the outcome of their gains to those of the state," the same great
landowners, the same church, and the same social class which had made the
rise of totalitarianism possible. And if that were to happen, it would be only
a matter of time before a new form of totalitarianism, a new "capitalist
imperialist" political ideology, attempted to seize control of Europe, from
which would inevitably follow a still more bloody civil war.[80]

In the struggles that Spinelli believed would probably break out after the
end of the war between democrats and communists (whom, however, he

urged to make a common cause) on one hand, and those whom he calls "the reactionary forces" on the other, the tactics of the latter, would be precisely to attempt to reconstruct the pre-war "national state." This would allow them to mobilize in their interests the most widespread of all "popular sentiments," the one "most easily adapted to reactionary ends," namely patriotism. It did not really matter what political form these new nation-states might initially acquire. Spinelli was fully aware that both Nazism and Fascism had begun as socialist movements. They might perfectly well be Marxist or socialist. For in the end, while he clung to the belief that the true socialist was neither "militarist nor nationalist," Marxism, in particular in the shape of Stalin and Bukharin's "socialism in one country," had in fact led only to the creation of what he called the "barrack society."[81] In every case, so long as what was being ruled over was the nation-state, so long as the prime popular political sentiment was nationalism, "the return to the hands of the reactionaries would only be a matter of time." Once the old antagonisms between nations had been re-established, then the people would once again allow themselves to be transformed into soldiers, "the generals would return to power, the monopolist would profit from autarchy, the bureaucratic bodies would swell, and the priest would ensure that the masses remain docile."[82]

In 1941 Spinelli might perhaps have been forgiven for believing that history would in this way be capable of simply repeating itself. Entombed on Ventotene, it was perfectly reasonable for him to assume that any future threat to European peace and stability would, as it had been in the early twentieth century and again in the 1930s, come from the military. He had also, however, seen more clearly than most that the underlying cause of all the internecine conflicts which had erupted within Europe ever since the late nineteenth century had been the betrayal of that liberal "prophetic vision" of Mazzini, Cattaneo, Hugo, and Proudhon, whom he singled out as the originators of a new internationalism, in favor of a narrow sectarianism.[83] The League of Nations and the " Franco-German politics of rapprochement of Briand and Stresemann" had done very little, if anything, to check this process when it had failed—or had simply refused—to acknowledge that it had been this, and not the mere fact of German aggression, which had been the underlying cause of the Great War. By attempting to uphold the authority of international law while failing to create any means of enforcing it, and by "respecting the absolute sovereignty of the participating states," the League had only helped to accelerate and aggravate the

descent into the barbarism of nationalism. Absurd too had been the principle of nonintervention, an underhand attempt to protect the sovereignty of
the victors of the war, as if the "internal constitution of each individual
state" was not of "vital interest for all the other countries of Europe." The
only possible solution was a federal Europe. Like Kant, however, Spinelli
firmly believed that this would only be possible if all the member states
adopted broadly republican democratic constitutions, and when all had shed
their previous imperial antagonisms or at least found what he called a
"European arrangement" for their overseas empires (although quite what
that would entail for the colonized peoples he does not say). It was also, he
believed, crucial that both the armed forces and the economy—"the back-
bone of totalitarian regimes"—should be placed under the control of the
federal government and that this should also be provided with what he
called "the organs and the sufficient means . . . to carry out its decisions and
to maintain a common order." No matter how the forces of reaction might
struggle to regain their authority, he was confident that once the war was
over, they would find that, in the eyes of the majority, they had been "dis-
qualified by the disastrous experience of the past twenty years." Then would
be the time of the "new men, of the MOVEMENT FOR A FREE AND
UNITED EUROPE."[84]

Yet for all his reiterated recognition of the role that what he called the
"incandescent lava of popular passions" had played in the rise of Fascism and
National Socialism, for all that he recognized that his "free and United
Europe" could only be achieved by the "empowerment" of that "modern
civilization" which "totalitarianism had brought to a halt," Spinelli had little
trust in democracy per se as a pacifying force. You would, he wrote, have to
be very naive to suppose that "once national democracies had been restored
[throughout Europe], there would be the least probability that these would
remain for long on the pathway of peaceful interaction [convivenza]." The
best that such states, when aroused by "a moment of nausea at the horrors
of war," would be capable of thinking up would be, yet again, some version
of the League of Nations.[85] Leagues, however, had had a dismal record.
Throughout history the most effective means by which some peace and
stability had been introduced into the "international order" had been
empires. In 1941 he was witnessing yet another attempt "carried out with
great style and great coherence" to create yet another empire—in fact
two—within Europe itself, and if this were to be resisted successfully, it
would be because those who were threatened by it could see only too

clearly that it would lead inexorably to the creation of a state that would be "based upon violence, upon inequality of peoples, on the exploitation by the dominant power, on the exaltation of the mystique of empire, on the ultimate tendency toward universal domination and on its persistent military nature."

In Spinelli's opinion, federation was the sole means by which the virtues of imperial rule might be created in a manner which was "in accord with our fundamental requirements." One of the key distinctions between empires and federations, however, was that while the former were created by force, the latter could only be the outcome of consent. The real problem, therefore, became not how to preserve a federation, but how to create one in the first place, given that, as Spinelli admitted, with the exception of Switzerland, federations "lay outside the European tradition."[86] Even the most progressive forces within Europe were trapped by the conviction that their political struggle, like that of their opponents, could only be conducted in nationalist terms. There were always those who claimed that what has never been could never be. The reactionaries and the nationalists would always insist that the only "secure road would be to follow that of one's ancestors."[87] "Alas for thee," he wrote, quoting, somewhat incongruously in the circumstances, Goethe's *Faust*, "that thou a grandson art" [*Weh dir, dass du ein Enkel bist!*]. Needless to say, there were indeed many at the time, and there have been many since, who have echoed these sentiments. One was Jean Monnet, another of the "Founding Fathers" of the EU. Writing on August 6, 1943, from Algeria, where he was serving as a member of the French Committee for National Liberation, Monnet warned that "there will be no peace in Europe if states rebuild themselves on the basis of national sovereignty which brings with it the politics of prestige and protectionisms . . . . European states are too small [*étroits*] to be able to guarantee their peoples the prosperity that modern conditions make possible and consequently necessary."[88]

The underlying fear with which both Spinelli and Monnet looked upon reactionary nationalists was, in fact, Kant's fear—as it had been both Hugo and Benda's assumptions—that, in any larger assembly of states, one more powerful and supposedly more "gifted" would eventually come to dominate all the others, and in that direction, as Kant had said, lay only despotism, "universal monarchy," and the "graveyard of freedom."[89] Spinelli, however, was optimistic that it might, nevertheless, be possible to persuade even the most reluctant reactionaries that the crucial distinction between an empire and a federation, or at best between an empire and the kind of federation he had in mind, lay in the fact that while in an empire ultimate sovereignty, however it might choose to share it with others, lies with the imperial nation, in a federation by contrast it is located in a coalition of member states governed by a common body of "international laws to which all must be subject equally." The powers of the central organization responsible for ensuring that these laws are observed must also be sufficient to "guarantee the definitive end to exclusivist national politics." To make this a possibility, he envisioned the creation of federal armed forces, a federal magistracy, and a federal administrative system, which would be independent of those of the member states, together with some kind of federal parliament. There would be open borders, a common currency, and a common foreign policy capable of satisfying the "fundamental demands" of the federated states (and to stifle any emergence of what he called "the absurd formula of the right to self-determination," which was "irreconcilable with the very idea of federation").[90] Most of the initial post-war hopes for what was intended to become the European Union, from the ill-fated European Defence Force to the European Court of Justice to the Commission and the European Parliament, reflect one or another of Spinelli's objectives, albeit in most cases in often radically compromised forms.

Spinelli was also convinced that the restraining power of the institutions within a new federated Europe would have no impact upon the political, cultural, and social life of the individual European nations, and these should, therefore, be allowed to develop "according to the individual characteristics of the various peoples."[91] The upsurge of nationalism which had preceded both world wars had been an alien, manufactured ideology manipulated by powerful economic interests and the omnipresent military establishment. In reality, European culture had long possessed "a cosmopolitan character" which a federation would both protect and enhance.[92] The only way forward, then, would be to detach culture, language, identity, all that gave to the nation Hegel's "spirit in its substantial rationality and immediate actuality," from the source of sovereignty which since 1648 had defined the state. As T. S. Eliot concluded in a lecture he gave in 1949 on the unity of European culture, "there can be no 'European' culture if the several countries are isolated from each other...there can be no European culture if these countries are reduced to identity. We need variety in unity: not unity in variety." It was message which, in their several ways, all those who have subsequently helped to create the European Union have taken very much to heart.[93]

Spinelli, himself, had grand hopes for his "United States of Europe" that went well beyond the simple creation of a peaceful post-war continent. Since, in his view, Europe occupied a preeminent position as "the center for the spread of civilization" and yet had also, because of its perennial internal squabbles, always been "the epicenter of all international conflicts," the continent's reconstitution as a federation would offer light to the entire globe: "the greatest step toward the pacification of the world which can be achieved in current circumstances."[94] Then, and only then, might it be possible, he hoped, to develop a peaceful and collaborative relationship between Europe and the peoples of the Americas and Asia, and "in a distant future the possibility of the political union of the entire globe."[95]

In May 1944 representatives of the non-communist resistance movements, Spinelli among them, met in Geneva to launch an appeal to "overcome the dogma of absolute sovereignty" and "create a federal union." Only this, they insisted, would secure peace in Europe, and only peace in Europe would secure a world peace. Only a European federation would "permit the German people to take part in European life without being a menace to other people," and only a federation would solve the problems of national minorities.[96]

In December 1946, together with two other prominent Europeanists, Henri Brugmans and Alexandre Marc, Spinelli set up the Union of European Federalists, which promised to usher in what they called, in a phrase which has subsequently been used to describe a wide and often contradictory range of political positions, a "Third Way" in interstate relations.

That way was, of course, to become in time what is today the European Union, and it is not insignificant that in 1980 Spinelli, as a member of the European Parliament, began work on a "Draft Treaty Establishing a European Union." "I have merely practiced the art of maieutics, after the manner of Socrates," Spinelli told the parliament on introducing the final version of the draft on (appropriately) February 14, 1984. "I am the midwife who has delivered Parliament of this infant. Now we must nurture it."[97]

The treaty was passed by the parliament and although it was not adopted by the member states, and Spinelli himself died two years later, it had considerable influence on the negotiations which led finally to the creation in 1992 of the "Treaty on European Union"—or the Maastricht Treaty, as it has subsequently come to be called—which remains to this day the most foundational of all the EU treaties.[98] If anyone was not the "father" of Europe, but in his ironic self-description, only its midwife, it was Spinelli.

6

Refashioning Europe

I

The final defeat of Germany on May 8, 1945—that "moment of Liberation"—had, claimed the historian and future rector of the College of Europe in Bruges Henri Brugmans, persuaded an entire generation that the continent was about to undergo a "regeneration" and that now "everything was possible."[1] Buoyed up by this wave of optimism, in September of the following year Brugmans, together with Altiero Spinelli, Denis de Rougemont, Henri Frenay, and Alexandre Marc, and some seventy deputes from sixteen European nations, founded the Union of European Federalists, with Brugmans as its president. The optimism did not, however, last long. In less than a year, the visionary, often seemingly impossible projects of Spinelli and the other members of the wartime resistance for the creation of a European federation had all but collapsed. The "European idea," lamented Brugmans, "which had enjoyed such widespread support," seemed "to have disappeared from the political scene." It was, he reflected, possibly inevitable, since "The joy of liberation had taken national, often even nationalist forms, far more than it had served to inspire any European endeavors."[2] In the eyes of so many of those who picked their way through the rubble of the cities in which they had been imprisoned by an alien, hated regime for so long, for those who had contributed so much to make the longed-for Liberation possible, it was France, Belgium, Holland, and Denmark which had been liberated, not "Europe."

Brugmans, however, was being unduly pessimistic. Even amid the nationalist fervor which followed May 8, there were still many who could see that whatever form the defeat of Germany might have taken, post-war reconstruction, if it were to be lasting, could only possibly be a collaborative, continent-wide effort. In the immediate aftermath of the war, a plethora of small committees intended to promote some degree of European union sprang up, including an attempt by Gaston Riou to revive Briand's customs union and then, in 1946, to set up a rather more ambitious "European Economic and Federal Union."[3] None of these, however, lasted long or achieved anything very much, in no small part because reconstruction was dominated less by the Europeans themselves than by the two superpowers and the two major victors of the war, the Soviet Union and the United States, and both of these were, in the American case initially, in the Soviet unflinchingly, opposed to any idea of European unification. For the Soviets, anything resembling a "United States of Europe" could only be yet another attempt to create—as Stalin had described the Briand Plan in 1930—a "bourgeois movement for intervention against the Soviet Union."[4] Russian hostility to European unification has remained consistent from one regime to another, save for a brief interlude in the 1980s. Ever since Napoleon's bid to "liberate" Russia and Hitler's "crusade" against the USSR, the Russians have looked upon a unified Europe as little more than a strategy meant to contain, if not destroy, the Russian Empire, be it tsarist or Soviet. For Putin, no less than for Stalin, a liberal democratic and united Europe is understood as a continuing threat to Russia's very existence, politically, culturally, and economically, although Stalin's grounds for believing this to be the case were far more secure than Putin's.

The United States in the closing years of the war had been similarly unsympathetic to the idea of a federal Europe. It was widely believed in Washington that since a war with the Soviet Union was unthinkable and almost certainly unwinnable, and a permanent American military presence in Europe would be unacceptable to the American electorate, it was only by handing Europe over to the Soviet Union that a lasting peace between the two now reigning superpowers could be achieved. What William C. Bullitt, the first US ambassador to the Soviet Union and later ambassador to France, called President Franklin Roosevelt's "grand design" had been "to enroll the Soviet Union as a sincere and willing collaborator in post-war settlements," no matter what the consequences for the "smaller nations of Europe" might turn out to be.[5] In September 1943 Roosevelt himself, in a private conversation, had laid out plans for the post-war world as a division of the entire globe into four "spheres of influence": the USA, Britain, the Soviet Union, and China. The USA would get the Pacific, China the Far East, while Britain and Russia would be given Europe and Africa; but "because Great Britain's interests are mainly colonial, it must be assumed that Russia will predominate in Europe." This might, he acknowledged, turn out to be tough on the Europeans, but they would simply have to outlast Soviet domination in the hope of being able to "live on good terms with the Russians in ten or twenty years' time."[6]

Winston Churchill, however, thought otherwise. He was convinced that once the war was over, "Europe and European civilisation," which did not, however, include Great Britain, "must rise again from the chaos and carnage into which it has been plunged," and he believed firmly that the only way to achieve that would by means of a federal union.[7] In October 1942, he had written to Anthony Eden, then British foreign secretary, that "it would be a measureless disaster if Russian bolshevism overlaid the culture and independence of the ancient states of Europe. Hard as it is to say, I trust that the European family may act unitedly as one, under a Council of Europe."[8] In March, the following year he outlined a proposal for this "Council of Europe" to be created "under a world institution embodying or representing the United Nations"—the analogy with the Briand Plan was inescapable— and that a "world council" should be set up consisting of the "Big Three"— Britain, the US, and the Soviet Union—with representatives from smaller unions to be created in both Europe and Asia. The future European union was to consist of about twelve states, which would then form a "council of the United States of Europe."[9]

At the time all of this fell on largely deaf ears in Washington. When, however, two years later and with an Allied victory all but certain, the "Big Three" met in Yalta in February 1945, Roosevelt had come to recognize that the Soviet Union could not be allowed to seize effective control of the entire continent and that whatever shape the future balance of world power might finally take, a democratic Western European alliance (at the very least) would be the necessary condition of Soviet containment. Similarly, the Marshall Plan (or European Recovery Program), signed into effect by President Truman three years later on April 3, 1948, was intended not only to help the individual nations of Europe to rebuild their economies and to restore, in the words of the US Secretary of State George Marshall, "the confidence of the people of Europe in the economic future of their own countries and of Europe as a whole"; it was also meant to direct them toward eventual economic, and (possibly) political unification. This was evident from the plan's demands that the European nations should begin dismantling trade barriers between them and that a pan-European organization should be established to oversee the process of economic recovery.[10] The plan was in effect a far-reaching bid to refashion Europe, economically at least in, the image of the US. It was also an admittedly heavily disguised attempt to encourage the creation of some not very clearly defined version of the "United States of Europe"—an attempt in the words of the historian Michael Hogan "to remake Western Europe in the image of 'God's own country.'"[11]

Churchill, himself, seemingly had grander ambitions. In November 1945 in a passionate address to the Belgian parliament, he conjured up a vision of a new Europe which would be far more than a mere bulwark against communist expansionism. The "United States of Europe," he declared would "unify this Continent in a manner never known since the fall of the Roman Empire, and within which all its peoples may dwell together in prosperity, in justice and in peace."[12] And on September 19 of the following year he delivered a now famous and characteristically rambunctious speech at the University of Zurich.

"If Europe were once united," he began, "in the sharing of its common inheritance, there would be no limit to the happiness, to the prosperity and glory which its three or four hundred million people would enjoy." But notoriously, and for centuries, they had known only conflict and discord. Battered by "the frightful nationalistic quarrels" which had already resulted in two world wars, "a vast quivering mass of tormented, hungry, care-worn and bewildered human beings gape at the ruins of their cities and homes." It was only the intervention of "that great Republic across the Atlantic Ocean," which had now finally awoken to the fact that "the ruin and enslavement of Europe would involve their own fate as well," that had saved the continent from a return to "the cruelty and squalor" of the "Dark Ages." But he warned, "They may still return." There could be only one sure means to prevent any future resurgence of the ancient animosities, something which would make "all of Europe, or the greater part of it, as free and happy as Switzerland is today." And that was to "build a kind of United States of Europe." Many subsequently wondered just what this last phrase was supposed to mean. What exactly were the limits of this "kind of United States of Europe" intended to be? When later his colleague Robert ("Bob") Boothby questioned Churchill about just what he meant by "a kind of," he remained evasive and remarked irritatedly, "We are not making a machine, we are growing a living plant."[13]

A "kind of United States of Europe" had, in fact, been very close to just what the League had been intended to provide. And it is not hard to see behind almost all of Churchill's utterances on Europe the lurking shadow of the Briand Plan. The League had failed not, in Churchill's view "because of its principles or conception," but because these had been "deserted by those States who had brought it into being." For all that Churchill urged his listeners to look forward, not back, to unite the "European family" in an "act of oblivion against all the crimes and follies of the past," his vision was still, much as Briand's had been, of a "regional organization of Europe" under the broader influence of a world organization, with the United Nations now in place of the League.

The model he apparently had in mind for the new European order, however, was not, despite his repeated invocation of the "United States of Europe," the United States of America, or even the Swiss Federation. It was instead the British Commonwealth of Nations, which he claimed was the "main support" of what he referred to repeatedly as the "world organization." The "European group" within this organization would give a "sense of enlarged patriotism and common citizenship to the distracted peoples of this mighty and turbulent continent." And if anyone should have been in any doubt as to the distance which separated Britain and its Commonwealth from "Europe," he concluded with the hope that "Great Britain, the British Commonwealth of Nations, mighty America and, I trust, Soviet Russia" would together be the "friends and sponsors of the new Europe and must champion its right to live and shine."[14] As Rougemont observed later, the British had always been concerned primarily with the survival of their empire—now disguised as the British Commonwealth of Nations. "For us continentals," he wrote, "it was Europe which was at stake. For the English it was rather the empire; and the unification of Europe might be able to save the empire if only it was not too much here or there, too precise, or too continental."[15]

Whatever misgivings Rougemont and others might have had about it, Churchill's speech was greeted by a great many federalists with widespread, if often cautious enthusiasm. "There is probably no European federalist," wrote the Franco-Swiss journalist, *littérateur*, and activist Léon vanVassenhove, "who is not grateful to Churchill for the fact that, in what may be a decisive hour, he has indicated to the peoples of Europe that union is the only road to salvation, and has insisted on the necessity of their uniting at once." Brugmans was more cautious but no less approving. "For the first time in modern history," he remarked, to the Reuters' special correspondent in February 1947, with obvious relief, "Britain seems interested in strengthening Europe instead of weakening it."[16]

Not everyone, however, was quite so keen on Churchill's characterization of the "kind of United States of Europe" as some kind of new *Grossraum* to be allied with those of the United States and the British Commonwealth of

Nations in order to restrain the rising power of the Soviet Union. It was, said the antifascist politician, historian, and Harvard professor Gaetano Salvemini at a gathering in the Teatro Eliseo in Rome, an "attempt to draw Europe into a conflict between the Soviet and Anglo-American systems." Churchill's call for European unity was described in similar terms, with heavy sarcasm, by Hans Bauer, president of the federal *Europa-Union*, as nothing other than an "invitation to European countries to be kind enough to form a safety zone protecting the British Isles from bombs and air attack from Soviet-controlled central Europe."[17]

This view of the true motives behind the creation of a united Europe, whatever form it might eventually take, persisted throughout much of the Cold War. Those on the left often saw it as an American-sponsored strategy to strengthen Germany as a counterweight to the USSR. The economic neoliberals on the right, the followers of the brilliant, if quixotic Austrian economist Freidrich Hayek, looked upon the possibility of European integration as a threat to the Atlantic Community. In their view what was needed was not a future United States of Europe but a return to what some of them at least imagined to have been the golden years before 1914, when the world economy had, on their reckoning, been a unitary one, when, as Benedetto Croce had written wistfully in 1932, "old Europe" had been a place of "riches ... flourishing trade, [an] abundance of goods ... ease of life, [a] bold sense of security."[18]

Even in Britain, Churchill's speech was received with a certain amount of icy contempt. In a book published in the United States with the apt title *You Can't Turn the Clock Back* (every chapter of which was prefaced by a passage from *Alice in Wonderland*), R. W. G. Mackay pointed out that the much-vaunted Commonwealth of Nations was now, in effect, a thing of the past and that "it cannot continue as a political and economic entity in the modern world, because it does not have sufficient power to defend itself in all parts of the world." Britain, he argued, had to "face its responsibilities" to Europe and become a "foundation member" of any future European federation, and this "marks the end of the British Commonwealth as understood in the past." Mackay was also as certain as Bauer that Churchill's main object was to create a common front against the Soviet Union, and that no arrangement that would involve the surrender of "sufficient sovereignty to establish ... a federation" could possibly be "founded upon such a negative conception."[19] What Mackay also recognized, although he was hardly alone in this, was that the war had indeed marked the beginning of the end for the

British Empire, even in the much-attenuated shape of the Commonwealth, and the way ahead could only be as an effective—which also meant committed—member of a new European union, whatever form that might take. For Churchill, a veteran of the Anglo-Sudan and the Boer Wars, who had famously taken part in the cavalry charge at the Battle of Omdurman in September 1898, that future was all but invisible.

For all that, "Churchill the European," as the Swiss journal *Europa* called him, despite his defeat at the hands of the British electorate in 1945, was a statesman who enjoyed immense international stature. The speech also drew attention, at a moment of confusion and uncertainty, to the possibility that a new united Europe might yet become a reality and that the peoples of Western Europe might not only help to secure the frontier against a communist East, but might also live henceforth if not exactly "in a manner never known since the fall of the Roman Empire," then possibly in one in which, instead of being locked into incessant combat with each other, they might indeed "dwell together in prosperity, in justice, and in peace."

Two years later, in May 1948, Churchill led a gathering in The Hague of what one observer referred to as the "Estates General of Europe." Some eight hundred delegates attended, including over sixty government ministers; the future West German chancellor Konrad Adenauer; a future French prime minister, François Mitterrand (then "War Veterans Minister"); a former French prime minister, Édouard Daladier; Altiero Spinelli; Harold Macmillan; and over two hundred members of the parliaments of Europe. Rougemont, who was present, left a vivid, overwrought account of the events. He sat under the grand arched wooden roof of the "Hall of Knights," the seat of the Dutch parliament, resting his cheek against the pleats of a vast purple velvet curtain, behind "two rows of backs and fascinating necks which projected above the backs of their armchairs. That large red neck was Paul Ramadier [another former French prime minister], the calm pale one was Paul van Zeeland [former prime minister of Belgium]; and that neckless head was Paul Reynaud [prime minister of France at the time of the German invasion in 1940]. . . . A white puffy neck emerged from out of a black morning coat—Winston Churchill." To the left and right of him were old friends and old companions in the struggle for a new Europe: the "slit eyes of Coudenhove, the Voltairean smile of Lord Layton, someone with the profile of the carpenter from *Alice in Wonderland*, who could only be Bertrand Russell, . . . English socialist members of parliament, a jolly Italian anarchist, some German ministers in rimless glasses." "Where am I?," he asked himself,

"In which epoch? In a dream? What is happening?" Someone then spoke into a microphone, and his voice reverberated around the room. "The task before us at this congress," he declared, "is not only to raise the voice of Europe as a united home.... We must here and now resolve that a European Assembly be constituted."

Yes, Rougemont concluded, it was indeed a dream: "a dream become reality and one which I had been dreaming for twenty years."[20] Emotions ran high. "We have seen," enthused Paul Ramadier, that "the reactionary idea of national sovereignty was defended by practically no one."[21] There was talk of the "birth of a new era," of a "Saint Bartholomew's Day massacre of national sovereignty" (an unfortunate allusion perhaps) or a new "Tennis Court Oath." The British however were, as before, hesitant, skeptical, urging caution: "Remember your own French proverb," Harold Macmillan, who in 1957 would become British prime minister, told Paul Reynaud, "hurry slowly" (*hâte-toi lentement*). To which Reynaud replied, "A strange remark to come from someone who is drowning!"[22] For all that, what Churchill had dubbed "this historic moment" generated such a "climate of enthusiasm and fervor" that Churchill had tears in his eyes as he spoke. It all culminated, in Brugmans's words, in "a unanimous elan." But it finished ominously in a thunderstorm so loud that it drowned out even Churchill's booming voice.[23]

The meeting ended with a resolution supported, albeit reluctantly, even by Britain to create a "European Assembly," and it set up a working party to that end under the supervision of Ramadier. The negotiations which took place between July 1948 and January 1949 were, however, predictably contentious and inconclusive. The British, in particular, wanted to ensure that nothing resembling a European popular assembly—a "chamber of echoes where cranks could make their voices heard" in the words of Ernest Bevin, then foreign secretary—might be made into a reality.[24] The French government, in contrast, wished to see something far closer to what the European Parliament has subsequently become, whose members would have been elected rather than nominated by their respective governments and would have been free to vote as they wished. In the end and after a great deal of wrangling, which resulted in a French threat to create its own assembly unilaterally and in an awkward comprise which made no one happy, it was agreed to divide the council into a committee of ministers representing the governments of the member states and a consultative assembly representing their parliaments. On May 5, 1949, by means of the Treaty of London, the

Council of Europe, comprising France, Germany, Italy, Belgium, the Netherlands, Sweden, Demark, Norway, Ireland, and the ever reluctant United Kingdom (later joined by Greece and Turkey), finally came into being. Three months later, on August 10, 1949, with the Belgian foreign minister Paul-Henri Spaak as its president, the Consultative Assembly met in Strasbourg for its first plenary session, which lasted nearly a month. It was attended by Adenauer, Schuman, Mitterrand, Churchill, Georges Bidault (the former president of the National Council of the Resistance), and, as observers, Rougemont and Salvador de Madariaga (now in self-imposed exile from Franco's Spain), among others. Its charter declared that the aim of the council was "to achieve a greater unity between its members for the purpose of safeguarding and realising the ideals and principles which are their common heritage and facilitating their economic and social progress." Those ideals, although left suitably vague, were broadly characterized as "the spiritual and moral values which are the common heritage of their peoples and the true source of individual freedom, political liberty and the rule of law, principles which form the basis of all genuine democracy."[25] The Council is still in existence. But it did not, as its founding members had so passionately hoped, mark the first step on the path to a United States of Europe. It created the flag and the anthem subsequently adopted by the EU. No state has joined the EU without first becoming a member, and it is responsible for the European Court of Human Rights. But for all that, and for all its obvious influence, it was never incorporated into the governing structure of the EU.

II

There were many who could see, even well before the end of the war, that the state system which had made the entire period of the "Great European Civil War" possible would have to change substantially if the process were not merely to repeat itself in a seemingly limitless conflict. As early as 1941, E. H. Carr warned that, as in 1919, "legalistic discussions about sovereignty, leagues and federations may serve as a red herring to divert public opinion from those practical issues of co-operation and interdependence, military and economic, on which the future depends."[26] Many of those who would later become the founders of the EU were broadly in agreement. The creation of the council was in itself hardly insignificant, but it had, in fact, come up with no clear institutional project for the future and had indeed proved to be little more than Bevin's "chamber of echoes." "At the Council of Europe in Strasbourg that summer," Jean Monnet wrote later, "spectacular resolutions had been passed amid great acclaim," but once pronounced, they had "disappeared without trace." The whole affair had, he reflected, merely confirmed his belief that "this approach would end nowhere." Monnet—a former cognac salesman (for his father's company), deputy secretary general of the League of Nations, an international financier, an adviser to President Roosevelt, and minister for armaments in the National Liberation Committee, de Gaulle's government in exile during World War II (among many other roles)—was nothing if not a pragmatist.

In Monnet's view, The Hague and Strasbourg had been little more than overwhelming manifestations of enthusiasm and goodwill. Even Rougemont, for all his impulsive enthusiasm, concluded that although "the hardest battles for the unity of Europe had been won at The Hague," and that the congress had set out to create "a shock, to change opinion," and had, indeed, "awoken the conscience of Europe," nevertheless its most "spectacular conclusions... were only realized much later or elsewhere."[27] Certainly, Churchill had got his council; but instead of being the precursor of a new European parliamentary assembly, it had rapidly become little more than a "talking shop." Despite all the ambitious rhetoric, "amid these vast groupings of countries," Monnet observed, "the common interest was too indistinct, and common disciplines were too lax."[28] Public opinion was focused on what he referred to dismissively as "magic spells," which the eager federalists and their allies continued to "refine" while persistently failing to understand why "reality resisted them so stubbornly."[29] It was also perhaps Europe's greatest missed opportunity.

Within a few years Monnet's pessimism about the possible outcomes to be expected from The Hague and Strasbourg had spread across most of Europe. As Brugmans remarked gloomily in 1952, "We [now] concluded somberly that it would be difficult to organize political life in Europe." After the war, at "the moment of Liberation" many had come to believe that they were living through a moment of "regeneration," that "everything was possible," something which the euphoria generated by The Hague conference seemed to have abundantly confirmed. Now, however, he lamented, "We have had to disappoint ourselves." Even so, and for all his supposed pessimism, he believed that he could still see that "little by little, in nearly every country, a new political theory is taking shape." He was not sure what form it would finally assume, but he remained convinced that it would inevitably be "conditioned by the presence of federalist thought, supple, coherent, organized but open."[30]

All the projects for some kind of united Europe had worked with the assumption that the only way to create a unified Europe had to begin with politics and law. Monnet thought otherwise. What was now needed, he said, was a secure way forward by means of something that would be at once both more "practical and more ambitious" than any of the "spells" touted at The Hague, or the encouraging, but ultimately amorphous talk of European values as a bulwark against the threat of communism. Crucially, it had to be something which would confront the problem of "national sovereignty," which both The Hague and Strasbourg had effectively buried under gesture and allusion, "more broadly and on a narrower front."[31] In Monnet's view, and he was certainly not alone, the only way to achieve this, at least initially, would be by means of some kind of economic alliance, something akin to Aristide Briand's customs union, which had been intended to pave the way for his *lien fédéral*. Once this had been secured, all the rest, all that was essentially "political" (all the way to an eventual "United States of Europe"), would inevitably and painlessly follow.

In the early 1950s, however, full customs union was believed, even by Monnet, to be impracticable. Something still narrower, more feasible, and yet highly symbolic was clearly required. The form this finally took was the proposal for a "European Coal and Steel Community" drawn up by the French prime minister Robert Schuman, with Monnet's assistance, and the enthusiastic support of the West German chancellor Konrad Adenauer, and the Italian prime minister Alcide De Gasperi, who thereby became known colloquially and not unironically, in yet another allusion to the USA, as the "Founding Fathers" of the future EU. The creation of this new international entity was announced by Schuman on May 9, 1950, in a declaration from the Quai d'Orsay, and less than a year later, on April 18, 1951, it was signed into existence in Paris by France, West Germany, Italy, Belgium, Luxembourg, and the Netherlands. (Britain, which had only just succeeded in nationalizing both these industries, saw no reason to immediately surrender them to a transnational organization with an uncertain future and, from their point of view, uncertain objectives. The British government, therefore, attempted, discreetly, to sabotage the entire process in the hope that when the plan had failed, a far less extensive one, more favorable to British interests, and one which, crucially, would involve no transfer of sovereignty, could be set up in its place.[32])

To achieve its objectives, the ECSC was to be equipped, as no previous purely economic alliance had ever been, with a high council, referred to as the "first European government," composed of independent appointees whose first president was to be Monnet himself. It was to have a common assembly made up of parliamentarians from the member states, a special council of ministers, also from the member states, and a court of justice—described by the German–American political scientist Ernst Haas in 1958, when disputes over the true nature of the Community were still running high, as "the most typical federal aspect of the Community."[33] These were the forerunners of four of the seven institutions of the European Union: the European Commission, the Parliament, the Council of the European Union (and the European Council), and the European Court of Justice.

Schuman and Monnet were pragmatists. They had little or no professional concern for grand moral, cultural, or even political schemes beyond a commitment to the basic rule of democracy. Both believed that economics, the substance of all "concrete achievements," could and should lead eventually to politics, not—as had so often been the case in the long history of Europe from the French Wars of Religion of the sixteenth century until 1945—the other way around. If the war had taught them anything, it was the potential truth of the argument that progress, security, and happiness could only be found where all citizens could acquire what they most wanted in peace and without interference from government. The good of the individual took precedence over the good, the greatness, the glory—or whatever other properties it was assumed to possess—of the state. This approach was, in Monnet's view, the only one that was likely to work in the long run. They offered no model for a future state system of the kind that thinkers from the duc de Sully to Saint-Pierre, to Proudhon, to Lorimer and Bluntschli or Scelle had envisaged. But for all that much-vaunted "realism," Monnet and his fellow founders were in fact no less committed to the ultimate creation of a truly federal Europe than any of their more utopian predecessors had been. It was not the overall objectives discussed so enthusiastically at The Hague to which they objected. It was the "federalist methods" by which these were supposedly to be implemented which were in Monnet's view totally "alien to the crude and violent traditions of European international politics." The administrative institutions created by

the Treaty of Paris seemingly posed no (or at least very little) long-term
threat to the sovereign power of the signatories. In the end the Community
failed to live up to the promises made in the treaty. It was dogged by
administrative and personal difficulties which finally drove Monnet to
resign from the High Council, and then to found the "Action Committee
for the United States of Europe."[34] It was abundantly clear from all this that
the ultimate objective of the founders was not merely economic or merely
to prevent future war among the European states. It was, in effect, to create
a new European political order. "Monnet's barely hidden plan," remarked
Altiero Spinelli sardonically in 1978,

> was not to create mere agencies tamely tied to particular tasks, but to establish
> one or more European administrations around which "concrete interests"
> would concentrate with such force that the multi-headed sovereign would
> delegate more and more administrative tasks. At a certain point quantity
> would become quality: the originally functional institution would become a
> fully fledged political power. After all, had not France been created in this way?

"Of course," he went on, "only a French high official could believe that if
the *commis du roi* had founded the French state, the Commissioners of the
Council could establish the United States of Europe."[35] Thus was born what
has come to be called *le méthode Monnet*—the "Monnet method." It was, said
the great Austro-American political scientist Stanley Hoffmann in 1966, "a
gamble on the possibility of substituting motion as an end in itself for agreement on ends." In the course of all this, the idea of national sovereignty,
forever the single most persistent threat to any species of international
cooperation, would be "chewed up leaf by leaf like an artichoke"[36]

Spinelli was, of course, right. For all that the ECSC was firmly grounded
in an economic alliance with predominantly economic institutions, it was
still to be a "community" (a word that was used to describe every subsequent
common European body until it became a union in 1992). "Europe,"
Schuman had declared, "will not be made all at once, or according to a single
plan. It will be built through concrete achievements which first create a de
facto solidarity." The first of these achievements was clearly a final and lasting
peace, in particular between France and Germany. Since coal and steel had
for long been the sinews of war, it was widely assumed that if these were to
be placed under a common intergovernmental body, "any war between
France and Germany becomes not merely unthinkable, but materially
impossible." And it should never be forgotten that, however checkered the

subsequent history of the EU, however it might now seem to some to be fragmenting irrevocably, it has unquestioningly fulfilled that single function. Not only has there been no conflict between Germany and the other nations of Europe in the past seventy-six years. The only other war within what might broadly be thought of as "Europe"—at least geographically—was the conflict in Bosnia-Herzegovina between 1992 and 1995. But this, although it revealed the Union's inability to mount a cooperative military operation, or even to agree upon a common foreign policy, was a war between former client states of the Soviet Union exacerbated by ethnic and religious animosities which years of Soviet subjugation had managed to contain but never to resolve. Not even the far-right populist movements in Germany and Italy which have attempted to vindicate rather than atone for the actions of their Nazi and Fascist antecedents, believe that any future conflict within Europe might be possible or desirable, despite murmurs about "worrying echoes of Weimar" following the success of the Alternative for Germany (Alternative für Deutschland) at the elections in Thuringia in 2020. Germany and France have also forged economic, political, and cultural bonds—which extend through a Franco-German Youth Office, a Franco-German Ministerial Council which meets twice a year, a joint television channel (Arte), and the development of a Franco-German history textbook—which despite differences, sometimes severe, over the speed and manner of European integration and monetary policies, now seem, in particular since the election of Emmanuel Macron to the French presidency, to have gone some way to fulfilling Victor Hugo's Carolingian vision of a united Europe with France and Germany at its core.[37]

The ECSC, however, was explicitly intended to achieve something far more than a simple peace, no matter how remarkable that was likely to be in the continent's long history of ceaseless conflict. It was intended to be, in Schuman's words, "the leaven from which may grow a wider and deeper community between countries long opposed to one another by sanguinary divisions" which would inevitably result in "the first step in the federation of Europe."[38] The ECSC itself was, of course, a community made up of only six European states. It was, however, Monnet made clear from the start, to be "no less dependent than any previous bid for a united Europe upon a vision of something far beyond itself, of once again, in whatever form it might finally take, the United States of Europe." And as he told the Common Assembly of the Council of Europe in Strasbourg on June 19, 1953, it was now incumbent upon those states that still remained outside the Coal and

Steel Community to "accept this same revolutionary principle and to hand over a portion of the national sovereignty to a common authority" so that in the rest of Europe,

> which has been divided for so many centuries and brought by the conflicts of the last fifty years to the brink of disaster, the parliaments will at last consent to give to those common authorities, which make the people of Europe into one people, the power to apply these same rules, so that this continent, which has sufficient resources, and probably men and brains and imagination up to—perhaps above—those to be found anywhere else in the world, can at last use them for its prosperity and happiness instead of turning them, as it has done for so long, to its destruction.[39]

The preamble to the Treaty of Paris itself, although seemingly modest in its objectives, spelled these larger ambitions out in greater detail. The signatories, it declared, while "RECOGNIZING that Europe can be built only through practical achievements which will first of all create real solidarity, and through the establishment of common bases for economic development," were nonetheless "CONVINCED that the contribution which an organized and vital Europe can make to civilization is indispensable to the maintenance of peaceful relations" and were thus "RESOLVED . . . to create, by establishing an economic community, the basis for a broader and deeper community among peoples long divided by bloody conflicts; and to lay the foundations for institutions *which will give direction to a destiny henceforward shared*" (emphasis added).

"Europe is born," Monnet telegraphed Konrad Adenauer on the day the German Bundestag had ratified the treaty. "Long Live Europe." This Europe was to be what was often referred to, only half-ironically, as "Little Europe." But it was also, as Schuman said at the time, a "leap into the unknown."[40] Little wonder, perhaps, that May 9, the day on which Schuman unveiled his original plan, has since become "Europe Day."

No one, however, least of all Schuman (for all his otherwise confident rhetoric), was inclined to underestimate the challenge. "We cannot," he warned, "hide the fact that the integration of Europe is an immense and arduous task which has never before been attempted." It required, he went on, "that we undertake it together, on a basis of absolute equality, with mutual esteem and confidence, after our generation has experienced the highest degree of suffering and hatred."[41] It was the first time that the signatory powers had shown any willingness to surrender a degree of their hitherto zealously guarded sovereignty to an intergovernmental institution.[42] It was also the first time that France and Germany, which had been in a state of near perpetual conflict since 1871, agreed not merely to bury their differences, but to form an alliance, at least temporarily, in the pursuit of a common objective. And when, in 1955, Monnet published a collection of his speeches from 1952 to 1954, he entitled it, not unrealistically at the time, "The United States of Europe Has Begun."

From the moment that the Treaty of Paris came into effect until today, European unification and integration have progressed by means of a series of interlocking treaties which have in effect created a system of European public law. It is, significantly, the outcome of a process which, ever since at least the eighteenth century, has been seen as the formal expression of the European capacity for creating alliances between peoples, and as such has been a crucial aspect of the European civilizing process.[43]

For Monnet, as for all of those who had tried to imagine what the future of a peaceful, unified Europe might look like, all of this was under threat from a persistent and recurrent nationalism. It was nationalism which had been the undoing of whatever precariously uncertain unity the European peoples had once been able to achieve through international agreement and cooperation. He was convinced too that, even though "the world has changed a great deal . . . its future always depends largely on what is happening in Europe." A fragmented Europe would be forever a "constant source of conflict," and thus he believed could not but be a threat to the entire world. "Exposed to nationalist ambitions, [Europeans] will be forced, as happened in the past, to look for outside guarantees in order to protect themselves against each other."[44] A united Europe would secure peace not only for the continent but ultimately for the entire world; Europe would too, as he told the members of the National Press Club in Washington in 1952, at a basic practical level, be able to "do her part in the common defense without having to rely on the continuation of your contributions."[45]

Acutely hostile though Monnet, together with the other founders, was to the more recent manifestations of nationalism, he was not seeking to abolish national distinctions as such. The future USE which the new community was intended to usher into existence, whatever final form it might eventually take, was clearly intended to be a Mazzinian structure of independent, but also interdependent, states.[46] Hence Monnet's insistence that East and West Germany should be once again united, but united only "within a united Europe."

As the English historian (and dogmatic, if also nicely ironic "realist") Alan Milward insisted in 1990, it was, paradoxically perhaps, "Europe" that had in this way "saved" the nation-state. But Milward also in effect reversed Monnet's claims. It was not, as Monnet had imagined, economics which would eventually lead politics, but politics which had always led economics. The member states of the new Europe had in effect and very effectively mobilized the ideal and the institutions of economic integration to prevent the post-war collapse of the nation-state, which in most places in Europe was in a condition of economic disarray and had lost much of its political credibility. The new Europe helped save France, Germany, Italy, and the Benelux countries in particular from possible chaos or revolution. There is something to be said for this argument, at least as far as the initial phases of the integration process were concerned. But like most "realist" accounts of the creation of the new Europe, it fails utterly to grasp the full ideological force of the convictions of what Milward sneeringly calls the "European saints," and is unable to see that they were not simply deceptively pragmatic statesmen concerned exclusively with the preservation of their own national interests.[47]

It is certainly true that if the ECSC had not been conceived as a cleverly nefarious device to preserve the status quo, it had certainly been conceived as a peace project and sold as such. But peace was but one objective; for peace depended not only on economic and eventually political union; it depended also on prosperity and a further, deeper, more elusive sense of unity among the various peoples of the continent. "A unified Europe," declared Monnet,

> has a meaning for civilization that is deeper even than security and peace. Europe was the source of the cultural achievements from which we all benefit, and Europeans are now, as they have always been, capable of enriching the world by the creative effort which has been Europe's historic contribution.[48]

A coal and steel community, Monnet told the graduating class of 1961 at Dartmouth University in the United States, might have seemed to outside observers, in particular from the distance of the United States, to be little more than "technical"; but in the ten years since its creation, its "new methods and its common institutions had brought about a profound change of heart. France and Germany have been reconciled after great wars. What a revolution has taken place in these years! Today it is by French invitation that German troops enter French soil."[49] This was not only a real and pressing necessity if the still precarious security acquired after 1945 was to be sustained; it was also the inescapable destiny of both Europe and the wider world. For now all problems had become universalized. The individual states of Europe could no longer hope to live, as the British had tried to do for so long, in "splendid isolation" from one another. "The United States," he told his audience at Dartmouth, "has already felt the need to unite. Europe today is uniting; and in the same way the West should move toward a sort of union. This is not an end in itself. It is the beginning of a better organization of the world which will allow us to prevent its destruction." And, he went on, just as the West was only able to achieve a present "political and moral equilibrium" by facing the problems of those within its midst who had been "disinherited," so the great traditions of the West would only with difficulty be able to survive in a world in which "the oppositions between rich and poor, between black, yellow, and white had not been overcome."[50] It was now time for the Europeans to bring "our institutions and our economies into harmony with modern times." And that, of course would only be possible through unification.[51]

For all that Monnet's dream of a "United States of Europe" made frequent explicit allusions to and often drew fairly close analogies with the United States of America, it had become vividly obvious by the end of the war, if not earlier, that the analogy was a strained, unworkable one. Europe might well still become a "United States," but it would have to be united in quite different ways and by quite different means than those which the USA had employed. The question, of course, was, and many would argue still is: What should these be?

The first attempt to find an answer to this question, to lay the foundations for what might well have become a truly federal Europe, took place within a year of the signing of the Treaty of Paris. On May 27, 1952, in response to the US Secretary of State's declaration that in view of her industrial capacity and the fact that Germans were "able fighters," Germany should be rearmed in order to be able to defend "Free Europe" from the "threat of Bolshevism," the six members of the ECSC signed a "Treaty of the European Defence Community."[52] This was meant to give the new Europe a centralized transnational army which would have required a supranational authority, common training procedures, a common uniform and procurement policies, a joint military research initiative, and a fully integrated armament industry.[53] All of this would inevitably have entailed a massive surrender of state sovereignty in precisely that area where all the member states were most sensitive. The Community, which was crucially said to possess a "juridical personality," would have represented the member states in the international arena, which would have made it all but impossible for the individual states to pursue their own independent foreign policies.[54] The treaty would, in effect, have created an embryonic federal authority, complete with a council of ministers, a common assembly, a commissariat—"vested with executive and supervisory powers"—and a court of justice.[55] As the signatories fully recognized, they were "conscious that they are thus taking a new and essential step on the road to the formation of a united Europe."[56] For if the federalization of the means to make war had only been the first step, it was clear the federalization of the entire war machine should inevitably have been the second.

Three months later, at the very first meeting of the Council of the ECSC in September 1952, on the prompting of a proposal from Schuman and the Italian prime minister Alcide De Gasperi to "draw up . . . a draft Treaty setting up a European Political Community," the council appointed a constitutional committee, under the chairmanship of the German Foreign Minister Heinrich von Brentano, charged with drafting a still more ambitious "Draft Treaty Embodying the Statute of the European Community," which the former Belgian prime minister and ardent federalist Guy Verhofstadt considered to be the "blueprint" for a future European constitution which would "rebuild the European Union."[57] Brentano's proposal was for a traditional bicameral system consisting of a "Peoples' Chamber" and a senate, "a supranational executive organ . . . in the form of the European Executive Council," and a European court. The "European Political Community" which the treaty would have brought into being would have taken over the "power and competencies" of the both the ECSC and the European Defence Community.

Although the constitutional committee wished to make it clear that while they had no intention of establishing a European "super-State in place of the six participating national States," it was indeed their objective to design a "Community . . . that will be able to take on a more and more precise form, according to its own laws, until it develops, by a natural process into a real Federal State or Confederation."[58] This was to be based upon "the contribution which a living, united free Europe can bring to civilization and to the preservation of our common spiritual heritage" and was intended to foster "through the expansion of our production in improving the standard of living and furthering the works of peace" the determination "to safeguard by our common action the dignity, freedom and fundamental equality of men of every condition, race or creed."

III

In August 1954, this now largely forgotten bid to create the very first constitution for a truly united Europe was rejected, along with the Treaty for the European Defence Community, by the French National Assembly. This effectively put an end not only to the EDC and the European Political Community, but seemingly also to the larger aspirations of the federalists. As the Anglo–Czech social scientist Jan Zielonka has wryly observed, the whole affair made it clear that European policymakers were in effect presented by the national governments with a stark choice: "integration in disguise or no integration."[59]

At a conference held in the Sicilian city of Messina in June 1955, representatives from the six ECSC member governments, led by the Belgian foreign minister Paul-Henri Spaak, agreed to limit their future efforts to create a European customs union and a common market, and to avoid, or at least to disguise as far as possible, any longer-term ambitions to create a lasting political union. The final communiqué urged Europe to "regain influence and prestige" in the world and to work for a "continued increase in the standard of living of her people." Later, at a dinner for a meeting of the Organization for European Economic Cooperation, the British Chancellor of the Exchequer Rab Butler dismissed the conference as "some archaeological excavation." There was, he added, "not the slightest possibility of the Messina 'common market' coming into existence…the only troublesome point was whether we should strive to kill it or let it collapse of its own weight."[60]

Despite Butler's skepticism and hostility, the outcome, two years and many rounds of negotiations (in which Britain played no significant role) later, was the "Treaty Establishing the European Economic Community" or the Treaty of Rome, which was signed on March 25, 1957. To commemorate the events, children on the streets of Rome waved miniature flags of the six signatory states, while the newsstands of the city carried posters depicting six farm girls dancing in circles in blouses decorated with the national colors of the Six. The treaty has now come to be widely looked upon as a foundational document for what would eventually become the European Union.[61] It begins with the resounding and often repeated declaration of its determination to "lay the foundations of an ever-closer union among the peoples of Europe." The new entity still employed the word "community," and like the now abandoned European Political Community, it too was to have a "legal personality." It also carried over many of the institutional arrangements of the ECSC, most notably an assembly, a European parliament, a council of ministers, a commission, and a court of justice. In the longer term, the most politically far-reaching innovations were the (relatively) extensive powers given to the ECJ in Articles 164–88, and Article 52, which grants what subsequently became one of the key sources of contention in the Brexit disputes, the "right of establishment" throughout the community to all citizen of its member states.

The political objectives of the treaty were also clear to those who could see them; so too was the hope that a unified Europe would be able to exercise a far greater influence in world affairs than any of the individual states could assert on their own. To emphasize this last point, at the close of his speech to the French National Assembly in which he asked for—indeed, pleaded for—the ratification of the treaty, the secretary to the French foreign minister Maurice Faure remarked pointedly:

> See, my dear friends, we live with a fiction which consists of saying that there are four "Great Powers." Well there are not now four Great Powers, there are two: America and Russia. There will be a third by the end of the century: China. It depends on you whether there will also be a fourth: Europe.[62]

Few utterances of the past century could, in particular as we move forward in the third decade of the twenty-first, have been more poignant, more prophetic, and more challenging.

The idea that the individual European states were now no longer powerful enough individually to play a significant role in the world or to prevent themselves from ultimately being crushed—economically, culturally, even possibly eventually politically—by the far greater power of the United States on one side, and the Soviet Union on the other, remained a powerfully persuasive one throughout much of the Cold War. The Copenhagen Declaration on European Identity of 1973, for instance, stated that "International developments and the growing concentration of power and responsibility in the hands of a very small number of great powers mean that Europe must unite and speak increasingly with one voice if it wants to make itself heard and play its proper rôle in the world."[63] A French poster from 1960 depicted a determined, square-jawed, muscular (and male) Europe forcing apart two blocks, one bearing the Soviet, the other the US flag. "The United States of Europe" the caption ran, "will prevent you from being crushed [*vous éviteront l'écrasement*]."

The Treaty of Rome's declared objectives, however, were explicitly and narrowly to create a "common market" for the purposes of a "European Economic Community."[64] Any further suggestion that this should contain within it the elements from which a future federal state might eventually be constructed had been carefully hidden from sight.

But they could not be for long. The Rome Treaty may indeed have, as the committee members at Messina hopefully phrased it, "relaunched" Europe; but there was never any doubt in the minds of most of them that it was but the beginning of a long and potentially hazardous road toward a federal Europe.[65] The true relaunching—and the renaming—of the European project took place with the signing in 1992 of the "Treaty Establishing a European Union"—or the Maastricht Treaty, as it has come to be known, after the town in the Netherlands in which it was signed. This not only transformed the "Community" into the far more resonant, if still somewhat ambiguous "Union"; it also significantly altered the political identity of Europe, bringing it (institutionally, at least) far closer to the federal ideals of the "Founders."[66]

The long, hazardous negotiations which preceded Maastricht, beginning with the Single European Act of 1986, had all taken place during the closing years of the Cold War, which would radically change the geopolitical landscape of Europe. The states of Central and Eastern Europe, which since 1945 had disappeared behind the Iron Curtain, to be glimpsed only fleetingly from the West, once during the Hungarian Revolution of 1956 and then in the "Prague Spring" of 1968, had emerged after 1989 fully into the light as European nations in the eyes of most of their citizens, and thus potentially members of the new European Union. Since 1957 "Europe" had expanded from six to twelve. It was now faced with the certainty that before long it would have to expand from twelve to a possible twenty-eight. This was made clear by Helmut Kohl, the chancellor of a soon to be newly unified Germany, in a speech he gave on October 20, 1989 at the College of Europe in Bruges. "Europe at this time," he said, "happens to be more than the Twelve of the European Community. It is not only London, Rome, The Hague, Dublin and Paris that belong to Europe. But Warsaw, Budapest, Prague and Sofia, and, of course, Berlin, Leipzig and Dresden as well."[67]

It is against this background that the opening phrase of the new treaty should be read. It declared that its signatories were "RESOLVED to mark a new stage in the process of European integration [a word that does not appear anywhere in the Treaty of Rome] undertaken with the establishment of the European Communities."[68] It insisted upon the attachment of all the member states to the principles of "liberty, democracy and respect for human rights and fundamental freedoms and the rule of law," and it made democracy and the rule of law conditions of membership. It created a European Central Bank and prepared the way for the creation of a single currency. It greatly extended the powers of the European Parliament, whose members were now to be elected directly from among the citizens of the member states and not appointed by their respective governments, as had previously been the case. This, for the first time, gave the union a fully functioning, fully integrated, democratic institution, even if its actual powers still fell well below those of any national parliament. Although it made no attempt to revive the defunct European Defence Community, it did claim that one of its principal objectives was to "assert its identity on the international scene, in particular through the implementation of a common foreign and security policy," which, it was hoped, would in time lead to a common defense policy and ultimately even "to a common defence."[69]

It did not. What did follow, however, was the creation in 1999 of a single currency, the euro. This could perhaps be counted—against all the predictions of a final calamitous failure which began when the project was first introduced in the 1960s, and continues, all evidence to the contrary, to this day—as the final step in the Monnet method.

The idea of a single European currency has a long history. Éméric Crucé's *New Cyneas* of 1623 had one, the abbé de Saint-Pierre's "European Union" predictably had one, so too did Victor Hugo's "United States of Europe"; and in 1921 the German chancellor Gustav Stresemann had called for the creation of single currency as part of the "Briand Plan" (although it was not included in the final *Memorandum for the organization of a European Federal Order*.)[70] It had also been obvious to the founders that no future integration would be possible without it.

Although the principal objective of the creation of the euro was clearly economic, there could be no mistaking the fact that this was also seen by its creators as yet another step toward the realization of a future federal state. The German chancellor at the time, Helmut Kohl, who had gone so far as to declare that the success of the single currency was nothing less than "a question of war and peace," and Joschka Fischer, then a Green Party leader in the Bundestag and subsequently foreign minister, warned that the only alternative to an early start of the euro was a return to the European past of power balancing and nationalism.[71] True, the long-term benefits of the euro are still a matter of bitter dispute, and the common financial and fiscal policies which it was hoped would follow ineluctably from its creation, thus establishing a set of supranational authorities with real political powers strongly reminiscent of those of the United States, never materialized (or at least they have not yet). For some European nations, for Greece and Spain and Portugal, which had for decades lived under oppressive military regimes, and for the former satellite states of the USSR, joining the euro was (and is, for those which are still excluded) the final stage in a process of acceptance into what is perceived as being not merely a democratic, but also a modern European state system.[72] There is also a deeply emotive aspect to the euro. It is unmistakably a *European* currency. With the array of images of monuments, buildings, celebrities, political icons, flags, maps, stars, every note and coin proclaims the currency to be the economic incarnation of "unity in diversity" that it was intended to be, and to some degree remains: a prime symbol of European unity. Unsurprisingly, it was seen, in particular by the populists of the right, as a blow at what many looked upon as a major bearer of national sovereignty. It could hardly not be. As Monnet had observed of an earlier proposal for monetary union in 1969, currency is "still regarded as an almost magical expression and weapon of national sovereignty."[73] Certainly the protestations which preceded the creation of the euro demonstrated just how attached many of the peoples of Europe were to their currency, not only as one of the more tangible "marks" of sovereignty, but also as a vital prop to any national identity. Even today, the Alternative für Deutschland vows to bring an end to "the euro project" and calls for the government to put the matter to a national referendum.[74] The far-right Italian League still hankers after the lira, a currency which in 1999 was trading at nearly 1,800 to the dollar; and until recently Marine Le Pen promised the French people not only a withdrawal from the EU but a return to the supposedly beloved franc (a promise which has subsequently been silently dropped, although recently in response to the COVID-19 crisis she has said that France would be far better placed to deal with the economic fallout from the pandemic if it were not beholden to the European Central Bank). Yet most Europeans have in the past twenty years come quietly to accept the new currency, which could be interpreted as meaning that, for all the protestations, a currency is not, after all, so central to a person's cultural identity; or, alternatively, that one aspect of what it might mean to become a European has been largely realized. It is also obviously the case that a whole generation is growing up for whom the lira, the franc, or the German mark are about as familiar and symbolically resonant as the guilder or the florin.

Politically and legally, Maastricht also introduced into law two lastingly consequential innovations. The first, in an attempt to quell mounting fears among the member states about the new union's potential threat to their individual sovereignty, was "conferral, subsidiarity, and proportionality" as the key legal principle on which the division of power within the union has subsequently been based. Of the three, subsidiarity was by far the most significant. (Conferral meant merely that "the EU acts only within the limits of the competences that EU countries have conferred upon it in the Treaties," and Proportionality that "the action of the EU must be limited to what is necessary to achieve the objectives of the Treaties.")[75] The treaty stated that:

> In areas which do not fall within its exclusive competence, the Community shall take action, in accordance with the principle of subsidiarity, only if and in so far as the objectives of the proposed action cannot be sufficiently achieved by the Member states and can therefore, by reason of the scale or effects of the proposed action, be better achieved by the Community.[76]

Although the basic principle derives from the Roman *ius commune* ("common law"), subsidiarity was first articulated in the manner in which it is used today in the late nineteenth century by the Catholic bishop of Mainz, a theologian and former jurist, Wilhelm Emmanuel von Ketteler. In 1891, it was incorporated into Pope Leo XIII's encyclical *Rerum novarum* as a means of combating what the pope saw as the rising threat of liberalism and industrialization, and subsequently into Pope Pius XI's encyclical of 1931, *Quadragesimo anno*, in protest against the centralizing tendencies of both National Socialism and communism.[77]

Needless to say, this has had the effect of greatly limiting the democratic potential of the Union, and of placing obvious limitations on any bid for an "ever closer union."[78] It also bears a—perhaps unintended—resemblance to the Tenth Amendment of the US Constitution, which similarly states, "The Powers not delegated to the United States by the Constitution, nor prohibited by it to the States are reserved to the States respectively or to the peoples." (Even after the massive extension of federal power which has taken place over the past three centuries, it is still true that federal law is "designed to accomplish limited objectives," is "built upon legal relationships established by the states," and applies only "so far as necessary for special purposes.")[79] As Lord Mackenzie Stuart (president of the European Court of Justice from 1984 until 1988) complained, subsidiarity involved what was, in effect, a political decision which "places that responsibility" as to what do and what do not count as objectives which "cannot be sufficiently achieved by the Member states acting on their own" "squarely on the shoulders" of the court. Anyone, he concluded acidly, who regards this "chosen formula as a constitutional safeguard shows great optimism."[80]

The manner in which subsidiarity was presented in the treaty itself also introduced by stealth the claim that the community did, in fact and in law, enjoy some measure of "exclusive competence" and that this, although the treaty does not say just what it might involve, would appear to raise the Union, potentially at least, somewhere close to the level of a federal state.[81] This was taken even further by the European Court of Justice, which stated first that "An international treaty is to be interpreted not only on the basis of its wording, but in the light of its objectives," and then that "As the Court of Justice has consistently held, the Community treaties established a new legal order for the benefit of which the States have limited their sovereign rights, in ever wider fields, and the subjects of which comprise not only the Member-States *but also their nationals*."[82]

The second innovation in the treaty was the creation of a European citizenship to be held by "every person holding the nationality of a Member State," but that "citizenship of the Union shall be additional to and not replace national citizenship." Exactly what this means was and still remains unclear, and at least some of the key provisions of the original treaty—the right, for instance, of all citizens of the union "to vote and stand as a candidate in municipal elections" in any state in which they reside—have never been consistently respected, while others, such as the right to travel and to settle in any of the other member states, were rights already enjoyed by the *members* of the EEC. A declaration of *citizenship*, with all the centuries-old implications of belonging which the term carries with it, as distinct from mere membership, was clearly, however, a major symbolic act in the continuing bid to construct a European *imaginaire*.[83] Indeed, the European parliamentary committee convened in November 1989 to study the question of citizenship stated clearly that the intention was to "strengthen its citizens' feelings of belonging to one legal community." (It carefully avoided, however, any suggestion that this might also constitute one political body.)[84] And although the treaty makes no allusion to the United States of Europe, the invention of an unanchored category of "European citizen" was clearly intended to persuade the citizens of the member states that they were indeed now citizens of a place called "Europe" and that, as James Lorimer had imagined it, there now indeed existed, in law at least,

> two nations in the world, every citizen of each...must *eo ipso* be an interna-
> tional man, and cannot *eo ipso* be only an international man. In order that he
> may be either national or international, he must be both; and must be gov-
> erned, or must govern himself, in both capacities.[85]

It was in something like this spirit that in 2001 the European Court of Justice, always eager to push the implications of the treaties toward a more radical conclusion than their drafters had intended, insisted that "Union citizenship is destined to be the fundamental status of nationals of the Member States."[86] What the court believed that it had created was, in effect, a true transnational constitution, which meant that no member state was wholly and completely sovereign and that European law consequently became something more than international law.

EU citizenship does indeed carry with it certain rights and possible duties which played no role in national citizenship—most notably perhaps the right to be "directly represented *at Union level* in the European Parliament" (emphasis added), and the corresponding right to appeal directly to the parliament and to the European Ombudsman. Yet if citizenship is to be something more than a simple legal category, it surely implies a degree of commitment to, and understanding of, a political and social order. In reality, however, European Citizenship, as it is currently conceived, is only a legal concession which confers upon Europeans a number of very limited rights, all of which, although upheld by the European Court of Justice, are, in fact, endorsed and protected by national governments and national courts.[87] This is further underlined by the statement that "Citizenship of the Union shall be additional to national citizenship and shall not replace it."[88] For all the very considerable symbolic implications and the hallowed position which the very notion of citizenship has always played in all European political discourse, ever since the Romans invented the term, for many Europeans it must seem to be little more than one further layer of abstraction (as, indeed, the language in which it is defined strongly suggests it is).

This perception is further underlined by the insistence that whatever rights European citizenship might confer, they are not absolute but "shall be exercised in accordance with the conditions and limits defined in the Treaties," a clause which might appear superfluous did it not imply that subsequent treaties might, in effect, revoke citizenship, something which the

Treaty of Lisbon has basically to happen to the entire population of the United Kingdom.[89] As the English political theorist Richard Bellamy says, the "value of EU citizenship consists in its enabling the mutual concern and respect that operates among sovereign polities to apply to the citizens of those polities in moving and trading between them." This—which significantly makes no mention of rights—is surely what the drafters of the treaties had in mind, even if they were constrained to express it in the language of a status which had hitherto only been conceived as a part of the life of a political and social body.[90]

Citizenship, however, as it has been traditionally understood, supposes the existence of the *civitas*, the state, at least as an imaginary, fictive person capable of uniting its members into a common body bound by a shared commitment to a set of laws and customs, habits, and associations. Ancient forms of citizenship were created to serve very small communities, city states whose populations were no larger than that of a modern village, all of whom spoke the same language (and, at least in the case of the Greek *poleis*, all of whom could fit into a single city square and listen to, if not always participate directly in, public debate). Modern citizenship has long since shed its association with direct democracy; but there still exists a conviction that citizenship demands that the bearer be granted a right to some degree of immediate participation. In the modern state that participation may well, as Benjamin Constant had already foreseen as early as 1814, be an illusion, but illusory or not, it remains the case that all the citizens of modern democracies look upon their presumed capacity to influence the direction of the political entity to which they belong as a sacred right. And if they are to be asked to dilute their attachment to the nation-state which claims to protect that right by placing themselves under the aegis of another political body, then that other has to provide a far stronger sense of participation than the right to vote for a European Parliament which, at present, still has only very limited legislative powers. Democratic processes, as Jürgen Habermas has observed "have hitherto functioned, imperfectly to be sure," and they have done so "only inside national boundaries."[91] To operate beyond them requires more than the superimposition of one layer of citizenship upon another.

In creating a European citizenship, Maastricht also carefully avoided the obvious question: What allegiance do I choose if my European persona finds himself or herself in conflict with my persona as, say, French or German? We might all finally come to share a set of common institutions, even a common set of political objectives; we might all agree on the need for the rule of law and democratic government, human rights, equality between men women, between all genders and ethnicities, because we all already shared, *mutatis mutandis*, those values *before* we found ourselves to be citizens of the union. (It is not insignificant that, with the exception of Spain and Portugal, those states where those values were less prevalent, most obviously Hungary and Poland, are the ones which are now the most fiercely opposed both to the EU as it has become and to liberal democracy, which led the Hungarian prime minister Viktor Orbán infamously to call for the creation of a new "illiberal" democracy.) But how do I stand as a citizen of Europe, if I am, say, Hungarian when the policies of my government on, for instance, immigration, blatantly violate the basic principles of the citizenship of the EU which I also hold? In the absence of any clear answer it would appear that "European citizenship" amounts to little more than a means of emphasizing the degree to which the treaties have constituted a community, even an "ethical life," to which all Europeans have access.[92] Ultimately, it does not confer binding rights, quite explicitly *not* rights that can be said to "trump"—to use the American jurist Ronald Dworkin's term—national laws.[93]

The only attempt to provide some more precise meaning to the claim that the citizens of every member state of the union were now "citizens of Europe" was the ill-fated "Treaty Establishing a European Constitution" of 2004, which would have replaced all the former treaties by a single document, something which Habermas looked upon at the time as a "unique medium of transnational communication."[94] This was to be what some called "an emphatic constitution" which would replace the unwritten, unspecific, and decidedly " unemphatic" constitution which some constitutional lawyers and the European Court of Justice believed the treaties had already created.[95] It was to be enacted like the US Constitution in the name of "We the People," acting as "an original constituent power [*pouvoir constituant originaire*]," and, like the US constitution, it was to create a "founding moment."[96] In reality, however, the actual document was a glorified tidying-up operation. None of the articles was entirely new, and none of the changes it intended to introduce would, in fact, have altered greatly the actual government of the union, although as the historian Harold James has pointed out, while it "aimed at cementing Europe's new identity," it also stressed the centrality of the market, and the first of its "Fundamental Freedoms" was "the free movement of persons, services, goods and capital, and freedom of establishment," which had been there since the Treaty of Rome.[97] Nor did it attempt to do what the US Constitution of 1789 had done, that is, to create a form of government. For all that, its larger objectives and its significance, at least in the eyes of those who drafted it, were far grander. Its declared purpose was nothing less than to "reflect" what it assumed to be the "will of the citizens and States of Europe to build a common future," although it then hurried on to reassure the individual states that it also meant to respect "the diversity of the cultures and traditions of the peoples of Europe as well as the national identities of the Member States and the organisation of their public authorities at national, regional and local levels."[98] The union was, it declared,

> founded on the indivisible, universal values of human dignity, freedom, equality and solidarity; it is based on the principles of democracy and the rule of law. It places the individual at the heart of its activities, by establishing the citizenship of the Union and by creating an area of freedom, security and justice.[99]

Most significantly of all perhaps, and despite the fact that it was still officially described as a treaty (and at over 400 pages, the longest to date), there was little doubt in most people's minds that this was intended to be a true constitution, and since hitherto only sovereign states had had constitutions, it was, like the creation of a European citizenship, of immense symbolic importance, no matter what its actual political and legal content might be. Had it ever in fact come into being, it would, legally and symbolically, have transformed the union from an assembly of states bound by a form of international law into a constitutional political body. As Habermas said at a moment when the document was still in embryo, the project had "put the unsolved end and suppressed problem of the final goal of the unification process on the political agenda."[100]

That it certainly did. It was, indeed, meant to be Europe's true "Philadelphia moment." At a dinner held at the Finnish Parliament in Helsinki, the former French president Valéry Giscard d'Estaing, the chairman of the convention charged with drafting the new constitution, asked his colleagues over dessert: "What about the name of the new union? What would you think about the United States of Europe?" He then regaled his apparently astounded listeners with a series of far-fetched analogies between the drafters of the US Constitution and the solemn bureaucrats sitting around the table. "If I am George Washington," he declared, "then you, Giuliano

[Amato, the vice president of the convention], are James Madison. But who is Alexander Hamilton? Well, António [Vitorino, a former member of the commission], of course."[101]

For all Giscard's bravura, the constitution, although it was initially signed by all twenty-five of the then member states, was finally only ratified by eighteen of them, and was rejected in a referendum in France on May 29, 2005 and in another held in the Netherlands—which had not held a referendum since 1797—three days later. Opposition came for different reasons, from both the extreme left and the right. Both, however sought to exploit fear and uncertainty in those areas dominated by the twinned menace of immigration and unemployment—just as the Brexit campaign was later to do. As one member of the French Socialist Party put it later, the "Yes" campaign had attempted to employ "reason and political appreciation," while the "No" party had merely appealed to "people's guts."[102] The French National Front, unsurprisingly, claimed in the words of one of its manifestos that saying yes to the constitution meant saying yes to Turkish entry into Europe. *Je garde la France* ("I protect France"), it proudly proclaimed. The far left-wing "No Committee," for its part, stated that the constitution "encourages the cancer of liberalism" (meaning economic neoliberalism). Very much the same divisions and the same anxieties surfaced in the Netherlands, reinforced by the fear that the Netherlands because of its size was steadily losing its influence within Europe, and ruthlessly exacerbated by the claims from the far right that the Netherlands' famously tolerant policies, in particular toward immigrants, were responsible for a steady erosion of Dutch culture and Dutch political and moral values. The Dutch, as Gert Wilders, founder of the far-right "Party for Freedom," phrased it, have been "too tolerant with intolerance."[103] To make matters worse for the "Yes" campaigners, the country was still under the shadow of the murder in 2004 of the filmmaker Theo Van Gogh by a Muslim extremist for his film *Submission*, which represented, in often explicit detail, violence perpetrated against Muslim women by Muslim men.[104]

After this, the entire project was laid to rest, never—to date, at least—to be resurrected. The significance of the failure was considerable. This may have been in form a treaty; but it was intended to be a true *constitution*, and it was as a constitution that had been rejected. It led Habermas—who had initially greeted the prospect of a Europe-wide referendum on the constitution as an opportunity to "touch off a large-scale debate throughout Europe" which had the "potential to become a self-fulfilling prophecy"—to

conclude gloomily that the rejection had demonstrated that "European citizens lack any sense of mutual political belonging, and that the member
states are as far away as ever from pursuing a common project."[105] It perhaps
also demonstrated that constitutions, like treaties, are too complex and too
demanding in their implementation, and their potential long-term consequences too significant, to be subjected to a random public plebiscite.
Constitutions have to be capable of meeting the needs of entire populations
over time, for which reason they must allow for constant emendation, not
just the approval of (often very slender) majorities at one particular inevitably highly contentious moment. Neither the constitution of the United
States nor that of France in 1791 nor many of the constitutions which have
constituted the states of post-war Europe would have survived a popular referendum, least of all the sectarian and willfully ill-informed treatment to
which the European Constitution was submitted.

Despite the considerable symbolic significance of the rejection and the
glee with which the news was greeted by Euroskeptics, it did not in fact do
very much to halt the actual process of integration. Many of the significant
changes to the nature of the EU proposed by the constitution were incorporated, silently and without significant protest, into the Treaty of Lisbon,
which passed into law in 2007. "The route to a politically workable and
democratically legitimized (core) Europe is by no means blocked," wrote
Habermas in 2011. "Indeed, with the Lisbon Treaty the longest stage of the
journey has already been completed."[106]

Lisbon also added the "Charter of Fundamental Rights of the European
Union"—fundamental rights being, of course, one of the core principles of
constitutionalism—which previously had only been "proclaimed" in
December 2000. Although these were fundamental rights of the EU, they
were also declared to "have the meaning and scope" of and to be "the same
as" those guaranteed by the "Convention for the Protection of Human
Rights and Fundamental Freedoms" of 1950, which, if taken together with
the frequent insistence, repeated in every treaty, that Europe was a standard
bearer for human rights, greatly—and for those states which zealously
guarded their sovereignty, alarmingly—extended the potential range of
EU law.[107]

The claim that "human rights" constituted the key to those values on
which the identity of Europe depended had been there since the beginning.
But the treaties and conventions from Maastricht through to Lisbon have
come to place ever greater emphasis on the concept. The understanding of

just what "human rights" are and their status in international law is, at best, problematical. Despite decades of wrangling and disputes, ever since the Universal Declaration of Human Rights was issued in 1948, their status in EU law has been, if anything, even more opaque.[108] The earliest declaration of the "rights of man," issued by the French National Assembly in 1789, made it clear that these were linked indissolubly to those of the citizen, and in general, subsequent declarations of human rights were similarly dependent upon specifically political attachments.[109] Although indissolubly "human" and thus unequivocally universal, human rights may nevertheless be interpreted very differently by different national and political cultures without necessarily thereby undermining their status as "human."[110] It is also true that the EU Charter insists on the indivisibility of the "universal" and the "European" and proclaims its "due regard" for the "principle of subsidiarity" and "the rights as they result, in particular, from the constitutional traditions and international obligations common to the Member States."[111]

One of the reasons why each of the EU treaties has insisted so heavily upon the inclusion of human rights among the core "European values" (although historically this may be a sleight of hand depending on what view you take of the history of human rights) is precisely that, whatever they may actually be, to be "human," they can only be judged and defended by an international body; indeed, as Habermas has argued, that they can only logically be "implemented on a global scale." At present, no effective global polity exists which is capable of achieving these ends, but the EU might plausibly be seen to be "an important stage along the route to a politically constituted world society."[112] For any declaration of what are in fact universal rights, if they do not, of logical necessity, override it, nevertheless certainly pose a serious threat to the sovereign authority of national domestic law.[113]

It was for this reason, if for no other, that Britain and Poland both insisted on a protocol to the "Charter of the Fundamental Rights of the European Union," which, in the somewhat contorted language the EU treaties habitually employ, prevented the European Court of Justice (now renamed the Court of Justice of the European Union) from declaring any of the "laws, regulations or administrative provisions, practices or actions" of those two countries to be "inconsistent with the fundamental rights, freedoms and principles that it [the Charter] reaffirms." Which was to say that, whatever domestic laws Britain and Poland chose to enact were to be considered *eo ipso* consistent with the fundamental rights of the Union as a whole.[114] In addition, a "Protocol on the Application of the Principles of Subsidiarity and Proportionality" gave national parliaments a formal role in the scrutiny of EU legislation, allowing each chamber to issue a reasoned opinion if it considered that a proposal breached the principle of subsidiarity, something which clearly enhanced the power of the governments of the member states at the expense of the union, or at least of the ECJ. The Treaty of Lisbon also attempted to extend the democratic accountability of the EU; but this too it did largely at a national, not at the transnational level.[115] Whatever else it might be, the Treaty of Lisbon marked the seeming abandonment of the idea of a far-reaching and all-embracing European constitutional order—what the legal philosopher Joseph Raz has called "thick" constitutionalism—which so many Europeanists (and Europeans) had been hoping for.[116]

As Chris Patten, former chairman of the British Conservative Party, last British governor of Hong Kong, and a member of the European Commission remarked, astutely, in 2005, the rejection of the constitution "had sought to draw a line in the sand as far as further integration was concerned." It had, he believed, demonstrated that "voters dislike the feeling that Europe is made over their heads" and that in many places

> there is clearly a sense that the European project has gone too far, too fast for many of Europe's citizens; there is a sense too that Europe's political leaders have allowed the institutions that they themselves have created to drift away from the citizens whose interests those same institutions are supposed to serve.[117]

What in fact he meant was that the long-term project for European unification had finally shown signs of becoming a reality, and that many Europeans at that time, and not only the British, had been alarmed by the possible consequences.

One other feature of both the Constitution and of the Treaty of Lisbon is the now celebrated—or notorious—Article 50 (Article I-59 of the Constitution), which for the first time, introduced the possibility that a member state might, if it so chose, secede from the union, "in accordance with its own constitutional requirements." This not only suggested that the declared objective of an "ever closer union" repeated in the preamble of every treaty since 1957 might in fact be reversible; but since a right to secede has very rarely, if ever, been written into the constitution of any nation state, federal or otherwise, the presence of Article 50 also implied that the EU was indeed only an intergovernmental arrangement with no ultimate ambition to become anything more (even if such an ambition was still implied).[118] Most strikingly of all, perhaps—although this, too, is something that the treaty passes over in silence—Article 50 gives to the member states the implicit right to deprive its citizens of their European citizenship without their consent. In this respect the Lisbon Treaty ran directly counter to what most identified as being one of the fundamental ambitions of the Constitution of 2004, namely the creation of a union which "places the individual at the heart of its activities, by establishing the citizenship of the Union and by creating an area of freedom, security and justice." This was substantially reinforced by the "Protocol on the Application of the Principles of Subsidiarity and Proportionality" of the Treaty of Lisbon of 2009, which gave national parliaments a formal role in the scrutiny of EU legislation, allowing each chamber to issue a reasoned opinion if it considered that a proposal breached either of these principles.

The intention of the drafters of the treaty seems, however, to have been merely to create a let-out clause in order to assure all future potential members of the Union, anxious about what the consequences of membership might be for their national sovereignty, that their decision could, *in extremis*, be reversed; and it is unlikely that any of the drafters seriously expected that any existing member state would actually ever have recourse to it, as Britain was to do in 2016, least of all one which had been a member since 1973. Only this can explain the paucity of detail provided by the treaty as to what steps would have to be taken were it to be activated. This, of course, proved to be disastrous for the people of Britain. It not only allowed the then British prime minister David Cameron, in an ill-judged attempt to gain control of the Euroskeptic, Europhobic elements in his government, to subject the people to a hasty, poorly explained, and ideologically vacuous plebiscite. It also enabled two successive governments, in a series of desperate attempts to control the damage unleashed by the decision taken on June 23, 2016, while respecting—or at least appearing to respect—the supposed "will of the people," to subject the state to a prolonged series of negotiations, which has, as of 2021, left the country poorer, more divided, more uncertain of its future than it has perhaps ever been in any period of its history since the Glorious Revolution of 1688.

Lisbon was the most recent move in what has been called the "functionalist integration" process. There is no knowing for certain whether it will also be the last, or what will follow next. For all that it might ultimately have "drawn a line in the sand"—though, like all lines in sand, it can easily be redrawn—each successive treaty, from Rome to Lisbon, has succeeded in strengthening and extending the reach of the economic and political institutions of the union, and in increasing both its legal powers and its democratic accountability. In this, the nature and ultimate goals of the "European project" have remained remarkably consistent, as has the progress toward them, although halting and often uncertain, and achieved through a series of successes, half-successes, crises, mishaps, and setbacks which often seemed to many as if they would finally bring an end to the entire enterprise. For all the qualifications, for all that the principle of subsidiarity would seem to have placed a very considerable object in its path, the wider, more general ambition expressed in the Treaty of Rome of 1957 as a determination—"to lay the foundations of an ever closer union among the peoples of Europe... and to ensure the economic and social progress of their countries by common action to eliminate the barriers which divide Europe"—has never been entirely lost to sight. For all its defects, for all the vicissitudes it has endured and continues to endure, the European Union is still undoubtedly the most sustained, most far-reaching, most successful attempt to unite the peoples of Europe there has ever been—with the possible exception of the Roman Empire. It is the closest thing yet to the realization of what Voltaire called "the Great Republic of Europe." Europe has, indeed, come a very long way since Napoleon effectively, if inadvertently, set in motion the process which would eventually transform the political identity of the continent.

7

The Once and Future Europe

I

Every one of the treaties which have contributed to the making of the EU has insisted upon the existence of a common European identity rooted, in the words of the Treaty of Lisbon, in the "cultural, religious and humanist inheritance of Europe from which have developed the universal values of the inviolable and inalienable rights of the human person, freedom, democracy, equality and the rule of law."[1] But what exactly is that inheritance?

In 1835 the great Italian liberal Carlo Cattaneo declared—suitably in a tract against anti-Semitism—that Europe had always possessed four unifying features: the power of the former imperial authority, the Roman Law, Christianity, and the Latin language.[2] As the authority of the Roman Empire (and of the papacy) is no more and English has replaced Latin as the lingua franca of the continent (ironic in view of the fact that the only place to which it is native now lies outside "Europe"), the list may today seem to be simply a historical curiosity. But the "imperial authority," if only as an analogy, still lingers persuasively in the European imagination, and the other two items on Cattaneo's list have exercised and continue to exercise a profound and lasting, if often indirect influence over any possible understanding of what now constitutes "Europe."

Christianity—and more significantly the Christian intellectual legacy—remains a persistent, often submerged, and ceaselessly contested, but also inextricable component of whatever identity Europe might have possessed ever since the Roman Empire became a Christian state in the fourth century. By the seventeenth century, if not earlier, Christianity, for all its irreducible Asian origins and Hebraic foundations, had come to be looked upon as a resolutely European religion. "Jesus Christ, who is the way, the truth and the life," wrote the English propagandist for the settlement of America Samuel Purchas in 1625, "has long since given the Bill of Divorce to ingrateful Asia where he was born and of Africa, the place of his flight and refuge, and has become almost wholly European."[3]

Christianity has also been far more present in the slow construction of Europe since 1945 than the language of the treaties, which makes every effort to accommodate the substantial number of those of non-Christian origin who now have a claim to being European, would suggest. Despite the fact that, for centuries, Christianity had been by far the most divisive ideological force in the continent, it was seen by many of the earlier European federalists in broadly irenic terms, as a heritage which favored stability, equanimity, equality, and social justice for all—even for non-believers.

The Congress of the Hague ended with this claim:

> Believing that this true unity, [which] states the final resolution, even in the midst of our national, ideological and religious differences, consists of *a common heritage of Christian civilisation*, of spiritual and cultural values and a common loyalty to the fundamental rights of man, especially freedom of thought and expression.[4]

Three of the "Founding Fathers" of the EU—Schuman, Adenauer, and De Gasperi—were all practicing Catholics, and even spent some time together in a prayer retreat in a Benedictine Monastery on the Rhine—they were also all German-speaking—before signing the Treaty of Paris in 1951. ("The Triple Alliance of Adenauer, Schuman, and De Gasperi," quipped Vincent Auriol, the French president at the time, was "three tonsures beneath the same biretta."[5]) Schuman, in particular, was convinced that the rebuilding of the European community would only be possible "by forming a democratic model of governance which through reconciliation develops into a 'community of peoples' in freedom, equality, solidarity and peace, and which is deeply rooted in basic Christian values."[6] Little wonder that the origins of the future EU have been described, or derided, as being the creation of a "Christian Club." It is also significant that Mazzini, whose liberal democratic vision of the future Europe has had such a lasting, if indirect influence on all subsequent visions of a united Europe, was also profoundly convinced that this was to be the inescapable outcome of the "mission which God has entrusted to the races, to the families of Humanity."[7] There can also be no doubt that Christian Democracy, although now all but spent as a political movement, played a formative role in the creation of the Union.

However, the Schuman Plan itself, the Copenhagen Declaration on European Identity of 1973, and the preambles to all the subsequent treaties have all scrupulously avoided any direct reference to religion. All have simply repeated, with slightly different wording, the Copenhagen Declaration's identification of the "fundamental elements of the European Identity" in the highly generalized, uncontentious "principles of representative democracy, of the rule of law, of social justice—which is the ultimate goal of economic progress—and of respect for human rights."

This did not mean, however, that the recognition of some Christian influence, however disguised, on the subsequent formation of the European project was entirely suppressed. The most contentious struggle over the place of Christianity in what by then had been established as a strictly secular union occurred in 2003, when Valéry Giscard d'Estaing attempted to preface the "Treaty Establishing a European Constitution" with a far more elaborate preamble than that of any previous treaty. This began with a passage from the Greek historian Thucydides' account of Pericles' famous *Funeral Oration* of 431 BCE. "Our Constitution," claimed Pericles (in Giscard's version), "is called a democracy because power is in the hands not of a minority but of the whole people." This was to remind its readers of Europe's origins in classical Athens.[8] It then offered a somewhat long-winded summary of what Giscard took to be the principle features of a common European identity:

> Drawing inspiration from the cultural, religious and humanist inheritance of Europe, which, nourished by the civilizations of Greece and Rome, characterized by the spiritual impulse always present in its heritage, and later by the philosophical currents of the Enlightenment, has embedded within the life of society its perception of the central role of the human person and their inviolable and inalienable rights, and of respect for law.[9]

The allusion to Europe's "spiritual impulse" was immediately met with numerous demands for a direct and explicit reference to "the Christian heritage of Europe." These came, inevitably, from all the more obvious quarters: from the Irish, the Poles, the Hungarians, the Slovaks; from Gianfranco Fini, leader of Italy's now defunct neofascist *Movimento Sociale Italiano-Destra Nazionale*; and, of course, from Pope John Paul II, who feared that, "with the slow and steady advance of secularism," the "prestigious symbols of the Christian presence" risked "becoming a mere vestige of the past."[10] In a more thoughtful, yet more robustly censorious tone, his successor Benedict

XVI—who was, after all, a better theologian—castigated the "failure to mention Christian roots" in the constitution as nothing less than the expression "not of a superior tolerance that respects all cultures," but as "a dogmatism that believes itself in possession of the definitive knowledge of human reason, with the right to consider everything else merely as a stage in human history."[11] Giscard himself claimed later, in a more reconciliatory tone, that, in fact, "It would have been absolutely natural to make a clear reference to Europe's Christian origins, for it was clear, if you take Europe from the 6th to the 18th century, it was Christian...It's not a value judgement, it's not saying it's good or bad. It's just how it is."[12] The other members of the convention responsible for drafting the treaty had, however, prevented him from so doing, claiming that Europe was a secular society and that any direct reference to Christianity among its founding values, even if historically irrefutable, would alienate the substantial non-Christian, above all Muslim populations who now make up a small but significant and growing part of the population of Europe.

In the end, under pressure from all sides, the quotation from Thucydides was removed, much to the regret of the Greek delegation, and the preamble replaced by the far more anodyne, more familiar, and far less informative allusion to "the cultural, religious and humanist inheritance of Europe, from which have developed the universal values of the inviolable and inalienable rights of the human person, freedom, democracy, equality and the rule of law."

Since then, every attempt has been made at an official level to avoid any trace of Christianity and Christian symbols or generalized Christian values in any official document. At times this has been met with outrage, mostly from Catholic organizations and states from the former Soviet bloc eager to assert their hitherto repressed allegiances. When, for instance, in 2013 the Slovak government adorned the images of the national Saints Cyril and Methodius on their newly minted 2-euro commemorative coins with halos, the European Monetary and Economic Department of the European Commission, after having received protestations from a number of (unnamed) member states, asked politely that they be removed. The Slovak government complied without protest. The church, however, characterized this as "yet another attack on our common Christian heritage" by "the secular reformation of Europe...under the guise of religious neutrality." (The whole affair, inevitably also conjured up uncomfortable memories of the old communist regime which had banned the use of halos on the images of

Cyril and Methodius, and it fueled a populist claim that the EU was little more than Moscow in a new set of clothes.)

For all that the Union is truly committed to a respect for religious diversity, to the strictly secular status of its political institutions, and to the values which underpin them, it remains the case that to date all the member states, although themselves in fact now wholly secular, were originally, and had been for centuries, officially Christian. Europe as it is conceived today corresponds roughly, as the French political scientist Olivier Roy has pointed out, to the geographical extent of eleventh-century Latin Christendom.[13] It is also true that a vaguely allusive language which echoes a generalized understanding of an essentially Christian past still permeates much of the official language of the Union. The preamble to the "Charter of the Fundamental Rights of the European Union" of 2012, for instance, while it respects "the diversity of the cultures and traditions of the peoples of Europe," which are all implicitly secular ones, nevertheless remains "conscious of its *spiritual* and moral heritage," a heritage which can only ultimately be a Christian one.[14]

The older underlying tensions between Christianity the other religions which exist within Europe, in particular of course Islam, continue to exercise a powerful and largely unacknowledged influence on the shaping not only of the ever-evasive "European identity," but of the polices of the Union itself. This has been most obviously the case with the question of Turkey's eligibility for membership in the Union.[15]

Ever since the Treaty of Paris in 1856, when it was formally "admitted to participate in the advantages of the Public Law and System (Concert) of Europe," the Ottoman Empire had been tacitly accepted by the "Great Powers," legally and politically at least, as a part of some broad, vaguely conceived, conception of "Europe." When in 1923 the empire, now shorn of most of its non-Turkic populations, was replaced by the Republic of Turkey under the fiercely secularist, if hardly democratic Mustafa Kemal, known as "Atatürk," "Father of the Turks," it became in effect a modern European state, one which also—although in the contemporary calculation of "Europeanness" geography is rarely mentioned—shares a common border with Bulgaria and Greece. It has been a member of the Council of Europe since its creation in 1949, and it is, of course, also a member of NATO. There are those too who, despite the enduring conflict between Christendom and Islam, are prepared to argue, as the Swiss Islamic scholar Tariq Ramadan did in 2009, that "the Ottoman Empire shared and shaped the political and strategic future of the continent [of Europe]" and that "Islam is, de facto, a

European religion, culturally, politically and economically."[16] The first of these statements is unquestionably true. The second, however, is not.

Turkey's bid to join the EU has been persistently thwarted since it first applied for membership in what was then the EEC in 1987. The objections have for the most part been on the grounds that modern Turkey has consistently failed to meet "the Copenhagen criteria" for entry established by the Copenhagen European Council in 1993 and strengthened by the Madrid European Council in 1995. What was most frequently singled out was Turkey's generally poor record with regard to human rights and the rule of law, something which has further deteriorated since the accession to power of Recep Tayyip Erdoğan and his overtly Islamic Justice and Development Party in 2003. It is also hardly inconsequential—although rarely voiced as such, at least officially—that with a population of some seventy million, Turkey, if admitted, would become the Union's second most populous state. This would make it, on entry, the second most powerful in terms of voting power on the Council of Ministers and the second largest net recipient of the EU Budget. Many would have agreed with the senior German diplomat who, in 1993, declared bluntly that admitting Turkey into Europe "would dilute the EC's Europeanness," although few have expressed it so openly.[17] There is too the question of the "Turkish Republic of Northern Cyprus," a state created in 1974 by Turkish military intervention in a flagrant violation of international law and subsequently recognized by no state other than Turkey. After considering all these factors, the General Affairs Council of the EU decided in June 2018 that until Turkey's government was prepared to demonstrate greater commitment to the shared values of the other peoples of Europe as set out in the treaties, accession negotiations with Turkey were effectively frozen.

All of the arguments against membership have carefully avoided any direct discussion of the fact that, despite being constitutionally a secular democratic republic, Turkey remains a predominantly Muslim society, and under its present government is becoming increasingly so.[18] Whatever interpretation one gives to the sacred texts of Islam, they cannot be assumed to follow unquestioningly "the spiritual and moral heritage" which the other European states were presumed to possess. Islam, whatever else it might be, is certainly not "a European religion" and has not been since the Arabs were driven out of Spain in 1492 and the Ottomans out of Hungary in 1686. And as Olivier Roy has argued, any attempt at a purely theological dialogue between the two religions as a method of eliminating conflict has only ever, and could only ever, lead to an impasse. "Interfaith dialogue," although it may sound promising is, in fact, as pointless now as it was between the warring Christian sects in the sixteenth century. Potential conflicts between religious factions can only be resolved, as they were in Europe in 1648, by placing politics above religion, the state above the church or the mosque.[19]

Turkey's religious heritage has, however, never surfaced openly in any of the official objections to EU membership, precisely because religious *belief* as such has never played any significant role in the formation of the values espoused by the Union, nor, of course does in have any place in the thirty-five "Chapters of the *acquis*" (the heading under which entry will be considered) except to insist on the "right to freedom of thought, conscience and religion" and the right of every individual to change his or her religion at will—something which is, of course, denied by all monotheistic religions.

The long history of the struggle between Turkey's Ottoman predecessors and the Christian world has also rarely been mentioned as a possible reason for exclusion. Yet it might seem absurd even to imagine that the heir to the Ottoman Empire—the greatest threat to their existence the states of Europe have ever faced, "the present terror of the world," as the English historian Richard Knolles nicely and accurately called them in 1603, the "Perpetual Enemy" of Christendom—which for over three hundred years occupied so much of Eastern Europe should now be thought of as a potential European state.[20] Turkey had clearly played no part in the "spiritual and moral heritage" supposedly shared with the other formerly Christian nations of Europe. It also, except for a brief period of largely legal and military reform, known as the *Tanzimat* or "Reordering" under Sultan Abdülmecid I in the mid-nineteenth century, took no part in what is undeniably the principal source of all "European values": the European Enlightenment.

When the then French president Nicolas Sarkozy declared bluntly in 2007 that no matter what its outward appearances might be, geographically Turkey was simply not a part of Europe, and the idea of it joining the Union was unthinkable, it was clearly this history he had in mind. Ever since antiquity, the frontier between Europe and Asia, between the "West" and the "East," had been drawn at the Bosporus, the narrow stretch of water which connects the Black Sea to the Sea of Marmara. By this measure, 96 percent of Turkey's land mass technically lies in Asia. The unspoken assumption, however, is that "Europe" is that region of Paul Valéry's "Peninsula of Asia" which lives by the legacy of the values and assumptions about human identity and human freedom once embedded in the Greco-Judeo-Christian tradition.[21] The German existentialist philosopher Karl Jaspers made this point in 1946, when, in response to Valéry's image, he asked whether Europe was really only "a small peninsula which the Asiatic continent pushed out into the Atlantic Ocean? Or is it rather a spiritual principle in the peninsula, the principle of the West." "Christendom," he concluded, "is Europe."[22] It is also inescapably the case that for over a thousand years Europe and Christendom, the *orbis Christianus*, were thought of as synonymous. As late as 1761, such a relatively hostile witness as Jean-Jacques Rousseau was prepared to concede that "Europe, even now, is indebted more to Christianity than to any other influence for the union...which survives among her members."[23] It was a union he frequently abhorred, but from which he could never quite escape.

Giscard's allusion in 2009 to the "religious" inheritance of Europe, bracketed as it was in his text between the Greco-Roman "humanist" tradition and the Enlightenment, also made the point that the cosmopolitanism which was central to the European Enlightenment was inextricably associated with Christian universalism. The Enlightenment idea which now lies at the heart of the European Union's repeated insistence on the existence of an "identity" based not on ethnicity, or on a common religion, or on a common language, but upon a set of common goals and values was also obviously and exclusively a European phenomenon. It is shared only with Europe's former overseas settler populations and could never have arisen except in a broadly Christian world. The (final) preamble to the ill-fated constitution unhesitatingly makes the point that while "the inviolable and inalienable rights of the human person, freedom, democracy, equality and the rule of law" may now indeed be universal, their origins are to be found exclusively in "the cultural, religious and humanist inheritance of Europe."

The same is true of what the German sociologist Claus Offe has described as the "capacity and propensity for self-revision and *autocritique*," which is as much a European creation as capitalism or the steam engine. It is the consequence of what Kant intended by saying that to be "enlightened" meant making "use of one's own understanding without the guidance of another."[24] It meant thinking for oneself. And thinking for oneself inevitably meant casting a cold and critical eye on all that one's people, one's ethnos, one's society, or one's nation had, or claimed to have, achieved. And this, Offe claims, has "no parallel...in any of the non-European civilizations." Certainly none of the other great civilizations of the world; not China, Japan, India, or Turkey, much less Iran or the heirs of the Umayyad and Abbasid Caliphates, has shown any inclination to express doubts about the value of their historical pasts, much less to feel guilty or to apologize for them. It is also true, however, that, as Offe also says, "Europe has plentifully supplied itself with the 'real' objects of its self-critical normative scrutiny...from the Crusades to colonial rule to the Holocaust."[25] (Not, of course, that China and Turkey, Iran and Japan have not also an abundance of objects of potential "self-critical normative scrutiny," should they care to look for them.) Without this capacity to repudiate part of one's own history when that history has, in the case of the Crusades, colonial rule, and the Holocaust, come to seem morally reprehensible, no cohesion based on the acceptance of the supposedly universal values of inviolable and inalienable rights of the human person, freedom, democracy, equality, and the rule of law "would have been possible." What Jürgen Habermas rightly describes as the "egalitarian, individualistic universalism which continues to shape our normative self-understanding" is not the least of the achievements of modern Europe.[26] That said, autocritique can all too easily slip into a form of destructive self-hatred. What Albert Camus once called the "secular confessional" may all too often slide into little more than a form of self-flagellation which has more to do with the self-image of the flagellator than it has with any real recognition or any real regret for the crimes his or her culture is supposed to have committed. Since the 1960s, in many academic circles, and not only there, the "secular confessional" has sought to replace reasoned argument and rational inquiry with strident, generally ill-informed denunciation. And in all this what is entirely overlooked is any recognition that if Europe may justifiably be excoriated for having practised colonialism (although it was hardly alone in this), it was also responsible for bringing it to an end—albeit slowly and painfully, and perhaps in too many places incompletely; that if Europeans can rightly be denounced for having benefited massively from the enslavement of Africans (although they were not alone in that), they were also responsible for abolishing slavery. As the contemporary French *philosophe* Pascal Bruckner has written in a vivid denunciation of what he calls "Occidental masochism," these things constituted "a double advance in both civilization and law.... We should be proud of ourselves *despite* our crimes precisely because we have recognized and rejected them."[27]

This capacity, to recognize past crimes and not merely to denounce ourselves to the world for having committed them, but to attempt to do something to reduce their more damaging consequences, we owe broadly to the legacy of the Enlightenment. And the Enlightenment, for all its rejection of unexamined beliefs and of any kind of unchallenged religious faith, for all that it insisted that every individual must, in Kant's famous definition, abandon his "self-incurred minority" and make use of his "own understanding without the guidance of another"—including crucially his (or her) "pastor"—was the outcome of the secularization of the Stoic-Christian tradition.[28] At the same time, however, it is important to insist that this was indeed a true *secularization*, that no matter what the values and the arguments which the Christian-Stoic tradition might have transmitted to modern Europe, they did not carry with them a mythology or a system of belief. Europe, as Bruckner nicely observed, "is a desperately secular [*profane*] construction."[29] Pope John Paul II rightly summed this up in 2003, when he complained that "European culture gives the impression of 'silent apostasy' on the part of people who have all that they need and who live as if God does not exist."

The position of this transformed version of Christianity at the center of all attempts to construct a universal European identity in part explains the place that human rights now plays in the current account of European values. Today human rights have become the common currency of Western liberal democracies, in particular in their dealings with the non-Western world. The term "human right" is, however, a very recent one. It does not seem to have appeared before the 1940s, although "Rights of Man" had, of course, been in existence since 1789. But as the term came to be understood in the post-war period, its origins were to be found deeply embedded in the idea of a law of nature whose sources had been Stoic, then Christian. By transforming rights that were "natural" into ones that were exclusively "human" and thus irreproachably secular, it became possible to salvage with impunity some measure of an originally Christian universalism to which many forms of (European) cosmopolitanism are inextricably indebted.[30]

It is also the case that there exists within Europe the acceptance of a sharp and unquestionable division between the institutions of religion—and of the supposed laws of any deity—and those of the state. Ever since the Christian church, in the West at least (the situation with the Greek and Russian Orthodox Churches is more complex), lost the battle to transform the Roman Empire from a polytheistic, multicultural, and strictly secular polity into a theocracy, the laws by which all Europeans have lived their communal lives have been human, positive ones administered by the government of the state. It is indubitably true, as so many have insisted, that the values—or at least some of them (free speech has no place in any monotheistic religion)—which the European Union now professes to uphold are deeply embedded in a centuries-old Christian tradition. But that does nothing to invalidate them, for it is also the case that those values exist today as *rights* entirely because of the secular political, social, and above all *legal* system which enforces them.

II

This brings me to the last of Cattaneo's "unifying forces" for Europe: the Roman law. That law now, of course, occupies only a very small place in the legal systems of modern Europe; but it was the source of the conception of a universal, overarching transnational legal order which, although it now reaches far beyond Europe, is perhaps the most significant defining feature of the European Union. As Edmund Burke remarked in 1796, "The whole polity of Europe, and the economy of every country in Europe, has been derived from the same sources. . . . It was drawn from the old Germanic or Gothic customary [law] . . . improved and digested into system . . . by the Roman law."[31] However remote European community law and international law may now be from their origins, they would never have been possible without the great corpus of law composed shortly after the turn of the sixth century on the orders of the (Byzantine) Roman emperor Justinian and known as the *Corpus iuris civilis*—the Corpus of Civil Law. It was seen, as Aldo Schiavone has phrased it, as something apart, independent, "detached . . . from religion, morals, even politics," and that "separateness came to be regarded as a peculiar feature of the West," around which an "extraordinary ideological discourse quickly took shape . . . making it one of the underlying values of our [European] civilization."[32] Like the Roman Empire itself, the Union is essentially a legal creation. But it is also the case that neither Roman law nor EU law, dynamic, diverse, and innovative though it is, offers an easy route to a political, much less cultural or social collective identity.

There is, however, another way of conceiving the place of law in in the construction of identity which has proved to be immensely fruitful, and that is what Habermas has called, following Dolf Sternberger, the German political theorist and close associate of Karl Jaspers, "constitutional patriotism."[33] The project is to relocate the attachment to the nation, the *patria*, to a constitution, and the values which sustain it. In place of the ethnic nation or the imaginary kinship group constituted by the older understanding of the word *patria* comes an "entirely new, abstract and legally mediated form of social solidarity."[34]

It was, Sternberger believed in 1970, precisely this love of the *res publica*, of just laws and common liberties, that post-war Germany should attempt to revive. It was to be the final stage in the evolution of a way of thinking about the true identity of the nation which had begun with Aristotle's conception of the *politeia*.[35] For unlike the members of Plato's ideal city, the Aristotelian citizens had no need to be persuaded by a falsehood, noble or otherwise, into believing that they all belonged to one great family. For them the *polis* is not defined by its territory or by the men and women who live on it, but by its constitution (*politeia*), which is its form (*eidos*) or substance. If that changes, so does it. "For, since," in Aristotle's words,

> the state is a partnership, and is a partnership of citizens in a constitution, when the form of government changes, and becomes different, then it may be supposed that the state is no longer the same, just as a tragic differs from a comic chorus, although the members of both may be identical.[36]

The *patria* thus becomes a wholly intellectual, free-floating, imaginary—and an exclusively *juridical-political*—one. No mention is made of culture or religion or language or even of collective values beyond the reach of the constitution itself. It needs neither a family nor a location. It could be anywhere, among anyone where the laws and the constitution are worthy of devotion. And it was hoped that the participation by the citizens of individual states in the processes by which constitutions are created and evolve over time, "in the light," in Habermas's words, of each nation's "own national history," might indeed "take the place originally occupied by nationalism."[37]

Historically, this owes much to Montesquieu's and Kant's conception of republican patriotism which we encountered in Chapter 2. But as a possibly viable political ideal, Kant's "cosmopolitan right" had, as we saw, been swept aside in the nineteenth century, first by Mazzinian liberal nationalism and then by the rise of post-Hegelian nationalism, both of which, in their very different ways, replaced any notion of a *patriotic* constitution by the ideal of ethnically defined territory in which the nation and the state were now the focus of an unquestioning adherence. The German (Saxon) philosopher Johann Gottlieb Fichte, who came to be looked upon as the architect of German nationalism and champion of the idea of a superior German *Kultur*, dismissed what he called the "spirit of calm civic love [*bürgerliche Lieb*] for the constitution and the laws" as poor stuff limited to the "level of the understanding" and therefore devoid of passion, incapable of uniting a people, incapable of becoming the animating spirit of the nation. Only what Fichte called the "blazing flame of the higher love of the fatherland" could achieve that end, for that alone had the "undisputed right to command everyone who may be concerned, whether he wants to or not, to compel the objector, to jeopardise everything, even his own life."[38]

To this it has been objected that while the "spirit of calm civic love for the constitution and the laws" might indeed be the antithesis of the murderous nationalism of the kind of ethnic state imagined by Fichte, few, if any modern nations bear much resemblance to Fichte's ideal "fatherland." Most today are, in fact, pluralist, multicultural at least at some level, and broadly open to outside influences, something which makes them more capable, in Mazzini's image, of living harmoniously together with other nations; and many have, in fact, proven to be capable, as the steady process of European integration has shown, of sharing, at a number of different levels, a common existence.[39] It might also be objected that while constitutional patriotism may, indeed, have some appeal within a single state such as Germany, it can hardly be expected to work in a semi-federation of states with different cultures, different religions, different ethnicities, different languages, and different legal traditions. To this Habermas has replied that multicultural societies like Switzerland and the United States have, in fact, demonstrated that all that was necessary to bind them together, even through moments of extreme crisis, was the existence of a shared liberal political culture. For although it was true that, in what he called in 1990 "a future Federal Republic of European States," all existing laws would have to be interpreted from the "perspectives of different national traditions and histories," the legal *principles* sustaining the federal constitution would in all cases be the same.[40] What this meant was that each purely national tradition "must in each case be relativized by the perspectives of other traditions, and appropriated in such a manner that it can be brought into a transnational, Western European constitutional culture."

For constitutional patriotism to work at a European level, however, for it to be able to offer the kind of cohesion that the Roman law once arguably did, Europe would need what at the moment it still most conspicuously lacks: a constitution capable of giving some recognizable substance to the "Western European constitutional culture" and to which the would-be European constitutional patriot can make his or her attachment—however "reflective, critical, or sometimes even ambivalent" that might turn out in practice to be. Each EU treaty, every act of European unification, has stated the values for which Europe now stands. They are familiar enough to all and are sustained by a substantial and increasingly complex body of law. But as yet there is no document, no foundational act, capable of giving to those laws—opaque and largely invisible to all but EU lawyers—a political—even a cultural—substance. It may well be true, as the political theorist Jan-Werner Müller claims, that constitutional patriots are happy to look upon "their constitutional culture as always open and incomplete."[41] But even assuming this to be the case, it demands a great deal more intellectual invest-ment than most average citizens are willing (or able) to give it. Crucially, no "constitutional culture" without a constitution, since it must clearly be open to multiple and possibly competing interpretations, can offer an alternative focus of loyalty to the symbolic nation in the way that the US constitution does.

The European Court of Justice has claimed repeatedly that the EU trea-ties themselves add up to what it has called a "constitutional charter."[42] This resembles, if anything, the famously unwritten British constitution Montesquieu had so admired because it had created what he called a "mod-erated monarchy" by placing real limits upon the monarch's powers, but had made no attempt to establish a new or independent social order, and this, for Montesquieu, constituted the ideal *res publica*.[43] Edmund Burke in 1782, when arguing against any form of popular sovereignty, had praised the British constitution for being one "made by what is ten thousand times better than choice, it is made by the peculiar circumstances, occasions, tem-pers, dispositions, and moral, civil, and social habitudes of the people, which disclose themselves only in a long space of time."[44] Yet it is precisely for this reason that, in today's democratic environment, the British constitution exists, in the words of the Anglo-American political theorist Larry Siedentop, in a "kind of ideological vacuum." It is based not upon those inalienable rights which have become the defining feature of modern states, but on a set of agreements "between gentlemen." Its voice is "an essentially upper-class voice, ironic and private rather than assertive and public."[45] The European Court of Justice's "constitutional charter," although short on irony, could be said to be similarly private rather than public.

"Constitutional patriotism" may not require, as so many other forms of identity politics supposedly do, an enemy, an "other," or even a sentimen-tal return to a premodern attachment to the *patria* as the enlargement of a—now imaginary—kin group.[46] It does, however, demand, in Müller's words, that "citizens...reflect critically upon particular traditions and group identities in the name of shared universal principles."[47] And that, it might be objected, is a lot to ask of the citizens of any modern representative democracy, who, in the majority, will tend to take such matters for granted, to assume that the customs and values by which they live their lives are true and valid precisely because they are simply *theirs* and, therefore, in no need of "continuous civil self-interrogation." This certainly is the attitude of most of the citizens of the United States toward their constitution, which is symbolically the most heavily weighted of any. Yet as F. A. Hayek argued in 1960, for the very reason that the US constitution is the oldest surviving and had been "crystalized at so early a stage in the understanding of the meaning of a constitution," and because, furthermore, so little subsequent use has been made of "the emending power to embody in the written document the [lessons to be] learned" from subsequent experience—not to mention the vastly changed nature of every aspect of political, legal, and social reality since the late eighteenth century— "the unwritten parts are more important than the text."[48] Written constitutions, even if open to subsequent modifications and interpretation, as the American founders insisted the US constitution should indeed be, have a dangerous potential for becoming, as the US constitution has so often in painful reality become, a means of impeding or preventing change, when change is urgently needed.

It could also be argued that if, for the constitutional patriot, the *patria* is *not* to be understood as a place, a culture, a way of life, much less an ethnos or a race, then it can offer little with which to harness the loyalties and expectations—or even to arouse the interest—of those for whom a constitution is probably little more than a dimly understood highly technical term, and for whom anything which is "legally mediated" is entirely remote from their understanding and experience. It is also the case that associating the term "patriotism" with a constitution—though it might well have served to unite a severely fractured post-war Germany—can still not entirely disguise the disquieting militaristic and potentially ethnic and tribal implications of the term *patria*. As E. H. Carr pointed out in 1945, "It was...a 19th-century American democrat [Stephen Decatur Jr.] who coined the slogan 'My country right or wrong.'"[49] It could also be said that it was precisely a form of "constitutional patriotism"—with its insistence upon the inviolable sovereignty of that particular constitution—which has served as the principal ideological force behind Brexit.

What any possible "spirit of calm civic love for the constitution and the laws" of the European Union needs most urgently, as not only the Union itself but so many of the values for which it stands are under attack from populists on both the left and the right, is something powerful enough to douse the "blazing flame" of nationalism before it reduces us and all our best-meant efforts to cinders.

III

But what? Making Italians in 1861 or Greeks in 1830 or Germans in 1871—or for that matter Americans in 1789—proved to be a very hard task. It demanded not only a complete subjugation of the former subjects of old empires to their new communities; it also required that at least a sizable part of the population had some understanding of what Italy or Greece or Germany or the USA was beyond a new label for a new political and territorial space. In nearly every case there had, of course, been some common features to which the nationalists could make appeal: most obviously a common mutually intelligible language, or at least series of these, most often too a religion, and in the Greek, Italian, and German cases a shared, if often remote and partly imaginary, historical past. The links between classical Greece and modern Greece, between ancient Rome and modern Italy, between the Carolingian Empire and modern Germany were, in great part, a fabrication of canny nationalists; but they had—and in some quarters continue to have—immense symbolic value and coercive power.

Making Europeans has proved to be not only a far harder, but also an utterly different kind of task. True Europe, taken as whole, can lay claim to a shared and immensely rich common history, not least because every one of its current member states has at one time been part of the ancient Roman Empire. This might in itself offer a compelling imaginary, however fictionalized, something which has not been lost even on the popular imagination. (It might also, as I shall suggest, provide an analogy, a better means of understanding what the Union has become than any other currently available.) But for all that it is fanciful to suppose that this shared past might, in reality, become something which any individual can easily experience *as a European*—rather than as a Greek, an Italian, or a German. Europe—or at least a Europe capable of attracting the devotion, loyalty, trust, affection even, to anything like the degree that the nation has—still lacks even the specificity that Italy, or Germany, or Greece was believed to have in the nineteenth century.

The tacit assumption is that if the EU is to evolve into something other than the economic and administrative bloc it is currently so often perceived as being, then it has to do so by analogy with the nation. It has, in Habermas's words, to offer something which could "appeal more strongly to the [people's] hearts and minds than the dry idea of popular sovereignty and human rights" which is, in effect, all that any form of the modern democratic state has had to offer.[50] It has effectively to fabricate the illusion of a shared identity. Hence the sometimes initially encouraging, but ultimately inconsequential and dispiriting trappings of nationhood with which generations of well-meaning federalists have supplied the Union: the flag, the national day, the national anthem, all of which—with the exception of the flag—are symbols created specifically by nation states, and all of which suppose some measure of collective behavior. National anthems are intended to be sung by groups of citizens, or at least citizens are supposed to stand reverently by while they are being played. ("God Save the Queen" was still being played at the end of the film in some British cinemas into the 1970s, while the audience—or most of them—stood dutifully to attention.) But it is impossible to sing Beethoven's "Ode to Joy" because it has been deprived of Schiller's lyrics (which, in any case, make no allusion to Europe). National days—the fourteenth of July in France, the second of June in Italy, or the twelfth of October in Spain (which, perhaps significantly, commemorates Columbus's landfall in the Americas)—are all holidays and are all, at least nominally, occasions for a common celebration of a moment which most at least recognize to have been crucial in the creation of the modern nation. Europe Day, which, as we have seen, only celebrates the declaration of a treaty and of which very few have even heard, is neither of these things. Then there are the regular processes of identity re-enhancement from the national educational systems, which in most cases include instruction in national (and often openly nationalist) history and state propaganda to remind all citizens of who they are and what they owe to their place of origin. But there is still, even in the most Europhile of European states, very little such attention paid to the collective history of *Europe*. Julien Benda had urged his fellow European patriots (or nationalists) to replace one set of myths with another, one set of idols with another, for, he insisted, "you will only vanquish the nationalist passion with another passion."[51] But that, of course, is precisely what the European Union was never meant to do.

"No nation," as the Nobel Prize-winning Peruvian novelist and (briefly) politician Mario Vargas Llosa said in 1993, "has emerged by natural and spontaneous generation from an ethnic religious or cultural tradition. All have been born from political negotiation, invasion, imperialist intrigue, brute economic interest, and brute force combined with chance."[52] "Unity," as Ernest Renan phrased it "was always achieved brutally," which was why the "act of forgetting, I would even say, historical error is an essential factor in the creation of a nation."[53] The EU, in contrast, was not only not created in this manner, *out of* war internal or external. It was created *after* war to sustain a supposedly fragile peace and a common order of justice, and it has, as I have tried to show, been the outcome—or at least *an* outcome—however hazardous, of a long, deeply felt, carefully studied, patiently reflected-upon *project*. Indeed, one of the most powerful arguments for the creation of a single united European community that was neither a state *nor* a nation was precisely that a European federation or confederation was a means, perhaps the only means, of combating the murderous consequences of post-Hegelian, anti-liberal nationalism.[54] "Consolidating European unification," it was said during the controversy over the Maastricht Treaty, "is a modern way of limiting the damaging propensity of nations to become nationalist."[55] Or, as the Anglo-Romanian functionalist David Mitrany expressed it in 1949, "the problem of our time is how to break away from the modern lining up of authority with territory," but to do so in such a way "as not to do violence to national feeling."[56]

This Europe, therefore, can have no founding moment, no founding event, and the closest thing it has to a founding document, the Maastricht Treaty, as Habermas has rightly pointed out, lacks "the symbolic power which can only be generated by a political founding act."[57] It was, after all, rejected by what sour English Euroskeptics called "the plucky Danes"—an allusion to the Danish resistance to the Nazis—who voted against it in a national referendum, and it was only passed through the French National Assembly by the narrowest of margins.[58] Under such circumstances it is hardly surprising that there was no public occasion to mark its signature, nothing to match the signing of the Declaration of Independence or the Tennis Court Oath, no Jacques-Louis David, not even a John Trumbull, at hand to immortalize the moment. It offered, that is, no project of future liberation—none of the treaties has—and a promise of some future liberation, as Claus Offe has written, is the only "benefit . . . which has historically driven . . . the territorial reorganization of states."

All that the Treaty of Maastricht did was to transform, legally at least, a "community" into a "union" and, as we have seen, to provide the members of that union with a very restricted, highly ambiguous form of citizenship. At the same time, it carefully played down any suggestion that this union it had brought into being was or was intended ever to become a new federal or confederal state. It is hardly surprising, then, that it and all subsequent treaties have failed to create what Habermas has called a "pan-European political public sphere that all EU citizens can share."[59] That was perhaps the predicable outcome of Monnet's belief that a federal state could be created by stealth; that, one morning, the Europeans from the Mediterranean to the Urals would wake up and find themselves in something called the "United States of Europe"—and that they would then spontaneously rejoice in it.[60] Neither citizenship nor identity, however, can be fabricated by fiat—which is what the Maastricht Treaty in effect attempts to do. If the "United States of Europe" were ever to become a reality, then, like the United States of America, it would have to be created in full sight of all its would-be citizens and as a self-declared project *for* unification. That possibility, however, died at The Hague in 1948, and for all Monnet's sincerest hopes, nothing by way of an economic and administrative union has subsequently been capable of reviving it. For Monnet's integrationist method never provided an answer to the question of how a "European" people was to be made out of a collection of Germans, French, Spanish, Swedes, Danes, etc. How were they to be persuaded to adopt the identity of Lorimer's "international man"? How were they to be persuaded not, indeed, to abandon their old allegiances to their national states, but ultimately to adopt a new allegiance to a multistate confederation so that, as J. R. Seeley had insisted in 1871, they might, when called upon to do so, "prefer the Union to the State," "take up a completely new citizenship," and take as much pride "in calling [themselves] Europeans" as "Englishmen, Frenchmen, Germans."[61]

It is significant that the areas of Europe which have shown the highest degree of collective enthusiasm for the Union have been those—the Ukraine, Slovenia, Croatia—where the nation-state was previously very unstable or of very recent creation, and which had only very recently emerged from the most bitter and prolonged conflict within Europe itself since 1945. For the former satellites of the Soviet Union, membership, "invited not coerced," of the European Union did indeed offer a promise of further liberation from a restricted and penurious way of life inflicted by an oppressive and foreign ruler. The émigré Czech novelist Milan Kundera begins his essay "The Tragedy of Central Europe" by recalling that in 1956, shortly before his office was flattened by Soviet artillery fire, the director of the Hungarian News Agency sent a message to the entire world: "We are going to die for Hungary *and* for Europe."[62] It was a sentiment which survived until the crisis of 2007, and survives still among those in Hungary who continue valiantly to resist Viktor Orbán's attempts to transform their country into his "illiberal democracy."

The French veto in October 2019 on discussions over the entry into the EU of the recently renamed "North Macedonia" until any further enlargement of the Union had been reconsidered—a move denounced by Jean-Claude Juncker and Donald Tusk, presidents of the Commission and of the European Council, as a "historical error"—led the prime minster of North Macedonia, Zoran Zaev, to warn that this might result precisely in the resurgence of "nationalism and radicalism"—something which his fledgling nation would be unlikely to survive—and of the impending "open conflict inside the countries again . . . and open conflict between countries again."[63] The decision, he declared, had left him "breaking inside" and "destroyed personally and psychologically." There was no reason to doubt him. For similar reasons potentially secessionist states, Scotland, Catalonia, the (Spanish) Basque country, and Corsica, have turned to independent membership in the EU as the possible means of fulfilling their objectives. Even in such circumstances as these, however, the attachment can be precarious and short-lived, unless the Union fulfills most of what is expected of it, which, given that those expectations are inevitably very high, is hard to do in the condition in which it now is. As the Franco-Polish sociologist Georges Mink remarked on the thirtieth anniversary of the fall of the Berlin Wall, the populist elites of Poland and Hungary in particular, who had once seen membership in the Union as a way to escape from their previous dependence upon Moscow and as opening a route to a more prosperous, more modern world—who had indeed once be prepared to die *for Europe*—had now, after the economic crisis of 2007 and its aftermath, come to look upon the EU "as a sort of new Moscow, as a Franco-German coalition imposing diktats from Brussels and Strasbourg."[64] Persuading the citizens of long-established states with firmly embedded nationalist attachments to adopt a new form of belonging to a multicultural, multinational entity which is not intended to arouse anything resembling nationalist fervor is a still more daunting task.

It is also true that today, most peoples, even minorities, particularly in the long-established nation-states of which for the most part the EU is made up, have multiple, shared identities. As Daniel Cohn-Bendit (at the time—2012—co-president of the Greens/European Free Alliance in the European Parliament) and Guy Verhofstadt have indignantly argued, the whole discourse of identity, as far as modern Europe is concerned, is ultimately vacuous. There are, they believe, within Europe as many "identities as there are individuals," each is multifaceted rather than "uniform as the nationalists would have us believe." For each individual identifies himself or herself with reference to a collectivity, a community, a nationality, or an ethnic group depending on who or where they are. "In Edinburgh you're from Glasgow, in Manchester you're Scottish, in Berlin you're British, in America you're European."[65]

The trouble with this is that while it may well be true of the first three, it is only ever partly true, if true at all, of the fourth, because whereas the first three of these examples are forms of local attachment, the fourth is not. And this for modern Europe is precisely the problem. For whereas most forms of contemporary identity politics, when applied to political communities, add up to little more than a revised version of the old nationalism, the kind of identity now being sought for Europe is of a much less distinctive kind, if only because it quite clearly defies any easy association with place, language, religion, or even—except in the most generalized kind which will fall apart on closer examination—an ethnos. (It does not even always work at a national level. In 2007, with the succession of Nicholas Sarkozy to the presidency, France—"a nation," in the scathing observation of the classicist Marcel Detienne, "which is a part of Europe like all the others"—created a "Ministry of National Identity."[66] It was met with howls of protest and derision and silently dissolved three years later.)

Even assuming that a European identity does indeed exist—even assuming that it needs to exist—where is it now to be found? "Europe" may well carry some meaning as the embodiment of a set of values or of achievements. But as the German political scientist Thomas Risse has pointed out, it is "the EU [that] not only regulates the daily lives of individuals in various respects; it also constitutes 'Europe,' as a political and social space in people's beliefs and collective understandings."[67] Little wonder, then, that a great intellectual effort has been made to provide a compelling and comprehensive description of just what the European Union claims to be—or what it might eventually become. As it currently is, however, it remains conceptually and ideologically something of a "contested project," what the French Marxist Étienne Balibar has called "the name of an *unresolved political problem*" or, in the oft-repeated, offhand remark of the sometime president of the European Commission and French finance minister Jacques Delors, an "unidentified political object."[68]

In addition to these somewhat derogatory epithets, it has been called a "performance-based polity," a "regulatory state," a "form of government beyond the nation-state," an "intragovernmental organization," a "multilevel system of governance," an "international regime," and a "consociational state."[69]

It has also been suggested by Jan Zielonka, although he is not the first to make this analogy, that the EU, if it is not yet, might still become a "post-modern" version of a "neo-medieval empire," one that expands, on his account, through invitation and incentive, whose form of governance is "polycentric," and which governs in accordance with a shared body of laws and through bureaucratic (and democratic) institutions, not military might.[70] But what the English theorist of international relations Hedley Bull in the 1970s dubbed "new medievalism" takes no account of the fact that the medieval empires were all what have been called "composite monarchies" and that most were held together through dynastic alliance—"matrimonial imperialism," as one historian has called it.[71] They were, in other words, kin groupings closer to tribal federations than to modern or even postmodern empires. They were also hardly very inspiring and certainly did not "offer institutionalized forms of collaboration and identity."[72] No one could ever have claimed to be a citizen of the Holy Roman Empire (or even, except for the Free Imperial Knights, a *subject* of the emperor). The emperor's task was to mediate between local autocrats; it was not to protect the rights, such as they were, or the welfare of the peoples.[73] It also fails to offer much by way of encouragement for those "good Europeans" of Nietzsche's imagination, whom he urged "actively to work towards the amalgamation of all nations" to which they might attach themselves.[74]

One thing the EU clearly at present is not is what so many of the earlier champions of European unification hoped and supposed that it would become, namely a federal state; and given the checks—if not balances—inscribed in the Treaty of Lisbon, it is unlikely to become one, in the near future at least, without some very substantial transformation. For all that the Brexiters and their like have claimed airily that the EU had "robbed" them of their national sovereignty, the EU, as the American political scientist Andrew Moravcsik has pointed out, in fact exercises very few recognizable sovereign powers. It has only limited diplomatic, military, and policing capabilities. It does not provide social welfare, "the major activity of advanced industrial societies," for its citizens; and although EU law does impinge in often significant ways upon the domestic law of the member states, thanks to the policy of "subsidiarity" it does so only in very specific and limited cases. The Union has no single unified pension scheme.[75] It has, as the signatories of the "Manifesto for the Democratization of Europe" led by the highly visible French economist Thomas Piketty continue stridently to insist, no common system of taxation or of fiscal control capable, as they express it, of fulfilling the promise of the Treaty of Rome, to bring about an "equalization in the progress of conditions of life and work."[76]

It also has very few common health policies or common medical institutions, a failing which has proved to be potentially disastrous when it is confronted, as it is as I write, by a deadly and unpredicted pandemic of a hitherto unknown disease which is only poorly understood.

IV

In 2009 Claus Offe ironically and aptly described the relationship between the various member states of the EU as a "peaceful state of nature."[77] At that time, it could be said to have been the closest we have come in over three hundred years since the abbé de Saint-Pierre apparently coined the term to creating a functioning, sustainable "European Union." Over a decade later, however, the European state of nature has become increasingly less peaceful, more Hobbesian. Nasty and brutish in too many places—and many fear, and some hope, inevitably short. It has been buffeted by one crisis after another, most not or not directly of its own making. The financial crisis of 2007–8, which, in the words of the (resolutely pro-European) Nobel Prize-winning economist Joseph E. Stiglitz, "morphed almost seamlessly" into the awaited crisis of the euro and the austerity measures that followed, unleashed wave after wave of protests from the weaker economies of the member states, and in particular Greece, although these were directed more at Germany as the perceived master state within the Union, than at the Union itself.[78] (Indeed, as the American economist and another Nobel laureate Paul Krugman protested in July 2015, the German measures were a "grotesque betrayal of everything the European project was supposed to stand for."[79]) That same year a seemingly unstoppable flow of refugees from the war-torn regions of the Middle East and Africa began to pour across Europe's borders, provoking a very varied reception. There was outrage and often openly racist hostility on the immediate front line in Greece, Romania, Hungary, and even in Italy, while farther to the north the German Chancellor Angela Merkel's hotly contested and now largely abandoned policy of open borders had begun with the cry *Wir schaffen das!* ("We can do it"), and enthusiasts carrying placards reading "Refugees Welcome" and "No Person Is Illegal" crowded Vienna's Westbahnhof railway station to welcome the immigrants.

And then, after two years of acrimonious debate, on January 31, 2020, the United Kingdom, finally, after months of bitter and inconclusive wrangling, became the first state ever to leave the Union.

Brexit has inevitably cast a long shadow over the future of Europe. The markedly sharp response from the more Europhile of the leaders of Europe, in particular Emmanuel Macron, has been that, sad though this day was both for Europe and for Britain, it should serve to encourage the remaining twenty-seven states not only not to surrender so readily to their own populist minorities, but also to embark on a major revision of the policies and the structure of the Union, and to consider carefully what the future of the European project should now become.

In this way, Britain's exit may indeed bring about a new era in the history of European unification. It will almost certainly give pause to any other of the member states whose geopolitical positions and economies are very unlike and in some cases considerably weaker than Britain's from attempting anything similar. Yet it does not really offer much of a parallel to what might befall any other European state if it too were to secede. For if we look back over the history of the European project since it first emerged in the years following the defeat of Napoleon, Britain's exit looks like an event foreseen. Britain's relationship with the continent has always been, at best, an uneasy one. For Victor Hugo, Europe, after the final defeat of Napoleon, had found itself sandwiched between two great and sometimes friendly, more often hostile, but always menacing, imperial powers: Russia to the east and Britain to the west. It was an image which was to linger on until, after 1945, Russia was replaced by the Soviet Union and Great Britain by the United States.[80] When in 1963 and again in 1967, the French president Charles de Gaulle vetoed Britain's membership of the community (urged on apparently by Alexandre Kojève), he did so for some very sound economic reasons: the state of the pound, the country's reliance on "cheap food," her massive external debt. In large part, however, he did so because he believed that Britain would always place the "special relationship" with

the US before any possible commitment to Europe. Britain might, for economic reasons, have wished to be part of the Common Market; but it was
also clear that it wished to hang on to what still remained of its position as
an Atlantic power, and as the leader of the Commonwealth—and those
positions were clearly incompatible with being a major member of a potential confederal state.[81] "The nature, the structure, the very situation [conjunc-
ture]," declared de Gaulle, that are Britain's "differ profoundly from those of
the continentals." The majority of the British people looked upon the
Common Market simply as what its name misleadingly suggested that it was
and intended to remain—a trading block and an enlarged customs union—
and few Britons, outside the passionately vocal, but also shrinking number
of British federalists, had any commitment to, or any real understanding of,
the European project. Britain, said de Gaulle, would have to engineer, on its
own, "a radical transformation" before she would be able to "join the continental states." "Everything depends," he concluded, on whether Britain
"might manage to transform herself sufficiently to become part of the
European Community, without restriction, without reserve and preference
for anything whatsoever."[82]

When Britain, together with Ireland and Denmark, did finally join in
1973, the prime minister Edward Heath declared that his country had finally
"taken our rightful place in a truly United Europe." Britain, he now believed,
would "be able once again to play a worthy role in the world"; and he
orchestrated a two-week-long cultural festival, "Fanfare for Europe," to cel-
ebrate the event. The Queen attended a gala opening at the Royal Opera
House, conducted by Benjamin Britten and Colin Davis, and Herbert von
Karajan brought the Berlin Philharmonic to the Royal Albert Hall (to play
Beethoven's fourth and fifth symphonies). There was a televised service of
thanksgiving at Coventry Cathedral, famously rebuilt out of the rubble of
the Blitz, while a Festival of European Art displayed treasures from across the
continent. There was also a vintage car rally from London to Brussels, a
beauty contest won by the Dutch model Sylvia Kristel, rock concerts, and
a "friendly" football match between "the Three," made up of players from
Denmark, Ireland, and Britain, on one side, and "the Six," from the founder
members of the EEC, on the other. (The new members won by two goals
to nil.)

For all the noise, membership of the EEC was seen by most on both the
left and the right not, as in Heath's jubilant words, "a change so radical, a
revolution so quiet and yet so total, that it will go far beyond the programme

for a Parliament," but as a purely economic move carrying with it no real commitment to any greater union with the rest of Europe. The government's campaign during the referendum which followed in 1975 did little to threaten this illusion, and the result was the biggest mandate ever achieved in a national election. The Labour prime minister Harold Wilson told reporters triumphantly that the European debate was now closed. "Fourteen years of national argument," he proclaimed, "are over." But this was the first national referendum in British history, and as the referendum was an institution alien to the traditions of British representative democracy, it was declared by many (including the *Sun* newspaper, which was such a fervent supporter of the 2016 referendum) to be unconstitutional and was condemned by Margaret Thatcher, in her first major speech as Leader of the Opposition, as "a device of dictators and demagogues."[83] Few voters can have had any very clear idea of all that it implied and just what was at stake. When asked later why the British electorate had voted in favor of membership, Roy Jenkins, Labour Chancellor of the Exchequer between 1967 and 1970, and subsequently president of the European Commission, who had led the "In" campaign, tellingly replied that he supposed that it was because "they took the advice of the people they were used to following."[84] (It could be said that the precise opposite took place in 2016; but on that occasion, and in striking contrast with 1975, an overconfident government failed to offer very much by way of advice or guidance to a still more divided electorate.) Although it was obvious to many that membership in the community spelled the beginning of the end for the special economic relationship that Britain enjoyed with its former overseas colonies—the source of all that cheap food—few believed that it contained any significant political aspects or aspirations that might pose a real threat to UK sovereignty, something which ever since the rumblings in The Hague in 1948 had been of paramount concern for successive British governments.[85]

Britain has always been seen, in particular by the British themselves, as unique among European nations—partly for cultural reasons; partly because Britain is an island, culturally and politically proud of its insularity; partly because England (if not Britain) had developed a form of nationalism expressed as a sense of belonging to a territorial state before most of the other nations of Europe.[86] As Carl Schmitt said, while Britain was a part of Europe, it would never be *of* Europe. In 1930, Winston Churchill made much the same observation—echoing the words of Imogen, the ancient British Princess, heroine of Shakespeare's *Cymbeline*: "In the world's volume / Our Britain seems as of it, but not in it." "We are with Europe," said Churchill, "but not of it. We are linked but not compromised. We are interested and associated but not absorbed."[87] This led him to develop his three circles theory, which made the point with even greater emphasis. The circles were the British Commonwealth, the "English-Speaking World"— which meant primarily the United States—and a united Europe. As the only nation with a role to play in all three, Britain, in the future decolonized world, would, in Churchill's imagination, be able to retain her status as a world power, while not actually being one.[88] As this also makes clear, what most often divided Britain from her continental neighbors was the existence of its massive overseas empire and the strong ties which Britain has always maintained with its present or former overseas settler populations. (Her former empire, in particular in Africa, is also of great and lasting concern to France. But the French Empire was never as extensive, did not last so long, and has never occupied so prominent a place in the national imagination as Britain's.)

The central importance of the empire to Britain's conception of itself and of its continuing role in world politics has been a constant refrain. As the disgraced director general of the International Monetary Fund Dominque Strauss-Kahn wrote in April 2019, at the height of the Brexit crisis (under the somewhat ironic byline "I am a sad Brexiter"), while recognizing that British history was inextricably bound up with that of the continent and that the British shared at least some of the values which made up the EU—"the rights of man, culture as a means of emancipation, a durable model of development and a vision of the international order based upon multilateralism"—the British, he concluded, "heirs to a vast empire and the undisputed victors of two world wars, have never overcome the nationalism and the geopolitics which derive from it."[89]

The empire is, of course, no more, and the dominions have now all gone save in name only; but the lingering memory and the nostalgia for empire and the great-power status which accompanied them—the "nationalism and the geopolitics"—still survive, if sometimes only faintly, as reflected for instance in the historian Niall Ferguson's almost offhand remark that "the world we know today is in large measure the product of Britain's age of empire." Of course, he admits, that age is now well past, and "British imperialism was not without a blemish." However, the real question is "whether there could have been a less bloody path to modernity. Perhaps in theory there could have been. But in practice?" (a remark that raises so many questions of definition that it is difficult to know where to begin).[90] Add to this the conviction within Britain which seems to have arisen in the mid-nineteenth century that Europeans were obsessed by uniformity and insufficiently liberal by British standards. Add to this the fact that the country was the first European nation capable of creating, in a remarkably short space of time, a far-reaching welfare state system which demanded between 1945 and 1951 a 50 percent increase in public spending over the level of 1938. Add to this that Britain, unlike all the nations of the EU, has undergone no major constitutional change since 1832; and just as it did not, ultimately, suffer the humiliation of defeat in 1945, so it was not obliged to rethink, rebuild, and reconstruct its constitution, and with it its entire political identity, after World War II.[91] Add all of that together, and the outcome has been the emergence of a deeply entrenched, isolationist political culture which continues to look across the Atlantic more often than it does across the Channel.

Britain may be, in these and in many other respects, the exception among the nations of Europe. But Brexit itself, although perhaps a catastrophe waiting to happen, was only made possible by that wave of populism which, on the whole, has not in the past been a characteristic of British politics and which now has become very much a European, indeed, a worldwide phenomenon. It has been responsible for an unsteady rise across the entire European Union of xenophobic anti-European sentiments and the emergence or consolidation of far-right and sometimes far-left populist parties—on the right France's National Rally, Hungary's Fidesc ("Hungarian Civic Alliance"), Poland's PiS ("Law and Justice Party"), Italy's League and Five-Star Movement, Austria's Freedom Party, Germany's AfD, the Dutch Party for Freedom, the Danish People's Party, the Finns Party; and, on the left, "Unbowed France" (*La France insoumise*), Greece's Syriza, Spain's Podemos—the list goes on and on. All of these have been united in their endeavors in one way or another to dissolve, overthrow, abandon, or severely limit the powers of the Union.[92] Anti-Europeanism has indeed become, as the French political theorist Pierre Rosanvallon has observed, one of the "essential features" of European populism, since it gives to the populist message "a more modern and more easily acceptable tone to what is otherwise a traditional form of nationalism."[93]

More recently, in particular as the possibly deleterious consequences for Britain of Brexit have become more evident, parties such as the French National Rally and the AfD have declared that rather than leaving the Union and allowing their nations to drift away, increasingly impoverished and irrelevant, but "free," they would instead seek to create, in the words of the AfD, "a new European economic union" of their own.[94] There have also been still more aggressive, more alarming suggestions, especially from the prime minister and now virtual dictator of Hungary Viktor Orbán and Italy's former deputy prime minister Matteo Salvini, that the populists might instead be able to transform the Union from within into something more to their liking. "Twenty-seven years ago," declared Orbán, in a speech in July 2017, "here in Central Europe, we believed that Europe was our future; today we feel that we are the future of Europe"—a future to be made up of closely knit communities of fiercely Eurocentric nation-states, based on a vision, in Orbán's words "of our two-thousand-year Christian culture" and of the way to a "life beyond globalism." His was an image of a Europe closed in upon itself, white and autocratic, in which liberal democracy has become—as indeed it already has in Hungary and Poland—a mere shadow of respectability, a medieval Europe, backward-looking, and inevitably in a condition of semipermanent economic, cultural, and political decline, a thoroughly Putinized Europe. In 2011, Vladimir Putin too fantasized about a "Eurasian Union" with Russia at its center, a de facto empire made up of all those states deemed unfit to be members of the EU, and all those which he confidently expected would soon be exiting the EU. It was to be based not upon cooperation and "ever greater union," much less human rights and their like, but upon what Putin, like Orbán, calls "civilization." Eventually this "Eurasian Union" would overwhelm the European one in a larger, Russian-controlled, "Union of Europe," a "space between the Atlantic and the Pacific," from "Lisbon to Vladivostok."[95] It was to be Russia's very own, *Neuordnung Europas*. As Emmanuel Macron told a massed audience at the Sorbonne in Paris in September 2017, "we are indeed witnessing a European civil war"—or, at least, being threatened with one.[96] Two years later he warned that as the Union had been "founded on internal reconciliation," an objective which until very recently it seemed to have fulfilled, it had all but "forgotten the realities of the world." And those realities now called for interconnected efforts on the part of all the member states to reform and strengthen the Union, to ward off the efforts of the Orbáns and Putins and their allies within Western Europe itself. "It is up to you to decide," Macron went on, "whether Europe and the values of progress that it embodies are to be more than a passing episode in history."[97]

Populism has taken many different forms. All of these, however, share a common hostility to the existing institutions of government, which the populists claim are run by elites exclusively in their own interests rather than in the interests of an amorphous and ill-defined "people." Populists argue that that this people constitutes an often imaginary majority which is always sovereign. There can, therefore, be no place for minorities, no concept of a "loyal opposition"—on which representative democracy has been built—and most criticism is dismissed as "fake news." There is, therefore, no easily identifiable populist ideology and no easily identifiable populist policies—and indeed populists have supported a number of often startlingly contradictory political positions. All of this makes the EU, which has been constructed precisely out of governmental institutions in an attempt to harmonize under a single set of European values various political positions, particularly vulnerable.

The EU is also, of course, an international institution, and populists from Britain to the Philippines share a profound dislike and distrust of all the many forms of internationalism which currently exist, and a hatred—in particular after the financial crisis of 2007–8—of the international "experts" responsible for managing them. In Europe much of this political anger has been directed against the Union as the embodiment of a form of unaccountable technocratic globalism. Increasingly, it is claimed, decisions are made not by "us," the people of each national state, but by a nebulous unspecified international cosmopolitan "they" living for the most part in Brussels—a foreign city to all but the Belgians, and thus a site to all others of indifference and animosity. The claims made by most populists about the supposedly untrammeled power exercised by "Brussels" are, inevitably, inflated and distorted: the EU cannot abolish Christmas as one Brexiter claimed. Nor, as the British electorate was assured by the then prime minister Theresa May in January 2017, are the laws of the UK "interpreted by judges . . . in Luxembourg" instead of "in courts across this country." But in a condition of anxiety over other issues, presumed also to be the fault of Brussels—the economic crisis, the austerity measures imposed in the attempt to overcome it, and the supposed threat to jobs of continuing immigration—such claims fell on all-too-eager ears.

At the core of all this is the fear of what all populists rightly perceive to be the steady erosion of national sovereignty across all the democratic nations of the world. Sovereignty, as we have seen, lay at the core of that nationalism against which all the federalists, unionists, and various shades of internationalists have fought since at least 1918. The conception of sovereignty has been the defining feature of the modern state on which the old Westphalian order had been built. It had been the only way to counter what Thomas Hobbes in the mid-seventeenth century had seen as the prime source of "all such calamities as may be avoided by human industry," namely civil war, and "for the avoiding thereof Civil Government was ordained."[98] It alone had the power to place politics above religion.[99] And not only, of course, religion, which is no longer quite the divisive threat it had been in Hobbes's day. It was also, as Habermas has argued, a device which made the state capable both "of prevailing over *all* the competing powers within its borders and of asserting itself in the international arena as a competitor with equal standing"[100] (emphasis added). The creation of what, in the nineteenth century, Henry Maine called "*national* sovereignty" had, in this way, secured itself against civil conflict by creating a single undisputed source of power. But it had also necessarily involved what he called an "endeavor to climb within the region of an equal law"—that is, a domestic civil law—so as to escape from "the common law of the world."[101] Today, however, the "common law of the world" has reasserted itself, in the form of ever-increasing universalism, globalization, the proliferation of transnational agencies, modern trade mechanisms, modern technologies, modern systems of policing, even, or perhaps most particularly, modern warfare, and, of course, the information networks on which even the most isolated populations in the developed world rely, together with the conceptions of "international justice," "geo-governance," "global civil society," transnational conceptions such as "crimes against humanity," and such border-transgressing legal principles as "the responsibility to protect." In the face of all these, any idea of a strong version of national sovereignty along the Hobbesian lines the Brexiters and their likes have always claimed to be able to deliver has become increasingly impossible even to imagine.[102] It is also clearly the case that no modern state is a fully "unitary" one, and has not been for a very long time. National sovereignty, as it is frequently evoked today by those who fear its erosion, is largely a nineteenth-century concept. All modern democratic states are in practice "disaggregates"—to borrow a term from the American international lawyer and foreign policy analyst Anne-Marie Slaughter—in that the powers of government are divided up between a large number of different interconnected institutions, many of which share their authority with comparable institutions beyond the state.[103]

It is obvious too that in the world as it is today the resources at the disposal of any modern state, even if it attains the size of the United States or China, are insufficient to solve most of the problems with which the modern globalized world confronts it. Going it alone is not an option. Even the most diehard Brexiters only envisaged a move from the membership in a union over whose actions they had, albeit unknown to many of them, a very considerable degree of control, to the economic grasp of the USA over which, should it ever choose to embrace them, they will have next to none.[104]

"Sovereignty and sovereign states," wrote the great Scottish jurist and member of the European Parliament Neil MacCormick in 1993, "have been the passing phenomenon of a few centuries [and] their passing is by no means regrettable."[105] With hindsight it is clear that he was being unduly optimistic. In the EU as it is currently constituted, no one of the member states is, in MacCormick's words, "in a position such that all the power exercised internally in it, whether politically or legally, derives from purely internal sources." On the other hand, nor does the EU—or at least not yet—possess sufficient "plenitude of power" that it could be said to "resemble in itself a sovereign state or sovereign federation of states." The simple conclusion for MacCormick was that there are no longer any "sovereign states left within the European Community"; but then nor does there exist "a sovereign super-state, a sovereign Community." This does not, of course, mean that within their own realms of competence the nation-states of which the EU is composed do not exercise a very considerable degree of state sovereignty. Different legal systems can, pace Hobbes, Schmitt, et al., easily overlap and interact without, in MacCormick's words, "necessarily requiring that one be subordinate or hierarchically inferior to the other or to some third system."[106] Nor, of course, does it mean that the nations have ceased to exercise real influence at the social and cultural level. Nation-states are more than simply "artificial men," and even a Hobbesian sovereign cannot hope to survive for long in the modern world without a high degree of support from the educational, cultural, and emotive components which make up the society as a whole being. Distributing sovereignty between states or to supra-state institutions, which are, as is the EU, always made up of citizens of those same states—"sharing" in other words—does not, as the opponents of the EU persistently protest, diminish civil society in any way. As MacCormick also pointed out, this participation in a collective sovereignty meant that the sovereignty of each of the member states had not been lost, but instead "subjected to a process of division and combination internally, and hence in a way *enhanced externally*" (emphasis added). Such a division of sovereign power gives each state, as a member of the collective, a greater ability to manage its own place within the international arena to which it belongs than it could ever enjoy if it were wholly independent. The ability of each member state to participate in the Union's massive global power over trade and standards, consumer health and safety, environmental protection, and the like is a case in point. Brexiters boast how they will now no longer be subjected to the tiresome rules and regulations—the butt of many ill-informed jokes about the shape of bananas and the like—imposed by "Brussels." But, of course they will, to exactly the same degree that Google and Microsoft for instance, both of which have been the subject of EU antitrust suits, are. Only now, having regained their national sovereignty and surrendered the share they once had in the sovereignty of the Union, *they will have no control over the creation of any future regulations*.[107] Shared or divided, sovereignty is also perhaps the best means to protect the kind and degree of liberty the modern citizen has come to expect, the kind of liberty which most populists, most of the defenders of unalloyed national sovereignty would, once they themselves were in power, rapidly overthrow.[108]

Wherever Europe might ultimately be going, it is certainly not, for all the noise they make, in the direction chosen by the Le Pens, the Salvinis, the Orbáns, and their like. Which is not to say that they will not continue to do a great deal of damage as they slowly but inexorably fade away, nor that they might not well take the EU, as it is currently constituted, with them. And although the often observed parallels between today and the 1930s may often seem far-fetched, they do serve to remind us that, even when history seems to be on your side, things can always get a lot worse before they get any better.[109]

V

In this changing world of interlocking, overlapping shared sovereignties it makes sense to think of the EU itself as a new kind of post-sovereign international organization, one which, as the Franco-Greek-British—and wholly European—political theorist Kalypso Nicolaidis has suggested, is composed not of a single and for the time being at least illusory "European demos," but of a multiplicity of *demoi* who have come together to form, not a democracy but a "demoicracy" and that consequently the EU should be understood not as a state, even a confederal one, but as "a union of peoples who govern together but not as one." This, Nicolaidis believes, "holds the promise of escape from the tyranny of dichotomies which still dominate EU debates" by constituting a "third way" between the Scylla of the sovereigntists and the Charybdis of the federalists. But to be a demoi-cracy the Union "should remain an open-ended process of transformation which seeks to accommodate the tensions inherent in the pursuit of rad-ical mutual opening between separate peoples."[110] What this means in effect is that the member states share their sovereignty in much the same way that any transnational body has to, but that the Union itself becomes not a simple union of *states*, but instead a union of "peoples."

To compliment this general theory of democracy, Richard Bellamy has come up with the conception of the EU as an association of "republics"—a term which should be understood as describing a particular kind of citizen body, not a constitution—bound together in a relationship of reciprocal "non-domination"—a condition in which all citizens are free from "power imbalance, dependency and personal rule" to exercise their will in collabo-ration and deliberation with others. (It is, in short, the very antithesis of the Hobbesian state.) This, Bellamy argues, will be capable of delivering what he calls "statist cosmopolitanism."[111] Bellamy believes that democracies have good compelling reasons for cooperating with one another at the interstate level, but that this does not necessarily require any transfer of state sover-eignty, something which the historical record, brief though it is, would seem to bear out. This will be broadly true, however, only if the level of cooperation required is limited to those things, most of them economic, in which all the states have similar concerns. It clearly does not work when, as if often the case, their interests are in conflict at the all-important level of, for instance, immigration, military activities, or diplomacy, or, as has now seemingly become apparent, healthcare.

Both of these ways of conceiving the EU suggest that it is not suffering from any crisis, or at least not from any potentially lethal one. It may indeed harbor a great many internal dissidents, but if we take its overall conception to be that of multiple demoi governing together, it can be made to work to the satisfaction both of those who still cling to a belief in the possible exist-ence of some responsible version of national sovereignty, as Bellamy does, and for the more exacting demands of the "thick" cosmopolitans who would wish to see a complete devolution of sovereignty to the interstate level. Both Nicolaidis and Bellamy, however, fully recognize that for all their optimism, if the EU, as it is currently constituted, is to achieve these ends, it is in need of reform. It needs, for instance, a "banking union" and a "genuine European Monetary Fund."[112] It requires a constitutional overhaul, a reform of its governing institutions so as to remedy or address the "democratic deficit," and a coherent foreign policy. In the wake of the current COVID-19 pandemic it obviously requires a common policy on healthcare. If, however, it were to acquire all these things, it is not clear whether this would not, at least over time, bring the EU far closer to a federal state, which the concepts of both "demoicracy" and "statist cosmopolitanism" are seeking to replace.[113]

Both demoicracy and statist cosmopolitanism are attempts to redescribe—rather than suggestions as to how to transform—the Union, in the hope of being able to lay finally to rest the persistent federal ideal, and to raise up in its place the vision of a new kind of transnational society which would serve its citizens far better than the old state system has. They are both also, as Bellamy tacitly acknowledges, means of "saving the nation-state," which he, at least, also believes to be the only way to preserve true democracy and thus "non-domination" as it currently exists.[114] Neither Bellamy nor Nicolaidis has much to say about identity or social and political values beyond the latter's claim that demoicracy would be a more accurate reflection of "the deep texture of European history, law and politics" than any existing perception of the Union.[115] Neither also really addresses the question of how and on what terms each individual demos is supposed to govern together with all the rest—other, that is, than in a slightly extended version of the highly institutionalized manner in which they do so already, with a number of modifications and improvements, and in which ultimate sovereign power would still lie with the member states, not with the Union. Both are also committed to an open-ended notion of just where all this is going. On this account the Union becomes not a project—which suggests some definitive final goal—so much as a process, which like Kant's *Völkerbund* must always remain a condition of future time, "Ever closer union," in other words, means just that, never a true union, always an eternal becoming.[116]

Not everyone, of course, is quite so optimistic or so confident that redescription amounts to prescription. In the aftermath of the financial crisis of 2007–8, a species of gleeful doom has prevailed over much of the reflection on Europe, its possible future, and probable demise, punctuated by books with titles such as *After Europe*; *Is the EU Doomed?*; *What's Wrong with the European Union and How to Fix It*; and *The End of Europe*.[117] Some twenty years ago, at the beginning of the new millennium, the picture had looked very different. Then, Europe could be said, by the historian Tony Judt, to be "a paragon of the international virtues: a community of values and a system of inter-state relations, held up by Europeans and non-Europeans alike as an exemplar for all to emulate."[118] Back then the books had titles like *The European Dream: How Europe's Vision of the Future Is Quietly Eclipsing the American Dream*; *Why Europe Will Run the Twenty-First Century*; and *The United States of Europe: The New Superpower and the End of American Supremacy*.[119]

The beliefs implied by these titles were clearly overstated, and few really assumed that the Union would emerge as a global superpower in the course of the century. But the current wave of overeager pessimism is still more unwarranted. For all its obvious structural institutional shortcomings, for all that the Monnet method has failed to produce a coherent political project, there can be little doubt that the states of Europe have indubitably done far better, by any conceivable measure, since 1945 together than they would have done separately. Their economic performance has grown in ways which it is very unlikely that they would have achieved on their own. Even those, in particular Norway and Switzerland, which have chosen to stand alone have nevertheless benefited directly from the success, economic and social, of their neighbors and from their membership in the European Economic Area. In other respects too the Union has indeed become, as Jean Monnet predicted for it in 1947, a "civilian great power." Civility within the member states—the rise of the populists notwithstanding—has increased immeasurably. For the most part, in most regions, the states of Europe are fairer, juster, healthier (despite the present pandemic), more peaceful, more educated, more prosperous places than they were even forty years ago. Greater interaction between their populations and their cultures has made for far greater diversity—in the full meaning of that now much-abused term. The enlargement of the Union since the early nineties, described as its "most successful foreign policy instrument," has brought stability, prosperity, the rule of law, and liberal democracy to large areas of Europe which had little or no prior experience of these things; and while some of these, Hungary, Romania, and Poland in particular, may now be beginning to revert to their former selves, others, most notably Spain, Portugal, and Greece, have proved to be, despite all their economic difficulties, strong, committed, "good Europeans."

Greater social and geographical mobility in Europe, immigration both across the various European states and now increasingly from beyond them, have significantly altered the cultural and ethnic mix on which ethnic nationalism so heavily relies. The experience of movement, of interaction, and of cooperation, however limited it might be in some areas, for which the Union has been largely responsible, has also greatly lessened the substance and the persuasiveness of the old nationalism. As Stanley Hoffmann remarked over forty years ago, most European nationalism today is not "a daily plebiscite *for* something. It is...a daily routine," and what the nationalists have in effect created is the image of "a community based on habit rather than on common tasks, an identity that is received rather than shaped."[120] A more deeply entrenched, far more reactionary nationalism has emerged since then, but it is still the case that the Germans, the French, the Italians, the Dutch, the Swedes, the Danes, even the British have now a far closer affinity with each other than they had even a decade ago. In these respects, at least, the EU is surely, in Jan-Werner Müller's words, "arguably the most successful institutional experiment since the invention of the welfare state."[121] It is certainly no utopia, and we have far to go before the full range of social injustices are eliminated and the fully potential of the continent's immense human resources realized for the benefit of all its citizens. But certainly few people in human history have succeeded in creating a better place to live.

The Union also exercises another kind of soft power, which, as the Finish-American jurist Anu Bradford has argued in her remarkable book *The Brussels Effect* (significantly subtitled *How the European Union Rules the World*), is steadily transforming not only the states of Europe, but much of the globe. Ever since the 1990s, the EU has been playing an ever-increasing role in global governance by building "a European regulatory state" based upon a system of intergovernmental networks.[122] As the Monnet method had focused on the creation of a single market as a means toward ultimate federalization, the institutions of the EU, as they developed over time, had to ensure that they created standards that were enforceable across all the member states. It was these regulatory norms that the European Court of Justice and the General Court were created in large part to enforce. And it is, of course, these norms which the subsidiarity clause in the Maastricht Treaty describes as falling within "the exclusive competence of the Community." While ensuring that trade remains free, they have also ensured that it becomes honest and safe for both practitioners and beneficiaries. For, as the American economist Dani Rodrik succinctly puts it, "if you want markets to expand, you need governments to do the same." The need for the expansion of government, as the exercise of political and legal control over the activities of free citizens, is not, he added,

> just because governments are necessary to establish peace and security, protect property rights, enforce contracts, and manage the macro economy. It is also because they are needed to preserve the legitimacy of markets by protecting people from the risks and insecurities markets bring with them.[123]

He was speaking of national governments. But what applies to them applies with even greater force to the kind of multi-governance polity the EU has become, because, as Rodrik also points out, the larger the dependence on international trade, the greater the risks, and the greater the insecurities.

The EU's extensive regulatory measures—condemned as "environmental cultural imperialism" in the eyes of its predominantly US opponents—have also extended the EU's effective reach across the globe, since they allow the Union to regulate activities which, although they occur beyond its territorial borders, nevertheless have significant consequences for what happens within them, with regulations governing hazardous substances, electric waste, animal welfare, and above all climate change, in which Europe has emerged as the world leader. All these have resulted in the introduction of regulatory changes in countries over which the EU has no sovereign authority, thus making it an effective global economic power.[124] The "Green Deal" endorsed by the member states in December 2019, which aims to make Europe climate-neutral by 2050, will, if it can overcome the political and economic fallout of the COVID-19 pandemic, inevitably have a massive impact even on those "many international partners," who, in the measured words of the Commission, "do not share the same ambition as the EU."[125] In Warsaw on October 7, 2000, as the EU prepared to expand eastward, the then British prime minster Tony Blair declared that Europe, "a civilised continent united in defeating brutality and violence, a continent joined in its belief in social justice . . . whose vision of peace is matched by its vision of prosperity," was poised to become "a superpower, but not a superstate." And that, in the intervening twenty years, is precisely what it has become.[126]

The benefits which all of these aspects of the Union have brought to the populations of the member states—not to mention to the rest of the world—vary greatly from nation to nation, and are far more marked among the richer, better-educated sectors of the population than among the poorer, less well-educated (the people who gave us Brexit), more marked in the cities than in the countryside. It still, of course, lacks what Johann Caspar Bluntschli in 1895 described as "a new independent state personality, endowed with its own will and its own organs"; but succeeding generations are likely to come increasingly closer to being a European *people*, varying perhaps as little in their cultural assumptions and political and social aspirations between the citizens of the various member states as two centuries ago they did between the villages and parishes within a single nation.[127]

Whatever future political form it might evolve into—and it is clear that in the coming years, in the wake of first Brexit and now the COVID-19 pandemic, a great many changes will have to be made—the Union is still unlikely to be a federal or even a properly confederal state of the kind imagined by so many over the years since 1815. Nor is it likely to be the quasi-empire dominated by one European nation that Napoleon, Hugo, and Benda had in mind, still less the hegemonic state dreamed up by Hitler and Mussolini. It might seem to be closer to Carl Schmitt's *Grossraum* in that each of the European nations is possessed by the same political idea—in this case liberal democracy. But despite the geographical connotations of the word "Europe," neither ancient nor modern Europe has set itself many clear geographical boundaries of the kind which Schmitt's *Grossraum* demands. And it quite clearly is not dependent upon the presence of "a certain enemy in mind." For that same reason it cannot sensibly be described as what some Russians and some Chinese, in a bid to revitalize the imaginary of their old empires, have called a "civilizational state," for this too can only find expression in opposition to some "other," and in both the Russian and Chinese cases that "other" is precisely that congeries of Western liberal values that the EU claims as its own.[128]

The EU cannot, however, rely on economic power alone if it is to survive indefinitely into the future. It may, as Blair said, be a "superpower," but its power is indeed very "soft" and as such it is also vulnerable. If it is to remain fully intact, to continue to be an effective agent for global change, if it is to resist the damage which the populists within and its economic and political rivals without would inflict upon it, the Union will need some significant restructuring, which will probably have to go beyond those limited modifications suggested by Nicolaidis and Bellamy. There have been recent demands for the revival of the European Defence Force (although within the wider embrace of NATO), calls for a common fiscal policy, for, in Emmanuel Macron's words, "a common border force and a European asylum office," and for a "European Agency for the Protection of Democracies" to prevent cyberattacks on the electoral process.[129] There is now a commissioner for "Promoting Our European Way of Life" charged with launching a "European Rule of Law Mechanism" which will ultimately be responsible for revising security policies, creating stronger external borders, safeguarding rights, and, potentially most far-reaching of all, "creating a European area of justice by linking the different national legal systems."[130] As Bluntschli had seen in 1878, there should also be a European parliament with real legislative powers whose representatives would all be expected to vote in accordance with their individual political convictions and in the interests of Europe as whole rather than those of the nation from which they come.[131] Furthermore it should, as Thomas Piketty has argued, have direct control over a common budget and a common system of taxation.[132] In the Union as it is currently constituted the parliament plays only a secondary role in a system devised solely, in Piketty's words, "to regulate a very large market, and to reach agreements between governments. It was certainly not designed to create fiscal or social policies."[133] To bring about any of these changes, however, there would have of course to be a constitution. Nothing so fiercely totemic as that of the United States, but certainly more assured, more accessible, more legible, something more capable of *constituting* the basis for a true citizenship than the accumulated force of the treaties of unification.

The problem, however, is that these are all merely suggestions. From 1951 until 2009 there was the Monnet Plan. It moved by steady increments from treaty to treaty. Each step was never as carefully planned or executed as many might have hoped, and none, perhaps, has turned out exactly as originally expected. And although ever since Maastricht the larger objective, the "United States of Europe," has been less often spoken of, it remained obvious that this was still to be the final political goal, just as it had first been announced in 1950. Now, however, the Monnet method has come to a halt. Henceforth, the way forward can only be a truly political one. But to date no one seems to know which, and nobody, not even Emmanuel Macron, seems to be willing or able to take the first step.

VI

As we have seen, the EU has been described as many things and likened to many others, none of which, however suggestive, has been entirely satisfactory. Let me end, therefore, with yet another analogy. Today, although it is improbable that "the disintegration of the Union is one of the most likely outcomes" of the current crisis (or crises), as the Bulgarian political scientist and journalist Ivan Krastev confidently predicted in 2017, it is obvious that in its present form the EU is very far from secure.[134] It now seems unlikely that there will be, at least in the near future, further "exits" following Brexit, given the alarming precedent that that has already set. But the Union may yet disintegrate in other ways. The fact that the return to something like the old Westphalian tradition seems unimaginable, that Europe is highly unlikely to dissolve back into anything resembling the parts from which it was originally created, does not exclude the possibility that it might split into a western and an eastern half, or, to use the current language, into a "two-track Europe," leaving a shrunken western part, while most of Eastern Europe becomes a new *Mitteleuropa* under the sway of Russia's "civilizational state."

If something like that were to happen, then the EU—this "unprecedented, anti-imperial empire," as Timothy Garton Ash has nicely called it[135]— the first successful attempt to unite Europe since the ninth century, will have followed quite closely in the steps not of the Carolingian Empire or of the Holy Roman Empire, with which it has so often been compared, but of the predecessor of both, the ancient Roman Empire. And that empire, rather than its successor, may offer another way of imaging what a unified Europe might ultimately come to represent. The assumption that something like the Holy Roman Empire could serve as an illuminating analogy with the EU relied primarily on the fact that, like the Union, the Holy Roman Empire had acquired its territories by invitation and had no single source of sovereignty, the emperor himself being, as we have seen, merely a useful arbiter, a "first among equals." Its historic predecessor, by contrast, was deemed to have expanded through conquest and to have been dominated by a single sovereign who exercised unfettered control over a single source of law. This account is, broadly speaking, true of the Holy Roman Empire, at least before the accession of Charles V in 1519. It is not true, however, of the ancient Roman Empire, which, while it did, of course, possess a single source of sovereign authority—*imperium*—in the person of the emperor, was in fact a complex web of polities which were bound together not so much by the imperial authority itself as by an interconnected body of laws and administrations, some Roman, some not. It was, in effect, the supreme exercise in that shared sovereignty that the EU now practices.

True, most of the lands of which this world was composed had indeed originally been acquired by conquest or coercion rather than any form of

invitation. But by the end of the first century CE, this had become of relatively little importance to most of their inhabitants. What this vast *imperium*
had become by the time the Antonines took control in the middle of the
first century CE was a multiracial, multicultural, polytheistic polity governed
by a species of interstate law which also respected local law and custom. It
was dedicated to the preservation of peace—the celebrated *Pax Romana*—
and to a particular way of life, what the early Christian theologian Tertullian
called "Romanness" [*Romanitas*], which allowed all its various peoples the
right to pursue their own cultural preferences so long as these did not disrupt the good and tranquility of the whole. Within its borders, declared the
Greek orator Aelius Aristides on the occasion of the anniversary of the birth
of the Eternal City in the spring of 143 or 144 CE, "a clear and universal
freedom from all fear has been granted both to the world and to all who live
in it."[136] Aristides was perhaps being unduly sycophantic to his rulers. But
his views were widely shared. Rome was more than an empire. It was, as
Ernest Renan said of it in 1882, "a great association, a synonym for order,
peace, and civilization."[137] It was a society which, although it had always
looked to the city of Rome itself, the "mother" and the "prince" of cities,
had no fixed place, and in the mind of its citizens was destined one day to
gather all humanity into what Cicero called a single community "of gods
and men." In this way it depended, in practice, upon a process of reciproca-
tion and assimilation. As Cicero said of the imperial republic which he
served, "we could more truly have been titled a protectorate [*patrocinium*]
than an empire of the world."[138]

   It was, in short, a true cosmopolitan order. Of course, it clearly did not
always seem that way to all its citizens and subjects. It was, after all, a society
based on slave labor in which fathers had absolute authority over their
families and in which women were utterly subservient to their husbands.
Its emperor was indeed the supreme lawmaker who considered himself
to be "not bound by the law." And, of course, the celebrated *Pax Romana*
had not only been acquired through war, but was also sustained by war.
There is, of course, no parallel with any of this in any modern state. The
analogy with modern Europe, however, lies elsewhere, in the ideal of a single
legal order resting upon a single body of norms, even if those of ancient
Rome often bore very little resemblance to the ones characterized as the
basis of "Our European Way of Life." The crucial similarity between the two
is that Rome, like Europe today, did not describe itself in terms of geographical spaces, but in legal, political, and ethical ones. It was a vast interpersonal

culture. It had a law, the "law of peoples"—*ius gentium*—which linked its citizens to the populations which lay beyond its constantly shifting borders. It had achieved whatever political unity it possessed through the creation of a juridical union, and through this it had, ever since its mythical foundation, prided itself on its ability to assimilate new peoples into its midst.[139] "No one," enthused Aristides, "worthy of rule or trust remains an alien, but a civil community of the world has been established as a free republic under one, the best, ruler and teacher of order; and all come together as into a common civic center; in order to receive each man his due."[140]

Although the EU does currently set geographical limits to "Europe," these merely coincide with the national borders of its (now) twenty-seven member states. They are descriptive, not prescriptive. Membership is determined by citizenship—however indeterminate EU citizenship may currently be. The conditions for admission to the Union as set out in the "Copenhagen criteria" of 1993 are wholly tautological in that the only definition offered of a "European state" is that it respects "its [Europe's] common values and is committed to promoting them." Similarly, the thirty-five "Chapters of the *acquis*" do not impose any geographical or historical condition upon membership. As we have already seen, it has been precisely on these grounds that, until recently, Turkey has sought entry. In 1987, King Hassan II of Morocco applied for membership of what was then the EEC on the grounds that the French Protectorate between 1912 and 1956 had made of his county an "interpenetrated civilization" which now, despite being ethnically Arab and religiously Muslim, was "more European than Greece."[141] Hassan had perhaps understood the possible future significance of the Union better than many of its own statesmen. Europe is today, and always has been, a truly "interpenetrated civilization" which, like Rome in theory at least, might eventually come to embrace the entirety of the cosmos. It is, as Lucien Febvre said of it in 1944, "an expanse of territory, of ever-expanding territory."[142]

We have not yet come even close to anything akin to the world federation or world government envisaged by the League of Nations, or to Kant's "Federation of Peoples"; but it is entirely possible that the EU might well be the beginnings of such a process. For even if it is hard to imagine a future EU spreading, as the Roman world had, east into Turkey and south into Africa, it is possible to imagine similar interstate groupings—true "civilizational states," not merely old empires redescribed—growing up to replace the ramshackle, constantly dissolving nation-states of Africa and the Middle East, all of which were thrown together, some after 1919, others after the 1960s, in the image of the only state form then available, and one which has dismally failed to serve their purposes. As Anne-Marie Slaughter has written, the EU, while it may not be, nor perhaps is any longer intended to become, a federation, is a genuine "transgovermental system," which indeed makes it "such an extraordinary model for other regions of the world."[143]

It is here, perhaps, that the analogy with ancient Rome—and the lessons to be learned from it—becomes most compelling. For one of the principal weapons in the populist armory is the claim that it is only by re-establishing the borders between the European states that their cultural integrity can be preserved against the threat currently posed by immigration, or what has subsequently become, in effect, a *migration* of peoples unseen since the third century. If one of the consistent features of Europe over the centuries has been the ability of its peoples to resolve their differences when needed and to form alliances and leagues with one another, another was the perception that every people has an obligation to extend hospitality to those who require it. Ever since antiquity, within Europe, hospitality had been looked upon as a semi-sacred practice. (There is even a saying in Sanskrit that "The guest is god."[144]) Hospitality, said Kant, was the *right* that all persons possessed, as persons "to try to establish community with all and, to this end, to visit all regions of the world," for "all men are entitled to present themselves in the society of others by virtue of the right to communal possession of the earth's surface."[145]

But although such a conception of hospitality as a human duty offered a way of imaging the conditions required for a peaceful international community, it clearly also posed a serious threat to the idea of the state as it came to be conceived after the Treaty of Westphalia in 1648. Furthermore, the nation-state, as it emerged in the nineteenth century, although an artificial legal and political creation, an "imagined community," was believed to be rooted in a place, a culture, and a language. It was composed of a single people, however they were constituted. It had no place in its conception of itself for immigrants, and therefore little use for the ancient ideal of hospitality. Legitimate immigrants could only be refugees, persons who had no real choice but to leave their place of origin and who were expected to integrate, to "melt in." As the great Saxon jurist Samuel Pufendorf argued in 1672, although all states have a moral obligation to accept such refugees, it was only on their own terms. "Such persons," he concluded, "must recognize the established government of that country, and so adapt themselves to it so that they may be the source of no conspiracies and revolts."[146]

The same general principle—and thinking which underlies it—still applies today. A consistent effort is made to distinguish between "genuine" refugees—which in effect means those classified as such by the Geneva Convention Relating to the Status of Refugees of 1951—and those loosely referred to as "economic migrants," those who come to Europe not because they have to in order to survive, but because they are looking for a better life than they could hope for in their place of origin.[147] Many today, like the English political theorist David Miller, would argue, as Pufendorf would have, that the state can have no obligations toward this latter category. The distinction, however, can never be so simple. Miller himself is prepared to make an exception for those who have been described as "survival" migrants, those, that is, whose "rights cannot be secured so long as they remain in their countries of origin"—most obviously, of course, their basic human right to survival.[148] In recent years, the sheer numbers have begun to overwhelm even these nice distinctions; and most groups of migrants are now, in fact, generally lumped together as "mixed-flow."

The circumstances have also changed dramatically since the seventeenth century—indeed since 1951. Pufendorf was thinking of refugees from other European Christian states whose values, ways of life, and systems of law would all have been comparable to those of their host societies. Today, however, the refugees invariably come from very different kinds of societies, and most come from societies which once formed part of the wider orbit of the European world, many, although not all of them, former European colonies. From the early sixteenth century until well into the twentieth, many European nations had been *migrant* nations, sending out to their distant colonies all those of their citizens who had little prospect of success at home, a process described by the nineteenth-century colonial reformer Charles Buller with disgust, as "shoveling out your paupers to where they might die without shocking their betters with the sight and sound of their last agony."[149] Now, however, the direction of travel has been reversed.

Before the financial crisis of 2007–8, immigration was running at around 2–3 million per year. It then increased substantially, until peaking in 2016. Subsequently, it seems to have been significantly curtailed—largely by means at odds with the European Union's declared intent "in its relations with the wider world...to uphold and promote its values...and [to] contribute to...solidarity and mutual respect among peoples, free and fair trade, eradication of poverty and the protection of human rights."[150] But all of the current measures in place, in particular between Turkey and the EU, are at best uncertain and temporary. And even if the migration only continues at the present diminished rate, it cannot but change the nature of the continent. According to one prediction, in thirty years from now 20–25 percent of Europe's population could be of African origin, compared to a mere 1.5–2.0 percent in 2015.[151] Of course, like all predictions, this one will almost certainly turn out to be wrong. But while the numbers will probably be far lower, they could also be far greater, and no matter what they are, the impact on the cultures we call European cannot fail to be significant. In many areas of Europe, the steady flow of formerly colonized peoples from North Africa and the Indian subcontinent has already transformed small but significant regions of the continent, and there is little reason to suppose that it will not continue to do so.[152]

VII

This is not, however, the first time in the history of Europe that something like this has happened. From the third century CE waves of Germanic tribes—the Visigoths, the Ostrogoths, later to be joined by the Lombards—semi-nomadic tribesman from northern Europe, came to occupy huge swaths of what was then the Roman Empire of the West. They came not to conquer or to destroy—although they would eventually do both—but to be a part of it, to benefit from all that Roman culture had to offer: Roman political stability, and, above all perhaps, the Roman law, which was the most lastingly consequential of those institutions in which, in Edward Gibbon's words, "the nations of the empire insensibly melted away into the Roman name and people."[153] All of these things spoke a universal language which had, for centuries, persuaded non-Romans from Africa to Scotland to identify themselves with the empire.[154] As James Wilson observed in 1790, echoing Francis Bacon, while musing upon the possible future of the United States as the new Rome in the West, "it might be said, not that the Romans extended themselves over the whole globe, but that the inhabitants of the globe poured themselves upon the Romans."[155] As with Rome, he prophesied—correctly, as it turned out—so would it be with the United States, and so may it become for the new Europe. It was, in Bacon's words, "the securest method of extending an empire." It is also the surest method of securing any coalition of diverse peoples.[156]

In the fourth century, however, the Romans, who previously had prided themselves on their willingness to welcome outsiders into their midst (who, in Gibbons' words, had adopted "virtue and merit for their own wheresoever they were to be found, among slaves or strangers, enemies or barbarians"), now turned in upon themselves.[157] As Julien Benda remarked in 1933, Rome perished "when in defiance of the principle of extension with which it had nourished itself for centuries, it refused the Barbarians the right to enter its orbit."[158]

Like that Rome, modern Europe is a "persistent plurality of peoples," and if it is to avoid collapsing under populist pressure into some enclosed version of its former self, it will need, as the ancient Roman Empire had done, to engage with the populations who live within its borders to a far greater degree than it has succeeded in doing so far. For the peoples who have flooded into Europe from her former march lands and colonies in search of the better life that Europe has to offer cannot easily be "melted in." Even when they are willing to embrace the external trappings of their adopted country, they may never—or not easily, at least not for several generations—become fully German or French or Italian or Spanish or Danish, in part because of entrenched hostilities from their host countries, in part because they themselves tend, often in bewilderment or self-defense, to cling to the ways of life and beliefs they have carried with them, even when these are incompatible with those of the peoples among whom they have now chosen to live and frequently also at odds with their own personal interests. "Guest workers," as they were once called, while they may have been integrated economically, socially, and politically, still all too often find themselves looked upon as alien. The German journalist Ferda Ataman (whose parents came to Germany from Turkey) captured this in a recent (2019) book whose title says it all: *Ich bin von hier: Hört auf zu fragen!* ("I Am from Here: Stop Asking!"). In her own eyes, Ms. Ataman is obviously a "German." Many "ethnic" Germans, however, clearly do not agree. And many of her fellow former immigrant contemporaries, in so many instances precisely because of the hostilities they have encountered, remain stubbornly, angrily corralled within their own communities, even sometimes on to the second generation.[159] Both they and she would surely find it far more compelling to claim not "I am German," but "I am European."

The time has come for the member states of European Union to detach their specific historical and ethnic cultures from the political, legal, and ethical project which now sustains them all. Then, perhaps, subsequent generations of immigrants and the children of immigrants might well find in the very idea of *Europe* not only a place of greatly enhanced opportunities, but also one of refuge from their previous inward-looking, archaic, repressive, and restraining ways of life.[160] Women, in particular, who count among the largest number of victims, might chose to find in European law, in European political and social expectations—in precisely "Our European Values"—release from the constraints that the patriarchy placed upon them in those societies to which they originally belonged. Instead of being asked to exchange the narrow confines of their original communities for those of the frequently no less confining host communities— which is what integration is often reduced to—they would be free to abandon altogether the limitations imposed by community, *patria*, or nation. Then, perhaps, it might be possible for the many migrants who will continue to flow across Europe's borders to identify themselves as individuals not with Germany or France or Sweden, but simply with "Europe," much as the Gauls, the Britons, or the Dacians came eventually to see themselves as collective "Romans."

Alexandre Kojève had a similar intuition in 1945. "It is even possible," he wrote

> that it is in this unified Latino-African world, the Muslim problem (and perhaps the "colonial" problem in general) can one day be resolved. For . . . there is no reason to believe that, within a true Empire, this synthesis of opposites could not be freed of its internal contradictions, which are really irreducible *only with respect to purely national interests.*[161]

Kojève's concern had been with the need to integrate, politically and culturally, Muslim populations under French rule into his imaginary "Latin Empire" of the future. But what was said for that might now, perhaps, be said for the entirety of the EU.

"Hitherto, history has granted the empires that have come and gone but *one* appearance on the world stage," Jürgen Habermas wrote in 1990. "This is just as true of the modern states—Portugal, Spain, England, France, Russia—as it was for the empires of antiquity. By way of an exception, Europe as a whole is now being given a *second* chance." "But" he went on, "it will be able to make use of this opportunity not on the terms of its old-style power politics but only under the changed premises of a non-imperialist process of reaching understanding with, and learning from, other cultures."[162] Being a part of this Europe will demand of its adherents the conception of something unlike the older attachment to the *patria* or the nation. For the older ideals of nationalism and patriotism, both of which rested upon the idea that one could "love" a given place or collection of peoples, can, for obvious reasons, have little place in the kind of diverse society modern Europe is becoming. We do not need to *love* Europe. Nor should we be asked to, although we may, perhaps must, certainly like it, take pleasure in it, be saddened and angered by the corruption of its values or its cultures, the pollution of its air and waters, the graffiti on its walls. The nation-state borrowed the language, and the trappings—the hymns, the anthems, the banners, the oaths, and the slogans that went with them—from the older patriarchal society it hoped to have left behind in a misguided attempt to lend to its new imaginary political order a substance and the corresponding affective commitment it was believed to require. But it was a false move. Love is an emotion which exists only between individuals and within families. Loving nations has turned out, all too often, to be a murderous enterprise.

In 1745, in that notebook of reflections he called "My Thoughts," Montesquieu argued that because, as he said, he was "a man before I am a Frenchman, or rather because I am of necessity a man but only a Frenchman by chance":

> If I knew something useful to me, and harmful to my family, I would reject it from my mind. If I knew something useful to my family, and not to my country, I would try to forget it. If I knew of something useful to my country, and harmful to Europe, or useful to Europe and harmful to Mankind, I would look upon it as a crime.[163]

In this way we too, like Montesquieu, might retain the idea of an allegiance to a set of values or a way of life while shedding the militaristic, paternalistic overtones which still cling, however hard we might try to ignore them, to the word "patriotism."[164] No one here is being asked to *love*, or fight, or die. "Utility" and "harm" are the key terms. Some form of Montesquieu's conception of what that involves as a means of minimizing pain and providing the best possible condition for human life—which one may even indeed, if necessary, be asked to fight to preserve—is probably the best way to understand the possible benefits the future Europe might hold for all its citizens.

This is to say that some form of "constitutional patriotism" might well be possible at the level of Europe which would be impossible at the level of any of the nations of which it is composed.

To make this a reality, however, Europe will have to devise a more robust and compelling form of citizenship. For citizenship is the only means of creating a form of legal solidarity, and the only means of conferring upon the Union a lasting form of what Habermas has called a "secular source of *legitimation*."[165] Citizenship itself was, after all, a Roman imperial conception, intended precisely to bring together myriad peoples who had very little else in common but their place within the empire; no shared culture, no single religion, nothing in effect but an adherence to a common set of laws and aspirations. (The fact that it was also a device for levying taxes on what Gibbon called "reluctant provincials" does not alter the force of the concept.)[166] At the present moment, however, all that the EU citizen is offered is something akin to membership of an international corporation, something which really only applies to the citizens of the member states "in moving and trading between them." Just as, for instance, every member state insists on taxing all residents no matter what their national citizenship, so they should be bound to allow every resident not only to benefit from its health and welfare provisions but also to vote in elections, both local and national, and to run for public office. For if we discard the rituals and trumperies of citizenship, the oaths and swearing before the flag, and all those other trappings of the old nationalism, citizenship amounts to nothing more than a number of reciprocal obligations and commitments. European citizenship should indeed *count*. And it should, as the European Court has so often insisted it should, in the last appeal trump the demand imposed by the member states. It should, in short, be a true *transnational* citizenship, and it should be underpinned by an enforceable constitution—not, in Edmund Burke's memorable phrase, a "vestment which accommodates itself to the body," but instead one truly capable of creating a "body politic."

This might bring Europe far closer to the vision of "a community of others" or "persistent plurality of peoples." To do that, however, it can only ever be in a perpetual state of becoming. The catchphrase "ever greater union" will mean just that, "ever *greater* union"—with no specific limit set upon its possible growth or on its capacity to change.[167]

As Karl Jaspers put it in 1946, if Europe were to describe its "character" as "the impulse to freedom, as real history, as the source of universal knowledge," this could only "signify Europe's fundamental imperfectibility. For freedom, history, and knowledge never reach their goal; thus Europe is not complete, and thus it is still to appear what we, from our basic life, can be."[168] This, it is true, might be said of all political systems, at least in the West. Since their citizens live in time, so must the societies to which they belong. Their health and survival depend upon it. Were they to cease to evolve, were they to come to believe that they have reached some level of perfection, they would surely begin to decay and finally collapse.[169] Freedom, as Karl Jaspers said, "keeps Europeans in unrest and movement."[170]

From the beginning and at almost every significant moment of its creation and recreation, in 1815, in 1919, in 1950, the European project has been an attempt to find a means of putting an end to warfare within Europe and a way of containing and eventually of overcoming "the damaging propensity of nations to become nationalist," and, in the process, of fulfilling, however imperfectly, Giuseppe Mazzini's vision of "Young Europe" as a transnational "family" of nations living peacefully together in the ecumenical pursuit of a common body of political objectives and governed by a single, if diverse, order of justice. It will be the eventual realization of Kojève's "true Empire."

Now, however, is not the time for irenic complacency. For precisely because of its undeniable success and its economic influence, Europe can ill afford to adhere too unwaveringly to its long-declared ambition for an entirely tranquil, amicable relationship with the world beyond its borders, which, in the words of the *Declaration on European Identity* of 1973, is "not directed against anyone, nor is it inspired by a desire for power."[171] For, threatened by an aggressive and subversive Russia and the ruthlessly expansionist economic power of China, it faces radical diminution if it does not.[172] As Emmanuel Macron told the French people on the evening of June 14, 2020, echoing, consciously or not, the remarks of Maurice Faure fifty-three years earlier, the response to the COVID-19 pandemic might now usher in

> a new phase in our European adventure, and the consolidation of an independent Europe which will now equip itself with the means to assert its identity, its culture, its individuality in the face of China, the United States, and the disorder which we are experiencing across the globe. It will be a stronger, more united, more authoritative Europe.[173]

Now it depends on us—all of us—to ensure that this does indeed happen. Europe may have been given a second chance. It is unlikely that we will be given a third.

Notes

INTRODUCTION

1. Quoted in John Hale, *The Civilization of Europe in the Renaissance* (London: Harper Collins, 1993), 3.
2. See Chapter 4, pp. 160–1.
3. Quoted in Larry Wolff, *Inventing Eastern Europe: The Map of Civilization on the Mind of the Enlightenment* (Stanford, CA: Stanford University Press, 1994), 41.
4. Lucien Febvre, *L'Europe: Genèse d'une civilisation: Cours professé au Collège de France en 1944–1945* (Paris: Perrin, 1999), 132–3.
5. See pp. 312–13.
6. Edmund Gibbon, "General Observations on the Fall of the Roman Empire in the West," in *The History of the Decline and Fall of the Roman Empire*, vol. 2, ed. David Womersley (London: Penguin Books, 1995), 511.
7. Charles de Secondat, baron de Montesquieu, *Pensée*, no. 318, in *Pensées; Le Spicilège*, ed. Louis Desgraves (Paris: Robert Laffont, 1991), 281.
8. Edmund Burke, "First Letter on a Regicide Peace," ed. R. B. McDowell, in *The Writings and Speeches of Edmund Burke*, vol. 9, ed. Paul Langford (Oxford: Oxford University Press, 1981–91), 250.
9. Johann Gottfried Herder, *Outlines of a Philosophy of the History of Man* [*Ideen zur Philosophie der Geschichte der Menschheit*], ed. David G. Payne, trans. T. O. Churchill (New York: Bergman Publishers, 2016), 418. Emphasis original. I would like to thank Roey Reichert for drawing my attention to this passage.
10. Aldo Schiavone, *The Invention of Law in the West*, trans. Jeremy Carden and Antony Shugar (Cambridge, MA: Harvard University Press, 2012), 11–12.
11. Strabo, *Geography* 2.5.26.
12. Gibbon, *Decline and Fall*, vol. 1, 413.
13. Febvre, *L'Europe*, 38.
14. Johann Gottfried Herder, *Another Philosophy of History for the Education of Mankind* [*Auch eine Philosophie der Geschichte zur Bildung der Menschheit*] [1774], in *Another Philosophy of History and Selected Political Writings* ed. Ioannis D. Evrigenis and Daniel Pellerin (Indianapolis, IN, and Cambridge: Hackett, 2004), 23.
15. Gibbon, *Decline and Fall*, vol. 1, 107.
16. Gibbon, *Decline and Fall*, vol. 1, 103.
17. Herder, *Another Philosophy of History for the Education of Mankind*, 23–4; Gibbon, *Decline and Fall*, vol. 1, 28–9. Emphasis original.

18. Gibbon, *Decline and Fall*, vol. 1, 107. See also the comments by J. G. A. Pocock, *Barbarism and Religion*, vol. 3 (Cambridge: Cambridge University Press, 2003), 447.

19. Francis Bacon, *Advancement of Learning* [1605], ed. Joseph Devey (New York: P. F. Collier and Son, 1901), 390–1. The image subsequently became a popular one. See pp. 153, 309.

20. Cicero, *De Officiis*, II. 27. See p. 305.

21. *De Republica* III, 35.

22. David Hume, "Of the Populousness of Ancient Nations", in *Essays: Moral, Political, and Literary*, ed. Eugene F. Miller (Indianapolis, IN: Liberty Fund, 1985), 383.

23. For the history of the attempt to "conquer" peace as a central part of the processes of European integration, see the brilliant and comprehensive account by Stella Ghervas, *Conquering Peace: From the Enlightenment to the European Union* (Cambridge, MA: Harvard University Press, 2021).

24. On this, see the pioneering study by Donald Kelley, *The Beginning of Ideology: Consciousness and Society in the French Reformation* (Cambridge: Cambridge University Press, 1981).

25. Quoted in Paul Hazard, *La Pensée européene du XVIIIᵉ siècle* (Paris: Libraire Arthème Fayard, 1963), 395.

26. See pp. 126–8.

27. Peter Schroder, *Trust in Early-Modern International Political Thought, 1598–1713* (Cambridge: Cambridge University Press, 2017), 5–68.

28. Éméric Crucé, *Le Nouveau Cynée ou Discours d'état représentant les occasions et moyens d'établir une paix générale et liberté du commerce par tout le monde*, ed. Astrid Guillaume (Rennes: Presses Universitaires de Rennes, 2004).

29. Jeremy Bentham, *Principles of International Law*, in *The Works of Jeremy Bentham*, 11 vols., ed. John Bowring (Edinburgh, 1843), 11, 546, 557. For selections from all of these, see Esref Asku, ed., *Early Notions of Global Governance: Selected Eighteenth-Century Proposals for "Perpetual Peace"* (Cardiff: University of Wales Press, 2008).

30. See Ghervas, *Conquering Peace*, 51–6.

31. Voltaire, *De la paix perpétuelle par le docteur Goodheart* (Geneva, 1769).

32. Gottfried Wilhelm Leibniz, "On the Works of the Abbé de Saint-Pierre" (1715), in *The Political Writings of Leibniz*, ed. Patrick Riley (Cambridge: Cambridge University Press 1972), 183.

33. Jean-Jacques Rousseau, "Jugement sur le projet de paix perpétuelle," in *Œuvres complètes*, vol. 3, ed. Bernard Gagnebin and Marcel Raymond (Paris: Gallimard, Bibliothèque de la Pléiade, 1959–95), 591.

34. Rousseau, "Jugement sur le projet de paix perpétuelle," in *Œuvres complètes*, 394–600.

35. Charles-Irénée Castel, abbé de Saint-Pierre, *Projet pour rendre la paix perpétuelle en Europe* (Paris: Fayard, 1986), 22–3.

36. Immanuel Kant, *Toward Perpetual Peace*, in *Practical Philosophy*, ed. and trans. Mary J. Gregor (Cambridge: Cambridge University Press, 1996), 317. Emphasis original.

37. Immanuel Kant, *Idea for a Universal History with Cosmopolitan Aim*, in *Anthropology, History and Education*, ed. Günter Zöller and Robert B. Louden (Cambridge:

Cambridge University Press, 2007), 114–15; see also Immanuel Kant, "On the Common Saying: 'This may be true in theory, but it is of no use in practice,'" in *Practical Philosophy*, 309. On the arguments of Saint-Pierre's *Projet* and its relationship to Kant's *Toward Perpetual Peace*, see Massimo Mori, *La pace e la ragione: Kant e le relazioni internazionali: Diritto, politica, storia* (Bologna: Il Mulino, 2004), 23–35.

38. Immanuel Kant, "Kant on the Metaphysics of Morals: Vigilantius' lecture notes," in *Lectures on Ethics*, ed. Peter Heath and J. B. Schneewind (Cambridge: Cambridge University Press, 1997), 339.

39. Rousseau, "Jugement," in *Œuvres complètes*, vol. 3, 595.

40. Kant, *Toward Perpetual Peace*, in *Practical Philosophy*, 327.

41. Kant, *Toward Perpetual Peace*, in *Practical Philosophy*, 323 n. See also Arthur Ripstein, *Force and Freedom: Kant's Legal and Political Philosophy* (Cambridge, MA: Harvard University Press, 2009), 182–231.

42. Kant, *The Metaphysics of Morals*, in *Practical Philosophy*, 481, and "On the Common Saying," in *Practical Philosophy*, 296–7. Emphasis original.

43. Kant, *The Metaphysics of Morals*, in *Practical Philosophy*, 584.

44. Kant, *Toward Perpetual Peace*, in *Practical Philosophy*, 335.

45. Kant, *Toward Perpetual Peace*, in *Practical Philosophy*, 323–4.

46. For this reason, Kant has frequently been cited as one of the inspirations behind democratic peace theory—the claim that democracies do not go to war against each other. See Zeev Maôz and Bruce Russett, "Normative and Structural Causes of Democratic Peace, 1946–1986," *American Political Science Review* 87 (1993), 624–38; and Otfried Höffe, *Kant's Cosmopolitan Theory of Law and Peace*, trans. Alexandra Newton (Cambridge: Cambridge University Press, 2006), 177–81.

47. On Kant's often contradictory uses of these terms, see Andrew Hurrell, "Kant and the Kantian Paradigm in International Relations," *Review of International Studies* 16 (1990), 183–205, and Mori, *La pace e la ragione*, 103–14.

48. Kant, *Idea for a Universal History with a Cosmopolitan Aim*, in *Anthropology, History and Education*, 114.

49. Kant, *Toward Perpetual Peace*, in *Practical Philosophy*, 336.

50. On Kant's three categories of *lex*, see Sharon B. Byrd and Joachim Hruschka, "Lex iusti, lex iuridica und lex iustitiae in Kants *Rechtslehre*," *Archiv für Rechts- und Sozialphilosophie*, 91 (2005), 484–500.

51. Immanuel Kant, *Critique of Pure Reason*, ed. and trans. Paul Guyer and Allen W. Wood (Cambridge: Cambridge University Press, 1998), 397. Cf. Immanuel Kant, *The Conflict of the Faculties*, in *Religion and Rational Theology*, ed. and trans. Allen W. Wood and George di Giovanni (Cambridge: Cambridge University Press, 1996), 307.

52. Kant, *Conflict of the Faculties*, in *Religion and Rational Theology*, 297.

53. See Pauline Kleingeld, "Approaching Perpetual Peace: Kant's Defence of a League of States and his Ideal of a World Federation," *European Journal of Philosophy* 12 (2004), 304–25. Emphasis original.

54. Kant, *Toward Perpetual Peace*, in *Practical Philosophy*, 337.

55. Kant, *Anthropology from a Pragmatic Point of View*, in *Anthropology, History, and Education*, 419. Emphasis original.

56. Kant, *Toward Perpetual Peace*, in *Practical Philosophy*, 329–331.

57. Quoted in Jeanne Morefield, *Covenants without Sword: Idealist Liberalism and the Spirit of Empire* (Princeton, NJ: Princeton University Press, 2005), 99. On Zimmern's role in the creation of the League of Nations and subsequently of the United Nations, see Mark Mazower, *No Enchanted Palace: The End of Empire and the Ideological Origins of the United Nations* (Princeton, NJ: Princeton University Press, 2009), 66–103.

58. Kant, *The Metaphysics of Morals*, in *Practical Philosophy*, 488. In the next paragraph, however, he denies that the league can be a federation since it is "only a voluntary coalition of different states which can be dissolved at any time," whereas as federation like the United States is "based on a constitution and can therefore not be dissolved."

59. Marie-Jean-Antoine-Nicolas de Caritat, marquis de Condorcet, *Esquisse d'un tableau historique des progrès de l'esprit humain*, ed. Alain Pons (Paris: Flammarion, 1988), 288.

60. Kant, *Conflict of the Faculties*, in *Religion and Rational Theology*, 303.

61. Condorcet, *Esquisse*, 236.

62. Kant, *The Metaphysics of Morals*, in in *Practical Philosophy*, 481. For a more detailed account of Kant's views on revolution and what he called the "law of continuity" (*lex continuo*), see my *The Enlightenment and Why It Still Matters*. (Oxford: Oxford University Press, 2013), 309–11.

I. REMAKING THE GREAT EUROPEAN FAMILY

1. Emmanuel de Las Cases, *Mémorial de Sainte Hélène ou journal où se trouve consigné, jour par jour, ce qu'a dit et fait Napoléon durant dix-huit mois*, vol. 1 (Paris, 1824), 417.

2. Las Cases, *Mémorial*, vol. 1, 417.

3. François René de Chateaubriand, *Mémoires d'outre-tombe*, vol. 1, ed. Maurice Levaillant and Georges Moulinier (Paris: Gallimard, Bibliothèque de la Pléiade, 1951), 223.

4. Chateaubriand, *Mémoires*, vol. 1, 1005.

5. Chateaubriand, *Mémoires*, vol. 1, 1008.

6. Johann Wolfgang von Goethe, Johann Peter Eckermann, and Frédéric Jacob Soret, *Conversations of Goethe with Eckermann and Soret*, vol. 2, trans. John Oxenford, (London, 1850), 40.

7. Quoted in Judith Shklar, *Freedom and Independence: A study of the political ideas of Hegel's "Phenomenology of Mind"* (Cambridge: Cambridge University Press, 1976), 119.

8. Quoted in David A. Bell, *The First Total War: Napoleon's Europe and the Birth of Warfare as We Know it* (Boston, MA, and New York: Houghton Mifflin, 2007), 241.

9. See Jürgen Habermas, *The Inclusion of Ohers: Studies in Political Theory*, ed. Ciaran Cronin and Pablo De Greiff (Cambridge, MA: MIT Press, 2000), 114: "Since

the French Revolution, general conscription has gone hand in hand with civil rights; the willingness to fight and die for one's country is supposed to express both national consciousness and republican virtue."

10. See Biancamaria Fontana, *Germaine de Staël: A Political Portrait* (Princeton, NJ: Princeton University Press, 2016), 201.

11. E. H. Carr, *Nationalism and After* (New York: Macmillan, 1945), 8.

12. Chateaubriand, *Mémoires*, vol. 1, 1005.

13. Thomas Carlyle, *On Heroes, Hero-Worship, and the Heroic in History* [1840], ed. Michael K. Goldberg, Joel J. Brattin, and Mark Engel (Berkley, Los Angeles, Oxford: University of California Press, 1993), 206.

14. Ralph Waldo Emerson, "Napoleon; Man of the World" in *Representative Men: Seven Lectures* [1850] (Boston, MA: William Sampson and Co., 1952), 247.

15. Quoted in Biancamaria Fontana, "The Napoleonic Empire and the Europe of Nations" in *The Idea of Europe: From Antiquity to the European Union*, ed. Anthony Pagden (Cambridge: Cambridge University Press, 2002), 123, n.16.

16. Las Cases, *Mémorial*, vol. 2, 360.

17. Las Cases, *Mémorial*, vol. 2, 419.

18. Richard von Coudenhove-Kalergi, *Europe Must Unite* (Glarus, Switzerland: Paneuropa Editions, 1939), 80–1.

19. I would like to thank Mike Rapport for suggesting this definition to me.

20. Quoted in Fontana, "Napoleonic Empire," 123.

21. William Burke, *Additional Reasons for our Immediately Emancipating Spanish America* (London, 1808), 10–11. On Mill's authorship of this work, see Mario Rodríguez *"William Burke" and Francisco de Miranda: The Word and the Deed in Spanish America's Emancipation* (London and Lanham, MD: University Press of America, 1994), 123–53.

22. Madame (Anne-Louise-Germaine) de Staël, *Dix Années d'exil: Fragment d'un ouvrage inédit*, in *Œuvres complètes de Mme. la baronne de Staël*, vol. 5 (Paris, 1820–1), 89. On Napoleon's attempts to administer his empire according to the principle "Ce qui est bon pour les français est bon pour tout le monde," see in particular Michael Boers, *Napoleon: The Spirit of the Age* (London: Faber and Faber, 2018).

23. Napoléon Bonaparte, "Au sénat conservateur," in *Œuvres de Napoléon Bonaparte*, ed. C. L. F. Panckoucke, vol. 4 (Paris, 1821), 26.

24. Armand Augustin Louis de Caulaincourt, *With Napoleon in Russia: The Memoirs of General de Caulaincourt, Duke of Vicenza* (New York: William Morrow and Co., 1935), 277–8.

25. See, in general, Charles Esdaile, *Napoleon's Wars: An International History 1803–1815* (London: Allen Lane, 2007), who argues persuasively that the Napoleonic Wars should be understood, at least as far as objectives were concerned, "in terms of the dynastic wars of the eighteenth century" (p. 6).

26. Staël, *Dix Années d'exil*, 255.

27. The creation of the code and its relationship with Justinian's is discussed by Donald Kelley, "'What Pleases the Prince': Justinian, Napoleon and the Lawyers," *History of Political Thought*, 23 (2002), 288–302.

28. Quoted in Frank McLynn, *Napoleon* (New York and London: Random House, 2002), 664.

29. Steven Englund, *Napoleon: A Political Biography* (Cambridge, MA: Harvard University Press, 2004), 399–422.

30. For a more detailed account of the Congress, see Mark Jarrett, *The Congress of Vienna and its Legacy: War and Great Power Diplomacy after Napoleon* (London and New York: I. B. Tauris, 2014).

31. Jarrett, *Congress of Vienna*, 94.

32. Napoléon Bonaparte, "Réflexions sur la conduite des souverains coalisés," in *Commentaires de Napoléon Premier*, ed. Anselm Petetin, vol. 5 (Paris: Imprimerie Impériale, 1867), 444.

33. Las Cases, *Mémorial*, vol. 2, 384–5.

34. Sudhir Hazareesingh, *The Legend of Napoleon* (London: Granta Books, 2004), 7, 162–3.

35. Chateaubriand, *Mémoires*, vol. 1, 1005.

36. *Acte additionnel aux Constitutions de l'Empire du 22 avril 1815*, http://www.conseil-constitutionnel.fr/conseil-constitutionnel/francais/la-constitution/les-constitutions-de-la-france/acte-additonnel-aux-constitutions-de-l-empire-du-22-avril-1815.5103.html, accessed February 3, 2021. See also L. Lacché, "Coppet et la percée de l'état libéral constitutionnel," in *Coppet, creuset de l'esprit libéral: Les Idées politiques et constitutionnelles du groupe de Madame de Staël*, ed. Lucien Jaume (Marseilles and Paris: Presses Universitaires d'Aix-Marseille and Economica, 2000), 135–55.

37. Quoted in Adam Zamoyski, *Rites of Peace: The Fall of Napoleon and the Congress of Vienna* (London: Harper Press, 2007), 464.

38. Quoted in Zamoyski, *Rites of Peace*, 464.

39. See Bernard Bailyn, *The Ideological Origins of the American Revolution* (Cambridge, MA: Harvard University Press, 1967), 213.

40. James Wilson, "Of Man as Member of a Confederation," *Lectures on Law*, in *The Collected Works of James Wilson*, vol. 1, ed. Mark David Hall and Kermit L. Hall (Indianapolis, IN: Liberty Fund, 2007), 646–7; and see David J. Bederman, *The Classical Foundations of the American Constitution: Prevailing Wisdom* (Cambridge: Cambridge University Press 2008).

41. James Madison, *Federalist XVIII*, in James Madison, Alexander Hamilton, and John Jay, *The Federalist Papers*, ed. Isaac Kramnick (London and New York: Penguin Books, 1987), 160.

42. Las Cases, *Mémorial*, vol. 1, 720.

43. Quoted in Brendan Simms, *Europe: The Struggle for Supremacy from 1453 to the Present* (New York: Basic Books, 2013), 166.

44. Friedrich Nietzsche, *The Gay Science* [1882], ed. Bernard Williams, trans. Josefine Nauckhoff (Cambridge: Cambridge University Press, 2012), 362.

45. Quoted in Simms, *Europe*, 307.

46. Richard von Coudenhove-Kalergi, *Pan-Europe* (New York: Alfred A. Knopf, 1927), 27.

47. All mentioned in Hazareesingh, *The Legend of Napoleon*, 7.

48. Paul Johnson, *Napoleon* (London: Orion Books, 2003), 17.

49. Dominique de Villepin, *Les Cent-jours, ou l'esprit de sacrifice* (Paris: Perrin, 2001), 584.

50. Lionel Jospin, *Le Mal napoléonien* (Paris: Éditions du Seuil, 2014), 228.

51. Ernest Renan, "What is a Nation?" *Qu'est-ce qu'une nation?* [1882], in *What is a Nation? And Other Political Writings*, ed. and trans. M. F. N. Giglioli (New York: Columbia University Press, 2018), 261.

52. Napoléon Bonaparte, "Dix-sept notes sur l'ouvrage intitulé *Considérations sur l'art de la guerre*," in *Commentaires de Napoléon Premier*, vol. 6, 61 and 178.

53. John Robert Seeley, *A Short History of Napoleon the First* (Boston, MA: Roberts Brothers, 1886), 306–7.

54. Johann Caspar Bluntschli, *The Theory of the State* [*Lehre vom Modernen Staat*, 1895] (Freeport, NY: Books for Libraries Press, 1971), 30–1.

55. Benjamin Constant, *The Spirt of Conquest and Usurpation and their Relation to European Civilization* in *Political Writings*, ed. and trans. Biancamaria Fontana (Cambridge: Cambridge University Press, 1988), 72–3.

56. Constant, *Political Writings*, 79.

57. Constant, *Political Writings*, 100–1.

58. Quoted in Duncan Bell, *Reordering the World: Essays on Liberalism and Empire* (Princeton, NJ: Princeton University Press, 2018), 276–7.

59. See Étienne Balibar, *We the Peoples of Europe? Reflections on Transnational Citizenship* (Princeton, NJ: Princeton University Press, 2004), 11–30.

60. Giuseppe Mazzini, "Principles of International Politics" [1871, written in Italian], in *A Cosmopolitanism of Nations: Giuseppe Mazzini's Writings on Democracy, Nation Building and International Relations*, ed. and trans. Stefano Recchia and Nadia Urbinati (Princeton, NJ: Princeton University Press, 2009), 225.

61. Nietzsche, *Gay Science*, 362. See also, in general, Don Dombowsky, *Nietzsche and Napoleon: The Dionysian Conspiracy* (Chicago: Chicago University Press, 2014).

2. THE BIRTH OF THE NATION

1. Adam Zamoyski, *Rites of Peace: The Fall of Napoleon and the Congress of Vienna* (London: Harper Press, 2007), 356–7.

2. Mark Jarrett, *The Congress of Vienna and its Legacy: War and Great Power Diplomacy after Napoleon* (London and New York: I. B. Tauris, 2014), 376.

3. Quoted in Jarrett, *Congress of Vienna*, 465.

4. See Mathew Levinger, *Enlightened Nationalism: The Transformation of Prussian Political Culture, 1806–1848* (Oxford: Oxford University Press, 2000), 150–2 and Jarrett, *Congress of Vienna*, 166.

5. Giuseppe Mazzini, "Towards a Holy Alliance of Peoples" [1849, originally written in Italian], in *A Cosmopolitanism of Nations: Giuseppe Mazzini's Writings on Democracy, Nation Building and International Relations*, ed. and trans. Stefano Recchia and Nadia Urbinati (Princeton, NJ: Princeton University Press, 2009), 117.

6. Sir Travers Twiss, *Le Congrès de Vienne et la conférence de Berlin* (Brussels and Leipzig, 1888), 4 (an extract from the *Revue de droit international*).

7. Edmund Burke, "Letters on a Regicide Peace," in *The Writings and Speeches of Edmund Burke*, vol. 9, ed. Paul Langford (Oxford: Oxford University Press, 1981–91), 248–9.

8. Friedrich von Gentz, *On the State of Europe before and after the French Revolution* (London, 1802), 11–15. This was written in response to Hauterive's *L'État de la France à la fin de l'an VIII*. See Isaac Nakhimovsky, "The 'Ignominious Fall of the European Commonwealth': Gentz, Hauterive, and the Debate of 1800," in *Trade and War: The Neutrality of Commerce in the Inter-State System*, ed. Koen Stapelbroek (Helsinki: University of Helsinki, 2011), 212–28, and Carsten Holbraad, *The Concert of Europe: A Study in German and British International Theory 1815–1914* (London: Longman, 1970), 18–19.

9. Friedrich von Gentz, *Fragments upon the Balance of Power in Europe* [1800] (London, 1806), 61.

10. Gentz, *Fragments*, 69.

11. Quoted in Holbraad, *Concert of Europe*, 17–18.

12. J. R. Seely, "The United States of Europe" *Macmillan's Magazine* 23 (1871), 436–48.

13. Jarrett, *Congress of Vienna*, 177, and Stella Ghervas, *Conquering Peace: From the Enlightenment to the European Union* (Cambridge, MA: Harvard University Press, 2021), 109–10, who points out that, in addition to their aversion to "absolute" monarchy, the British were committed to the balance of power, "which required a modicum of disunity among the continental states," something which effectively persisted until after World War II.

14. Paul W. Schroeder, *The Transformation of European Politics 1763–1848* (Oxford: Clarendon Press, 1994), 559.

15. Mazzini, "Holy Alliance" in *A Cosmopolitanism of Nations*, 117–19.

16. Giuseppe Mazzini, "On Public Opinion and England's International Leadership" [1847], in *A Cosmopolitanism of Nations*, 201.

17. Jarrett, *Congress of Vienna*, 376–7.

18. Quoted in Andreas Osiander, *The States System of Europe 1640–1990: Peacemaking and the Conditions of International Stability* (Oxford: Clarendon Press, 1994), 248.

19. "On the Common Saying: 'This may be true in theory, but it is of no use in practice,'" in *Practical Philosophy*, ed. and trans. Mary J. Gregor (Cambridge: Cambridge University Press, 1996), 309.

20. Claude Henri de Saint-Simon, *De la réorganisation de la société européenne, ou de la nécessité et les moyens de rassembler les peuples de l'Europe en un seul corps politique en conservant à chacun son indépendance nationale* [1814], ed. Alfred Pereire, intro. Henri de Jouvenel (Paris: Les Presses Françaises, 1925), 10; and see Richard Swedberg, "Saint-Simon's vision of a united Europe," *European Journal of Sociology* 35 (1994), 145–69.

21. Saint-Simon, *De la réorganisation*, 10.

22. Saint-Simon, *De la réorganisation*, 26.

23. Saint-Simon, *De la réorganisation*, 57–8.
24. Holbraad, *Concert of Europe*, 62.
25. Holbraad, *Concert of Europe*, 21, n.14.
26. "The Ideologues and Their Day," *The Speaker:The Liberal Review* 7 (1902), 223.
27. Heinrich von Treitschke, *Politics*, vol. 1, trans. Blanche Dugdale and Torben de Bille (New York: Macmillan, 1916), 271–2.
28. Friedrich Meinecke, *Weltbürgertum und Nationalstaat: Studien zur Genesis des deutschen Nationalstaates*, (Munich: R. Oldenbourg, 1922), 3–22.
29. Claus Offe, "Is There, or Can There Be, a 'European Society'?" in *Demokratien in Europa: Der Einfluss der europäischen Integration auf Institutionenwandel und neue Konturen des demokratischen Verfassungsstaates*, ed. Ines Katenhusen and Wolfram Lamping (Wiesbaden: Springer, 2003), 71–89.
30. Émile Durkheim, *Les Règles de la méthode sociologique* (Paris: Felix Alcan, 1938), 124–38.
31. See Rogers Brubaker, *Nationalism Reframed: Nationhood and the National Question in the New Europe* (Cambridge: Cambridge University Press, 1996), who believes that it is "so central and protean a category of modern political and cultural thought, discourse and practice, that it is hard to imagine a world without nationalism." For a broad overview which argues that, rather than being the consequence of the assertion of or quest for identity, nationalism was indeed the creation of the state, or, as he puts it, "nationalism as a form of politics," see John Breuilly, *Nationalism and the State* (Manchester: Manchester University Press, 1982).
32. Jürgen Habermas, "The European Nation-State: On the Past and Future of Sovereignty and Citizenship," *The Inclusion of Others: Studies in Political Theory*, ed. Ciaran Cronin and Pablo De Greiff (Cambridge MA: MIT Press, 2000), 110.
33. Charles de Secondat, baron de Montesquieu, *De l'esprit des lois* (XXIX, 16–17), in *Œuvres complètes*, vol. 2, ed. Roger Caillois (Paris: Gallimard, Bibliothèque de la Pléiade, 1951), 876–82; David Hume, "Of National Characters," in *Essays. Moral, Political, and Literary* ed. Eugene F. Miller (Indianapolis, IN: Liberty Fund, 1985), 197–215.
34. Johann Gottfried von Herder, *Outlines of a Philosophy of the History of Man* [*Ideen zur Philosophie der Geschichte der Menscheit*], ed. David G. Payne, trans. T. O. Churchill (New York: Bergman Publishers, 2016), 288.
35. Jürgen Habermas, *Between Facts and Norms: Contribution to a Discourse Theory of Law and Democracy*, trans.William Rehg (Cambridge, MA: MIT Press, 1998), 494.
36. Hans Kelsen, "Foundations of Democracy," *Ethics* 66 (1955), 1–101. Autocracy, by contrast "is by its very nature a paternal community. The child–father relationship is its corresponding category."
37. Richard J. Evans, *The Pursuit of Power: Europe 1815–1914* (London: Penguin Books, 2017), 28–9.
38. John Dunn, *Western Political Theory in the Face of the Future* (Cambridge: Cambridge University Press, 1979), 55.

39. Thomas Hobbes, *Leviathan* [1651] (II, 18), ed. Richard Tuck (Cambridge: Cambridge University Press, 1991), 127.

40. For a compelling and passionate defense of liberal nationalism, see Yael Tamir, *Why Nationalism?* (Princeton, NJ: Princeton University Press, 2019).

41. Liah Greenfeld, *Nationalism: Five Roads to Modernity* (Cambridge, MA: Harvard University Press, 1992), and Azar Gat with Alexander Jacobson, *Nations: The Long History of Political Ethnicity and Nationalism* (Cambridge: Cambridge University Press, 2103).

42. Anthony Smith, *The Ethnic Origins of Nations* (Oxford: Blackwell, 1989) and Anthony Smith, *Myths and Memories of the Nations* (Oxford: Oxford University Press, 2000).

43. Most persuasively by Ernest Gellner, *Nations and Nationalism* (Oxford: Blackwell, 2006) and Benedict Anderson, *Imagined Communities. Reflections on Nationalism* (New York: Verso, 1991).

44. Ernest Renan, "What is a Nation?" [*Qu'est ce qu'une nation?*, 1882], in *What is a Nation? And Other Political Writings*, ed. and trans. M. F. N. Giglioli (New York: Columbia University Press, 2018), 261–2.

45. Gellner, *Nations and Nationalism*, 6–7.

46. Émile Durkheim, "Débat sur le nationalisme et le patriotisme," in *Textes* III: *Fonctions sociales et institutions* (Paris: Les Éditions de Minuit, 1975), 180.

47. Plato, *Republic*, 414–15.

48. Henry Maine, *Ancient Law: Its Connection with the Early History of Society, and its Relation to Modern Ideas* [1861], (London: Dent, 1917), 82, 85.

49. Émile Durkheim, "Moral civique et patrie," 1909, in *Textes* III, 224.

50. In David Wotton, ed. *Divine Right and Democracy: An Anthology of Political Writings in Stuart England* (London: Penguin Books, 1986), 107.

51. John Stuart Mill, "The Subjugation of Women" [1869], in *On Liberty and Other Writings*, ed. Stefan Collini (Cambridge: Cambridge University Press, 1989), 130.

52. David A. Bell, *The Cult of the Nation in France: Inventing Nationalism, 1680–1800* (Cambridge, MA; Harvard University Press, 2001), 51–4, who provides a brilliant evocation of the setting and an analysis of the oration. See also Peter Campbell, "The Language of Patriotism in France, 1750–1770," *e-France* 1 (2007), 14, and Peter Campbell, "The Politics of Patriotism in France (1770–1788)," *French History* 24 (2010), 550–75.

53. See pp. 274–9.

54. Montesquieu, *De l'esprit des lois* (IV, 5), in *Œuvres Complètes*, vol. 2, 267.

55. Oliver Goldsmith, *Letters from a Citizen of the World to his Friends in the East* [1762] (London: Bungy, 1820), I, 19.

56. Quoted in Biancamaria Fontana, "The Shaping of Modern Liberty: Commerce and Civilisation in the Writings of Benjamin Constant," *Annales Benjamin Constant* 5 (1985), 2–15.

57. Charles Lemonnier, *Les États-Unis d'Europe* (Paris: Librairie de la Bibliothèque Démocratique, 1872), 165.

58. Or what the French historian Claude Nicolet calls "juridic" patriotism: see *L'Idée républicaine en France: Essai d'histoire critique (1789–1924)* (Paris: Gallimard, 1982).

59. Jürgen Habermas, "Citoyenneté et identité nationale," in *L'Europe au soir du siècle: Identité et démocratie*, ed. Jacques Lenoble and Nicole Dewandre (Paris: Éditions Esprit, 1992), 20.

60. See pp. 16–18.

61. Michael Walzer, "Spheres of Affection" in Martha C. Nussbaum (with respondents), *For Love of Country: Debating the Limits of Patriotism*, ed. Joshua Cohen (Boston, MA: Beacon Press, 1996), 125. For an analysis and a critique of what she calls the cosmopolitan "tradition," which emphasizes what she sees as its applicability to the "challenges of today's world" (before turning into yet another plea for her "Capabilities Approach"), see Martha C. Nussbaum, *The Cosmopolitan Tradition: A Noble but Flawed Ideal* (Cambridge, MA: Harvard University Press, 2019).

62. This is a reference to the celebrated "Stoic circles." See my *The Enlightenment and Why It Still Matters* (Oxford: Oxford University Press, 2013), 246–7.

63. Giuseppe Mazzini, "Nationality and Cosmopolitanism" [1847], in *Cosmopolitanism of Nations*, 58. *Ubi bene, ibi patria* is a parody of the slogan *ubi libertas, ibi patria* attributed to James Otis and Benjamin Franklin.

64. Quoted in Elie Kedourie, *Nationalism* (London: Hutchinson, 1960), 73.

65. Roger Scruton, *A Dictionary of Political Thought* (Houndmills: Palgrave-Macmillan, 2007), 146.

66. *The Meditations of the Emperor Marcus Aurelius Antoninus*, 6. 50. 58.

67. Mazzini, "Nationality and Cosmopolitanism", in *Cosmopolitanism of Nations*, 59.

68. Giuseppe Mazzini, "From a Revolutionary Alliance to the United States of Europe" [1850, originally written in Italian], in *Cosmopolitanism of Nations*, 134. Emphasis original.

69. Denis Mack Smith, *Mazzini* (New Haven, CT, and London: Yale University Press, 1994), 24 and 183.

70. Quoted in H. S. Jones, "The Idea of the National in Victorian Political Thought" *European Journal of Political Theory* 5 (2006), 12–21.

71. Nietzsche to Matilda van Meyerberg, quoted in Julian Young, *Friedrich Nietzsche: A Philosophical Biography* (Cambridge: Cambridge University Press, 2010), 307; see also Mack Smith, *Mazzini*, 215. For Mill's association with Mazzini, see Marcella Pellegrino Sutcliffe, *Victorian Radicals and Italian Democrats* (Woodbridge: Royal Historical Society and Boydell Press, 2015).

72. Quoted in Stefano Recchia and Nadia Urbinati, "Introduction: Giuseppe Mazzini's International Political Thought," in *A Cosmopolitanism of Nations*, 1.

73. Alfred Zimmern, *Europe in Convalescence* (London: Mills and Boon, 1922), 38.

74. Mack Smith, *Mazzini*, 219; see also Fabrizio De Donno, "The Gandhian Mazzini: Democratic Nationalism, Self-Rule, and Non-Violence," in *Giuseppe Mazzini and the Globalization of Democratic Nationalism 1830–1920*, ed. C. A. Bayly and Eugenio F. Biagini (Oxford: Oxford University Press, 2008), 375–98.

75. Quoted in Mack Smith, *Mazzini*, 221.

76. *Thoughts upon Democracy in Europe* (1846–1847): *Un "manifesto" in inglese*, ed. Salvo Mastellone (Florence: Centro editoriale toscano, 2001), 72.

77. On Fichte's attempt to blend nationalism with a kind of internationalism, see Hans Kohn, "The Paradox of Fichte's Nationalism," *Journal of the History of Ideas* 10 (1949), 319–43.

78. Quoted in Johann Gottlieb Fichte, *Addresses to the German Nation*, ed. and trans. Gregory Moore (Cambridge: Cambridge University Press, 2008), xxii.

79. Mazzini, "Nationality and Cosmopolitanism," in *A Cosmopolitanism of Nations*, 60. Emphasis original.

80. Giuseppe Mazzini, "Humanity and Country" [1839, originally written in French], in *A Cosmopolitanism of Nations*, 55.

81. Renan, "What is a Nation?," in *What is a Nation?*, 247.

82. J. R. Seely, *Introduction to Political Science: Two Series of Lectures* (London: Macmillan, 1923), 88. See also Duncan Bell, *Reordering the World: Essays on Liberalism and Empire* (Princeton, NJ: Princeton University Press, 2018), 279.

83. Mazzini, "Nationalism and Nationality," in *A Cosmopolitanism of Nations*, 62–3.

84. Pierre Joseph Proudhon, *Du Principe fédératif et de la nécessité de reconstituer la parti de la révolution* [1863], in, *Œuvres complètes de P.-J. Proudhon* (Paris: Librairie Marcel Rivière et Cie, 1959), 263. For Proudhon's views on Mazzini and Italian unification, see "La Féderation et l'unité en Italie" in Proudhon, *Œuvres complètes*, 79–202.

85. For a wide-ranging, persuasive, and highly readable account of the revolutions, see Mike Rapport, *1848: Year of Revolution* (New York: Basic Books, 2008).

86. Quoted in Rapport, *1848: Year of Revolution*, 358.

87. Alexis de Tocqueville, *The Recollections of Alexis de Tocqueville* [1893], trans. Alexander Teixeira de Mattos (New York, 1896), 93–4.

88. Friedrich Nietzsche, *Beyond Good and Evil* [1886], ed. and trans. Rolf-Peter Horstmann and Judith Norman (Cambridge: Cambridge University Press, 2002), 132–3. Emphasis original.

89. Mazzini, "Humanity and Country," in *A Cosmopolitanism of Nations*, 56. Emphasis original.

90. Duncan Bell and Casper Sylvest, "International Society in Victorian Political Thought: T. H. Green, Herbert Spencer and Henry Sidgwick," *Modern Intellectual History* 3 (2006), 1–31.

91. Giuseppe Mazzini, *Statuto della "Giovine Europa"* [1843] in *Scritti editi ed inediti di Giuseppe Mazzini*, vol. 4 (Imola: Cooperativa Tipografico-Editrice, Paolo Galeati 1908), 12. Emphasis original. For an exhaustive account of *La Giovine Europa*, see Franco della Peruta, *Mazzini e i rivoluzionari italiani: Il "partito d'azione" 1830–1845* (Milan: Feltrinelli, 1974), 161–219.

92. Giuseppe Mazzini, *Aux patriotes suisses!* [1843], in *Scritti editi ed inediti*, 47. Emphasis original.

93. Mazzini, *Aux patriotes suisses!*, in *Scritti editi ed inediti*, 35–7.

94. Renan, "What is a Nation?," in *What is a Nation?*, 262.

95. Mazzini, "Nationalism and Nationality," in *A Cosmopolitanism of Nations*, 63.

96. Johann Gottfried von Herder, *Letters for the Advancement of Humanity (1793–1797)*, 6n *Philosophical Writings*, ed. Michael N. Forster, (Cambridge: Cambridge University Press, 2002), 378–9. Emphasis original.

97. Johann Caspar Bluntschli, *The Theory of the State* [*Lehre vom modernen Staat*, 1895] (Freeport, NY: Books for Libraries Press, 1971), 68. Emphasis original.

98. *D'una letteratura europea e altri saggi*, ed. Paolo Maria Sipala (Fasano: Schena, 1991), 67.

99. Bluntschli, *Theory of the State*, 67.

100. Nietzsche, *Beyond Good and Evil*, 132, 148. Emphasis original.

101. Robert Gascoyne-Cecil, 3rd Marquess of Salisbury, *Essays of the Late Marquess of Salisbury* (London: Murray, 1905), 184–5.

102. Friedrich Nietzsche, *The Will to Power: Selections from the Notebooks of the 1880s*, ed. and trans. R. Kevin Hall and Michael A. Scarpitti (New York: Penguin Books, 2017), 421–2. Emphasis original.

103. Friedrich Nietzsche, *Human All Too Human: A Book for Free Spirits*, trans. R. J. Hollingdale (Cambridge: Cambridge University Press, 1986) 174–5. Emphasis original.

104. Julien Benda, *Discours à la nation européenne* (Paris: Gallimard, 1933), 118–20.

105. *Entretiens: L'Avenir de l'esprit européen.* (Paris: Institut International de Coopération Intellectuelle, 1934), 64–6.

106. Benda, *Discours à la nation européenne*, 126–7. The best account of Benda's project is Jan Werner Müller, "Julien Benda's Anti-Passionate Europe," *European Journal of Political Theory* 5 (2006),125–37.

107. Charles Taylor, *Hegel* (Cambridge: Cambridge University Press, 1975), 387–8.

108. Georg Wilhelm Friedrich Hegel, *Elements of the Philosophy of Right*, trans. H. B. Nisbet (Cambridge: Cambridge University Press, 1991), 288–9 (para. 268).

109. See Quentin Skinner, "The Sovereign State: A Genealogy," in *Sovereignty in Fragments: The Past, Present and Future of a Contested Concept*, eds. Hant Kalmo and Quentin Skinner (Cambridge: Cambridge University Press, 2010), 26–46.

110. Hobbes, *Leviathan*, (II, 17), 120–1.

111. For a devastating account of Kant's views on marriage and their subsequent legacy in modern discourses on sexuality, see Giulia Sissa, *Jealousy: A Forbidden Passion* (Cambridge: Polity, 2018), 112–17.

112. Hegel, *Elements of the Philosophy of Right*, 105 (para. 75), and on marriage as "the *immediate ethical relationship*," 200–1 (para. 162).

113. Hegel, *Elements of the Philosophy of Right*, 277–8 (para. 258). Emphasis original.

114. Georg Wilhelm Friedrich Hegel, *The Philosophy of Mind*, trans. William Wallace 4nd A. V. Miller (Oxford: Clarendon Press, 1970), 256 (para. 522): "the family is only a single person."

115. See John Dunn, "The Contemporary Political Significance of John Locke's Conception of Civil Society," in *Civil Society: History and Possibilities*, ed. Sudipta Kaviraj and Sunil Khilnani (Cambridge: Cambridge University Press, 2001), 39–57.

116. Hegel, *Elements of the Philosophy of Right*, 220 (para.182).

117. Hegel, *Elements of the Philosophy of Right*, 263–4 (paras 238–40).

118. Hegel, *Elements of the Philosophy of Right*, 233 (para. 199).

119. Hegel, *Elements of the Philosophy of Right*, 222 (para. 185).

120. Hegel, *Elements of the Philosophy of Right*, 375 (para. 349). Emphasis original.

121. Hegel, *Elements of the Philosophy of Right*, 367, 368 (paras 331, 335). Emphasis original.

122. Hegel, *Elements of the Philosophy of Right*, 277 (para. 258).

123. Georg Wilhelm Friedrich Hegel, *The Philosophy of History*, trans. J. Sibree (New York: Dover Publications, 1959), 250.

124. Hegel, *Elements of the Philosophy of Right*, 366–7 (para. 331).

125. Hegel, *Elements of the Philosophy of Right*, 366–7 (para. 331).

126. Hegel, *Elements of the Philosophy of Right*, 368 (para. 333).

127. Hegel, *Elements of the Philosophy of Right*, 368 (para. 333).

128. Quoted in Pierre Hassner, *La Revanche des passions : Métamorphoses de la violence et crises du politique* (Paris: Fayard 2015), 150.

129. Hegel, *Elements of the Philosophy of Right*, 366–7 (para. 331). Emphasis original.

130. Hegel, *Elements of the Philosophy of Right*, 362 (para. 324, Addenda G). See Jens Bartelson, *A Genealogy of Sovereignty* (Cambridge: Cambridge University Press, 1995), 210–18.

131. Hegel, *Elements of the Philosophy of Right*, 360 (para. 324).

132. Hegel, *Elements of the Philosophy of Right*, 361 (para. 324). On China, see my *Enlightenment and Why It Still Matters*, 235–46.

133. Hegel, *Elements of the Philosophy of Right*, 371 (para. 339).

134. Hegel, *Philosophy of Mind*, 45 (para. 393).

135. Hegel, *Philosophy of Mind*, 47 (para. 394).

136. Hegel, *Philosophy of Mind*, 47 (para. 394).

137. Hegel, *Elements of the Philosophy of Right*, 319, (para. 279). Emphasis original.

138. Desiderius Erasmus, *The Education of a Christian Prince* [1516], trans. Lester K. Born (New York: Octagon Books, 1963), 255. I owe this reference to Giulia Sissa.

139. Heinrich Heine, *The Romantic School and Other Essays*, ed. Jost Hermand and Robert C. Holub (New York: Continuum, 2002) 51.

140. See Jan-Werner Müller, *Constitutional Patriotism* (Princeton, NJ: Princeton University Press, 2007), 82.

141. Hegel, *Philosophy of History*, 341.

142. Hegel, *Philosophy of History*, 417.

143. Hegel, *Philosophy of Mind*, 51 (para. 394).

144. Treitschke, *Politics*, vol. 1, 232–3.

145. *Central-Europe* [*Mitteleuropa*], trans. Christabel M. Meredith (New York: Alfred A. Knopf, 1917), 41. On Naumann, see pp. 195–6.

146. Tomáš Garrigue Masaryk, *The New Europe (The Slav Standpoint)* (Lewisburg, PA: Bucknell University Press, 1972). 26, 28. I am grateful to Roey Reichert for this reference.

147. Treitschke, *Politics*, vol. 2, 588.

148. Treitschke, *Politics*, vol. 1, 65, and vol. 2, 599.

149. Treitschke, *Politics*, vol. 2, 599.

150. Treitschke, *Politics*, vol. 1, 68.

151. Émile Durkheim, *"L'Allemagne au dessus de tout": La Mentalité allemande et la guerre* (Paris: Armand Colin, 1915), 3–4. The title is an allusion to the anthem *Deutschland über alles*, which, although Durkheim interprets it as symptomatic of the culture of nationalist bellicosity he is denouncing, was, in fact, written in 1841 on behalf of the liberal nationalists in favor of a united Germany. On the place of this tract in Durkheim's other writings, see Frédéric Ramel, "Durkheim au-delà des circonstances: Retour sur *L'Allemagne au-dessus de tout. La mentalité allemande et la guerre*," *Revue française de sociologie* 45 (2004), 739–51.

152. Durkheim, *"L'Allemagne au dessus de tout,"* 3–4. Emphasis original.

153. Durkheim, *"L'Allemagne au dessus de tout,"* 30–1.

154. Durkheim, *"L'Allemagne au dessus de tout,"* 34.

155. Durkheim, *"L'Allemagne au dessus de tout,"* 57.

156. Durkheim, *"L'Allemagne au dessus de tout,"* 40.

3. THE SCRAMBLE FOR THE WORLD

1. Henry Sumner Maine, *International Law* (London: John Murray, 1888), 7.

2. Claude Henri de Saint-Simon, *De la réorganisation de la société européenne, ou de la nécessité et les moyens de rassembler les peuples de l'Europe en un seul corps politique en conservant à chacun son indépendance nationale* [1814], ed. Alfred Pereire, intro. Henri de Jouvenel (Paris: Les Presses Françaises, 1925), 52.

3. Georg Wilhelm Friedrich Hegel, *Elements of the Philosophy of Right*, trans. H. B. Nisbet (Cambridge: Cambridge University Press, 1991), 334 (para. 369).

4. Paul Leroy-Beaulieu, *De la colonisation chez les peuples modernes*, vol. 1 (Paris: Guillaumin, 1902, 5th edition), viii. First published 1874.

5. Carl Schmitt, "The *Grossraum* Order of International Law [*Völkerrechtlichegroßraumordnung*] with a Ban on Intervention for Spatially Foreign Powers: A Contribution to the Concept of *Reich* in International Law [*Völkerrecht*] (1939–1941)," in *Carl Schmitt, Writings on War*, ed. and trans. Timothy Nunan (Cambridge: Polity Press, 2011), 117. See pp. 198–205.

6. See the comments by Étienne Balibar, *We the People of Europe? Reflections on Transnational Citizenship* (Princeton, NJ: Princeton University Pres, 2004), 57.

7. Richard von Coudenhove-Kalergi, *Europe Must Unite* (Glarus, Switzerland: Paneuropa Editions, 1939), 104–5.

8. *Treaty Establishing the European Economic Community* (Rome, 25 March 1957) Part 4, Art. 141, https://www.cvce.eu/content/publication/1999/1/1/cca6 ba28-0bf3-4ce6-8a76-6b0b3252696e/publishable_en.pdf, 46–8/72. See also Quinn Slobodian, *Globalists: The End of Empire and the Birth of Neoliberalism* (Cambridge, MA: Harvard University Press, 2018),183, 191–2.

9. See Slobodian *Globalists*, 194–5, and Kaye Whiteman, "The Rise and Fall of *Eurafrique*: From the Berlin Conference of 1884–1885 to the Tripoli EU–Africa Summit of 2010," in *The EU and Africa: From Eurafrique to Afro-Europa*, ed. Adekeye Adebajo and Kaye Whiteman (New York: Columbia University Press, 2012), 23–44. On the Treaty of Rome, see pp. 247–9.

10. Slobodian *Globalists*, 192–5.

11. H. G. Wells, Salvador de Madariaga, J. Middleton Murray, and C. E. M. Joad, *The New World Order* (London: National Peace Council, 1940), 19.

12. Richard von Coudenhove-Kalergi, *Pan-Europe*, (New York: Alfred A. Knopf, 1926), 33–4.

13. Vladimir Ilyich Lenin, "On the Slogan for a United States of Europe," in *Lenin Collected Works*, vol. 21 (Moscow: Progress Publishers, 1974), 339–43. See also Antoine Leca, "Lénine et les États-Unis d'Europe," in *L'Europe entre deux tempéraments politiques : Idéal d'unité et paticularisme régionaux* (Aix-en-Provence: Presses Universitaires d'Aix, 1994), 207–15.

14. Quoted in Brendan Simms, *Britain's Europe: A Thousand Years of Conflict and Cooperation* (London: Allen Lane, 2016), 173.

15. John Stuart Mill, *Principles of Political Economy with Some of their Applications to Social Philosophy* [1848] (London: Longmans, 1920), 791.

16. Ernest Renan, "Intellectual and Moral Reform of France" [1871, *La Réforme intellectuelle et morale de la France*], in *What is a Nation? And Other Political Writings*, trans. and ed. M. F. N. Giglioli (New York: Columbia University Press, 2018), 232.

17. John Darwin, *After Tamerlane: The Global History of Empire* (London: Allen Lane, 2007), 256–69. The data is from Paul Kennedy, *The Rise and Fall of the Great Powers* (New York: Random House 1987), 148–9.

18. Johann Caspar Bluntschli, *The Theory of the State* [1895, *Lehre vom modernen Staat*], vol. 1 (Freeport, NY: Books for Libraries Press, 1971), 71.

19. Quoted in J. P. Daughton, *An Empire Divided: Religion, Republicanism, and the Making of French Colonialism 1880–1914* (Oxford: Oxford University Press, 2006), 10.

20. Friedrich Nietzsche, *Daybreak: Thoughts on the Prejudices of Morality*, trans. R. J. Hollindale (Cambridge: Cambridge University Press, 1982), 127. Emphasis original.

21. The phrase "doux commerce," although frequently attributed to Montesquieu, is in fact Montaigne's and was later taken up by Albert Hirschman in his classic *The Passions and Interests: Political Arguments for Capitalism before Its Triumph* (Princeton, NJ: Princeton University Press, 1977), 61. Montesquieu himself did not claim that commerce itself was "sweet" but that it created customs or habits—*mœurs*—that were. On this, see Anoush Terjanian, *Commerce and Its Discontents in Eighteenth-Century French Political Thought*, (Cambridge: Cambridge University Press, 2013) 12–14.

22. Benjamin Constant, *The Spirit of Conquest and Usurpation and their Relation to European Civilization*, in *Political Writings*, ed. and trans. Biancamaria Fontana (Cambridge: Cambridge University Press, 1988), 64.

23. Constant, *Political Writings*, 79. On the central role of public opinion in Constant's liberalism, see Artuur Ghins, "Benjamin Constant and Public Opinion in Post-Revolutionary France," *History of Political Thought* 40 (2019), 484–514, and Biancamaria Fontana, *Benjamin Constant and the Post-Revolutionary Mind* (New Haven, CT, and London, Yale University Press, 1991), 81–97.

24. Rabindranath Tagore, *Nationalism* [1917] (n.p.: Alpha Editions, 2017), 12.

25. George Nathaniel Curzon, *Speeches by Lord Curzon of Kedleston, Viceroy and Governor General of India*, vol. 1 (Calcutta: Office of the Superintendent of Government Printing, India, 1900), ii.

26. Alexis de Tocqueville, "Essay on Algeria" [October 1841], in *Writings on Empire and Slavery*, ed. and trans. Jennifer Pitts, (Baltimore, MD: Johns Hopkins University Press, 2001), 59. See also Jennifer Pitts, *A Turn to Empire: The Rise of Imperial Liberalism in Britain and France* (Princeton, NJ: Princeton University Press, 2005), 204–39.

27. Quoted in Pierre Guillen, *L'Expansion 1881–1898* (Paris: Imprimerie Nationale, 1984), 101.

28. Quoted in Javier Krauel, *Imperial Emotions: Cultural Responses to Myths of Empire in Fin-de-Siècle Spain*, (Liverpool: Liverpool University Press, 2013), 60.

29. Schmitt, *Writings on War*, 117.

30. Quoted in Brendan Simms, *Europe: The Struggle for Supremacy from 1453 to the Present* (New York: Basic Books, 2013), 392.

31. Joseph Schumpeter, *Imperialism and Social Classes* [*Zur Soziologie der Imperialismen*], trans. Heinz Norden (New York: Meridian Books, 1955), 6–7.

32. Georg Wilhelm Friedrich Hegel, *The Philosophy of History*, trans. J. Sibree (New York: Dover Publications, 1959), 80.

33. Georg Wilhelm Friedrich Hegel, *Enzyklopädie der philosophischen Wissenschaften* (Heidelberg, 1817), § 393 Z., 63.

34. Hegel, *Elements of the Philosophy of Right*, 475–6 (paras 349, 351).

35. Leroy-Beaulieu, *De la colonisation*, 605–6.

36. The theoretical foundations for some version of "indirect rule" had, however, already been laid by Henry Maine in India a generation earlier. See Karuna Mantena, *Alibis of Empire: Henry Maine and the Ends of Liberal Imperialism* (Princeton, NJ: Princeton University Press, 2010), 148–78.

37. J. S. Furnivall, *Netherlands India: A Study of Plural Economy* (Cambridge: Cambridge University Press, 1939), 291.

38. Quoted in Mark Mazower, *No Enchanted Palace: The End of Empire and the Ideological Origins of the United Nations* (Princeton, NJ: Princeton University Press, 2009), 32.

39. Edmund Burke, "Speech on Nabob of Arcot's Debts, 28 February 1785" in *The Writings and Speeches of Edmund Burke*, vol. 5, *India: Madras and Bengal 1774–1785*, ed. P. J. Marshall (Oxford: Clarendon Press, 1981), 519. He also refers to "the sufferings of our fellow creatures and fellow subjects in that oppressed part of the world" (p. 549). For the later uses of the concept of the "sacred trust of civilization," see C. H. Alexandrowicz, "The Juridical Expression of the Sacred Trust of Civilization" in *The Law of Nations in Global History*, ed. David Armitage and Jennifer Pitts (Oxford: Oxford University Press, 2017), 336–46.

40. "Great Britain, Palestine and the Jews. Jewry's Celebration of Its National Charter," https://archive.org/stream/greatbritainpaleooworlrich/greatbritain-paleooworlrich_djvu.txt, accessed February 7, 2021.

41. Livy, *Ab urbe condita* 8.13.16.

42. F. D. Lugard, *The Dual Mandate in British Tropical Africa* (Edinburgh and London: William Blackwood and Sons, 1923), 97–8.

43. Rudyard Kipling, *The Recessional*, line 22.

44. See http://avalon.law.yale.edu/20th_century/leagcov.asp, accessed February 7, 2021. For a brilliantly acerbic account of how the architects of the League

manipulated the concept of "self–determination" as an instrument for extend-
ing and securing a new post-war imperial order, see Adom Getachew,
Worldmaking after Empire: The Rise and Fall of Self-Determination (Princeton, NJ:
Princeton University Press, 2019), 41–52. See also Erez Manela, *The Wilsonian
Moment. Self-Determination and the International Origins of Anti-Colonial
Nationalism* (Oxford: Oxford University Press, 2007), 56–62.

45. For an account, mostly in the secondary literature, of this view as it has played
out from the sixteenth to the twentieth centuries, see Brett Bowden, *The
Empire of Civilization: The Evolution of an Imperial Idea* (Chicago and London:
University of Chicago Press, 2009).

46. Giuseppe Mazzini, "Principles of International Politics" [1871 written in
Italian], in *A Cosmopolitanism of Nations: Giuseppe Mazzini's Writings on Democracy,
Nation Building and International Relations*, ed. and trans. Stefano Recchia and
Nadia Urbinati (Princeton, NJ: Princeton University Press, 2009), 238.

47. See in general, Leon Poliakov, *The Aryan Myth: A History of Racist and Nationalist
Ideas in Europe*, trans. E. Howard (New York: Basic Books, 1974).

48. Friedrich Max Müller, *Biographies of Words and the Home of the Aryas* (London,
1888), 245. See also the comments by Julian Huxley and A. C. Haddon in *We
Europeans: A Survey of "Racial" Problems* (New York and London: Harper and
Brothers, 1936), 120–1.

49. Bluntschli, *Theory of the State*, 84.

50. Quoted in Martti Koskenniemi, *The Gentle Civilizer of Nations: The Rise and Fall
of International Law 1870–1960* (Cambridge: Cambridge University Press, 2001),
104. And for an extended account of the international lawyer's racist approach
to empire, see Koskenniemi, *Gentle Civilizer of Nations*, 98–178.

51. John Burrow, *The Crisis of Reason: European Thought, 1848–1914* (New Haven,
CT, and London: Yale University Press, 2000), 106–7.

52. For a further account of European racism in this context see Shane Weller, *The
Idea of Europe: A Critical History* (Cambridge: Cambridge University Press,
2021), ch. 5.

53. John Stuart Mill, *On Liberty*, in *On Liberty and Other Writings*, ed. Stefan Collini
(Cambridge: Cambridge University Press, 1989), 72.

54. Renan, "Two Letters to Mr. Strauss," in *What is a Nation?*, 176.

55. Renan, "What is a Nation?," in *What is a Nation?*, 256.

56. Mill, *On Liberty*, in *On Liberty and Other Writings*, 14.

57. Henry Sumner Maine, *Ancient Law: Its Connection with the Early History of
Society, and Its Relation to Modern Ideas* [1861] (London: Dent, 1917), 104.

58. Renan, "Two Letters to Mr. Strauss," in *What is a Nation?*, 175.

59. François Guizot, *The History of Civilization in Europe, from the Fall of the Roman
Empire to the French Revolution*, trans. William Hazlitt (Indianapolis, IN: Liberty
Fund, 1997), 10–11. For Guizot's achievements and the wide influence of the
History, see the introduction by Larry Siedentop, vii–xl.

60. Guizot, *History of Civilization in Europe*, 16–17.

61. For Kant's "unsocial sociability," see Immanuel Kant, *The Idea for a Universal History with a Cosmopolitan Aim*, in *Anthropology, History, and Education*, ed. Günter Zöller and Robert B. Louden (Cambridge: Cambridge University Press, 2007), III.

62. John Stuart Mill, "Civilization," in *Essays on Politics and Society*, vol. 18, ed. J. M. Robson (Toronto: University of Toronto Press, 1977), 117–48.

63. R. G. Collingwood, "What Civilization Means," in *The New Leviathan or Man, Society, Civilization and Barbarism*, ed. David Boucher (Oxford: Clarendon Press, 1992), 283, 326.

64. Quoted in Gerrit W. Gong, *The Standard of "Civilization" in International Society* (Oxford: Oxford University Press, 1984), 17.

65. Maine, *Ancient Law*, 152.

66. Maine, *Ancient Law*, 170.

67. Thomas Babbington Macaulay, "A Speech Delivered in the House of Commons on the 10th of July, 1833," in *Speeches of Lord Macaulay Corrected by Himself* (London: Longman, Green, Longman, and Roberts, 1869), 162–3. See also Ronald Hyam, *Britain's Imperial Century 1815–1914: A Study of Empire and Expansion* (London: B. T. Batsford, 1976), 220.

68. Quoted in Duncan Bell, *Reordering the World: Essays on Liberalism and Empire* (Princeton, NJ: Princeton University Press, 2018), 56.

69. Bell, *Reordering the World*, 55.

70. Victor Hugo, "Congrès de la Paix de Paris, Discours d'ouverture," in *Œuvres complètes*, vol. 7, édition chronologique publiée sous la direction de Jean Massin (Paris : Le Club français du livre, 1951), 218–22 at p. 220.

71. Hugo, "Congrès de la Paix," in *Œuvres complètes*, vol. 7, 222.

72. Denis de Rougemont, *Écrits sur l'Europe, 1948–1961*, in *Œuvres complètes*, vol. I (Paris: Éditions de la Différence, 1994), 85.

73. It was, he said, an appropriate replacement for the "law of nations," which he regarded as wholly inadequate, partly because this was too close to the "law of nature," which in his view was no law at all, partly because, if it described anything, it described the relationships between individuals not states. See M. W. Janis, "Jeremy Bentham and the Fashioning of 'International Law,'" *The American Journal of International Law* 78 (1984), 405–18.

74. The translation of "*ius gentium*" as "law of nations," although conventional is not unproblematical. *Ius* can mean both "right" and "law" and *gens* can mean a "nation" in something like the modern sense of the term, but also a "people."

75. Article 39 of the Statute of the International Court of Justice.

76. See Jennifer Pitts, *Boundaries of the International: Law and Empire* (Cambridge, MA: Harvard University Press, 2018), 118–47.

77. Henry Wheaton, *Elements of International Law: With a Sketch of the History of the Science* (Philadelphia, PA, 1836), 51.

78. Wheaton, *Elements of International Law*, 45, 30.

79. William E. Hall, *A Treatise on International Law*, 3rd edn. (Oxford: Clarendon Press, 1890), 42–3 See also Gong, *Standard of "Civilization,"* 55.

80. For a wider discussion of Hall's position, see Koskenniemi, *Gentle Civilizer of Nations*, 81–3.

81. Émile Durkheim, *The Division of Labour in Society* [1893], trans. W. D. Halls (New York: Free Press, 1984), 121. This was based on his doctoral thesis and was Durkheim's first major publication. See Gerard Delanty, "Social Theory and European Transformation: Is there a European Society?" *Sociological Research Online* 3, no. 1 (1998), 103–17.

82. Quoted in Koskenniemi, *Gentle Civilizer of Nations*, 41–42. Koskenniemi points out that the French original "conscience juridique" could mean either the "juridical conscience" or the "juridical *consciousness*."

83. Lass Oppenheim, quoted in Gong, *Standard of "Civilization,"* 30.

84. T. J. Lawrence, *Principles of International Law* (London: Macmillan, 1895), 58. See also Pitts, *Boundaries of the International*, 175.

85. Quoted in Carsten Holbraad, *The Concert of Europe: A Study in German and British International Theory 1815–1914* (London: Longman, 1970), 166.

86. Mark Mazower, *Governing the World: The History of an Idea* (New York: Penguin, 2012), 67.

87. Quoted in Andrew Fitzmaurice, *Sovereignty Property and Empire 1500–2000* (Cambridge: Cambridge University Press, 2014), 295.

88. Francis Lieber, *Fragments of Political Science on Nationalism and Inter-Nationalism* (New York: Charles Scribner, 1868) 20–2. See Koskenniemi, *Gentle Civilizer of Nations*, 67, and on Bluntschli, see Betsy Röben, *Johann Caspar Bluntschli, Francis Lieber und das moderne Völkerrecht 1861–1881* (Baden-Baden: Nomos, 2003).

89. With regard to Kant's highly tendentious understanding of the events which led up to the declaration of the French Republic in 1792, it had been Louis XVI himself, who, by calling the Estates-General in an attempt to resolve a financial crisis, had voluntarily, if inadvertently, surrendered the "supreme authority" within the French state to the people, and "the consequence was that the monarch's sovereignty wholly disappeared (it was not merely suspended) and passed to the people." Once anything like this has happened, a situation is created in which "the united people does not merely represent the sovereign: it is itself the sovereign." In other words the Revolution had been no revolution at all, but only a legal transfer of power. For a further discussion of this point, see my *The Enlightenment and Why It Still Matters* (Oxford: Oxford University Press, 2013), 310–11.

90. Marie-Jean-Antoine-Nicolas de Caritat, marquis de Condorcet, *De l'influence de la révolution d'amérique sur l'europe*, in *Œuvres de Condorcet*, (Paris, 1847), 11–12.

91. Condorcet, *De l'influence de la révolution d'amérique*, in *Œuvres de Condorcet*, 97.

92. Carlo Cattaneo, "Cosiderazioni sulle cose d'Italia nel 1848," in *Scritti storici e geografici*, vol. 2, ed. Gaetano Salvemini and Ernesto Sestan (Florence: Felice le Monnier, 1957), 147; see also Filippo Sabetti, *Civilization and Self-Government: The Political Thought of Carlo Cattaneo* (Lanham, MD: Rowman and Littlefield, 2010), 152.

93. Carlo Cattaneo, *L'insurrezione di Milano nel 1848 e la successiva guerra*, in *Scritti storici e geografici*, vol. 4, 329.
94. Lenin, "Slogan for a United States of Europe," in *Lenin Collected Works*, vol. 21, 339–43.
95. Quoted in Élisabeth Du Réau, *L'Idée d'Europe au XXe siècle : Des mythes aux réalités* (Brussels : Éditions Complexe, 2008), 101.
96. Jean Monnet, *Les États-Unis d'Europe ont commencé: La Communauté européenne du charbon et de l'acier: Discours et allocutions 1952–1954* (Paris: Robert Laffont, 1955). See also Chapter 6, pp. 241–3.
97. Guy Verhofstadt, *Europe's Last Chance: Why the European States Must Form a More Perfect Union* (New York: Basic Books, 2017), 259–68.
98. For a subtle and sympathetic account of Hugo's understanding of Europe see Weller *Idea of Europe*, ch. 5.
99. Victor Hugo, "Préface," in *Œuvres complètes*, vol. 6, 574.
100. For an account of the Congress, see, W. H. van der Linden, *The International Peace Movement 1815–1874* (Amsterdam: Tilleul Publications, 1987), 328–39.
101. William Wells Brown, *The American Fugitive in Europe: Sketches of Places and People Abroad* (New York, 1855), 75.
102. Hugo, "Congrès de la Paix de Paris," in *Œuvres complètes*, vol. 7, 218–22 at p. 219.
103. Wells Brown, *American Fugitive in Europe*, 59.
104. Quoted in Dina Gusejnova, *European Elites and Ideas of Empire 1919–1957* (Cambridge: Cambridge University Press, 2016), 81.
105. Charles Lemonnier, *Les États-Unis d'Europe* (Paris: Librairie de la Bibliothèque Démocratique, 1872), 116.
106. Victor Hugo, *Le Rhin*, in *Œuvres complètes*, vol. 6, 518–20.
107. Victor Hugo, "Anniversaire de la Révolution de 1848" [February 24, 1855], in *Œuvres complètes*, vol. 9, 560–63.
108. Hugo, "Anniversaire de la Révolution de 1848," in *Œuvres complètes*, vol. 9, 561.
109. Victor Hugo, "Révision de la Constitution," in *Œuvres complètes*, vol. 7, 329–31.
110. John Stuart Mill, *Considerations on Representative Government*, in *The Collected Works of John Stuart Mill*, vol. 19, ed. John M. Robson (Toronto: University of Toronto Press, 1977), 549–51.
111. Mill, *Considerations on Representative Government*, in *Collected Works of John Stuart Mill*, vol. 19, 554.
112. Simms, *Europe*, 246–48.
113. Victor Hugo, "Pour la guerre dans le présent et pour la paix dans l'avenir" [Address to the National Assembly, March 1, 1871], in *Œuvres complètes*, vol. 15, 1261–3.
114. Victor Hugo, "L'Avenir de l'Europe" [September 20, 1872], in *Œuvres complètes*, vol. 15, 1338–9.
115. Hans Kelsen, *Peace through Law* [1944] (New York and London: Garland Publishing Inc., 1973), 11–12.
116. See pp. 10–12.

117. John Jay, *Federalist* II, in James Madison, Alexander Hamilton, and John Jay, *The Federalist Papers*. Edited by Isaac Kramnick (Harmondsworth: Penguin Books, 1987), 91.

118. Gustave Rolin-Jaequemyns, "De la nécessité d'organiser une institution scientifique permanente pour favoriser l'étude et le progrès du droit international," *Revue de droit international et de législation comparée* 5 (1873), 463–91, at 478.

119. James Madison, *Federalist* XX, in Madison, Hamilton, and Jay, *Federalist Papers*, 172. Madison was describing the government of the United Netherlands. The Articles of Confederation were drafted in 1771 but not ratified until March 1, 1781.

120. Alexis de Tocqueville, *Democracy in America*, vol. 1 [1835–40], trans. James T. Schleifer (Indianapolis, IN: Liberty Fund, 2012), 91–2.

121. Lemonnier, *Les États-Unis d'Europe*, 137.

122. J. R. Seely, "The United States of Europe," *Macmillan's Magazine* 23, (1871) 436–48.

123. Tocqueville, *Democracy in America*, vol. 2, 605.

124. See David Armitage, *Civil Wars: A History in Ideas* (New York: Alfred A. Knopf, 2017), 161.

125. Jürgen Habermas, "Does Europe Need a Constitution?," in *Time of Transitions*, ed. and trans. Ciaran Cronin and Max Pensky (Cambridge: Polity Press, 2006), 90.

126. See, in particular, the claims of Jonathan Israel, *The Expanding Blaze: How the American Revolution Ignited the World 1775–1848* (Princeton, NJ: Princeton University Press, 2017).

127. J. R. Seeley, "The United States of Europe," *Macmillan's Magazine* 23 (1871), 436–48, at 448.

128. James Lorimer, *The Institutes of the Law of Nations: A Treatise of the Jural Relations of Separate Political Communities*, vol. 1 (Edinburgh and London, 1884), 93. See also Koskenniemi, *Gentle Civilizer of Nations*, 70.

129. Lorimer, *Institutes of the Law of Nations*, vol. 1, 131.

130. Lorimer, *Institutes of the Law of Nations*, vol. 2, 225.

131. James Lorimer, "Proposition d'un congrès international basé sur le principe *de facto*," *Revue de droit international et de législation comparée* 3 (1871), 1–11.

132. See Bruno Arcidiacono, "La Paix par le droit international dans la vision de deux juristes du XIXᵉ siècle: Le Débat Lorimer–Bluntschli," *Relations internationales* 149 (2012), 13–26.

133. Lorimer, *Institutes of the Law of Nations*, vol. 2, 288.

134. Lorimer, *Institutes of the Law of Nations*, vol. 2, 196.

135. Lorimer, *Institutes of the Law of Nations*, vol. 2, 184.

136. James Lorimer, "Proposition d'un congrès international basé sur le principe *de facto*," in *Institutes of the Law of Nations*. vol. 2, 181–299.

137. Lorimer, "Proposition d'un congrès international," in *Institutes of the Law of Nations*. vol. 2, 198.

138. Johann Caspar Bluntschli, "Die Organisation des europäischen Staatenvereines" (1878) in *Gesammelte kleine Schriften*, vol. 2 (Nördlingen: C. H. Beck, 1879), 293. For the distinctions between Lorimer's and Bluntschli's projects, see Arcidiacono,

"La Paix par le droit international ," and Ingrid Rademacher, "Johann Caspar Bluntschli: Conception du droit international et projet de Confédération européenne (1878)," *Études Germaniques* 254, no. 2 (2009), 309–28; and for the background to Bluntschli's project, see Georg Cavallar, "Johann Caspar Bluntschlis europäischer Staatenbund in seinem historischen Kontext," *Zeitschrift der Savigny-Stiftung für Rechtsgeschichte* 121 (2004), 504–18.

139. Lorimer, *Institutes of the Law of Nations*, vol. 2, 266.

140. Lorimer, *Institutes of the Law of Nations*, vol. 2, 266.

141. Lorimer, *Institutes of the Law of Nations*, vol. 2, 279–87.

142. Lorimer, *Institutes of the Law of Nations*, vol. 2, 287.

143. Lorimer, *Institutes of the Law of Nations*, vol. 2, 284.

144. Lorimer, *Institutes of the Law of Nations*, vol. 2, 285.

145. Lorimer, *Institutes of the Law of Nations*, vol. 2, 264–7.

146. See pp. 252–3.

147. Lorimer, *Institutes of the Law of Nations*, vol. 2, 273.

148. Johann Caspar Bluntschli, "Die Gründung der Amerikanischen Union von 1787" in *Gesammelte kleine Schriften*, vol. 2, 61.

149. Bluntschli, "Die Organisation des europäischen Staatenvereines," 229.

150. Bluntschli, "Die Organisation des europäischen Staatenvereines," 239–34.

151. Bluntschli, "Die Organisation des europäischen Staatenvereines," 299.

152. Lorimer, *Institutes of the Law of Nations*, vol. 2, 273.

153. Lorimer, *Institutes of the Law of Nations*, vol. 2, 261.

154. They are Germany, Italy, France, Austria, Britain, Russia, Spain, Denmark, Portugal, Sweden, Norway, Belgium, Switzerland, the Netherlands, Turkey, Romania, Greece, Serbia, and Montenegro. In addition there are what he calls "semi-sovereign" states—Bulgaria, Liechtenstein, San Marino, Monaco, and Andorra—which are "obliged to be joined to one of the other European states like moons to the planets."

155. Bluntschli, "Die Organisation des europäischen Staatenvereines," 308.

156. Bluntschli, "Die Organisation des europäischen Staatenvereines," 305. The cost of the institutions of the union would, however, be borne by "the states in accordance with their voting rights."

157. Bluntschli, "Die Organisation des europäischen Staatenvereines," 310.

158. Alexander Hamilton, *Federalist* XI, in Hamilton, Madison, and Jay, *Federalist Papers*, 133–4.

159. Anatole Leroy-Beaulieu, *Congrès des sciences politiques: Séance du mardi 5 Juin, 1900: Rapport général de M. Anatole Leroy-Beaulieu. Les États-Unis d'Europe* (Paris: L. Faraut, 1900), 6.

160. Charles Albert, *L'Angleterre contre l'Europe* (Paris: Denoël, 1941), 28–9.

161. Michel de Montaigne, "Of Coaches" in *The Complete Essays*, ed. and trans. M. A. Screech (Harmondsworth: Penguin Books, 1993), 1031.

162. See p. 105.

163. Richard Coudenhove-Kalergi, "Das Pan-Europa Programm," *Paneuropa* 2 (1924), 4–20.

164. Edgar Morin, *Penser l'Europe* (Paris: Gallimard 1987), 146–7. See also Jan-Werner Müller, *Contesting Democracy: Political Ideas in Twentieth-Century Europe* (New Haven, CT, and London: Yale University Press, 2011), 156–7.

165. Fondation Robert Schuman, "Declaration of 9th May 1950 delivered by Robert Schuman," *European Issue* 204 (May 10, 2011), 2, https://www.robert-schuman.eu/en/doc/questions-d-europe/qe-204-en.pdf, accessed February 8, 2021. See also Chiara Bottici and Benoît Challand, *Imagining Europe: Myth, Memory and Identity* (Cambridge: Cambridge University Press, 2013), 172.

166. For the claim that the unification of Europe after 1945 is merely a device for continuing colonialism by other means, see Immanuel Wallerstein, *Africa: The Politics of Independence and Unity* (Lincoln, NE, and London: University of Nebraska Press, 2005) and Peo Hansen and Stefan Jonsson, *Eurafrica: The Untold Story of European Integration and Colonialism* (London: Bloomsbury, 2014).

167. Jan-Werner Müller, *Constitutional Patriotism* (Princeton, NJ: Princeton University Press, 2007), 123.

168. J. A. Hobson, *Imperialism: A Study* [1902] (Cambridge: Cambridge University Press, 2010), 29–10.

169. Hobson, *Imperialism*, 4.

170. Quoted in Pitts, *Boundaries of the International*, 184.

4. THE WAR THAT WILL END WAR

1. Quoted in Christopher Clark, *The Sleepwalkers: How Europe Went to War in 1914* (London: Allen Lane, 2012), 470.

2. Clark, *Sleepwalkers*, 536.

3. Richard von Coudenhove-Kalergi, *Crusade for Pan-Europe: Autobiography of a Man and a Movement* (New York: G. P. Putnam, 1943), 54–5.

4. Emer de Vattel, *The Law of Nations, or Principles of the Law of Nature, Applied to the Conduct and Affairs of Nations and Sovereigns* [1757], ed. and trans. Béla Kapossy and Richard Whatmore (Indianapolis, IN: Liberty Fund, 2008), 496.

5. Benjamin Constant, *The Spirit of Conquest and Usurpation and Their Relation to European Civilization*, in *Political Writings*, ed. and trans. Biancamaria Fontana. (Cambridge: Cambridge University Press, 1988), 53–5.

6. Norman Angell, *The Great Illusion: A Study of the Relation of Military Power to National Advantage* (New York: Putnam, 1913), xii and 49.

7. René Brunet, "En réalité, l'Europe est la véritable vaincue de la guerre," in *La Société des Nations et la France* (Paris: Librairie de la Société Recueil Sirey, 1921), 8.

8. On the "short war" debate, see Clark, *Sleepwalkers*, 561.

9. H. G. Wells, *The War That Will End War* (London: Frank and Cecil Palmer, 1914), 8, 54.

10. André Gide, *The Journals of André Gide*, vol. 2 II: (1914–27), trans. Justin O'Brien (New York: Alfred A. Knopf, 1948), 56.

11. Carl H. Pegg, *The Evolution of the European Idea, 1914–1932* (Chapel Hill, NC, and London: University of North Carolina Press, 1983), 9.

12. Benedetto Croce, "Postille," *La Critica* 14 (1916), 103.

13. Quoted in Mark Mazower, *Governing the World: The History of an Idea* (New York: Penguin, 2012), 124.

14. Alfred Zimmern, "True and False Nationalism," in *Nationality and Government, with Other Wartime Essays*, (New York: Robert McBride and Company, 1918), 64–6.

15. Wilson's claims, however, were not quite so unambiguous as they have often been presented as being. See David Raic, *Statehood and the Law of Self Determination* (The Hague, London, and New York: Kluwer Law International, 2002), 180–4, and the comments by Andreas Osiander, *The States System of Europe 1640–1990: Peacemaking and the Conditions of International Stability* (Oxford: Clarendon Press, 1994), 242–61.

16. Coudenhove-Kalergi, *Crusade for Pan-Europe*, 5–6.

17. Quoted in Stella Ghervas, *Conquering Peace: From the Enlightenment to the European Union* (Cambridge, MA: Harvard University Press, 2021), 149.

18. Quoted in David Fromkin, *A Peace to End All Peace: The Fall of the Ottoman Empire and the Creation of the Modern Middle East* (New York: Henry Holt and Company, 1989).

19. Martti Koskenniemi, *The Gentle Civilizer of Nations: The Rise and Fall of International Law 1870–1960* (Cambridge: Cambridge University Press, 2001), 425–6. In 1950 Schmitt elaborated on the substance of his objection to this and a number of other clauses relating to the criminality of war in the treaty in his better-known work, *Der Nomos der Erde im Volkerrecht des Jus Publicum Europaeum*. See Carl Schmitt, *The Nomos of the Earth in International Law and the Jus Publicum Europeaum* [1950], trans. G. L. Ulmen (New York: Telos Press, 2003), 259–65.

20. Wolfgang J. Mommsen, "Max Weber and the Peace Treaty of Versailles," in *The Treaty of Versailles: A Reassessment after 75 Years*, ed. Manfred F. Boemeke, Gerald D. Feldman, and Elisabeth Glaser (Cambridge: Cambridge University Press, 1998), 535–46.

21. John Maynard Keynes, *The Economic Consequences of the Peace* (New York: Harcourt, Brace, and Howe, 1920), 5–10.

22. Keynes, *Economic Consequences of the Peace*, 226.

23. Keynes, *Economic Consequences of the Peace*, 10.

24. Zara Steiner, *The Lights That Failed: European International History 1919–1933* (Oxford: Oxford University Press, 2005), 65–7.

25. Jacques Bainville, *Les Conséquences politiques de la paix* (Paris: Nouvelle Librairie Nationale, 1920), 24–5.

26. Quoted in Mark Mazower, *No Enchanted Palace: The End of Empire and the Ideological Origins of the United Nations* (Princeton, NJ: Princeton University Press, 2009), 52, who also makes the point about Smuts's ambition to secure the future of the British Empire through first the League and then the United Nations. See also Adom Getachew, *Worldmaking after Empire: The Rise and Fall of Self-Determination* (Princeton, NJ: Princeton University Press, 2019), 41–52, and on the League more broadly, see Mazower, *Governing the World*, 116–53.

27. Georges Scelle, *Le Pacte des nations et sa liaison avec la traité de paix* (Paris: Librairie du Recueil Sirey, 1919), 15.

28. Alfred Zimmern, *The League of Nations and the Rule of Law, 1918–1935* (London: Macmillan, 1936), 495. At the beginning of his book, Zimmern confessed that he did not know "whether I was writing a history of an experiment that had reached its conclusion or describing the early phases of a living and developing institution" (xii–xiii).

29. E. H. Carr, *The Twenty-Years' Crisis 1919–1939: An Introduction to the Study of International Relations* (London: Macmillan, 1939), 307. These are, significantly, the closing words of the book.

30. Quoted in Pegg, *Evolution of the European Idea*, 15.

31. Carl Schmitt, *Concept of the Political* [1932], trans. George Schwab (Chicago and London: University of Chicago Press, 1996), 55–8.

32. Thomas Hobbes, *Leviathan* [1651] (I,14), ed. Richard Tuck (Cambridge: Cambridge University Press, 1991), 94.

33. Quoted in Mazower, *Governing the World*, 139.

34. Henry Cabot Lodge, *The Senate and the League of Nations* (New York: C. Scribner's Sons 1925), 185.

35. Jean Bodin, *The Six Bookes of a Commonweal*, ed. Kenneth Douglas McRae and trans. Richard Knolles (Cambridge, MA: Harvard University Press, 1962) 1, 84. The best account of Bodin's conception of sovereignty and its subsequent influence on the evolution of the theory of the state is Daniel Lee, *The Right of Sovereignty* (Oxford: Oxford University Press, forthcoming).

36. Carl Schmitt, *Constitutional Theory*, ed. and trans. Jeffrey Seitzer (Durham, NC, and London: Duke University Press, 2008), 101.

37. Hobbes, *Leviathan* (II, 18), 127.

38. For a further discussion of the definition of sovereignty, see pp. 277–8 and 296–8.

39. Luigi Einaudi, "La Società delle Nazioni è un ideale possibile?," *Corriere della Sera*, January 5, 1918, and reprinted in *La guerra e l'unità europea* (Florence: Le Monnier, 1984), 1–8. The full range of Einaudi's ideas on federation and their limits are discussed in Matthew D'Auria, "Junius and the 'President Professor,'" in *Europe in Crisis: Intellectuals and the European Idea 1917–1957*, ed. Mark Hewitson and Matthew D'Auria (New York and Oxford: Berghahn, 2012), 289–304.

40. See pp. 6–7.

41. Luigi Einaudi, "Contro il mito dello stato sovrano," *Risorgimento liberale*, January, 3 1945, https://www.inasaroma.org/wp-content/uploads/EINAUDI-Contro-il-mito-dello-stato-sovrano.pdf, accessed February 9, 2021.

42. James W. Garner, "Des limitations à la souveraineté nationale dans les relations extérieures," *Revue de droit international et de législation comparée* 52 (1925), 36–58.

43. Hans Kelsen, *Peace through Law* [1944] (New York and London: Garland Publishing Inc., 1973), 10.

44. Kelsen, *Peace through Law*, 14, 49–50. Kelsen had, as he said in 1941, tried to persuade the world that "the establishment of a court with compulsory

jurisdiction is the first and indispensable step to an effective reform of international relations" (49–50).

45. Hans Kelsen, *General Theory of Law and State*, trans. Anders Wedberg (Cambridge
MA: Harvard University Press, 1945), 318–20. And on centralization and decentralization, see Hans Kelsen, *Pure Theory of Law*, trans. Max Knight (Berkeley
and Los Angeles, CA: California University Press, 1967), 313.

46. See Hidemi Suganami, "Understanding Sovereignty through Kelsen/Schmitt,"
Review of International Studies 33 (2007), 511–30.

47. Jan-Werner Müller *A Dangerous Mind: Carl Schmitt in Post-War European Thought*
(New Haven, CT, and London: Yale University Press, 2003), 3.

48. Schmitt, *Constitutional Theory*, 390.

49. On Scelle, see Koskenniemi, *Gentle Civiliszer of Nations*, 316–17.

50. Scelle, *Pacte des nations*, 94–5.

51. Scelle, *Pacte des nations*, 98–9.

52. Scelle, *Pacte des nations*, 100–1.

53. Herman Heller, *Sovereignty: A Contribution to the Theory of Public and International
Law*, ed. David Dyzenhaus (Oxford: Oxford University Press, 2019), 74–5.

54. See Jean-Michel Guine, "'Société universelle des nations' et 'sociétés continentales': Les Juristes internationalistes euro-américains et la question du régionalisme européen dans les années 1920," *Siècles* 41 (2015), https://journals.
openedition.org/siecles/2584?lang=en, accessed February 8, 2021.

55. Léon Bourgeois, "The Reasons for the League of Nations," https://www.
nobelprize.org/nobel_prizes/peace/laureates/1920/bourgeois-lecture.html,
accessed February 9, 2021. Bourgeois had written a glowing preface to Scelle's
Pacte des nations.

56. Henry Sumner Maine, *International Law* (London: John Murray, 1888), 58. And
in general on the issue of divided sovereignty, see Edward Keene, *Beyond the
Anarchical Society: Grotius, Colonialism and Order in World Politics* (Cambridge:
Cambridge University Press, 2002).

57. R. W. G. Mackay, *Federal Europe: Being the Case for European Federation together
with a Draft Constitution of a United States of Europe* (London: Michael
Joseph, 1940).

58. Alfred Zimmern, *Europe in Convalescence* (London Mills and Boon, 1922), 126.
On Zimmern, see Mazower, *No Enchanted Palace*, 66–103. On the wider issue
of the sovereignty of the Great Powers, in particular over their mandatory
territories, see Susan Pedersen, *The Guardians: The League of Nations and the
Crisis of Empire* (Oxford: Oxford University Press, 2015), 204–32.

59. Paul Valéry, "La Crise de l'esprit" [1924], in *Œuvres complètes*, vol. 1, *Variétés*
(Paris: Gallimard, Bibliothèque de la Pléiade 1957), 988.

60. Paul Valéry, "Note (ou L'Européen)" [1924], in *Œuvres complètes* I, 1412–15.

61. Albert Demangeon, *Le Déclin de l'Europe*, (Paris: Payot, 1920), 313–14.

62. Henri Massis, *Defence of the West*, trans. F. S. Flint, with a preface by
G. K. Chesterton (London: Faber and Gwyer, 1927), 167, 19. See also Jan
Ifversen, "The Crisis of European Civilization after 1918," in *Ideas of Europe since*

1914: The Legacy of the First World War, ed. Menno Spiering and Michael Wintle (Houndmills: Palgrave Macmillan, 2002), 14–31.

63. Quoted in Mark Hewitson, "Inventing Europe and Reinventing the Nation-State in a New World Order," in *Europe in Crisis*, ed. Hewitson and D'Auria, 64.

64. Edmund Husserl, *Phenomenology and the Crisis of Philosophy: Philosophy as Rigorous Science and Philosophy and the Crisis of European Man* [1935], trans. Quentin Lauer (New York: Harper and Row, 1965), 150, 157.

65. Husserl, *Phenomenology*, 155.

66. Husserl, *Phenomenology*, 189.

67. Oswald Spengler, *The Decline of the West: Form and Actuality*, vol. 1, trans. Charles Francis Atkinson (New York: Alfred Knopf, 1927), 2, 335.

68. Friedrich Nietzsche, "Aus dem Nachlass der achtziger Jahre," quoted in Jean Starobinski, "Le Mot civilisation," in *Le Remède dans le Mal : Critique et légitimation de l'artifice à l'âge des Lumières* (Paris: Gallimard, 1989), 11–59, at p. 43.

69. Spengler, *Decline of the West*, vol. 1, 31.

70. Northrop Frye, "*The Decline of the West* by Oswald Spengler," *Daedalus* 103, (1974), 1–13.

71. Spengler, *Decline of the West*, vol. 1, 415.

72. Spengler, *Decline of the West*, vol. 1, 417.

73. Denis de Rougemont, *Vingt-huit siècles d'Europe* (Paris: Payot, 1961), 213.

74. Miguel de Unamuno, "L'Avenir de l'Europe: Le Point de vue d'un Espagnol," *La Revue de Genéve* (1 January, 1923), 20.

75. See Joshua Foa Dienstag, *Pessimism: Philosophy, Ethic, Spirit* (Princeton, NJ: Princeton University Press, 2006).

76. It was clear, he wrote in May 1917, that since the Russian Revolution "This enormous war is itself going to be swallowed up by social questions. I have ceased despairing of seeing Germany as a republic. Well then, England too? All the states of Europe as republics; the war will not end otherwise" (Gide, *André Gide*, 205).

77. André Gide, "L'Avenir de l'Europe: Le Point de vue d'un Français," *La Revue de Genève* 6 (1923) 1–9. One of a number of such comments by leading European intellectuals including Miguel de Unamuno (see n. 27), Hermann von Keyserling, John Middleton-Murray, and Vilfredo Pareto. For the context and history of the *Revue*, see Jean-Pierre Meylan, *La Revue de Genève* (Geneva: Droz, 1969), 252–5.

78. Georges Scelle, "Essai relatif a l'Union européenne," *Revue générale de droit international public* 38 (1931), 521–63. This was, in fact, one of a number of essays by Alejandro Álvarez, Albert de Lapradelle, Yves de La Brière, the Greek diplomat Nicolaos Politis, Louis Le Fur, Henri Truchy, and Joseph Barthélemy, among others, concerning what was referred to as the "regionalization" of the League. For a general account, see Guine, "'Société universelle des nations'."

79. José Ortega y Gasset, *The Revolt of the Masses* (New York: W. W. Norton, 1952), 176–83.

80. Zimmern, *Europe in Convalescence*, 139.

81. For a detailed account of Coudenhove-Kalergi's project, see Anita Ziegerhofer, *Botschafter Europas: Richard Nikolaus Coudenhove-Kalergi und die Paneuropa-Bewegung in den zwanziger und dreißiger Jahren* (Vienna: Böhlau, 2004).

82. Richard von Coudenhove-Kalergi, *Praktischer Idealismus* (Vienna: Paneuropa-Verlag, 1925), 22.

83. Richard von Coudenhove-Kalergi, *The Totalitarian State against Man* (Glarus, Switzerland: Paneuropa Editions, 1938), 104–5.

84. Coudenhove-Kalergi, *Crusade for Pan-Europe*, 79. In an open letter to Benito Mussolini, February 22, 1923.

85. Richard von Coudenhove-Kalergi, *Europe Must Unite* (Glarus, Switzerland: Paneuropa Editions, [1939]), 17–18.

86. Coudenhove-Kalergi, *Europe Must Unite*, 26.

87. Coudenhove-Kalergi, *Europe Must Unite*, 84, and Richard von Coudenhove-Kalergi, *Europe Seeks Unity* (New York: Institute of Public Affairs and Regional Studies, 1948), 8.

88. Coudenhove-Kalergi, *Europe Must Unite*, 104.

89. Coudenhove-Kalergi, *Europe Must Unite*, 97.

90. Coudenhove-Kalergi, *Europe Must Unite*, 87 and Richard von Coudenhove-Kalergi, *Pan-Europe* (New York: Alfred A. Knopf, 1927), 24–6.

91. Coudenhove-Kalergi, *Pan-Europe*, 90; Coudenhove-Kalergi, *Europe Seeks Unity*, 12–14.

92. Coudenhove-Kalergi, *Europe Must Unite*, 133.

93. Coudenhove-Kalergi, *Crusade for Pan-Europe*, 78–80 On Schmitt's use of the Monroe Doctrine, see pp. 200–2.

94. Coudenhove-Kalergi, *Crusade for Pan-Europe*, 170–2. See also Marco Duranti, *The Conservative Human Rights Revolution: European Identity, Transnational Politics, and the Origins of the European Convention* (Oxford: Oxford University Press, 2017), 73–6.

95. Coudenhove-Kalergi, *Europe Must Unite*, 117–25.

96. Coudenhove-Kalergi, *Europe Must Unite*, 18–20.

97. Coudenhove-Kalergi, *Europe Must Unite*, 119.

98. "Turkey excepted, Europe is nothing more than a province of the world. When we battle, we engage in nothing more than a civil war." David Armitage, *Civil Wars. A History in Ideas*, 196–7. There are, as Armitage points out, many previous instances of all wars being described as civil wars. This, however, seems to have been the first case of all wars between *Europeans* being so called.

99. Coudenhove-Kalergi, *Pan-Europe*, 33–4.

100. Gaston Riou, *The Diary of a French Private: War-Imprisonment 1914–1915*, trans. Eden Paul and Cedar Paul (London: Allen and Unwin, 1916), 221.

101. Mark Mazower, *Dark Continent: Europe's Twentieth Century* (New York: Vintage Books, 2000), 19.

102. Ortega y Gasset, *Revolt of the Masses*, 17–18.

103. Gaston Riou, *Europe, ma patrie*, édition revue et augumentée (Paris: Éditions Baundinière, 1938), 30–1. This edition includes both *Europe, ma patrie* and *S'unir ou mourir*.

104. Riou, *Europe, ma patrie*, 144–5.

105. Riou, *Europe, ma patrie*, 31–2.

106. Riou, *Europe, ma patrie*, 36.

107. Riou, *Europe, ma patrie*, 63–70.

108. Riou, *Europe, ma patrie*, 33.

109. Riou, *Europe, ma patrie*, 57–9.

110. Riou, *Europe, ma patrie*, 147–9.

111. Riou, *Europe, ma patrie*, 180–1.

112. Quoted in Peter M. R. Stirk, "Introduction: Crisis and Continuity in Interwar Europe," in *European Unity in the Interwar Period*, ed. Peter M. R. Stirk (London and New York: Pinter Publishers, 1989), 13. On the British attitudes toward and limited understanding of ideas for European union at the time, see Robert Boyce, "British Capitalism and the Idea of European Unity between the Wars," in Stirk, *European Unity*, 65–83.

113. Arthur Salter, *The United States of Europe and Other Papers* (New York: Reynal and Hitchcock, 1933), 89.

114. Riou, *Europe, ma patrie*, 35.

115. Riou, *Europe, ma patrie*, 169.

116. Riou, *Europe, ma patrie*, 38.

117. Riou, *Europe, ma patrie*, 103.

118. On this aspect of Riou's work and of that of many of his contemporaries, see Bernard Bruneteau, *"L'Europe nouvelle de Hitler": Une Illusion des intellectuels de la France de Vichy* (Monaco: Éditions du Rocher, 2003) and Jean-Luc Chabot, "Le Primat de la civilisation occidentale au principe des premiers plans d'Europe unie," in *L'Europe communautaire au défi de la hiérarchie*, ed. Bernard Bruneteau and Youssef Cassis (Brussels: P. I. E. Peter Lang, 2000), 37–56.

119. On Briand's career, see Gérard Unger, *Aristide Briand: Le Ferme Conciliateur* (Paris: Fayard, 2005).

120. Text in David Hunter Miler, *The Peace Pact of Paris: A Study in the Briand–Kellogg Treaty* (New York and London: G. P. Putnam, 1928), 25. The "High Contracting Parties" were Germany, USA, Belgium, France, the United Kingdom, Canada, Australia, New Zealand, South Africa, Ireland, India, Italy, Poland, and Czechoslovakia. For a lively account of the creation and subsequent history of the Pact, see Oona A. Hathaway and Scott J. Shapiro, *The Internationalists and Their Plan to Outlaw War* (London: Penguin Books, 2018).

121. See Steiner, *The Lights That Failed*, 572–3.

122. Quoted in Mazower, *Dark Continent*, 109.

123. Aristide Briand, "Déclaration d'Aristide Briand," in *Europe, ma patrie*, 9.

124. Coudenhove-Kalergi, *Crusade for Pan-Europe*, 131.

125. Coudenhove-Kalergi, *Europe Seeks Unity*, 27.

126. These words are repeated verbatim in Briand's "Déclaration," in *Europe, ma patrie*, 10. For a full discussion of the drafting of the speech, see Élisabeth Du Réau, *L'Idée d'Europe au XXe siècle: Des mythes aux réalités* (Brussels: Éditions Complexe, 2008), 97–108.

127. Quoted in Mark Hewitson "The United States of Europe: The European Question in the 1920s" in *Europe in Crisis*, ed. Hewitson and D'Auria, 26.

128. Gustav Stresemann, *The Times*, December 2, 1921, p. 16.

129. Ortega y Gasset, *Revolt of the Masses*, 179.

130. Jean Monnet, *Memoirs*, trans. Richard Mayne (New York: Doubleday, 1978), 300.

131. Alexis Léger, *Mémorandum sur l'organisation d'un régime d'union fédérale européenne*, https://gallica.bnf.fr/ark:/12148/bpt6k5613159m/f5.image, 11.

132. Léger, *Mémorandum*, 16.

133. Scelle, "Essai relatif à l'union européenne," 530–2.

134. Scelle, "Essai relatif à l'union européenne," 537.

135. "Can Europe Unite ?" *Political Science Quarterly*, 46 (1931), 428–9.

136. Coudenhove-Kalergi, *Crusade for Pan-Europe*, 135. See also Marco Duranti, *The Conservative Human Rights Revolution*, 73–6.

137. Léger, *Mémorandum*, 8.

138. Scelle, "Essai relatif à l'union européenne," 535. Emphasis original.

139. Léger, *Mémorandum*, 14.

140. Mackay, *Federal Europe*, 98.

141. Brunet, *Société des Nations*, 49–50. See also Koskenniemi, *Gentle Civilizer of Nations*, 270–4. For the "Grand Design," see pp. 10–11.

142. Quoted in Hewitson, "United States of Europe," in *Europe in Crisis*, ed. Hewitson and D'Auria, 16.

143. For a detailed account of the responses from the various European nations, see Antoine Fleury with Lubor Jílek, eds., *Le Plan Briand d'union fédérale européenne: Perspectives nationales et transnationales, avec documents: Actes du colloque international tenu à Genève du 19 au 21 septembre 1991* (Berne and Berlin: Peter Lang, 1991).

144. See Élisabeth Du Réau, "La France et l'Éurope d'Aristide Briand à Robert Schuman: Naissance, déclin et redéploiement d'une politique étrangère (1919–1950)," *Revue d'histoire moderne et contemporaine* 42 (1995), 556–67.

145. Saint-Jean Perse, *Anabasis: A poem by St-J. Perse with a translation into English by T. S. Eliot*, (London: Faber and Faber, 1930), VIII.

146. Scelle, "Essai relatif a l'Union européenne," 521–63.

147. Émile Durkheim, *The Division of Labour in Society*, trans. W. D. Halls (New York: Free Press, 1984), 405–6. See also F. Callegaro and N. Marcucci, "Europe as a Political Society: Emile Durkheim, the Federalist Principle and the Ideal of a Cosmopolitan Justice." *Constellations* 25 (2018), 542–55. doi: 10.1111/1467-8675.12352.

148. Scelle, "Essai relatif a l'Union européenne," 523.

149. Émile Durkheim, *Professional Ethics and Civic Morals*, trans. Cornelia Brookfield (London and New York: Routledge, 1957), 74.

150. Scelle, "Essai relatif a l'union européenne," 523.

151. Keynes, *Economic Consequences of the Peace*, 34.

152. Scelle, "Essai relatif à l'union européenne," 521–2.

153. Scelle, "Essai relatif à l'union européenne," 522–3.

154. Scelle, "Essai relatif à l'union européenne," 256–7.

155. See Chapter 2, Section VIII, pp. 69–70.

156. Scelle, "Essai relatif à l'union européenne," 256–7. Scelle's "ideological type" is clearly indebted to Max Weber's "ideal type."

5. A NEW ORDER FOR EUROPE

1. Georges Duhamel, *L'Avenir de l'esprit europénne* (Paris: Société des Nations, Institut international de coopération intellectuelle, 1934), 127–9. See also Jean-Luc Chabot *L'Idée d'Europe unie* (Grenoble: Presses Universitaires de France, 2005), 204.

2. Raymond Aron, "L'Aube de l'histoire universelle," in *Penser la liberté, penser la démocatie* (Paris: Gallimard, 2005), 1795–6.

3. E. H. Carr, *The Twenty-Years' Crisis 1919–1939: An Introduction to the Study of International Relations* (London: Macmillan, 1939), 287.

4. For a brilliant historical analysis of the period as a struggle between these three competing ideologies, see Mark Mazower, *Dark Continent*.

5. Zara Steiner, *The Lights That Failed: European International History 1919–1933* (Oxford: Oxford University Press, 2005), 65–6.

6. Carl Schmitt, "The *Grossraum* Order of International Law [*Völkerrechtliche Großraumordnung*] with a Ban on Intervention for Spatially Foreign Powers: A Contribution to the Concept of *Reich* in International Law [*Völkerrecht*] (1939–1941)," in *Carl Schmitt, Writings on War*, ed. and trans. Timothy Nunan (Cambridge: Polity Press, 2011), 89. For the complicated publishing history of this text, see *Carl Schmitt, Writings on War*, 73–4. As William Hooker points out, *Völkerrecht* is a difficult term to translate. The most obvious English version would be not "international law," but "law of peoples," itself a rendering of the Roman *ius gentium*, usually translated as "law of nations," that is, not so much a universal law to which all states agree to be bound as a set of rules agreed upon by certain states in order to regulate their relationship between each other. Schmitt himself, however, insists that "international law [*Völkerrecht*] is, as *jus gentium*, as a law of nations first and foremost a personal concrete order.... The principle of order assigned to the concept of nation in international law is the right of national self-determination," which must mean that no international law can impinge upon the sovereignty of the individual state. (Schmitt, "*Grossraum* Order of International Law," in *Carl Schmitt, Writings on War*, 77). The term "law of peoples" has, however, been widely used in American jurisprudence in quite a different sense by John Rawls and his followers to capture Rawls's conception of a well-meaning liberal order, what Rawls called the law of "decent" (but not necessarily democratic) peoples, which is clearly very far from what Schmitt had in

mind. See William Hooker, *Carl Schmitt's International Thought: Order and Orientation* (Cambridge: Cambridge University Press, 2009) 128, n. 6.

7. See Martti Koskenniemi, "International Law as Political Theology: How to Read *Nomos der Erde?*," *Constellations* 11 (2004), 492–511.

8. Quoted in Brendan Simms, *Europe: The Struggle for Supremacy from 1453 to the Present* (New York: Basic Books, 2013), 322.

9. See in general, Birgit Kletzin, *Europa aus Rasse und Raum: Die nationalsozialistische Idee der Neuen Ordnung* (Münster: Lit, 2000).

10. Joseph J. Bendersky, *Carl Schmitt: Theorist for the Reich* (Princeton, NJ: Princeton University Press, 1983), 250–55; on Haushofer, see Holger H. Herwig, *The Demon of Geopolitics: How Karl Haushofer "Educated" Hitler and Hess* (Lanham, MD: Rowman and Littlefield, 2016).

11. See Peter M. R. Stirk, "The Idea of Mitteleuropa," in *Mitteleuropa: Idea and Prospects* (Edinburgh: Edinburgh University Press. 1994), 1–20.

12. Friedrich Naumann, *Central Europe [Mitteleuropa]*, trans. Christabel M. Meredith (New York: Alfred A. Knopf, 1917), 179.

13. See Bo Stråth, "Mitteleuropa: From List to Naumann," *European Journal of Social Theory* 11 (2008), 171–83. See also Patrick Pasture, *Imagining European Unity since 1000 AD* (London: Palgrave Macmillan, 2015), 91–4.

14. Naumann, *Central Europe*, 46.

15. Jan-Werner Müller, *Contesting Democracy: Political Ideas in Twentieth-Century Europe* (New Haven, CT, and London: Yale University Press, 2011), 122.

16. Quoted in Mark Mazower, *Hitler's Empire: How the Nazis Ruled Europe* (New York: Penguin, 2008), 43.

17. Jan-Werner Müller *A Dangerous Mind: Carl Schmitt in Post-War European Thought* (New Haven, CT, and London: Yale University Press, 2003), 3.

18. Schmitt, "*Grossraum* Order of International Law," in *Carl Schmitt, Writings on War*, 114.

19. Carl Schmitt, "Völkerbund und Europa," in *Positionen und Begriffe im Kampf mit Weimar-Genf-Versailles, 1923–1939* (Berlin: Duncker and Humboldt, 1940), 91. See also Gopal Balakrishnan, *The Enemy: An Intellectual Portrait of Carl Schmitt* (London and New York: Verso, 2000), 85.

20. Carl Schmitt, *The Nomos of the Earth in International Law and the Jus Publicum Europaeum* [1950], trans. G. L. Ulmen (New York: Telos Press, 2003), 257–8, and cf. 241. On Schmitt's views on the League, see Müller, *Dangerous Mind*, 26.

21. Schmitt, "*Grossraum* Order of International Law," in *Carl Schmitt, Writings on War*, 81, quoting the nineteenth-century Italian philosopher, Luigi Valli.

22. Schmitt, "*Grossraum* Order of International Law," in *Carl Schmitt, Writings on War*, 107. Schmitt attributes the "organisation"/"organism" distinction to the Nazi constitutional lawyer and SS-Oberführer Reinhard Höhn.

23. Carl Schmitt, *Constitutional Theory*, ed. and trans. Jeffrey Seitzer, (Durham, NC, and London: Duke University Press, 2008), 101, 127–8.

24. Schmitt, "*Grossraum* Order of International Law," in *Carl Schmitt, Writings on War*, 99.

25. Schmitt, "*Grossraum* Order of International Law," in *Carl Schmitt, Writings on War*, 103–4.

26. Schmitt, "*Grossraum* Order of International Law," in *Carl Schmitt, Writings on War*, 113.

27. Schmitt, "*Grossraum* Order of International Law," in *Carl Schmitt, Writings on War*, 119–20. Emphasis added.

28. Schmitt, "*Grossraum* Order of International Law," in *Carl Schmitt, Writings on War*, 101.

29. Schmitt, "*Grossraum* Order of International Law," in *Carl Schmitt, Writings on War*, 88.

30. Carl Schmitt, "Cambio de estructura del derecho internacional," *Revista de estudios políticos* 5 (1943), 3–36. This also paid tribute to the Franco regime.

31. Schmitt, "*Grossraum* Order of International Law," in *Carl Schmitt, Writings on War*, 87. See also Hooker, *Carl Schmitt's International Thought*, 133–4 and Bendersky, *Carl Schmitt*, 258–9.

32. Bendersky, *Carl Schmitt*, 252–9.

33. Quoted in Oona A. Hathaway and Scott J. Shapiro, *The Internationalists and Their Plan to Outlaw War* (London: Penguin Books, 2018), 242–3.

34. Quoted in Mark Mazower, *Governing the World: The History of an Idea* (New York: Penguin, 2012), 184.

35. Schmitt, "*Grossraum* Order of International Law," in *Carl Schmitt, Writings on War*, 82–3.

36. Schmitt, "*Grossraum* Order of International Law," in *Carl Schmitt, Writings on War*, 87–8.

37. Schmitt, "*Grossraum* Order of International Law," in *Carl Schmitt, Writings on War*, 101.

38. Schmitt, "*Grossraum* Order of International Law," in *Carl Schmitt, Writings on War*, 116.

39. Schmitt, "*Grossraum* Order of International Law," in *Carl Schmitt, Writings on War*, 102.

40. Schmitt, "*Grossraum* Order of International Law," in *Carl Schmitt, Writings on War*, 111.

41. On Schmitt's understanding and use of the Holy Roman Empire, see Ionut Untea, "New Middle Ages or New Modernity? Carl Schmitt's Interwar Perspective on Political Unity in Europe," in *Europe in Crisis. Intellectuals and the European Idea 1917–1957*, ed. Mark Hewitson and Matthew D'Auria (New York and Oxford: Berghahn, 2012), 169–82.

42. Mazower, *Hitler's Empire*, 580.

43. Timothy Snyder, *The Road to Unfreedom: Russia, Europe, America* (New York: Tim Duggan Books, 2018), 81–3.

44. Quoted in Benjamin G. Martin *The Nazi-Fascist New Order for European Culture* (Cambridge, MA: Harvard University Press, 2016), 1.

45. Clifton J. Child, "The Concept of the New Order" in *Hitler's Europe: Survey of International Affairs 1939–1946*, ed. Arnold Toynbee and Veronica M. Toynbee (London: Oxford University Press, 1954), 47–51.

46. Bertrand de Jouvenel, *Après la défaite* (Paris: Plon, 1941), 129–32.

47. Bertrand de Jouvenel, "Quelle Europe voulons-nous" [May 1945], in *Quelle Europe?* [A collection of Jouvenel's newspaper articles] (Paris: Le Portulan, n.d.), 90–3.

48. Bertrand de Jouvenel, "Un Gouvernement mondial?" [December 1945], in *Quelle Europe?*, 143.

49. Bertrand de Jouvenel, *L'Amérique en Europe: Le Plan Marshall et la coopération intercontinentale* (Paris: Plon, 1948), 12.

50. Bernard Bruneteau, *"L'Europe nouvelle de Hitler": Une Illusion des intellectuels de la France de Vichy* (Monaco: Éditions du Rocher, 2003), 37–8.

51. Joseph Goebbels, "Directive on the Treatment of the European Nation" [February 15, 1943], in *Documents on the History of European Integration*, vol. 1: *Continental Plans for European Union 1939–1945*, ed. Walter Lipgens (Berlin and New York: Walter de Gruyter, 1985), 120.

52. Joachim von Ribbentrop, "Joachim von Ribbentrop: Europa Confederation 21 March, 1943," in *Documents on the History of European Integration*, vol. 1, ed. Walter Lipgens, 123–4.

53. Quoted in Simms, *Europe*, 307.

54. Quoted in Mazower, *Dark Continent*, 147–9.

55. Quoted in Martin, *Nazi-Fascist New Order*, 184.

56. Alexandre Kojève, *Outline of a Phenomenology of Right* [1943], ed. and trans. Bryan-Paul Frost and Robert Howse (Lanham, MD: Rowman and Littlefield, 2000), 327. Written in 1943, although only published in 1982, this is Kojève's most extensive and perhaps most original work; and it prefigures and explains much of what he subsequently wrote about and did for the European Union. On this, see the "Introductory Essay" by Robert Howse and Bryan-Paul Frost (1–27).

57. "Outline of a Doctrine of French Policy" [1945] *Policy Review* 3/4 (2004), 3–40. Kojève died on June 4, 1968, shortly after having delivered a speech to the EEC on behalf of the French government.

58. Giovanni Gentile, *Origini e dottrina del fascismo* (Rome: Libreria del Littorio, 1929), 26.

59. Reprinted in Gabriele D'Annunzio, *La Carta del Carnaro e altri scritti su Fiume* (Rome: Castelvecchi, 2009). And see Dominique Kircher Reill, "Fiume Crisis: Life in the Wake of the Habsburg Empire" (Cambridge , MA: Harvard University Press, 2020). Available at: https://www.hup.harvard.edu/catalog. php?isbn=9780674244245, accessed February 13, 2021.

60. Ruth Ben-Ghiat, *La cultura fascista* (Bologna: Il Mulino, 2000), 207–11.

61. Quoted in MacGregor Knox, *Common Destiny: Dictatorship, Foreign Policy and War in Fascist Italy and Nazi Germany* (Cambridge: Cambridge University Press, 2000), 61.

62. Quoted in Emilio Gentile, *La Grande Italia: Il mito della nazione nel XX secolo* (Rome and Bari: Laterza, 2006), 193–4.

63. The phrase "bloodthirsty recluse" is MacGregor Knox's; *Common Destiny*, 61.

64. See Davide Rodogno, *Fascism's European Empire: Italian Occupation during the Second World War* (Cambridge: Cambridge University Press, 2006), 44–6.

65. Emilio Gentile, *I profeti del risorgimeno italiano* (Florence: Vallecchi Editore, 1923), 35–7. Gentile claimed to believe that the "philosophy" of Fascism was "not a

philosophy that thinks, but one that does, and that reveals itself not in formulas but in actions" (Gentile, *Origini*, 58).

66. Quoted in Giovanni Gentile, *Il culto del littorio* (Rome and Bari: Laterza, 1994), 115–16.

67. Emilio Gentile, *Fascismo, storia e interpretazione* (Rome and Bari: Laterza, 2002), 214–15 and *Il culto del littorio*, 111–17. On Giovanni Gentile and Mazzini see Claudio Fogu, *The Historic Imaginary: Politics of History in Fascist Italy* (Toronto, Buffalo, and London: University of Toronto Press, 2003), 25–7.

68. Quoted in Emilio Gentile, *La Grande Italia*, 153–4.

69. Quoted in Davide Rodogno, "Le Nouvel Ordre fasciste en Méditerranée, 1940–1943: Présupposés idéologiques, visions et velléités," *Revue d'histoire moderne et contemporaine* 55 (2008), 138–56.

70. Quoted in Marco Duranti, *The Conservative Human Rights Revolution: European Identity, Transnational Politics, and the Origins of the European Convention* (Oxford: Oxford University Press, 2017), 77.

71. Oswald Mosley, *Europe: Faith and Plan* (n.p.: Euphorion Books, 1958), 135–6; 2–3.

72. Jean-Paul Sartre, *Qu'est-ce que la littérature* [1948], (Paris: Gallimard, 2008), 280.

73. Peter Jay, "Europe: Periclean League of Democracies, Bonaparte's Third French Empire or Carolingian Fourth Reich?," in *The Pursuit of Europe: Perspectives from the Engelsburg Seminar*, ed. Kurt Almqvist and Alexander Linklater (Stockholm: Axel and Margaret Ax:son Johnson Foundation, 2012), 63–72, whose title says it all.

74. H. G. Wells, Salvador de Madariaga, J. Middleton Murry, and C. E. M. Joad, *On the New World Order* (London: National Peace Council, 1940), 4 and 26.

75. Kojève, "Outline of a Doctrine of French Policy," 3–40.

76. Anson Rabinbach and Sandra L. Gilman, eds., *The Third Reich Source Book* (Berkeley, Los Angeles, and London: University of California Press, 2013), 865–6. See also Harold James *The Roman Predicament: how the rules of international order create the politics of empire* (Princeton, NJ: Princeton University Press, 2006), 123. And on Moltke, see Ger van Roon, *German Resistance to Hitler: Count Moltke and the Kreisau Circle* (London, New York: Van Nostrand Reinhold Co., 1971).

77. Altiero Spinelli, *La mia battaglia per un'Europa diversa* (Maduria: Lacaita editore, 1979), 7, 25.

78. Spinelli is buried in the local cemetery on Ventotene and, on August 22, 2016, the Italian prime minister Matteo Renzi, the German chancellor Angela Merkel, and the French president François Hollande met on the island, which had subsequently become a holiday resort, to work out a coordinated reaction to a possible Brexit.

79. Altiero Spinelli, *Il manifesto di Ventotene con un saggio di Norberto Bobbio* (Bologna: Il Mulino, 1991), 37.

80. Spinelli, *Il manifesto di Ventotene*, 42–7.

81. Altiero Spinelli, "Politica marxista e politica federalista" [written between 1942 and 1943], in Spinelli, *Il manifesto di Ventotene*, 137–8.

82. Spinelli, *Il manifesto di Ventotene*, 49.

83. Altiero Spinelli, "Sviluppo del moto per l'unità europea dopo la seconda guerra mondiale" [1957], in *Il Progetto europeo* (Bologna: Il Mulino, 1985), 163.

84. Spinelli, *Il manifesto di Ventotene*, 48–50.

85. "Gli stati uniti d'Europa e le varie tendenze politiche," a pamphlet written in late 1942 and printed in Spinelli, *Il manifesto di Ventotene*, 71–2.

86. Spinelli, *Il manifesto di Ventotene*, 92–3.

87. Spinelli, *Il manifesto di Ventotene*, 93, quoting *Faust*, 1977. Mephistopheles is, in fact, condemning customary law as resembling an "eternal disease."

88. Jean Monnet, "Note de réflexion de Jean Monnet (Alger, 5 août 1943)," https://www.cvce.eu/obj/note_de_reflexion_de_jean_monnet_alger_5_aout_1943-fr-b61a8924-57bf-4890-9e4b-73bf4d882549.html, accessed February 11, 2021.

89. See p. 82.

90. Spinelli, *Il manifesto di Ventotene*, 86–7.

91. Spinelli, *Il manifesto di Ventotene*, 51.

92. Spinelli, *Il manifesto di Ventotene*, 89.

93. T. S. Eliot, *Notes towards the Definition of Culture* (New York: Harcourt, Brace, and Company, 1949), 123–4.

94. Spinelli, *Il manifesto di Ventotene*, 88.

95. Spinelli, *Il manifesto di Ventotene*, 49–50.

96. Quoted in Walter Lipgens, *The Formation of the European Unity Movement* [vol. 1 of *A History of European Integration 1945–1947*] (Oxford: Clarendon Press, 1982), 57.

97. Altiero Spinelli, *Altiero Spinelli: From Ventotene to the European Constitution*, ARENA Report No 1/07, RECON Report No 1, ed. Agustín José Menéndez (Oslo: Centre for European Studies University of Oslo, 2007), 72, http://www.reconproject.eu/main.php/RECONreport0107.pdf?fileitem=50487350, accessed February 11, 2021. I would like to thank Mike Raapport for drawing the history of the Draft Treaty to my attention.

98. See pp. 249–56.

6. REFASHIONING EUROPE

1. Henri Brugmans, *Pour un gouvernement européen* (n.p.: Éditions de la Campagne Européenne de la Jeunesse, 1952) 29–30.

2. Henri Brugmans, *L'Idée européenne 1920–1970* (Bruges: De Tempel, 1970), 102–5.

3. Bertrand Vayssière, *Vers une Europe fédérale?: Les Espoirs et les actions fédéralistes au sortir de la Seconde Guerre Mondiale* (Brussels: Peter Lang, 2006), 109–17.

4. Quoted in Walter Lipgens, *The Formation of the European Unity Movement* [vol. 1 of *A History of European Integration 1945–1947*] (Oxford: Clarendon Press, 1982), 70–1.

5. William C. Bullitt, *The Great Globe Itself: A Preface to World Affairs* (New York: Charles Scribner's Sons, 1946).

6. Quoted in Lipgens, *Formation of the European Unity Movement*, 74.

7. Winston Churchill, "Speech to a Joint Meeting of the Senate and Chamber, Brussels, 16 November, 1945," in *The Sinews of Peace: Post-War Speeches by Winston Churchill* (London: Cassell, 1948), 41–2.

8. Quoted in Tony Judt, *A Grand Illusion? An Essay on Europe* (London: Penguin Books, 1995), 5.

9. Lipgens, *Formation of the European Unity Movement*, 67.

10. Alan S. Milward, *The Reconstruction of Western Europe 1945–1951* (London: Methuen, 1984), 392.

11. Michael Hogan, *The Marshall Plan: America, Britain and the Reconstruction of Western Europe 1947–1952* (Cambridge: Cambridge University Press, 1987), 427. See also Stanley Hoffman and Charles Maier, eds. *The Marshall Plan: A Retrospective* (Boulder, CO: Westview Press, 1984) Perhaps the most recent exploration of the claim that the plan was actually intended to foster collaboration and eventual integration among the nations of Europe is Michael Holm, *The Marshall Plan: A New Deal for Europe* (New York: Routledge, 2016).

12. Quoted in Lipgens, *Formation of the European Unity Movement*, 318.

13. Quoted in Marco Duranti, *The Conservative Human Rights Revolution: European Identity, Transnational Politics, and the Origins of the European Convention* (Oxford: Oxford University Press, 2017), 189.

14. Winston Churchill, "Speech at Zurich University 19 September, 1946," in *Sinews of Peace*, 198–202.

15. Denis de Rougemont, *L'Europe en jeu*, in *Œuvres complètes*, vol. 3 (Paris: Éditions de la Différence, 1994), 58.

16. Lipgens, *Formation of the European Unity Movement*, 342.

17. Both quoted in Lipgens, *Formation of the European Unity Movement*, 343–4.

18. Benedetto Croce, "Of Liberty," *Foreign Affairs* 11 (1932), 1–7. I would like to thank Roey Reichert for bringing this very interesting article to my attention. On Hayek and his followers, see Quinn Slobodian *Globalists: The End of Empire and the Birth of Neoliberalism* (Cambridge, MA: Harvard University Press, 2018), 184–7.

19. R. W. G. Mackay, *You Can't Turn the Clock Back* (New York and Chicago: Ziff Davis, 1948), 264–6. The book was published in the same year in London with the no less telling title *Britain in Wonderland*.

20. Rougemont, *L'Europe en jeu*, in *Œuvres complètes*, vol. 3, 53–6.

21. Quoted in Brugmans, *L'Idée européenne*, 136.

22. Rougemont, *L'Europe en jeu*, in *Œuvres complètes*, vol. 3, 57.

23. Quoted in Brugmans, *L'Idée européenne*, 132–4.

24. Quoted in Milward, *Reconstruction of Western Europe*, 393 n. 68.

25. *Statute of the Council of Europe* (London, 5.V.1949), https://www.coe.int/en/web/conventions/full-list/-/conventions/rms/0900001680935bdo, accessed February 12, 2021.

26. E. H. Carr, *The Future of Nations: Independence or Interdependence?* (London: Kegan Paul, 1941), 60–1.

27. Rougemont, *L'Europe en jeu*, in *Œuvres complètes*, vol. 3, 56.

28. Jean Monnet, *Memoirs*, trans. Richard Mayne (New York: Doubleday, 1978), 281–2, 495.

29. Monnet, *Memoirs*, 283.

30. Brugmans, *Pour un gouvernement européen*, 29–30.

31. Monnet, *Memoirs*, 274.

32. Milward, *Reconstruction of Western Europe*, 404–6; see also the comments in Andreas Staab, *The End of Europe? The Five Dilemmas of the European Union* (London: EPIC Publishing, 2020), 87–8.

33. Ernst Haas, *The Uniting of Europe: Political Social and Economic Forces, 1950–1957* (Stanford, CA: Stanford University Press, 1958), 44.

34. Giandomenico Majone, *Dilemmas of European Integration: The Ambiguities and Pitfalls of Integration by Stealth* (Oxford: Oxford University Press, 2005), 4.

35. Altiero Spinelli, "Reflections on the Institutional Crisis of the European Community," *West European Politics* 1 (1978), 77–88. The *commis* were medium-level civil servants under the *ancien régime*.

36. Stanley Hoffmann, "Obstinate or Obsolete? The Fate of the Nation State and the Case of Western Europe," *Daedalus* 95 (1966), 892–908.

37. See pp. 114–18.

38. "The Schuman Declaration—9 May 1950," https://europa.eu/european-union/about-eu/symbols/europe-day/schuman-declaration_en, accessed February 12, 2021. Schuman also called it "a midway between 'international' and 'federal' organisation," quoted in Henry Mason, *The European Coal and Steel Community* (The Hague: Nijhoff, 1955), 121. See also John Gillingham, *Coal, Steel, and the Rebirth of Europe, 1945–1955* (Cambridge: Cambridge University Press, 2004).

39. Jean Monnet, *Les États-Unis d'Europe ont commencé: La Communaute européenne, du charbon de l'acier: Discours et allocutions 1952–1954* (Paris: Robert Laffont, 1955). There is an English translation, Jean Monnet, *The United States of Europe Has Begun. The European Coal and Steel Community Speeches and Address 1952–1954* (University of Pittsburgh Archive of European Integration, 2010), 28, http://aei.pitt.edu/14365/, accessed February 12, 2021.

40. Quoted in Henri Brugmans, *La Pensée politique du fédéralisme* (Leiden: A. W. Sijthoff, 1969), 66.

41. Robert Schuman, *Pour l'Europe* (Paris: Les Éditions Nagel, 1964), 106 (from an undated speech).

42. Milward, *Reconstruction of Western Europe*, 407.

43. On this see Marc Belissa, *Fraternité universelle and intérêt nationale 1713–1795: Les Cosmopolitiques du droit des gens* (Paris: Éditions Kimé, 1998). On the rapid growth of treaties and international organizations from the mid-nineteenth century until 1945, see Mike Rapport, "Alliances and Treaties: Cooperation and Exchange in War and Peace, " *European History Online* (2016), http://ieg-ego.eu/en/threads/alliances-and-wars/alliances-and-treaties/mike-rapport-alliances-and-treaties-cooperation-and-exchange-in-war-and-peace/?searchterm=&set_language=en, accessed February 12, 2021.

44. *The United States of Europe Has Begun*, 61.

45. *The United States of Europe Has Begun*, 61, 58.

46. See pp. 65–7.

47. Alan, S. Milward, assisted by George Brennan and Federico Romero, *The European Rescue of the Nation State* (Berkeley, Los Angeles: University of California Press, 1992).

48. Monnet, *The United States of Europe Has Begun*, 58.

49. Jean Monnet, *La Communauté européenne et l'unité de l'Occident* (Lausanne: Centre de Recherches Européennes, 1961), 7.

50. Monnet, *La Communauté européenne*, 9.

51. Monnet, *La Communauté européenne*, 58.

52. Quoted in Josef L. Kunz, "Treaty Establishing the European Defense Community," *The American Journal of International Law* 47 (1953), 275–81.

53. For the intricate relationship between the EDC and the European Political Community, see Michael Burgess, *Federalism and European Union: The Building of Europe, 1950–2000* (London and New York: Routledge, 2000), 67–71.

54. *Treaty Constituting the European Defense Community* [unofficial translation of *Traité instituant la Communauté européenne de defense*], Article 7, p. 168, http://aei.pitt.edu/5201/1/5201.pdf, accessed February 12, 2021.

55. *Treaty Constituting the European Defense Community*, Article, 8, p. 169.

56. *Treaty Constituting the European Defense Community*, 167. For a more detailed account, see Edward Fursdon, *The European Defence Community: A History* (London: Macmillan, 1980), and Kevin Ruane, *The Rise and Fall of the European Defence Community: Anglo-American Relations and the Crisis of European Defence* (Basingstoke: Macmillan, 2000).

57. Guy Verhofstadt, *Europe's Last Chance: Why the European States Must Form a More Perfect Union* (New York: Basic Book, 2017), 259.

58. *Draft Treaty Embodying the Statute of the European Community* (Secretariat of the Constitutional Committee: Paris, 1953), 50–1, http://aei.pitt.edu/991/, accessed February 12, 2021.

59. Jan Zielonka, *Europe as Empire: The Nature of the Enlarged European Union* (Oxford: Oxford University Press, 2006), 5.

60. See Andrew Moravscik, *The Choice for Europe: Social Purpose and State Power from Messina to Maastricht* (Ithaca, NY: Cornell University Press 1997), 139–42.

61. Slobodian, *Globalists*, 191. The treaty was renamed in 2009 by the Treaty of Lisbon: "Treaty on the Functioning of the European Union."

62. Quoted in Miriam Camps, *Britain and the European Community, 1955–1963* (Princeton, NJ: Princeton University Press, 1964), 88, n.5 9.

63. *Declaration on European Identity* (Copenhagen, 14 December 1973), 3–4, https://www.cvce.eu/content/publication/1999/1/1/02798dc9-9c69-4b7d-b2c9-f03a8db7da32/publishable_en.pdf, accessed February 12, 2021. The declaration went on to insist, however, that "The Europe of the Nine is aware that, as it unites, it takes on new international obligations. European unification is not directed against anyone, nor is it inspired by a desire for power."

64. *The Treaty of Rome*, March 25, 1957. There were, in fact, two treaties. The second, which was far less controversial, established "Euratom," the European Atomic Energy Community.

65. Quoted in Milward, *The European Rescue of the Nation State*, 215.

66. See Perry Anderson, "Under the Sign of the Interim," in *The Question of Europe*, ed. Peter Gowan and Perry Anderson (London and New York: Verso, 1997), 51.

67. Quoted in Burgess, *Federalism and European Union*, 191.

68. *Treaty on European Union* (Luxembourg: Office for Official Publications of the European Communities, 1992), Preamble p. 3, https://europa.eu/european-union/sites/europaeu/files/docs/body/treaty_on_european_union_en.pdf, accessed February 12, 2021. This was replaced in the Treaty of Amsterdam in 1999 by: "This Treaty marks a new stage in the process of creating an ever closer union among the peoples of Europe, in which decisions are taken as openly as possible and as closely as possible to the citizen," https://eur-lex.europa.eu/legal-content/EN/TXT/HTML/?uri=CELEX:11997D/TXT&from=EN, Art. 1, p. 7, accessed February 12, 2021.

69. *Treaty on European Union*, Title 1, Art. B, p.8.

70. See pp. 183–4.

71. Thomas Risse and Daniela Engelmann-Martin, "Identity Politics and European Integration: The Case of Germany," in *The Idea of Europe: From Antiquity to the European Union*, ed. Anthony Pagden (Cambridge: Cambridge University Press, 2002), 287–316.

72. Martin Sandbu, *Europe's Orphan: The Future of the Euro and the Politics of Debt* (Princeton, NJ: Princeton University Press, 2015), 49–50.

73. Monnet, *Memoirs*, 495.

74. Alternative für Deutschland, *Manifesto for Germany: The Political Programme of the Alternative for Germany* (2017), 17–20, https://www.afd.de/wp-content/uploads/sites/111/2017/04/2017-04-12_afd-grundsatzprogramm-englisch_web.pdf, accessed February 12, 2021.

75. For the debates preceding and surrounding the introduction of subsidiarity, see Burgess, *Federalism and European Union*, 228–41.

76. Article 3b. This was substantially reinforced by the "Protocol on the Application of the Principles of Subsidiarity and Proportionality" of the Treaty of Lisbon of 2009. See pp. 262–3.

77. See Martin J. O'Malley, "Currents in Nineteenth-Century German Law and Subsidiarity's Emergence as a Social Principle in the Writings of Wilhelm Ketteler," *Journal of Law, Philosophy and Culture* 2 (2008), 23–53.

78. See Trevor Latimer, "The Principle of Subsidiarity: A Democratic Reinterpretation," *Constellations* 25 (2018), 586–601.

79. Quoted in Francis G. Jacobs and Kenneth L. Kars, "The 'Federal' Legal Order: The USA and Europe Compared," in *Integration through Law: Europe and the American Federal Experience*, vol. 1, ed. Mauro Cappelletti, Monica Seccombe, and Joseph Weiler (Berlin and New York: Walter de Gruyter, 1986), 169–243, at 240.

80. Quoted in Burgess, *Federalism and European Union*, 235.

81. See David Mackay, *Federalism and European Union: A Political Economy Perspective* (Oxford: Oxford University Press, 1999).

82. Opinion 1/91 (EAA) [1991] ECR – 6079, paras. 17–18. Emphasis added.
83. For a scathingly brilliant account—although it has been somewhat overtaken by events—of the creation and signification of European citizenship, see Joseph Weiler, "To Be a European Citizen: Eros and Civilization," in *The Constitution of Europe: "Do the New Clothes Have an Emperor?" and Other Essays on European Integration* (Cambridge: Cambridge University Press, 1999), 334–57.
84. Quoted in William Maas, *Creating European Citizens* (New York: Rowman & Littlefield, 2007), 47.
85. See pp. 131–2.
86. *Judgment of the Court of 20 September 2001—Rudy Grzelczyk v Centre public d'aide sociale d'Ottignies-Louvain-la-Neuve*, Preamble and para. 31. See also the comments by Richard Bellamy, *A Republican Europe of States: Cosmopolitanism, Intergovernmentalism and Democracy in the EU* (Cambridge: Cambridge University Press, 2019), 133 that this formula has "been ritually repeated in all but the most recent subsequent citizenship cases."
87. For this reason, it is hard to see it as, in James Bohman's words, an "arrangement" which is truly "transnational rather than intergovernmental in form" (*Democracy across Borders* (Cambridge, MA: MIT Press, 2007), 136).
88. *Treaty on European Union* [Maastricht], Article 9, and quoted in Bellamy, *Republican Europe of States*, 134–5.
89. Quoted in Bellamy, *Republican Europe of States*, 134–5.
90. Bellamy, *Republican Europe of States*, 133. "In many respects," he adds, "Union citizenship ought not to be conceived as if it were offering citizenship of a quasi EU polity" (p. 136).
91. Jürgen Habermas, *Between Facts and Norms: Contribution to a Discourse Theory of Law and Democracy*, trans. William Rehg (Cambridge, MA: MIT Press, 1998), 502–3.
92. See Jan-Werner Müller, "The Promise of 'Demoi-cracy': Democracy, Diversity, and Domination in the European Public Order," in *Political Theory of the European Union*, ed. Jürgen Neyer and Antje Wiener (Oxford: Oxford University Press, 2011), 187–203.
93. Ronald Dworkin, *Taking Rights Seriously* (London: Duckworth 1977).
94. Jürgen Habermas, "Does Europe need a Constitution?" in *Time of Transitions*, ed. and trans. Ciaran Cronin and Max Pensky (Cambridge: Polity Press, 2006), 101.
95. See Mattias Kumm, "Beyond Golf Clubs and the Judicialization of Politics: Why Europe Has a Constitution Properly so Called," *The American Journal of Comparative Law* 54 (2006), 505–30: "The ECJ has long claimed that the EU Treaties establish a constitution in the strong sense. It referred to the Treaties as the EU's 'constitutional charter' and has claimed that national courts must set aside all national laws in conflict with it, including national constitutional law" (511–12). All of this however is clearly in conflict with the principle of subsidiarity.
96. Jan-Werner Müller, *Constitutional Patriotism* (Princeton, NJ: Princeton University Press, 2007), 97.

97. Harold James, *The Roman Predicament: How the Rules of International Order Create the Politics of Empire* (Princeton, NJ: Princeton University Press, 2006), 126–7.

98. *Draft Treaty Establishing a Constitution for Europe (Not Ratified)* (*Official Journal of the European Union*), Part I, Title I, Art 1, https://eur-lex.europa.eu/legal-content/EN/TXT/?uri=OJ:C:2004:310:TOC, accessed February 12, 2021.

99. *Draft Treaty Establishing a Constitution for Europe*. Part II, *The Charter of Fundamental Rights of the Union*, Preamble.

100. Jürgen Habermas, "Is the Development of a European Identity Necessary, and Is It Possible?," in *The Divided West*, ed. and trans. Ciaran Cronin (Cambridge: Polity Press, 2006), 71. At the same time, however, it also lacked the "symbolic power which can only be generated by a political founding act" (Habermas, "Does Europe Need a Constitution?," in *Time of Transitions*, 90).

101. As recorded by Kimmon Kiljunen, the Finnish member of the European Convention responsible for drafting the Constitution (Kimmon Kiljunen, *The European Constitution in the Making* (Brussels: Centre for European Policy Studies, 2004), 1–2.

102. Pierre Kanuty, as quoted in an interview in 2008, in Ece Ozlem Atikcan, *Framing the European Union: The Power of Political Arguments in Shaping European Integration* (Cambridge: Cambridge University Press, 2015), 112.

103. For a detailed account of both campaigns, see Atikcan, *Framing the European Union*, 94–166.

104. On this, see Ian Buruma. *Murder in Amsterdam: The Death of Theo van Gogh, and the Limits of Tolerance* (London and New York: Penguin Press, 2006).

105. Habermas, "Does Europe Need a Constitution?," in *Time of Transitions*, 101, and Habermas, "Is the development of a European identity necessary?," in *Divided West*, 67.

106. Jürgen Habermas, *The Crisis of the European Union: A Response*, trans. Ciaran Cronin (Cambridge: Polity, 2012), 11.

107. Article 52, *Charter of the Fundamental Rights of the European Union*, https://eur-lex.europa.eu/legal-content/EN/TXT/HTML/?uri=CELEX:12012P/TXT&from=EN#d1e35-391–391, accessed February 12, 2021.

108. See Andrew Williams, *EU Human Rights Policies: A Study in Irony* (Oxford: Oxford University Press, 2004) and Andrew Williams, *The Ethos of Europe: Values, Law and Justice in the EU* (Cambridge: Cambridge University Press, 2010), 110–53.

109. See my *The Burdens of Empire: 1539 to the Present* (Cambridge: Cambridge University Press, 2015) and Samuel Moyn, *The Last Utopia: Human Rights in History* (Cambridge, MA: Harvard University Press, 2012).

110. See Joseph Weiler, "Fundamental Rights and Fundamental Boundaries: On the Conflict on Standards and Values in the Protection of Human Rights in the European Legal Space," in *The Constitution of Europe*, 102–29. "Human rights constitute . . . both a source of, and an index for, cross-national differentiation and not only cross-national assimilation" (p. 105).

III. *Charter of the Fundamental Rights of the European Union*, Preamble.

II2. Habermas, *Crisis of the European Union*, xi–xii, 2.

II3. *Charter of the Fundamental Rights of the European Union*, Preamble.

II4. *Charter of the Fundamental Rights of the European Union, Protocol on the Application of the Charter of Fundamental Rights of the European Union to Poland and the United Kingdom*, Art I (I).

II5. See, Christine Reh, "The Lisbon Treaty: De-Constitutionalizing the European Union," *Journal of Common Market Studies* 47 (2009), 625–50, who argues that in terms of "the separation of powers, the protection of fundamental rights and democratic participation ... the domestic–supranational gap has widened rather than narrowed post-Lisbon." See also the comments of Bellamy, *Republican Europe of States*, 197–9.

II6. Joseph Raz, "On the Authority and Interpretation of Constitutions: Some Preliminaries," in Larry Alexander ed., *Constitutionalism: Philosophical Foundations* (Cambridge: Cambridge University Press, 1988), 152–93.

II7. Chris Patten, *Not Quite the Diplomat: Home Truths about World Affairs* (London: Allen Lane, 2005), 130. See also Christopher J. Bickerton, *European Integration: From Nation-States to Member States*, 45.

II8. I have learnt a lot from a forthcoming essay by Anthony Norton, "Integration from Disintegration: Article 50 and the European Project." See also David Raic, *Statehood and the Law of Self-Determination* (The Hague, London, and New York: Kluwer Law International, 2002), 313–6, and Majone, *Dilemmas of European Integration*, 215, who believed in 2005 that the clause was "unlikely to be a serious problem in practice."

7. THE ONCE AND FUTURE EUROPE

I. *Treaty of Lisbon Amending the Treaty on European Union and the Treaty Establishing the European Community, Signed at Lisbon, 13 December 2007* (Official Journal of the European Union), Art. 1, https://eur-lex.europa.eu/legal-content/EN/TXT/?uri=CELEX%3A12007L%2FTXT, accessed February 13, 2021.

2. Carlo Cattaneo, *Sulle interdizioni isrealitiche*, ed. G. A. Belloni (Rome: Sestante, 1944), 56–8.

3. Samuel Purchas, *Hakluytus Posthumus or Purchas his Pilgrimes, contayning a History of the World, in Sea Voyages and lande-Travells by Englishmen & others*, vol. I (London, 1625), 45.

4. Antonin Cohen, "The Future of Europe: Past and Present: From the Hague Congress to the Convention on the Future of Europe" (emphasis added), in *Whose Europe? National Models and the Constitution of the European Union*, Papers of a Multi-Disciplinary Conference held in Oxford in April 2003, ed. Kalypso Nicolaidis and Stephen Weatherill (2003), 39–47, at 4, https://europaeum.org/wp-content/uploads/2017/09/Whose-Europe.pdf, accessed February 13, 2021.

5. Quoted in Philippe Chenaux, *De la chrétienté à l'Europe: Les Catholiques et l'idée européenne au XXe siècle* (Tours: CDD Éditions, 2007), 105.

6. See Joseph Weiler, "A Christian Europe? Europe and Christianity: Rules of Commitment," *European View* 6 (2007), 143–50. The claim made by several Catholic websites that the twelve stars of the European flag symbolizing the ideal of unity, solidarity, and harmony among the peoples of Europe derives from the Virgin Mary's crown of twelve stars is, however, false. The number of stars has everything to do with geometry, nothing with religion.

7. Giuseppe Mazzini, *Aux patriotes suisses!* [1843], in *Scritti editi ed inediti di Giuseppe Mazzini*, vol. 4 (Imola: Cooperativa Tipografico-Editrice Paolo Galeati, 1908), 36.

8. Thucydides, *History of the Peloponnesian War* 2.37. The famous declaration reads: "Our constitution does not copy the laws of neighboring states; we are rather a pattern to others than imitators ourselves. Its administration favors the many instead of the few; this is why it is called a democracy."

9. Quoted by Guy Milton, "God and the Constitution," in *God and the EU: Retrieving the Christian Inspiration of the European Project*, ed. Jonathan Chaplin and Gary Wilson (London and New York: Routledge, 2016), 191–207, at 201.

10. Post-Synodal Apostolic Exhortation, *Ecclesia in Europa* of his Holiness Pope John Paul II, http://w2.vatican.va/content/john-paul-ii/en/apost_exhortations/documents/hf_jp-ii_exh_20030628_ecclesia-in-europa.html, accessed February 13, 2021.

11. Quoted, with evident approval, by Paul E. Kerry. "The Quarrel over the Religious Roots of European Identity in the European Constitution and the Nature of Historical Explanation: A Catholic Coign of Vantage," in *The Religious Roots of Contemporary European Identity*, ed. Lucia Faltin and Melanie Wright (London and New York: Continuum, 2007), 168–78, at 175.

12. Transcription of the Interview with Valéry Giscard d'Estaing (Paris, 17 November 2008), 16, https://www.cvce.eu/content/publication/2011/3/3/b3e39520-70b9-4bda-9ad2-02d83be29649/publishable_en.pdf, accessed February 13, 2021.

13. Oliver Roy, *Is Europe Christian?*, trans. Cynthia Schoch (Oxford: Oxford University Press, 2020), 7.

14. *Charter of the Fundamental Rights of the European Union*, Preamble (emphasis added), https://eur-lex.europa.eu/legal-content/EN/TXT/HTML/?uri=CELEX:12012P/TXT&from=EN, accessed February 13, 2021.

15. See José Casanova, "Religion, European Secular Identities and European Integration," in *Religion in an Expanding Europe*, ed. Timothy A. Byrnes and Peter J. Katzenstein (Cambridge: Cambridge University Press, 2006), 65–92.

16. Tariq Ramadan, "Turkey is Part of Europe: Fear Keeps It out of the EU," *The Guardian* (August 6, 2009), https://www.theguardian.com/commentisfree/2009/aug/06/turkey-eu-membership, accessed February 13, 2021. See also Rieke Trimçev, Gregor Feindt, Félix Krawatzek, and Friedemann Pestel, "Europe's Europes: Mapping the Conflicts of European Memory," *Journal of Political Ideologies* (2019), 51–77. doi: 10.1080/13569317.2019.1696925, accessed February 13, 2021.

17. Quoted by Talal Asad, "Muslims and European Identity: Can Europe represent Islam?," in *The Idea of Europe: From Antiquity to the European Union*,

ed. Anthony Pagden (Cambridge: Cambridge University Press, 2002), 211 quoting a *Time* magazine article of October 19, 1991.

18. See François Foret, *Religion and Politics in the European Union: The Secular Canopy* (Cambridge: Cambridge University Press, 2015), 244–9 on Turkey as the "gate-keeper of European Identity."

19. Roy, *Is Europe Christian?* 15.

20. See Noel Malcolm, *Useful Enemies: Islam and the Ottoman Empire in Western Political Thought, 1450–1750* (Oxford: Oxford University Press, 2019).

21. See Grace Davie, *Religion in Modern Europe: A Memory Mutates* (Oxford: Oxford University Press, 2000), 125: "There are memories," she claims of the Siege of Vienna of 1683 which marked the end of the Ottoman advance into Christian Europe, "which persist in the European mind, albeit latently."

22. Karl Jaspers, *Vom europäischen Geist* (Munich: R. Piper, 1947), 7–8.

23. Jean-Jacques Rousseau, *Écrits sur l'abbé de Saint St. Pierre*, in *Œuvres complètes de Jean-Jacques Rousseau*, ed. Bernard Gagnebin and Marcel Raymond, vol. 3 (Paris: Gallimard, Bibliothèque de la Pléiade, 1964), 566.

24. Immanuel Kant, *An Answer to the Question: "What is Enlightenment?"* in *Practical Philosophy*, trans. and ed. Mary J. Gregor (Cambridge: Cambridge University Press, 1996), 17.

25. Claus Offe, "Is There or Can There Be a 'European Society'?," in *Civil Society: Berlin Perspectives*, ed. John Keane (New York and Oxford: Berghahn Books, 2006), 169–88. Oddly, however, he then goes on to cite as examples of other "non-European civilizations" the United States, China, and Japan. But the United States is in this respect a wholly "European" civilization and does indeed have a marked propensity for "self-revision and *autocritique*." See also Claus Offe, *Europe Entrapped* (Cambridge: Polity, 2015), 63–5.

26. Jürgen Habermas, "Does Europe Need a Constitution?," in *Time of Transitions*, ed. and trans. Ciaran Cronin and Max Pensky (Cambridge: Polity Press, 2006), 105.

27. Pascal Bruckner, *La Tyrannie de la pénitence: Essai sur le masochisme occidental* (Paris: Grasset, 2006), 121.

28. See my *The Enlightenment and Why It Still Matters* (Oxford: Oxford University Press, 2013), 83.

29. Bruckner, *Tyrannie de la pénitence*, 109.

30. The most influential theorist of this association was the French neo-Thomist Jacques Maritain, who was one of the framers of the "Universal Declaration of Human Rights" of 1948. See Samuel Moyn, *Christian Human Rights* (Philadelphia, PA: University of Pennsylvania Press, 2015), 82–4. For the sources of the concept of a human right in an enlightened concern with what in the eighteenth century was called "sympathy," see Lynn Hunt, *Inventing Human Rights: A History* (New York and London: W. W. Norton, 2007).

31. Edmund Burke, "First Letter on a Regicide Peace," in *The Writings and Speeches of Edmund Burke*, vol. 9, ed. Paul Langford (Oxford: Oxford University Press, 1981–91), 250. On Burke's invocation in this context of the Roman law of

vicinity, see Jennifer M. Welsh, "Edmund Burke and the Commonwealth of Europe: The Cultural Bases of International Order," in *Classical Theories of International Relations*, ed. Ian Clark and Iver B. Neumannn (London: Macmillan, 1996), 173–92.

32. Aldo Schiavone, *The Invention of Law in the West*, trans. Jeremy Carden and Antony Shugar (Cambridge, MA: Harvard University Press, 2012), 4. See also the essays in Kaius Tuori and Heta Bjorklund, eds., *Roman Law and the Idea of Europe* (London: Bloomsbury Academic, 2019).

33. The French historian Claude Nicolet called this "juridical patriotism" to distinguish it from "geographical patriotism." See Jean-Marc Ferry, *La Question de l'état européen* (Paris: Gallimard, 2000), 165–9.

34. Habermas, "Does Europe Need a Constitution?," in *Time of Transitions*, 100.

35. Jan-Werner Müller, *Constitutional Patriotism* (Princeton, NJ: Princeton University Press, 2007), 20–2.

36. Aristotle, *Politics*, 1276b.

37. Jürgen Habermas, "The European Nation-State: On the Past and Future of Sovereignty and Citizenship," in *The Inclusion of Others: Studies in Political Theory*, ed. Ciaran Cronin and Pablo De Greiff (Cambridge, MA: MIT Press, 2000), 118.

38. Johann Gottlieb Fichte, *Addresses to the German Nation*, ed. and trans. Gregory Moore (Cambridge: Cambridge University Press, 2008), 107.

39. See, in particular, Craig J. Calhoun, "Imagining Solidarity: Cosmopolitanism, Constitutional Patriotism, and the Public Sphere," *Public Culture* 14 (2002), 147–71, at p. 149: "Nations have often had ethnic pedigrees and employed ethnic rhetorics, but they are modern products of shared political, cultural, and social participation, not mere passive inheritances."

40. Jürgen Habermas, *Between Facts and Norms: Contribution to a Discourse Theory of Law and Democracy*, trans. William Rehg (Cambridge, MA: MIT Press, 1998), Appendix II, 500.

41. Müller, *Constitutional Patriotism*, 61.

42. See, in general, Karen Alter, *Establishing the Supremacy of European Law: The Making of an International Rule of Law in Europe* (Oxford: Oxford University Press, 2001).

43. Charles de Secondat, baron de Montesquieu, *De l'esprit des lois* (XI, 6), in *Œuvres complètes*, vol. 2, ed. Roger Caillois (Paris: Gallimard, Bibliothèque de la Pléiade, 1951), 396–7. For this reason England was, he said, "a republic which hides beneath a monarchy."

44. Edmund Burke, "Speech on Reform of Representation," in *On Empire, Liberty and Reform: Speeches and Letters*, ed. David Bromwich (New Haven, CT, and London, 2000), 274.

45. Larry Siedentop, *Democracy in Europe*, (New York: Columbia University Press, 2001), 72.

46. Siedentop, *Democracy in Europe*, 43. We are a long way from the understanding of patriotism espoused by, for instance, Mauricio Viroli, *For Love of Country: An Essay on Patriotism and Nationalism* (Oxford: Oxford University Press, 1995).

47. Müller, *Constitutional Patriotism*, 34.

48. F. A. Hayek, *The Constitution of Liberty* [1960], in *The Collected Works of F. A. Hayek*, vol. 17, ed. Ronald Hamowy (Chicago: University of Chicago Press, 2011), 285.

49. E. H. Carr, *Nationalism and After* (New York: Macmillan, 1945), 4.

50. Habermas, "The European Nation-State," in *Inclusion of Others*, 113.

51. Julien Benda, *Discours à la nation européenne* (Paris: Gallimard, 1933), 2–21. See also Müller, *Constitutional Patriotism*, 144–5 on what he calls the European need for "substituting one passion for another, one absolute attachment for another," although it must be admitted that the proponents of a species of Euro-nationalism have never sought the exclusion of local national attachments. On Benda, see pp. 69–70.

52. Quoted in Dominique Schnapper, *La Communauté des citoyens: Sur l'idée moderne de nation* (Paris: Gallimard, 1994), 104.

53. Ernest Renan, "What is a Nation?" in *What is a Nation? And Other Political Writings*, trans. and ed. M. F. N. Giglioli (New York: Columbia University Press, 2018), 251.

54. See pp. 79–81.

55. Quoted by Ariane Chebel d'Appolonia, "European Nationalism and European Union," in *Idea of Europe*, ed. Anthony Pagden, 172–90.

56. Quoted in Or Rosenboim, *The Emergence of Globalism: Visions of World Order in Britain and the United States, 1939–1950* (Princeton, NJ: Princeton University Press, 2017), 28.

57. Habermas, "Does Europe Need a Constitution?," in *Time of Transitions*, 90.

58. See William I. Hitchcock, *The Struggle for Europe: The Turbulent History of a Divided Continent 1945–2002* (New York: Doubleday, 2003).

59. Habermas, "Does Europe Need a Constitution?," in *Time of Transitions*, 101.

60. See Giandomenico Majone's comments that even if such a thing had happened, the new USE thus constituted would have to respect "the absolute primacy of the territorial state over all competing principles of social cohesion" (Giandomenico Majone, *Dilemmas of European Integration: The Ambiguities and Pitfalls of Integration by Stealth* (Oxford: Oxford University Press, 2005), 184–5).

61. See p. 282.

62. Milan Kundera, "The Tragedy of Central Europe," trans. Edmund White, *The New York Review of Books* (April 26, 1984), 31. Emphasis original.

63. "Macron accusé d'"erreur historique' pour avoir fermé la porte de l'UE à la Macédoine du Nord et à l'Albanie," *Le Monde* (October 29, 2019), and "Now We Are without a Vision': An EU Setback in the Balkans," *New York Times*, November 20, 2019.

64. "Trente ans après la chute du mur de Berlin: 'Les Élites populistes perçoivent l'UE comme un nouveau Moscou,'" *Le Monde* (November 9, 2019). See also Ivan Krastev and Stephen Holmes, *The Light That Failed: Why the West Is Losing the Fight for Democracy* (New York and London: Pegasus Books, 2019), 75.

65. Daniel Cohn-Bendit and Guy Verhofstadt, *For Europe! Manifesto for a Postnational Revolution in Europe* (Munich: Carl Hanser Verlag, 2012), 57–9.

NOTES TO PAGES 284–286

66. Marcel Detienne, *L'Identité nationale, une énigme* (Paris: Gallimard, 2010), 12. The full title of the ministry was "Immigration, Integration, National Identity, and Codevelopment," and it was, of course, primarily concerned with integrating predominantly African immigrants into French society.

67. Thomas Risse, "Social Constructivism and European Integration," in *European Integration Theory*, ed. Antje Wiener, Tanja Börzel, and Thomas Risse (Oxford: Oxford University Press, 2019) 138.

68. Zenon Bankowski and Emilios Christodoulidis, "The European Union as an Essentially Contested Project," *European Law Journal* 4 (1998), 341–54 and Étienne Balibar, *We the People of Europe?: Reflections on Transnational Citizenship* (Princeton, NJ: Princeton University Press, 2004), 2. Emphasis original.

69. Glyn Morgan, *The Idea of a European Superstate: Public Justification and European Integration* (Princeton, NJ: Princeton University Press, 2005), 112.

70. Cf. Pasquale Pasquino, "Conceptualizing Europe," in *Whose Europe?*, ed. Nicolaidis and Weatherill, 124–9, at 126–7: "It is a complex, composite organism that uses economic and administrative tools to produce peace, rather than war; an organism that looks from a legal point of view more like the Holy Roman Empire, than like a modern territorial political unit or nation-state." Jan Zielonka *Europe as Empire: The Nature of the Enlarged European Union* (Oxford: Oxford University Press, 2006), 17, denies that he, in fact, intends any analogy with the Holy Roman Empire. But it would indeed be hard to find any other actual medieval empire which fits Zielonka's criteria. No European empire was created by "invitation" unless marriage is to be considered as such.

71. Hedley Bull, *The Anarchical Society: A Study of Order in World Politics*, 4th edn. (London: Macmillan, 2012), 154–56; Geoffrey Parker, *Emperor: A New Life of Charles V* (New Haven, CT, and London: Yale University Press, 2019), 4. As was said of the Habsburgs *Bella gerant alii, tu felix Austria nube*— "Let others wage war: you happy Austria, marry."

72. Harold James, *The Roman Predicament: How the Rules of International Order Create the Politics of Empire* (Princeton, NJ: Princeton University Press, 2006), 120.

73. See the comments by Martha C. Nussbaum, *The Cosmopolitan Tradition: A Noble but Flawed Ideal* (Cambridge, MA: Harvard University Press, 2019), 137–40.

74. The full quotation from *Human, all Too Human* appears as the epigraph for this book.

75. Andrew Moravcsik, "Federalism in the European Union: Rhetoric and Reality," in *The Federal Vision: Legitimacy and Levels of Governance in the United States and the European Union*, ed. Kalypso Nicolaidis and Robert Howse (Oxford: Oxford University Press, 2001), 159–87. Moravcsik also cites the lack of a single educational policy and cultural policy. Although it is still true that nothing very robust exists in these areas, they have made significant advances since 2001. They are also matters on which many truly federal states have divergent policies at the state level, not least the United States and Canada. Educational and cultural policies are remarkably weak even within at least some of the member states themselves.

76. "Manifeste pour la démocratisation de l'Europe," http://tdem.eu/, accessed February 14, 2021.
77. "Is there or can there be a 'European Society'?," in *Civil Society: Berlin Perspectives*, 168–9.
78. Joseph E. Stiglitz, *The Euro: How a Common Currency Threatens the Future of Europe* (New York and London: Norton Publishers, 2016), 7. Stiglitz, despite the gloomy title of his book, was, however, convinced that the "euro can be saved, should be saved, but saved in a way which creates the shared prosperity and solidarity that was part of the promise of the euro, for the good not only of Europe, but for that of the entire world" (p. 323). For the argument that the introduction of the single currency was not responsible for the crisis, although it substantially altered the form which it took, see Martin Sandbu, *Europe's Orphan: The Future of the Euro and the Politics of Debt* (Princeton, NJ: Princeton University Press, 2015).
79. Quoted in Markus K. Brunnermeier, Harold James, and Jean-Pierre Landau, *The Euro and the Battle of Ideas* (Princeton, NJ: Princeton University Press, 2016), 266, and see pp. 262–7 for the "Grexit" fear.
80. For a larger view of this, see Brendan Simms, *Britain's Europe: A Thousand Years of Conflict and Cooperation* (London: Allen Lane, 2016), who concludes that what "Europe" needs to become is a "single Eurozone state" constructed along "Anglo-American constitutional lines in confederation with Great Britain." This he believes would be in everyone's interest and "compatible with British sovereignty." He carefully avoids, however, saying not only how this could be achieved but what actual constitutional form this new state or the "confederation" with Britain might take (p. 240). For Hugo's distrust of Britain, see pp. 115–16.
81. See Stanley Hoffmann, "De Gaulle, Europe and the Atlantic Alliance," *International Organization* 18 (1964), 1–25 and Andrew Moravcsik, *The Choice for Europe: Social Purpose and State Power from Messina to Maastricht* (Ithaca, NY: Cornell University Press 1997), 122–4.
82. "French President Charles DeGaulle's Veto on British Membership of the EEC 14 January 1963," https://www.files.ethz.ch/isn/125401/1168_DeGaulleVeto.pdf, accessed February 13, 2021.
83. Robert Saunders, *Yes to Europe! The 1975 Referendum and Seventies Britain* (Cambridge: Cambridge University Press, 2018), 1–26.
84. As quoted by the theater critic Kenneth Tynan in Christopher J. Bickerton, *European Integration: From Nation-States to Member States* (Oxford: Oxford University Press, 2012), 5.
85. The EEC did not, however, replace the ECSC, which survived until 2002, when its founding treaty expired. By the European Communities Act of 1967 the EEC, the ECSC, and Euratom were united into one body called the "European Communities."
86. See Liah Greenfeld, *Nationalism: Five Roads to Modernity* (Cambridge, MA: Harvard University Press, 1992), 30–87, who identifies the emergence of a "national sentiment" in England in the early sixteenth century. One piece of

evidence she cites for this is a riot in 1517 against the presence of foreign artisans who had deprived native Englishmen of their right to make a living (p. 42).

87. Quoted in Walter Lipgens, *The Formation of the European Unity Movement* (Oxford: Clarendon Press, 1982), 318.

88. See Roxanne Lynn Doty, "Sovereignty and the Nation: Constructing the Boundaries of National Identity," in *State Sovereignty as Social Construct*, ed. Thomas J. Biersteker and Cynthia Weber (Cambridge: Cambridge University Press, 1996), 121–47, at 125.

89. Dominque Strauss-Kahn, *Les Échos*, April 11, 2019.

90. Niall Ferguson, *Empire: The Rise and Demise of the British World Order and the Lessons for Global Power* (London: Allen Lane, 202), xxv. On the impact of the experience of empire in both Britain and France, see Robert Gildea, *Empires of the Mind: The Colonial Past and the Politics of the Present* (Cambridge: Cambridge University Press, 2019).

91. See Georgios Varouxakis, "Mid-Atlantic Musings. The 'Question of Europe' in British Intellectual Debates, 1961–2008," in *European Stories: Intellectual Debates on Europe in National Context*, ed. Justine Lacroix and Kalypso Nicolaidis (Oxford: Oxford University Press, 2010), 147–66.

92. Not all modern European nationalist movements are, however, anti-European. The Scottish National Party, for instance, is left-leaning and far from xenophobic; the same was true of most of the Catalan secessionists, all of whom, in one way or another, support the Union. But then, as all of these are also secessionist parties which look to Europe not as threat but as a potential savior, they might be thought to be exceptions that only go to prove the rule.

93. Pierre Rosanvallon, *Le Siècle du populisme: Histoire, théorie, critique* (Paris: Seuil, 2020), 61.

94. Alternative für Deutschland, *Manifesto for Germany: The Political Programme of the Alternative for Germany* (2017), 15, https://www.afd.de/wp-content/uploads/sites/111/2017/04/2017-04-12_afd-grundsatzprogramm-englisch_web.pdf, accessed February 12, 2021.

95. Brilliantly described by Timothy Snyder, *The Road to Unfreedom: Russia, Europe, America* (New York: Tim Duggan Books, 2018), 82–4.

96. "Discours d'Emmanuel Macron pour une Europe souveraine, unie, démocratique," 26 septembre, 2017, https://www.elysee.fr/front/pdf/elysee-module-795-fr.pdf, accessed February 13, 2021.

97. Emmanuel Macron, "Dear Europe, Brexit is a Lesson for All of Us: It's Time for Renewal," *The Guardian* (March 4, 2019). https://www.theguardian.com/commentisfree/2019/mar/04/europe-brexit-uk, accessed February 14, 2021.

98. Thomas Hobbes, *De Corpore*, 1.7. See also David Armitage, *Civil Wars: A History in Ideas* (New York: Alfred A. Knopf, 2017), 106–12.

99. See Olivier Christin, *La Paix de religion. L'Autonomisation de la raison politique au XVIᵉ siècle* (Paris: Seuil, 1997).

100. Habermas, "The European Nation-State," in *Inclusion of Others*, 108.

101. Henry Sumner Maine, *Ancient Law: Its Connection with the Early History of Society, and its Relation to Modern Ideas* [1861] (London: Dent, 1917), 28. Emphasis added.

102. On "R2P," see Anne Orford, *International Authority and the Responsibility to Protect* (Cambridge: Cambridge University Press, 2011).

103. Anne-Marie Slaughter, *A New World Order*, (Princeton, NJ: Princeton University Press, 2004), 12–15.

104. See Anu Bradford, *The Brussels Effect: How the European Union Rules the World* (Oxford: Oxford University Press, 2020), 277–8.

105. Neil MacCormick, "Beyond the Sovereign State," *Modern Law Review* 56 (1993), 1–18. See also Neil MacCormick, *Questioning Sovereignty: Law, State, and Nation in the European Commonwealth* (Oxford: Oxford University Press, 1999), 133: "Despite the rhetoric of politicians it cannot be credibly argued that any member of the European Union remains, politically or legally, a sovereign state in the strict sense of the terms."

106. MacCormick, "Beyond the Sovereign State."

107. See pp. 300–1.

108. Cf. Jan-Werner Müller, *Populism* (London: Penguin Books, 2016), 63: "positive or constructive constitutionalism is followed by negative or restraining constitutionalism."

109. Christopher Coker, *The Improbable War: China, the United States, and the Logic of Great Power Conflict* (Oxford: Oxford University Press, 2015), 9, is surely right in dismissing what he calls the "liberal assumption that inter-state war has become 'extinct' or 'anachronistic'" as both absurdly complacent and "exactly the kind of thinking that could lead to another conflict in the near future." But while war has not been eliminated by internationalism, wars between nation-states as we know them may well have been.

110. Kalypso Nicolaidis, "Our European Demoï-cracy: Is This Constitution a Third Way for Europe?," in *Whose Europe?*, ed. Nicolaidis and Weatherill, 137–52; Kalypso Nicolaidis, "The Idea of European Demoicracy" in Julie Dickson and Pavlos Eleftheriadis eds. *Philosophical Foundations of EU Law* (Oxford: Oxford University Press, 2012), 247–74. See also Kalypso Nicolaidis, "European Demoicracy and Its Crisis," *Journal of Common Market Studies* 51 (2013), 351–69. On the concept of Demoï-cracy, see also James Bohman, *Democracy across Borders* (Cambridge, MA: MIT Press, 2007), 29–55.

111. Richard Bellamy, *A Republican Europe of States: Cosmopolitanism, Intergovernmentalism and Democracy in the EU* (Cambridge: Cambridge University Press, 2019), 21. The term is a play on Lea Ypi's "Statist Cosmopolitanism," *Journal of Political Philosophy* 16 (2008), 48–71. The concept of non-domination is from Philip Pettit's *Republicanism: A Theory of Freedom and Government* (Oxford: Oxford University Press, 1997).

112. Bellamy, *Republican Europe of States*, 206–7.

113. But see Jan-Werner Müller, "The Promise of 'Demoi-cracy': Democracy, Diversity and Domination in the European Public Order," in *Political Theory of*

the European Union, ed. Jürgen Neyer and Antje Wiener (Oxford: Oxford University Press, 2011), 196, who is generally critical of the notion of a "demoi-cracy" on the grounds that "What is lacking...is any strong evidence from transitional forums, where deliberation could be initiated outside state or quasi-state structures, but with eventual noticeable effect on nation-states and the EU.".

114. Bellamy, *Republican Europe of States*, 39–40.

115. Nicolaidis, "European demoicracy and Its Crisis."

116. Müller, "The Promise of 'Demoi-cracy,'" 197.

117. For a sample of similarly worded articles from newspapers and journals, see Bradford, *The Brussels Effect*, xiii–xiv. See also Gerda Falkner and Patrick Muller, eds., *EU Policies in a Global Perspective* (London and New York: Routledge, 2014).

118. Tony Judt, *Postwar: A History of Europe since 1945* (London: Penguin Books, 2005), 799.

119. By Jeremy Rifkin, Mark Leonard, and T. R. Reid respectively.

120. Stanley Hoffmann, "Obstinate or Obsolete? The Fate of the Nation State and the Case of Western Europe," *Daedalus* 95, (1966), 862–915, at 890. Emphasis original.

121. Müller, "The Promise of 'Demoi-cracy,'" 189.

122. On these, see Renaud Dehousse, "Regulation by Networks in the European Community: The Role of European Agencies," *Journal of European Public Policy* 4 (1997) 246–61.

123. Dani Rodrok, *The Globalization Paradox: Democracy and the Future of the World Economy* (New York and London: W. W. Norton and Company, 2012), 18–19.

124. Bradford, *The Brussels Effect*, 221–2, 248–9.

125. *Communication from the Commission: The European Green Deal (Brussels, 11.12.2019)*, https://eur-lex.europa.eu/legal-content/EN/TXT/HTML/?uri=CELEX:52019DC0640&from=EN, accessed February 13, 2021.

126. Tony Blair, "A Superpower, but not a Superstate," *The Guardian* (October 7, 2000), https://www.theguardian.com/politics/2000/oct/07/uk.tonyblair, accessed February 13, 2021.

127. Johann Caspar Bluntschli, "Die Gründung der Amerikanischen Union von 1787," in *Gesammelte kleine Schriften*, vol. 2 (Nördlingen: C. H. Beck, 1879), 61.

128. See Christopher Coker, *The Rise of the Civilizational State* (Cambridge: Polity Press, 2019). Coker, although he has a great many, largely derogatory things to say about it, does not identify the EU as a possible "civilizational state." But see Charlemagne, "Huntington's Disease and the Clash of Civilization-States," *The Economist* (January 2, 2020), https://www.economist.com/europe/2020/01/02/huntingtons-disease-and-the-clash-of-civilisation-states, accessed February 14, 2021, who does. (I would like to thank Roey Reichert for this reference.) The term "civilizational" owes its existence to the American political scientist Samuel Huntington's widely read (and widely reviled, and widely misunderstood) 1996 book *The Clash of Civilizations*, which argued that, in the post-Cold War world, conflicts would no longer be between power

groupings or even ideologies but between what Huntingdon called "civilizations," that is, peoples organized according to their political and social values, their aspirations, and their (predominantly religious) beliefs.

129. Macron, "Dear Europe."

130. See https://ec.europa.eu/info/strategy/priorities-2019-2024/promoting-our-european-way-life_en, accessed February 19, 2021.

131. p. 132.

132. Thomas Piketty, *Capital et idéologie* (Paris: Seuil, 2019), 1034–5. Piketty's prime concern is how to make the government of the Union more democratic in order to redress the unequal distribution of wealth throughout the continent. His proposal is for the creation of a bicameral system made up of the European Parliament and a European Assembly, 20 percent of which would be drawn from the existing European Parliament and 80 percent from the national parliaments.

133. Piketty, *Capital et idéologie*, 1030.

134. Ivan Krastev, *After Europe* (Philadelphia: University of Pennsylvania Press, 2017), 109.

135. Timothy Garton Ash, "Europe (and Yes, That Includes Britain) Can Still Be a Superpower," *The Guardian*, March 2, 2020 https://www.theguardian.com/world/commentisfree/2020/mar/02/europe-britain-superpower-european, accessed February 13, 2021.

136. Aelius Aristides, "The Roman Oration," in James H. Oliver, "The Ruling Power: A Study of the Roman Empire in the Second Century after Christ through the Roman Oration of Aelius Aristides," *Transactions of the American Philosophical Society*, n.s., 23 (1953), 103.

137. Renan, "What is a Nation?," in *What is a Nation?*, 249.

138. Cicero, *De Officiis*, II. 27.

139. Although he does not mention Rome as any kind of "federated state," this is very much the kind of unification which Alexandre Kojève, *Outline of a Phenomenology of Right*, [1943], ed. and trans. Bryan-Paul Frost and Robert Howse (Lanham, MD: Rowman and Littlefield, 2000) 326–7, had envisaged for the ultimate future of the world, See also pp. 219–20.

140. Aristides, "The Roman Oration," 59–60.

141. Quoted in Volkan Ipek, *North Africa Colonialism and the EU* (Cham: Palgrave Pivot, 2019) 57–9.

142. See p. 2.

143. Slaughter, *New World Order*, 134.

144. Émile Benveniste, *Indo-European Language and Society*, trans. Elizabeth Palmer (London: Faber and Faber, 1973), 71–83.

145. On what Kant understands by this, see Pauline Kleingeld, *Kant and Cosmopolitanism: The Philosophical Ideal of World Citizenship* (Cambridge: Cambridge University Press, 2012), 81–2. And Georg Cavallar *The Rights of Strangers: Theories of International Hospitality, the Global Community, and Political Justice since Vitoria* (Aldershot: Ashgate, 2002).

146. Samuel Pufendorf, *De iure naturae et gentium libri octo*, trans. C. H. Oldfather and W. A. Oldfather, vol. 2 (Oxford: Clarendon Press, 1934), 364–6.

147. Article 18 of the *Charter of Fundamental Rights of the European Union* guarantees a right to asylum based on the Geneva Convention of 1951, as amended by the New York Protocol of January 1967 "Relating to the Status of Refugees" and defines a refugee as a person who, "owing to well-founded fear of being persecuted for reasons of race, religion, nationality, membership of a particular social group or political opinion, is outside the country of his nationality and is unable or, owing to such fear, is unwilling to avail himself of the protection of that country; or who, not having a nationality and being outside the country of his former habitual residence as a result of such events, is unable or, owing to such fear, is unwilling to return to it." *Acte final de la Conférence de plénipotentiaires des Nations Unies sur le statut des réfugiés et des apatrides.* Tenue à Genve du 2 juillet 1951 au 25 juillet 1951 Cap. I Art. 1 (2), https://perma.cc/A6MN-JB7K, accessed February 13, 2021.

148. David Miller, *Strangers in Our Midst: The Political Philosophy of Immigration* (Cambridge, MA: Harvard University Press, 2016), 166–73.

149. Quoted in Duncan Bell, *Reordering the World: Essays on Liberalism and Empire* (Princeton, NJ: Princeton University Press, 2016), 43–4.

150. *Treaty of Lisbon Amending the Treaty on European Union and the Treaty Establishing the European Community*, Art. 2.

151. Stephen Smith, *The Scramble for Europe: Young Africa on Its Way to the Old Continent* (Cambridge: Polity Press, 2019).

152. See the comments by Anthony Giddens. *Turbulent and Mighty Continent: What Future for Europe?* (Cambridge: Polity, 2014), 124–38.

153. Edmund Gibbon, *The History of the Decline and Fall of the Roman Empire*, vol. 1, ed. David Womersley (London: Penguin Books, 1995), 67.

154. See Clifford Ando, *Imperial Ideology and Provincial Loyalty in the Roman Empire* (Berkeley, Los Angeles, and London: University of California Press, 2000), 67.

155. James Wilson, "Lectures on Law: XI Citizens and Aliens" [1790–1], in *The Collected Works of James Wilson*, vol. 2, ed. Mark David Hall and Kermit L. Hall (Indianapolis, IN: Liberty Fund, 2007), 1048. See also pp. 6, 163.

156. See p. 6.

157. Gibbon, *Decline and Fall*, vol. 1, 61.

158. Benda, *Discours à la nation européenne*, 126.

159. See Casanova, "Religion, European Secular Identities and European Integration," 74: "Can the European Union open new conditions for the kind of multiculturalism that its constituent national societies find so difficult to accept?"

160. For instance, Bassam Tibi, emeritus Professor for International Relations at the University of Gottingen, and an Arab immigrant to Germany "who has not been accepted by the society in which he lives," has argued that the "Europeanization" of Islam holds out the possibility for a new form of belonging to a Europe which, as he insists, is not Christian, and most certainly not Muslim, but secular. From the contact of Islam with a secular Europe a new

more tolerant brand of Islam might emerge. See Bassam Tibi, "Europeanising Islam or the Islamisation of Europe: Political Democracy versus Cultural Difference" in *Religion in an Expanding Europe*, ed. Byrnes and Katzenstein, 204–24. For similar reasons, the historian Harold James, *Roman Predicament*, 124, argued in 2006 that Turkey should be admitted to the EU, "as a model for the rest of the Islamic world." (It is not, however, any longer a model with which most of the states of the EU would wish to be associated.)

161. Alexandre Kojève, "Outline of a Doctrine of French Policy" [1945], *Policy Review* 3/4 (2004), 3–40. (emphasis added). Francis Fukuyama, *Identity: The Demand for Dignity and the Politics of Resentment* (New York: Farrar, Strauss, and Giroux, 2018), 196, n. 4, has pointed out that after the Act of Union of 1707 the Scots, although they still preserve a strong sense of their individual identity, began to use the term "Briton" or, as David Hume and others called themselves, "North Briton" to characterize their now collective English/Scottish identity. "Britain" came to describe the United Kingdom of England, Scotland, Ireland, and Wales. Similar, while the word *russkiy* indicates an ethic Russian, *rossiyskiy* refers to any citizen of the current Russian Federation.

162. Habermas, *Between Facts and Norms*, 507.

163. Montesquieu, *Pensées*, nos 250, 741, in *Pensées; Le Spicilège*, ed. Louis Desgraves (Paris: Robert Laffont, 1991), 285, 341.

164. See the comments on this by Joseph Weiler, "Federalism without Constitutionalism: Europe's *Sonderweg*," in *Federal Vision*, ed. Nicolaidis and Howse, 54–70, at 64.

165. Habermas, "The European Nation-State," in *Inclusion of Others*, 112.

166. See Frederick Cooper, *Citizenship, Inequality, and Difference: Historical Perspectives* (Princeton, NJ: Princeton University Press, 2018), who describes the EU as "one of the world's most innovative citizenship regimes" (p. 1). I would like to thank Mike Rapport for bringing this book to my attention.

167. See Müller, "The Promise of 'Demoi-cracy,'" 197: "Above all it is not a fixed institutional arrangement, but a process: 'ever-closer union' is never-achieved union: it is about eternally becoming, and never just being."

168. Jaspers, *Vom europäischen Geist*, 16.

169. This, it has been argued, is what befell the Roman Empire after the end of the second century, when its citizens had persuaded themselves that what they had created was the most perfect political union humanity could devise. See Aldo Schiavone, *The End of the Past: Ancient Rome and the Modern West*, trans. Margaret J. Schneider (Cambridge, MA, and London: Harvard University Press, 2000).

170. Jaspers, *Vom europäischen Geist*, 10.

171. See p. 248.

172. Timothy Garton Ash, "Europe (and Yes, That Includes Britain) Can Still Be a Superpower," has recently made the same claim: "Faced with an increasingly powerful and authoritarian China, global heating, the challenge of AI, not to mention an aggressive Russia, chaotic Middle East and Trumpian United

States, this argument is more compelling than ever. In a world of giants, you need to be a giant yourself. If we Europeans don't hang together, we will hang separately."

173. Adresse aux Français, 14 juin de 2020, https://www.elysee.fr/front/pdf/elysee-module-15667-fr.pdf, accessed February 19, 2021. For Faure's remarks on the occasion of the signing of the Treaty of Rome. See p. 248.

Bibliography

This is a list of all those works cited in the endnotes. It does not, however, include sources in Greek and Latin, which are cited according to convention.

Albert, Charles. *L'Angleterre contre l'Europe*. Paris: Denoël, 1941.

Alexander, Larry, ed., *Constitutionalism: Philosophical Foundations*. Cambridge: Cambridge University Press, 1988.

Alexandrowicz, C. H. *The Law of Nations in Global History*. Edited by David Armitage and Jennifer Pitts. Oxford: Oxford University Press, 2017.

Almqvist, Kurt, and Alexander Linklater, eds. *The Pursuit of Europe: Perspectives from the Engelsburg Seminar*. Stockholm: Axel and Margaret Ax:son Johnson Foundation, 2012.

Alter, Karen. *Establishing the Supremacy of European Law: The Making of an International Rule of Law in Europe*. Oxford: Oxford University Press, 2001.

Alternative für Deutschland. *Manifesto for Germany: The Political Programme of the Alternative for Germany* (2017), https://www.afd.de/wp-content/uploads/sites/111/2017/04/2017-04-12_afd-grundsatzprogramm-englisch_web.pdf, accessed February 12, 2021.

Anderson, Benedict. *Imagined Communities: Reflections on Nationalism*. New York: Verso, 1991.

Ando, Clifford. *Imperial Ideology and Provincial Loyalty in the Roman Empire*. Berkeley, Los Angeles, and London: University of California Press, 2000.

Angell, Norman. *The Great Illusion: A Study of the Relation of Military Power to National Advantage*. New York: Putnam, 1913.

Arcidiacono, Bruno. "La Paix par le droit international dans la vision de deux juristes du XIXᵉ siècle: Le Débat Lorimer-Bluntschli." *Relations internationales* 149 (2012): 13–26.

Aristides, Aelius. "The Roman Oration." In James H. Oliver, "The Ruling Power: A Study of the Roman Empire in the Second Century after Christ through the Roman Oration of Aelius Aristides." *Transactions of the American Philosophical Society*, n.s., 23 (1953): 103.

Armitage, David. *Civil Wars: A History in Ideas*. New York: Alfred A. Knopf, 2017.

Aron, Raymond. *Penser la liberté, penser la démocratie*. Paris: Gallimard, 2005.

Asad, Talal. "Muslims and European Identity: Can Europe Represent Islam?" In *The Idea of Europe: From Antiquity to the European Union*. Edited by Anthony Pagden, 209–27. Cambridge: Cambridge University Press, 2002.

Asku, Esref, ed. *Early Notions of Global Governance: Selected Eighteenth-Century Proposals for "Perpetual Peace."* Cardiff: University of Wales Press, 2008.

Atikcan, Ece Ozlem. *Framing the European Union: The Power of Political Arguments in Shaping European Integration.* Cambridge: Cambridge University Press, 2015.

Bacon, Francis. *Advancement of Learning* [1605]. Edited by Joseph Devey. New York: P. F. Collier and Son, 1901.

Bailyn, Bernard. *The Ideological Origins of the American Revolution.* Cambridge, MA: Harvard University Press, 1967.

Bainville, Jacques. *Les Conséquences politiques de la paix.* Paris: Nouvelle Librairie Nationale, 1920.

Balakrishnan, Gopal. *The Enemy: An Intellectual Portrait of Carl Schmitt.* London and New York: Verso, 2000.

Balibar, Étienne. *We the People of Europe?: Reflections on Transnational Citizenship.* Princeton, NJ: Princeton University Press, 2004.

Bankowski, Zenon, and Emilios Christodoulidis. "The European Union as an Essentially Contested Project." *European Law Journal* 4 (1998): 341–54.

Bartelson, Jens. *A Genealogy of Sovereignty.* Cambridge: Cambridge University Press, 1995.

Bayly, C. A., and Eugenio F. Biagini, eds. *Giuseppe Mazzini and the Globalization of Democratic Nationalism 1830–1920.* Oxford: Oxford University Press, 2008.

Bederman, David J. *The Classical Foundations of the American Constitution: Prevailing Wisdom.* Cambridge: Cambridge University Press, 2008.

Belissa, Marc. *Fraternité universelle and intérêt national 1713–1795: Les Cosmopolitiques du droit des gens.* Paris: Éditions Kimé, 1998.

Bell, David A. *The Cult of the Nation in France: Inventing Nationalism, 1680–1800.* Cambridge, MA: Harvard University Press, 2001.

Bell, David A. *The First Total War: Napoleon's Europe and the Birth of Warfare as We Know It.* Boston, MA, and New York: Houghton Mifflin, 2007.

Bell, Duncan. *Reordering the World: Essays on Liberalism and Empire.* Princeton, NJ: Princeton University Press, 2018.

Bell, Duncan, and Casper Sylvest. "International Society in Victorian Political Thought: T. H. Green, Herbert Spencer and Henry Sidgwick." *Modern Intellectual History* 3 (2006): 1–31.

Bellamy, Richard. *A Republican Europe of States: Cosmopolitanism, Intergovernmentalism and Democracy in the EU.* Cambridge: Cambridge University Press, 2019.

Benda, Julien. *Discours à la nation européenne.* Paris: Gallimard, 1933.

Benda, Julien. *Entretiens: L'Avenir de l'esprit européen.* Paris: Institut International de Coopération Intellectuelle, 1934.

Bendersky, Joseph J. *Carl Schmitt: Theorist for the Reich.* Princeton, NJ: Princeton University Press, 1983.

Ben-Ghiat, Ruth. *La cultura fascista.* Bologna: Il Mulino, 2000.

Bentham, Jeremy. *The Works of Jeremy Bentham.* 11 vols. Edited by John Bowring. Edinburgh, 1843.

Benveniste, Émile. *Indo-European Language and Society.* Translated by Elizabeth Palmer. London: Faber and Faber, 1973.

Bickerton, Christopher J. *European Integration: From Nation-States to Member States.* Oxford: Oxford University Press, 2012.

Biersteker, Thomas J., and Cynthia Weber, eds. *State Sovereignty as Social Construct.* Cambridge: Cambridge University Press, 1996.

Blair, Tony. "A Superpower, but not a Superstate." *The Guardian* (October 7, 2000), https://www.theguardian.com/politics/2000/oct/07/uk.tonyblair, accessed February 13, 2021.

Bluntschli, Johann Caspar. *Gesammelte kleine Schriften.* Nördlingen: C. H. Beck, 1879.

Bluntschli, Johann Caspar. "Die Organisation des europäischen Staatenvereines" [1878]. In *Gesammelte kleine Schriften*, vol. II, 279–312. Nördlingen: C. H. Beck, 1879.

Bluntschli, Johann Caspar. *The Theory of the State* [*Lehre vom modernen Staat*, 1895]. Freeport, NY: Books for Libraries Press, 1971.

Bodin, Jean. *The Six Bookes of a Commonweal.* Edited by Kenneth Douglas. Translated by Richard Knolles McRae. Cambridge, MA: Harvard University Press, 1962.

Boemeke, Manfred F., Gerald D. Feldman, and Elisabeth Glaser, eds. *The Treaty of Versailles: A Reassessment after 75 Years.* Cambridge: Cambridge University Press, 1998.

Boers, Michael. *Napoleon: The Spirit of the Age.* London: Faber and Faber, 2018.

Bohman, James. *Democracy across Borders.* Cambridge, MA: MIT Press, 2007.

Bonaparte, Napoléon. *Œuvres de Napoléon Bonaparte.* Edited by C. L. F. Panckoucke. 5 vols. Paris, 1821.

Bonaparte, Napoléon. *Commentaires de Napoléon Premier.* Edited by Anselm Petetin. 6 vols. Paris: Imprimerie Impériale, 1867.

Bottici, Chiara, and Benoît Challand. *Imagining Europe: Myth, Memory and Identity.* Cambridge: Cambridge University Press, 2013.

Bourgeois, Léon. "The Reasons for the League of Nations," https://www.nobel-prize.org/nobel_prizes/peace/laureates/1920/bourgeois-lecture.html, accessed February 9, 2021.

Bowden, Brett. *The Empire of Civilization: The Evolution of an Imperial Idea.* Chicago and London: University of Chicago Press, 2009.

Boyce, Robert. "British Capitalism and the Idea of European Unity between the Wars." In *European Unity in the Interwar Period.* Edited by Peter M. R. Stirk, 65–83. London and New York: Pinter Publishers, 1989.

Bradford, Anu. *The Brussels Effect: How the European Union Rules the World.* Oxford: Oxford University Press, 2020.

Breuilly, John. *Nationalism and the State.* Manchester: Manchester University Press, 1982.

Brubaker, Rogers. *Nationalism Reframed: Nationhood and the National Question in the New Europe.* Cambridge: Cambridge University Press, 1996.

Bruckner, Pascal. *La Tyrannie de la pénitence: Essai sur le masochisme occidental.* Paris: Grasset, 2006.

Brugmans, Henri. *Pour un gouvernement européen.* n.p.: Éditions de la Campagne Européenne de la Jeunesse, 1952.

Brugmans, Henri. *La Pensée politique du fédéralisme.* Leiden: A. W. Sijthoff, 1969.

Brugmans, Henri. *L'Idée européenne 1920–1970.* Bruges: De Tempel, 1970.

Brunet, René. *La Société des Nations et la France*. Paris: Librairie de la société Recueil Sirey, 1921.

Bruneteau, Bernard. *"L'Europe nouvelle de Hitler": Une Illusion des intellectuels de la France de Vichy*. Monaco: Éditions du Rocher, 2003.

Bruneteau, Bernard, and Youssef Cassis, eds. *L'Europe communautaire au défi de la hiérarchie*. Brussels: P. I. E. Peter Lang, 2000.

Brunnermeier, Markus K., Harold James, and Jean-Pierre Landau. *The Euro and the Battle of Ideas*. Princeton, NJ: Princeton University Press, 2016.

Bull, Hedley. *The Anarchical Society: A Study of Order in World Politics*. 4th edn. London: Macmillan, 2012.

Bullitt, William C. *The Great Globe Itself: A Preface to World Affairs*. New York: Charles Scribner's Sons, 1946.

Burgess, Michael. *Federalism and European Union: The Building of Europe, 1950–2000*. London and New York: Routledge, 2000.

Burke, Edmund. *The Writings and Speeches of Edmund Burke*. Vol. 5, *India: Madras and Bengal 1774–1785*. Edited by P. J. Marshall. Oxford: Clarendon Press, 1981.

Burke, Edmund. *On Empire, Liberty and Reform: Speeches and Letters*. Edited by David Bromwich. New Haven, CT, and London: Yale University Press, 2000.

Burke, William. *Additional Reasons for Our Immediately Emancipating Spanish America*. London, 1808.

Burrow, John. *The Crisis of Reason: European Thought, 1848–1914*. New Haven, CT, and London: Yale University Press, 2000.

Buruma, Ian. *Murder in Amsterdam: The Death of Theo van Gogh, and the Limits of Tolerance*. London and New York: Penguin Press, 2006.

Byrd, Sharon B., and Joachim Hruschka. "Lex iusti, lex iuridica und lex iustitiae in Kants *Rechtslehre*." *Archiv für Rechts- und Sozialphilosophie* 91 (2005): 484–500.

Byrnes, Timothy A., and Peter J. Katzenstein, eds. *Religion in an Expanding Europe*. Cambridge: Cambridge University Press, 2006.

Calhoun, Craig J. "Imagining Solidarity: Cosmopolitanism, Constitutional Patriotism, and the Public Sphere." *Public Culture* 14 (2002): 147–71.

Callegaro, F., and N. Marcucci. "Europe as a Political Society: Émile Durkheim, the Federalist Principle and the Ideal of a Cosmopolitan Justice." *Constellations* 25 (2018): 542–55. doi: 10.1111/1467-8675.12352.

Campbell, Peter. "The Language of Patriotism in France, 1750–1770." e-*France* 1 (2007): 1–43.

Campbell, Peter. "The Politics of Patriotism in France (1770–1788)." *French History* 24 (2010): 550–75.

Camps, Miriam. *Britain and the European Community, 1955–1963*. Princeton, NJ: Princeton University Press, 1964.

Cappelletti, Mauro, Monica Seccombe, and Joseph Weiler, eds. *Integration through Law: Europe and the American Federal Experience*. Berlin and New York: Walter de Gruyter, 1986.

Carlyle, Thomas. *On Heroes, Hero-Worship, and the Heroic in History* [1840]. Edited by Michael K. Goldberg, Joel J. Brattin, and Mark Engel. Berkley, Los Angeles, and Oxford: University of California Press, 1993.

Carr, E. H. *The Twenty-Years' Crisis 1919–1939: An Introduction to the Study of International Relations.* London: Macmillan, 1939.

Carr, E. H. *The Future of Nations: Independence or Interdependence?* London: Kegan Paul, 1941.

Carr, E. H. *Nationalism and After.* New York: Macmillan, 1945.

Casanova, José. "Religion, European Secular Identities and European Integration." In *Religion in an Expanding Europe.* Edited by Timothy A. Byrnes and Peter J. Katzenstein, 65–92. Cambridge: Cambridge University Press, 2006.

Cattaneo, Carlo. *Sulle interdizioni israelitiche.* Edited by G. A. Belloni. Rome: Sestante, 1944.

Cattaneo, Carlo. *Scritti storici e geografici.* Edited by Gaetano Salvemini and Ernesto Sestan. Florence: Felice le Monnier, 1957.

Caulaincourt, Armand Augustin Louis de. *With Napoleon in Russia: The Memoirs of General de Caulaincourt, Duke of Vicenza.* New York: William Morrow and Co., 1935.

Cavallar, Georg. *The Rights of Strangers: Theories of International Hospitality, the Global Community, and Political Justice since Vitoria.* Aldershot: Ashgate, 2002.

Cavallar, Georg. "Johann Caspar Bluntschlis europäischer Staatenbund in seinem historischen Kontext." *Zeitschrift der Savigny-Stiftung für Rechtsgeschichte* 121 (2004): 504–18.

Chabot, Jean-Luc. "Le Primat de la civilisation occidentale au principe des premiers plans d'Europe unie." In *L'Europe communautaire au défi de la hiérarchie.* Edited by Bernard Bruneteau and Youssef Cassis, 37–56. Brussels: P. I. E. Peter Lang, 2000.

Chabot, Jean-Luc. *L'Idée d'Europe unie.* Grenoble: Presses Universitaires de France, 2005.

Charlemagne. "Huntington's Disease and the Clash of Civilization-States." *The Economist* (January 2, 2020), https://www.economist.com/europe/2020/01/02/huntingtons-disease-and-the-clash-of-civilisation-states, accessed February 13, 2021.

Chateaubriand, François René de. *Mémoires d'outre-tombe.* Edited by Maurice Levaillant and Georges Moulinier. Paris: Gallimard, Bibliothèque de la Pléiade, 1951.

Chenaux, Philippe. *De la chrétienté à l'Europe: Les Catholiques et l'idée européenne au XXe siècle.* Tours: CDD Éditions, 2007.

Child, Clifton J. "The Concept of the New Order." In *Hitler's Europe: Survey of International Affairs 1939–1946.* Edited by Arnold Toynbee and Veronica M. Toynbee, 47–51. London: Oxford University Press, 1954.

Christin, Olivier. *La Paix de religion: L'Autonomisation de la raison politique au XVIe siècle.* Paris: Seuil, 1997.

Churchill, Winston. *The Sinews of Peace: Post-War Speeches by Winston Churchill.* London: Cassell, 1948.

Clark, Christopher. *The Sleepwalkers: How Europe Went to War in 1914*. London: Allen Lane, 2012.

Clark, Ian, and Iver B. Neumann, eds. *Classical Theories of International Relations*. London: Macmillan, 1996.

Cohen, Antonin. "The Future of Europe: Past and Present: From the Hague Congress to the Convention on the Future of Europe." In *Whose Europe? National Models and the Constitution of the European Union*. Papers of a Multi-Disciplinary Conference held in Oxford in April 2003. Edited by Kalypso Nicolaidis and Stephen Weatherill (2003), 36–48, https://europaeum.org/wp-content/uploads/2017/09/Whose-Europe.pdf, accessed February 13, 2021.

Cohn-Bendit, Daniel, and Guy Verhofstadt. *For Europe! Manifesto for a Postnational Revolution in Europe*. Munich: Carl Hanser Verlag, 2012.

Coker, Christopher. *The Improbable War: China, the United States, and the Logic of Great Power Conflict*. Oxford: Oxford University Press, 2015.

Coker, Christopher. *The Rise of the Civilizational State*. Cambridge: Polity Press, 2019.

Collingwood, R. G. *The New Leviathan or Man, Society, Civilization, and Barbarism*. Edited by David Boucher. Oxford: Clarendon Press, 1992.

Condorcet, Marie-Jean-Antoine-Nicolas de Caritat, marquis de. *Œuvres de Condorcet*. Paris, 1847.

Condorcet, Marie-Jean-Antoine-Nicolas de Caritat, marquis de. *Esquisse d'un tableau historique des progrès de l'esprit humain*. Edited by Alain Pons. Paris: Flammarion, 1988.

Constant, Benjamin. *Political Writings*. Edited and translated by Biancamaria Fontana. Cambridge: Cambridge University Press, 1988.

Cooper, Frederick. *Citizenship, Inequality, and Difference: Historical Perspectives*. Princeton, NJ: Princeton University Press, 2018.

Coudenhove-Kalergi, Richard von. "Das Pan-Europa Programm." *Pan-Europa* 2 (1924): 4–20.

Coudenhove-Kalergi, Richard von. *Praktischer Idealismus*. Vienna: Paneuropa-Verlag, 1925.

Coudenhove-Kalergi, Richard von. *Pan-Europe*. New York: Alfred A. Knopf, 1927.

Coudenhove-Kalergi, Richard von. *The Totalitarian State against Man*. Glarus, Switzerland: Paneuropa Editions, 1938.

Coudenhove-Kalergi, Richard von. *Europe Must Unite*. Glarus, Switzerland: Paneuropa Editions, 1939.

Coudenhove-Kalergi, Richard von. *Crusade for Pan- Europe: Autobiography of a Man and a Movement*. New York: G. P. Putnam, 1943.

Coudenhove-Kalergi, Richard von. *Europe Seeks Unity*. New York: Institute of Public Affairs and Regional Studies, 1948.

Croce, Benedetto. "Postille." *La Critica* 14 (1916): 103.

Croce, Benedetto. "Of Liberty." *Foreign Affairs* 11 (1932): 1–7.

Crucé, Éméric. *Le Nouveau Cynée ou Discours d'état représentant les occasions et moyens d'établir une paix générale et liberté du commerce par tout le monde*. Edited by Astrid Guillaume. Rennes: Presses Universitaires de Rennes, 2004.

Curtin, Deidre. *Postnational Democracy: The European Union in Search of a Political Philosophy.* The Hague: Kluwer Law International, 1997.

Curzon, George Nathaniel. *Speeches by Lord Curzon of Kedleston, Viceroy and Governor General of India.* Calcutta: Office of the Superintendent of Government Printing, India, 1900.

D'Annunzio, Gabriele. *La Carta del Carnaro e altri scritti su Fiume.* Rome: Castelvecchi, 2009.

Darwin, John. *After Tamerlane: The Global History of Empire.* London: Allen Lane, 2007.

Daughton, J. P. *An Empire Divided: Religion, Republicanism, and the Making of French Colonialism 1880–1914.* Oxford: Oxford University Press, 2006.

D'Auria, Matthew. "Junius and the 'President Professor.'" In *Europe in Crisis: Intellectuals and the European Idea 1917–1957.* Edited by Mark Hewitson and Matthew D'Auria, 289–304. New York and Oxford: Berghahn, 2012.

Davie, Grace. *Religion in Modern Europe: A Memory Mutates.* Oxford: Oxford University Press, 2000.

Deák, Francis. "Can Europe Unite?" *Political Science Quarterly* 46 (1931): 428–9.

Dehousse, Renaud. "Regulation by Networks in the European Community: The Role of European Agencies." *Journal of European Public Policy* 4 (1997): 246–61.

Delanty, Gerard. "The Frontier and Identities of Exclusion in European History." *History of European Ideas* 22 (1996): 93–103.

Delanty, Gerard. "Social Theory and European Transformation: Is there a European Society?" *Sociological Research Online* 3, no. 1 (1998): 103–17.

Deluermoz, Quentin. "L'Europe, une réalité globale du XIXe siècle." In *Histoire du monde au XIXe siècle.* Edited by P. Singaravélou and S. Venayre, 621–5. Paris: Fayard, 2019.

Demangeon, Albert. *Le Déclin de l'Europe.* Paris: Payot, 1920.

Detienne, Marcel. *L'Identité nationale, une énigme.* Paris: Gallimard, 2010.

Dickson, Julie, and Pavlos Eleftheriadis, eds. *Philosophical Foundations of EU Law.* Oxford: Oxford University Press, 2012.

Dienstag, Joshua Foa. *Pessimism: Philosophy, Ethic, Spirit.* Princeton, NJ: Princeton University Press, 2006.

Dombowsky, Don. *Nietzsche and Napoleon: The Dionysian Conspiracy.* Chicago: Chicago University Press, 2014.

Doty, Roxanne Lynn. "Sovereignty and the Nation: Constructing the Boundaries of National Identity." In *State Sovereignty as Social Construct.* Edited by Thomas J. Biersteker and Cynthia Weber, 121–47. Cambridge: Cambridge University Press, 1996.

Duhamel, Georges. *L'Avenir de l'esprit europénne.* Paris: Société des Nations, Institut international de coopération intellectuelle, 1934.

Dunn, John. *Western Political Theory in the Face of the Future.* Cambridge: Cambridge University Press, 1979.

Duranti, Marco. *The Conservative Human Rights Revolution: European Identity, Transnational Politics, and the Origins of the European Convention.* Oxford: Oxford University Press, 2017.

Du Réau, Élisabeth. "La France et l'Europe d'Aristide Briand à Robert Schuman: Naissance, déclin et redéploiement d'une politique étrangère (1919–1950)." *Revue d'histoire moderne et contemporaine* 42 (1995): 556–67.

Du Réau, Élisabeth. *L'Idée d'Europe au XXe siècle: Des mythes aux réalités.* Brussels: Éditions Complexe, 2008.

Durkheim, Émile. *"L'Allemagne au dessus de tout": La Mentalité allemande et la guerre.* Paris: Armand Colin, 1915.

Durkheim, Émile. *Les Règles de la méthode sociologique.* Paris: Felix Alcan, 1938.

Durkheim, Émile. *Professional Ethics and Civic Morals.* Translated by Cornelia Brookfield. London and New York: Routledge, 1957.

Durkheim, Émile. *Textes III: Fonctions sociales et institutions.* Paris: Les Éditions de Minuit, 1975.

Durkheim, Émile. *The Division of Labour in Society.* Translated by W. D. Halls. New York: Free Press, 1984.

Dworkin, Ronald. *Taking Rights Seriously.* London: Duckworth, 1977.

Einaudi, Luigi. "La Società delle Nazioni è un ideale possibile." *Corriere della Sera* (January 5, 1918).

Einaudi, Luigi. "Contro il mito dello stato sovrano." *Risorgimento liberale* 204 (January 3, 1945), https://www.inasaroma.org/wp-content/uploads/EINAUDI-Contro-il-mito-dello-stato-sovrano.pdf, accessed February 9, 2021.

Einaudi, Luigi. *La guerra e l'unità europea.* Florence: Le Monnier, 1984.

Eliot, T. S. *Notes towards the Definition of Culture.* New York: Harcourt, Brace, and Company, 1949.

Emerson, Ralph Waldo. *Representative Men: Seven Lectures* [1850]. Boston, MA: William Sampson and Co., 1952.

Englund, Steven. *Napoleon: A Political Biography.* Cambridge, MA: Harvard University Press, 2004.

Erasmus, Desiderius. *The Education of a Christian Prince* [1516]. Translated by Lester K. Born. New York: Octagon Books, 1963.

Esdaile, Charles. *Napoleon's Wars: An International History 1803–1815.* London: Allen Lane, 2007.

Evans, Richard J. *The Pursuit of Power: Europe 1815–1914.* London: Penguin Books, 2017.

Falkner, Gerda, and Patrick Muller, eds. *EU Policies in a Global Perspective.* London and New York: Routledge, 2014.

Faltin, Lucia, and Melanie Wright, eds. *The Religious Roots of Contemporary European Identity.* London and New York: Continuum, 2007.

Febvre, Lucien. *L'Europe: Genèse d'une civilisation: Cours professé au Collège de France en 1944–1945.* Paris: Perrin, 1999.

Ferguson, Niall. *Empire: The Rise and Demise of the British World Order and the Lessons for Global Power.* London: Allen Lane, 2002.

Ferry, Jean-Marc. *La Question de l'état européen.* Paris: Gallimard, 2000.

Fichte, Johann Gottlieb. *Addresses to the German Nation*, Edited and translated by Gregory Moore. Cambridge: Cambridge University Press, 2008.

Fitzmaurice, Andrew. *Sovereignty, Property and Empire 1500–2000*. Cambridge: Cambridge University Press, 2014.

Fleury, Antoine, with Lubor Jílek, eds. *Le Plan Briand d'Union fédérale européenne: Perspectives nationales et transnationales, avec documents: Actes du colloque international tenu à Genève du 19 au 21 septembre 1991*. Berne and Berlin: Peter Lang, 1991.

Fogu, Claudio. *The Historic Imaginary: Politics of History in Fascist Italy*. Toronto, Buffalo, and London: University of Toronto Press, 2003.

Fondation Robert Schuman. "Declaration of 9th May 1950 Delivered by Robert Schuman." *European Issue* 204 (May 10, 2015), https://www.robert-schuman.eu/en/doc/questions-d-europe/qe-204-en.pdf, accessed February 8, 2021.

Fontana, Biancamaria. "The Shaping of Modern Liberty: Commerce and Civilisation in the Writings of Benjamin Constant." *Annales Benjamin Constant* 5 (1985): 2–15.

Fontana, Biancamaria. *Benjamin Constant and the Post-Revolutionary Mind*. New Haven, CT, and London: Yale University Press, 1991.

Fontana, Biancamaria. *Germaine de Stäel: A Political Portrait*. Princeton, NJ: Princeton University Press, 2016.

Foret, François. *Religion and Politics in the European Union: The Secular Canopy*. Cambridge: Cambridge University Press, 2015.

Fromkin, David. *A Peace to End All Peace: The Fall of the Ottoman Empire and the Creation of the Modern Middle East*. New York: Henry Holt and Company, 1989.

Frye, Northrop. "*The Decline of the West* by Oswald Spengler." *Daedalus* 103 (1974): 1–13.

Fukuyama, Francis. *Identity: The Demand for Dignity and the Politics of Resentment*. New York: Farrar, Strauss, and Giroux, 2018.

Furnivall, J. S. *Netherlands India: A Study of Plural Economy*. Cambridge: Cambridge University Press, 1939.

Fursdon, Edward. *The European Defence Community: A History*. London: Macmillan, 1980.

Garner, James W. "Des limitations à la souveraineté nationale dans les relations extérieures." *Revue de droit international et de législation comparée* 52 (1925): 36–58.

Garton Ash, Timothy. "Europe (and Yes, That Includes Britain) Can Still Be a Superpower." *The Guardian* (March 2, 2020), https://www.theguardian.com/world/commentisfree/2020/mar/02/europe-britain-superpower-european, accessed February 13, 2021.

Gat, Azar, with Alexander Jacobson. *Nations: The Long History of Political Ethnicity and Nationalism*. Cambridge: Cambridge University Press, 2103.

Gellner, Ernest. *Nations and Nationalism*. Oxford: Blackwell, 2006.

Gentile, Emilio. *Il culto del littorio*. Rome and Bari: Laterza, 1994.

Gentile, Emilio. *Fascismo, storia e interpretazione*. Rome and Bari: Laterza, 2002.

Gentile, Emilio. *La Grande Italia: Il mito della nazione nel XX secolo*. Rome and Bari: Laterza, 2006.

Gentile, Giovanni. *I profeti del risorgimeno italiano*. Florence: Vallecchi Editore, 1923.

Gentile, Giovanni. *Origini e dottrina del fascismo*. Rome: Libreria del Littorio, 1929.

Gentz, Friedrich von. *On the State of Europe before and after the French Revolution.* London, 1802.

Gentz, Friedrich von. *Fragments upon the Balance of Power in Europe* [1800]. London, 1806.

Getachew, Adom. *Worldmaking after Empire: The Rise and Fall of Self-Determination.* Princeton, NJ: Princeton University Press, 2019.

Ghervas, Stella. *Conquering Peace: From the Enlightenment to the European Union.* Cambridge, MA: Harvard University Press, 2021.

Ghins, Arthur. "Benjamin Constant and Public Opinion in Post-Revolutionary France." *History of Political Thought* 40 (2019): 484–514.

Gibbon, Edmund. *The History of the Decline and Fall of the Roman Empire.* Edited by David Womersley. London: Penguin Books, 1995.

Giddens, Anthony. *Turbulent and Mighty Continent: What Future for Europe?* Cambridge: Polity, 2014.

Gide, André. "L'Avenir de l'Europe: Le Point de vue d'un Français." *La Revue de Genève* 6 (1923): 1–9.

Gide, André. *The Journals of André Gide.* Translated by Justin O'Brien. New York: Alfred A. Knopf, 1948.

Gildea, Robert. *Empires of the Mind: The Colonial Past and the Politics of the Present.* Cambridge: Cambridge University Press, 2019.

Gillingham, John. *Coal, Steel, and the Rebirth of Europe, 1945–1955.* Cambridge: Cambridge University Press, 2004.

Goebbels, Joseph. "Directive on the Treatment of the European Nation" [February 15, 1943]. In *Documents on the History of European Integration.* Vol. 1, *Continental Plans for European Union 1939–1945.* Edited by Walter Lipgens, 120. Berlin and New York: Walter de Gruyter, 1985.

Goethe, Johann Wolfgang von, Johann Peter Eckermann, and Frédéric Jacob Soret. *Conversations of Goethe with Eckermann and Soret.* Translated by John Oxenford. London, 1850.

Goldsmith, Oliver. *Letters from a Citizen of the World to his Friends in the East* [1762]. Vol. 1. London: Bungy, 1820.

Gong, Gerrit W. *The Standard of "Civilization" in International Society.* Oxford: Oxford University Press, 1984.

Gowan, Peter, and Perry Anderson, eds. *The Question of Europe.* London and New York: Verso, 1997.

Greenfeld, Liah. *Nationalism: Five Roads to Modernity.* Cambridge, MA: Harvard University Press, 1992.

Guillen, Pierre. *L'Expansion 1881–1898.* Paris: Imprimerie Nationale, 1984.

Guine, Jean-Michel. "'Société universelle des nations' et 'sociétés continentales': Les Juristes internationalistes euro-américains et la question du régionalisme européen dans les années 1920." *Siècles* 41 (2015), https://journals.openedition.org/siecles/2584?lang=en, accessed February 9, 2021.

Guizot, François. *The History of Civilization in Europe, from the Fall of the Roman Empire to the French Revolution.* Translated by William Hazlitt. Indianapolis, IN: Liberty Fund, 1997.

Gusejnova, Dina. *European Elites and Ideas of Empire 1919–1957*. Cambridge: Cambridge University Press, 2016.

Haas, Ernst. *The Uniting of Europe: Political Social and Economic Forces, 1950–1957*. Stanford, CA: Stanford University Press, 1958.

Habermas, Jürgen. "Citoyenneté et identité nationale." In *L'Europe au soir du siècle: Identité et démocratie*. Edited by Jacques Lenoble and Nicole Dewandre, 17–38. Paris: Éditions Esprit, 1992.

Habermas, Jürgen. *Between Facts and Norms: Contribution to a Discourse Theory of Law and Democracy*. Translated by William Rehg. Cambridge, MA: MIT Press, 1998.

Habermas, Jürgen. *The Inclusion of Others: Studies in Political Theory*. Edited by Ciaran Cronin and Pablo De Greiff. Cambridge, MA: MIT Press, 2000.

Habermas, Jürgen. *The Divided West*. Edited by translated by Ciaran Cronin. Cambridge: Polity Press, 2006.

Habermas, Jürgen. *Time of Transitions*. Edited and translated by Ciaran Cronin and Max Pensky. Cambridge: Polity Press, 2006.

Habermas, Jürgen. *The Crisis of the European Union: A Response*. Translated by Ciaran Cronin. Cambridge: Polity, 2012.

Hall, William E. *A Treatise on International Law*. 3rd edn. Oxford: Clarendon Press, 1890.

Hansen, Peo, and Stefan Jonsson. *Eurafrica: The Untold Story of European Integration and Colonialism*. London: Bloomsbury, 2014.

Hassner, Pierre. *La Revanche des passions: Métamorphoses de la violence et crises du politique*. Paris: Fayard 2015.

Hathaway, Oona A., and Scott J. Shapiro. *The Internationalists and Their Plan to Outlaw War*. London: Penguin Books, 2018.

Hay, Denys. *Europe: The Emergence of an Idea*. Edinburgh: Edinburgh University Press, 1968.

Hayek, F. A. *The Constitution of Liberty* [1960]. In *The Collected Works of F. A. Hayek*. Vol. 17. Edited by Ronald Hamowy. Chicago: University of Chicago Press, 2011.

Hazard, Paul, *La Pensée européene du XVIIIe siècle*. Paris: Libraire Arthème Fayard, 1963.

Hazareesingh, Sudhir. *The Legend of Napoleon*. London: Granta Books, 2004.

Hegel, Georg Wilhelm Friedrich. *Enzyklopädie der philosophischen Wissenschaften*. Heidelberg, 1817.

Hegel, Georg Wilhelm Friedrich. *The Philosophy of History*. Translated by J. Sibree. New York: Dover Publications, 1959.

Hegel, Georg Wilhelm Friedrich. *The Philosophy of Mind*. Translated by William Wallace and A. V. Miller. Oxford: Clarendon Press, 1970.

Hegel, Georg Wilhelm Friedrich. *Elements of the Philosophy of Right*. Translated by H. B. Nisbet. Cambridge: Cambridge University Press, 1991.

Heine, Heinrich. *The Romantic School and Other Essays*. Edited by Jost Hermand and Robert C. Holub. New York: Continuum, 2002.

Heller, Herman. *Sovereignty: A Contribution to the Theory of Public and International Law*. Edited by David Dyzenhaus. Oxford: Oxford University Press, 2019.

Herder, Johann Gottfried von. *Philosophical Writings*. Edited by Michael N. Forster. Cambridge: Cambridge University Press, 2002.

Herder, Johann Gottfried von. *Another Philosophy of History and Selected Political Writings*. Edited by Ioannis D. Evrigenis and Daniel Pellerin. Indianapolis, IN, and Cambridge: Hackett, 2004.

Herder, Johann Gottfried von. *Outlines of a Philosophy of the History of Man* [*Ideen zur Philosophie der Geschichte der Menschheit*]. Edited by David G. Payne. Translated by T. O. Churchill. New York: Bergman Publishers, 2016.

Herwig, Holger H. *The Demon of Geopolitics: How Karl Haushofer "Educated" Hitler and Hess*. Lanham, MD: Rowman and Littlefield 2016.

Hewitson, Mark. "Inventing Europe and Reinventing the Nation-State in a New World Order." In *Europe in Crisis: Intellectuals and the European Idea 1917–1957*. Edited by Mark Hewitson and Matthew D'Auria, 63–82. New York and Oxford: Berghahn, 2012.

Hewitson, Mark. "The United States of Europe. The European Question in the 1920s." In *Europe in Crisis: Intellectuals and the European Idea 1917–1957*. Edited by Mark Hewitson and Matthew D'Auria, 15–34. New York and Oxford: Berghahn, 2012.

Hewitson, Mark, and Matthew D'Auria, eds. *Europe in Crisis: Intellectuals and the European Idea 1917–1957*. New York and Oxford: Berghahn, 2012.

Hirschman, Albert. *The Passions and Interests: Political Arguments for Capitalism before Its Triumph*. Princeton, NJ: Princeton University Press, 1977.

Hitchcock, William I. *The Struggle for Europe: The Turbulent History of a Divided Continent 1945–2002*. New York: Doubleday, 2003.

Hobbes, Thomas. *Leviathan* [1651]. Edited by Richard Tuck. Cambridge: Cambridge University Press, 1991.

Hobson, J. A. *Imperialism: A Study* [1902]. Cambridge: Cambridge University Press, 2010.

Höffe, Otfried. *Kant's Cosmopolitan Theory of Law and Peace*. Translated by Alexandra Newton. Cambridge: Cambridge University Press, 2006.

Hoffmann, Stanley. "De Gaulle, Europe and the Atlantic Alliance." *International Organization* 18 (1964): 1–25.

Hoffmann, Stanley. "Obstinate or Obsolete? The Fate of the Nation State and the Case of Western Europe." *Daedalus* 95 (1966): 862–915.

Hoffmann, Stanley, and Charles Maier, eds. *The Marshall Plan: A Retrospective*. Boulder, CO: Westview Press, 1984.

Hogan, Michael. *The Marshall Plan: America, Britain and the Reconstruction of Western Europe 1947–1952*. Cambridge: Cambridge University Press, 1987.

Holbraad, Carsten. *The Concert of Europe: A Study in German and British International Theory 1815–1914*. London: Longman, 1970.

Holm, Michael. *The Marshall Plan: A New Deal for Europe*. New York: Routledge, 2016.

Hooker, William. *Carl Schmitt's International Thought: Order and Orientation*. Cambridge: Cambridge University press, 2009.

Hugo, Victor. *Œuvres complètes*. Edited by Jean Massin. Paris: Le Club français du livre, 1951.

Hume, David. *Essays: Moral, Political, and Literary*. Edited by Eugene F. Miller. Indianapolis, IN: Liberty Fund, 1985.

Hunt, Lynn. *Inventing Human Rights: A History*. New York and London: W. W. Norton, 2007.

Hunter Miler, David. *The Peace Pact of Paris: A Study in the Briand–Kellogg Treaty*. New York and London: G. P. Putnam, 1928.

Hurrell, Andrew. "Kant and the Kantian Paradigm in International Relations." *Review of International Studies* 16 (1990): 183–205.

Husserl, Edmund. *Phenomenology and the Crisis of Philosophy: Philosophy as Rigorous Science and Philosophy and the Crisis of European Man* [1935]. Translated by Quentin Lauer. New York: Harper and Row, 1965.

Huxley, Julian, and A. C. Haddon. *We Europeans: A Survey of "Racial" Problems*. New York and London: Harper and Brothers, 1936.

Hyam, Ronald. *Britain's Imperial Century 1815–1914: A Study of Empire and Expansion*. London: B. T. Batsford, 1976.

Ifversen, Jan. "The Crisis of European Civilization after 1918." In *Ideas of Europe since 1914: The Legacy of the First World War*. Edited by Menno Spiering and Michael Wintle, 14–31. Basingstoke: Palgrave Macmillan, 2002.

Ipek, Volkan. *North Africa, Colonialism and the EU*. Cham: Palgrave Pivot, 2019.

Israel, Jonathan. *The Expanding Blaze: How the American Revolution Ignited the World 1775–1848*. Princeton, NJ: Princeton University Press, 2017.

Jacobs, Francis G., and Kenneth L. Kars. "The 'Federal' Legal Order: The USA. and Europe Compared." In *Integration through Law: Europe and the American Federal Experience*. Vol. 1. Edited by Mauro Cappelletti, Monica Seccombe, and Joseph Weiler, 287–316. Berlin and New York: Walter de Gruyter, 1986.

James, Harold. *The Roman Predicament: How the Rules of International Order Create the Politics of Empire*. Princeton, NJ: Princeton University Press, 2006.

Janis, M. W. "Jeremy Bentham and the Fashioning of 'International Law'." *The American Journal of International Law* 78 (1984): 405–18.

Jarrett, Mark. *The Congress of Vienna and Its Legacy: War and Great Power Diplomacy after Napoleon*. London and New York: I. B. Tauris, 2014.

Jaspers, Karl. *Vom europäischen Geist*. Munich: R. Piper, 1947.

Jaume, Lucien. ed. *Coppet, creuset de l'esprit libéral: Les Idées politiques et constitution-nelles du groupe de Madame de Staël*. Marseilles and Paris: Presses Universitaires d'Aix-Marseille and Economica, 2000.

Jay, Peter. "Europe: Periclean League of Democracies, Bonaparte's Third French Empire or Carolingian Fourth Reich?" In *The Pursuit of Europe: Perspectives from the Engelsburg Seminar*. Edited by Kurt Almqvist and Alexander Linklater, 63–72. Stockholm: Axel and Margaret Ax:son Foundation, 2012.

Jennings, W. I. *A Federation for Western Europe*. Cambridge: Cambridge University Press, 1940.

Johnson, Paul. *Napoleon*. London: Orion Books, 2003.

Jones, H. S. "The Idea of the National in Victorian Political Thought." *European Journal of Political Theory* 5 (2006): 12–21.

Jospin, Lionel. *Le Mal napoléonien*. Paris: Éditions du Seuil, 2014.

Jouvenel, Bertrand de. *Après la défaite*. Paris: Plon, 1941.

Jouvenel, Bertrand de. *L'Amérique en Europe: Le Plan Marshall et la coopération inter-continentale*. Paris: Plon, 1948.

Jouvenel, Bertrand de. *Quelle Europe?* [A Collection of Jouvenel's Newspaper Articles]. Paris: Le Portulan, n.d.

Judt, Tony. *A Grand Illusion? An Essay on Europe*. London: Penguin Books, 1995.

Judt, Tony. *Postwar: A History of Europe since 1945*. London: Penguin Books, 2005.

Kalmo, Hant, and Quentin Skinner, eds. *Sovereignty in Fragments: The Past, Present and Future of a Contested Concept*. Cambridge: Cambridge University Press, 2010.

Kant, Immanuel. *Kant's gesammelte Schriften*. Berlin: Walter de Gruyter, 1902–19.

Kant, Immanuel. *Practical Philosophy*. Edited and translated by Mary J. Gregor. Cambridge: Cambridge University Press, 1996.

Kant, Immanuel. *Religion and Rational Theology*. Edited and translated by Allen W. Wood and George di Giovanni. Cambridge: Cambridge University Press, 1996.

Kant, Immanuel. *Lectures on Ethics*. Edited by Peter Heath and J. B. Schneewind. Cambridge: Cambridge University Press, 1997.

Kant, Immanuel. *Critique of Pure Reason*. Edited and translated by Paul Guyer and Allen W. Wood. Cambridge: Cambridge University Press, 1998.

Kant, Immanuel. *Correspondence*. Edited and translated by Arnulf Zweig. Cambridge: Cambridge University Press, 1999.

Kant, Immanuel. *Critique of the Power of Judgment*. Edited and translated by Paul Guyer and Eric Mathews. Cambridge: Cambridge University Press, 2000.

Kant, Immanuel. *Anthropology, History and Education*. Edited by Günter Zöller and Robert B. Louden. Cambridge: Cambridge University Press, 2007.

Katenhusen, Ines, and Wolfram Lamping, eds. *Demokratien in Europa: Der Einfluss der europäischen Integration auf Institutionenwandel und neue Konturen des demokratischen Verfassungsstaates*. Wiesbaden: Springer, 2003.

Kaviraj, Sudipta, and Sunil Khilnani, eds. *Civil Society: History and Possibilities*. Cambridge: Cambridge University Press, 2001.

Keane, John, ed. *Civil Society: Berlin Perspectives*. New York and Oxford: Berghahn Books, 2006.

Kedourie, Elie. *Nationalism*. London: Hutchinson, 1960.

Keene, Edward. *Beyond the Anarchical Society: Grotius, Colonialism and Order in World Politics*. Cambridge: Cambridge University Press, 2002.

Kelley, Donald. *The Beginning of Ideology: Consciousness and Society in the French Reformation*. Cambridge: Cambridge University Press, 1981.

Kelley, Donald. "'What Pleases the Prince': Justinian, Napoleon and the Lawyers." *History of Political Thought* 23 (2002): 288–302.

Kelsen, Hans. *General Theory of Law and State*. Translated by Anders Wedberg. Cambridge, MA: Harvard University Press, 1945.

Kelsen, Hans. *Pure Theory of Law*. Translated by Max Knight. Berkeley and Los Angeles: California University Press, 1945.

Kelsen, Hans. "Foundations of Democracy." *Ethics* 66 (1955): 1–101.

Kelsen, Hans. *Peace through Law* [1944]. New York and London: Garland Publishing Inc., 1973.

Kennedy, Paul. *The Rise and Fall of the Great Powers*. New York: Random House, 1987.

Kerry, Paul E. "The Quarrel over the Religious Roots of European Identity in the European Constitution and the Nature of Historical Explanation: A Catholic Coign of Vantage." In *The Religious Roots of Contemporary European Identity*. Edited by Lucia Faltin and Melanie Wright, 168–78. London and New York: Continuum, 2007.

Keynes, John Maynard. *The Economic Consequences of the Peace*. New York: Harcourt, Brace, and Howe, 1920.

Kiljunen, Kimmon. *The European Constitution in the Making*. Brussels: Centre for European Policy Studies, 2004.

Kircher Reill, Dominique. "Fiume Crisis: Life in the Wake of the Habsburg Empire." Cambridge, MA: Harvard University Press, 2020. Available at: https://www.hup. harvard.edu/catalog.php?isbn=9780674244245.

Kleingeld, Pauline. "Approaching Perpetual Peace: Kant's Defence of a League of States and His Ideal of a World Federation." *European Journal of Philosophy* 12 (2004): 304–25.

Kleingeld, Pauline. *Kant and Cosmopolitanism: The Philosophical Ideal of World Citizenship*. Cambridge: Cambridge University Press, 2012.

Kletzin, Birgit. *Europa aus Rasse und Raum: Die nationalsozialistische Idee der Neuen Ordnung*. Münster: Lit, 2000.

Knox, MacGregor. *Common Destiny: Dictatorship, Foreign Policy and War in Fascist Italy and Nazi Germany*. Cambridge: Cambridge University Press, 2000.

Kohn, Hans. "The Paradox of Fichte's Nationalism." *Journal of the History of Ideas* 10 (1949): 319–43.

Kojève, Alexandre. *Outline of a Phenomenology of Right* [1943]. Edited and translated by Bryan-Paul Frost and Robert Howse. Lanham, MD: Rowman and Littlefield, 2000.

Kojève, Alexandre. "Outline of a Doctrine of French Policy" [1945]. *Policy Review* 3/4 (2004): 3–40.

Koskenniemi, Martti. *The Gentle Civilizer of Nations: The Rise and Fall of International Law 1870–1960*. Cambridge: Cambridge University Press, 2001.

Koskenniemi, Martti. "International Law as Political Theology: How to Read *Nomos der Erde*?" *Constellations* 11 (2004): 492–511.

Krastev, Ivan. *After Europe*. Philadelphia, PA: University of Pennsylvania Press, 2017.

Krastev, Ivan, and Stephen Holmes. *The Light That Failed: Why the West Is Losing the Fight for Democracy*. New York and London: Pegasus Books, 2019.

Krauel, Javier. *Imperial Emotions: Cultural Responses to Myths of Empire in Fin-de-Siècle Spain*. Liverpool: Liverpool University Press, 2013.

Kumm, Mattias. "Beyond Golf Clubs and the Judicialization of Politics: Why Europe Has a Constitution Properly so Called." *The American Journal of Comparative Law* 54 (2006): 505–30.

Kundera, Milan. "The Tragedy of Central Europe." Translated by Edmund White. *The New York Review of Books* (April 26, 1984): 31.

Kunz, Josef L. "Treaty Establishing the European Defense Community." *The American Journal of International Law* 47 (1953): 275–81.

Lacché, L. "Coppet et la percée de l'état libéral constitutionnel." In *Coppet, creuset de l'esprit libéral: Les Idées politiques et constitutionnelles du groupe de Madame de Staël*. Edited by Lucien Jaume, 135–55. Marseilles and Paris: Presses Universitaires d'Aix-Marseille and Economica, 2000.

Lacroix, Justine, and Kalypso Nicolaidis, eds. *European Stories. Intellectual Debates on Europe in National Context*. Oxford: Oxford University Press, 2010.

Las Cases, Emmanuel de. *Mémorial de Sainte-Hélène ou journal où se trouve consigné, jour par jour, ce qu'a dit et fait Napoléon durant dix-huit mois*. 8 vols. Paris, 1824.

Latimer, Trevor. "The Principle of Subsidiarity: A Democratic Reinterpretation." *Constellations* 25 (2018): 586–601.

Laurens, Henry. *Les Origines intellectuelles de l'expédition d'Égypte: L'Orientalisme islamisant en France (1698–1798)*. Istanbul: Éditions Isis, 1987.

Lawrence, T. J. *Principles of International Law*. London: Macmillan, 1895.

Leca, Antoine. "Lénine et les États-Unis d'Europe." In *L'Europe entre deux tempéraments politiques: Idéal d'unité et paticularismes régionaux*, 207–15. Aix-en-Provence: Presses Universitaires d'Aix-Marseille, 1994.

Lee, Daniel. *The Right of Sovereignty*. Oxford: Oxford University Press, forthcoming.

Léger, Alexis. *Mémorandum sur l'organisation d'un régime d'union fédérale européenne*, https://gallica.bnf.fr/ark:/12148/bpt6k5613159m/f5.image, accessed February 10, 2021.

Leibniz, Gottfried Wilhelm. *The Political Writings of Leibniz*. Edited by Patrick Riley. Cambridge: Cambridge University Press, 1972.

Lemonnier, Charles. *Les États-Unis d'Europe*. Paris: Librairie de la Bibliothèque Démocratique, 1872.

Lenin, Vladimir Ilyich [Ulyanov]. *Lenin Collected Works*. Moscow: Progress Publishers, 1974.

Leroy-Beaulieu, Anatole. *Congrès des sciences politiques: Séance du mardi 5 juin, 1900: Rapport général de M. Anatole Leroy-Beaulieu: Les États-Unis d'Europe*. Paris: L. Faraut, 1900.

Leroy-Beaulieu, Paul. *De la colonisation chez les peuples modernes*. Paris: Guillaumin, 1902.

Levinger, Mathew. *Enlightened Nationalism: The Transformation of Prussian Political Culture, 1806–1848*. Oxford: Oxford University Press, 2000.

Lieber, Francis. *Fragments of Political Science: On Nationalism and Inter-Nationalism*. New York: Charles Scribner, 1868.

Linden, W. H. van der. *The International Peace Movement 1815–1874*. Amsterdam: Tilleul Publications, 1987.

Lipgens, Walter. *The Formation of the European Unity Movement* [Vol. 1 of *A History of European Integration 1945–1947*]. Oxford: Clarendon Press, 1982.

Lipgens, Walter, ed. *Documents on the History of European Integration*. Vol. 1, *Continental Plans for European Union 1939–1945*. Berlin and New York: Walter de Gruyter, 1985.

Lodge, Henry Cabot. *The Senate and the League of Nations*. New York: C. Scribner's Sons 1925.

Lorimer, James. "Proposition d'un congrès international basé sur le principe *de facto*." *Revue de droit international et de législation comparée* 3 (1871): 1–11.

Lorimer, James. *The Institutes of the Law of Nations: A Treatise of the Jural Relations of Separate Political Communities.* Edinburgh and London, 1884.

Lugard, F. D. *The Dual Mandate in British Tropical Africa.* Edinburgh and London: William Blackwood and Sons, 1923.

Maas, William. *Creating European Citizens.* New York: Rowman and Littlefield, 2007.

Macaulay, Thomas Babbington. *Speeches of Lord Macaulay Corrected by Himself.* London: Longman, Green, Longman, and Roberts, 1869.

MacCormick, Neil. "Beyond the Sovereign State." *Modern Law Review* 56 (1993): 1–18.

MacCormick, Neil. *Questioning Sovereignty: Law, State, and Nation in the European Commonwealth.* Oxford: Oxford University Press, 1999.

Mackay, David. *Federalism and European Union: A Political Economy Perspective.* Oxford: Oxford University Press, 1999.

Mackay, R. W. G. *Federal Europe: Being the Case for European Federation together with a Draft Constitution of a United States of Europe.* London: Michael Joseph, 1940.

Mackay, R. W. G. *You Can't Turn the Clock Back.* New York and Chicago: Ziff Davis, 1948.

MacKitterick, Rosamund. *Charlemagne: The Formation of a European Identity.* Cambridge: Cambridge University Press, 2008.

McLynn, Frank. *Napoleon.* New York and London: Random House, 2002.

Mack Smith, Denis. *Mazzini.* New Haven, CT, and London: Yale University Press, 1994.

Macron, Emmanuel. "Dear Europe, Brexit Is a Lesson for All of Us: It's Time for Renewal." *The Guardian* (March 4, 2019), https://www.theguardian.com/commentisfree/2019/mar/04/europe-brexit-uk, accessed February 14, 2021.

Madison, James, Alexander Hamilton, and John Jay. *The Federalist Papers.* Edited by Isaac Kramnick. Harmondsworth: Penguin Books, 1987.

Maine, Henry Sumner. *International Law.* London: John Murray, 1888.

Maine, Henry Sumner. *Ancient Law: Its Connection with the Early History of Society, and Its Relation to Modern Ideas* [1861]. London: Dent, 1917.

Majone, Giandomenico. *Dilemmas of European Integration: The Ambiguities and Pitfalls of Integration by Stealth.* Oxford: Oxford University Press, 2005.

Malcolm, Noel. *Useful Enemies: Islam and the Ottoman Empire in Western Political Thought, 1450–1750.* Oxford: Oxford University Press, 2019.

Manela, Erez. *The Wilsonian Moment: Self-Determination and the International Origins of Anti-Colonial Nationalism.* Oxford: Oxford University Press, 2007.

Manners, Ian. "Global Europa: Mythology of the European Union in World Politics." *Journal of Common Market Studies* 48, no. 1 (2009): 67–87. doi: 10.1111/j.1468-5965.2009.02042.x.

Mantena, Karuna. *Alibis of Empire: Henry Maine and the Ends of Liberal Imperialism.* Princeton, NJ: Princeton University Press, 2010.

Maôz, Zeev, and Bruce Russett. "Normative and Structural Causes of Democratic Peace, 1946–1986." *American Political Science Review* 87 (1993): 624–38.

Martin, Benjamin G. *The Nazi-Fascist New Order for European Culture.* Cambridge, MA: Harvard University Press, 2016.

Masaryk, Tomáš Garrigue. *The New Europe (The Slav Standpoint)*. Lewisburg, PA: Bucknell University Press, 1972.

Mason, Henry. *The European Coal and Steel Community*. The Hague: Nijhoff, 1955.

Massis, Henri. *Defence of the West*. Translated by F. S. Flint, with a preface by G. K. Chesterton. London: Faber and Gwyer, 1927.

Mazower, Mark. *Dark Continent: Europe's Twentieth Century*. New York: Vintage Books, 2000.

Mazower, Mark. *Hitler's Empire: How the Nazis Ruled Europe*. New York: Penguin, 2008.

Mazower, Mark. *No Enchanted Palace: The End of Empire and the Ideological Origins of the United Nations*. Princeton, NJ: Princeton University Press, 2009.

Mazower, Mark. *Governing the World: The History of an Idea*. New York: Penguin, 2012.

Mazzini, Giuseppe. *Scritti editi ed inediti di Giuseppe Mazzini*. Imola: Cooperativa Tipografico-Editrice Paolo Galeati, 1908.

Mazzini, Giuseppe. *D'una letteratura europea e altri saggi*. Edited by Paolo Maria Sipala. Fasano: Schena, 1991.

Mazzini, Giuseppe. *Thoughts upon Democracy in Europe (1846–1847): Un "manifesto" in inglese*. Edited by Salvo Mastellone. Florence: Centro editoriale toscano, 2001.

Mazzini, Giuseppe. *A Cosmopolitanism of Nations: Giuseppe Mazzini's Writings on Democracy, Nation Building and International Relations*. Edited and translated by Stefano Recchia and Nadia Urbinati. Princeton, NJ: Princeton University Press, 2009.

Meinecke, Friedrich. *Weltbürgertum und Nationalstaat: Studien zur Genesis des deutschen Nationalstaates*. Munich: R. Oldenbourg, 1922.

Meylan, Jean-Pierre. *La Revue de Genève*. Geneva: Droz, 1969.

Mill, John Stuart. *Principles of Political Economy with Some of Their Applications to Social Philosophy* [1848]. London: Longmans, 1920.

Mill, John Stuart. *The Collected Works of John Stuart Mill*. Edited by John M. Robson. Toronto: University of Toronto Press, 1977.

Mill, John Stuart. *On Liberty and Other Writings*. Edited by Stefan Collini. Cambridge: Cambridge University Press, 1989.

Miller, David. *Strangers in Our Midst: The Political Philosophy of Immigration*. Cambridge, MA: Harvard University Press, 2016.

Milton, Guy. "God and the Constitution." In *God and the EU: Retrieving the Christian Inspiration of the European Project*. Edited by Jonathan Chaplin and Gary Wilson, 13–32. London and New York: Routledge, 2016.

Milward, Alan S. *The Reconstruction of Western Europe 1945–51*. London: Methuen, 1984.

Milward, Alan S. assisted by George Brennan and Federico Romero. *The European Rescue of the Nation State*. Berkeley and Los Angeles: University of California Press, 1992.

Mommsen, Wolfgang J. "Max Weber and the Peace Treaty of Versailles," in *The Treaty of Versailles: A Reassessment after 75 Years*. Edited by Manfred F. Boemeke, Gerald D. Feldman, and Elisabeth Glaser, 535–46. Cambridge: Cambridge University Press, 1998.

Monnet, Jean. "Note de réflexion de Jean Monnet (Alger, 5 août 1943)," https://www.cvce.eu/obj/note_de_reflexion_de_jean_monnet_alger_5_aout_1943-fr-b61a8924-57bf-4890-9e4b-73bf4d882549.html, accessed February 11, 2021.

Monnet, Jean. *Les États-Unis d'Europe ont commencé: La Communauté européenne du charbon et de l'acier: Discours et allocutions 1952–1954.* Paris: Robert Laffont, 1955.

Monnet, Jean. *La Communauté européenne et l'unité de l'Occident.* Lausanne: Centre de Recherches Européennes, 1961.

Monnet, Jean. *Memoirs.* Translated by Richard Mayne. New York: Doubleday, 1978.

Monnet, Jean. *The United States of Europe Has Begun. The European Coal and Steel Community Speeches and Address 1952–1954.* Pittsburgh, PA: University of Pittsburgh Archive of European Integration, 2010.

Montaigne, Michel de. *The Complete Essays.* Edited and translated by M. A. Screech. Harmondsworth: Penguin Books, 1993.

Montesquieu, Charles de Secondat, baron de. *Œuvres Complètes.* Edited by Roger Caillois. Paris: Gallimard, Bibliothèque de la Pléiade, 1951.

Montesquieu, Charles de Secondat, baron de. *Pensées; Le Spicilège.* Edited by Louis Desgraves. Paris: Robert Laffont, 1991.

Moravcsik, Andrew. *The Choice for Europe: Social Purpose and State Power from Messina to Maastricht.* Ithaca, NY: Cornell University Press 1997.

Moravcsik, Andrew. "Federalism in the European Union: Rhetoric and Reality." In *The Federal Vision: Legitimacy and Levels of Governance in the United States and the European Union.* Edited by Kalypso Nicolaidis and Robert Howse, 159–87. Oxford: Oxford University Press, 2001.

Morefield, Jeanne. *Covenants without Sword: Idealist Liberalism and the Spirit of Empire.* Princeton, NJ: Princeton University Press, 2005.

Morgan, Glyn. *The Idea of a European Superstate: Public Justification and European Integration.* Princeton, NJ: Princeton University Press, 2005.

Mori, Massimo. *La pace e la ragione: Kant e le relazioni internazionali: Diritto, politica, storia.* Bologna: Il Mulino, 2004.

Morin, Edgar. *Penser l'Europe.* Paris: Gallimard 1987.

Morin, Edgar. *Culture et barbarie européennes.* New edn. Montrouge: Bayard, 2009.

Morin, Edgar. *L'Europe à deux visages: Humanisme et barbarie.* Paris: Lemieux, 2015.

Mosley, Oswald. *Europe: Faith and Plan.* n.p.: Euphorion Books, 1958.

Moyn, Samuel. *The Last Utopia: Human Rights in History.* Cambridge, MA: Harvard University Press, 2012.

Moyn, Samuel. *Christian Human Rights.* Philadelphia, PA: University of Pennsylvania Press, 2015.

Müller, Friedrich Max. *Biographies of Words and the Home of the Aryas.* London, 1888.

Müller, Jan-Werner. *A Dangerous Mind: Carl Schmitt in Post-War European Thought.* New Haven, CT, and London: Yale University Press, 2003.

Müller, Jan-Werner. "Julien Benda's Anti-Passionate Europe." *European Journal of Political Theory* 5 (2006): 125–37.

Müller, Jan-Werner. *Constitutional Patriotism.* Princeton, NJ: Princeton University Press, 2007.

Müller, Jan-Werner. *Contesting Democracy: Political Ideas in Twentieth-Century Europe.* New Haven, CT, and London: Yale University Press, 2011.

Müller, Jan-Werner. "The Promise of 'Demoi-cracy': Democracy, Diversity, and Domination in the European Public Order." In *Political Theory of the European*

Union. Edited by Jürgen Neyer and Antje Wiener, 187–203. Oxford: Oxford University Press, 2011.

Müller, Jan-Werner. *Populism*. London: Penguin Books, 2016.

Nakhimovsky, Isaac. "The 'Ignominious Fall of the European Commonwealth': Gentz, Hauterive, and the Debate of 1800." In *Trade and War: The Neutrality of Commerce in the Inter-State System*. Edited by Koen Stapelbroek, 212–28. Helsinki: University of Helsinki, 2011.

Naumann, Friedrich. *Central Europe [Mitteleuropa]*. Translated by Christabel M. Meredith. New York: Alfred A. Knopf, 1917.

Neyer, Jürgen, and Antje Wiener, eds. *Political Theory of the European Union*. Oxford: Oxford University Press, 2011.

Nicolaidis, Kalypso. "Our European Demoï-cracy: Is This Constitution a Third Way for Europe?." In *Whose Europe? National Models and the Constitution of the European Union*. Papers of a Multi-Disciplinary Conference held in Oxford in April 2003. Edited by Kalypso Nicolaidis and Stephen Weatherill (2003), 137–52, https://europaeum.org/wp-content/uploads/2017/09/Whose-Europe.pdf, accessed February 13, 2021.

Nicolaidis, Kalypso. "European Demoicracy and Its Crisis." *Journal of Common Market Studies* 51 (2013): 351–69.

Nicolaidis, Kalypso, and Robert Howse, eds. *The Federal Vision: Legitimacy and Levels of Governance in the United States and the European Union*. Oxford: Oxford University Press, 2001.

Nicolaidis, Kalypso, and Stephen Weatherill, eds. *Whose Europe? National Models and the Constitution of the European Union*. Papers of a Multi-Disciplinary Conference held in Oxford in April 2003, https://europaeum.org/wp-content/uploads/2017/09/Whose-Europe.pdf, accessed February 13, 2021.

Nicolet, Claude. *L'Idée républicaine en France: Essai d'histoire critique (1789–1924)*. Paris: Gallimard, 1982.

Nietzsche, Friedrich. *Daybreak: Thoughts on the Prejudices of Morality*. Translated by R. J. Hollindale. Cambridge: Cambridge University Press, 1982.

Nietzsche, Friedrich. *Human, All Too Human: A Book for Free Spirits*. Translated by R. J. Hollingdale. Cambridge: Cambridge University Press, 1986.

Nietzsche, Friedrich. *Beyond Good and Evil [1886]*. Edited and translated by Rolf-Peter Horstmann and Judith Norman. Cambridge: Cambridge University Press, 2002.

Nietzsche, Friedrich. *The Gay Science [1882]*. Edited by Bernard Williams. Translated by Josefine Nauckhoff. Cambridge: Cambridge University Press, 2012.

Nietzsche, Friedrich. *The Will to Power: Selections from the Notebooks of the 1880s*. Edited and translated by R. Kevin Hall and Michael A. Scarpitti. New York: Penguin Books, 2017.

Nussbaum Martha C. (with respondents). *For Love of Country: Debating the Limits of Patriotism*. Edited by Joshua Cohen. Boston, MA: Beacon Press, 1996.

Nussbaum Martha C. *The Cosmopolitan Tradition: A Noble but Flawed Ideal*. Cambridge, MA: Harvard University Press, 2019.

Offe, Claus. "Is There, or Can There Be, a 'European Society'?" In *Demokratien in Europa: Der Einfluss der europäischen Integration auf Institutionenwandel und neue Konturen des demokratischen Verfassungsstaates*. Edited by Ines Katenhusen and Wolfram Lamping, 71–89. Wiesbaden: Springer, 2003.

Offe, Claus. "Is There or Can There Be a 'European Society'?" In *Civil Society: Berlin Perspectives*. Edited by John Keane, 169–88. New York and Oxford: Berghahn Books, 2006.

Offe, Claus. *Europe Entrapped*. Cambridge: Polity, 2015.

O'Malley, Martin J. "Currents in Nineteenth-Century German Law and Subsidiarity's Emergence as a Social Principle in the Writings of Wilhelm Ketteler." *Journal of Law, Philosophy and Culture* 2 (2008): 23–53.

Orford, Anne. *International Authority and the Responsibility to Protect*. Cambridge: Cambridge University Press, 2011.

Ortega y Gasset, José. *The Revolt of the Masses*. New York: W. W. Norton, 1957.

Osiander, Andreas. *The States System of Europe 1640–1990: Peacemaking and the Conditions of International Stability*. Oxford: Clarendon Press, 1994.

Pagden, Anthony, ed. *The Idea of Europe: From Antiquity to the European Union*. Cambridge: Cambridge University Press, 2002.

Pagden, Anthony. *Worlds at War: The 2,500 Year Struggle between East and West*. Oxford: Oxford University Press, 2008.

Pagden, Anthony. *The Enlightenment and Why It Still Matters*. Oxford: Oxford University Press, 2013.

Pagden, Anthony. *The Burdens of Empire: 1539 to the Present*. Cambridge: Cambridge University Press, 2015.

Parker, Geoffrey. *Emperor: A New Life of Charles V*. New Haven, CT, and London: Yale University Press, 2019.

Pasquino, Pasquale. "Conceptualizing Europe." In *Whose Europe? National Models and the Constitution of the European Union*. Papers of a Multi-Disciplinary Conference held in Oxford in April 2003. Edited by Kalypso Nicolaidis and Stephen Weatherill (2003), 124–9, https://europaeum.org/wp-content/uploads/2017/09/Whose-Europe.pdf, accessed February 13, 2021.

Pasture, Patrick. *Imagining European Unity since 1000 AD*. London: Palgrave Macmillan, 2015.

Patten, Chris. *Not Quite the Diplomat: Home Truths about World Affairs*. London: Allen Lane, 2005.

Pedersen, Susan. *The Guardians: The League of Nations and the Crisis of Empire*. Oxford: Oxford University Press, 2015.

Pegg, Carl H. *The Evolution of the European Idea, 1914–1932*. Chapel Hill, NC, and London: University of North Carolina Press, 1983.

Pellegrino Sutcliffe, Marcella. *Victorian Radicals and Italian Democrats*. Woodbridge: Royal Historical Society and Boydell Press, 2015.

Perse, Saint-Jean [Alexis Léger]. *Ananbasis: A Poem by St.-J. Perse with a Translation into English by T. S. Eliot.* London: Faber and Faber, 1930.

Peruta, Franco della. *Mazzini e i rivoluzionari italiani: Il "partito d'azione" 1830–1845.* Milan: Feltrinelli, 1974.

Piketty, Thomas. *Capital et idéologie.* Paris: Seuil, 2019.

Pettit, Philip. *Republicanism: A Theory of Freedom and Government.* Oxford: Oxford University Press, 1997.

Pitts, Jennifer. *A Turn to Empire: The Rise of Imperial Liberalism in Britain and France.* Princeton, NJ: Princeton University Press, 2005.

Pitts, Jennifer. *Boundaries of the International: Law and Empire.* Cambridge, MA: Harvard University Press, 2018.

Pocock, J. G. A. *Barbarism and Religion.* 6 vols. Cambridge: Cambridge University Press, 2003–15.

Poliakov, Leon. *The Aryan Myth: A History of Racist and Nationalist Ideas in Europe.* Translated by E. Howard. New York: Basic Books, 1974.

Proudhon, Pierre Joseph. *Du Principe fédératif et de la nécessité de reconstituer la parti de la révolution* [1863]. In *Œuvres complètes de P.-J. Proudhon.* Paris: Librairie Marcel Rivière et Cie, 1959.

Pufendorf, Samuel. *De iure naturae et gentium libri octo.* Translated by C. H. Oldfather and W. A. Oldfather. Oxford: Clarendon Press, 1934.

Purchas, Samuel. *Hakluytus Posthumus or Purchas his Pilgrimes, contayning a History of the World, in Sea Voyages and lande-Travells by Englishmen & others.* 5 vols. London, 1625.

Rabinbach, Anson, and Sandra L. Gilman, eds. *The Third Reich Source Book.* Berkeley, Los Angeles, and London: University of California Press, 2013.

Rademacher, Ingrid. "Johann Caspar Bluntschli: Conception du droit international et projet de Confédération européenne (1878)." *Études Germaniques* 254, no. 2 (2009): 309–28.

Raic, David. *Statehood and the Law of Self Determination.* The Hague, London, and New York: Kluwer Law International, 2002.

Ramadan, Tariq. "Turkey is Part of Europe: Fear Keeps It out of the EU." *The Guardian* (August 6, 2009), https://www.theguardian.com/commentisfree/2009/aug/06/turkey-eu-membership, accessed February 13, 2021.

Ramel, Frédéric. "Durkheim au-delà des circonstances: Retour sur *L'Allemagne au-dessus de tout. La mentalité allemande et la guerre.*" *Revue française de sociologie* 45 (2004): 739–51.

Rapport, Mike. *1848: Year of Revolution.* New York: Basic Books, 2008.

Rapport, Mike. "Alliances and Treaties: Cooperation and Exchange in War and Peace." *European History Online* (2016), http://ieg-ego.eu/en/threads/alliances-and-wars/alliances-and-treaties/mike-rapport-alliances-and-treaties-cooperation-and-exchange-in-war-and-peace/?searchterm=&set_language=en, accessed February 12, 2021.

Reh, Christine. "The Lisbon Treaty: De-Constitutionalizing the European Union." *Journal of Common Market Studies* 47 (2009): 625–50.

Renan, Ernest. *What is a Nation? And Other Political Writings*. Edited and translated by M. F. N. Giglioli. New York: Columbia University Press, 2018.

Ribbentrop, Joachim von. "Joachim von Ribbentrop: Europa Confederation 21 March, 1943." In *Documents on the History of European Integration*. Vol. 1. *Continental Plans for European Union 1939–1945*. Edited by Walter Lipgens, 123–4. Berlin and New York: Walter de Gruyter, 1985.

Riou, Gaston. *The Diary of a French Private: War-Imprisonment 1914–1915*. Translated by Eden Paul and Cedar Paul. London: Allen and Unwin, 1916.

Riou, Gaston. *Europe, ma patrie*. Rev. edn. Paris: Éditions Baundinière, 1938.

Ripstein, Arthur. *Force and Freedom: Kant's Legal and Political Philosophy*. Cambridge, MA: Harvard University Press, 2009.

Risse, Thomas. "Social Constructivism and European Integration." In *European Integration Theory*. Edited by Antje Wiener, Tanya Börzel, and Thomas Risse, 128–48. Oxford: Oxford University Press, 2019.

Risse, Thomas, and Daniela Engelmann-Martin. "Identity Politics and European Integration: The Case of Germany." In *The Idea of Europe: From Antiquity to the European Union*. Edited by Anthony Pagden, 287–316. Cambridge: Cambridge University Press, 2002.

Röben, Betsy. *Johann Caspar Bluntschli, Francis Lieber und das moderne Völkerrecht 1861–1881*. Baden-Baden: Nomos, 2003.

Rodogno, Davide. *Fascism's European Empire: Italian Occupation during the Second World War*. Cambridge: Cambridge University Press, 2006.

Rodogno, Davide. "Le Nouvel Ordre fasciste en Méditerranée, 1940–1943: Présupposés idéologiques, visions et velléités." *Revue d'histoire moderne et contemporaine* 55 (2008): 138–56.

Rodrígue, Mario. *"William Burke" and Francisco de Miranda: The Word and the Deed in Spanish America's Emancipation*. London and Lanham, MD: University Press of America, 1994.

Rodrok, Dani. *The Globalization Paradox: Democracy and the Future of the World Economy*. New York and London: W. W. Norton, 2012.

Rolin-Jaequemyns, Gustave. "De la nécessité d'organiser une institution scientifique permanente pour favoriser l'étude et le progrès du droit international." *Revue de droit international et de législation comparée*, 5 (1873): 463–91.

Roon, Ger van. *German Resistance to Hitler: Count Moltke and the Kreisau Circle*. London and New York: Van Nostrand Reinhold Co., 1971.

Rosanvallon, Pierre. *Le Siècle du populisme: Histoire, théorie, critique*. Paris: Seuil, 2020.

Rosenboim, Or. *The Emergence of Globalism: Visions of World Order in Britain and the United States, 1939–1950*. Princeton, NJ: Princeton University Press, 2017.

Rougemont, Denis de. *Vingt-huit siècles d'Europe*. Paris: Payot, 1961.

Rougemont, Denis de. *The Idea of Europe*. Translated by Norbert Guterman. Cleveland, OH, and New York: Meridian Books, 1968.

Rougemont, Denis de. *Œuvres complètes*. Paris: Éditions de la Différence, 1994.

Rousseau, Jean-Jacques. *Œuvres complètes*. Edited by Bernard Gagnebin and Marcel Raymond. Paris: Gallimard, Bibliothèque de la Pléiade, 1959–95.

Roy, Oliver. *Secularism Confronts Islam*. Translated by George Holoch. New York: Columbia University Press, 2007.

Roy, Oliver. *Is Europe Christian?* Translated by Cynthia Schoch. Oxford: Oxford University Press, 2020.

Ruane, Kevin. *The Rise and Fall of the European Defence Community: Anglo-American Relations and the Crisis of European Defence*. Basingstoke: Macmillan, 2000.

Sabetti, Filippo. *Civilization and Self-Government: The Political Thought of Carlo Cattaneo*. Lanham, MD: Rowman and Littlefield, 2010.

Saint-Pierre, Charles-Irénée Castel, abbé de. *Projet pour rendre la paix perpétuelle en Europe*. Paris: Fayard, 1986.

Saint-Simon, Claude Henri de. *De la réorganisation de la société européenne, ou de la nécessité et les moyens de rassembler les peuples de l'Europe en un seul corps politique en conservant à chacun son indépendance nationale* [1814]. Edited by Alfred Pereire with an introduction by Henri de Jouvenel. Paris: Les Presses Françaises, 1925.

Salisbury, Robert Gascoyne-Cecil, 3rd Marquess of. *Essays of the Late Marquess of Salisbury*. London: Murray, 1905.

Salter, Arthur. *The United States of Europe and Other Papers*. New York: Reynal and Hitchcock, 1933.

Sandbu, Martin. *Europe's Orphan: The Future of the Euro and the Politics of Debt*. Princeton, NJ: Princeton University Press, 2015.

Sartre, Jean-Paul. *Qu'est-ce que la littérature?* [1948]. Paris: Gallimard, 2008.

Saunders, Robert. *Yes to Europe! The 1975 Referendum and Seventies Britain*. Cambridge: Cambridge University Press, 2018.

Scelle, Georges. *Le Pacte des nations et sa liaison avec la traité de paix*. Paris: Librairie du Recueil Sirey, 1919.

Scelle, Georges. "Essai relatif à l'Union européenne." *Revue générale de droit international public* 38 (1931): 521–63.

Schiavone, Aldo. *The End of the Past: Ancient Rome and the Modern West*. Translated by Margaret J. Schneider. Cambridge, MA, and London: Harvard University Press, 2000.

Schiavone, Aldo. *The Invention of Law in the West*. Translated by Jeremy Carden and Antony Shugar. Cambridge, MA: Harvard University Press, 2012.

Schmitt, Carl. *Positionen und Begriffe im Kampf mit Weimar-Genf-Versailles, 1923–1939*. Berlin: Duncker and Humboldt, 1940.

Schmitt, Carl. "Cambio de estructura del derecho internacional." *Revista de estudios políticos* 5 (1943): 3–36.

Schmitt, Carl. *Concept of the Political* [1932]. Translated by George Schwab. Chicago and London: University of Chicago Press, 1996.

Schmitt, Carl. *The Nomos of the Earth in International Law and the Jus Publicum Europaeum* [1950]. Translated by G. L. Ulmen. New York: Telos Press, 2003.

Schmitt, Carl. *Constitutional Theory*. Edited and translated by Jeffrey Seitzer. Durham, NC, and London: Duke University Press, 2008.

Schmitt, Carl, *Carl Schmitt, Writings on War*. Edited and translated by Timothy Nunan. Cambridge: Polity Press, 2011.

Schnapper, Dominique. *La Communauté des citoyens: Sur l'idée moderne de nation.* Paris: Gallimard, 1994.

Schroder, Peter. *Trust in Early-Modern International Political Thought, 1598–1713.* Cambridge: Cambridge University Press, 2017.

Schroeder, Paul W. *The Transformation of European Politics 1763–1848.* Oxford: Clarendon Press, 1994.

Schuman, Robert. *Pour l'Europe.* Paris: Les Éditions Nagel, 1964.

Schumpeter, Joseph. *Imperialism and Social Classes [Zur Soziologie der Imperialismen].* Translated by Heinz Norden. New York: Meridian Books, 1955.

Scruton, Roger. *A Dictionary of Political Thought.* Basingstoke: Palgrave-Macmillan, 2007.

Seely, J. R. "The United States of Europe." *Macmillan's Magazine* 23 (1871): 436–48.

Seeley, J. R. *A Short History of Napoleon the First.* Boston, MA: Roberts Brothers 1886.

Seely, J. R. *Introduction to Political Science: Two Series of Lectures.* London: Macmillan, 1923.

Shklar, Judith. *Freedom and Independence: A Study of the Political Ideas of Hegel's "Phenomenology of Mind."* Cambridge: Cambridge University Press, 1976.

Siedentop, Larry. *Democracy in Europe.* New York: Columbia University Press, 2001.

Simms, Brendan. *Europe: The Struggle for Supremacy from 1453 to the Present.* New York: Basic Books, 2013.

Simms, Brendan. *Britain's Europe: A Thousand Years of Conflict and Cooperation.* London: Allen Lane, 2016.

Sissa, Giulia. *Jealousy: A Forbidden Passion.* Cambridge: Polity, 2018.

Skinner, Quentin. *Hobbes and Republican Liberty.* Cambridge: Cambridge University Press, 2008.

Slaughter, Anne-Marie. *A New World Order.* Princeton, NJ: Princeton University Press, 2004.

Slobodian, Quinn. *Globalists: The End of Empire and the Birth of Neoliberalism.* Cambridge, MA: Harvard University Press, 2018.

Smith, Anthony. *The Ethnic Origins of Nations.* Oxford: Blackwell, 1989.

Smith, Anthony. *Myths and Memories of the Nations.* Oxford: Oxford University Press, 2000.

Smith, Stephen. *The Scramble for Europe: Young Africa on Its Way to the Old Continent.* Cambridge: Polity Press, 2019.

Snyder, Timothy. *The Road to Unfreedom: Russia, Europe, America.* New York: Tim Duggan Books, 2018.

Spengler, Oswald. *The Decline of the West: Form and Actuality.* Translated by Charles Francis Atkinson. New York: Alfred Knopf, 1927.

Spiering, Menno, and Michael Wintle, eds. *Ideas of Europe since 1914: The Legacy of the First World War.* Basingstoke: Palgrave Macmillan, 2002.

Spinelli, Altiero. "Reflections on the Institutional Crisis of the European Community." *West European Politics* 1 (1978): 77–88.

Spinelli, Altiero, *La mia battaglia per un'Europa diversa.* Maduria: Lacaita editore, 1979.

Spinelli, Altiero. *Il progetto europeo.* Bologna: Il Mulino, 1985.

Spinelli, Altiero. *Il manifesto di Ventotene con un saggio di Norberto Bobbio*. Bologna: Il Mulino, 1991.

Spinelli, Altiero. *Altiero Spinelli: From Ventotene to the European Constitution*. ARENA Report No 1/07, RECON Report No 1. Edited by Agustín José Menéndez and Alexander Linklater. Oslo: Centre for European Studies University of Oslo, 2007, http://www.reconproject.eu/main.php/RECONreport0107.pdf?fileitem= 50487350, accessed February 11, 2021.

Staab, Andreas. *The End of Europe? The Five Dilemmas of the European Union*. London: EPIC Publishing, 2020.

Staël, Madame (Anne-Louise-Germaine) de. *Œuvres complètes de Mme. La Baronne de Staël*. 17 vols. Paris, 1820–1.

Stapelbroek, Koen, ed. *Trade and War: The Neutrality of Commerce in the Inter-State System*. Helsinki: University of Helsinki, Helsinki Collegium for Advanced Studies, 2011.

Starobinski, Jean. *Le Remède dans le Mal: Critique et légitimation de l'artifice à l'âge des Lumières*. Paris: Gallimard, 1989.

Steiner, Zara. *The Lights That Failed: European International History 1919–1933*. Oxford: Oxford University Press, 2005.

Stiglitz, Joseph E. *The Euro: How a Common Currency Threatens the Future of Europe*. New York and London: Norton Publishers, 2016.

Stirk, Peter M. R., ed. *European Unity in the Interwar Period*. London and New York: Pinter Publishers, 1989.

Stirk, Peter M. R. *Mitteleuropa: Idea and Prospects*. Edinburgh: Edinburgh University Press. 1994.

Stråth, Bo. "Mitteleuropa: From List to Naumann." *European Journal of Social Theory* 11 (2008): 171–83.

Suganami, Hidemi. "Understanding Sovereignty through Kelsen/Schmitt." *Review of International Studies* 33 (2007): 511–30.

Swedberg, Richard. "Saint-Simon's Vision of a United Europe." *European Journal of Sociology* 35 (1994): 145–69.

Tagore, Rabindranath. *Nationalism* [1917]. n.p.: Alpha Editions, 2017.

Tamir, Yael. *Why Nationalism?* Princeton, NJ: Princeton University Press, 2019.

Taylor, Charles. *Hegel*. Cambridge: Cambridge University Press, 1975.

Terjanian, Anoush. *Commerce and Its Discontents in Eighteenth-Century French Political Thought*. Cambridge: Cambridge University Press, 2013.

Tibi, Bassam. "Europeanising Islam or the Islamisation of Europe: Political Democracy versus Cultural Difference." In *Religion in an Expanding Europe*. Edited by Timothy A. Byrnes and Peter J. Katzenstein, 204–24. Cambridge: Cambridge University Press, 2006.

Tocqueville, Alexis de. *The Recollections of Alexis de Tocqueville* [1893]. Translated by Alexander Teixeira de Mattos. New York, 1896.

Tocqueville, Alexis de. *Writings on Empire and Slavery*. Edited and translated by Jennifer Pitts. Baltimore, MD: Johns Hopkins University Press, 2001.

Tocqueville, Alexis de. *Democracy in America* [1835–40]. Translated by James T. Schleifer. Indianapolis, IN: Liberty Fund, 2012.

Toynbee, Arnold, and Veronica M. Toynbee, eds. *Hitler's Europe: Survey of International Affairs 1939–1946*. London: Oxford University Press, 1954.

Treitschke, Heinrich von. *Politics*. Translated by Blanche Dugdale and Torben de Bille. New York: Macmillan, 1916.

Trimçev, Rieke, Gregor Feindt, Félix Krawatzek, and Friedemann Pestel. "Europe's Europes: Mapping the Conflicts of European Memory." *Journal of Political Ideologies* (2019): 51–77. doi: 10.1080/13569317.2019.1696925, accessed February 13, 2021.

Tuori, Kaius, and Heta Bjorklund, eds. *Roman Law and the Idea of Europe*. London: Bloomsbury Academic, 2019.

Twiss, Sir Travers. *Le Congrès de Vienne et la conférence de Berlin*. Brussels and Leipzig, 1888.

Unamuno, Miguel de. "L'Avenir de l'Europe. Le Point de vue d'un Espagnol." *La Revue de Genéve* 6 (1923): 20–4.

Unger, Gérard. *Aristide Briand: Le Ferme Conciliateur*. Paris: Fayard, 2005.

Untea, Ionut. "New Middle Ages or New Modernity? Carl Schmitt's Interwar Perspective on Political Unity in Europe." In *Europe in Crisis: Intellectuals and the European Idea 1917–1957*. Edited by Mark Hewitson and Matthew D'Auria, 169–82. New York and Oxford: Berghahn, 2012.

Valéry, Paul. *Œuvres complètes*. Paris: Gallimard, Bibliothèque de la Pléiade, 1957.

Varouxakis, Georgios. "Mid-Atlantic Musings: The 'Question of Europe' in British Intellectual Debates, 1961–2008." In *European Stories: Intellectual Debates on Europe in National Context*. Edited by Justine Lacroix and Kalypso Nicolaidis, 147–66. Oxford: Oxford University Press, 2010.

Vattel, Emer de. *The Law of Nations, or Principles of the Law of Nature, Applied to the Conduct and Affairs of Nations and Sovereigns* [1757]. Edited and translated by Béla Kapossy and Richard Whatmore. Indianapolis, IN: Liberty Fund, 2008.

Vayssière, Bertrand. *Vers une Europe fédérale?: Les Espoirs et les actions fédéralistes au sortir de la Seconde Guerre Mondiale*. Brussels: Peter Lang, 2006.

Verhofstadt, Guy. *Europe's Last Chance: Why the European States Must Form a More Perfect Union*. New York: Basic Books, 2017.

Villepin, Dominique de. *Les Cent-jours, ou l'esprit de sacrifice*. Paris: Perrin, 2001.

Viroli, Mauricio. *For Love of Country: An Essay on Patriotism and Nationalism*. Oxford: Oxford University Press, 2005.

Voltaire [François-Marie Arouet]. *De la paix perpétuelle par le docteur Goodheart*. Geneva, 1769.

Wallerstein, Immanuel. *Africa: The Politics of Independence and Unity*. Lincoln, NE, and London: University of Nebraska Press, 2005.

Weiler, Joseph. *The Constitution of Europe: "Do the New Clothes Have an Emperor?" and Other Essays on European Integration*. Cambridge: Cambridge University Press, 1999.

Weiler, Joseph. "Federalism and Constitutionalism: Europe's *Sonderweg*." Harvard Jean Monnet Working Paper No.7/99 (2000): 10/100, https://jeanmonnetprogram.org/2000-jean-monnet-working-papers/, accessed February 12, 2021.

Weiler, Joseph. "Federalism without Constitutionalism: Europe's *Sonderweg*." In *The Federal Vision: Legitimacy and Levels of Governance in the United States and the European Union*. Edited by Kalypso Nicolaidis and Robert Howse, 159–87. Oxford: Oxford University Press, 2001.

Weiler, Joseph. "A Christian Europe? Europe and Christianity: Rules of Commitment." *European View* 6 (2007): 143–50.

Weller, Shane. *Idea of Europe: A Critical History*. Cambridge: Cambridge University Press, 2021.

Wells, H. G. *The War That Will End War*. London: Frank and Cecil Palmer, 1914.

Wells, H. G., Salvador de Madariaga, J. Middleton Murry, and C. E. M. Joad. *The New World Order*. London: National Peace Council, 1940.

Wells Brown, William. *The American Fugitive in Europe: Sketches of Places and People Abroad*. New York, 1855.

Welsh, Jennifer M. *Edmund Burke and International Relations: The Commonwealth of Europe and the Crusade against the French Revolution*. New York: St. Martin's Press, 1995.

Welsh, Jennifer M. "Edmund Burke and the Commonwealth of Europe: The Cultural Bases of International Order." In *Classical Theories of International Relations*. Edited by Ian Clark and Iver B. Neumann, 173–92. London: Macmillan, 1996.

Wheaton, Henry. *Elements of International Law: With a Sketch of the History of the Science*. Philadelphia, PA, 1836.

Whiteman, Kaye. "The Rise and Fall of Eurafrique: From the Berlin Conference of 1884–1885 to the Tripoli EU–Africa Summit of 2010." In *The EU and Africa: From Eurafrique to Afro-Europa*. Edited by Adekeye Adebajo and Kaye Whiteman, 23–44. New York: Columbia University Press, 2011.

Wiener, Antje, Tanja Börzel, and Thomas Risse, eds. *European Integration Theory*. Oxford: Oxford University Press, 2019.

Williams, Andrew. *EU Human Rights Policies: A Study in Irony*. Oxford: Oxford University Press, 2004.

Williams, Andrew. *The Ethos of Europe: Values, Law and Justice in the EU*. Cambridge: Cambridge University Press, 2010.

Wilson, James. *The Collected Works of James Wilson*. 2 vols. Edited by Mark David Hall and Kermit L. Hall. Indianapolis, IN: Liberty Fund, 2007.

Wolff, Larry. *Inventing Eastern Europe: The Map of Civilization in the Mind of the Enlightenment*. Stanford, CA: Stanford University Press, 1994.

Wotton, David, ed. *Divine Right and Democracy: An Anthology of Political Writings in Stuart England*. London: Penguin Books, 1986.

Young, Julian. *Freidrich Nietzsche: A Philosophical Biography*. Cambridge: Cambridge University Press, 2010.

Ypi, Lea. "Statist Cosmopolitanism." *Journal of Political Philosophy* 16 (2008): 48–71.

Zamoyski, Adam. *Rites of Peace: The Fall of Napoleon and the Congress of Vienna.* London: Harper Press, 2007.

Ziegerhofer, Anita. *Botschafter Europas: Richard Nikolaus Coudenhove-Kalergi und die Paneuropa-Bewegung in den zwanziger und dreißiger Jahren.* Vienna: Böhlau 2004.

Zielonka, Jan. *Europe as Empire: The Nature of the Enlarged European Union.* Oxford: Oxford University Press, 2006.

Zimmern, Alfred. *Nationality and Government, with Other Wartime Essays.* New York: Robert McBride and Company, 1918.

Zimmern, Alfred. *Europe in Convalescence.* London: Mills and Boon, 1922.

Zimmern, Alfred. *The League of Nations and the Rule of Law, 1918–1935.* London: Macmillan, 1936.

Index